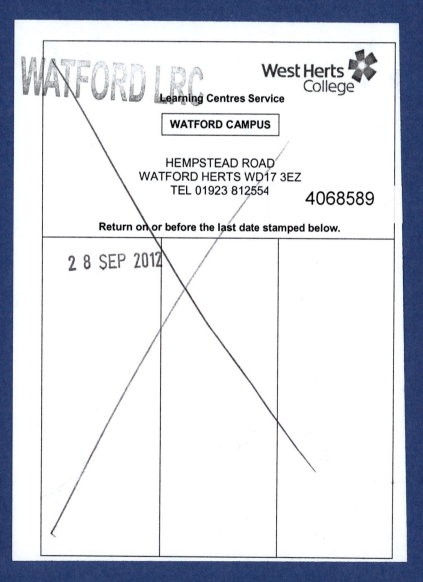

WATFORD LRC

West Herts College

Learning Centres Service

WATFORD CAMPUS

HEMPSTEAD ROAD
WATFORD HERTS WD17 3EZ
TEL 01923 812554

4068589

Return on or before the last date stamped below.

2 8 SEP 2012

Theatrical Design and Production

Theatrical Design and Production

An Introduction to
Scenic Design and Construction,
Lighting, Sound, Costume, and Makeup

SIXTH EDITION

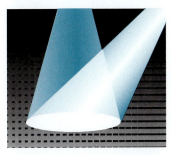

J. Michael Gillette

University of Arizona

McGraw-Hill
Higher Education

Boston   Burr Ridge, IL   Dubuque, IA   New York   San Francisco   St. Louis
Bangkok   Bogotá   Caracas   Kuala Lumpur   Lisbon   London   Madrid   Mexico City
Milan   Montreal   New Delhi   Santiago   Seoul   Singapore   Sydney   Taipei   Toronto

For Joyce Ann, who will always know why

THEATRICAL DESIGN AND PRODUCTION

Published by McGraw-Hill, an imprint of The McGraw-Hill Companies, Inc., 1221 Avenue of the Americas, New York, NY 10020. Copyright © 2008, 2005, 2000, 1997 All rights reserved. No part of this publication may be reproduced or distributed in any form or by any means, or stored in a database or retrieval system, without the prior written consent of The McGraw-Hill Companies, Inc., including, but not limited to, in any network or other electronic storage or transmission, or broadcast for distance learning.

This book is printed on acid-free paper.

4 5 6 7 8 9 0 DOW/DOW 0

ISBN: 978-0-07-351419-2
MHID: 0-07-351419-5

Editor in Chief: *Mike Ryan*
Publisher: *Lisa Moore*
Executive Editor: *Chris Freitag*
Marketing Manager: *Pamela Cooper*
Developmental Editor: *Caroline Ryan*
Production Editor: *Melissa Williams*
Production Service: *Margaret Pinette for Thompson Type*
Manuscript Editor: *Randy Stevens for Thompson Type*
Text Designer: *Susan Brietbard*
Cover Designer: *Cassandra Chu/Dog Eared Design*
Photo Research: *Inge King*
Senior Production Supervisor: *Tandra Jorgensen*
Composition: *9.5/12 Palatino Roman by Thompson Type*
Printing: *PMS 314C, 45# Pub Matte Plus, by R. R. Donnelley & Sons*

Cover: *In the Heights*, a musical about three days in the Washington Heights neighborhood in Upper Manhattan, was conceived by Lin-Manuel Miranda, who stars as Usnavi and also wrote the music and lyrics; book by Quiara Alegría Hudes, directed by Thomas Kail, choreographed by Andy Blankenbuehler, scenic design by Anna Louizos, costume design by Paul Tazewell, lighting design by Jason Lyons. Production photo by Sara Krulwich/The New York Times/Redux; costume renderings for "Graffiti Pete" and "Vanessa" printed with permission of Paul Tazewell; set model reproduced with permission of Anna Louizos.

Credits: The creidts section for this book begins on page 598 and is considered an extension of the copyright page.

Library of Congress Cataloging-in-Publication Data
Gillette, J. Michael.
   Theatrical design and production : an introduction to scenic design and construction, lighting, sound, costume, and makeup / J. Michael Gillette.—6th ed.
      p. cm.
   Includes bibliographical references and index.
   ISBN 0-07-256262-5 (alk. paper)
   1. Stage management. 2. Theater—Production and direction. 3. Theaters—Stage-setting and scenery. I. Title.

PN2085.G5 2008
792'.025—dc22   2007035218

www.mhhe.com

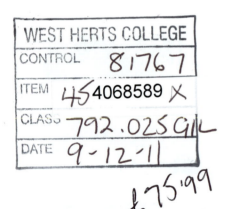

Preface

First courses in the world of theatrical design and production, like the art they introduce, come in a bewildering array of shapes, sizes, textures, and colors. Some students receive their introduction to this subject area in a general overview course that covers the design and production elements of scenery, costumes, lighting, and sound in a single semester. Other students may enjoy the luxury of an entire year in which to discuss the same material. Still others may take individual courses that specialize in the theory and craft of the separate areas that comprise the field of theatrical design and technical production. The course content is very flexible indeed.

To create a text that will serve the needs of all these courses is a distinct challenge. I've tried to rise to that challenge by organizing the material in two ways. The chapters appear in a logical sequence, but each chapter is also an island of information that can stand alone. My hope is that this organization will enable each instructor to pick and choose the type and amount of material that is appropriate for his or her particular course. This type of organization also makes the text a useful reference for students to keep throughout their design and technical production careers.

Organization and Content

Just as a play wouldn't start without the scenery being in place, this book doesn't delve into technical procedures without first setting the stage. Chapters 1 through 4, "Production Organization and Management," "The Design Process," "A Brief History of Theatre Architecture and Stage Technology," and "The Stage and Its Equipment," provide a grounding in real world issues and are appropriate for use in almost any type of technical production class.

Of special significance is Chapter 2, "The Design Process." It contains material new to beginning technical theatre texts. It is a problem-solving and conceptual-thinking model created specifically for theatrical practice. Its purpose is to increase each student's creative capacity by reducing the effects of two prime ingredients of creative dysfunction—fear and frustration. The mechanism used to effect this change is a seven-step procedure that enables students to make logical, rational, and considered decisions when making the myriad choices involved in creating a design or solving a technical challenge in any area of theatrical production.

Chapter 3, "A Brief History of Theatre Architecture and Stage Technology," provides a concise chronology, both pictorially and textually, of the history of theatre architecture. I've included this information for two reasons: the functional design of the environment in which a play is produced has always been a major factor in determining the type, style, and design of technical elements used in a production, and all too frequently student designers are not required to take courses in theatre history.

Chapters 7 and 8, "Mechanical Drafting" and "Perspective," contain specific how-to information on the drafting and mechanical perspective techniques most commonly used in theatrical production. These chapters have been moved to this location because it was suggested that it may be helpful for students to learn the grammar of graphic language before they encounter these types of drawings in the scenic and lighting design chapters. Chapter 7, "Mechanical Drafting," provides information about the materials and types of drafting used in the theatre, as well as helpful hints on the process of drafting. Chapter 8, "Perspective Drawing," offers a step-by-step procedure, with exercises, for creating accurate scale mechanical perspective drawings.

Chapter 15, "Electrical Theory and Practice," provides a concise explanation of the nature and function of electricity and electronics and the practical use of the power formula, as well as information on wiring practices and standards.

Chapter 22, "Drawing and Rendering," provides an overview of the types of paints, pastels, markers, and papers commonly used in theatrical rendering, as well as information on basic application techniques used with these media.

The remainder of the text provides an overview of the function and responsibilities of the scenic, lighting, costume, and sound designers. It also contains primary information about the tools and basic techniques that are used to bring each designer's concepts to the stage.

As with any art form, the basic element necessary for creating a successful design in theatre is an understanding of design principles and chosen medium. I hope that this text not only provides those basics but also offers encouragement and inspiration to create.

Features

In many ways, *Theatrical Design and Production* is a traditional introductory text for the various design and craft areas of theatrical production. With a number of features, however, I strive to set this text apart.

Philosophy   The underlying spirit of this text is firmly rooted in my belief that learning and creating in the various fields of theatrical design and production can be, and should be, fun. With that thought in mind, I've tried to make this text not only informative and practical but also motivating and inspirational.

Color Analysis   The sixteen-page color analysis section presents a discussion of the practical applications of color theory by analyzing the interactive effects of the color selections for the scenery, costumes, and lighting for two productions—one with a very narrow, muted palette and the other with a full-spectrum, heavily saturated color style.

Safety Tips   Safety tips are discussed throughout the text. They have been placed in special boxes adjacent to the relevant text to help readers integrate learning about a tool, material, or process with its safe use.

Running Glossary   To help students learn and remember the vocabulary of the theatre, new terms are defined in the margin on the page where they first appear.

Production Insights   Placed throughout the text, these newly named boxes identify material that provides further depth and practical information to the discussion.

Design Inspiration   Similar to the "Production Insights" boxes, but located only in design chapters, these include material that will enhance student understanding by providing insights and solutions to real theatrical problems.

Illustration Program   An extensive photo and illustration program provides a very strong adjunct to the textual information. Photos from professional theatre productions are used to provide a model that students can strive to emulate.

New to the Sixth Edition

The sixth edition has been extensively revised. While the basic features and organization of *Theatrical Design and Production* remain the same as previous editions, the chapters have been reordered. Chapters 7 and 8, "Mechanical Drafting" and "Perspective Drawing," have been moved from their former positions as Chapters 20 and 21 so that this grouping would form a natural block of information when combined with the material in Chapter 5, "Style, Composition, and Design," and Chapter 6, "Color." This placement might also help students comprehend the material in the various design chapters a little better by introducing them to the nomenclature and techniques of drafting and mechanical perspective prior to encountering the design chapters.

A continuing challenge of revising a design and production text is determining when a particular material, process, or type of technology should no longer be included in the text. Materials that are no longer manufactured or are in violation of current safety standards are relatively easy to identify and remove. But others, such as the soft-covering of flats, preset light boards, and production sound tapes are not so easy. Although most theatre practitioners younger than forty probably haven't seen, let alone built, muslin-covered, wooden-framed flats, the technology is still viable. Similarly, almost all theatres now have computer light boards and use computers for sound recording and playback. But the principles behind some of these older technologies, such as the logical processes involved in running preset light boards and the making of production sound tapes are still valid and, in fact, are still being used today. Some of these materials are still in the main body of the text, and some, such as soft-covering of flats, have been moved to appendixes. Their inclusion, or removal, may at first seem arbitrary but I'm sure there was some logic to it at the time that I did it.

Much of the technical information in the text has been extensively revised and updated. New tools, materials, processes, and techniques have been added; obsolete ones have been removed. To make these changes I have relied on the input of a number of practicing professional theatre artists/craftspeople. All of these people teach. They also practice their respective crafts at various professional theatres and venues around the country.

Specifically, I am sincerely indebted to Kimb Williamson, Scottscale College. Kimb is a practicing professional scenic artist who works and teaches at Cobalt Scenic in addition to her work as an educator. She made many excellent and delightfully detailed suggestions for the revisions to Chapter 12, "Scenic Painting." Almost every one of her comments has been included in this revision.

I am equally indebted to Sandra J. Strawn, University of Wisconsin-Milwaukee Peck School for the Arts (Theatre Arts), for her extensive contributions to the revision of Chapter 13, "Stage Properties." In addition to her work as an educator, Sandy is a professional property designer who works at numerous LORT and other professional theatres throughout the country. In what I think was a stroke of genius, Sandy volunteered to take the properties chapter to the annual SPAM conference, a meeting of professional property directors/designers. The membership and Sandy made dozens of excellent suggestions, most of which have been included in this revision.

I am likewise very appreciative of the work that Patrick Holt, University of Arizona School of Theatre Arts, did on his review of Chapter 18, "Costume Design," Chapter 19 "Costume Construction," and Chapter 20, "Makeup." In addition to his academic work, Patrick has designed costumes for numerous productions in a variety of professional theatres throughout the country. His valuable suggestions regarding updated costume and makeup processes, paperwork, techniques, and materials are genuinely appreciated.

Of no less significance are the contributions that Walter Clissen, University of Arizona School of Theatre Arts, made to Chapter 21, "Sound Design and Technology." In addition to his educational work, Walter has an extensive background in sound design in the professional theatre and the recording industry both in the United States and in Europe. His suggestions regarding current practices, procedures, techniques, and equipment have been invaluable for updating the information on sound in the theatre.

Finally, Tom Young, with J. R. Clancy, provided extremely valuable information on the use of synthetic rope in the theatre, as well as concise information about the evolution of motorized rigging systems. His information was excellent, and his help was enthusiastic. His input was greatly appreciated.

I would also like to sincerely thank development editor Caroline Ryan for bringing the changes that needed to be made to this new edition into clear focus for me. Her suggestions, counsel, and positive outlook were both helpful and genuinely appreciated.

Finally, I would like to thank those friends and colleagues who have offered suggestions for improving *Theatrical Design and Production.* In particular I would like to thank the following reviewers for their help in preparing the sixth edition of this text.

Chris Gray, Lincoln College, Illinois
Chris Jaehnig, New York University
Martha Marking, Appalachian State
Jonathan Middents, University of Houston
Louella Powell, University of Wisconsin-Milwaukee
Gordon Rice, University of Rochester
Mark Shanda, Ohio State University
Erin Slattery, New York University

Brief Contents

Contents

6. Color   88

7. Mechanical Drafting   113

8. Perspective Drawing   136

9. Scenic Design   161

10. Tools and Materials   186

11. Scenic Production Techniques   237

12. Scene Painting   281

Chapter 1

Production Organization and Management

"Great art conceals art." That statement has been attributed to Konstantin Stanislavski, founder of the Moscow Art Theatre and developer of Method acting. He was referring to the phenomenon that occurs when actors create brilliantly believable roles. Great actors don't seem to be working. They make us believe that they *are* the characters they are playing and that everything they say or do is happening spontaneously, without thought or effort. Stanislavski meant by his aphorism that a seemingly effortless job of acting is the end result of years of training, dedication, and just plain hard work.

Great art *does* conceal art, but not just the art of the actor. Imagine a male actor, wrapped in a heavy fur cape, standing in the middle of the stage and delivering a soliloquy. The stage resembles a craggy mountain peak, with an angular platform surrounded by an immense expanse of solemn purple and blue sky. The actor strides to a rocky outcropping. Under his weight the platform slowly starts to tip. The actor scrambles backward to save himself and catches the hem of his cape on another "rock." The cape comes off, and the **followspot** reveals the actor standing in his BVDs with his cape around his ankles. The spotlight operator, horrified, tries to turn off her light. But she doesn't hit the right lever and, instead of turning it off, changes its color from deep blue to brilliant white.

followspot: A lighting instrument with a high-intensity, narrow beam; mounted in a stand that allows it to tilt and swivel so the beam can "follow" an actor.

This unlikely scenario illustrates the fact that less-than-great art conceals little. It also demonstrates that Stanislavski's injunction can be just as true for the design and technical elements of the production as it is for the actors. Together, they can create the delicate illusionary reality that we call theatre. The illusion that the spectators see is just that. A great performance doesn't simply happen; it is the product of a great deal of organization, teamwork, talent, and dedication.

Theatre folk have always delighted in surrounding the process of putting on plays with an aura of mystery. This tradition stems from the probably accurate belief that a play's entertainment value increases if the audience thinks that the production just happens spontaneously. The Mickey Rooney and Judy Garland movies of the 1930s are perfect examples. Mickey, Judy, or one of their friends says, "Let's put on a show!" Someone chimes in that her uncle owns a barn. Amazingly, the barn happens to have a highly polished linoleum floor that is perfect for tap dancing, and the barn is equipped with a full orchestra, sets, lights, and spectacular costumes. The show is an astounding success.

The real world of theatrical production isn't like that. Getting a play from the written word to the stage requires a lot of challenging work. The result of all this

production team: Everyone working, in any capacity, on the production of the play.

production design team: The producer, director, and scenic, costume, lighting, sound, and other designers who develop the visual and aural concept for the production.

production concept: The creative interpretation of the script, which will unify the artistic vision of producer, director, and designers.

production meeting: A conference of appropriate production personnel to share information.

supernumerary: An actor, normally not called for in the script, used in a production; an extra; a walk-on.

effort, the **production team** hopes, will be artistic and artful, but the business of making a script come alive on the stage is a process that isn't all that mysterious.

 ## The Production Sequence

How does a play happen? What sequence of events must occur for it to move from the pages of a script to a live performance before an audience? Every play goes through several stages of development.

Script

The overwhelming majority of theatrical productions begin with a script. This is not true, however, for every theatrical performance. The production of some plays begins with just an idea. That idea may be developed by the performing group in a variety of interesting and creative ways. Some of these concepts may evolve into written scripts, and others may remain as conceptual cores that the actors use as guides when they improvise dialogue during the actual performance.

Concept, Design, and Construction

We will assume that our hypothetical production begins with a traditional script. After the script has been selected, the producer options it, or secures the legal rights to produce it, and hires the director, designers, and actors. The members of the **production design team** read the script and then develop the **production concept,** also referred to as the "production approach."

The production concept is the central creative idea that unifies the artistic vision of the producer, director, and designers. In many ways, any production concept originates with the personal artistic "points of view" of the members of the production design team. The personality, training, and prior experiences of each team member will shape and color his or her thoughts about the play. One of the primary jobs of the director is to mold these individual artistic ideas and expressions into a unified vision—the production concept—so that, ideally, each designer's work supports the work of the other designers as well as the central artistic theme of the production. Normally, the production concept evolves during the first few **production meetings** from the combined input of the members of the production design team. The principles of the production concept are best explained by example.

Let's assume that our hypothetical production team is working on a production of Shakespeare's *The Merchant of Venice.* Most productions of this play would probably be traditional: Elizabethan costumes and a set that mimics the appearance of the Globe Theatre, the theatre most scholars think was used by Shakespeare. However, some production groups might choose, for a variety of reasons, to develop a nontraditional production concept. In a production of this play directed by Cosmo Catellano at the University of Iowa, the performance was set inside a World War II Nazi concentration camp. In this production, all of the actors in the play were portrayed as Jewish interns of the camp. **Supernumeraries,** dressed as Nazi officers and their female companions, sat in the auditorium and watched the play alongside the paying audience. Additional extras, in the uniforms of concentration camp guards and carrying weapons, patrolled the stage throughout the performance. While the script wasn't altered, the radical production concept forced the audience to concentrate on the Jewish persecution themes that are very much a part of the script.

(1)

(2)

(3)

(4)

(5)

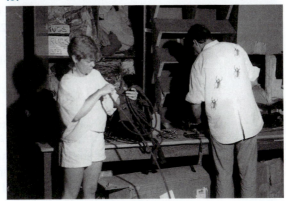

(6)

(7)

FIGURE 1.1
A great deal of backstage activity occurs before the production reaches the stage. Photo 1, 2 by Evon Photography, courtesy of the University of Arizona School of Theatre Arts. Photos 3–7 by author.

FIGURE 1.2
The director discusses a scene with the
actors.

FIGURE 1.3
Scene shifting must be carefully organized
and choreographed.

After the production concept is agreed on, the sets, props, lights, costumes,
and sound are designed. Then the various diagrams, sketches, and other plans
are sent to shops for construction, fabrication, or acquisition of the production
elements (see Figure 1.1).

While the various visual elements are being built, the director and actors are
busy rehearsing (see Figure 1.2). After the rehearsal and construction period,
which usually lasts three to seven weeks, the play moves into the theatre, and
the technical and dress rehearsals begin.

Rehearsals

Technical rehearsals are devoted to integrating the sets, props, lighting, and sound
with the actors into the action of the play. During this hectic period, the patterns
and timing for shifting the scenery and props are established. The movements
of any scenic or property elements (see Figure 1.3), regardless of whether those
movements happen in front of the audience or behind a curtain, have to be
choreographed, or **blocked,** just as are the movements of the actors. This ensures

technical rehearsals: Run-throughs in
which the sets, lights, props, and sound are
introduced into the action of the play.

blocking: Movement patterns, usually of
actors, on the stage.

FIGURE 1.4
FIGURE 1.4
Sound operator at work in a sound booth. Sound operators frequently run the sound board from a location in the auditorium as opposed to operating from the booth.

that each shift will be consistent in timing and efficiency for every performance. The shifts may be numerous or complex enough to warrant holding a separate **shift rehearsal,** in which the director, scene designer, technical director, and stage manager work with the scenery and prop crews to perfect the choreography and timing of all scenic and prop shifts.

The basic timing and intensity of the light **cues** will have been established during the **lighting rehearsal** (which precedes the first technical rehearsal). But during the tech rehearsals almost all of the light cues have to be adjusted in some way, since it is the rule rather than the exception that new lighting cues are added and old ones deleted or modified during this time. The lighting designer meets with the director and stage manager in the theatre to discuss the modifications and have a look at them. The intensity, timing, and nature of the sound cues are subjected to similar changes during the technical rehearsals (see Figure 1.4). Depending on the production schedule and the complexity of the show, there are generally one to three tech rehearsals over the course of a week or so.

The **dress rehearsals** begin toward the end of "tech week." During these rehearsals, which are a natural extension of the tech rehearsals, any adjustments to costumes and makeup are noted and corrected by the next rehearsal time (see Figure 1.5). Adjustments to the various sound, lighting, and shifting cues continue to be made during the dress rehearsals. Depending on the complexity of the

shift rehearsal: A run-through without actors to practice changing the scenery and props.

cue: A directive for action, for example, a change in the lighting.

lighting rehearsal: A run-through without the actors to look at the intensity, timing, and placement of the various lighting cues.

dress rehearsal: A run-through in which the actors wear costumes and makeup.

FIGURE 1.5
Costumes must be adjusted to fit properly. Photo by Evon Photography. Courtesy of University of Arizona School of Theatre Arts.

production and the number of costumes and costume changes, there may be one to three dress rehearsals.

After the last dress rehearsal, there are sometimes one to ten or more preview performances (with an invited audience and/or reduced ticket prices and no critics) before the production officially opens to the public and critics.

Theatre Organization

More than anything else good theatre requires good organization. Every successful production has a strong "artistic responsibility" organizational structure that follows a fairly standard pattern. Figure 1.6 depicts the organization of a hypothetical, but typical, theatrical production company. Each company's structure is unique to its own needs, and it is doubtful that any two companies would be set up exactly the same. One particular feature of Figure 1.6 should be noted. In this flowchart the director and the designers are symbolized as equals. This equality is essential to the collaborative process that is theatre art and will be discussed at greater length throughout this book. The functions of the various members of the company will be taken up in the next section. It should be reiterated that this is an artistic responsibility or "make happy" flowchart. This simply means that the work produced by someone "reporting" to a position higher on the flowchart must artistically satisfy the visual requirements stipulated by that higher position. To illustrate, the visual appearance of the properties must satisfy the scenic designer. It is also important to note what this chart is not: this is not a work responsibility flowchart. A "work responsibility" flowchart would look significantly different. In the real world property masters normally do not "work for" scenic designers. Most property masters work for—are accountable to—the production manager for the on-time, on-budget, as-designed production of properties.

The production meeting is probably the single most important device for ensuring smooth communication among the various production departments. The initial production conferences are attended by members of the production design team. Their purpose is to develop the production concept. After the designers begin to produce their drawings, sketches, and plans, the production meeting is used as a forum to keep other members of the team informed about the progress in all design areas. At this time, the stage manager normally joins in the discussions.

When the designs are approved and construction begins, the production meeting expands to include the technical director and appropriate crew heads. As construction starts, the director becomes heavily involved in rehearsals. At this time, a few adjustments are almost inevitably necessary in one or more of the design elements. These changes should be discussed and resolved at the production meeting so that all departments are aware of the progress and evolution of the production concept.

While the production concept is being developed, the production meetings are usually held as often as it is practicable and necessary—daily or less frequently. As the meetings become less developmental and more informational, their frequency decreases to about once a week. The last meeting is usually held just before the opening of the production.

Who participates in production meetings depends, to a great extent, on the nature of the producing organization. A single-run, Broadway-type professional conference usually includes only the members of the production design team and their assistants. A production conference at a regional professional theatre includes the production design team and some of the other members of the

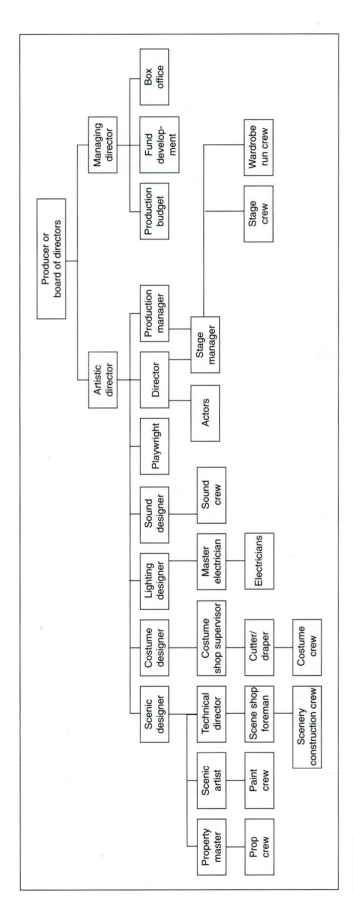

FIGURE 1.6
The organizational structure chart of a typical theatrical production company.

permanent production staff, such as the production manager and technical director. For a professionally oriented educational theatre, the staffing of the production meeting is generally the same as for the regional professional production group and ideally will include those faculty supervisors overseeing the work of student designers, technical directors, and crew heads.

The development of advanced communication technologies and the reality that most professional designers are working on more than one project at a time often necessitate that much of the direct communication between members of the production design team take place over great geographical distances. Designs can be sent by overnight express, forwarded as e-mail attachments, or faxed. Phone or video conferences can be used in place of face-to-face meetings. While these developments speed the transfer of data and information, the isolation of the design team members from each other may break down the necessary communication flow within the group. But if everyone is aware of this potential "communication gap," it doesn't have to become a problem. More and more designers are communicating electronically, and we can expect even more "remote conferencing" in the future.

 ## Production Job Descriptions

Although the organization of any company will fit its own needs, the duties of those holding the various positions will be much the same.

Producer

The producer is the ultimate authority in the organizational structure of a theatrical production. He or she is, arguably, the most influential member of the team. The producer secures the rights to perform the play; hires the director, designers, actors, and crews; leases the theatre; and secures financial backing for the play. The specific functions of the producer can vary considerably. In the New York professional theatre, most productions are set up as individual entities. As a consequence, the producer and his or her staff are able to concentrate their efforts on each production. They will sometimes be working on the preliminary phases of a second or third production while another show is in production or in the final stages of rehearsal, but in general they concentrate on one show at a time.

Regional professional theatres such as the Guthrie Theatre in Minneapolis, the American Conservatory Theatre (ACT) in San Francisco, the Arizona Theatre Company in Tucson, the Asolo Theatre in Sarasota, Florida, and others have been set up in every section of North America over the past forty years. Generally, these theatres produce a full seven- or eight-month season of limited-run productions. Some of them have active summer programs. Because of the sweeping responsibilities imposed on the producer within these organizations, the functions of the position are generally divided between two persons, the *managing director* and the *artistic director*. The business functions of the producer—contracts, fund-raising, ticket sales, box-office management—are handled by the managing director, and any artistic decisions—selection of directors, actors, and designers, for example—are made by the artistic director. The managing and artistic directors are hired by the theatre's board of directors, which is responsible for determining the long-range artistic and fiscal goals of the theatre.

In educational theatre, the department chair and administrative staff frequently function in the same capacity as the managing director. The duties of the artistic director are often assigned to a production committee, which selects the plays and is responsible for their artistic quality.

In other nonprofit theatres, such as community or church groups, the functions of the producer are usually carried out by a production committee or board of directors, which functions as previously described.

Playwright

The playwright is obviously a vital and essential link in the production chain. The playwright creates and develops the ideas that ultimately evolve into the written script. In the initial public performance of the play, he or she may be involved in the production process. The playwright frequently helps the director by explaining his or her interpretation of various plot and character developments. During this developmental process, the playwright often needs to rewrite portions of some scenes or even whole scenes or acts. If the playwright is not available for conferences or meetings, the production design team proceeds with the development and interpretation of the script on its own.

Director

The director is the artistic manager and inspirational leader of the production team. He or she coordinates the work of the actors, designers, and crews so that the production accurately expresses the production concept. Any complex activity such as the production of a play must have someone with the vision, energy, and ability to focus everyone else's efforts on the common goal. The director is this leader. He or she works closely with the other members of the production design team to develop the production concept and also works with the actors to develop their roles in a way that is consistent with the production concept. The director is ultimately responsible for the unified creative interpretation of the play as it is expressed in production.

Production Manager

Theatres with heavy annual production programs, such as regional professional theatres and many educational theatre programs, frequently mount several productions or production series simultaneously, often in multiple theatres or venues. In many of these situations the directors and designers are hired or assigned for only one production per year. At the same time the "construction people"—those who actually build the scenery, props, costumes, lights, and sound—are normally hired on an annual basis to work/supervise all of the shows that are produced by that organization. Typically, the technical director runs the scene shop and supervises the production of the scenery for every play in the company's season. Similarly, the property director runs the prop shop and supervises the creation/acquisition of the props used in each production. The same applies for the costume shop supervisor, master electrician, and so forth. Someone on the organization's permanent staff needs to be in control of, and facilitate communication between, the individual design teams and the "permanent" production staff. Enter the production manager.

The production manager is typically responsible for keeping the individual production teams on track, on budget, and on time. He or she oversees the transition from plans to performance for each production and is responsible for managing the producing organization's production budget, personnel, and calendar, and generally keeping everything moving smoothly.

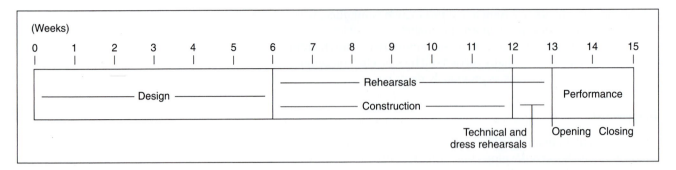

FIGURE 1.7
The production calendar shows the time line for each limited-run production from the initial production conference until the closing night.

limited run: A production run of predetermined length, for example, two weeks, six weeks, and so forth.

The production manager must be an adept mental gymnast, because this important position has the responsibility for coordinating the complex activities associated with a multishow season. Each production within the theatre's season requires its own logistical structure to bring it from concept to the stage. Figure 1.7 illustrates a typical period needed to develop a play from production concept to reality. Since most regional professional theatres or professionally oriented educational theatres produce eight to twelve **limited-run** plays a season, frequently on several different stages, they must develop rehearsal and performance schedules for all of them simultaneously.

The production calendar shown in Figure 1.8 is used by the production manager to help keep track of the various stages of development for each play in the season. This master calendar contains all pertinent information regarding tryouts, rehearsals, design and construction deadlines, technical and dress rehearsals, and performances. From the production calendar, the production manager gleans the

FIGURE 1.8
A sample production calendar.

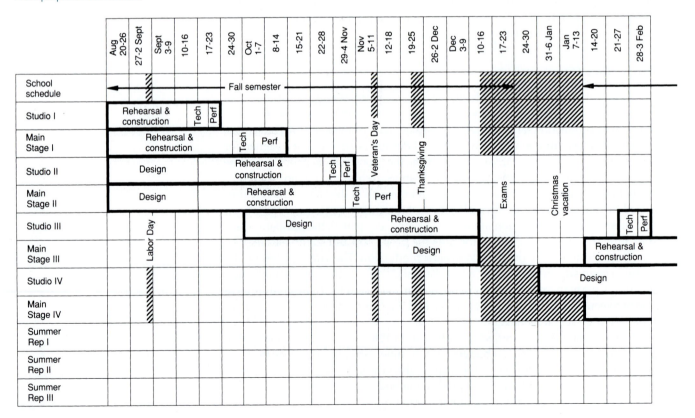

PRODUCTION INSIGHTS

Backstage Etiquette

Although every production company has specific rules that relate to its own production circumstances, some general rules of backstage etiquette are universal.

1. Don't talk to other crew members backstage during rehearsals or performances unless it is about the business of the production. Then talk only in a low whisper.

2. Don't talk to the actors backstage during rehearsals or performances unless it is about the business of the production. Their job — acting — takes a great deal of concentration, and they shouldn't be distracted.

3. Wear dark clothes, preferably dark blue or black, to minimize the distraction to the audience if you are seen. Wear sturdy rubber-soled shoes (no tennis shoes, cowboy boots, sandals, or flip-flops). Sturdy shoes will protect your feet, and the rubber soles will minimize noise.

4. Be sure to show up on time for your crew call (the time you are scheduled to arrive at the theatre ready for work). Sign the sign-in sheet, and check in with your crew head for work.

5. Don't smoke, eat, or drink backstage.

6. Do not touch props, costumes, or stage equipment that is not your responsibility.

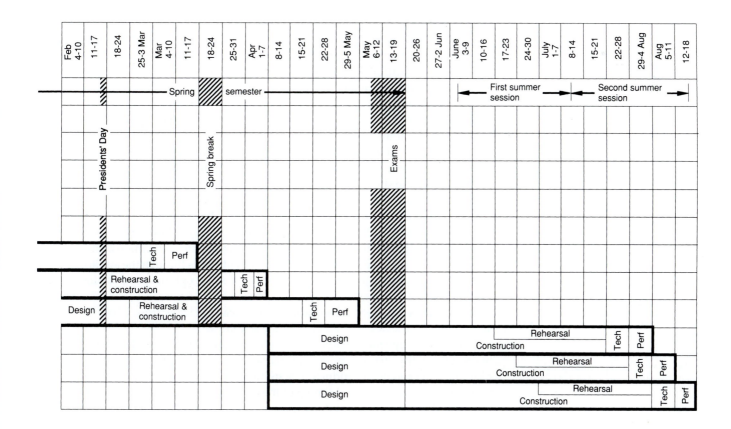

information necessary to coordinate the assignment of personnel and rehearsal space as well as the scheduling of the various production meetings and other necessary activities.

Stage Manager

The stage manager can be compared to a very gifted, slightly eccentric master mechanic who keeps a cantankerous, highly complex machine running at top efficiency by talking to it, soothing it, and lovingly fixing whatever is broken. The specific duties of the stage manager can be broken down into two primary categories: (1) assisting the director during rehearsals and (2) being responsible for all backstage activity after the show opens.

The stage manager is hired or assigned to the production at about the same time as the director. In the professional theatre, the stage manager must be a member of Actor's Equity, the actors' union. Sometimes the stage manager finds himor herself in an awkward position because he or she not only assists the director but also, if elected the Equity deputy by the union actors, functions as the enforcer of the Equity rules during rehearsals and performances. Since the Equity deputy can be viewed as enforcing the union rules to save money for the producer, some stage managers decline to serve as deputy because of the potential conflict of interest. Other stage managers elect to serve as deputy since they are already in a leadership position and do not see these activities as a conflict of interest.

The stage manager helps the director by taking responsibility for the majority of administrative details. They include such diverse activities as making sure that the ground plan of the set is taped or chalked on the floor of the rehearsal hall, arranging for rehearsal furniture (substitute furniture for the set) as well as tables and chairs for the director and other production personnel, and writing the blocking in the stage manager's **prompt book.**

The stage manager also assists the director by keeping information flowing among the director, the designers, and the various technical shops. During the rehearsal process, the director may decide to introduce a piece of **stage business** that requires the modification of some technical element. If the director decides that an actor should bounce a ball against one of the set walls, the stage manager needs to tell the set designer that this section of the wall must be sturdy.

Until the production moves into the theatre—or until the beginning of technical rehearsals, if the play has already been rehearsing in the theatre—the stage manager usually sits beside the director to facilitate communication. When technical rehearsals begin, the stage manager moves to the location from which he or she will **call** the show. The crew members will have previously recorded what to do on their cue sheets, but they don't start the action until they receive their "go" cue from the stage manager. Stage managers have traditionally called the show from backstage, because this location kept them in close contact with the cast and crew. However, the development of new theatre conventions, environments, and equipment enables the cast to make entrances through the auditorium and allows the lighting and sound operators to be in the optimal positions for seeing and hearing the stage action. This dispersion of the actors and crew from the backstage space has freed the stage manager to call the show from whatever position provides the best overall view of the action.

When the stage manager begins to call the show, the primary focus of his or her responsibility changes from administrative support for the director to technical coordination of all production activities. The director and various designers determine the nature and timing of the cues, but it is the stage manager who is responsible for seeing that those instructions are carried out. Figure 1.9 illus-

prompt book: A copy of the script with details about each actor's blocking as well as the location of all sets, props, lights, and sound cues.

stage business: A specific action, also known as a "bit," performed by an actor during the play.

call: To tell specific crew members when to perform their cues.

PRODUCTION INSIGHTS
Stage Manager's Prompt Book

The stage manager's prompt book is the bible of the production. The stage manager details all pertinent information about the production in a loose-leaf notebook as shown. Each page of the prompt book contains one page of the script. The blocking is usually indicated in the wide margins of the pages with arrows showing the movement of each actor. Some stage managers prefer to place a ground plan of the set on the facing page for each page of the script. The blocking and notes are then placed on this sheet.

The nature, location, and duration of each technical cue (lights, sound, shifting) are also written in the margins. Warning cues (to prepare the appropriate personnel for any forthcoming cues) are normally placed in the prompt book about half a page before the cue location.

The prompt book also contains a ground plan of the set(s), a prop schedule detailing the placement and conditions of props ("a half-full glass of milk on the coffee table"), and a "contact sheet" listing the phone numbers and addresses of all cast members, crew members, and other production personnel.

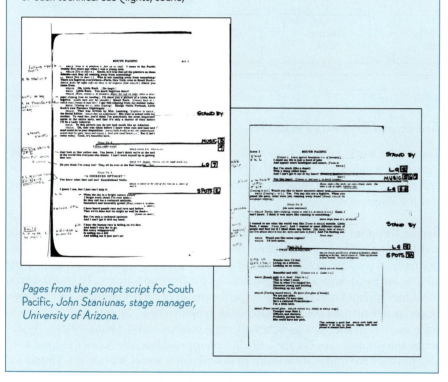

Pages from the prompt script for South Pacific, *John Staniunas, stage manager, University of Arizona.*

trates the change in organization that takes place when the play goes into technical and dress rehearsals and performances. The designers still discuss conceptual and aesthetic issues with the director, but they usually communicate specific information related to cues that will be called by the stage manager directly to the stage manager.

The stage manager calls the show from notes written in the prompt book. Preliminary locations for many of the cues will have been noted in the book during the rehearsal period. During the tech and dress rehearsals, the location, timing, and character of these cues are adjusted. When the last dress rehearsal or preview performance is finished, the prompt book will contain a complete and accurate set of instructions for running every cue in the production.

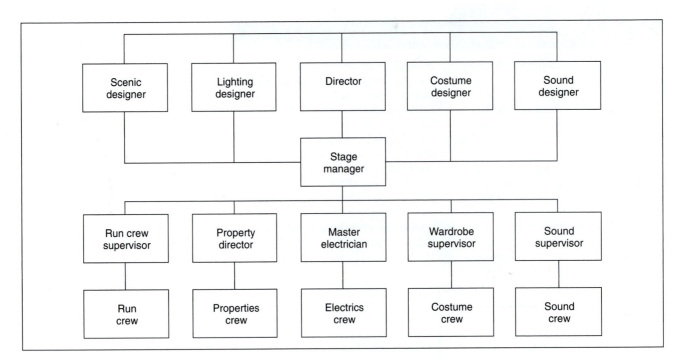

FIGURE 1.9
The organizational structure changes as a play goes from regular rehearsals into the tech/dress rehearsals and performances.

Scenic and Property Personnel

Those who work with the scenery and props in a production are the scenic designer, the scenic artist, the paint crew, the property master, or property director, and crew, the technical director, the scene-shop foreman, the construction crew, and the stage crew.

Scenic Designer The scenic designer is responsible for the visual appearance and function of the scenic elements used in the production. The scene designer, normally in collaborative partnership with the property director, shares responsibility for the design and function of the production's props. To translate the scenic design from concept to the stage, the designer produces either hand-drawn or computer-printed colored sketches or renderings of the sets and properties, scale models of the various sets, and scale mechanical drawings that fully describe the settings (see Figure 1.10). When appropriate, the scene designer may also produce computer animations to describe any scenic movement. The scenic designer's job will be explored in depth in Chapter 9, "Scenic Design."

Scenic Artist The scenic artist, under the supervision of the scenic designer, is responsible for the painting of the scenery. He or she needs to be an excellent craftsperson capable of working in a variety of media and styles. Although the scenic artist does a great deal of the actual scenic painting, he or she is also responsible for supervising the work of the paint crew.

Paint Crew The paint crew, under the supervision of the scenic artist, paints the sets and sometimes the **properties**. This challenging job involves painting the set (walls, floor, background, properties) to make it reflect the character of the design. Rarely do playwrights set their plays in freshly painted environments. More frequently than not the paint crew must make the set look old, tired, abused, and worn. Techniques for achieving these results are detailed in Chapter 12, "Scene Painting."

properties: Such elements as furniture, lamps, pictures, table linens, bric-a-brac, and window drapes that provide the finished set with visual character.

(A)

(B)

Property Master   The property master, also known as the property director, is a unique artisan in the theatre. He or she must be adept at a variety of skills ranging from, but not limited to, design, painting, sculpting, furniture construction and upholstery, welding, and electronics. The property master/director is responsible for the supervision of the prop shop personnel in the acquisition and construction of the various decorative and functional props in a collaborative design process with the scenic designer. The property director must also have a strong background in a wide range of areas: shop management—organization, personnel, budgeting, inventory; period research; the ability to turn the prop design sketches/ideas into working drawings that use appropriate construction techniques and materials. They obviously need to be skilled in all phases of property construction. Like all good technical/design folk, the property director also needs to be an effective collaborative communicator with directors, designers, actors, stage managers, and other area heads and personnel.

FIGURE 1.10
(A) *Look Back in Anger,* scenic design by A. S. Gillette, University of Iowa. (B) *The Petrified Forest,* scenic design by Peggy Kellner, University of Arizona.

running: Controlling or operating some aspect of production.

plate: A sheet of mechanical drawings, drawn to scale.

The property director used to work under the artistic supervision of the scenic designer. Within the past decade in many producing organizations this situation has changed to a more collaborative process. The twofold reasons for the change are logical: (1) many scene designers are hired for only one show out of an organization's season while property directors are typically hired to work all the shows in any given season; (2) e-mail communication has made it simple, fast, and effective to send notes, ideas, and sketches to literally anywhere in the world where a scene designer might be working on another show. Now the scene designer and the property director, functioning as a de facto on-site property designer, frequently collaborate on the design of the stage props.

The property director closely coordinates with the scenic, lighting, sound, and costuming departments when any technical needs overlap among those departments.

Chapter 13, "Stage Properties," contains additional information about the property director's duties, the organization and running of a prop shop, as well as the making and **running** of stage props during a production.

Property Crews   There are two types of property crews—construction and running. Under the supervision of the property master/director, the making and acquiring of properties is the responsibility of the property artisans. They are responsible for the creation and acquisition of all props used in a production. The skills needed to be a good property artisan are amazingly varied. Woodworking, furniture restoration/conservation/alteration and upholstery, welding, sewing, electronics, sculpting, graphics/drafting, special effects, and weaponry are but a few of the skills needed. And that's just for those artisans who *build* and decorate the props. Other prop artisans specialize in buying and renting props. Just about any craft and/or shopping skill you can think of is useful in properties construction and acquisition. The individual artisans are expected to be innovative, creative, and collaborative artists working to honor the specific intent of each prop design while making those props safe and stage worthy.

The property running crew, under the supervision of the stage manager, is responsible for tracking, placing, and maintaining all props during rehearsals and performances.

During technical rehearsals both crews work together to implement any changes/notes coming from the technical rehearsal, but when the show "opens" the running, or run, crew has control of the props for that production.

Technical Director   The technical director, also known as the TD, is responsible for purchasing construction materials, supervising the building of the scenery, transporting the sets from the shop(s) to the theatre stage, mounting the scenery onstage, overseeing the work of the scenic crews during rehearsals and performances, and maintaining the scene shop's equipment and supplies. To order the materials and build the scenery the TD reads scale plans supplied by the scene designer. These drawings may have to be supplemented with **plates** that the TD or an assistant draws that show the construction details and techniques that will be used to build the scenery.

An introduction to scenic and property production (the organization, tools, and construction techniques) is contained in Chapter 10 ("Tools and Materials") and 11 ("Scenic Production Techniques") and Chapter 12 ("Scenic Painting"), as well as Chapter 13 ("Stage Properties").

Scene-Shop Foreman   The scene-shop foreman or master carpenter, under the supervision of the technical director, is responsible for the construction, mounting, and rigging of the scenery. He or she usually supervises a crew of carpenters in the actual construction. The foreman is also normally responsible for the maintenance of the scene-shop equipment and supplies.

Construction Crew   The construction crew is composed of the people who build the various pieces of scenery and properties for the production. After the set has been built and painted, they move the sets from the shop to the theatre and assemble them on the stage.

Stage Crew   The stage crew **shifts** the set during technical and dress rehearsals and during the performances. This work is accomplished under the direct supervision of the stage manager.

shift: To change the position of the scenery, props, or stage equipment.

Lighting Personnel

The lighting staff is made up of the lighting designer, the master electrician, and other electricians.

Lighting Designer   The lighting designer is responsible for the design, installation, and operation of the lighting and special electrical effects used in the production. Because light is a nontactile sculptural medium, it is all but impossible to build a model or draw a sketch of what the lighting will look like.

To present their visual ideas, lighting designers frequently draw sketches or show visual examples—paintings, photographs, and so forth—that demonstrate the type and style of lighting that they intend to create. Various computer rendering/modeling/animation programs can now be used to create virtual examples of how the lighting is going to look. With currently available programs it is possible to scan in a rendering of the set, add a character or two, then add the lighting and print the result on a color printer. As computer technology continues to improve and rendering times are reduced, digital imagery will probably become the preferred method of demonstrating the lighting designer's concepts, simply because a computer image, whether printed or seen on the monitor, provides an extremely accurate, evocative visualization of the designer's intentions—one that was unavailable prior to the development of computer imaging.

To show where the lighting equipment will be placed, the lighting designer produces a light plot, which is a scale drawing that details the placement of the lighting instruments relative to the physical structure of the theatre and the location of the set. The techniques and materials that the lighting designer uses are discussed in Chapters 14 ("Lighting Design"), 15 ("Electrical Theory and Practice"), 16 ("Lighting Production"), and 17 ("Projections").

Assistant Lighting Designer   While the lighting designer's primary duty is to concentrate on the artistic elements of the lighting design, it is often said that a lighting design is only as good as its paperwork. Producing that paperwork is the role of the assistant lighting designer, also known as the lighting associate. This person is responsible for creating and continually updating the various types of paperwork that are an essential element of any good lighting design. That paperwork will be explained in Chapter 14, "Lighting Design." The assistant lighting designer may also, at the discretion of the designer, assist with focusing, organization of work, and so forth.

Master Electrician   The master electrician, under the supervision of the lighting designer, implements the lighting design. He or she is directly responsible for the acquisition, installation, and maintenance of all lighting equipment and the supervision of the crews who hang, focus, and run the lighting equipment.

hanging: Placing lighting instruments and equipment in the designated positions on the light plot.

focusing: Directing light from the lighting instruments to a specific area.

circuit: To connect a lighting instrument to a stage circuit.

patch: To connect a stage circuit to a dimmer circuit.

hookup sheet: A sheet containing pertinent information (hanging position, circuit, dimmer, color, lamp wattage, focusing notes) about every lighting instrument used in the production. Also known as an instrument schedule.

color media: The colored plastic, gel, or glass filters used in lighting instruments.

focus: To direct light from a lighting instrument to a specific location.

Programmer   Programmers are individuals who program the specialized consoles used to control automated lighting fixtures and projectors. They generally work under the aesthetic direction of the lighting designer. Programmers may be freelance technicians although they are also often associated with companies that manufacture or distribute automated fixtures or projectors. Programmers are usually hired for individual projects that use these highly specialized fixtures and projectors rather than being employed by a producing organization for the full run of a show or for an entire season. Programmers normally run the console for one-time performances such as television specials and concert events where making adjustments "on-the-fly" is frequently the norm rather than the exception. For events with more consistent performance expectations, such as theatre performances with multiweek (or longer) runs, programmers normally train other electricians to serve as board operators for the specialized consoles.

Electricians   The work of the electricians can be divided into three areas: **hanging, focusing,** and running. The *hanging crew* places the lighting instruments and associated equipment in the positions designated by the light plot. They also **circuit** and **patch** the instruments. The circuit and dimmer for each instrument are indicated on the light plot or **hookup sheet;** or the master electrician designates the appropriate circuit and dimmer during the hanging session. The hanging crew also puts the **color media** on the lighting instruments and, under the supervision of the lighting designer, **focuses** the instruments.

The *running crew* is responsible for the operation of the lighting equipment during the rehearsals and performances. Depending on the complexity of the production, as few as one or as many as five or more electricians are needed to run the lights.

Costume Personnel

Those staff members who are responsible for the production's costumes include the costume designer, costume shop supervisor, cutter/draper, and costume construction crew.

Costume Designer   The costume designer is responsible for the visual appearance of the actors. These responsibilities will include what isn't seen as well as what is. Clothes and accessories are seen. Undergarments aren't. But undergarments can be just as important. Corsets, hoops, and boning create the distinctive silhouette and appearance that tell us much about the costumes of specific periods. Additionally, character elements such as padded stomachs, sagging bosoms, and so forth add greatly to the audience's understanding of the nature of each character. The visible costume elements include the clothes, accessories (shoes, hats, purses, canes, parasols), jewelry, wigs, and makeup worn by the actors during the performance.

Designs for theatrical costumes consist of colored sketches depicting the clothing and accessories that will be worn by the actor. In the case of complex costume designs, sketches that show more than one view may be needed. In either case, the sketches, which can be either hand- or computer-drawn and painted, normally have appropriate construction notes jotted in the margins, and small swatches of the fabrics and trims from which the costumes will be made are usually attached to the sketches. Additional information about costume and makeup designs as well as costume production can be found in Chapters 18 ("Costume Design"), 19 ("Costume Construction"), and 20 ("Makeup").

Costume Shop Supervisor   The costume shop supervisor or manager, also known as the costumer or costume technician, is the person who, under the artistic supervision of the costume designer, builds or supervises the building of the costumes. The costume technician must be able to read and translate the costume designer's sketches into working garments, be skilled in all phases of costume construction, including pattern making, and be able to work with the designer and actors as well as supervise the shop personnel. In many operations, the costume shop supervisor is also responsible for maintaining the costume shop equipment and keeping the shop inventory of basic supplies current.

In larger costume operations, the duties of the costume shop supervisor are frequently divided into two parts — the costume shop and the craft shop. Each may have its own manager, although the craft shop sometimes is managed by an assistant to the costume shop supervisor. With this type of organization the duties are divided between the shops. The costume shop constructs the costumes — cuts, drapes, sews the fabric — while the craft shop generally creates "crafty" things — dyeing and painting fabric before it is cut and constructing shoes, accessories, millinery, jewelry, and specialty costumes such as animals, masks, and so forth.

Additional information about the work of the costumer and costume construction can be found in Chapter 19, "Costume Construction."

Costume Crew   The costume crew can be divided into several specialty areas. Depending on the type (professional or educational) and size of the costume operation, these areas may or may not have their own heads, assistant heads, and crew members.

The *cutter/draper* is responsible for actually translating the designer's sketches into reality. He or she devises an appropriate pattern using either draping or flat-patterning methods and, generally, cuts the fabric. This is an extremely important job because not only the shape of the pattern, but also how it is cut from the fabric — how the pattern is placed on the fabric in relation to the **warp and weft** or grain of the fabric — greatly affects the finished appearance of the costume. The *first hand* may also do some cutting from patterns developed by the cutter/draper, but this job is generally to supervise the construction of the costumes. Sewing of the costumes is done by *stitchers* who operate the machines and do the hand sewing that pieces the costumes together. Depending on the size of the production, there may be more than one cutter/draper on the show. If so, their responsibilities are frequently divided along gender lines, with one team (cutter/draper, first hand, stitchers) making the female costumes and another team making the male costumes.

Dyer/painters dye and paint the fabric. They select and mix the dyes to the costume designer's specifications, dye the fabric before it is cut, paint or embellish finished costumes to add dimension, and distress or age costumes to make them look old and worn.

Hats are an important accessory for many period and contemporary costumes. They are frequently made in the costume shop by the *milliner.* Wigs, like hats, are an important part of costuming. The *wigmaster* not only styles and arranges wigs but also makes them.

Although many theatres adapt modern footwear through the use of appliqúes that disguise the period of the footwear being worn, a complete costume shop frequently has the necessary equipment and expertise required to construct period footwear, or it has access to a company that produces this specialized work. The person who does this work is generally referred to as the *costume craftsperson.*

After the show moves into performances, the *wardrobe supervisor* is responsible for all costumes and accessories. Under the wardrobe supervisor's guidance, the costume crew cleans, presses, stores, and organizes the costumes, **dresses** any wigs or hairpieces to create a specific style or look, and makes any necessary

warp and weft: The vertical and horizontal threads in a fabric.

dress: In this context, dress refers to the process of curling, combing, teasing, and/or brushing necessary to maintain the style of a wig or hairpiece.

street makeup: Makeup worn in everyday life.

sound-reinforcement system: The amplification of sound coming from the stage.

wireless microphone: A microphone system that uses a short-range FM radio transmitter and receiver instead of a cable to send the signal from the microphone to the mixer.

costume-related repairs. The costume crew also places all costumes and accessories in their appropriate locations—actors' lockers, quick-change dressing rooms, and so forth—before and during the dress rehearsals and performances. During dress rehearsals and performances, *dressers* may assist the actors in getting into their costumes, quick changes, and so forth.

Makeup Personnel

The person responsible for the design and execution of makeup is the makeup designer. A small crew may be needed to assist the actors in the application of makeup, particularly if prosthetic devices such as three-dimensional pieces or beards and wigs are used.

Makeup Designer   The makeup designer is responsible for the visual appearance of any makeup worn by the actors. The makeup designer works closely with the costume designer to create a look for each actor that will visually support the character. Many times the makeup designer *is* the costumer designer. In the professional theatre actors may actually design their own makeup or work closely with the makeup designer in the creation of a character's makeup.

Makeup Crew   Actors are generally responsible for the application of their own makeup during a production, particularly if the design is basically **street makeup.** That said, if the design is unusual—for example, if it is fantasy-based or if it involves prosthetics or aging, or if some members of the cast are inexperienced in makeup application—a small crew may be needed to assist the actors in the proper execution of the designs.

Sound Personnel

Those who create the sound for a production include the sound designer and the sound crew.

Sound Designer   The sound designer is responsible for the design, recording, equipment setup, and playback of any sound used in the play. The sound designer is also responsible for any **sound reinforcement** used during the production. This would include placing any wired or **wireless microphones** as well as any associated playback equipment. The sound design can vary in complexity from simple recorded music used during intermissions to meticulously designed aural special effects used to underscore the entire production. This dynamic design field is one of the most challenging in theatre; it will be discussed in greater depth in Chapter 21, "Sound Design and Technology."

Sound Crew   Under the supervision of the sound designer, the sound crew does the actual recording, editing, and playback of sound during rehearsals and performances. The sound crew is also responsible for the running of any **sound-reinforcement systems** during the production.

Chapter 2

The Design Process

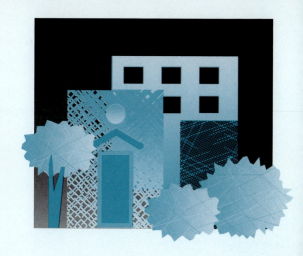

It may come as a rude shock, but design is more a process than an art. It is a series of steps through which we pursue the goal of creating what we hope will be a work of art—a scenic design, costume design, lighting design, or audio design—or the artistry of an efficiently coordinated production. The design process is a method for finding answers to questions. Although the examples and terms used in this chapter will direct your thinking toward theatrical design and production, the principles of the design process can be applied with equally productive results to acting, directing, and, for that matter, life in general. These principles and techniques can help you discover an appropriate and creative solution to virtually any design problem or challenge you may encounter. A problem-solving model for theatrical design and production consists of seven distinct phases: (1) commitment, (2) analysis, (3) research, (4) incubation, (5) selection, (6) implementation, and (7) evaluation.

Unfortunately, the design process isn't a simple, linear progression. As you move from step to step, you must check back on your previous steps to make sure that you are headed in the right direction with your proposed solution. Figure 2.1 shows the back-and-forth movement that occurs as you move through the various stages of the design process. Although Satchel Paige, the wise old pitcher, once advised, "Don't look back; something may be gaining on you," you would do well to look back during your progression through the design process, because the thing gaining on you could be a new thought, a better mousetrap.

A perceptive teacher/designer, Alison Ford, suggests that "perhaps good design is the intersection between the emotional and intellectual realms." While the process being discussed in this chapter is primarily intellectual, it is essential for you to understand that emotions are an equally important part of the design equation. Your emotional reaction to the script and the production concept will intuitively guide your design work on any project. Audience members strongly respond to the emotional content of a production—the story told by the script, the personalities of the characters and their interrelationships, as well as the scenic, costume, lighting, and sound designs. When working through any design process, you need to include your emotional reactions and personal life experiences as part of that process. This will greatly assist you in developing your own design ideas and your personal artistic point of view. Not coincidentally, your work probably will be better for it.

FIGURE 2.1
The design process is not simply a linear progression. As you move through the steps of the design process, you monitor your progress by continually checking back to see where you have been.

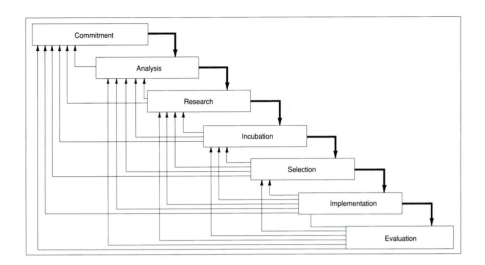

Commitment

Commitment is probably the most important step in the whole design process. If you wholeheartedly *commit* your energies to an assignment, you are promising yourself that you will do the best work you can possibly do.

A simple semantic game may help you commit yourself to an assignment. Use the word *problem* as infrequently as possible—it has a negative connotation—and substitute the word *challenge.* Everybody likes a challenge: The word itself hints at fun, games, and competition. When your problem has been transformed into a challenge, it automatically becomes more interesting and manageable.

Analysis

The analysis step in the design process has two objectives: (1) gathering information that will help clarify and refine the definition of the challenge you are facing and (2) identifying areas that will require further research. Analysis in theatrical production is primarily a search for information and an objective evaluation of the data you discover. Prime sources of this information are the script and other members of the production design team—the producer, director, and your fellow designers. In your discussions with them, you need to examine everything—production style, concepts, budgets, schedules—that is relevant to your design project. "*Who* is producing the play? *What* is the production budget? *Where* is the play being produced? *When* is the design due? *Why* are we doing this play? *How* is the scenery being moved from the shop to the theatre?" The answers to these questions will provide you with information that will further define and clarify your challenge. Each answer should also raise another question or two in your mind. Ask them. This **stream-of-consciousness questioning** can provide you with invaluable information about your challenge.

stream-of-consciousness questioning:
Asking whatever relevant questions pop into your mind in the course of a discussion.

At some point in your information gathering, you will read the script. Some designers prefer to read the script before they talk to other members of the production design team; others wait until later. Either way is fine. There isn't any rule about when you should read the script. Just make sure that you discuss it and share your ideas with the other members of the production design team.

Analyzing the Script

Although it is not at all unusual for designers to read scripts many times, they usually undertake the first three readings of the script with specific objectives in mind. The arbitrarily designated "first three readings" should be considered as a somewhat allegorical reference. Information can be gathered, and emotional or evocative reactions can occur, during any reading. The important point is that there are three related but distinct sets of information that any designer needs to glean from the script.

First Reading   The first time you sit down with the script, read it for fun. Discover the flavor of the play. Learn its general story line, the nature of its characters, their interrelationships, and your emotional response to the play. One of the first things you see when you open the script is the description of the physical environment of the play. Usually written in italics just before the opening lines, it describes the set and, occasionally, the costumes, sound, and lights. Unless you are working from an original script, these descriptions are normally taken from the stage manager's prompt book for the first major professional production of the play and explain the specific designs for that particular production. These descriptions shouldn't be thought of as the correct design solutions for the play; they are just one way that the show can be designed. Your production, along with your audience, is entitled to a fresh design treatment that will be appropriate to its personnel, time, place, and budget. To believe that you have to, or should, copy the original design is an insult to your creative ability. Use the descriptive information in the script along with the other information you gather to synthesize an original design concept.

Second Reading   During the metaphorical second reading of the script, you should be looking for specific moments and incidents within the play that stimulate your imagination and provide you with strong visual and textural images and feelings. These inspirations are random, often disconnected, thoughts, impressions, and emotions about the appearance of the various design elements. Jot them down. If they are more visual than verbal, sketch them. Carry a small notebook or **PDA** with you. Whenever a thought, idea, or emotion about the play pops into your mind, regardless of how inconsequential it seems, put it in your notebook or PDA. These thoughts and emotional responses can be anything relevant to the design challenge. A thought about a character's texture—"He is rough like burlap"—is an idea that should be noted. An impression that the atmosphere of the play is hot, heavy, and sticky is important. Your sense that the play is soft and curved, not sharp and hard, should also be noted.

> As you continue to reread the play, you will get more ideas. Ideas will also appear when you are not reading the script. They can materialize when you are talking to the director, discussing the play with another designer, eating breakfast, or walking to class. Don't judge the ideas at this point. Gather information now, and weed later.

PDA — personal digital assistant: A hand-held computer used for making/keeping notes, schedules, phone numbers, and similar functions.

Third Reading   In the metaphorical third reading, you are looking for specific mechanical information rather than broadly based concepts. For example, set designers look for such things as the number of sets, whether the scene changes are going to happen in front of the audience or behind the curtain, and specific requirements such as a closet door that needs to be hinged on the upstage side. Information that affects the budgets (time and fiscal) should also be noted at this time. Such notes include any special properties, construction, costumes, or effects that will require extra time or money.

The most unified production concepts are developed as a result of talking. In a production of *Cabaret* at the University of Arizona, the production design team began preliminary concept discussions in early January for a production that was to open on April 25.

The director indicated at the first meeting that he wanted to stress the decadence of Berlin society. Our initial informal discussions centered on what this decadence should look like. Someone said that the cabaret should appear to be below ground level (to subliminally support the idea of descending into the hell that was about to engulf Germany). Another person mentioned that it could be useful to have four towers onstage with followspots on top, because the audience might make a connection between them and the guard towers in a concentration

camp. The director said he wanted to have the cabaret audience watching the onstage action (cabaret and noncabaret scenes) at all times. He thought that this device would add an appropriately voyeuristic quality. Ideas just seemed to pop up as we all became more excited about the project.

Within a month, we developed the production concept through our discussions at these once-a-week meetings. We all brought rough sketches, photos, and ideas to every meeting. We discussed everything—acting style, acting areas, color, visual motifs, atmosphere, history. When the deadline for final designs arrived, we all knew what everyone else was thinking and doing.

This example shows what can happen when the production design team, under the leadership and coordination of the

director, works together to evolve the production concept. For a variety of reasons, however, it frequently isn't possible for the director and designers to sit around a table and work together to develop the production concept. When this happens, a good director usually adopts a more authoritarian posture in the development of the production concept. He or she develops a primary production concept and discusses it in individual meetings with the designers. The designers then work toward this concept.

The two methods work equally well. Quality productions can be achieved with either method. The common denominator is communication. A good production concept can evolve only if the director and designers talk to one another and share their ideas, thoughts, and imagination.

Information from the third reading is gathered not only from reading the script but also from conferences with other members of the production design team. As with the first and second readings, all of this information needs to be put in your notebook.

The Questioning Process

Questioning is one of the keys to creativity. Your drive to create is based, to a great extent, on your perceived need for change, or your creative discontent with the status quo. If you are satisfied with everything in your world, you will see no need to change, modify, or create anything.

To analyze effectively, it is necessary to shed fear—fear of criticism, fear of making mistakes, fear of seeming less than brilliant, fear of being thought a fool or somehow different. Fear inhibits thinking and makes us afraid to ask questions. All too frequently I hear students in my classes say, "I don't want to ask a dumb question, but . . ." As far as I am concerned, the only dumb question is one that isn't asked.

Analyze the script, question the director, question the other members of the production design team, and question the producer. Learn what they are thinking, feeling, and planning for the production. Analyze what they say. See how it fits in with your reactions and plans. The more information you receive, the more source material you will have to draw on when you finally begin to design.

Research

As you gather information, you will discover small pockets of knowledge in which your personal experience and background are weak. List them in your

How Did It Look?

A number of references are helpful in any search for visual information. Photo magazines such as *Life* and *National Geographic* contain excellent pictures of costumes, furniture, props, and decoration for plays set in the twentieth century. Department-store catalogs can provide additional visual information for the turn of that century and earlier. Visual information about earlier eras must usually be gleaned from paintings, sculpture, and engravings. Art history books have photographs of these items.

The ultimate use of these visual references is up to the individual designer. Some designers faithfully reproduce a costume or piece of furniture so that they can be sure the "look" they have achieved is authentic for the desired period. Other designers study a variety of sources and then design something new that reflects the general style of the period.

notebook or PDA as the areas in which research is necessary. You will be doing both background research and conceptual research.

Background Research

Designers have to study the historical background of each production they design. This type of research involves searching online and in the library for books, catalogs, paintings, periodicals, and other sources of information about the era.

A great deal of historical research can be accomplished online. For example, if you're designing the scenery for a play set in New York City in the late 1800s, you can conduct a search for interior and exterior photos, paintings, drawings, and so forth that will help you develop a comprehension of the look and feel of the period in that particular locale.

While online research is frequently the fastest way of obtaining information, it may not necessarily be the most detailed. The clarity of online images is sometimes a little fuzzy. Colors can be off a bit. You may be able to get a better feeling for the *detail* of a particular period by spending a few hours in the library browsing through a stack of books looking at pictures and reading the supporting text.

Your research may also involve using primary sources. If you are designing costumes for a period play and you're lucky enough to live near a museum that has a collection of historical clothing of that period, go look at them. See how they were made, think about how you could adapt the line and silhouette of those garments to the needs of your production design. Make both written and visual notes. Sketch details that interest you. Ditto for scenic design. If you live in an area similar to the locale of the environment you're designing, go look at buildings and houses that were constructed during the period of the play. Just look and observe. Again, make notes. Sketch things that interest you.

Your historical research may include reading about previous productions of the play and *might* include looking at photos, sketches, and models of those prior productions. But don't think that you *must* look at any visual references of prior productions. If you choose to look at them, simply use them as references for one way that the play was once produced. Don't fall prey to the temptation to copy someone else's work. That stifles your own creativity and, more pragmatically, is illegal in most states. While you shouldn't copy someone else's work, you should also be sure that you don't try to create something so original that it blinds you to the playwright's intention. Remember, the root of any viable design is based in the script.

> **PRODUCTION INSIGHTS**
> ## Historical Relevance for Design
>
> Although each visual designer (scenic, costume, lighting) must look at visual material relevant to his or her design area, all designers (including sound) should also study the history of the period. As an example, the costume designer needs to know the history and style of dress of the era of the play. This study could begin with a look at a text on costume history to get a general understanding of the style of the time. More detailed study will also be necessary. You can look at paintings, photos, museum displays, catalogs, and any other sources that illustrate the fashion of dress for the period.
>
> An understanding of the socioeconomic background of the play's environment is also useful, because clothing styles are usually a reflection of the morals and economics of the time. Throughout the major periods of fashion, there have been subtle, and sometimes not so subtle, shifts of style based on the socioeconomic status of the individual. Servants have rarely dressed like their employers, and it has usually been fairly easy to differentiate between classes based on the cut and quality of their clothes.
>
> Additional research into the arts (painting, sculpture, literature, music) and history of the playwright's era can provide information on the world that shaped the author's thinking. Essays and critical reviews of the playwright's work are another good source of background information.

Additional background research in the field of color will also be necessary for all designers. A thorough understanding of this extremely important area will enable the designer to match and blend colors in pigment and light. Additionally, by studying the psychology of color, you will be able to design color keys that help the audience understand the primary character motivations and relationships in the play. Color is discussed in Chapter 6.

Conceptual Research

Conceptual research involves devising multiple solutions to specific design challenges. In reading a script, for example, you may discover that the heroine leaves the stage at the end of Act I in a beautiful gown and reappears at the start of Act II with the same dress in tatters. Your conceptual research would be to figure out as many ways as possible to solve this challenge.

A snag frequently encountered during conceptual research is our apparently natural inability to conceive of any more than two or three possible solutions to any given challenge. Too often our brains go numb and refuse to dream up new ideas. In psychology this type of nonthinking state is referred to as a perceptual block. If the perceptual block can be eliminated, our ability to devise, or create, additional solutions to any given problem is greatly improved. In other words, the removal of perceptual blocks increases our personal creative ability.

 ## Incubation

How many times, having left the room after finishing an exam, have you suddenly remembered the answer to a question that eluded you while you were writing the test? How many times have you come up with the solution to a problem after having "slept on it"? In both of these cases, the information necessary to

PRODUCTION INSIGHTS
Unblocking Your Thinking

How can we get rid of our perceptual blocks? By eliminating the cause, we can usually eliminate the block. Proper identification of the real challenge is extremely important. Many times challenges are not what they first seem to be. If a play requires three sets, one of the design challenges would be to devise ways to shift among them. To most of us that would mean finding ways to move the sets. We see sets shifted in this way all the time—it's normal. But couldn't the challenge be solved just as well by putting all three locales on a unit set and shifting the audience's attention by lighting only the part of the set that we want it to see? or by using three separate theatres, each with its own set, and having the audience move? or by having two of the sets hidden behind the upstage wall of the third set and moving sections of the wall to reveal the appropriate set? These additional solutions to the challenge are the result of nothing more than a careful examination of the specific question being posed in the challenge.

Define Your Challenge More Broadly

If you thought about the traditional ways of shifting between sets in the previous problem, you were defining the challenge too closely. By unconsciously limiting your quest for possible solutions to the traditionally accepted methods, you were shutting off a whole realm of new, poten-

tially effective solutions to the challenge. Think creatively about the elements of the challenge, and don't accept only the commonplace answers to the questions posed in the challenge.

Overcome Tunnel Vision

When working on a design it is very easy, and egocentrically convenient, to fall into the trap of not seeing your assignment from the viewpoint of others involved in the challenge. When designing scenery, it is very easy to put a ceiling on the set without worrying about how this is going to affect the lighting design. Similarly, when determining the width of doors to be used on your set, it is easy to forget that the costume designer is planning to use hoop skirts that measure four feet in diameter at the hem.

Tunnel vision can be avoided if members of the production design team discuss their ideas in production meetings. By conferring on a regular basis, the director and designers can remain aware of everyone else's work as it progresses from conception to completion.

Avoid Visual Stereotyping

Visual stereotyping refers to seeing what you expect to see rather than what is actually in front of you. It limits your ability to conceive of existing elements in new combinations. If you expect to see casters attached to the bottom of a stage wagon, it may be difficult for you

to envision turning the casters upside down and attaching them to the stage floor. But that "inverted" thinking may provide an effective solution to the problem of shifting scenery for a complex show when you don't have enough casters to accomplish the task in the more conventional manner.

Remember Details Selectively

People remember things selectively. If we decide that something doesn't have great personal significance, we tend to forget it. To demonstrate this principle try to draw, from memory, a detailed sketch of the front door of your house, apartment, or dorm room. Most people can't do it. We see and use the door several times every day, but most of us never look at it very closely.

All of us remember details that we have determined will be important for us to recall. Albert Einstein was reputed not to have known his own telephone number. When asked why, he reportedly said that he didn't want to clutter up his mind with information he could look up.

Although it is very important for a designer or technician to have a thorough knowledge of the various subjects that make up his or her field of expertise, it is equally important to follow Einstein's dictum and not clutter up your mind with details that can be found fairly easily in a reference work in the library or on the Internet.

answer the questions was locked in your subconscious and only needed time and stress reduction to allow the answer to float into your consciousness.

Incubation provides you with time to let ideas hatch. During this time, you should basically forget about the project. Your subconscious mind will use the time to sort through the information you've gathered in the previous steps and may construct a solution to the challenge or point you in a valid direction.

Give yourself enough time to let your subconscious mind mull over the data that you have absorbed. How much time is enough? That depends on the scope or size of the project and, realistically, the amount of time remaining until the project is due. "Enough time" can be anywhere from a few hours to several days. It simply isn't possible to do your best work if you wait for the deadline and then rush through the assignment. You are more likely to produce quality work if you allow time for incubation.

FIGURE 2.2
Thumbnail sketches for the University of Arizona Department of Drama's production of *Nicholas Nickleby*, scenic design by Tom Benson, directed by Harold Dixon and Dianne Winslow. The first sketch (A) shows a basically symmetrical platform arrangement flowing from the upstage center high point down toward the edges of the proscenium. The set has an elaborate gridwork behind the platforms and a planked wooden floor. (B) The directors and designer made notes and sketches on a copy of the design as they discussed modifications to the set. (C) The stage right platforms were then opened to make the space underneath more usable, and the downstage left staircase was curled further onto the stage, making the set asymmetrical and more dynamic. The background gridwork was also abstracted, and the planked floor was eliminated to make the central floor more visually useful. In the final sketch (D), some of the background gridwork was angled to create a more dynamic line, and the lighting instruments were included as a scenic element.

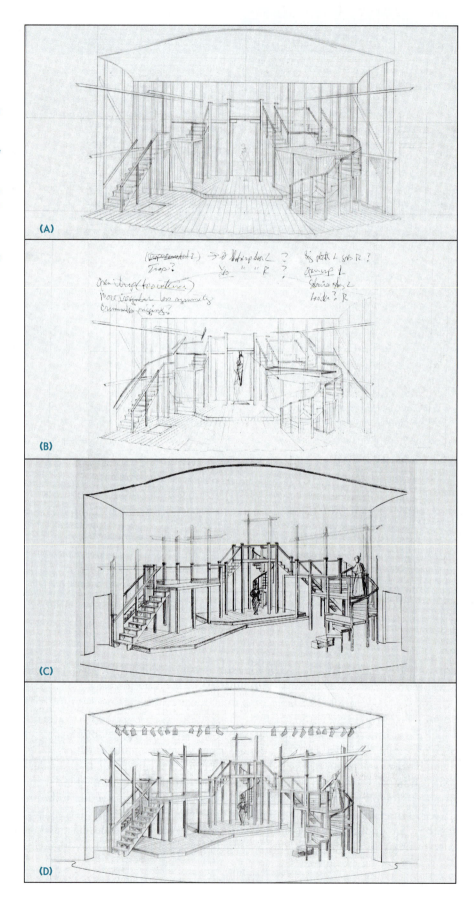

Selection

Selection is the step in the design process in which you sift through all of the data you've accumulated and decide on your specific design concept. Because the choices of each designer affect the work of all members of the production design team, everyone's designs need to be discussed in another production meeting.

The scenic designer draws as many **thumbnail sketches** as necessary to explain the scenic concepts for the production (see Figure 2.2). If the sets for the play are complex or the sketches do not fully explain the concepts, then a **functional model** of each set idea may be constructed. Alternatively, a computer model of the set can be constructed. These virtual models can be viewed from a variety of angles and help to fully communicate the scenic designer's intentions. If there is a lot of scenic movement — wagons sliding on and off stage, set elements rotating, drops flying in or out, and so forth — an animated computer presentation can be used to clearly show their timing and scope.

The scenic designer also provides an indication of the intended color scheme with the thumbnail sketches. This can be done by coloring on them or by accompanying them with color sample cards (paint chips).

The costume designer provides hand- or computer-drawn sketches or pictures of the intended costumes. Although the costume designer attaches fabric swatches to the final costume renderings, these preliminary sketches require only an indication of the color and type of fabric that will be used (see Figure 2.3).

thumbnail sketch: A small, quick, rough drawing, usually done in pencil, that shows the major outline, character, and feeling of the object but does not have much detail.

functional model: A three-dimensional thumbnail sketch of the scenic design; normally built on a scale of ½ or ¼ inch to 1 foot; usually made from illustration board, Bristol board, file folders or similar cardboard; also known as a white model.

FIGURE 2.3

The costume designer uses preliminary pencil sketches as a visual notebook to record ideas that may ultimately find their way into a finished costume design. Preliminary costume designs by Peggy Kellner for *Macbeth*, produced at the Old Globe Theatre, San Diego, California.

FIGURE 2.4
Finished scenic design for *Nicholas Nickleby.* (A) The production model, (B) the ground plan, (C) (on page 32) some construction drawings.

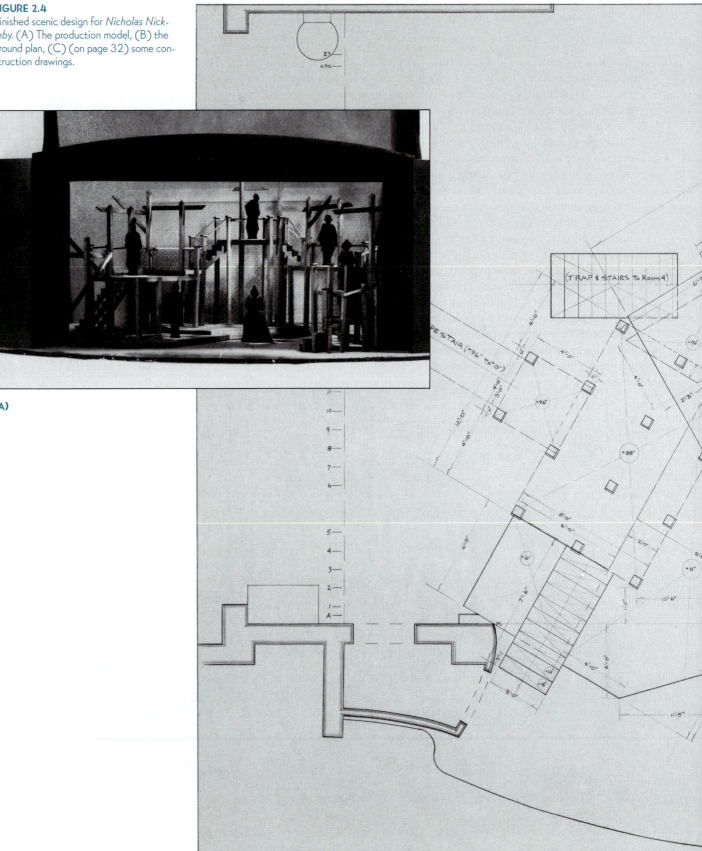

(A)

(B)

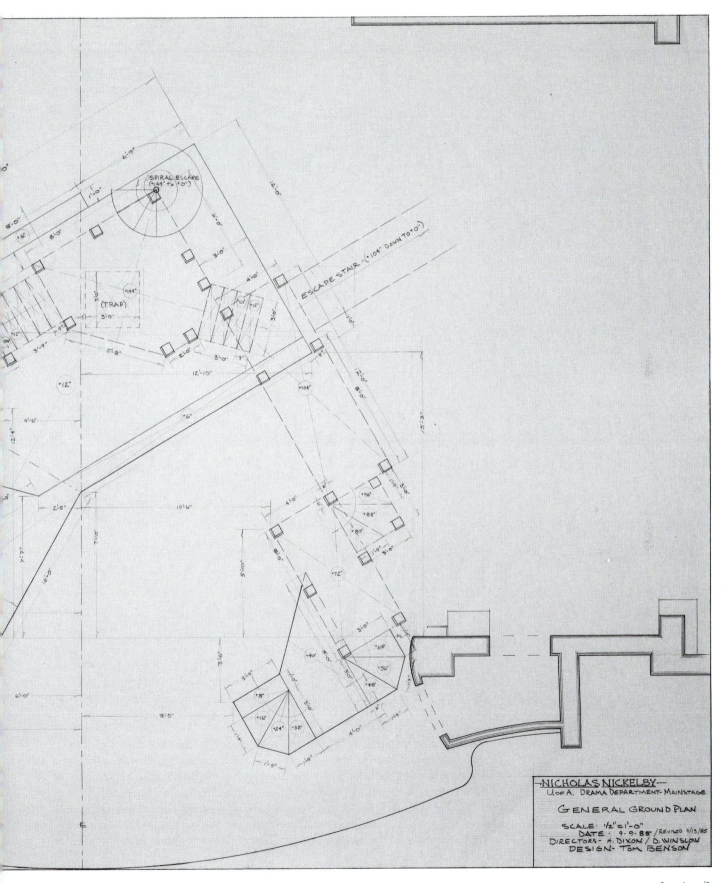

SPIRAL ESCAPE
(+144" TO +0")

(TRAP)

ESCAPE STAIR (+104" DOWN TO +0")

—NICHOLAS NICKELBY—
U. of A. Drama Department· Mainstage

GENERAL GROUND PLAN

SCALE· 1/2"=1'-0"
DATE· 9·9·85 / REVISED 9/13/85
DIRECTORS— H. DIXON / D. WINSLOW
DESIGN· TOM BENSON

(continued)

FIGURE 2.4
(continued)

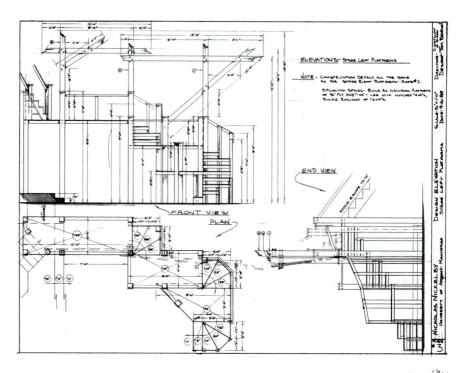

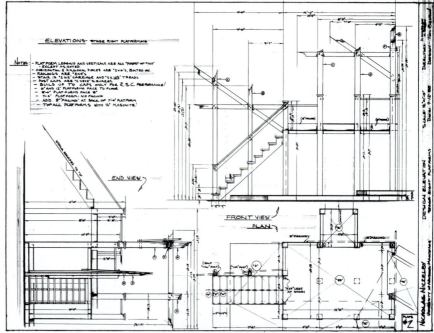

(C)

The lighting designer submits sketches or computer presentations showing the general characteristics of the concept for the lighting design, if such sketches are appropriate. At the least, he or she presents the intended palette and a verbal description of the atmospheric effect of the lighting during the production meeting. The sound designer discusses the sound scoring—the types of background and specific sound and musical effects—as well as the sound reinforcement equipment and the location and function of the various amplifiers, mixers, and speaker setups.

The selection phase of the design process is finished when the director feels satisfied that all design areas support the production design concept.

PRODUCTION INSIGHTS
The Gobo Trick

A lot of art is the result of happy accident. While sitting in the auditorium during technical rehearsals for some forgotten production, I noticed that one area of the stage floor seemed to have a rough texture. I went up on stage and looked more closely. The floor didn't have any texture; it was painted a smooth, flat color. Then I looked up at the lights. One of the instruments had a gobo (a thin metal template that creates a shadow pattern) left in it from a previous produc-

tion. That instrument was creating the texture. Although I took the gobo out of the instrument, I remembered the effect. Now whenever I want to create a textured atmosphere I put gobos in the instruments.

The moral? Always evaluate what you've done, even if you think it's a "mistake." Just because something isn't right for one situation doesn't mean it won't be right for another.

Implementation

The implementation phase begins when you stop planning and start doing. At this time the designers produce all drawings, models, plans, and instructions necessary to construct the scenic, lighting, costume, and sound designs.

The scenic designer makes the final color renderings for each set of the production and, if necessary, constructs **production models** of the sets. He or she also drafts the plans that describe, to scale, all the details of how the set should look (see Figure 2.4, pages 30–32). After completing the paperwork for the design, the scenic designer monitors the progress of the construction of the set(s) and properties to make sure that they are completed according to plan, on time, and within budget.

The lighting designer draws the light plot as well as the other paperwork associated with the lighting design (see Figure 2.5). He or she then supervises the hanging and focusing of the lights and determines the intensity levels and timing for all lighting cues.

The costume designer produces colored renderings for each costume, complete with notes and sketches that fully describe the accessories as well as the general style, period, and feeling of the costume (see Figure 2.6). Fabric samples and trims are attached to each sketch to indicate the various materials to be used. These designs are turned over to the costume shop. The costume designer maintains close contact with the shop to determine that the costumes are being built as planned and will be completed on time and within budget.

The sound designer completes the **sound plot** and begins gathering and recording the various musical and effects cues, as well as assembling the necessary reinforcement, and playback equipment, as well as the speaker systems. During the technical and dress rehearsals, the sound designer determines the appropriate loudness levels for each sound cue and does any necessary rerecording or reediting.

At this time, the technical director completes the production calendar, makes any necessary construction drawings, orders the materials for construction of all sets and props, organizes the crews, and begins construction. During rehearsals the director's view of the production concept will probably change or evolve as the actors become involved. Minor changes should be expected as part of the process of putting a production together. Production meetings during the implementation phase help to ensure that the information keeps flowing.

production model: A scale model, similar to the functional model but fully painted and complete with all furniture and decorative props.

sound plot: A list describing each sound cue in the production.

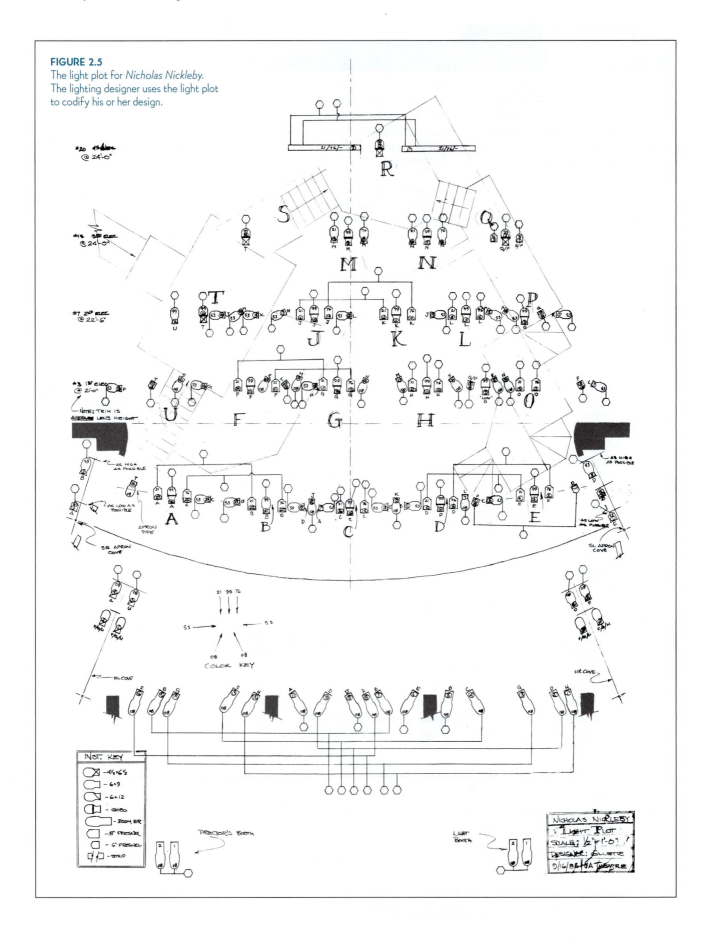

FIGURE 2.5
The light plot for *Nicholas Nickleby*.
The lighting designer uses the light plot
to codify his or her design.

Evaluation

Evaluation takes place within each step of the design process, and it also occurs when the project is completed. This final evaluation, or review, is not so much a back-patting session as an examination of the methods and materials used to reach the final design goal. All designers should evaluate their selections to see if they were appropriate and to determine if they could be used in the future in another context.

All members of the production design team should look objectively at the interchanges and communication process that took place inside and outside the various production conferences to see if they can improve the communication the next time around. The designers should also evaluate the judgments they made to see if anything that might have helped was left out, ignored, or rejected.

As you become more familiar with the design process, you will discover that your own work is more creative and that you can produce it faster and more easily. The design process described here is a valuable, efficient, time-saving, and frustration-reducing tool. Use it and enjoy.

FIGURE 2.6
The costume designer provides annotated colored sketches of the costumes, complete with samples of the fabrics to be used, to the costume shop for construction of the costumes. Costume design for *Two Gentlemen of Verona* by Peggy Kellner, Old Globe Theatre, San Diego, California.

Chapter 3

A Brief History of Theatre Architecture and Stage Technology

"Last night the curtain rose at the . . ." could have begun almost any theatrical critic's review during the 1940s or 1950s. Interestingly, the curtain rises on few productions these days, not for a lack of productions but because two of the three current styles of stage configuration normally don't use a front curtain. Of the three types of theatrical space used in the modern theatre — **proscenium, thrust, and arena** (see Figure 3.1) — only one, the proscenium, traditionally uses a front curtain. Each of these spaces has its own set of design and staging requirements, but they have all evolved from the same common heritage: the theatres of ancient Greece.

 ## Greek Theatre

Our knowledge of Greek or Roman theatres is based almost exclusively on archaeological studies and educated guessing. No one can say with authority that "this is the way it was." My summary offers the same disclaimers.

In practical reality, there was no single style or type of Greek theatre. A number of elements, however, seem to have been common to almost all the ones we know. The typical Greek amphitheatre illustrated in Figure 3.2 is a composite reconstruction based on a number of theatres dating from the fifth century B.C.

The steeply raked seating area for the audience, called the auditorium, or *theatron,* surrounded on three sides the circular playing area, known as the *orchestra.* Immediately in back of the orchestra was the *skene* (skee-nee), or stage house. The front wall of the skene probably had several doors or arches through which actors made their entrances. The exact purpose of the skene isn't known, but since it hid the actors from the audience's view and contained a number of rooms, it is assumed that it served various functions such as housing for stage machinery, storage for props, and possibly space for dressing rooms. The *paraskenia* were long, high walls that extended on either side of and parallel with the skene. It is believed that a low platform, about a foot high, extended across the front of the *paraskenia.* On later Greek theatres, they did not extend directly from the skene but were placed closer to the audience. A natural by-product of this relocation was to extend the low platform across the front of the skene to create a platformed stage. A columned arch, the *proskenium,* was located at the rear of this

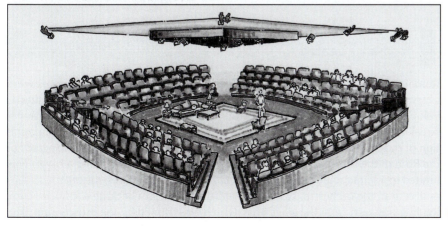

FIGURE 3.1
Examples of (A) proscenium, (B) thrust, and (C) arena theatres.

(A)

(B)

(C)

FIGURE 3.2
A typical Greek theatre.

stage and just in front of the skene. It served to support a porchlike projection from the second story of the skene.

Although most of the scenes in Greek plays were set outdoors, the Greeks used several devices to move or change scenery. The *eccyclema*, a wheeled platform, was apparently used in a variety of ways. If a scene called for a throne, the central doors in the *skene* were opened and the *eccyclema*, with a throne on top, was rolled forward. One of the Greeks' theatrical conventions dictated that violent deaths take place offstage, but the bodies were later revealed onstage. The *eccyclema*, this time piled with corpses, was again rolled onto the stage.

Periaktoi, which probably date from the fourth century B.C., were tall, three-sided forms that rotated on a central pivot. Each side was painted with a different scene. Although their exact use isn't known, they were probably placed in the background, and when a change of scene was desired, the *periaktoi* were rotated to reveal another face.

Possibly the most interesting machine was the *machina*. This was a basket or platform that was lowered to the orchestra level from the second story of the *skene*. Many plays called for intervention by the gods, and the *machina* was used to help the gods descend to, or rise from, the earth.

Pinakes were probably as close as the Greeks came to scenery. They were painted panels similar to modern flats. They were hung from the *skene*, but it is not known whether they were changed for each play or whether they were simply decorative.

 ## Roman Theatre

Roman architects tinkered with Greek designs, but most of their theatres were simply modifications of the basic Greek form. The most conspicuous Roman development was the compression of the three separate parts of the traditional Greek theatre (orchestra, auditorium, and skene) into one structure. The integration of these elements caused some interesting developments in the structure of the Roman theatre, as shown in Figure 3.3. The auditorium (called a *cavea*) was limited to a semicircular configuration. In many of the theatres, the *cavea* was separated from the orchestra by a short wall. The orchestra became a semicircle extending outward from the stage area, which was framed by the proscenium. The

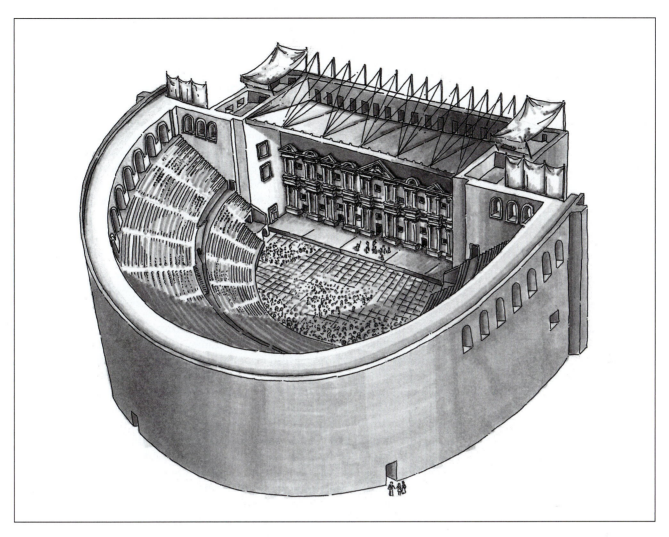

FIGURE 3.3
A typical Roman theatre.

skene was transformed into an elaborately decorated single facade called the *scaenae frons.* Its height generally matched the height of the *cavea.*

A number of subtle changes were also brought about by the development of the consolidated Roman theatre structure. The theatres were usually built on level ground instead of the hillside sites favored by the Greeks. In addition, a roofing system was developed for a number of the theatres. The roof extended from the *scaenae frons* to the edge of the proscenium. Some of the theatres even had an awning, known as a *velum,* covering the entire seating area.

Scenery in the Roman theatre differed little from the Greek. *Periaktoi* were used, but evidence indicates that the three faces were painted with thematic material—tragic, comic, and satiric scenes—rather than representative scenes of various locations. Two types of curtains were introduced by the Romans. The *auleum* was a front curtain that in early Roman theatres was lowered into a slot or trough in the floor and in later theatres was raised above the stage on ropes. The *siparium* was hung at the back of the stage. It provided a background for the action of the play and also concealed the backstage area. Entrances were probably made through slits in the curtain. Nothing is known about what, if anything, was painted on either curtain.

It is known that some Roman amphitheatres, such as the Colosseum, made extensive use of elevators, moving platforms, and trapdoors to raise animals, people, and scenery from the basements underneath the amphitheatre's floor to the arena level. There is also evidence of the use of complex moving scenery such as dancing trees, rocks, and other devices. While there is scant evidence that any of this stage machinery was used in the theatre, it does show that the Romans had developed a highly sophisticated collection of stage machinery that wouldn't be duplicated for at least another thousand years.

With the fall of Rome in A.D. 476 and the subsequent decline of the Roman Empire, these grand theatres, which were also the sites of circuses, gladiatorial fights, and lion feedings (Christians and slaves being the primary food), were essentially abandoned, silent relics of a lost era. For approximately five hundred years after the empire fell, the formal theatre was virtually dead. Yet the theatrical tradition was kept alive by bands of traveling entertainers, primarily actors and jugglers. These vagabonds surreptitiously performed wherever they could find an audience—in courtyards, village squares, and other temporary stage locations.

Medieval Theatre

During the Middle Ages, the suppression of theatrical activities was a direct result of the church's opposition to secular drama. Yet the same church that denied the sacraments to actors was also responsible for the revival of the theatre. Sometime during the tenth century, clerics began to use dramatized scenes to help convey their lessons and church doctrine to congregations. During the thirteenth century, many of these interludes became too complex to be staged inside the churches, so they were moved outdoors. Staging techniques naturally varied from church to church and location to location. Platform stages were generally constructed adjacent to the church, and the audience stood in the town square (see Figure 3.4). In some cases, the platforms were mounted on wagons, appropriately called *pageant wagons* (Figure 3.5), which were pulled from town to town to perform the plays.

All of these productions shared some common characteristics. The sets were identical, in concept if not detail, and followed the conventions that had been developed by the clergy for the church productions. The sets were composed of

FIGURE 3.4
A platform stage.

FIGURE 3.5
A pageant wagon.

small buildings called *mansions,* or stations, that depicted locations appropriate to the biblical stories dramatized in the productions (see Figure 3.6).

The mansions for heaven and hell were on opposite ends of the stage, with the other mansions sandwiched between them. There was a common playing area, called a *platea,* located in front of the mansions, where most of the play's action took place.

One interesting by-product of the medieval theatre was the development of a large number of relatively realistic special effects. Stage machinery, fittingly called *secrets,* included trapdoors and a wide variety of rigging that was used to move people and objects about the stages. In one account of "a play staged at Mons [a city in southwestern Belgium] in 1501, technicians were hired to construct the secrets, and seventeen people were needed to operate the hell machinery alone; five men were paid to paint the scenery, and four actor-prompters were employed both to act and to help with the staging."[1]

[1] Oscar G. Brockett, *The Theatre: An Introduction,* 4th ed. (New York: Holt, Rinehart and Winston, 1979), p. 106.

FIGURE 3.6
A typical medieval mansion stage.

forced perspective: A visual-distortion technique that increases the apparent depth of an object.

raked stage: A stage floor that is higher at the back than the front.

stock set: Scenery designed to visually support a generalized location (garden, city street, palace, interior) rather than a specific one; commonly used from the Renaissance through the early twentieth century and still in use today in some theatres.

drop: A large expanse of cloth, usually muslin or canvas, on which something (a landscape, sky, street, room) is painted.

1500–1650

With the Renaissance, the theatre became a central part of the cultural reawakening that quickly spread throughout Europe. Although church-sanctioned pageants continued, secular drama reemerged and became the dominant theatrical form. Theatres, which hadn't been permitted or constructed for over a thousand years, sprang up all over Europe. Because of the strong interest in classical forms and structures, the basic shape of almost all these theatres corresponded with the description of Greek and Roman theatres contained in the architectural writings of Vitruvius. Although the theatres were patterned after the classical forms, their designers made many interesting, and clever, adaptations.

The Teatro Olympico in Vicenza, Italy, was one of these theatres (see Figure 3.7). Built between 1580 and 1585, it was designed in the style of the ancient Roman theatres. Probably the most significant change was that the theatre finally moved indoors, with the entire structure enclosed in a building. The *cavea*, or auditorium, was designed not as an exact semicircle but as an ellipse, and this minor change dramatically improved the sight lines in the theatre. The *scaenae frons* was no longer a single decorated wall but was broken by several arches; elaborate permanent sets of street scenes were built, in **forced perspective,** on a **raked stage** floor in back of the arches. In many Renaissance theatres, the stage floors were raked to improve the visual effects of the scenery. The actors normally performed on a flat playing space in front of the raked stage.

A second minor Renaissance innovation in southern Europe was the introduction of elaborately painted, forced perspective, scenery. The use of **stock sets**—usually painted **drops** of the "comic scene," the "tragic scene," the "satyric scene," and so on—necessitated the evolution of the proscenium, or picture frame, stage. Drops, which greatly enhanced the feeling of depth created by the painted perspective, were usually hung at the upstage edge of the stage.

At this time, and the next several hundred years, stages were lit like any other indoor location—with varying arrangements of candles, lanterns, and torches. The first recorded use of a stage lighting effect occurred during the Re-

FIGURE 3.7
The Teatro Olympico.

naissance. In a treatise written in 1545, Sebastiano Serlio recommended "placing candles and torches behind flasks with amber- and blue-colored water."[2]

At approximately the same time, drama in England was being produced in a different type of structure. A number of theatres had been constructed just outside London by 1600. Probably the most famous was the Globe (1599–1632), the home theatre of William Shakespeare (see Figure 3.8). Although these theatres differed in detail, their basic shape was similar.

The stage of a typical Elizabethan theatre was a large, open-air platform generally raised from 4 to 6 feet off the ground (see Figure 3.9). The platform was surrounded by a yard, or *pit*, which served as the space for the lower-class audience—the groundlings—to stand. At the upstage end of the stage platform was the area that formed the *inner below*. There is some dispute about the shape of this structure. One theory maintains that it was a curtained alcove recessed into the upstage wall. Another hypothesis holds that it was a roofed structure, curtained on three sides, that projected a little way onto the stage platform. A final theory contends that there was no inner below at all. Depending on the theory to which you subscribe, the *inner above* was an area above the inner below on the back wall, or the acting area provided by the roof of the structure that projected onto the stage, or an area that didn't exist as a playing space. In any case, separate entrances apparently flanked either side of the inner below to provide access to the stage.

[2] "Stage Design." *Encyclopaedia Britannica.* 2003 (http://www.Britannica.com/eb/article?eu= 118829).

FIGURE 3.8
The Globe Theatre.

The stage, the pit, and the wall behind the stage were surrounded by the out-side of the building, a three-story structure that housed the galleries and private boxes for the wealthier patrons and nobles.

Little scenery seems to have been associated with Elizabethan productions, although contemporary records do indicate that a number of props—rocks, trees, and the like—were associated with the theatres.

In France staging conventions had changed little since medieval times. Man-sions were still in common use. Multiple mansions, each representing a specific location, were normally onstage simultaneously. If a play required additional lo-cations, painted coverings were removed from one or more of the mansions, or curtains were opened, to reveal the new locations. Perspective painting and other

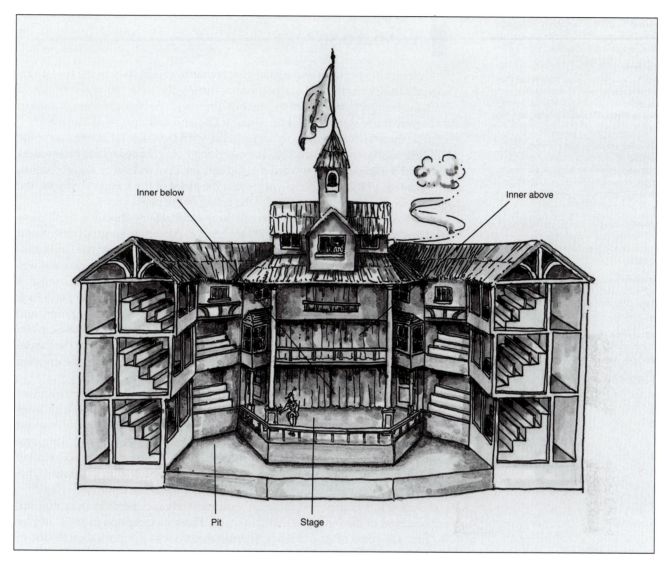

Inner below

Inner above

Pit

Stage

FIGURE 3.9
The stage of the Globe Theatre.

elements of the creative awakening that was developed in Italy began to be used in France toward the end of this period.

Stage machinery in Europe also had not evolved much since the 1300s. There are accounts of effects used for flying gods and other supernatural beings above the stage as well as boats with passengers moving across the stage. There are numerous indications that effects—smoke, fire, clouds, and sound—were in fairly common use. These effects had all been in existence for several hundred years. There wouldn't be any significantly new developments in stage machinery in Europe until the late nineteenth century.

Up until this time the primary challenge of lighting stages, and any indoor spaces, was simply providing enough light so people could see. Early efforts usually involved suspending candle-lit chandeliers over both the stage and auditorium. It took considerable effort to make the stage bright enough so the audience could easily see the actors. In the early 1600s reflectors began to be used to intensify the rather meager light output of both candles and oil lamps. About the same time footlights using candles and oil lamps began to be placed along the front edge of the stages. To provide additional light, vertical rows of lamps frequently were hidden behind the **wings** on either side of the stage.

wings: In scenic terms, either tall, cloth-covered frames or narrow, unframed drops placed on either side of the stage, parallel with the proscenium arch, to prevent the audience from seeing backstage; were usually painted to match the scene on the upstage drop.

apron: The flat extension of the stage floor that projects from the proscenium arch toward the audience.

borders: Wide, short, framed or unframed cloth drops suspended to prevent the audience from seeing above the stage; normally match the decorative treatment of the wings and drops in wing and drop sets.

elevator trap: A small elevator used to shift small pieces of scenery, or an actor, from the basement underneath the stage to the stage or vice versa. Usually no larger than 4 × 4 or 4 × 6 feet. Also known as a disappearance trap.

elevator stage: A large elevator used to shift large scenic elements or whole sets between the area beneath the stage and the stage.

revolving stage: A large, circular disk that pivots on its central axis. Built into the stage floor as part of the theatre's permanent equipment.

concentric revolving stages: A revolving stage with, usually, two sections, one rotating inside the other.

1650–1900

The interest in spectacle and visual effects that began in Italy in the mid-1500s moved rapidly northward across Europe during the next 100 years. By about 1660, the architectural style of theatre buildings and the types of scenery used in them were fairly standardized throughout England and the rest of Europe.

The theatres were primarily rectangular, with the stage set at one end of the building, as shown in Figure 3.10. The raked stage was framed by the proscenium arch, and the **apron** thrust toward the auditorium. Like its historical antecedents, the forestage of the Elizabethan stage and the *platea* of the medieval theatre, the apron was the site of the majority of the action of the play.

Although the scenery had become more elaborate by this time, with more locations depicted, it still followed the tradition of providing a visual background for the play rather than an environment in which the action of the play could happen. It was painted in perspective on movable drops, wings, and **borders** and was placed on the raked stage, where the inclined floor greatly added to the sense of depth created by the perspective painting of the scenery. Most of the plays took place in a generalized location (drawing room, courtyard, palace, garden, and so on), so each theatre owned stock sets that depicted these various scenes. When the action of the play took place in a library, the library set was used. If the theatre didn't happen to have a library set, another stock interior set, such as the drawing room, was substituted.

The auditoriums of these theatres also followed a traditional arrangement (see Figure 3.11): multitiered boxes (for dignitaries and other notables), galleries (for those who could afford the extra charge), and the pit (for those who wanted to see the play but couldn't afford, or weren't permitted, a better seat). This style of proscenium theatre was essentially modern. Some theatres continued to install raked stages, but more and more new structures were built with flat stages. Theatres were constructed in this style until the late nineteenth century.

During this time period the most significant advancements in stage machinery occurred in the Japanese Kabuki theatre. From its inception in 1603, and for the first 125 years of its existence, Kabuki theatre was performed outdoors. In 1724 the government gave permission for Kabuki troupes to build indoor roofed theatres. Shortly thereafter, highly sophisticated stage machinery began being developed. In 1736 **elevator traps** were introduced. This was followed less than twenty years later (1753) by **elevator stages.** Within five years (1758) Kabuki theatres began using **revolving stages** to shift scenery. The stage machinery became even more complex with the introduction of **concentric revolving stages** in 1827.[3]

There were no significant developments in stage lighting between 1630 and approximately the 1780s. Candles and oil lamps continued as the primary illumination source, and they were placed in locations—footlights, wings, overhead chandeliers—where they could get the most light on the stage. With the exceptions of the chandeliers, the sources were normally hidden from the audience's view. In 1783 a new lamp—the Argang oil lamp, was introduced. It had a cylindrical wick enclosed in a glass chimney that produced a brighter, whiter, and cleaner light than its floating wick predecessors.

In 1792 a Scottish engineer, William Murdock, developed a practical method of distilling gas from coal. This was the genesis of gas lighting. Gas lighting was a significant advancement over oil lamps and candles. It was much brighter and cleaner burning; and, of significant import to theatre practitioners, the intensity of

---

[3] Oscar G. Brockett, *History of the Theatre*, 6th ed. (Boston: Allyn and Bacon, 1991), p. 269.

gaslight was easily controlled. Within a relatively short period of time theatres throughout Europe and North America were equipped with gaslight. Distribution of gas throughout the stage and auditorium was accomplished with a maze of pipes and tubing. The gas panel or gas table, a centralized system of valves used to control the intensity of the various onstage gas lamps, was, in effect, the first light board. The group master control systems described in Chapter 16, "Lighting Production," are identical with the control methods utilized on these gas tables or panels. This flexible distribution system was a quantum leap in lighting control. Prior to its development, intensity control had primarily been accomplished by snuffing and relighting candles or lamps. Experiments with various mechanical systems that could control intensity and effect color changes by raising and lowering colored glass cylinders over the oil-lamp flames had not been particularly successful. Although gaslight offered a vast improvement over oil lamps, it was not without its challenges. Even when the flame was enclosed within a glass chimney, the open flame still posed a significant fire hazard. Additionally, gas lamps created a not insignificant amount of heat and unpleasant odors.

Thomas Drummond, a British engineer, invented limelight in 1816. Limelight is created when a sharp jet of flame is focused against a block of limestone. As the limestone incandesces, it produces a light that is both very bright and relatively soft. When coupled with a mirrored reflector, the limelight produced a relatively cohesive beam of light that was intense enough to reach the stage from the

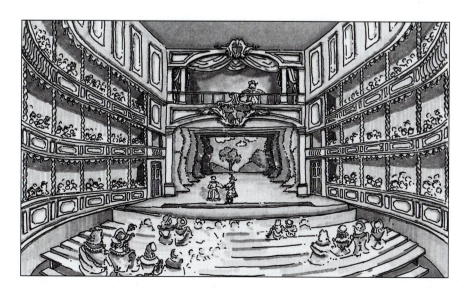

FIGURE 3.10
A typical Restoration theatre.

auditorium and still be significantly brighter than the other areas of the stage.
Thus was born the first followspot.

The first electric light used in the theatre was the carbon arc. This light, produced when electricity arcs between two electrodes, is extremely white and
bright. By 1860 the Paris Opera had developed a projector, a followspot, and several effects utilizing the carbon arc.

Thomas Edison's development of a practical incandescent lamp in 1879 and
the rapid electrification of Europe and North America were the next great advances in theatrical lighting. By 1900 almost all theatres throughout Europe and
North America had converted to electricity. Interestingly, the conversion to electricity did not immediately spawn any significantly new methods or techniques
of stage lighting. Stages continued to be lit as they had with gaslight. Conventional footlights, **borderlights,** and **winglights** were simply electrified. Intensity was
controlled with resistance dimmers utilizing the group master control methods
developed and refined with gas lighting control tables. Resistance dimmers continued to be the standard theatrical dimmer until the late 1940s.

 ## Twentieth Century

A revolution in the style of theatre began in the late 1800s and continued into the
early twentieth century. The work of a number of theatre artists was taking a de-
cidedly different turn from the declamatory style of earlier theatre. The new theatre was devoted to a more realistic and naturalistic type of drama and stressed
the previously unheard-of concepts of unity of style for all elements of the production. The Théâtre Libre, founded by André Antoine in Paris, and the Moscow
Art Theatre, founded by Konstantin Stanislavski and Vladimir Nemerovich-
Danchenko, were but two of the leading groups in this movement toward a more
naturalistic and unified style.

As the productions became more realistic, it was natural for the shape of the
theatres to change to support this new form. The new plays required that the settings become environments for the action of the drama rather than backgrounds.
Consequently, as the action of the play moved onto the stage from the apron, the

borderlights: Any lights hung above the
stage, behind the borders (horizontal masking pieces). In this context the borderlights
were striplights—long, narrow, troughlike
fixtures usually containing eight to twelve
individual lamps.

winglights: Lights hung on either side of
the stage, usually concealed by wings
(vertical masking pieces). In this context
the winglights were striplights—long,
narrow, troughlike fixtures usually containing eight to twelve individual lamps.

PRODUCTION INSIGHTS

From the Boxes to the Pits

Throughout history the various shapes of theatre have been determined, to a large extent, by the mores of the sponsoring society. In ancient Greece, everyone (except the slaves) was considered of equal rank, so the seating was similarly democratic and unsegregated. In the southern Renaissance and in Europe for the ensuing 200 years, the majority of theatres were built by the aristocracy for their own amusement. The visual illusions of forced-perspective scenery were best seen from a single point in the center of the auditorium. This ideal location, subsequently known as "the Duke's seat," was usually found in the second-level box at the back of the auditorium.

The theatres of Elizabethan England, such as the Globe, also had elevated boxes surrounding the stage. The aristocracy, and those others who could afford the higher ticket prices, sat in the boxes. The common people stood in the pit. About the time of the French Revolution, seats began to appear in the pit throughout European theatres as the various societies became more democratic.

depth of the apron shrank. When this happened, it became difficult to see all of the action from the boxes and gallery seats adjacent to the proscenium, so the shape of the auditorium began to evolve. The side seats were eliminated, and the remaining seats faced the stage.

Everything speeded up in the twentieth century. Almost as quickly as the realistic movement became the dominant mode of theatre, splinter groups broke off from it to create a number of antirealistic movements. These movements rose, fell, and evolved so rapidly that most of them didn't have a chance to develop distinctive types of theatre structures. Actually, most of these movements didn't need to change the basic shape of the proscenium theatre or its machinery, because the existing theatres provided a workable environment for their divergent styles.

In the United States, the Little Theatre movement of the 1920s and 1930s was an effort to establish quality productions outside of New York City. It also gave new playwrights a chance to improve their craft and have their works produced in an environment that was less critical than the supercharged atmosphere of Broadway. This movement continued and expanded throughout the country. Its crowning glory has been the establishment of a number of excellent contemporary regional professional theatre companies in such cities as San Francisco, Dallas, Denver, Hartford, Washington, San Diego, Minneapolis, Tucson, and Sarasota.

A ripple effect of the Little Theatre movement was that fledgling companies, funded more by inspiration and lofty intentions than money, began to produce theatre in "found" spaces. Existing barns; churches; feed stores; grocery stores; libraries; old movie houses; and other large, relatively open buildings were all candidates for takeover. Many of these groups relished the enforced intimacy between the actors and audience that shoehorning theatres into these cramped spaces provided. Whether by accident or design, many of these converted theatre spaces didn't have the room to erect a proscenium stage and auditorium. For whatever reasons, thrust and arena stages sprang up all over the country.

The form and structure of the physical theatre have gone through a great many developments. Any number of people have attempted to "improve" the spatial relationship between the stage and auditorium. It is doubtful, however, that anyone will ever devise any genuinely new developments in this relationship, simply because the theatrical experience is based on the premise that the actors need a space in which to perform and the audience must be in a position to see and hear them. When the form of the physical theatre is thought of in this context, it becomes apparent that there are no different types of theatre, only variations on a basic theme.

Like everything else, theatrical lighting began a rapid evolution in the early twentieth century that has continued unabated since that time.

Initially, the conversion from gas to incandescent lamps simply involved refitting extant gas fixtures for electricity. The first major technological development in stage lighting of the twentieth century resulted from refinements to the incandescent lamp that significantly increased the lamps' brightness and longevity. These improvements led to the development of incandescent spotlights, and steady progress in spotlight design continued throughout the twentieth century. Initial designs, such as the plano-convex spotlight, were a vast improvement over gaslight and electric arc technologies. Within a few decades the more efficient Fresnel and ellipsoidal reflector spotlights had largely replaced the plano-convex instruments. The tungsten-halogen (T-H) lamp was introduced in the early 1960s. It produced a whiter light, and its rated lamp life was minimally ten to twenty times longer than that of its predecessor. In the 1970s borosilicate lenses, which produced a much whiter light and were less susceptible to heat fracture than their Pyrex predecessors, became the industry standard.

The first electronic dimmer was the thyratron tube dimmer, developed by George Izenour in the late 1940s. For the first time the dimmers could be controlled from a remote location. Electronic control allowed development of the preset control system. Preset control was to remain the dominant method of dimmer control until it was supplanted by digital control in the 1980s. The principles of preset, as well as other control techniques, will be discussed in Chapter 16, "Lighting Production."

Sound effects had been a central part of theatre production since the Greeks. Until the development of electrically powered record players and amplified sound in the 1930s, any music used in the theatre was played live. Sound effects were also produced live, utilizing a fascinating array of mechanical devices, many of which had changed little in design or effect in, literally, centuries. The development of the tape recorder in the late 1940s ushered in the beginning of a period of experimentation and development in theatre sound that continues unabated. High fidelity sound—recorded sound that mimics the full range of human hearing—became commercially available in the early 1950s. Stereo sound followed almost immediately. High fidelity, stereo, tape-recorded sound had become the standard in effects sound in the theatre by the early 1960s. It continued to be the dominant technology until the introduction of a variety of digital storage, replay, and recording devices began in the early 1980s.

Since computers and digital technology were introduced to the world of technical theatre in the early 1980s, there has been a literal explosion of new developments in all areas of theatre technology. Specific uses of these new technologies will be explored in many of the chapters that follow.

Chapter 4

The Stage and Its Equipment

Theatrical performing spaces have undergone an interesting evolution since about 1960. Influenced by a number of experimental theatre movements as well as economic pressure to make theatres usable for dance groups, symphony concerts, and esoterica such as car, home, and boat shows, companies are changing the shapes of theatres and playing spaces.

Probably the most dominant trend in this evolution is the reduction of the physical and psychological barriers that separate the audience from the production. The New York production of *Cats* was indicative of this change. The set, a stylized representation of an incredibly cluttered junkyard, did not just sedately sit behind the proscenium arch. It negated the concept of the **picture frame stage** by placing elements of the set not only on the stage and apron but also in and on the **orchestra pit,** up the walls of the auditorium, around the balcony rail, and up into the ceiling of the auditorium (see Figure 4.1). The actors made entrances through the house, touched members of the audience, and talked directly to them. This exciting style of theatre doesn't let the audience simply sit and observe but directly involves them in the production.

Innovative productions like *Cats* have been happening with increasing regularity throughout the country, and the theatre spaces being designed today are reflecting these production trends. Although an ingenious production concept and large budget can radically alter the appearance of almost any stage-auditorium relationship, it is still true that three primary stage configurations—*proscenium, thrust,* and *arena*—dominate the world of theatre.

 ## Proscenium Stage

As we have seen, the proscenium stage is also known as the picture frame stage, because the spectators observe the action of the play through the frame of the proscenium arch (Figure 4.2). Although there is debate among theatre artists regarding the appropriateness of using what some describe as an aloof stage that forcefully separates the audience from the action, the fact remains that the proscenium stage and its machinery have, for more than 300 years, been the dominant mode of presentation. The reason is simple: Designs that work needn't be tinkered with.

Proscenium Arch

The proscenium arch, which gives this type of stage its name, is a direct descendant of the *proskenium* and *skene* of the Greek theatres (see Figure 4.3). This arch,

picture frame stage: A configuration in which the spectators watch the action of the play through a rectangular opening; synonym for proscenium-arch stage.

orchestra pit: The space between the stage and the auditorium, usually below stage level, that holds the orchestra.

51

FIGURE 4.1
Cats, New York production, produced by Cameron Mackintosh, The Really Useful Company Limited, David Geffen, and the Shubert Organization. Photo by Martha Swope.

FIGURE 4.2
Proscenium stage, Gammage Auditorium, Arizona State University, Tempe.

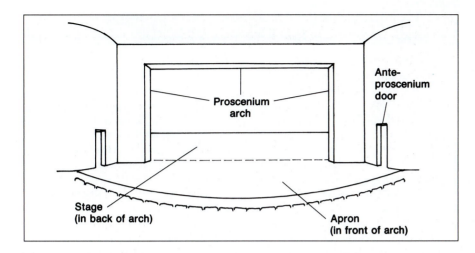

FIGURE 4.3
The parts of a proscenium stage.

which separates the stage from the auditorium, can vary in both height and width. The average theatre (with 300 to 500 seats) has a proscenium arch that is 18 to 22 feet high and 36 to 40 feet wide.

Stage

The playing area behind, or upstage, of the proscenium arch is referred to as the stage (see Figure 4.4). A stage floor is a working surface that serves a number of diverse functions. For the actors, it must provide a firm, resilient, nonskid (but not too sticky) surface that facilitates movement. For scenic purposes, a stage floor needs to be paintable. It should also be reasonably resistant to splintering and gouging caused by heavy stage wagons and other scenic pieces, and it should slightly muffle the sound of footfalls and shifting scenery.

Although many directors choose to move the action of their productions forward onto the apron to bring the play closer to the audience, the primary playing area for many proscenium productions is behind the proscenium arch.

Wings

The spaces on either side of the stage are called the wings. Wings are primarily used for storage. During a multiscene production, all sorts of scenic elements, props, and other equipment are stored in the wings until needed on stage.

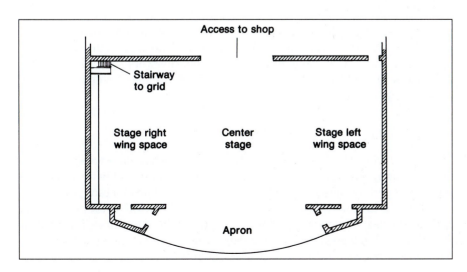

FIGURE 4.4
The proscenium stage and wings.

PRODUCTION INSIGHTS

Stage Directions

It can be frustrating trying to tell an actor what direction to move or telling a technician that "I want the sofa a little further to the left." "My left?" he asks. "No, that way. Over there." Through the years, a system of stage directions has evolved to help clear up these problems.

On the American proscenium and thrust stages, stage directions are understood to mean that you are standing on the stage and looking into the auditorium. Stage left is to your left and stage right is to your right. Upstage is behind you, and downstage is in front of you. The terms *upstage* and *downstage* probably evolved in the sixteenth or seventeenth century

during the era of raked stages, when you literally moved up the slope of the stage when moving upstage.

Stage directions in Europe are noted in a slightly different manner. Upstage and downstage are the same, but right and left are reversed from the American system, being given in reference to the auditorium rather than the stage.

Stage directions for arena stages cannot use this system, since the audience surrounds the stage. When this happens, it is much easier to describe the stage directions by referring to one direction as north, and then remaining directions are understood to be south, east, and west.

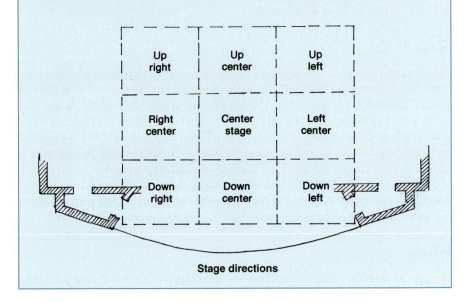

Stage directions

Apron

The apron, or forestage, is an extension of the stage from the proscenium arch toward the audience. It stretches across the proscenium arch to the walls of the auditorium and can vary in depth from a narrow sliver only 3 or 4 feet deep to as much as 10 or 15 feet. It generally extends for 5 to 15 feet beyond either side of the proscenium arch.

Orchestra Pit

Many proscenium theatres have an orchestra pit, which is almost always placed between the apron and the audience. It is used to hold the pit band, or orchestra, during performances that need live music. To hold an orchestra, the pit obviously needs to be fairly large. Most pits extend the full width of the proscenium, and their upstage-to-downstage dimensions are roughly 8 to 12 feet. The depth of the pit varies, but a good pit is deep enough so that the orchestra won't interfere with the spectators' view of the stage (see Figure 4.5).

FIGURE 4.5
The orchestra pit usually occupies part of the apron.

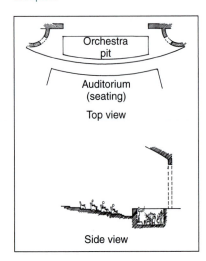

PRODUCTION INSIGHTS
Stage Floors

A good stage floor is actually composed of several layers. The subfloor should be made of soft wood such as pine or plywood. These materials are resilient and tough and will hold nails and other fasteners. Traditionally, a heavy, canvas groundcloth covered the subfloor. But a groundcloth can wrinkle or tear when heavy scenery is moved over it, can be painted only a few times before it starts to deteriorate, and is lousy for tap dancing. Quarter-inch tempered Masonite has all of the qualities needed for a good stage floor surface. It has the added advantage of being fairly inexpensive, and individual sections of the floor can be replaced as needed. The one drawback to this fiberboard floor is that it has a tendency to warp when first painted. This problem can be significantly reduced if the sheets are painted *on both sides* before being nailed to the subfloor. (Stand the fiberboard on edge, and paint both sides simultaneously.)

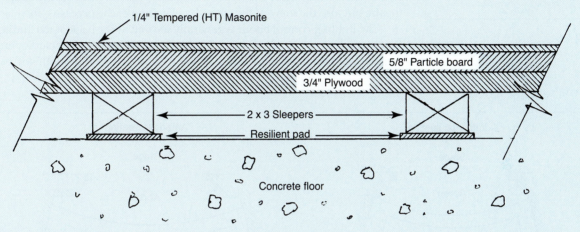

1/4" Tempered (HT) Masonite

5/8" Particle board

3/4" Plywood

2 x 3 Sleepers

Resilient pad

Concrete floor

Detail of a typical stage floor. The 2 × 3 sleepers are on 16-inch centers. Sleepers and sleeper pads are not attached to the concrete slab. Floor detail courtesy of Landry & Bogen, Theatre Consultants.

Obviously, the size of the orchestra pit imposes a formidable gulf between the audience and stage when it is not in use. Various solutions have been adopted to remedy this situation. In some theatres, the orchestra pit is hidden beneath removable floor panels under the apron; when the pit is needed for a production, the floor panels are removed. In other theatres, the pit is placed beneath the auditorium floor. When not in use it is covered with removable panels, and auditorium seats are placed on top. This method has the obvious advantage that additional tickets can be sold when the pit isn't being used.

In some theatres, the entire forestage area (apron, orchestra pit, front of the auditorium) is composed of one or more hydraulic lifts. With their great lifting power, it is possible to raise or lower whole sections of the stage. When more than one lift is used, they are able to shape the forestage into a variety of configurations, as shown in Figure 4.6.

Bally's Hotel in Las Vegas has created what may be the ultimate answer to the orchestra pit: There isn't any. In the Jubilee Room (a 2,500-seat theatre), the orchestra plays in a room in the basement of the theatre complex while watching the production on closed-circuit television. Each section of the orchestra is **miked,** and the sound is **mixed** and **balanced** with that of the singers before it is amplified and sent into the auditorium. Although this solution works well in the high-tech atmosphere of Las Vegas, it is doubtful that every musical director would feel comfortable working in this remote and disconnected manner.

mike: To place one or more microphones in proximity to a sound source (instrument, voice).

mix: To blend the electronic signals created by several sound sources.

balance: To adjust the loudness levels of individual signals while mixing, to achieve an appropriate blend.

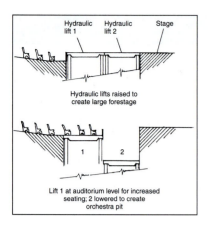

FIGURE 4.6
Hydraulic lifts can provide a variety of interesting auditorium/stage arrangements.

Auditorium

The shape of the typical proscenium theatre auditorium, or house, is roughly rectangular, with the proscenium arch located on one of the narrow ends of the rectangle (see Figure 4.7). Normally, each seat is approximately perpendicular to the proscenium arch. To reduce the reflection of sound waves in an auditorium, none of its finished surfaces (walls, ceiling, floor) should be parallel with any others. Thus, the side walls of most auditoriums angle out from the proscenium arch in the shape of a slightly opened fan. The rear wall of the auditorium is usually curved, and the ceiling generally slopes toward the rear of the house.

The floor of the auditorium is raked, or inclined, from the stage to the rear of the house. Angling of the house floor improves not only the acoustics of the theatre but also the view of the stage, by elevating each successive row.

The lighting control booth is generally located at the back of the auditorium. It normally has one or more large windows to provide the light-board operator(s) with an unobstructed view of the stage. Although a sound booth with a large

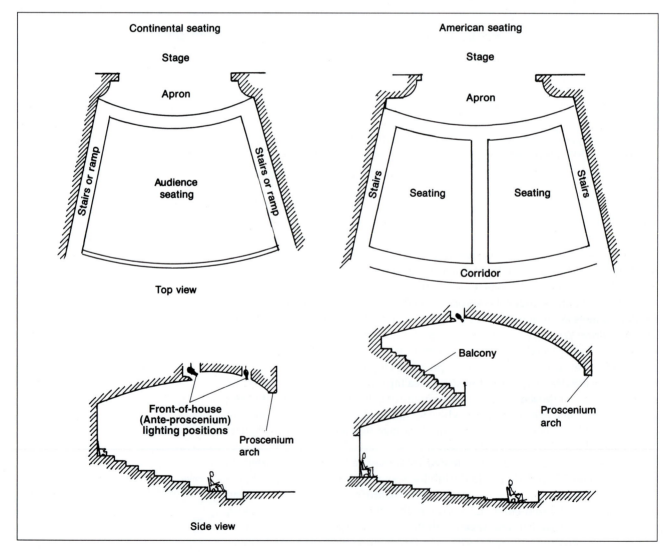

FIGURE 4.7
Types of seating configurations.

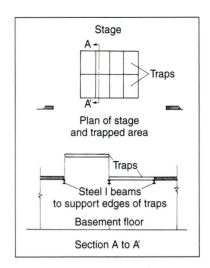

FIGURE 4.8
Stage traps provide access to the area beneath the stage.

window (which can be opened) is usually located in a similar back-of-house location, the sound operator frequently runs the **sound mixer** from a position in the auditorium so that he or she can hear what the audience is hearing and balance all the sound sources accordingly. The resulting sound "picture" has a focal point, usually the voice of the actor or singer.

Proscenium Stage Equipment

Several interesting pieces of permanent stage equipment are frequently associated with proscenium theatres.

Traps   Many theatres have traps cut into the stage floor. These removable sections provide access to the space beneath the stage (see Figure 4.8). These holes can be filled with stairs, an elevator, or a slide, or can be left open, depending on the desired visual and physical effect. Ideally, the majority of a stage floor is trapped. If only a few traps have been installed, Murphy's Law indicates that they will almost always be in the wrong places. Although traps are more frequently found in proscenium theatres, there is nothing to prevent this useful piece of equipment from being installed on either thrust or arena stages.

sound mixer: An electronic device used to adjust the loudness and tone levels of several sources, such as microphones and recorded sources (computer files/tape playback equipment).

Revolve   The revolve, also called a turntable or revolving stage, provides a visually interesting and efficient manner of shifting scenery (see Figure 4.9). Some theatres have revolves built into the stage floor. Depending on the size of the revolve, part or all of a multiset design can be fit onto it and rotated to bring other scenic elements into view.

Slipstage   The slipstage is a huge stage wagon large enough to cover the full width of the proscenium arch (see Figure 4.10). When not in use, the slipstage is stored in one of the wings. Entire sets can be mounted on the slipstage. When needed, it is simply rolled into place on stage.

Revolves and slipstages are permanent features of a theatre's stage. Smaller, temporary versions can be constructed to meet the needs of individual productions. Construction techniques for making these smaller versions are discussed in Chapter 11, "Scenic Production Techniques."

FIGURE 4.9
A revolving stage is sometimes built into the stage floor.

Fly Loft

The area directly over the stage is called the fly loft (see Figure 4.11). The fly loft, also referred to as "the flies," is usually quite tall, minimally two and a half times the height of the proscenium arch, to allow the scenery to be raised out of sight

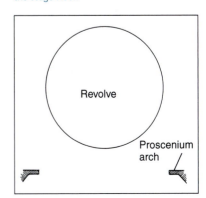

FIGURE 4.10
A slipstage is designed
to hold an entire set.

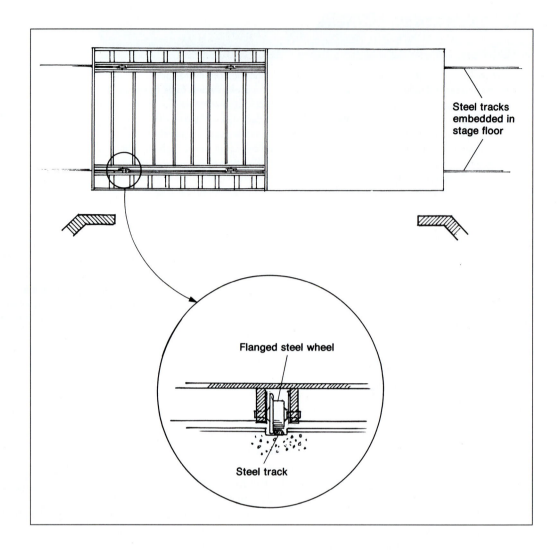

Steel tracks
embedded in
stage floor

Flanged steel wheel

Steel track

grid: A network of steel I beams supporting elements of the system used to raise and lower scenery.

fly: To raise an object or person above the stage floor with ropes or cables.

batten: A thick wooden dowel or metal pipe (generally 1¼ to 1½ inches in diameter) from which are suspended scenery and lighting instruments.

loft blocks: A grooved pulley, mounted on top of the grid, used to change the direction in which a rope or cable travels.

stage house: The physical structure enclosing the area above the stage and wings.

head block: A multisheave block with two or more pulley wheels, used to change the direction of all the ropes or cables that support the batten.

fly gallery: The elevated walkway where the pin rail is located.

pin rail: A horizontal pipe or rail studded with belaying pins; the ropes of the rope-set system are wrapped around the belaying pins to hold the batten at a specific height.

of the audience. The **grid,** or gridiron, is located just below the roof of the fly loft. It serves as a platform to hold some of the equipment used to **fly** scenery, as well as providing the primary support for the weight of the scenery and curtains being flown.

Fly Systems

Several systems are used to fly scenery. The two primary methods, rope set and counterweight, work on the same operating principle: counterbalancing.

The oldest method of flying is with rope and pulley. The pulley is attached to the grid, and the rope is fed through it and tied to the scenery. A stagehand pulls on the free end of the rope and raises the scenery. If the load is too heavy, a sandbag is tied to the free end of the rope as a counterbalance.

Rope Set   The rope-set system operates exactly like a rope and pulley, except it has three or more lines instead of one (see Figure 4.12). The ropes, usually ¾-inch manila, support a **batten.** From the batten they run to the grid, where they pass over **loft blocks,** which direct them toward the side of the **stage house.** At the edge of the grid, the lines pass over the **head block** and then down to the **fly gallery,** where they are tied off on the **pin rail.** The fly gallery is generally located 15 to 20 feet above the stage floor to give the flypersons, or operators of the flying system, a clear view of the stage.

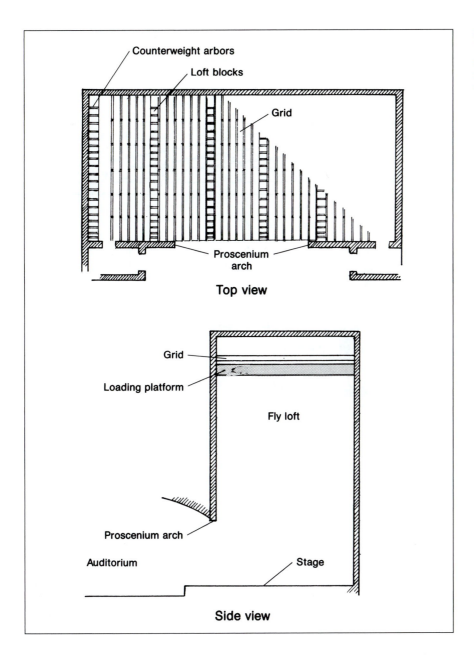

Top view

Side view

FIGURE 4.11
The fly loft and grid are integral parts of any flying system. Scenery and equipment can be flown for storage in the fly loft, while the grid supports the loft blocks.

The rope set is archaic and dangerous if not properly maintained and operated. For this reason it is rarely used today. Although seldom used, it is included here to show the evolution of flying techniques.

Counterweight System   The counterweight system works on the same principle as the rope-set system and is much safer. As shown in Figure 4.13, the support ropes for the battens have been replaced with steel cables. The cables are attached to the batten, and they run up to the loft blocks and over to the head block. But instead of being tied off at the pin rail, they are secured to the top of a **counterweight arbor,** or carriage. The counterweights in the arbor balance the weight of the scenery that is attached to the batten. When the batten is lowered to the stage level, the arbor raises to the level of the **loading platform** just below the grid. This allows the counterweights to be loaded onto the arbor while the scenery is still resting safely on the stage.

counterweight arbor: A metal cradle that holds the counterbalancing weights used in a counterweight flying system.

loading platform: A walkway, suspended just below the grid, where counterweights are loaded onto the arbor.

FIGURE 4.12
A rope set.

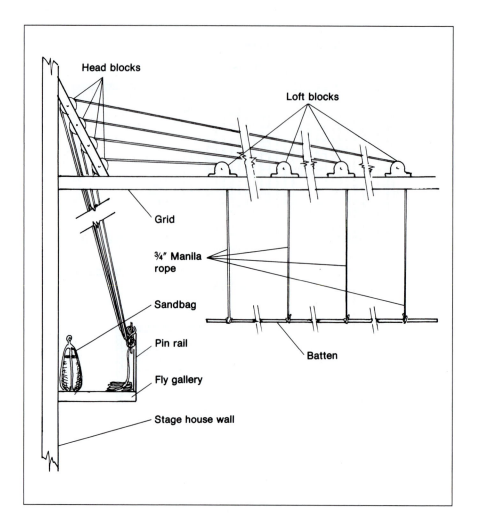

Head blocks

Loft blocks

Grid

¾" Manila rope

Sandbag

Pin rail

Fly gallery

Batten

Stage house wall

Safety Tip

Rope-Set Systems

Although the rope-set system is fairly simple, it is not particularly safe. The ropes, which are made from manila fiber, and sandbags, which are made of heavy-weight canvas, are subject to constant — and all but impossible to detect — stress and deterioration. They must be continually inspected for cuts, nicks, and other indications of wear. The ropes should be replaced as soon as any abrasions or cuts are noticed. Even if no deterioration is noted, they should be replaced at least once a year if the system is used with any frequency and more frequently if it is used heavily. The sandbags should also be replaced at least once every five years or immediately if any damage is noticed.

The scenery must be raised to its high trim mark (the height at which it will be stored) before the counterweight sandbag can be attached to the free end of the rope. Finally, the system must always be batten heavy (the scenery must always be heavier than the counterweight) so that the scenery can be lowered without having to attach special ropes to pull it down.

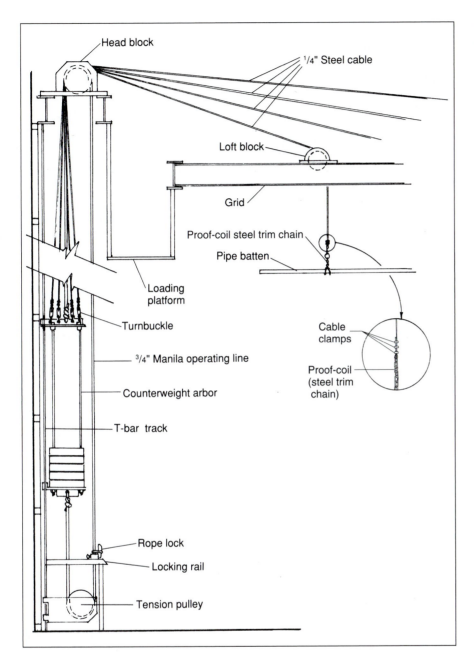

FIGURE 4.13
A counterweight system.

The system is controlled by an operating line of ¾-inch manila rope. (Parallel-core polyester rope can be used as a substitute for the manila operating line.) The operating line is attached to the top of the arbor, runs over a head block, down through a rope lock to a tension pulley, and then back to the bottom of the counterweight arbor. To lower the batten, you pull down on the part of the line that is closest to you. To raise the batten, you pull down on the offstage part of the line. The **locking rail** is located on the stage floor against the stage-house wall. Although this arrangement is convenient, it does take up floor space that could be used for other purposes.

In theatres with limited offstage space, the use of a multiple-speed counterweight system solves the problem by raising the locking rail off the stage floor. This type of system, shown in Figure 4.14, creates a mechanical advantage (2 to 1) that allows the batten to move twice as far as the counterweight arbor. The

locking rail: A rail that holds the rope locks for each counterweight set.

Safety Tip

Counterweight Systems

It isn't difficult to make a counterweight system safe to operate. A few basic rules need to be observed.

1. Make sure that everybody clears the stage area under the loading platform when counterweights are being loaded onto, or unloaded from, the arbor.

2. Don't stack counterweights above the lip of the loading platform or anywhere where they might be knocked off the platform.

3. When working on the grid, loading platform, or pin rail, don't carry anything in your pockets other than the tools you are going to use. Extra tools, pencils, or keys might fall on someone, causing serious injury.

4. Inspect all flying hardware, and repair or replace *any* defective equipment.

5. Bolt in place the hardware supporting all flown units. Nails or screws can pull out of the wood.

6. Always attach the scenery to the batten first, then load the counterweights.

7. When removing (striking) flown scenery, always unload the counterweights first, then remove the scenery from the batten.

8. Any unit other than a very light flat should be flown under compression. This means that the lines supporting the piece are attached to the bottom of the unit rather than the top.

The ¾-inch manila operating line should be inspected for abuse or unusual wear at least once a year. If any nicks or abrasions are noticed, replace the rope at once. Routinely replace the rope every five years. The cable clamps securing the cable to the batten and arbor should be inspected and tightened at least every six months. Any bent or otherwise broken or abused batten pipes should be replaced immediately. The entire rigging system should be inspected by a reputable professional rigger at least once every five years.

drawback to this system is that twice as much weight must be loaded onto the arbor to balance the weight of the scenery.

Motorized systems increasingly are being used for flying. These vary from simple systems that drive the operating line of a regular counterweight set to complex designs of great electronic sophistication.

Motorized Flying Systems   The process of flying and balancing scenery or stage equipment with a counterweight system is one of the more inherently dangerous activities in technical theatre. Loading heavy counterweights onto a counterweight arbor, often while leaning over the edge of a loading platform some 60 to 80 feet above the stage floor, poses a variety of obvious risks. After the arbor is loaded the scenery must be flown and its balance checked. It is often necessary to fly the scenery back in to load, or unload, counterweights from the arbor. This process has to be repeated until the scenery or equipment is in balance. Only then should the system be considered safe.

The convergence of an increased focus on safety, computer control, and technological advances in motorized rigging engineering have resulted in the development of a whole new class of affordable theatrical rigging systems. Prior to the last decade only theatres with very large budgets could afford the rather significant expense of a motorized rigging system. That is not the case anymore.

The Power Assist counterweight automation system from J. R. Clancy, Figure 4.15A, is a retrofit automation system intended for use with existing counterweight sets. The Power Assist system is designed for a lift capacity between 1,000 and 2,000 pounds. A load equal to 50 percent of the system's rated capacity is

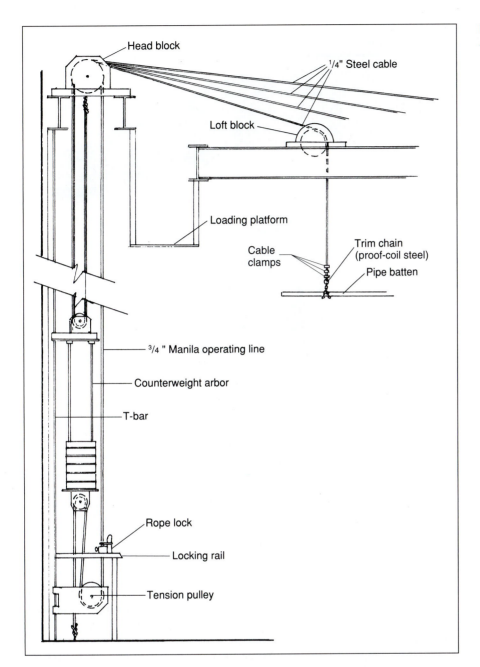

FIGURE 4.14
A multispeed counterweight system.

placed on the existing arbor during the installation process. That load is not changed regardless of how much, or how little, weight is placed on the batten. The system's electric winch is strong enough to safely operate the system with any batten weight from 0 to 100 percent of the system's rated capacity. The Power Assist is available in either fixed- or variable-speed configurations.

The Power Lift system, also from J. R. Clancy, Figure 4.15B, is a motorized rigging system designed for new installations or as a replacement for an existing counterweight system. Because the Power Lift system does not use a counterweight arbor, and because the lift unit is relatively compact, it can be hung on a theatre's wall as well as in the traditional "over stage" location. In this system, the steel cables that support the batten are attached to a moving drum. As the drum turns, cable is either taken up or paid out, thus raising or lowering the batten. The drum is driven by an electric motor through a transmission/gear box. Interestingly,

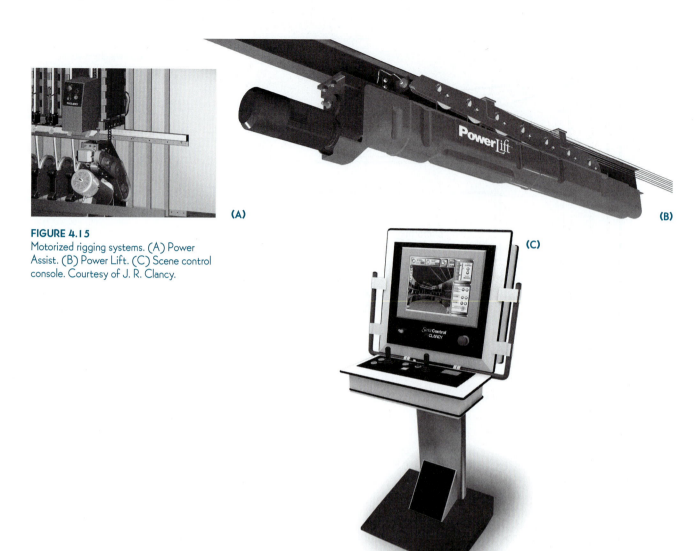

(A)

(B)

(C)

FIGURE 4.15
Motorized rigging systems. (A) Power Assist. (B) Power Lift. (C) Scene control console. Courtesy of J. R. Clancy.

because the system does not require a counterweight arbor nor its associated wall-mounted steel track and loading platform, the cost of this motorized system is very competitive with the cost of a traditional counterweight system.

Motorized rigging systems are typically controlled in two ways. The retrofit units, which are located at the counterweight locking rail, are readily available to an operator. These units normally have relevant control buttons on the units themselves. The remotely located systems—the ones that hang on the wall or above the grid—have to be remotely controlled. There are a variety of control consoles available. Some are designed to work with a few fixed-speed winches. Others, such as J. R. Clancy's Scene Control console, illustrated in Figure 4.15C, are used to control the variable speed motorized rigging systems typically installed in theatres with active production programs. These consoles record and playback all rigging movements for each motorized set in the system, which facilitates the synchronized movement of multiple battens, each with its own speed as well as its own starting and ending times.

Motorized rigging systems are becoming the new standard for flying scenery and equipment in the theatre. They are a safer alternative to existing counter-

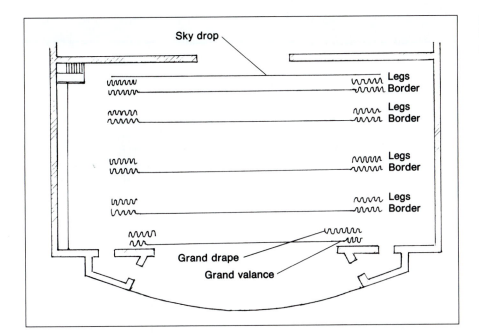

FIGURE 4.16
Standard hanging positions for stage draperies.

weight systems and they offer exact, and repeatable, control with their computer control consoles.

Stage Drapes

The proscenium stage uses more types of stage drapery than does either the thrust or arena stage. Although they have specific functions, all stage drapes are designed to **mask** backstage areas from the spectators. Stage drapes are usually made of black, light-absorbing material such as heavy-weight velour or similar material (commando cloth, duvetyn, rep). Typical hanging positions for the various types of stage drape are shown in Figure 4.16.

Grand Drape   The purpose of the grand drape (also known as the main curtain, main drape, or grand rag) is to cover the proscenium opening. In theatres that have a fly loft, the grand drape, which is usually made from heavy-weight velour, can normally be flown or **traveled.**

Grand Valance   The grand valance normally is located just downstage of the grand drape. It is made of the same material as the grand drape but is much shorter, usually only 8 to 12 feet high. It is used to mask the equipment and scenery that are flown immediately upstage of the proscenium.

False Proscenium   The false proscenium (Figure 4.17) is located immediately upstage of the grand drape and grand valance. It is normally mounted on a rigid framework. The **flat** structures of both the **hard teaser** and **tormentors** are usually covered with thin (⅛-inch to 3/16-inch) plywood, which is then covered with black velour or some similar type of black, light-absorbing material. The primary purpose of the false "pro" is to provide masking. The tormentors mask the sides of the stage, and the hard teaser provides primary masking for the flies. Since both the tormentors and hard teaser are movable, they can also be used to shrink the apparent size of the proscenium opening.

mask: To block the audience's view—generally, of backstage equipment and space.

travel: To move horizontally relative to the stage floor, as with a drape that opens in the middle and is pulled to the sides.

flat: A framework, normally made of wood or metal; frequently covered with fabric or thin plywood, although a variety of other covering materials may be used.

hard teaser: The horizontal element of the false proscenium; usually hung from a counterweighted batten so that its height can easily be adjusted.

tormentor: The vertical flats that form the side elements of the false proscenium.

PRODUCTION INSIGHTS
Mechanical Advantage

Certain mechanical systems can provide a power-multiplying effect known as mechanical advantage. A 2:1 mechanical advantage means that you can move twice the weight, with the same amount of force, that you can with a system providing no mechanical advantage.

The single whip illustrated in the first figure doesn't create any mechanical advantage, because it is just changing the direction of pull on the operating line. If, however, we attached one end of the rope to a strong beam in the ceiling, as shown in the second figure, attached the pulley to the weight we were trying to raise, and then pulled *up* on the rope, we would create a 2:1 mechanical advantage. This system is called a running block.

It is fairly easy to determine the mechanical advantage of any tackle-rigging configuration. Simply count the number of lines that pass through the block. Don't count the operating line if it is hanging down from the last pass through the block (the housing for the pulley wheels). The total number of lines will be equal to the mechanical advantage for that particular block-and-tackle system. Friction reduces the actual efficiency of any block-and-tackle arrangement by 10 percent for each pulley sheave in the system.

With block and tackle you create increased lifting power, but you do so by losing speed. For example, with a double whip (2:1 mechanical advantage), the load moves half the distance that the operating line travels, whereas the watch tackle (3:1 mechanical advantage) moves the load one-third the distance that the operating line travels.

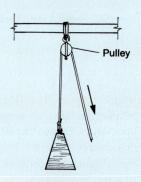

Single whip
(no mechanical advantage)

Running block
(2 to 1 mechanical advantage)

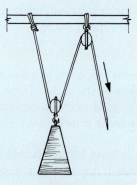

Double whip
(2 to 1 mechanical advantage)

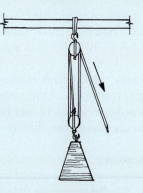

Watch tackle
(3 to 1 mechanical advantage)

Four common tackle rigs.

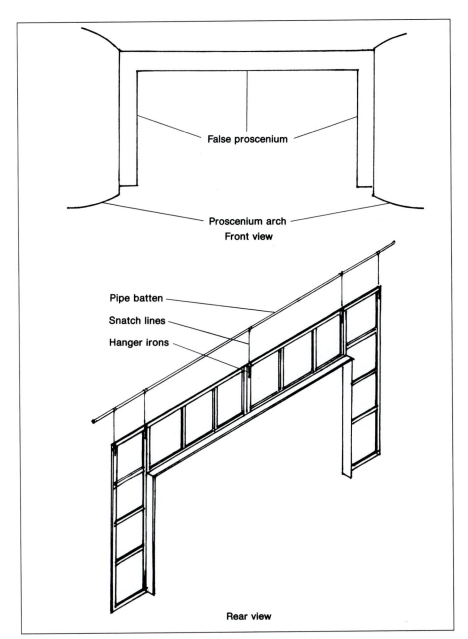

FIGURE 4.17
A false proscenium.

False proscenium

Proscenium arch
Front view

Pipe batten

Snatch lines

Hanger irons

Rear view

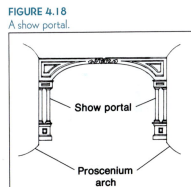

FIGURE 4.18
A show portal.

Show portal

Proscenium arch

A **show portal** (Figure 4.18) is a false proscenium designed for a specific production. It masks the stage and provides a picture frame for the set.

Legs and Borders   Legs are narrow, vertical stage drapes that are used to mask the sides of the stage upstage of the proscenium arch. They are generally made of the same light-absorbing material as other stage drapes. Borders, also called teasers, are short, wide, horizontal draperies, normally 4 to 10 feet tall, used to mask the flies. Legs and borders usually have long strings, called ties, either sewn to the jute tape at the top of the drape or slipped through brass **grommets,** which are fixed to the jute tape so that they can be tied to a supporting batten. Ties are usually made from 36-inch pieces of ½-inch-wide cotton tape, although 36-inch shoestrings work very well.

show portal: A false proscenium that visually supports the style and color palette of a particular production.

grommet: A circular metal eyelet used to reinforce holes in fabric.

FIGURE 4.19

Hanging positions for legs and teasers.

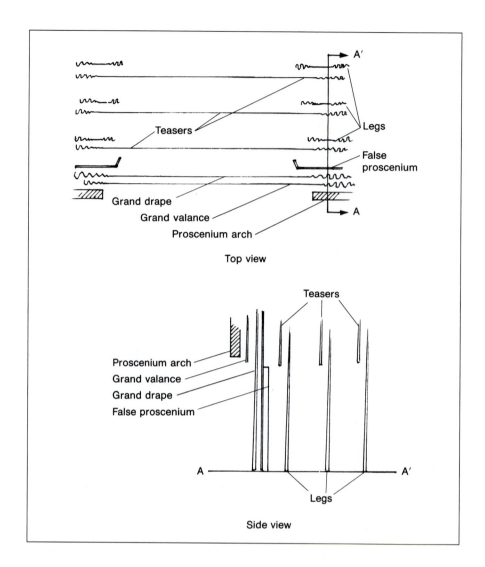

Borders are normally used in conjunction with a set of legs (two legs) to provide a complete framework of masking for the stage, as shown in Figure 4.19. If the theatre is equipped with a counterweight system, borders and legs are rarely hung on the same batten, because the trim height of the borders needs to be variable, whereas the legs should be trimmed so that the lower hem barely brushes the stage floor. Borders are generally hung on the batten immediately downstage of the one holding the legs. If the theatre doesn't have a counterweight or adjustable height rigging system, the legs and borders are frequently hung on the same batten.

Sky Drop   The sky drop (Figure 4.20), also known as a sky tab, is, as its name implies, used to simulate the sky. It is a large, flat curtain, without fullness, normally made of muslin or scenic canvas. It is usually hung on a batten as far upstage as possible.

Prior to the early 1960s, the sky drop was traditionally dyed a uniform blue to help simulate the color of the sky. Currently, sky drops are normally made from unbleached muslin, which is an off-white color. This neutral color allows the lighting designer to create a sky color that is appropriate to the mood and concept of the production.

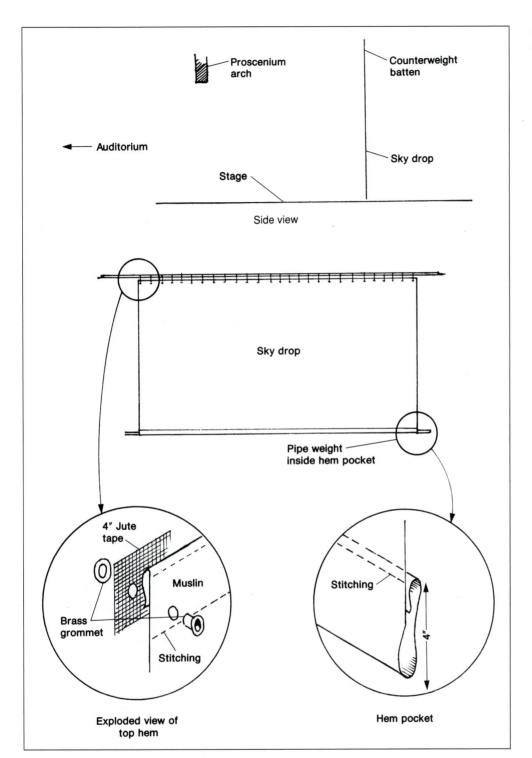

FIGURE 4.20
A sky drop.

Cyclorama   The cyclorama, or "cyc" (Figure 4.21), is an expansion on the concept of the sky drop. Although the sky drop (Figure 4.21A) works very well for productions that require only a small patch of sky, it doesn't surround the set with the illusion of vast expanses of open sky. Historically, when plays began making this type of scenic demand, technicians responded by hanging two more sky drops, or tabs, at almost right angles to the original curtain to provide

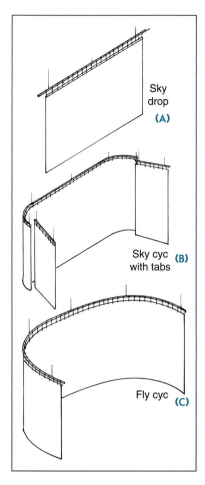

FIGURE 4.21
A sky drop and two types of cycloramas.

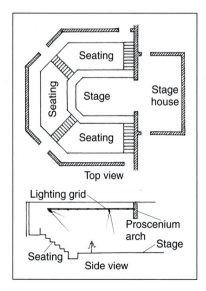

FIGURE 4.22
A typical thrust-stage arrangement.

a wraparound expanse of sky, as shown in Figure 4.21B. Where the drops met, they were overlapped to prevent gaps in the smooth expanse of simulated sky.

The **fly cyc** (Figure 4.21C) is made from one unbroken expanse of cloth. It is hung on a counterweighted pipe located outside the other counterweighted battens to reduce any possible interference between the two systems.

Sometimes sharkstooth **scrims** are used in conjunction with both sky drops and cycloramas. Sharkstooth scrim is a knit fabric that is actually composed of more open spaces than thread. Because of this structure, the fabric possesses some very interesting properties. When light is projected onto the front of sharkstooth scrim, it is reflected back toward the viewer, and the fabric appears to be opaque. When the front light is turned off and any objects behind the scrim are lit, the sharkstooth scrim becomes transparent, and the objects in back of it are clearly visible. When those same objects are lit, and light also strikes the scrim, it becomes translucent, and the objects, while still visible, are hazy and less distinct.

A white scrim hung in front of the cyc helps smooth out any wrinkles, dirty spots, and imperfections on the cyc. If the scrim is hung on a batten a foot or two downstage of the cyc, additional lights can be focused onto the scrim to provide very interesting, and sometimes spectacular, multilayer cyclorama lighting.

A black sharkstooth scrim can also be used to enhance the sky drop or cyc lighting. Used in the same manner as the white scrim, it improves aerial perspective by reducing the intensity and saturation of objects that are lit behind it.

A great deal of stage-lighting equipment could be considered a part of the permanent stage equipment. It will be discussed in Chapter 16, "Lighting Production."

Thrust Stage

As we saw in the last chapter, the thrust stage (see Figure 4.22) isn't a new development. Medieval audiences gathered on three sides of the pageant wagons

FIGURE 4.23
Thrust theatre. The Festival Theatre at the Stratford Festival. Courtesy of the Stratford Festival of Canada.

and platform stages to watch passion plays, and research indicates that the Globe Theatre also had a thrust stage. The thrust stage was rediscovered by directors who wanted to move the action of the play out of what they felt were the artificial and limiting confines of the proscenium stage. Thus, the mid–twentieth century saw the birth of a large number of thrust-stage theatres in the United States.

The stage of the thrust theatre projects into, and is surrounded on three sides by, the audience, so tall flats, drops, and vertical masking cannot be used where they would interfere with the spectators' view of the stage (see Figure 4.23). But on the fourth, or upstage, side of the stage, drops and flats can be placed to help describe the play's location. Entrances are frequently made through openings in the upstage wall, but the house is also used for this purpose.

The **lighting grid** in a thrust theatre is usually suspended over the entire stage and auditorium space, so instruments can be hung wherever necessary to effectively light the playing area. Lighting grids vary in complexity from designs that hide the lighting instruments from the spectators' view to simple pipe grids from which the lights are hung in full view, as shown in Figure 4.24.

Access to the simpler pipe grids is usually from a rolling ladder or scaffold placed on the stage. More complex grids frequently have access from above to a series of walkways or catwalks suspended adjacent to the pipes to allow the electricians relatively easy access to the lighting instruments.

A number of other creative solutions to grid access have been developed. One of the more ingenious, and effective, is the tension-mesh grid. This can be thought of as a transparent working platform hung underneath the grid. Strung

fly cyc: A single drop, hung on a U-shaped pipe, that surrounds the stage on three sides.

scrim: A drop made from translucent or transparent material.

lighting grid: A network of pipes from which lighting instruments are hung.

FIGURE 4.24
Lighting grids for thrust theatres are frequently exposed pipe grids. The Tom Patterson Theatre at the Stratford Festival. Photo courtesy of Stratford Shakespeare Festival, Canada.

FIGURE 4.25
A typical arena theatre configuration.

at a convenient working height beneath the grid, the tension-mesh grid is an interwoven series of ⅛-inch aircraft cables attached, under tension, to the sides of the grid or building. The weave of the cables is small enough so electricians can walk on it without falling through, but the cable diameter is small enough that they don't interfere with the light from the instruments. In addition to the grid, there are usually some additional **hanging positions** above the house, either open pipes or some type of semiconcealed location.

Some thrust theatres retain a vestigial proscenium arch on the upstage wall as well as a small backstage area. Although battens are frequently **dead hung** above this backstage space, some theatres have installed **ratchet winches**, rope sets, or counterweight sets so the battens can be raised and lowered.

The lighting and sound booths are generally located at the back of the house directly facing the stage, although nothing stronger than tradition prevents them from being placed at any location in the auditorium that provides an unobstructed view of the stage. Again, as in the proscenium theatre, and for the same reasons, the sound operator normally chooses to run the mixing board from a position in the house rather than from the sound booth.

FIGURE 4.26
Arena theatre. The interior of the 827-seat Arena Stage in Washington, D.C.

 Arena Stage

The arena stage (Figure 4.25), also called theatre-in-the-round, is another step in the development of an intimate actor-audience theatre. The audience surrounds the stage and is much closer to the action of the play than in either the proscenium or thrust theatres (see Figure 4.26).

The scenery used on an arena stage is extremely minimal. Because the audience surrounds the stage, designing for the arena theatre provides a challenge to all the designers. Anything used on an arena stage—sets, costumes, makeup, props—must be carefully selected to clearly specify the period, mood, and feeling of the play. Additionally, everything must be well constructed, because the audience sits almost on top of the stage and can see every construction detail.

As in the thrust stage theatre, the space above the arena stage has a lighting grid rather than a fly loft. The lighting grid frequently covers not only the stage but the auditorium as well.

hanging position: A location where lighting instruments are placed.

dead hang: To suspend without means of raising or lowering.

ratchet winch: A device, used for hoisting, with a crank attached to a drum; one end of a rope or cable is attached to the drum, the other end to the load; turning the crank moves the load; a ratchet gear prevents the drum from spinning backward.

The stage manager and the lighting and sound operators need to have a clear view of the stage. Many arena theatres have an elevated deck running around the perimeter of the auditorium to provide these people with a variety of potential work locations. Some arena theatres have a traditional lighting booth and sound-control booth rather than flexible work stations.

 ## Black Box Theatres

The flexible staging of black box theatres—so named because they are usually painted black and have a simple rectangular shape—encourages, and demands, ingenuity from the production design team. These design-it-yourself performance spaces are a direct result of a number of experimental theatre movements that sought to break down the visual and psychological barriers created by the proscenium stage.

In black box theatres the seating is generally located on movable bleacherlike modules that can be arranged in any number of ways around the playing space. Although the space can be set up in traditional proscenium, thrust, or arena configurations, it can also be aligned into excitingly different staging arrangements that support the production concept for particular productions. This type of theatre is fun to work in, and every production creates a challenge to the ingenuity of the production design team.

The black box theatre was developed partially as a reaction against the artistic confines of more formal types of stage space. Consequently, there isn't a great deal of specific stage equipment associated with it. However, there is a lighting grid, similar to that of the arena theatre, located above the stage and auditorium space, and there is usually a variety of additional hanging locations.

 ## "Found" Theatre Spaces

FIGURE 4.27
Converted theatre space. The stage/auditorium of the Yale Repertory Theatre, housed in a former church.

Found theatre spaces lend a great deal of credence to the statement that all theatre needs is "two boards and a passion." These theatres are housed in structures that were originally designed for some other purpose. Almost every conceivable type of space has been, or could be, converted for use as a theatre. In Tucson, Arizona between 1970 and 1985 a supermarket, movie house, lumberyard, feed store, office building, and restaurant were converted into theatres. The found theatre space conversions experienced in Tucson were not unique. The Lafayette Square Theatre in New York City houses five theatres in what used to be a library. The only criteria for conversion seem to be sufficient square footage to house a stage and its audience and nearby parking or public transportation.

Found theatre spaces are frequently converted into black box theatres, but a number of converting companies have opted for the more traditional arena or thrust stage configurations (see Figure 4.27). For some producing groups, the appeal of the converted space lies in the intimacy of the audience-actor relationship that is inherent in these generally small theatres. For others, the lower production costs of the smaller, more intimate theatre forms are an asset. For all of them, the fact that these spaces were considerably less expensive than building a new structure was a boon.

Chapter 5

Style, Composition, and Design

A designer needs to communicate, to share his or her information and ideas both verbally and visually. In Chapter 2, you were introduced to the verbal language of the designer—that is, the questioning process and the dynamics of group discussion, which are vital to the interaction among members of the production design team. In this chapter, you are introduced to the other, equally important language of the designer—the visual language.

Style and Stylization in Theatrical Design

What is style? In conversation we might refer to a particular "style" of clothing such as blue jeans or evening wear. When we refer to a "style" of car, we often use the word to differentiate between models that have significantly different appearances, such as sports cars and sedans. Narrowly defined, style refers to the compositional characteristics that distinguish the appearance of one type of thing from another. Style can be more generally defined as a "reflection of the social and political history of the times, . . . that . . . are eventually reflected in the patterns and shifting artistic trends of the period."[1] Combining both definitions provides a definition of style useful in theatrical design: a recognizable pattern of compositional elements that provides a distinctive reflection of the social and political history of the time. This definition can be used to identify particular compositional features that are reflective of a moment in history, such as the long, sweeping lines generally characteristic of women's clothing in the Late Gothic period (Figure 5.1) or the mechanistically based repetitive patterns of German expressionism.

Production Style

A definition of **production style,** while including the previously discussed definition of design style, must include acting and directing as well. Thus, production style can be viewed as the central stylistic theme on which the world of the production is based. It is a recognizable pattern of visual and intellectual elements,

production style: A manner of producing a play in which all production elements (costumes, scenery, lights, acting) adhere to a common set of artistic/philosophical characteristics (e.g., expressionism).

[1] Douglas A. Russell, *Stage Costume Design,* 2nd ed. (Englewood Cliffs, N.J.: Prentice-Hall, 1985), p. 170.

FIGURE 5.1
Long sweeping lines are a characteristic style of Late Gothic gowns.

based on social and political history, used to create the production environment for a particular play.

The identification of a particular production style, which derives in part from a careful and creative interpretation of the script, is the single most important step in the development of a play's production concept.

Design Styles and Design Periods

It is convenient to refer to specific design styles, such as romanticism or naturalism, and design periods, such as Elizabethan or Late Nineteenth Century. However, neither styles nor periods exist within narrowly prescribed time frames. They are merely indicative of major stylistic elements that are common during a particular period of time. Romanticism did not stop on one day and naturalism begin the next. Nor did the style of Elizabethan clothing abruptly begin with the coronation of Elizabeth I and end with her death. Both styles evolved from those that preceded them and into those that followed. Naturalism began as a reaction against what its practitioners viewed as the stylistic excesses of romanticism. As more artists followed the stylistic leaders of the naturalistic movement, naturalism became the dominant artistic style. Realism began as a reaction against what a few artists viewed as the rigid dictates of the naturalistic style. Again, a new style emerged and became dominant as another declined.

Stylization

It is difficult, if not impossible, and of no theatrical value, to create an absolutely accurate historical period or style on stage. The reasons are twofold: (1) the impact that contemporary stylistic and practical influences have on the designers and (2) the expectations of the audience. To illustrate the point, let's assume that we're producing a hypothetical play set in 1820 England. If contemporary fashion, which to a great extent determines audience reaction, dictates that the hair styles of 1820 England were ugly, silly, or funny looking, any costume designer would be ill-advised to insist on absolute historical accuracy of the hair design for the young female romantic lead in the play. Why? Simply because the audience is supposed to like her. If her hair style seems ugly or silly, it will be difficult for the audience to empathize with her character. Under these circumstances, a modification of the design, based on the historical research, would be more appropriate. It is frequently impossible to find historically accurate fabrics from which to make costumes. It is also a bit bizarre to think that the walls of the set for the library scene in our play would have to be made with historically accurate bricks, mortar, lath, and plaster; that the library shelves would have to be made from oak that has been painted with historically correct stains and varnishes; and that the books on those shelves would have to all have been published prior to 1820!

Instead of slavishly copying historical designs, designers stylize. Stylization refers to the use of specific compositional elements characteristic of a particular style or period to create the essence of that style or period. Designers use the degree of stylization of the scenic, costume, and lighting designs to communicate the level of reality of the production to the audience. Costumes, set, and furniture designs that are minimally stylized—that closely duplicate the line, mass, texture, and color of a particular style or period—normally will be interpreted by most audiences as being historically accurate and realistic. As designs depart further from visual reality—exaggerate or simplify line, shape, mass, texture, and/or color—audience interpretation becomes harder to project. A wide variety of demographic information, such as cultural background and values, as well as the audience's level of theatrical experience, come into play. A theatrically so-phisticated audience may think that heavily stylized scenic and costume designs reinforce the psychological reality of a play, while the same production may seem totally bizarre to others.

Literary Style and Theatrical Design

Another type of style that influences theatrical design is literary style. The style in which a script is written provides major clues for the designer. Verse drama has a majesty and sweep that cannot be duplicated in prose. The world of the verse play frequently seems more noble, simply because the story is written in verse. The scenic, costume, and lighting designs should mirror this noble quality. To reinforce this feeling, costume designers might choose to work in "noble" fabrics: rich velvets, brocades, and similar aristocratic materials and colors. Scenic de-signers would probably choose to work in a particular style that projects aristo-cratic, rather than middle-class, tastes.

The same criterion that visual style should respond to literary style can be ap-plied to plays in which the dialogue is written in short, choppy prose. To reflect the rough flavor of this literary style, the scenic and costume designers might choose to work with short, choppy lines and harsh angles to create realistic forms.

Elements of Design

Design can be described as the process of conceiving and executing a plan. In the theatre, design involves creating a stylistic plan for the production concept and developing the necessary sketches, patterns, and other visualizations of the de-sign concept(s), as well as overseeing the production of the sets, costumes, lights, and sound.

The drawings produced by every designer (scenic, costume, lighting, and to a certain extent, sound) need to be guided by the elements of design: line, shape, mass, measure, position, color, and texture.

This section provides a set of basic definitions, as well as discussion of the characteristics and functions, for each element of design—line, mass, shape, and so forth. The principles of composition, or how the elements of design are combined to create a picture or design, are discussed in the next section. An un-derstanding of how to use the elements of design to create a meaningful compo-sition—one that implies specific meaning to a viewer—begins with a thorough understanding of line, mass, shape, and so forth—the elements of design. After you've gone through the frequently annoying process of learning the individual characteristics of each element of design, and the principles that govern how those elements can be combined, you'll see how those elements were applied to create one particular design—the author's scene design for *The Kitchen*.

The following is another one of those "author's caveats" that I've sprinkled throughout this book. I urge you, gentle reader, to pay attention to the amazingly boring material in the following two sections and learn both the elements of de-sign and the principles of composition. A personal aside here: I *hate* learning def-initions/principles just for the sake of learning them. Always have, always will. But I've also learned the hard way that having a thorough understanding of these definitions and principles will actually make it easier for you to create more meaningful compositions. And creating "meaningful compositions"—scenic/costume/lighting designs that shape and influence audiences' understanding of the play that they're watching—is the reason that most people want to study this stuff in the first place. So hang in there, it'll get "funner" after awhile.

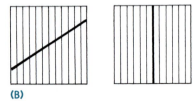

(A)

(B)

(C)

FIGURE 5.2
(A) Long lines are more noticeable than short ones. (B) Lines that contrast with their surroundings are more noticeable than those that don't. (C) Curved lines are more distinctive than straight lines of the same length.

value: Relative lightness or darkness.

FIGURE 5.3
The strongest line in a costume sketch is generally the one that outlines the silhouette. Costume design by Patrick Holt for The Hot Box girls chorus in the 2004 Arizona Repertory Theatre production of *Guys and Dolls.*

GUYS & DOLLS · "TAKE BACK YOUR MINK"

Line

Line can be defined as a mark that connects two points. The properties that define the characteristics of that "connecting mark" are dimension, quality, and character.

Dimension   Dimension refers to the length and width of a line.

Quality   The quality of a line refers to several intrinsic characteristics: its shape, its **value,** and its contrast with surrounding objects. Lines can be straight, curvilinear, angled, jagged, serpentine, or any combination of these characteristics.

Character   The character of a line refers to its emotionally evocative characteristics.

We notice lines because of their dimension and quality. We attach meaning to their character. Lines attract attention as their complexity increases, as shown in Figure 5.2. Long straight lines are more noticeable than short straight ones (Figure 5.2A). Lines that contrast strongly with their surroundings or backgrounds draw more attention than those that don't (Figure 5.2B). Curved lines are more distinctive than straight lines of the same length (Figure 5.2C). Scenic and costume designers understand and utilize these principles. Notice that the boldest lines in the costume design in Figure 5.3 are those that outline the silhouette of the gown. The lines revealing trim details are of lower value and contrast.

Shape

Any line that encloses a space creates a shape. The quality of the line creating the shape strongly influences the connotative meaning of that shape (Figure 5.4). In scenic design, shape defines the form of large elements such as walls, platforms, and so forth, as well as defining the outline of such details as windows, doors, and furniture (Figure 5.5A). Similarly, in costume design shape refers to the outline of the garment, whether it is the silhouette of the whole garment or the form of some trim element (Figure 5.5B).

Mass

Mass is the three-dimensional manifestation of shape. It creates an awareness of depth and spatial arrangements. Mass creates a feeling of depth in sketches of scenic elements such as platforms, walls, and furniture. Individual costume sketches depict the mass of each garment. While costume designers don't produce sketches depicting costumes in relation to the whole stage picture, they need to be aware of how their designs will function within the spatial arrangement of the stage.

Measure

Largely an intuitive skill, and closely related to proportion (discussed later in this chapter), measure refers to the ability to judge the size of objects and the relative distance between them without the aid of measuring devices.

Position

Position refers to the relative location of adjacent shapes or masses. This definition encompasses both the distance between objects and their placement relative to forms around them.

Color

Color is one of the most important and sophisticated of the design elements. It generates multiple, interwoven responses in the viewer based on psychological and cultural reactions. Because of its complexity, color will be discussed separately in Chapter 6.

Texture

Texture refers to the visual or tactile surface characteristics or appearance of an object. In costume, where the primary visual element is fabric, the texture of a fabric's surface plays a vital role in creating the audience's response to, and understanding of, the nature and personality of the character wearing the costume. Hard-surfaced fabrics, such as satins, taffeta, and metallics, reflect light. Soft, fuzzy-surfaced materials, such as wool, flannel, and velour, absorb light. Audience responses to specific fabric surfaces vary depending on the personalities of the individual audience members and the mix of textures in the design, so it is difficult to draw any generalizations about "meanings" for specific fabric surface textures. However, expensive cloth has always been the province of those who could afford it, such as the nobility and the upper class. Therefore, the surface textures, and light-reflective qualities, of expensive fabrics, such as satins and brocades, can be loosely associated with the wealthy and upper class. Similar comparisons can be drawn with those fabrics worn by the middle and lower classes.

In a similar manner, scenic designers have traditionally used texture to provide visual reference to the play's psychological environment. Although it is difficult to describe texture without reference to other design elements such as line, shape, and mass, certain associative reactions to texture are reasonably uniform. Generally speaking, smooth surfaces reflect a finished, orderly type of environment when compared with the harsher, less polished atmosphere created by rough textures.

In lighting design, **gobos** are used to create texture by breaking up the otherwise smooth output of the lighting instrument into shadow patterns. (See Chapter 16, "Lighting Production," for more information on gobos.) These patterns provide an effective tool to increase the dramatic tension in the lighting by providing the only effective means of creating texture in lighting.

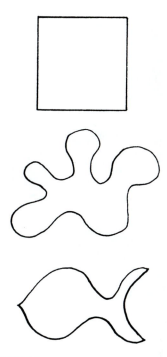

FIGURE 5.4
The quality of the line creating the shape determines the quality of the shape.

Principles of Composition

To be an effective designer you must understand the basic principles of composition. They can guide you to an understanding of how the elements of design are coordinated. Good composition usually results when the elements of design are arranged in a cohesive and unified manner according to the following guidelines.

Unity

Unity in design can be described as the creation of a stylistic plan to which all parts of the design subscribe. The production concept is that plan. It is the conceptual core of the production. In practice, unity in design means that each part of a design should have some type of logical connection with the production concept. In scenic design, unity is achieved when the arrangement of flowers on a table, the design of a door, or the library and living room sets for Act I and Act II

gobo: A thin metal template inserted into an ellipsoidal reflector spotlight to project a shadow pattern of light.

THE WINSLOW BOY — A.Gillette

(A)

FIGURE 5.5
Any line that encloses a space creates a shape such as a window, door, or wall. (A) *The Winslow Boy,* scenic design by A. S. Gillette. (B) Costume design by Patrick Holt for Amanda in the Playmaker's Repertory Company, Chapel production of *The Glass Menagerie.*

(B)

profile (silhouette): The outline of a form, which determines the form's quality and character.

of a hypothetical play all subscribe to the guiding principles of the production concept. Unity in costume design is achieved when the elements used in the design of individual costumes, as well as those groups of costumes that are on stage at the same time, have some type of logical connection to the production concept. Similarly, there must be a conceptual thread that ties together the various elements of the lighting and sound designs. That conceptual thread is the production concept.

Harmony

Harmony is the sense of blending and unity that is obtained when all elements of a design fit together to create an orderly, congruous whole. Harmony is achieved when a combination of design elements seem to naturally blend or flow together, avoiding discordant or incompatible contrasts.

Although harmony is primarily concerned with congruity, it doesn't require that all lines, forms, masses, values, and colors within a design be of one particular style, shape, or character. What it does mean is that those elements should be chosen to complement one another. For example, the **profile,** or **silhouette,** for the walls of the set of *The Member of the Wedding* (Figure 5.6) is actually composed of two basic lines. The more apparent is the slightly jagged silhouette of the short, vertical cuts. The second is the long, gentle sweep of the silhouette itself. The jagged line was chosen for two reasons, one aesthetic, the other logical. The jagged line is evocative of the emotional stress that is felt by Frankie, the play's main character. The more mundane reason for selecting this line is that the short, vertical breaks can be thought of as the ends of the clapboards that cover the outside of the house. The long, sweeping line was chosen to reinforce the romantic, nostalgic nature of the play.

Lest you think that harmony is a goal always to be sought, you need to realize that too much harmony can be monotonous, as when a motif, such as the harmony of angle and measure shown in Figure 5.7, is repeated too often. Monotonous har-

FIGURE 5.6
The profile, or cutout line, affects visual meaning. *The Member of the Wedding,* scenic design by J. Michael Gillette.

mony can also be achieved when too many closely related colors are used in the same design.

All designs don't necessarily have to be harmonious. Some designs might provide an accurate reflection of the mood and spirit of the play by being deliberately unharmonious. The degree of harmony to be pursued in the design depends on the designer's interpretation of the production concept.

Contrast

Contrast in composition can be defined as the juxtaposition of dissimilar design elements. To be effective, contrast must work in opposition to the major, or dominant, visual theme in a composition. But too much contrast can destroy that visual theme, and too little (too much harmony) will be monotonous. The obvious design ideal is to create compositions that provide a proper balance of harmony and contrast reflective of the production style. In scenic design, visual contrast frequently mirrors the psychological stress levels of the play—tragedies and plays with serious themes frequently have greater visual contrast than comedies do. In costume design, the personality of the character wearing the costume is a prime determinant of the amount of contrast used in the design of an individual costume. As a general guideline, the costumes of flamboyant characters employ greater contrast than do those of their more retiring compatriots.

Manipulation of contrast affects meaning. Note the change in "personality" between the two versions of the scenic design shown in Figure 5.8. The curved cutout lines used in Figure 5.8A create a new visual personality for the design by contrasting with the dominant vertical and horizontal lines of the "noncutout"

FIGURE 5.7
Too much harmony can be monotonous.

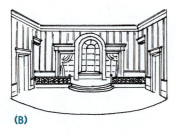

FIGURE 5.8
The use of an interesting silhouette can increase visual interest and connotative meaning in a scenic design.

symmetrical balance: Correspondence in size, form, and relative position of parts on either side of a center dividing line; mirror-image balance.

asymmetrical balance: A sense of equipoise achieved through dynamic tension created by the juxtaposition of dissimilar design elements (line, form, mass, value, color).

acting area: Those areas of the stage on which specific scenes, or parts of scenes, are played.

design pictured in Figure 5.8B. The sensuous line makes the entire design seem more relaxed, less formal and austere.

Variation

When too much harmony in a design produces monotony, variation of the monotonous elements can introduce visual interest. A simple pattern repeated many times (Figure 5.9A) can be monotonous, but by varying the shape of every second or third object in the design (Figure 5.9B) visual interest in the whole design is heightened. Similar effects are achieved by varying any of the design elements (line, shape, texture, and so forth) in a repetitive pattern, as shown in Figure 5.9C and D.

Balance

Balance can be achieved by arranging the design elements to give a sense of restfulness, stability, or equilibrium to the design. There are two types of balance: symmetrical and asymmetrical. In **symmetrical balance,** if you were to draw a line down the center of a design, the objects on the left side of a design would be the mirror image of the objects on the right, as shown in Figure 5.10. In **asymmetrical balance,** the left side of the design does not mirror the right. Balance is achieved by creating a pattern in which the juxtaposition of the various design elements creates a sense of restfulness, stability, or equilibrium, as shown in Figure 5.11. In this illustration, the white circle on the left of the design is dynamically balanced by the larger expanse of dark space to its right. This type of "nonmirror" balance presents many more ways for the designer to create dynamic balance through the manipulation of the elements of design.

The design of individual costumes is much more likely to involve the use of symmetrical balance (Figure 5.12A), in which the left side of the costume mirrors the right. However, a dynamic visual statement can be made about a character through the use of asymmetrical elements such as diagonal sashes, asymmetrical modular blocks of color, or asymmetrical draping (Figure 5.12B). Additionally, the overall balance of the costume design for the entire production is normally asymmetrical because the ebb and flow of the stage picture will rarely, if ever, contain any moments in which the left side of the stage picture will be a mirror image of the right. The majority of scenic designs employ asymmetrical balance because its dynamic nature presents more opportunities for the personality of the play to be visually described in the scenery, as shown in Figure 5.13.

Proportion

Proportion involves the harmonious relationship of the parts of an object to each other or to the whole. A significant portion of our understanding of beauty is based on proportion. Facial beauty, for example, is predominantly based on pro-

FIGURE 5.9
Variation creates visual interest. (A) Repetition of a simple pattern can be monotonous. (B) Varying the width of every second shape in the pattern creates visual interest. (C and D) Alternating patterns heighten visual interest.

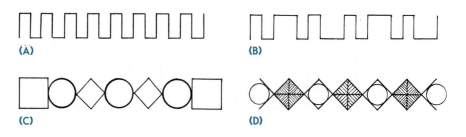

Terminal Accents

(A)

(B)

Carefully selected terminal accents—the lines that define the profile, or silhouette, of a form or mass—can be used to help portray emotional quality. In some productions, the upper parts of the set walls are cut off (Figure A). The quality and character of the line chosen to form this terminal accent on the upper edge of the wall (form) can help shape the audience's understanding of the emotional atmosphere of the play. If the play is a light comedy, a "fun" sort of curlicue line will reinforce the happy nature of the play. If the production is more romantic, a gentle, sensuous line may be more appropriate. If the play is serious and heavy, straight lines with sharp, angular corners are probably more appropriate.

The same effect can be achieved in costume design, where the character of the line chosen to create the silhouette of a costume helps shape the emotional quality of the gown (Figure B).

The emotional quality of the terminal accent can also be used to good advantage in costume design. The hems of the sleeves and skirts of witches' costumes are frequently designed with sharp points (dags) to visually support the menacing nature of the characters wearing those costumes. The unadorned neckline of a collarless smock provides a visual clue to the stiff, unyielding nature of its wearer. But add a soft, frilly, lace collar to that same dress, and our perception of its wearer will similarly be softened.

(A) Scenic design for The Birthday Party *by J. Michael Gillette. (B) Costume designs for Elise Darling in* Very Good Eddie *(left) and Queen Elinor in Shakespeare's* King John *(right) by Paul D. Reinhardt.*

portion. We normally think of a face as beautiful if all of its parts seem to "match" or "fit together." But if the nose or ears seem too big or too small, or if the spacing of the eyes is too wide or too narrow, what we are really discussing is proportion. The criteria that determine what is too big or too small are intuitive, culturally based, and vary considerably from person to person. This situation makes it all but impossible to create a definition of "proper proportion." But if some part of a scenic, costume, or lighting design appeals to our sense of beauty,

FIGURE 5.13
Asymmetrical balance helps create visual character. Scenic design by James Billings for the American Southwest Theatre Company production of *True West.*

placed in the downstage areas, which is where the majority of the play's action took place.

Contrasting surface textures — slick ceramic tiles, dull-black cast-iron stoves, brushed stainless steel, flat off-white and green walls, dull-red floor tiles — add to the visual interest of the design.

Variation

Repetition of a regular pattern produces monotony. Variation of that pattern introduces visual interest. This design exhibits several repetitive patterns: the door-and-window-trim motif, the height of the ceramic wainscoting, the shapes of the stoves. Variation is introduced in the door and window trim by varying the height and width of the openings. The horizontal line created by the top of the ceramic wainscoting would be visually boring if it were not interrupted by the door and window openings. While the design of the stoves remains the same on both sides of the stage, the pattern is varied by having three stoves on stage left and four on stage right. This variation is further enhanced by adding a double oven to the upstage end of the stoves on stage right.

Balance

Balance refers to the arrangement of design elements to provide a sense of restfulness, stability, or equilibrium. This design appears to be symmetrically balanced, but closer scrutiny reveals that it doesn't possess the requisite mirror-image balance. There are three stoves and a little work sink on the stage-left wall, while there are four stoves plus a double oven on the right. There are three work stations on stage left and only two on stage right. The center archway is slightly stage left of the center line of the set. While the set isn't symmetrical, the placement of the

FIGURE 5.14
The Kitchen, produced at the University of Arizona, directed by Robert C. Burroughs, scenic and lighting design by J. Michael Gillette.

various elements creates a sense of dynamic equilibrium. The "slightly asymmetrical" design was created to support the idea that everything in the world of *The Kitchen* is a little bit "off" — is not quite what it seems.

Proportion

Closely related to balance, proportion refers to the harmonious relationship of the parts of an object to each other or to the whole. There is a harmonious balance of mass and color in this design. The up-center wall creates a solid backdrop, and the walls, appliances, and work stations cascade out, down, and around to encircle the primary playing area. The layout of the major color blocks — the dirty off-white up-center wall, green and mahogany up-center hallway, black stoves, and silver work stations — is essentially symmetrical and provides a nice sense of balance and harmony to the design.

Emphasis

Emphasis refers to creating areas of visual interest that the audience will look at before they look at anything else. In scenic design, emphasis is normally placed on the acting area(s). In this design, emphasis was directed toward the primary down-center acting area in several ways. The black void surrounding the set doesn't give the audience anything to look at, effectively forcing them to direct their attention toward the set. The cutaway walls further reduce nonessential visual elements, requiring the audience to look at what remains. The essentially symmetrical design of the set dictates that a sense of equilibrium or balance is achieved only when you are looking at the approximate center of the set. The color design further focuses the audience's attention on the down-center area of the set. The dirty-white up-center wall provides an effective primary point of focus, but it was several shades darker than the white costumes of the cooks, so the wall didn't steal focus from the actors. The chrome and brushed stainless steel of the work stations provided two points of emphasis that effectively framed either side of the primary playing area. The stoves, placed further from the primary playing area, were finished in burnished metallic black to effectively recede into the black void surrounding the set. The medium green walls and dark mahogany doors of the up-center hallway diminished the visual importance of that prominent position, again focusing attention further downstage.

The foregoing example employed scenic design to explain the uses of the various principles of composition. An understanding of these tools of the designer will provide you with the basic artistic resources to be able to create effective designs in not only scenic design but costumes, lighting, and sound as well.

Chapter 6

Color

Color is easily the most noticeable of the design elements and is arguably the most dominant. It is also the least understood. We grow up with color all around us, and we see and use it every day. It is probably because of our constant contact with color that we accept it without really thinking about it. This chapter attempts to help you understand the complex subject of color.

 Defining Color

Color has a variety of definitions. It can be defined as a perception created in the brain as a result of stimulation of the retina by light waves of a certain length. It can also be thought of as the intrinsic physical properties of specific objects that allow those objects to reflect and absorb light waves of a certain length. The common denominator for any definition of color is light, because the visual perception of all color is derived from light. The phenomenon that we call light is actually the very narrow portion of the spectrum of electromagnetic radiation that is visible to the human eye. Figure 6.1 shows the position of visible light on this spectrum, as well as that of some of the other types of radiation. The visible spectrum stretches in frequency from approximately 750 nanometers to 400. (A nanometer is one billionth of a meter.) Figure 6.2 shows the approximate wavelengths for the various colors of the visible spectrum.

Color Terminology

Without a specific set of terms to describe the various properties of color, almost any discussion of it would quickly degenerate into rather meaningless comparisons. An example will help explain this phenomenon. If you provided each member of a group of twenty people with one hundred **paint chips,** all yellow, but each slightly different, and asked them to identify canary yellow, they would probably select twenty different chips. This is because the connection between the description of any specific color, such as canary yellow, and the brain's understanding of the physical appearance of that color differs, sometimes significantly, from person to person.

The terms that we will be using in our discussion of color are as follows:

Hue   Hue is the quality that differentiates one color from another, such as blue from green or red from yellow.

Saturation   Saturation, also known as chroma, refers to the amount, or percentage, of a particular hue in a color mixture. Fire-engine red has a high, or

paint chip: A small rectangle of paper or thin cardboard painted in a specific hue.

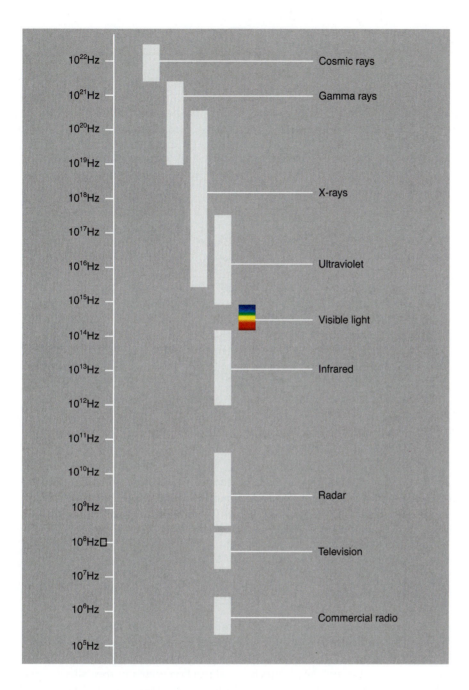

FIGURE 6.1
The frequency range of selected energy forms contained in the electromagnetic radiation spectrum.

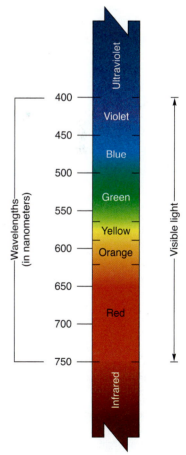

strong, saturation, because there is a lot of fully saturated color in the mixture. Dusty rose, in contrast, has a low, or weak, saturation, because there isn't a lot of fully saturated color in the mixture; instead, the majority is white or gray.

Value   The relative lightness or darkness of a color is referred to as value. Pale blue has a high value, and dark brown has a low value.

Tint   A color with a high value is referred to as a tint. It is usually achieved by mixing a hue with either white pigment or white light.

Shade   A color with a low value is known as a shade. It is usually created by a mixture of one or more hues and black.

FIGURE 6.2
The frequency range of visible light.

FIGURE 6.3
The color triangle is a visual representation of the relationships that exist among color, shade, tint, and tone.

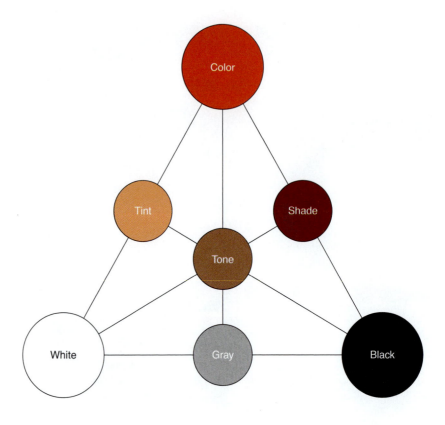

Tone   A color of middle value is frequently referred to as a tone. It is a mixture of a hue with black *and* white. The addition of a **complementary** hue tones a color.

The color triangle in Figure 6.3 shows the relationships among hue, white, black, gray (the product of mixing black and white), tint, shade, and tone.

 ## Seeing Color

Before we learn how color works, we should understand how we see color. Human sight comprises a complex series of events. When you look at an object, elements within your eye are stimulated by the light being emitted by, or reflected from, the viewed object. An electrochemical reaction occurs in specialized nerve cells in the retina. Two distinct types of light-receptor nerves, **rods** and **cones,** emit minute charges of electricity that are relayed to your brain, where the received data are interpreted as a "picture" that you have seen. The cones are divided into three primary groups: those that respond to the wavelengths of light that correspond to red, blue, and green, respectively.

If a red light enters the eye, the red-responsive cones are stimulated but the others are not. If a light that contains both red and blue wavelengths enters the eye, both the red- and blue-responsive cones are stimulated. In this case, the message that is sent to the brain corresponds to the ratio of red and blue light contained in the light mixture that the eye receives. If the light contains more red than blue light, that information is transmitted.

Notice that the eye can only send information to the brain corresponding to the input it has received. The brain is the organ that does the interpretative mix-

complementary: Two hues that, when combined, yield white in light or black in pigment; colors that are opposite each other on the color wheel.

rods: Nerve cells in the retina that are sensitive to faint light.

cones: Nerve cells in the retina that are sensitive to bright light; they respond to red, or to blue, or to green light.

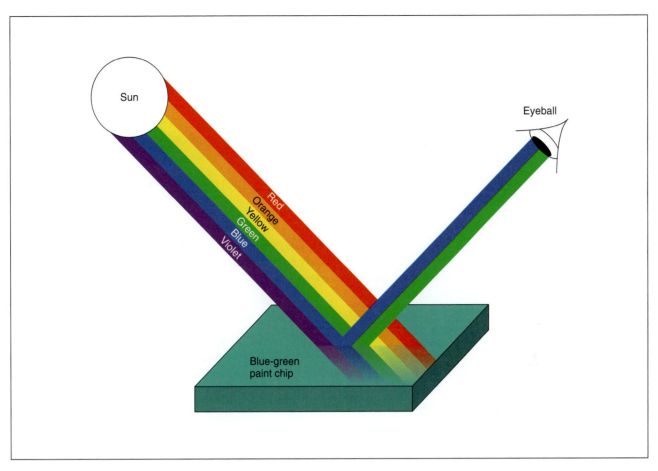

FIGURE 6.4
The brain interprets the neurological information it receives from the eye to be a specific hue.

ing of the colors. In the example of the red and blue light, the amount of red and blue in the mixture will be interpreted by the brain to be a particular color such as violet, magenta, or purple.

All perceived color is transmitted to the eye by light. If the light is dim, the cones (color sensors) do not function. The best way to demonstrate this effect is by standing outside on a moonlit night and looking at your surroundings. Everything you see will be a monochromatic gray, with perhaps a slight tint of blue or green if the moonlight is sufficiently bright. You will see no vibrant reds, blues, or greens, because the cones require more light than is being transmitted to your eye. If you look at the same scene during the daytime, the bright sunlight will activate the cones in your eye. Unless your eye has some physical dysfunction or the color-interpretative segment of your brain is impaired, you will see colors.

To further illustrate how the eye sees and the brain interprets color, let's assume that you are standing outside in the sunlight looking at a turquoise (blue-green) color chip, as shown in Figure 6.4. The sunlight, which contains all of the electromagnetic wavelengths of the visible spectrum, strikes the blue-green surface of the color chip. Some of that light is reflected, and some of it is absorbed by the pigment on the paint chip. The majority of those wavelengths of light that correspond to the color of the chip (blue and green) are reflected. The majority of all other wavelengths of light are absorbed by the paint chip. The reflected blue and green light is received by the eye. The blue and green cones are stimulated by the light, causing them to send electrical impulses to the brain. The relative strength of these signals from the blue and green cones is proportionate to the specific amount of blue and green in the color mix. When the color-sensitive area of the brain is stimulated by these impulses, it interprets that information as a specific color known to that particular brain as turquoise.

Color Mixing

Before examining color mixing, we must understand some additional terms.

Primary Colors

Primary colors are those hues that cannot be derived or blended from any other hues. In light, the primary colors are closely related to the color sensitivity of the red, blue, and green cones in the eye.

Secondary Colors

Secondary hues are the result of mixing two primary colors. In the color wheel for light (Figure 6.5A), the mixing of adjacent primaries creates the secondary hues yellow, magenta, and cyan (blue-green). The primary colors in **pigment** (Figure 6.5B) are red, blue, and yellow. The secondary colors in pigment are purple, green, and orange.

pigment: A material that imparts color to a paint or dye.

Complementary Colors

Complementary colors can be described as any two hues that, when combined, yield white in light or black in pigment. They can also be described as colors op-

FIGURE 6.5
Color wheels for (A) light and (B) pigment.

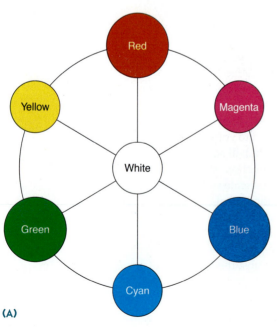

(A)

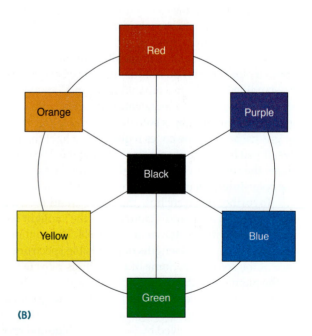

(B)

PRODUCTION INSIGHTS
Theoretical Versus Practical Color Mixing

According to color theory, the combination of complementary pigments yields black. The reason is straightforward. Each pigment reflects the wavelengths of light that correspond to its own hue and absorbs all others, as shown in Figure 6.6. Complementary hues are composed of one primary color and a secondary color. The secondary color is created from a mixture of the other two primary hues. The resultant blend of all three primaries should, theoretically, absorb all light that strikes it. This absence of reflected color means no light, which is the same as blackness.

In the practical mixing of pigments, you will be dealing with paints that are not pure colors. There are fillers, extenders, and impure colors in every commercially prepared paint. These impurities and surface diffusion—the scattering of light caused by the texture of the reflecting surface—will result in a deep gray instead of the theoretically correct black when mixing complementary hues.

posite each other on a color wheel. The color wheel for light (Figure 6.5A) shows that the complementary hue for red is cyan. When the two are combined, they form white light. In the color wheel for pigment (Figure 6.5B), the complementary of red is green. When the two are mixed, they form black.

FIGURE 6.6
Color reflection and absorption are determined by the hue of the pigment. Each hue will reflect its own color and absorb all others.

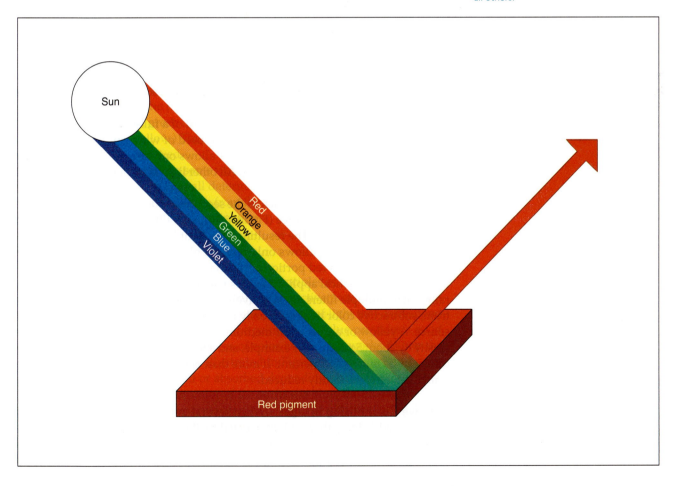

Sun

Red
Orange
Yellow
Green
Blue
Violet

Red pigment

FIGURE 6.14
The color of the set and sail (white) was selected for two reasons: (1) Antarctica is overwhelmingly white; (2) the highly reflective neutral color makes an excellent projection surface for the various colors and images that make up a large segment of the design concept.

nonspecific memory locations. It is essential for the continuity of the play that scenes flow smoothly from location to location without a break in the action.

The Scenic Design   The color design helped to create the cinematic flow required for the production. To bring to life the vast coldness of Antarctica, the set, which was a jumble of platforms arranged to create an abstraction of the ruptured surface of an ice floe, was painted an off-white (Figure 6.14). On the upstage side of the platforms a large expanse of unpainted, unbleached muslin was suspended from an abstracted ship's spar (Figure 6.15). This sail was used as a projection surface for color washes, visual effects, and photographic images of Scott's ill-fated expedition to the South Pole. The entire set was surrounded by a black cyclorama to help focus the audience's attention on the set and actors.

FIGURE 6.15
The sail was backlit with color washes (left) to provide primary atmospheric and psychological keys about the nature of the individual scenes. It was also used as a projection surface for black-and-white slides of Scott's actual expedition (right).

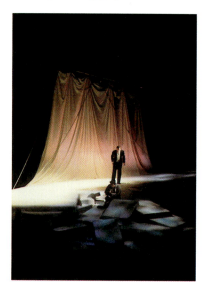

FIGURE 6.16
The warm floral-print fabric and diagonal hem of Scott's wife's summer dress provided a strong visual contrast with the vertical and horizontal patterns in the muted gray and brown fabrics of the men's suits.

The Costume Design   The costumes and properties were ultrarealistic. The natural earth tones (primarily shades of browns and grays) of the properties and the men's costumes stood out in strong contrast against the whiteness of the set. Scott's wife, the only woman in the play, was seen only in Scott's memory scenes of home. She was dressed in a floral print (Figure 6.16) to present a stark contrast with the muted patterns and solids that were worn by the men.

Lighting Design   The lighting used color as a primary device to create psychological keys in support of the emotional content of the various scenes. Figure 6.17 provides a color key of the lighting used in this production indicating the direction and color of the various light sources. (Note that the numbers indicate Roscolux color numbers.) Figures 6.18–6.21 show how the various design elements (scenic, costume, properties, lighting) blended to create the color impact of the production design.

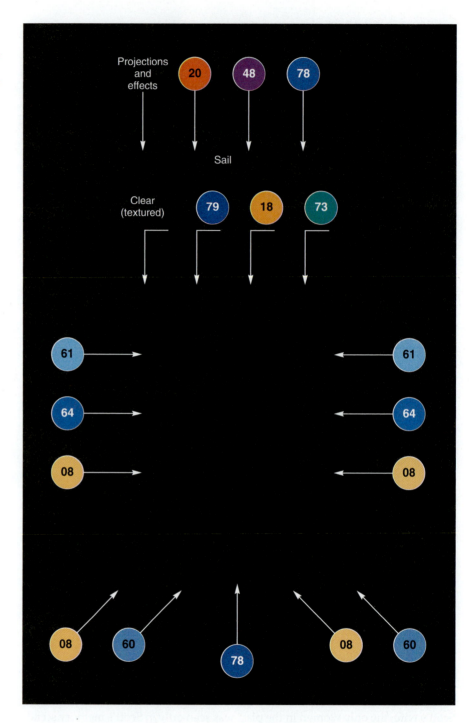

The scenes in Antarctica were lit with almost painfully brilliant white light
(Figure 6.18), which resulted in the colors of the costumes and properties being
portrayed very closely to their true hues.

The memory scenes were lit with textured top lights and color washes selected for their psychological impact: deep blue for Scott's heavier memories (Figure 6.19); soft pastels for the romantic memories of his wife (Figure 6.20); amber
candlelight for the banquet scene (Figure 6.21).

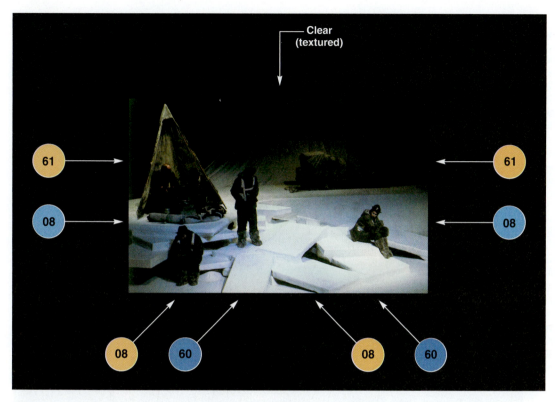

FIGURE 6.18
Complementary colors (Roscolux 08 and 60 from the front and 08 and 61 from the sides) were used at high (but equal) intensity to provide a white, very bright, slightly cool color mix. The clear (white) top light helped to edge the actors' heads and shoulders with white as well as wash out any color shadows created by the individual hues in the front and side lights. The rendering of the skin tones as well as costumes and property colors was slightly cooler than if white light (as opposed to the complementary mix) had been used. The "cooler" look was a desired effect.

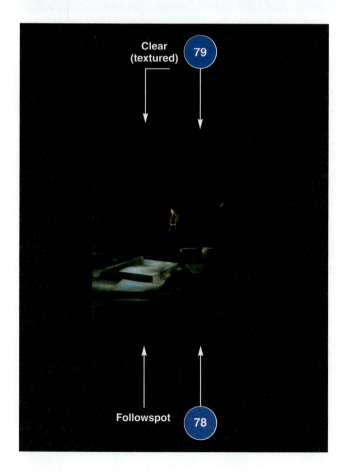

FIGURE 6.19
The textured light was created by bathing the stage with saturated blue (78 and 79) from the front and top. The texture was created by introducing the clear, textured top light at relatively low intensity. Scott's face was framed with a low-intensity followspot whose beam diameter was only shoulder wide. Skin tones and upper-torso costume colors were rendered naturally by the warm followspot (at low intensity the light from the uncolored beam is naturally warm) combining with, and overriding the effects of, the deep blue.

FIGURE 6.20
The atmosphere of England was created by using textured top lights colored in warm, soft hues (18 and 73) and the back lights on the sail (20 and 48) to provide a striking contrast with the blue-white coldness of the lights for Antarctica. Scott and his wife (down stage) were lit with warm-white combinations of 08 and 60 from the front and 08 and 61 from the sides. The figure in the background was side lit with a warm, dim, front/side light. The warm-white light on Scott and his wife provided accurate color rendering of their costumes. The warm light striking the background figure created a fairly accurate color rendering of his tuxedo.

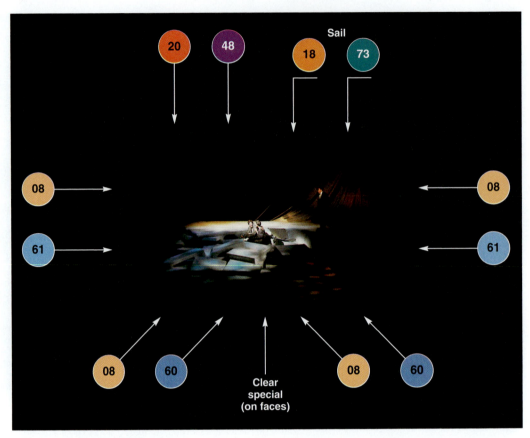

The use of low-saturation complementary colors to light the acting areas from the front and sides significantly reduced the color-shifting effects of the stage lights on costumes and skin tones. The clear, textured top lights, when used in conjunction with the heavily saturated top washes, created significant changes in the visual appearance of the set. These elements, working together, created a subtly effective color design that worked for the support of the production.

Explanations of how the color palettes of the various design elements (scenic, costume, property, and lighting) interacted are contained in the captions for each illustration.

Cabaret*

The Environment of the Play   The primary location of this musical is a seedy, second-rate night club, the Kit Kat Klub, in Berlin, Germany, in the years 1929–30. Additional scenes take place in several other locations: a railroad car, various rooms in a rooming house, and a fruit shop.

The Scenic Design   The scenic design for *Cabaret* created a startling contrast through the juxtaposition of line, color, and finish (Figure 6.22). The strong con-

---

*Director and choreographer: Richard Hanson; scenic design: Tom Benson; costume design: Peggy Kellner; lighting design: J. Michael Gillette.

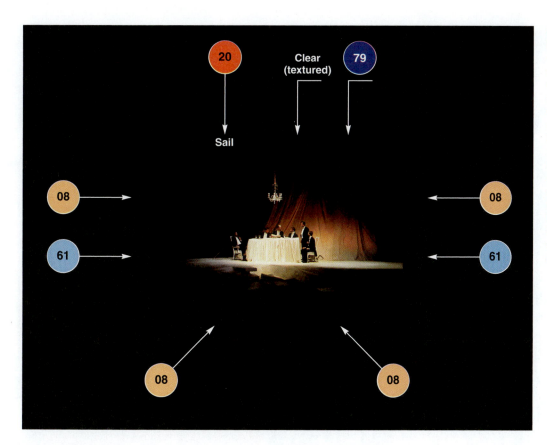

FIGURE 6.21
Primary color for this scene was provided by the warm amber (20) on the sail in the background. The banquet table was lit with a warm-white blend of 08 and 61 from the sides and 08 from the front and uncolored, textured top light. A little blue top light (79) was used to enhance the edging effect of the top light on the black tuxedos. This created a candlelit feeling with warm skin tones, tablecloth and floor, and black tuxedos.

trast was appropriate because it helped to heighten the dramatic tension inherent in the script and the production concept. The dominant element of the design was the Kit Kat Klub, which was painted in medium-saturation earth tones. However, the color was applied in an erratically angular pattern on the vertical face of the runway as well as on the floor of the audience portion of the nightclub. The zigzag motif was continued with the busy herringbone pattern on the floor of the runway and the rest of the stage.

The floor and four upstage columns were finished with a high-gloss glaze to heighten the contrast between those elements and the remainder of the set, which was painted with a traditional matte finish. The shimmering aluminized Mylar curtain (Figure 6.23) provided another dazzling type of contrast during one of the production numbers.

Small white light bulbs were used to spell CABARET and outline the arches. These little pinpoints of light played against the black void created by the surrounding black cyclorama to create another type of emphatic contrast.

The fully saturated secondary colors (amber, cyan, and magenta) used in the double rows of vertical striplights on either side of the stage, and the 6-inch Fresnel spotlights hung from the upper-level railings of the set, created another jarring note of color contrast.

The color and contrast treatment of the other locations, which slid in on a shuttle stage just upstage of the nightclub runway, were more muted than those of the Kit Kat Klub because, in general, scenes that took place in the other locations were emotionally "softer" and more intimate.

The Costume Design   Contrast was also readily evident in the costume design. The designs for the Kit Kat Girls were based on vibrant, fully saturated colors (Figure 6.24) and high-sheen fabrics. A powerful statement was made by the contrast between the actresses' pale skin and the skimpy, heavily saturated, highly reflective surfaces of the costumes.

The costumes for Sally (the two on the left and the two on the right in Figure 6.25) used a change in saturation and hue as a device to mirror her emotional progression through the play. In the beginning, she was dressed in the vibrant, shocking colors and styles of the Kit Kat Girls. As she fell in love with Cliff, she dressed in softer, more muted tones. When Sally chose to stay in Germany as Cliff left, her reimmersion in the world of the cabaret was mirrored in the high contrast of a floor-length black sequin evening dress that she wore in the final scene.

The men's costumes, while being faithful to the period, also mimicked the emotionally based use of high contrast employed for the women's costumes. The Master of Ceremonies and the cabaret ensemble men were costumed in black-

FIGURE 6.22
Scenic design for *Cabaret,* by Tom Benson.
A number of hues were used on this production,
but they were all in a fairly close tonal range.
Contrast was achieved primarily by pattern variation and gloss finish coats applied to selected
elements of the set.

and-white evening wear, while Cliff and Herr Schultz were dressed in suits of
muted hues selected to mirror their emotional warmth.

Lighting Design   The colors selected for the lighting design were dictated by
three primary considerations: (1) the full-spectrum colors of the costumes and set;
(2) the heavy, smoke-filled, sensuous atmosphere needed for the cabaret; and (3) the
need for a lighter, more realistic atmosphere for those scenes outside the cabaret
(Figure 6.26).

Complementary colors of light-to-moderate saturation (Roscolux 62 and 02)
were selected for the front lights for the acting areas because they would be appropriately neutral for both the cabaret scenes and those more intimate scenes
outside the cabaret. However, those colors had enough saturation to enhance
the costume and set colors in both locations. By balancing the color mix between
the 02 and 62, the stage could be made neutral, cool, or warm as appropriate. The
full saturation necessary for the scenes inside the cabaret was supplied by the
Roscolux 20, 57, and 93 used on the vertical striplights and Fresnels on either side

FIGURE 6.23
The aluminized Mylar curtain provided a startling contrast with the black background immediately upstage of the curtain and created a spectacular reflective surface for the fully saturated hues in the vertical strip-lights on either side of the stage.

of the stage. These saturated color washes, used in conjunction with the acting-area lights, enhanced the full-spectrum, strongly colored palettes of the costumes and scenery used in the cabaret scenes, as well as creating the heavy atmosphere necessary within the cabaret. (Specific hues of strongly saturated light create an impression of more vibrant color than do similar hues of less saturation. If two or more of these relatively saturated hues are additively mixed to create a white light, the resultant white light will create a similar vibrant color reaction from the full color spectrum.)

During production numbers, the set was generally lit with psychologically appropriate color washes, and the six followspots, using white or lightly tinted light, were used to highlight the various leads.

The downstage area of the cabaret audience was lit with a top wash of textured white light to support the concept that the area was lit by the individual table lamps. During the out-of-the-cabaret scenes, the textured top wash was combined with a deep blue wash to reduce the area's apparent visibility. (The deep blue looks like a shadow color but allows the "real" audience to see the shadow detail.)

The difference between the theory and practice of color mixing is only a matter of degree, not principle. Although an understanding of the laws of physics that govern the mixing of color is very helpful in using color in the theatre, the

FIGURE 6.24
Costume designs by Peggy Kellner. The full-saturation, high-contrast "glitzy" materials of the Kit Kat Girls' costumes were enhanced by the strongly saturated hues used to light the cabaret scenes.

FIGURE 6.25
Costume designs by Peggy Kellner. The color progression of Sally's costumes mirrored her emotional progression through the production. See text for details.

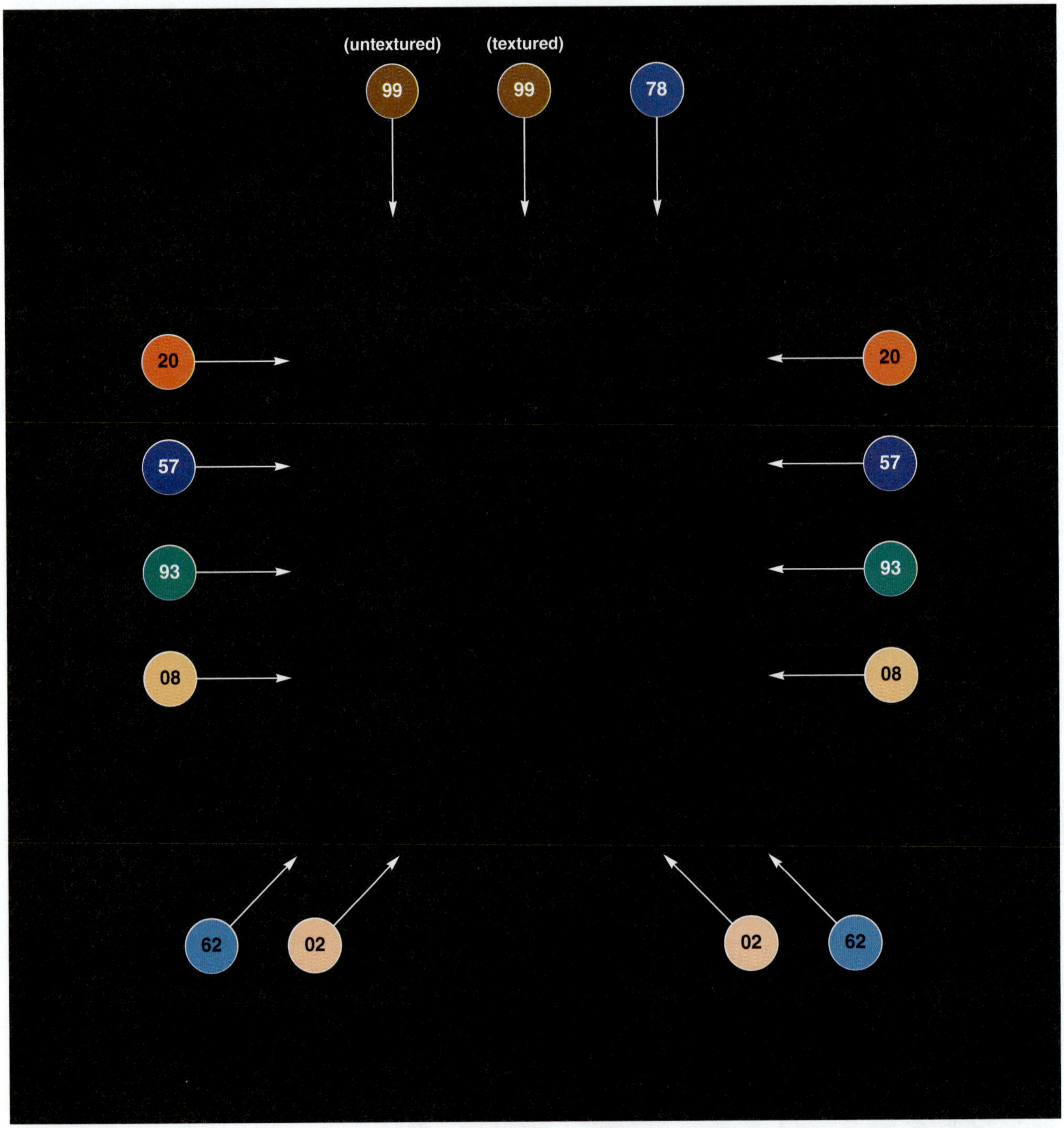

FIGURE 6.26
Color key for the lighting design. Low-saturation colors (02, 62, 08, 99) were used for general acting-area lights, while strong-saturation color washes (20, 57, 93, 78) were added for psychological emphasis. See text for details.

only way that a designer can develop any real understanding of, and facility in, the use of color is through experimentation and experience. Additional information on the practical application of color can be found in Chapters 12 ("Scene Painting"), 14 ("Lighting Design"), and 22 ("Drawing and Rendering").

Chapter 7

Mechanical Drafting

Diagrams, freehand drawings, and perspective sketches give a clear, general picture of what a proposed design or prop is supposed to look like, but they don't tell you how to build it. Similarly, sketches, notes, and verbal explanations describing the hanging location of the various instruments used to light a production are frequently more confusing than helpful. Fortunately, mechanical drawing, or drafting, provides a convenient, and efficient, solution to these challenges.

Mechanical drafting can be done by hand or with a computer. Hand drafting involves the use of a drafting instrument, such as a T square or drafting machine, triangle, compass, or template, to draw each line. Computer drafting requires a computer equipped with an appropriate drafting program. Computer drafting will be discussed a little later in this chapter. Regardless of which method is used, the object being illustrated is **drawn to scale** and is shown from as many views as necessary to provide a clear understanding of the shape of the finished object. Mechanical drawings, when accompanied by **specifications,** provide a complete visual and verbal description of the object.

In theatrical drafting, the scale used for the mechanical drawings needed for most scenic construction is ½ inch to 1 foot. This means that each ½ inch measured on a drawing represents 1 foot on the corresponding full-scale object. The width of the flat drawn to scale in Figure 7.1 is indicated to be 3 feet, but if you measured the drawing, you would find that the flat was only 1½ inches wide.

Mechanical drawings, and the ability to produce them, are extremely important in technical theatre. The scenic designer uses them to accurately describe every element of the setting(s) so that those elements can be built as he or she envisioned them. The technical director uses them to show how each object is to be constructed. For the lighting designer, mechanical drafting provides the accurate scale "road map" that the electricians will use as a guide for hanging the lighting instruments. The sound designer uses mechanical drafting to show, in exact scale representation, the location of the equipment that will be used in support of the production. The scenic technicians, electricians, and sound technicians must be able to read and understand the information contained on the mechanical-drafting sheets, or plates.

 ## Drafting Materials and Instruments

The list of equipment used in hand-drawn mechanical drawing isn't extensive. It includes a drafting board minimally 24 inches high by 36 inches wide (a larger board of approximately 30 by 42 inches will be better if you are also going to be

draw to scale: To produce a likeness that is a proportional reduction of an object.

specifications: Clarifying notes that explain the building materials, textures, or special effects to be used in a design or other project.

113

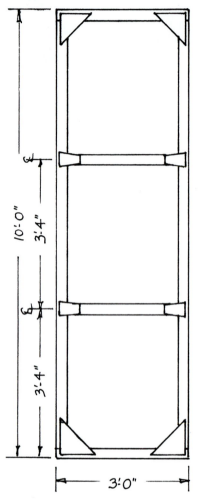

FIGURE 7.1
A flat drawn to scale.

drawing light plots); a good T square with a shaft long enough to reach across the width of the drafting board; one 8-inch 45-45-90-degree triangle and one 12-inch 30-60-90-degree triangle; a pencil compass; an architect's scale rule; an eraser; 2H, 3H, and 4H drafting pencils; and drafting tape.

All hand drafting should be done on good-quality, translucent drafting paper such as Clearprint or a brand of similar quality. Drawings made on this type of paper can be easily **bluelined** for use by other members of the production design team and the various construction shops. Cheap tracing paper tears easily when an erasure is attempted and becomes brittle and unusable with age. Tracing paper with grids shouldn't be used, as the lines will interfere with the drawings that you will be making on the paper.

Drafting Board

The size of the drafting board is not too important provided that the board is large enough to accept the dimensions of the stage for which you will be designing drawn to a scale of ½ inch to 1 foot. The board is usually made of white pine and may be covered with a plastic laminate. The ends of the board should be finished smoothly or, preferably, covered with a metal or plastic cap strip. The edges of the board must be absolutely straight so that the head of the T square will ride evenly on them. (See Figure 7.2.)

If the face of the drafting board is not covered with a plastic laminate, it should be padded with either a sheet of heavy white paper or drafting board padding material. The padding not only makes the drawing easier to see but also prevents sharp pencil points from scoring the wooden surface of the board.

T Square

The accuracy of any hand-produced mechanical drawing depends, to a great extent, on the condition of the T square. All horizontal lines are made by placing the head of the T square snuggly against the edge of the drawing board and guiding a pencil along the upper edge of the leg of the T square, as shown in Figure 7.3A. Vertical lines are drawn by placing the base of the triangle against the leg or shaft of the T square and guiding a pencil along the vertical edge of the triangle, as shown in Figure 7.3B. If the head of the T square is not firmly attached to the shaft at a true right angle, neither vertical nor horizontal lines will be accurate. Other types of equipment, such as the Mayline parallel (Figure 7.3C),

FIGURE 7.2
Drafting equipment.

(A)

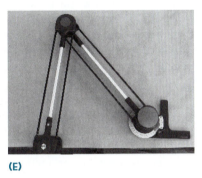
(B)

(C)

(D)

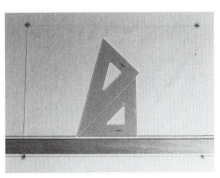
(E)

FIGURE 7.3
How to use a T square. (A) Pull on the leg to keep the head of the T square flush with the edge of the board when drawing horizontal lines. (B) Hold the triangle snuggly to the leg of the T square when drawing vertical lines. (C) A Mayline parallel rule. (D) A track drafting machine. Courtesy of Alvin & Company, Inc. (E) An elbow drafting machine. Courtesy of Vemco Drafting Products Corporation.

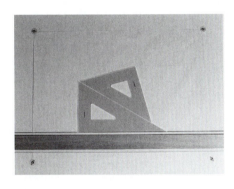

FIGURE 7.4
How to draw 15- and 75-degree angles.

the track drafting machine (Figure 7.3D), and the elbow drafting machine (Figure 7.3E), perform the same function as the T square but are considerably more expensive. As might be expected, the parallel and drafting machines are generally easier to use and more accurate than the T square.

Triangles

Triangles can be purchased in many different sizes, but the 8-inch 45-45-90-degree and the 12-inch 30-60-90-degree triangles are ideally suited for most drafting purposes. Triangles any smaller than these necessitate shifting both the T square and triangles to a new position to draw a long vertical line. By placing one triangle against another, as shown in Figure 7.4, and guiding both with the T square, angles of 15 and 75 degrees can be drawn.

The set square, shown in Figure 7.5, is an adjustable triangle with two parts joined by a plastic protractor reading from 0 to 45 degrees. A threaded bolt and thumbscrew allow the two halves of the triangle to be locked in any desired position.

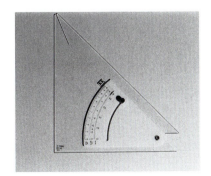

FIGURE 7.5
A set square.

(A)

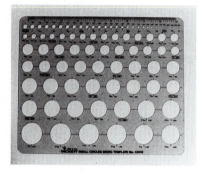

(B)

FIGURE 7.6
(A) A compass and (B) a circle template.

Compass and Circle Template

A medium-quality compass (Figure 7.6A) is needed for drawing circles and arcs. A substitute preferred by many drafters is a circle template, shown in Figure 7.6B. When purchasing a circle template, select one with a large number of circle diameters, because a template will almost invariably have every size except the one you want to use.

Architect's Scale Rule

The key to making all scaled mechanical drawings is the use of an architect's scale rule. The scales found on the rule make the process of allowing a fraction of a foot to represent a full foot practically painless.

The architect's rule (Figure 7.7) is made in two shapes, triangular and flat. The triangular rule (which is less expensive) has a standard foot measure on one edge and ten different scales, two on each of the remaining five edges: 1 foot to $\frac{3}{32}$, $\frac{1}{8}$, $\frac{3}{16}$, $\frac{1}{4}$, $\frac{3}{8}$, $\frac{1}{2}$, $\frac{3}{4}$, 1, $1\frac{1}{2}$, and 3 inches. The flat rule may be a little more convenient to use, but it has only eight scales and is more expensive.

The one-half-inch scale, as noted, is the most frequently used in theatrical drafting. This scale reads from right to left on the architect's scale shown in Figure 7.8A. At the extreme right of the rule is a $\frac{1}{2}$-inch space that has been divided into twelve spaces representing inches, with each scale inch subdivided into halves by shorter lines. Foot measurements are indicated in multiples of two; they read 0, 2, 4, 6, and so on. Odd-numbered foot measurements, not indicated by a numeral, are found by using the marks for the 1-inch scale. These marks fall midway between the numerals of the $\frac{1}{2}$-inch scale. On the $\frac{1}{2}$-inch scale the foot measurements are read to the left of the zero, and the inches are read to the right.

Figure 7.8B shows how the architect's scale rule is used to measure a line. One end of the line is placed on a full-foot mark, and the other end of the line projects into the inch breakdown of the scale foot. The length of the line is read by counting the number of feet to the right of the zero point on the scale and the number of inches to the left.

Drawing Pencils

Most drafting for theatrical work is done with drafting pencils marked 2H (soft), 3H (medium), and 4H (hard). Drawing pencils (those designated by the letter *B*) leave a blacker line, but they smudge easily and quickly leave both the drafter's hands and drawing instruments covered with graphite. It is much easier to

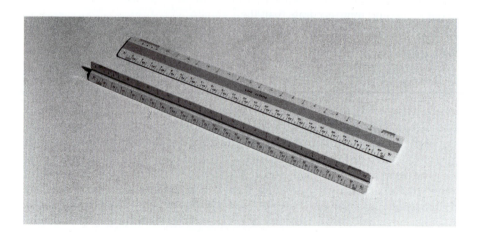

FIGURE 7.7
Architect's rules.

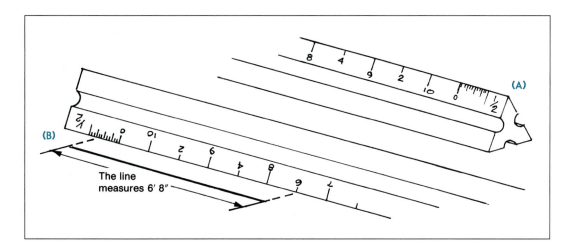

FIGURE 7.8
(A) A half-inch rule.
(B) How to measure
the scale length of
a line.

The line
measures 6' 8"

handle and manipulate a long drafting pencil than one that has been worn down to a stub. A sharp pencil is essential for accurate drafting, because only a sharp point can draw a clean, crisp line of unvarying width. The mechanical push-point drafting pencils, which use leads of diameters that correspond to the widths of the various drafting lines—approximately 0.3 mm for thin lines and 0.5 mm for thick lines—solve a lot of the problems with dull points that seem to plague neophyte drafters. However, whether you choose mechanical or wood pencils is strictly up to you; the two work equally well.

FIGURE 7.9
Auxiliary drafting equipment.

Eraser

A soft, pliable, pink eraser or a kneadable eraser (Figure 7.9) is the best choice for correcting penciled mistakes. Each removes the graphite without discoloring or damaging the paper.

Powdered eraser, contained in either a shaker can or a bag called a **pig,** can be sprinkled on the drafting paper while the drawing is being made. The movement of the T square and triangles over these particles keeps the underside of the instruments clean and prevents a graphite "shadow" from forming on the paper.

pig: A bag of loosely woven fabric containing powdered eraser material.

plotter: A printer used to produce computer-generated drafting sheets and drawings on large paper.

Drafting Tape

Drafting tape is used for holding the paper in place on the drafting board. Drafting tape and masking tape look alike. However, drafting tape will not leave a sticky residue on your drawings, whereas masking tape will.

To tape the paper to the board, you will need to adjust it until the upper or lower edge of the paper is parallel with the T square shaft. Use 2- to 3-inch strips of drafting tape to hold down the four corners of the paper, as shown in Figure 7.10. Commercially available small circular taping tabs can also be used to tape the paper to the drawing board.

Computer Drafting

One of the most common use of computers in theatrical production is in the area of drafting. There are numerous excellent two- and three-dimensional drafting programs. Two of the more commonly used are Vectorworks by Graphsoft (for Macs and PCs) (Figure 7.11) and AutoCad by Autodesk (for PCs).

An additional piece of hardware that is necessary for use when computer drafting is a **plotter** that will print on sheets of paper up to approximately

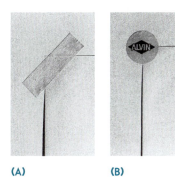

(A)   (B)

FIGURE 7.10
(A) Use of drafting tape. (B) Taping tabs.

24 × 36 inches. These machines are relatively expensive, but access to them is frequently available through local quick-copy centers, blueprint shops, or university computing labs or centers. You simply take the disk containing your drafting file(s) to the shop and it prints the file(s) at a nominal fee.

Scenic Drawings   Software drafting programs facilitate the rapid production of scale ground plans, sections, elevations, and other drawings used to describe scenery and properties. Depending on the skill and experience of the draftsperson and the complexity of the object being drawn, it may take longer to draft an object on the computer than by hand (or vice versa). For most draftspersons, once the basic principles of computer drafting have been mastered, use of these pro-

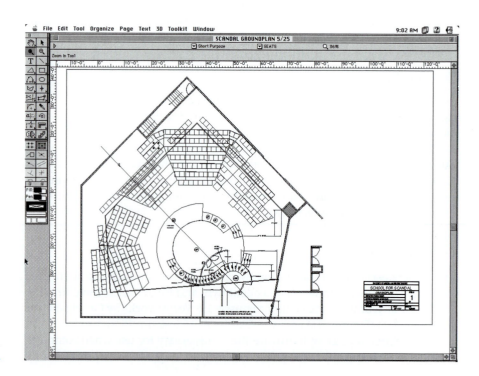

FIGURE 7.11

On-screen view of ground plan for *School for Scandal,* scenic design by Peter Beudert. Software: MiniCad by Diehl Graphsoft, Inc.

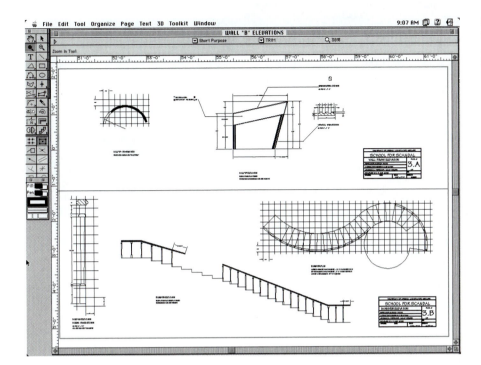

FIGURE 7.12
On-screen view of elevation for *School for Scandal,* scenic design by Peter Beudert. Software: MiniCad by Diehl Graphsoft, Inc.

grams reduces the overall time spent drafting. Computer drafting certainly reduces the time required to make corrections or changes on previously drafted plates. When making a change you simply recall the file, redraft only those sections of the plate that need to be altered, and print out a new copy of the full plate. Figure 7.12 is an example of computer drafting for scenery.

Drafting programs also are ideal for those situations in which you want or need to change the scale of a particular drawing. All you need to do is select the new scale. The computer recalculates the data and prints out a copy of the rescaled drawing.

Light Plots   There are a number of programs available to assist the designer in drafting the light plot and creating associated paperwork such as the instrument schedule/hook-up sheet, gel **cut list,** circuit to dimmer patch reports, and so forth.

Some examples of the types of computer-generated drafting for lighting are shown in Figure 7.13. Drafting programs for lighting design generally allow you to import CAD files of the scenic design drawings as well as those drawings that detail the stage and auditorium. Conceptually, you can think of the imported plates as a stack of acetate drawings. Stack them the way you want; select needed graphic information from each layer; then, building on that base, create your own drawing—the light plot layout or sectional.

After creating the basic layout, including any permanent and temporary hanging positions, you start placing your instruments. Most programs have an extensive symbol library from which you can "click and drag" the appropriate type and size of fixture or scenic element such as drapes, trusses, and so forth. After placing the instrument symbol on the plot, you assign notational—instrument number, color, circuiting, focus, and so forth—to each unit. Every time you select/place/edit an instrument or create any of the associated notational information, most programs will list that information in the embedded database. That information can be selectively extracted from the database to create the various lists needed to organize and track the equipment. Most drafting programs allow

cut list: A list of the color media required for the lighting design for a particular production categorized by hue and size; used to assist in ordering and cutting the color media for a lighting design.

PRODUCTION INSIGHTS
You Still Need to Know Both

While many of the computer drafting software programs contain excellent features, computer drafting does not negate the need to know the craft of drafting by hand. It can be argued that learning to draft by hand, as opposed to using a computer, is a better way to understand this type of graphic communication: that learning hand drafting makes understanding computer drafting much easier. There is an equally vocal camp that declares that students who've grown up in the "computer culture" learn drafting more easily if they first approach it on the computer. The reality is that some people learn drafting more easily if they first hand draft, while others find it easier to first learn on the computer. What is irrefutable is that you need to learn both ways. At some time you may be caught in a situation where you have to draft something and either you don't have access to a computer or you don't know how to operate the particular drafting program on the computer. Therefore, you still need to be able to read an architect's rule, operate a T square and triangle, draw a straight line, and perform the other hand-drafting skills. However, computer drafting is the current method of choice, and you absolutely need to know how to do it.

you to export data to specialized database programs such as Lightwright for more sophisticated paperwork management. Two of the more popular lighting design drafting programs are Vectorworks' Spotlight and Crescit Software's MacLux Pro.

There are two types of data management programs for lighting design. The first is the sophisticated spreadsheet/database program used to organize the data associated with lighting design—instrument, circuiting, dimmer control, and cueing information—into seemingly endless lists that are a necessary evil in lighting design. The second type is a utility. These programs provide some type of information not normally included in drafting programs.

Lightwright is a popular data management program for lighting design. Available for both Mac and PC, it provides advanced features not generally available in the data management portion of most drafting programs. "It can find mistakes, compare two sets of paperwork, figure your circuit and dimmer needs, automatically renumber a pipe, renumber or rearrange your channels or dimmers, or even assign dimmers automatically based on your channels."[1] Database information generated by a drafting program such as Vectorworks' Spotlight is imported into Lightwright for manipulation, organization, and printing.

Utility programs are generally stand-alone products that provide some type of information not available in a drafting program. Vectorworks' Beamwright is a program that helps the designer choose the correct instrument for a given situation. For example, if you input the distance from a fixture to a lighting area and the size of that lighting area, the software develops a list of fixtures that would provide an effective solution in those circumstances. Another utility, Rosco Labs' LightShop, provides photometric data for the 1,500 instruments in its inventory. On the basis of lamp used, the gel color, the trim height of the fixture, and its floor distance from the subject, the program will tell you the resultant beam diameter, throw, and light output.

Additional information about currently available software for lighting design can be found online and in articles and advertisements in trade magazines such as *Entertainment Design, Pro Lights & Staging News,* and *Lighting Dimensions.*

[1] John McKernon Software, "What Is Lightwright?" http://www.mckernon.com/whatis.htm (accessed April 25, 2004).

SoftPlot Report for file: C:\LITDES\USERINFO\SHOWS\GUYS\GUYSPLOT.LDP

Venue: Meadowvale Theatre
Production: Guys & Dolls
Director: Bob Ridell
Lighting Designer: Glen Miller
Date: 06-02-1996

Instrument Inventory Listing

Stock	Used	Hire	Type	Watts	Notes
44	44		STRAND ZOOM Lekolite 2206	1000	
18	18		STRAND 6 x 9 Lekolite 2209	1000	
15	15		STRAND 6 x 9 LEKO 40 - 12240	1000	
8	8		STRAND 6 x 16 LEKO 20 - 12220	1000	
2	2		STRAND 6 x 22 LEKO 15 - 12215	1000	
6	6		STRAND 6 x 12 Lekolite 2212	1000	
4	4		ALTMAN 6 x 12 360Q 6x12	750	
24	25	1	STRAND 8" Fresnel 3480	1000	
15	14		STRAND 6" Fresnel 3380	1000	
6	0		STRAND CODA 500/1 MkII - 5801	500	
6	0		STRAND Iris 1- 5911	1500	
4	2		STRAND 14" 4271	1000	
38	35		PAR-64 Q1000		
2	4	2	STRAND FLOODLIGHT	2000	

End of Report

(A)

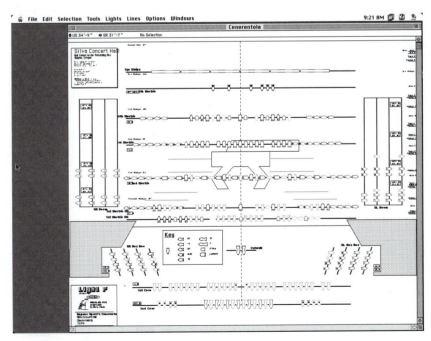

(B)

FIGURE 7.13
(A) Example of paperwork, in this case an Instrument Inventory Listing, produced with Soft Plot by Crescit Software. Lighting design by Glen Miller. (B) On-screen view of a portion of a light plot on the MacLux Pro demo disk. Software: MacLux Pro v. 1.5 by Aladdin Systems, Inc., and Raymond Lau.

Computer drafting for lighting design is clearly the way of the future. What is equally clear is that at the present time, as well as in the foreseeable future, lighting designers will need to know how to do both—draft by hand and draft on a computer.

horizontal offset section: >A section drawing with a horizontal cutting plane, which does not remain fixed but varies to provide a view of important details.

Drafting Symbols and Conventions

The information in this section has been extracted from the United States Institute for Theatre Technology's (USITT) recommendations for standard graphic language in scenic design and technical production. The concept of a standard must evolve from some logical base. In this case, that base is the only inflexible rule of technical drawing—that any graphic communication must be clear, consistent, and efficient. Although the USITT recommendations do not contain specific guidelines for the spacing of objects on a plate, any graphic presentation needs to adhere to the general recommendation of clarity: Do not crowd or unevenly space individual items on a plate. Equally important, all line weights, line types, symbols, conventions, and lettering should be consistent from plate to plate in a given set of drawings. This does not mean that everyone will be expected to letter in the same manner or draw arrowheads in precisely the same way. It means that each drafter should be able to establish his or her style within the guidelines of the recommended standards and conform to that style throughout the drawings for a particular project or production. Finally, the standards and symbols used in any recommended guide should be efficient, both in ease of drawing and in ease of comprehension for the reader.

A great deal of technical theatre drafting is directly related to the ground plan. A modification of the USITT-recommended definition of a light plot provides a good working definition for a ground plan: A ground plan is a **horizontal offset section** in which the cutting plane intersects the theatre at whatever level gives the most descriptive view of the set and stage configuration (Figure 7.14).

FIGURE 7.14

A ground plan for Arizona Summer Arts Festival, production of *K2*, designed by K. Pistor.

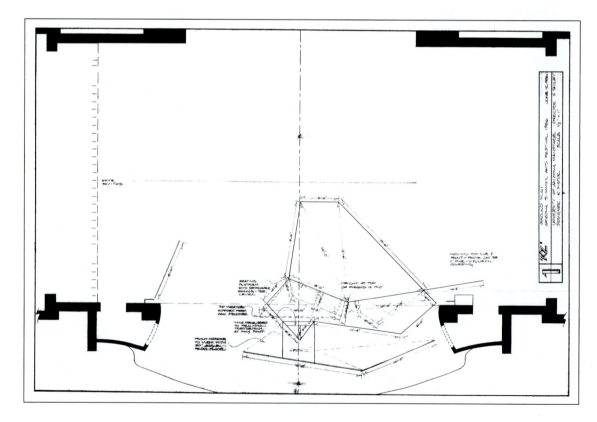

Line Weights

The USITT's adopted line weight standards for light plot drafting, which, in lieu of a specific standard for general theatrical drafting can be used as a guide for scenic drafting, are as follows: Line widths for pencil are 0.3 mm for a thin line and 0.5 mm for a thick line. For ink, the line weights are 0.010 inch to 0.0125 inch for a thin line and 0.020 inch to 0.025 inch for a thick line.[2] The standards for ink are broad enough to be inclusive of the parameters for both DM / PL and HPGL plotters. For scenic drafting, an extra-thick line (0.9 mm in pencil) may also be used to provide additional emphasis, as for a plate border, suitable section cutting plane line, and so on.

Drafting Conventions

The drawing on the ground plan of standard theatrical units such as chandeliers, shelves, fireplaces, and the like should be made using a sectional cutting plan at whatever height is appropriate to provide the most descriptive view of the object. Using this guideline, an item such as a chandelier would be indicated by a circle utilizing a hidden line style (see Table 7.1), because it is not in contact with the stage floor. The circle should be drawn, in scale, as the actual diameter of the chandelier at its widest point. This graphic would be placed in its appropriate location on the floor plan.

Other suspended objects such as ceiling beams or drops not in contact with the stage floor (for example, an Act II drop on an Act I floor plan) would be drawn in the appropriate outline using the hidden line type.

The USITT's guidelines for object emphasis—using the darkness or lightness of a line to direct attention to objects on the plate—for light plot drafting (see the box "Drafting for Lighting Design" in Chapter 14) provides an effective basis for similar standards in scenic drafting. In scenic drafting, the object definition lines—those lines used to define the shape of an object—and any notes/dimensions associated with them should be the darkest or most prominent, architectural lines should be of relatively medium darkness, and dimension lines should be the lightest.

Another recommended convention involves the drafting of flats on the ground plan. They should be drawn in scale thickness and should have the space darkened between the two visible lines that outline the thickness of the flat.

Lettering

Hand lettering should be legible, and the style should allow for easy and rapid execution. Characters that generally conform to the single-stroke Gothic style shown in Figure 7.15 meet these requirements. The criteria for computerized drafting are the same as for hand-drawn lettering. Fonts which are clearly legible and consistent within a set of drawings meet the USITT guidelines. As font names and their appearances vary, often quite a bit, from manufacturer to manufacturer, it is advisable to look through the available fonts on your computer and find one that generally looks like the aforementioned single-stroke Gothic and that pleases your aesthetic taste. Then use it.

[2] Patrick Gill, Chair of USITT Lighting Graphic Standards Committee, "A Revised Standard Graphic for Lighting Design," *Theatrical Design and Technology,* Fall 1991, p. 61.

TABLE 7.1

Drafting Conventions

Type	Style	Notes and Line Weights
Plate border		Extra thick Thick two lines
Cutting plane	A A'	Thick
Section outline		Thick
Visible outline		Thick
Hidden construction		Thin
Plaster ceiling and set line	Plaster line	Thin—note indicates type
Center line (all applications)		Thin—label C̶L̶ on axis
Leader line	To dimension Within outline To outline	Thin
Extension and dimension lines		Thin—full arrowhead preferred
Section interior		Thin—evenly spaced at 45° angle to edge of paper or as clarity requires
Break line	Short Long	Thin—both applications
Phantom line		Thin—used when an object repeats between position line. Also used to designate location of adjacent parts

Any special lines not listed above should be noted in the legend of each sheet.

ABCDEFGHIJKLM
NOPQRSTUVWXYZ
1234567890

FIGURE 7.15
Single-stroke Gothic lettering.

Title Block

The title block should be in the same location on all drawings of a single project. It should be located in either the lower left- or right-hand corner of the drawing or in a strip along the bottom of the drawing. In either case, the block should include the following information:

1. name of producing organization or theatre
2. name of production, act, and scene, if appropriate
3. drawing title
4. drawing number of drawings in the set: for example, ²⁄₁₀
5. predominant scale of the drawing
6. date the drawing was drafted
7. designer of the production
8. drafter, if different from the designer
9. approval of drawing, if applicable

Dimensions

Use of the following guidelines will help to ensure that your drawings are easily understood by everyone who must read them.

1. Dimensions must be clear, consistent, and easily understood.
2. Dimensions should be oriented to read from the bottom or the right-hand side of the plate.
3. Dimensions less than one foot are given in inches without a foot notation (for example, 6″, 9½″).
4. Dimensions one foot and greater include the whole foot with a single prime mark followed by a dash and then inches followed by a double prime mark (for example, 7′-0½″, 18′-5¼″, 1′-3′).
5. Metric dimensions less than one meter should be noted as zero, decimal point, and portion of meter in numerals (for example, 0.25 m, 0.90 m). All measurements one meter and greater should be given as a whole meter number, decimal point, and portion of meter (for example, 1.5 m, 2.35 m).
6. Dimensions that require more space than available between extension lines are placed in proximity to the area measured, parallel with the bottom edge of the sheet, and directed to the point of reference by means of a leader line (see Table 7.1), as shown in Figure 7.16A.
7. Platform and tread heights are given in inches above the stage floor. Such heights are placed in circles at or near the centers of the platform or tread, as shown in Figure 7.16B.

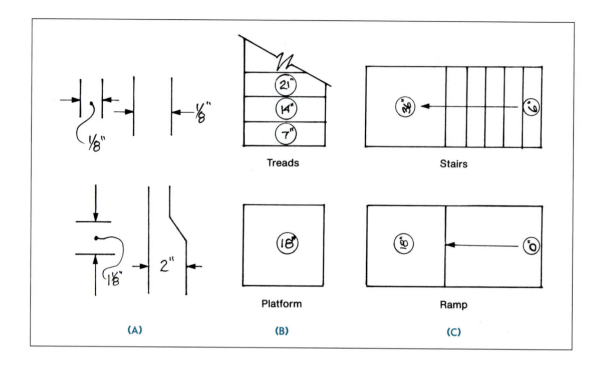

(A)   (B)   (C)

FIGURE 7.16
(A) Methods of indicating dimension.
(B) Heights above or below the stage level are placed in circles near the center of the tread or platform. (C) Arrows are used to indicate change of elevation point away from the primary level of the drawing.

8. Directions of arrows (when used to indicate elevation change on stairs, ramps, and the like) point away from the primary level of the drawing, as shown in Figure 7.16C.

9. A number of acceptable ways to indicate radii, diameters, centers, and angles are detailed in Figure 7.17.

Symbols

Figure 7.18 shows the standard symbols used in theatrical drafting. These symbols should be used as substitutions for drawings of the actual objects.

Objects of nonstandard size, such as doorways, windows, platforms, archways, stairs, and ramps, should be drawn in their actual scale size using the

FIGURE 7.17
Methods of indicating radii, diameters, centers, and angles.

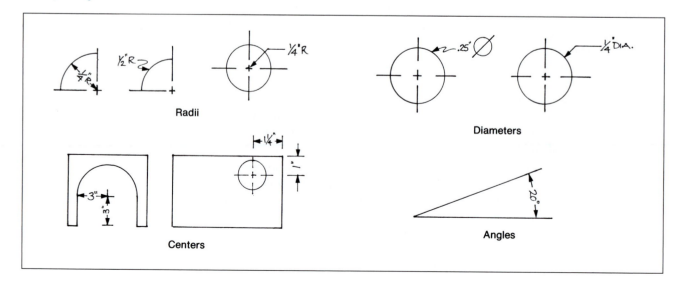

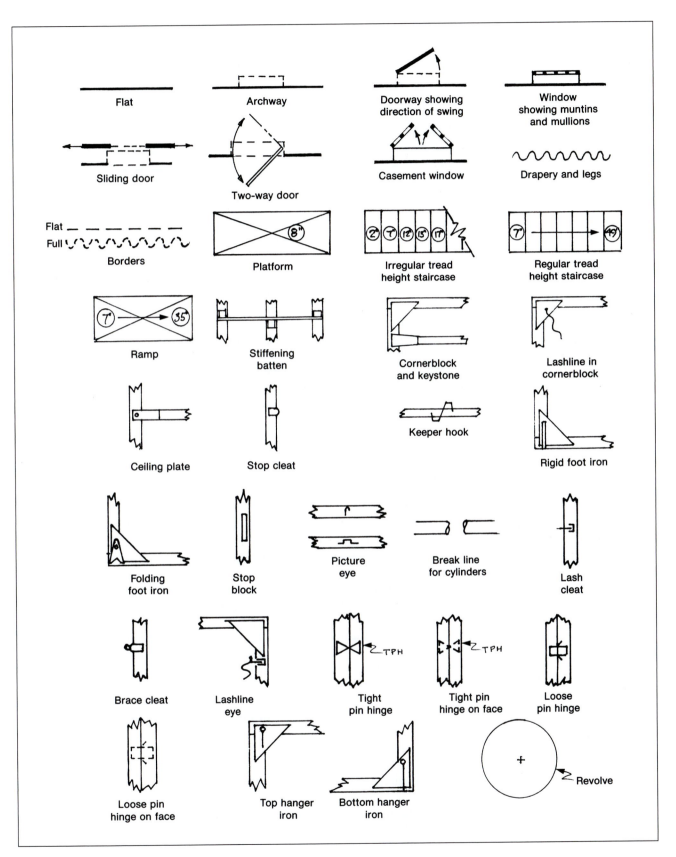

FIGURE 7.18
Technical production symbols.

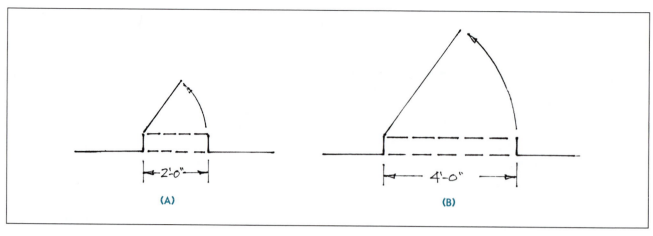

FIGURE 7.19
(A) A 2-foot doorway and (B) a 4-foot doorway. Notice that the symbol is the same, only the width varies.

conventions indicated by the symbols for those objects. According to this principle, a 2-foot-wide doorway would use the convention for a doorway, but the width of the doorway would be drawn in scale to 2 feet, as shown in Figure 7.19A. In a similar manner, a 4-foot-wide doorway would use the same convention, as shown in Figure 7.19B, but the scale width of the door would measure 4 feet. In both cases, the depth of the door casing would be drawn to its actual scale depth. Decorative detail on either the door or the door casing need not be indicated on the ground plan unless it alters the depth or width of the door or casing.

 ## Types of Drawings

Ground Plan

The ground plan is probably the single most important mechanical drawing used in the theatre. Created by the scenic designer, it is a top view of the setting and shows the position of the set in relation to the physical structure of the stage and auditorium.

Depending on the complexity of the production, there may be one or several ground plans. If the play requires a simple single-set interior, a single plan may be able to show the three requirements of any ground plan: (1) the shape of the set, (2) the position of the set within the physical structure of the theatre, and (3) the location of the furniture and set pieces within the set. If the play is a complex multiset show, such as a musical, it may be necessary to have a separate ground plan for each set as well as a composite plan indicating the relationship of one plan to another. There is no hard and fast rule that dictates the number of ground plans necessary for any given production. The guideline that should be followed is that every drawing needs to be clear, consistent, and efficient.

Ground plans are usually drawn in a scale of ½ inch to 1 foot. Drawings in this scale are easy to read, and the size of the paper, usually 24 by 30 inches, is convenient for use in the shop. If you are working in a very large, or very small, theatre, it might be appropriate to use a larger or smaller scale for the ground plan. The ground plan shown in Figure 7.20 illustrates all the pertinent data that need to be included for a proscenium production.

The set line is a leader line that extends, parallel with the proscenium arch, across the farthest downstage point(s) of the set. The plaster line is a leader line that extends across the opening of the proscenium arch. The fixed point from

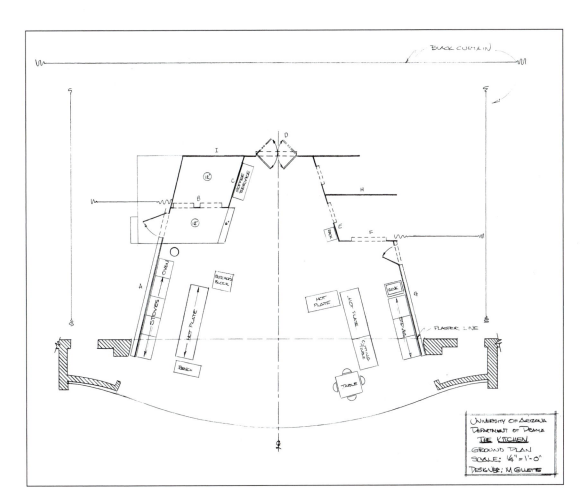

FIGURE 7.20
Ground plan of
The Kitchen.

which this line normally extends is the upstage edge of the proscenium arch, although any other permanent or semipermanent physical element of the stage or its equipment, such as the edge of the false proscenium, could also be used. The center line runs perpendicularly to the set line from the midpoint, or center, of the opening of the proscenium arch. It extends from the apron to the upstage wall of the stage. The margin line is an aesthetically pleasing line that is placed around the border of the plate approximately a ½ inch from the edge of the paper. The margin line can be functionally useful as well. When computer drafting and printing on small paper, you'll know that something isn't missing if the margin line is neatly encircling your entire plate.

Procedurally, it is normally advisable and convenient to draw the structure of the theatre first, then draw the scenery, and finish the plate by drawing the furniture and the margin line. If you are designing for a thrust or arena stage, you will not have a proscenium arch to serve as a reference for your set line and center line. In this case, you still need to establish two reference lines that have an identifiable connection with some permanent element of the stage or auditorium space, as shown in Figure 7.21. Most designers prefer to establish two intersecting lines that cross in the relative center of the set and then extend those lines until they intersect some element of the physical structure of the theatre. It then becomes a relatively simple matter to measure from that point of intersection to an identifiable element of the theatre's structure such as a door frame or exposed water pipe. On a proscenium, thrust, or arena stage, these intersecting lines (set and center) are used as the base lines for transferring the scenic designer's ground plan from the drawings to the actual stage floor.

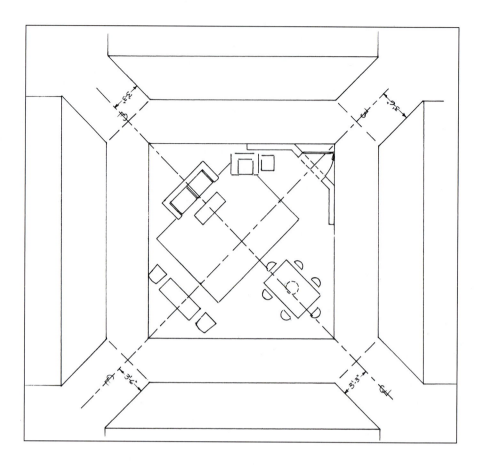

Sectional Drawings

A sectional drawing provides a view of an object as though it had been cut along some imaginary plane. A scenic sectional, also called a hanging plot (Figure 7.22A), shows a sectional view of the stage with the cutting plane of the section being on the center line of the stage. This drawing is used to show the relative position of the set, masking, and various lighting instruments. It is used to help determine trim heights for masking, the heights of various scenic pieces, and similar tasks. A sectional drawing frequently provides the best way of explaining a shape with irregular surfaces, as shown in Figure 7.22B.

Other sectional drawings are used for a variety of purposes. The vertical and horizontal sectional drawings that are used for determining sight-line drawings are discussed in Chapter 8, "Perspective Drawing," and the sectional drawings used in lighting design are discussed in Chapter 14, "Lighting Design."

Front Elevations

A front elevation is a front view of the setting as it would appear if it were flattened out until it was in a single plane and viewed as though the observer were standing exactly at right angles to it. The purpose of these drawings, usually drafted in a scale of ½ inch to 1 foot, is to show the location and measurements of all objects that cannot be recorded on the ground plan. As shown in Figure 7.23, the position, size, and arrangement of all structural elements such as walls, doors, and windows, as well as the location of any built-in items, are given on the front elevations. Decorative and trim features on the walls, such as pictures, base-

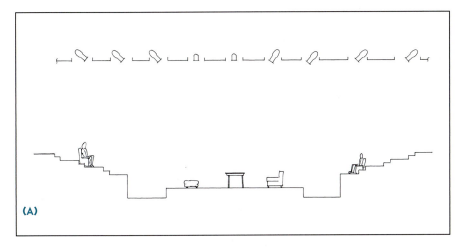

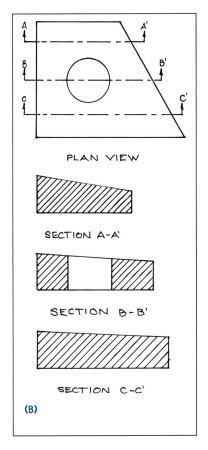

FIGURE 7.22
(A) Sectional drawing of a stage. (B) An irregularly shaped object can be explained with a sectional drawing.

boards, chair rails, wainscoting, cornices, and so on, are also indicated on the front elevations.

Rear Elevations

Rear elevations show the reverse side of objects depicted in the front elevations. This rear view allows the construction details—placement and dimensions of stiles, rails, toggles, and so forth—to be shown. Rear elevations, shown in Figure 7.24, are normally drawn in the same scale as their front-elevation counterparts. The outline of the flats for the rear elevations is easily produced by turning

FIGURE 7.23
Front elevations of *The Kitchen*.

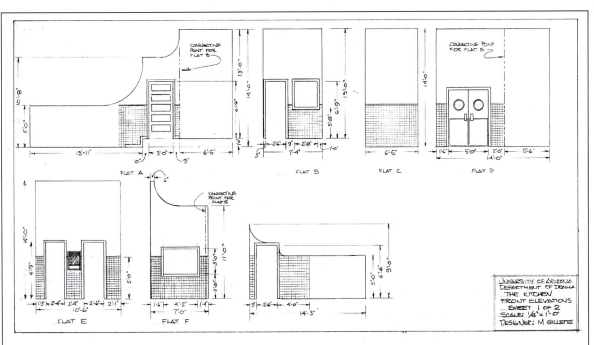

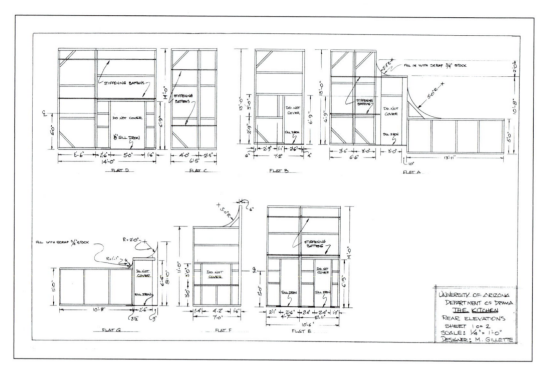

FIGURE 7.24
Rear elevations of *The Kitchen.*

over the tracing paper that contains the front elevations, covering it with another piece of tracing vellum, and tracing the outline using your T square and triangles.

Although the responsibility for producing rear elevations is one of the genuinely gray areas of theatrical production, the need for these drawings isn't. Rear elevations must be drawn when the construction crew is inexperienced or just learning how to build scenery. In the professional theatre, where the construction is done by trained theatrical carpenters, rear elevations are not normally drawn for ordinary construction items such as flats and platforms. They are made only when the object to be built is unusual enough to warrant the precise explanation that the rear elevation provides. In those instances, the drawings are usually done by the scene-shop foreman in consultation with the scenic designer.

In educational theatre, the responsibility for the production of the rear elevations becomes fuzzier. Generally speaking, the rear elevations are the responsibility of the technical director. Due to a variety of circumstances, however, the drawing may be accomplished by the scenic designer or student assistant designers. Regardless of who actually draws the rear elevations, they are vital, as previously noted, to give student carpenters a precise guide for building every element of the setting. Rewards will be reaped in terms of reduced construction errors, better training techniques, lower costs, better use of time, and less frustrated (therefore happier) students.

Detail Drawings

Many times the scale of ½ inch to 1 foot normally used in drawing the front elevations reduces the size of some of the smaller set features to the point that it is difficult, if not impossible, to include all of the dimensions and notes necessary for a complete understanding of the object. In these cases, a larger scale, such as 1 inch or 1½ inches to 1 foot, is frequently used.

If the smaller features of the set are intricately detailed, it is usually both easier and faster to draw them full scale. This would certainly be the case with the

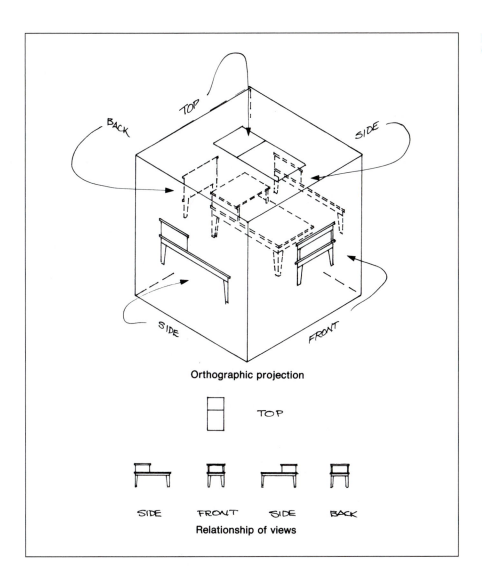

FIGURE 7.25
Orthographic projection.

design for a turned banister or the pattern for a wallpaper design. It is much easier to construct this type of object from a life-size drawing than from one that has been proportionally reduced to a smaller scale.

Many features of a setting cannot be fully described by drawing them in top and front views alone. Three-dimensional objects normally require a third (usually side) view to supplement the other two. Objects that cannot be fully described with only a front, top, and side view, such as an elaborate fireplace or an intricately designed stained-glass window, can usually be well described through the use of orthographic projection, isometric drawing, oblique drawing, or cabinet drawing.

Orthographic Projection   Orthographic projection describes an object with a series of scale elevations showing each side of the article, as shown in Figure 7.25.

The different views of the table are each represented by a separate drawing. Notice that each drawing shows the table as if the observer were standing at right angles to that side of the table.

Isometric Drawing   Isometric drawing provides a fast and easy way of representing an object pictorially without becoming involved with perspective. These

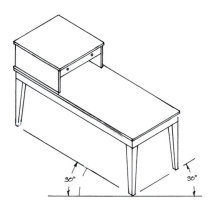

FIGURE 7.26
Isometric drawing.

FIGURE 7.27
Oblique drawing.

drawings are based on three lines called the isometric axes. Two of these axes, illustrated in Figure 7.26, are located at 30 degrees above the horizontal plane on either side of the third axis, which is perpendicular to the base line. Dimensions can be measured at their true length along any of the isometric axes or on lines parallel to them. Lines that are not located on or parallel to the isometric axes cannot be measured.

Since isometric drawing does not take into account the effects of foreshortening or the principles of perspective, it is inevitable that some finished drawings will appear to be distorted. This is especially true of large drawings; the larger the drawing, the more obvious the distortion becomes. Irregular shapes (those with non-square bases) are also difficult to draw and, if drawn, may seem to be misshapen.

Oblique Drawing   Oblique drawing is a combination of the principles of orthographic and isometric drawing. In oblique drawing, one of the faces of the object is placed at right angles to the observer's line of sight (as in orthographic projection), and the other faces subscribe to the tenets of isometric drawing, as shown in Figure 7.27.

If the most complicated surface of the object being drawn is placed in the front view, then the distortion problems encountered with isometric drawing are minimized. The remaining two sides of the object are drawn to the right or left of the front view at angles of 30 or 45 degrees.

Although the object being drawn will probably appear to be distorted, the advantage of the oblique-drawing technique is that it is possible to measure all elements of the drawing that are parallel to the vertical, horizontal, or base (30- or 45-degree) axes.

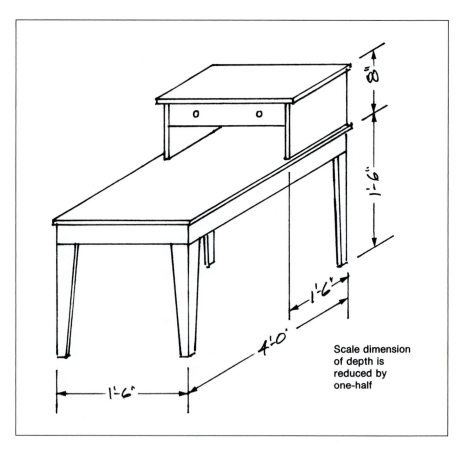

FIGURE 7.28
Cabinet drawing.

Cabinet Drawing   Cabinet drawing (Figure 7.28) and oblique drawing are similar in every detail except one: The depth or thickness measurements of a cabinet drawing are reduced by one-half or a similar ratio such as 1:4. This foreshortening is done in an attempt to reduce the pictorial distortion that occurs if the depth measurement is excessive.

Two precautions should be taken when using this drafting technique. Be sure to write the ratio of reduction in a conspicuous place on the drawing and to specify that the written depth dimension is its true length. The reversed figure **2** placed on either side of the dimension indicates that the length of the dimension line is not an exact scale measurement and that the stated figure is the correct dimension.

All mechanical drawings are created for one purpose—to provide clear, comprehensive visual communication. The standards and guidelines that have been suggested in this chapter are intended to help you reach that goal. But don't follow them blindly simply because they look like rules. Remember that it is the intended application of each drawing that dictates the appearance of that specific plate. For example, the general guidelines suggest that elevations are usually drawn in a scale of ½ inch to 1 foot. But common sense counsels that if another scale will provide a better representation of the object, that scale should be used. In addition to thinking about the purpose of each drawing, be sure to develop good drafting habits. Keep your work area and drafting equipment clean; use a "pig" to keep your drawings clean; practice and develop a clear and confident printing style based on single-stroke Gothic; apply consistent pressure to the pencil; and always, always keep your pencil sharp.

Chapter 8

Perspective Drawing

The process of perspective drawing provides a sketch with the illusion of realistic depth. The form of perspective drawing that will be discussed in this chapter provides you with an accurate, and fairly simple, method of sketching stage sets from a scale ground plan.

While computer drawing programs greatly simplify the process of creating accurate, scale perspective drawings, the reality is that you need to know how to hand draw in perspective. Knowing both methods is even better. This chapter provides you with one method of creating accurate, scale, hand-drawn perspective drawings.

 ## Principles of Perspective

The craft of drawing three-dimensional objects on a flat plane so that they will seem to have depth is based on an understanding of **foreshortening,** the principle that receding parallel lines apparently converge into a single point, as illustrated in Figure 8.1. In this scene, we seem to be looking at a desolate highway stretching into the empty flatness of west Texas. Telephone pole A seems to be closer than telephone pole B because it is taller. The portion of the road at the bottom of the picture appears to be closer to us than the road at the horizon because it is wider. The fence on the right side of the road seems to get smaller as it recedes toward its **vanishing point** (VP) on the horizon. The apparent depth in this drawing is caused by the converging of the parallel lines (the tops and bottoms of the telephone poles, the sides of the road, the barbed wire strung between the fence posts, and so on) to a single vanishing point on the horizon.

The basic principles of any perspective drawing can be further illustrated through the drawing of an everyday object such as a table (Figure 8.2). Again, notice how all of the parallel lines recede to the same vanishing points on the **horizon line** (HL).

To draw an accurate perspective sketch, you have to know the following basic information:

1. the distance from the observer to the object being drawn

2. the height of the observer's eye above the object being drawn

3. the size and shape of the object

Figure 8.3 illustrates the interrelationship among these three facts.

foreshortening: Representing the lines of an object as shorter than they actually are in order to give the illusion of proper relative size.

vanishing point: The point on the horizon to which a set of parallel lines recedes.

horizon line: A line in a perspective drawing representing the meeting of the earth and the sky; normally drawn parallel to the top or bottom edge of the paper.

136

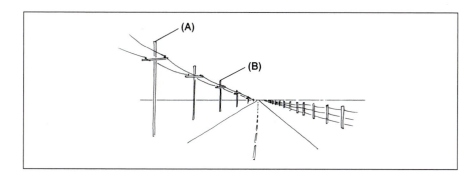

FIGURE 8.1
The principles of foreshortening.

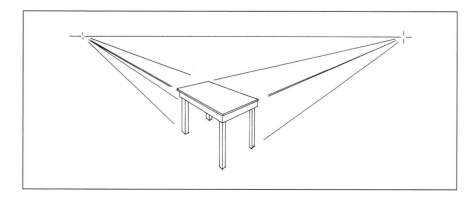

FIGURE 8.2
Parallel sets of lines recede to the same vanishing point.

You also need to know the relative position of the object in relation to a vertical plane that is placed between the observer and the object, as illustrated in Figure 8.4A. You might better understand the principles of this method of drawing if you think of this vertical plane as a transparent piece of glass. You are sitting in the auditorium looking through this "window" at the objects on the stage (in this case, the table illustrated in Figure 8.4B). A perspective drawing of this table would be created if its outline were to magically appear on this huge plate of glass, as shown in Figure 8.4C.

You don't need magic to create a perspective drawing; the following method provides you with the ability. It enables you to draw the outline of those objects on that vertical plane. The only significant differences are that the vertical plane is your drawing paper, not glass, and you don't have to be sitting in the auditorium looking at the stage to create the drawing.

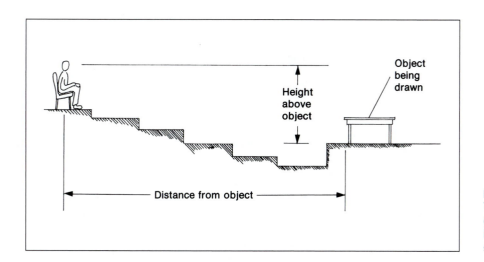

FIGURE 8.3
To draw in perspective, you need to know (1) the distance to the object, (2) your height above the object, (3) the size and shape of the object.

FIGURE 8.4
Perspective drawing is like drawing the outline of the object on a vertical pane of glass erected between you and the object you're observing.

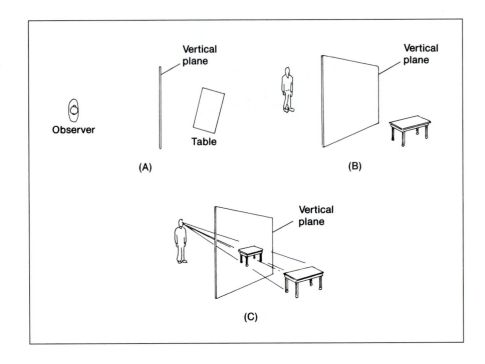

FIGURE 8.5
The vertical plane for the three forms of stage configuration is usually located in slightly different places.

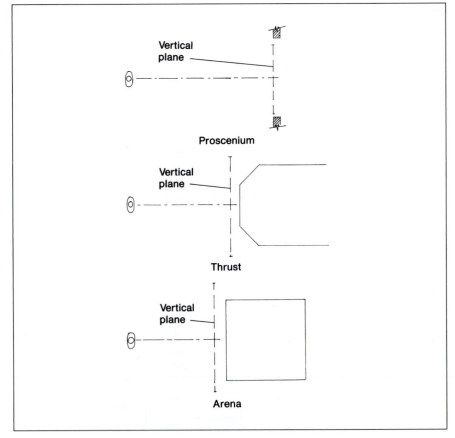

The location of this vertical plane is the only adjustment that needs to be made when applying this method of perspective drawing to proscenium, thrust, or arena theatres. As illustrated in Figure 8.5, the vertical plane in a proscenium theatre could be placed to coincide with the proscenium arch. For a thrust theatre,

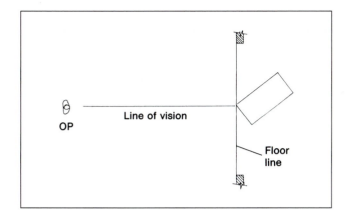 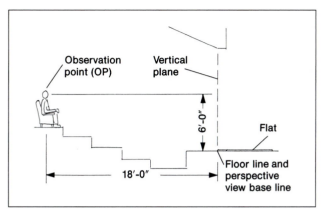

FIGURE 8.6
Plan and section layouts for the practice exercise.

it would be more appropriate to locate the vertical plane just outside the auditorium end of the thrust. For an arena stage, it could be erected in the aisle just beyond the edge of the stage that is closest to the observer.

Experience really *is* the best teacher, so the easiest way for you to develop a full understanding of drawing in perspective is to create a drawing in mechanical perspective. Later in this chapter we'll go step by step through several practice exercises.

Creating a Perspective Drawing

Imagine that you are sitting in a proscenium theatre looking at a flat lying on the stage floor, as shown in Figure 8.6. Your seat (observation point [OP]) is in the center of the auditorium, 18 feet from the proscenium arch, as shown. The flat is lying in the center of the stage floor with its near corner in contact with a line (the **floor line**) that has been drawn across the stage from the downstage edge of one side of the proscenium arch to the other. The sides of the flat make a 45-degree angle with the floor line. In this particular seat (OP), your eyes are 6 feet above the stage floor, which means that the horizon line (HL) is located 6 feet above the stage floor. Figure 8.7A shows how this information is used to lay out the basic grid used with this perspective method, which consists of only four lines—one vertical and three horizontal.

After you lay out the basic grid and the flat, the next thing you need to do is establish the vanishing points for the various sets of parallel lines. (Remember that in perspective drawing each set of receding parallel lines converges on a specific vanishing point located on the horizon line. The only exception to this rule is lines that are parallel to the floor line—they don't converge; they stay parallel to the floor line.) The flat in Figure 8.7A provides an example of this principle. There are two sets of parallel lines: AB and DC are parallel, and AD and BC are also parallel. Each of these systems of lines (AB/DC and AD/BC) has its own vanishing point on the horizon line.

To establish the vanishing point for lines AB/DC on the perspective grid, draw a very faint guide line, parallel to lines AB/DC, from OP until it intersects the floor line, as shown in Figure 8.7B. (Notice that this guide line for lines AB/DC angles to the right from OP.) From the point of intersection between the guide line for AB/DC and the floor line, drop a vertical line until it intersects the horizon line. This point of intersection between the dropped vertical and the horizon line establishes the vanishing point for line system AB/DC. The vanishing point for lines AD/BC is found in the same way. (The only difference is that the guide line for AD/BC angles to the left from OP.) Draw a very light guide line

floor line: The base of the vertical plane in a perspective drawing; for a proscenium sketch, usually drawn across the stage in contact with the downstage edge of the proscenium arch; in a thrust drawing, normally placed just outside the auditorium end of the thrust; in an arena sketch, usually placed in the aisle closest to the observer.

line of vision: The vertical line drawn from OP to the floor line in a perspective grid; represents the line of sight from the observer to the vertical plane.

perspective-view base line: The bottom edge of a perspective drawing.

from OP (parallel with lines AD/BC—which is the same as the angle of intersection between AD and the floor line) until it intersects the floor line. From this point of intersection, drop a vertical to the horizon line. This point of contact will be the vanishing point for lines AD/BC.

A basic rule of this perspective method is that any point in contact with the floor line is unaffected by the laws of perspective. Pragmatically, this means that a line can be dropped (a vertical line drawn parallel to the **line of vision**) from any point on the floor line until it contacts the **perspective-view base line.** The reason any point in contact with the floor line is unaffected by the laws of perspective is that the floor line and the perspective-view base line are simply different views of the same line. The floor line is a ground plan view of an imaginary line drawn across the stage at some easily identifiable location such as the upstage edge of the proscenium arch. The perspective-view base line is the bottom edge of a vertical plane that is erected from the floor line.

Since point A of the flat is in contact with the floor line, a vertical line can be dropped from point A until it contacts the perspective-view base line at point A' (the prime points—A', B', C', and so on—will establish the perspective view of the object), as shown in Figure 8.7C. In this particular case, point A happens to be located in the center of the floor line, so the dropped vertical coincides with the line of vision and point A' coincides with the observation point (OP).

To find the perspective view of line AB, extend a light guide line from A' to the vanishing point for the line system AB/DC, as shown in Figure 8.7D. This gives you a perspective view of line A'B' extended, but it doesn't show you the location of point B'.

FIGURE 8.7A
Sequential layout of the practice exercise. See text for explanation of each drawing.

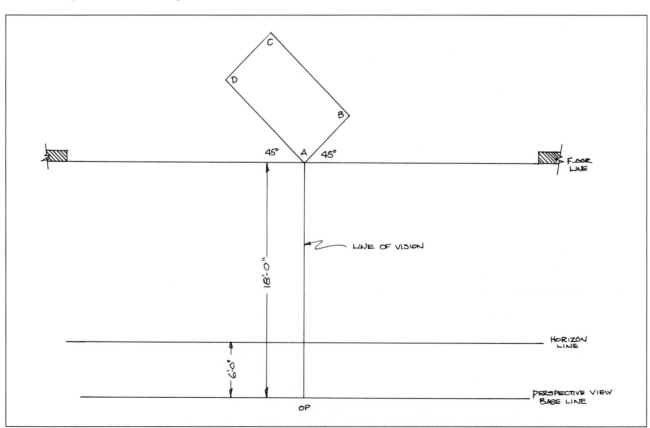

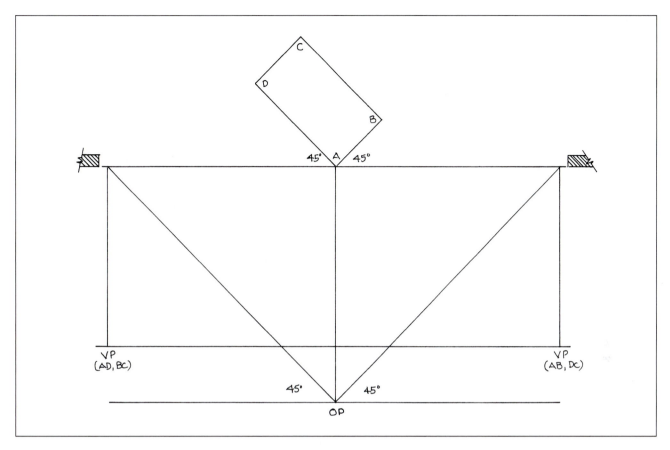

FIGURE 8.7B

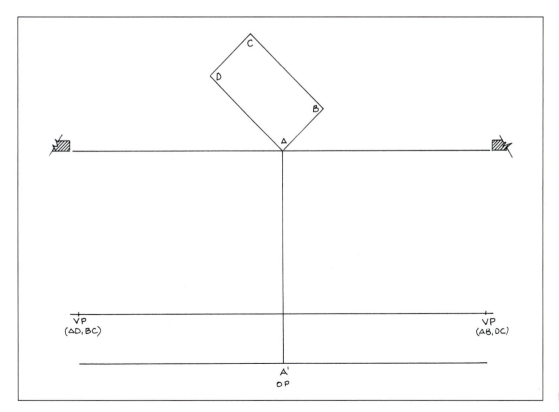

FIGURE 8.7C

FIGURE 8.7D

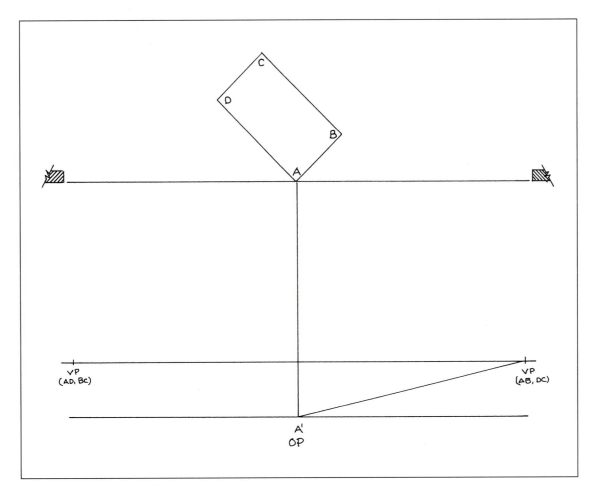

FIGURE 8.7E

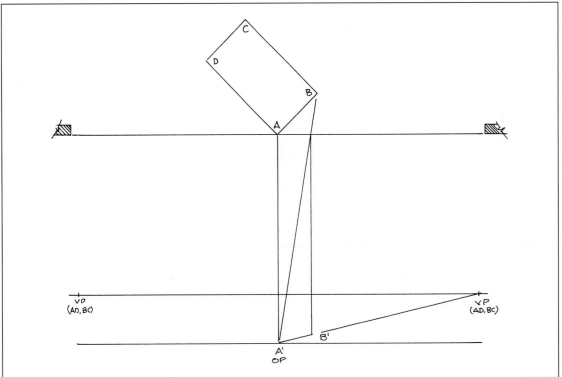

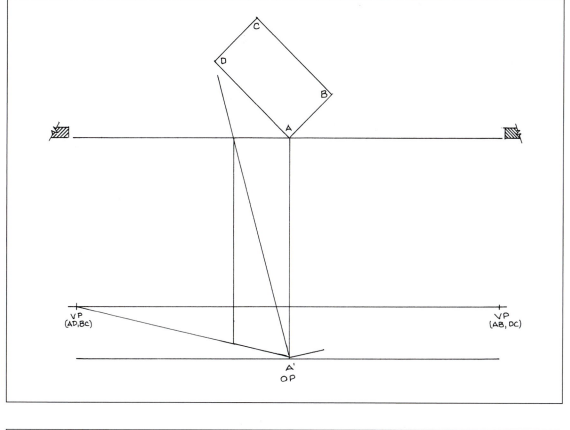

FIGURE 8.7F

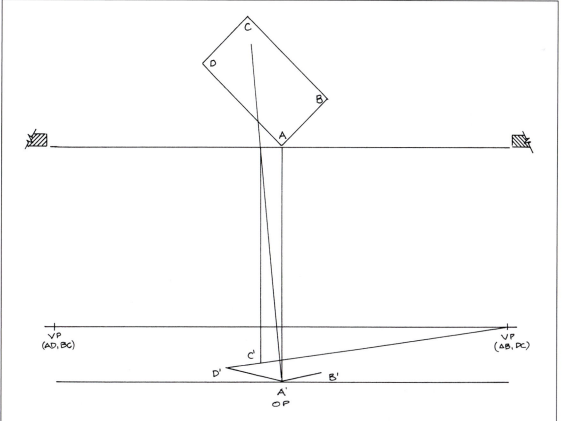

FIGURE 8.7G

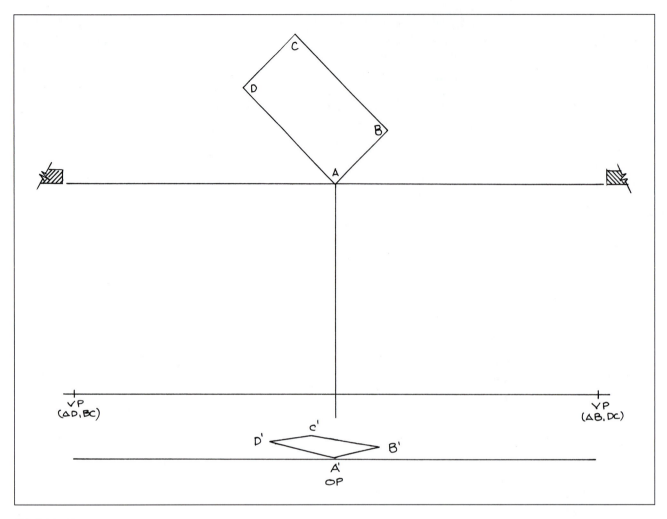

FIGURE 8.7H

To find the location of point B' on line A'B' extended, draw a light guide line between OP and corner B on the flat, as shown in Figure 8.7E. Where this guide line intersects the floor line, drop a vertical until it intersects line A'B' extended. This is the location of point B'. (Remember that any point in contact with the floor line is unaffected by perspective, so a line parallel with the line of vision can be dropped from that point on the floor line to the perspective-view base line.)

To find the perspective view of line A'D', repeat the process used to find the perspective view of line A'B', but this time use the vanishing point for the line system AD/BC. Draw a light guide line from A' to the vanishing point for line system AD/BC to form line A'D' extended, as shown in Figure 8.7F. Next draw a light guide line between OP and corner D on the flat. Where this line intersects the floor line, drop a vertical until it intersects line A'D' extended. This will be the location of point D'.

To find the perspective location of the last corner of the flat, point C', use the same process you used to find the location of B' and D'. Line D'C' is parallel to line A'B', so they have the same vanishing point (the vanishing point for line system AB/DC). To find line D'C' extended, draw a light guide line from point D' to the vanishing point for line system AB/DC, as shown in Figure 8.7G. To find the location of C' on line D'C' extended, draw a guide line from OP to C. Where that guide line intersects the floor line, drop a vertical until it intersects line D'C' extended. This point of intersection will be the location of point C'.

PRODUCTION INSIGHTS
Words of Encouragement

As you wade through the frequently frustrating complexities of learning to draw in mechanical scale perspective, take heart. Every major scenic designer has had the same kind of heartburn. They all had to learn how to draw in perspective. Some of them, such as Ming Cho Lee and Jo Mielziner, received their early training in art schools. Others, such as Peter Wexler, were formally trained as architects. Increasing numbers of rising designers are choosing university educational theatre training. All of them have a common bond — learning how to draw in perspective.

Assimilating the principles of any mechanical-perspective technique is difficult. But as with any craft, the more you practice, the easier it becomes.

In reality, the reason for learning any mechanical-perspective technique is to train your eye. As you practice, you learn how various objects are supposed to look when they are drawn. As you become adept at using mechanical perspective, you will also find that your freehand sketches will start to look better — more real. This is because you *are* training your eye. Eventually, you will find that you'll be able to sketch full sets freehand in accurate perspective, and you'll only occasionally need to use the perspective method to monitor or check your work. This kind of proficiency doesn't happen overnight; it comes with practice. But if you have a passion for drawing and designing, the practice won't be work, it'll be fun.

To complete the perspective view of the flat, you just need to play connect the dots between points B' and C', as shown in Figure 8.7H.

A Review of Perspective Procedure

Before moving on to the perspective exercises, you might want to review the procedure that is used to create these drawings.

1. All of the drawings are made on a basic grid composed of four lines, as shown in Figure 8.8A.

2. The vanishing point for any line or system of lines is determined by extending, from OP, a line parallel to the ground plan view of that particular line until it intersects the floor line, as shown in Figure 8.8B. From that point of intersection, a vertical line is dropped until it intersects the horizon line. That point of intersection is the vanishing point for that line system.

3. Any point in contact with the floor line is unaffected by the laws of perspective. Therefore, a line parallel to the line of vision can be dropped from that point to the perspective-view base line, as shown in Figure 8.8C.

4. A perspective view of a line can be established by extending a line from the point of contact with the perspective-view base line to the vanishing point for that particular line, as shown in Figure 8.8D.

5. To find the location of any point on the perspective view of a line, draw a sight line from the observation point (OP) to the ground plan view of that point, as shown in Figure 8.8E. From the point of intersection between that sight line and the floor line, drop a vertical until it intersects the extended line (A'B' extended and A'C' extended).

6. After all of the perspective points have been located using the techniques described above, connect those points to provide a perspective view of the object, as shown in Figure 8.8F.

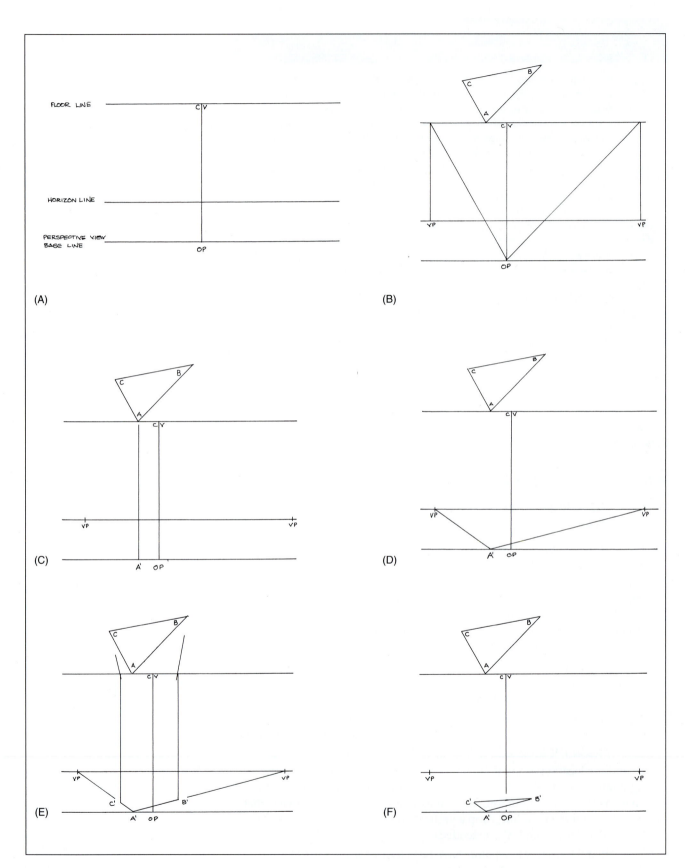

FIGURE 8.8
The perspective procedure.

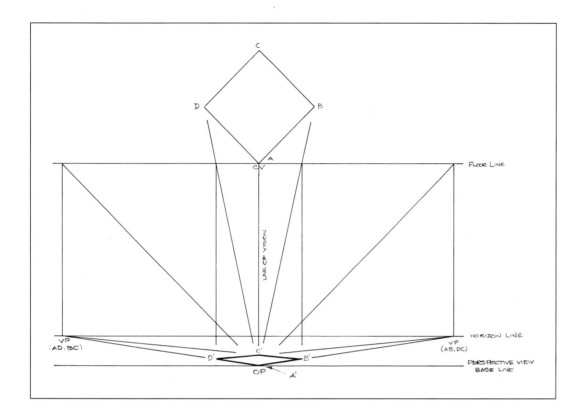

FIGURE 8.9
Exercise 1.

 Perspective Exercises

Craft is learned through doing. This perspective method is a craft. The following nine practice exercises, which are arranged in an ascending order of difficulty, provide specific examples of a variety of common situations and challenges frequently encountered in perspective drawing.

Exercise 1

The closer your eye level (horizon line) is to the stage floor in Exercise 1, Figure 8.9, the less you will see of the actual form of some object resting on the stage.

> **Scale:** ¼″ = 1′-0″
> **OP:** 36 -0″ right and 8′-0″ up[1]
> **Floor line:** 20′-0″ from **OP**
> **Horizon line:** 3′-0″ from **OP**
> **Perspective-view base line:** extends horizontally through **OP**
> **Object being drawn:** an 8′-0″ square resting on the stage floor with its sides at a 45-degree angle to the floor line and the near corner **(A)** in contact with the floor line at the line of vision.

[1] These dimensions are intended to help you center your drawing in the middle of a 12 × 18 sheet of paper. By measuring, in ¼-inch scale, 36′-0″ to the right of the lower left-hand corner and 8′-0″ up from the bottom edge of the sheet of paper, the observation point **(OP)** will be placed in a position that will center the perspective exercise in the middle of the paper. These dimensions don't have a thing to do with drawing in perspective; they just help to make the whole sheet look attractive and balanced. These exercises won't fit on a sheet smaller than 10 × 14, but if you are using paper larger than 12 × 18, just center the **OP** about one-quarter or one-third of the way up from the bottom of the sheet.

Procedure   No new challenges have been introduced here, so you can follow the procedure summarized in the previous section to do this exercise.

Exercise 2

The second exercise shows what to do if an object contacts the floor line in some location other than the point of intersection between the floor line and the line of vision.

> **Scale:** ¼″ = 1′-0″
> **OP:** 36′-0″ right and 8′-0″ up
> **Floor line:** 22′-0″ from **OP**
> **Horizon line:** 7′-0″ from **OP**
> **Perspective-view base line:** extends horizontally through **OP**
> **Object being drawn:** a flat 6′-0″ by 10′-0″ with its sides at a 45-degree angle to the floor line. The near corner **(A)** is in contact with the floor line and 7′-0″ to the left of the intersection between the line of vision and the floor line.

Procedure   Since the corner of the flat **(A)** is in contact with the floor line, it is unaffected by the laws of perspective. A vertical can be dropped from point **A** until it intersects the perspective-view base line, as shown in Figure 8.10. This point will be the perspective location of point **A′**.

After determining the location of **A′**, you can do the rest of the exercise using the procedure summarized in the previous section.

FIGURE 8.10
Exercise 2.

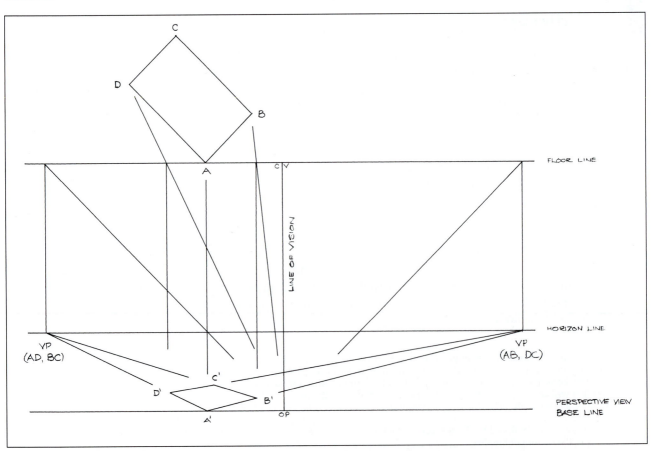

Exercise 3

Finding the perspective of an object that has height, as well as width and length, requires an additional step in the perspective procedure as illustrated in Figure 8.11.

Scale: ¼″ = 1′-0″
OP: 50′-0″ right and 8′-0″ up
Floor line: 23′-0″ from **OP**
Horizon line: 8′-0″ from **OP**
Perspective-view base line: extends horizontally through **OP**
Object being drawn: a platform 8′-0″ square by 3′-6″ high is placed on the stage with its sides forming 30- and 60-degree angles with the floor line. Corner **A** is in contact with the floor line and 12′-0″ to the left of the intersection of the floor line and the line of vision.

Procedure   Any point in contact with the floor line is unaffected by the laws of perspective. Corner **A** of the platform is in contact with the floor line, so a vertical can be dropped to the perspective-view base line to determine the perspective location of **A′**. Since this point (**A′**) is similarly unaffected by perspective, it is possible to determine the height of the platform by measuring the true vertical distance from **A′**.

Along a light vertical guide line erected from **A′**, lay out, in scale, the 3′-6″ height of the platform. This distance will determine the perspective location of point **A″**, which is the top of the front corner of the platform.

Draw guide lines from both **A′** and **A″** to the vanishing point for the **AB/DC** line system. The perspective location of corner **B** of the platform will be the point where these lines (the guide lines drawn between **A′** and **A″** and the vanishing point for the **AB/DC** line system) are intersected by the vertical dropped from

FIGURE 8.11
Exercise 3.

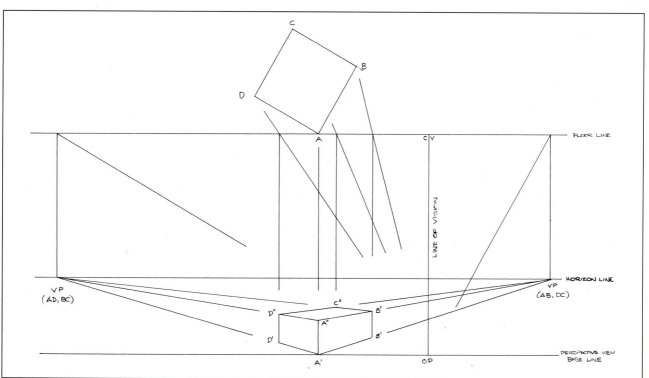

the point of intersection between the floor line and a sight line drawn between **OP** and **B.**

The perspective view of the other face **(A′D′/A″D″)** of the platform is determined in the same manner, except that you use the vanishing point for the line system **DA/BC.**

The perspective view of the two upstage edges of the platform (**B″C″** and **D″C″**) is determined by drawing lines between **D″** and the vanishing point for the **AB/DC** line system and between **B″** and the vanishing point for the **AD/BC** line system. Where these two lines intersect will be the location of **C″.**

Point **C″** can also be located in the conventional manner by drawing a sight line from **OP** to **C.** Where the sight line crosses the floor line, a vertical can be dropped until it intersects line **B″C″** extended or **D″C″** extended. This will be the location of **C″.**

Exercise 4

Drawing a perspective view of an object that is not in contact with the floor line adds one more step to the procedure but uses the same principles.

Scale: ¼″ = 1′-0″
OP: 40′-0″ right and 10′-0″ up
Floor line: 20′-0″ from **OP**
Horizon line: 8′-0″ from **OP**
Perspective-view base line: extends horizontally through **OP**
Object being drawn: a small flat, 6′-0″ by 10′-0″, lying on the stage floor with its sides at a 45-degree angle to the floor line. The near corner **A** is 4′-6″ to the left of the intersection between the floor line and the line of vision and 2′-6″ upstage of it (Figure 8.12).

FIGURE 8.12
Exercise 4.

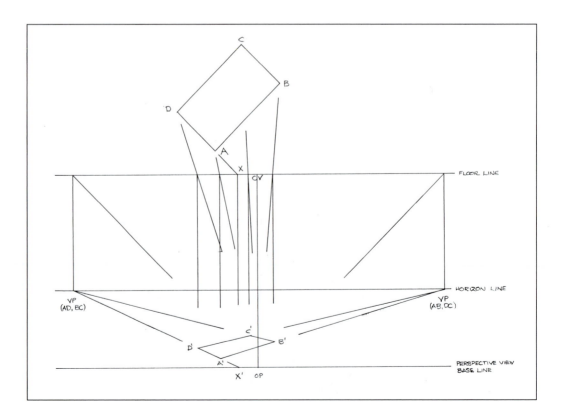

Procedure   Extend the line that forms one side of the flat **(DA)** until it intersects the floor line **(X)**. Since any point in contact with the floor line is unaffected by the laws of perspective, a vertical can be dropped to the perspective-view base line to determine the perspective location of point **X'**. Draw a light guide line between **X'** and the vanishing point for line system **AD/BC**. The locations of points **A'** and **D'** are determined in the usual manner. Sight lines are drawn between **OP** and points **A** and **D**. Where those sight lines cross the floor line, verticals are dropped until they intersect the guide line drawn between **X'** and the vanishing point for line system **AD/BC**.

The perspective view of the rest of the flat is determined using the same principles used in the previous exercises. Guide lines are drawn between **A'** and **D'** and the vanishing point for line system **AB/DC**. Sight lines are drawn between **OP** and points **B** and **C**. Where those sight lines cross the floor line, verticals are dropped until they intersect the guide lines drawn between **AD** and the vanishing point for line system **AB/DC**. These points of intersection will be the location of **B'** and **C'**.

Exercise 5

Drawing a perspective view of an object whose sides are either parallel with or perpendicular to the floor line doesn't differ in principle from the procedures that have been previously established.

> **Scale:** ¼″ = 1′-0″
> **OP:** 36′-0″ right and 8′-0″ up
> **Floor line:** 20′-0″ from **OP**
> **Horizon line:** 3′-0″ from **OP**
> **Perspective-view base line:** extends horizontally through **OP**
> **Object being drawn:** a large rectangular ceiling flat, 10′-10″ by 14′-0″, lying on the stage floor with its longer side parallel with, and 2′-0″ upstage from, the floor line. Notice that the floor line has been placed at the outer face of the proscenium arch to facilitate your creating a perspective drawing of the arch. The proscenium arch is 32′-0″ wide, 16′-0″ high, and 1′-0″ thick, as shown in Figure 8.13.

Procedure   Fortunately, creating a perspective drawing of objects whose sides are parallel with or perpendicular to the proscenium arch follows exactly the same procedure that has been used in the previous perspective exercises. First, find the vanishing point for the line system **AB/DC,** as shown in Figure 8.13A. From **OP** draw a line parallel to **AB** and **DC** until it intersects the floor line. From that point, drop a vertical until it intersects the horizon line. You will notice that this point happens to coincide with the intersection between the horizon line and the line of vision. Any line that is perpendicular to the floor line will always have this center vanishing point (CVP).

To find the perspective location of the lines that form the sides of the ceiling piece (**AB** and **DC**), extend those lines until they intersect the floor line. From those points, drop verticals until they intersect the perspective-view base line (points **X** and **Y**). From **X** and **Y,** draw light guide lines to the center vanishing point (vanishing point for line system **AB/DC**). You can determine the perspective location of points **A** and **B** or **D** and **C** in the usual manner and connect the dots to form a perspective view of the ceiling flat lying on the stage floor.

An alternative method: Instead of using the center vanishing point, you can draw diagonal lines between **CA** and **BD,** as shown in Figure 8.13B. Extend those diagonals until they intersect the floor line, and then locate the vanishing point for those lines in the usual manner. The rest of the exercise can be done using the procedure as previously outlined.

FIGURE 8.13
Exercise 5.

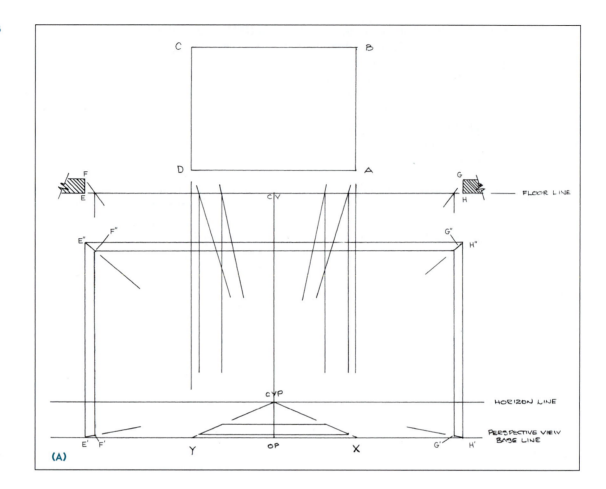

(A)

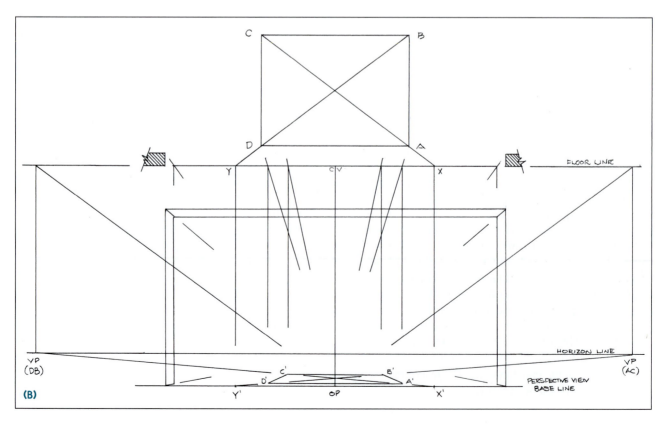

(B)

Determining the perspective location of the proscenium arch is fairly easy, since the downstage edge of the arch is in contact with the floor line. From points **E** and **H,** drop verticals to the perspective-view base line. The vertical height of the proscenium arch can be measured from **E′** and **H′**, since those points are in contact with the perspective-view base line and are consequently unaffected by the laws of perspective. Locating the top of the perspective view of the proscenium arch is done by connecting the dots between **E′** and **H′**.

The perspective view of the depth of the proscenium arch can be determined by using the methods previously described. To locate the base of the stage-right side of the arch, draw a light guide line from **E′** (the downstage edge of the proscenium arch) to the center vanishing point. To locate **F′**, draw a sight line from **OP** to **F.** Where that sight line crosses the floor line, drop a vertical until it intersects the guide line drawn from **F′** to the center vanishing point. This will be the location of **F′**.

The top of the stage-right side of the proscenium arch is found by drawing a guide line from **E″** to the center vanishing point. Where this line intersects the vertical erected from **F′** will be the location of **F″**.

The other side of the proscenium arch is determined in the same manner. The top of the proscenium arch can be determined by connecting **E″** and **H″** as well as **F″** and **G″**.

Exercise 6

This exercise synthesizes all of the previous material and allows you to draw a perspective view of a full stage set.

> **Scale:** ¼″ = 1′-0″
> **OP:** 36′-0″ right and 6′-0″ up
> **Floor line:** 22′-0″ from **OP**
> **Horizon line:** 6′-0″ from **OP**
> **Perspective-view base line:** extends horizontally through **OP**
> **Proscenium arch:** 16′-0″ high, 36′-0″ wide, 1′-0″ thick
> **Object being drawn:** a full stage setting, as illustrated in Figure 8.14

Procedure   Although the concept of drawing a full setting may, at first glance, be somewhat overwhelming, you can accomplish it by using the techniques described in this chapter. "Where do I begin?" is a logical first question. The answer isn't clear-cut and absolute. Drawing the proscenium arch first provides a visual framework and reference that makes most designers feel fairly comfortable. After you've drawn the proscenium (refer to the instructions for drawing the proscenium arch detailed in Exercise 5, if you need them), start on the set. It is usually easiest to begin by drawing the set at one corner of the ground plan. Point **A,** which is the downstage end of the bottom of flat **AB,** provides a convenient beginning place.

Flat AB   To find the location of point **A,** you will need to set up the vanishing point for flat **AB.** This can be done by measuring, with a protractor, the angle of intersection between **AB** extended and the floor line, and duplicating that angle from **OP,** to lay out the vanishing point. The full perspective view of flat **AB** can then be drawn using the techniques previously described. The sides and top of the door opening can be drawn by using the same techniques that are used to locate the sides and tops of the flat.

Flat BC   Since flat **BC** is parallel to the proscenium (and the floor line), horizontal lines can be extended from the top and bottom of the upstage end of flat **AB**

FIGURE 9.7
The production model is painted and furnished to provide an accurate miniature version of the finished set. (A) *Suddenly Last Summer,* scenic design by Darwin Reid Payne. (B) *The Member of the Wedding,* scenic design by J. Michael Gillette.

(A)

(B)

the audience from seeing backstage. Additionally, animation programs, either stand-alone or embedded, can be used to provide time-based visualizations of scene shifts and so forth. More information about graphic software programs and associated hardware is available in Chapter 22, "Drawing and Rendering."

Another caveat needs to be stated: An ever-increasing number of software programs do an admirable job of computer-based drawing, sketching, painting, rendering, and drafting. Ideally, you should be proficient in these technologies of the present and future. But you also need to know how to do these things the old-fashioned way—by hand. While it isn't quite as imperative to know how to sketch and paint both by hand and with a computer as it is to be able to draft by hand and with a computer, it will, in the long run, probably make your life a little easier if you know both techniques. You never can tell when you'll need to draw or paint

FIGURE 9.8
A computer-rendered scenic design for
The Quilters by Eric Fielding. Production
at Brigham Young University Theatre,
March 1998.

something and not have your own computer or access to a computer with your favorite program. In those situations, it really is good to know how to turn out a fast sketch or rendering by hand. So consider yourself forewarned.

Other Presentation Techniques

More traditional artistic techniques such as **collage** and **photomontage** can be used with either sketches/renderings or models. Copy machines produce excellent black-line reproductions of sketches on either white or colored stock. They can be colored with pencils or colored markers. If the copies are made on rag paper, water-based media can be used to color them. If these reproductions are printed in multiple copies, all appropriate personnel can be given a copy. Color copiers can also be used, although the color reproduction may not be totally accurate. If a sketch is made on **tracing paper,** blueline copies can be made using a blueprint machine. Some blueprint machines can print on **card stock,** which is available in a variety of colors. Like copy-machine prints, blueline copies can also be rendered with color using colored pencils, pastels, or markers.

These sketches and models are tools, not end products. The thumbnail sketches, renderings, and models that are made by the scenic designer help him or her discover workable solutions to specific design challenges. They are also the primary tools used to communicate those solutions to other interested members of the production team. They are, to a very real degree, working drawings.

collage: A picture made of various materials (e.g., paper, cloth) glued on a surface; can include drawn or photographic images as well.

photomontage: A composite picture made by combining several separate pictures; can include nonphotographic images as well.

tracing paper: Translucent paper used for drafting.

card stock: A thin cardboard, similar in thickness to 3 × 5 notecards and/or file folders.

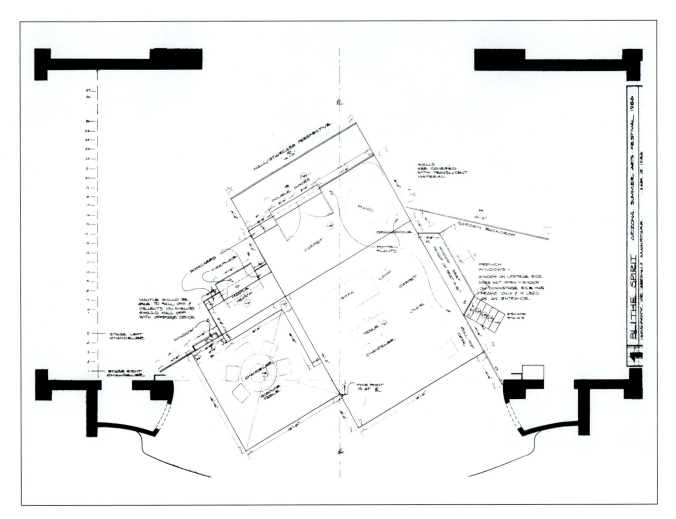

FIGURE 9.9
Ground plan for *Blithe Spirit,* produced at the University of Arizona; scenic design by K. Pistor.

Designer's Plans

The colored sketch or production model for a scenic design may be a thing of beauty, and it may give a clear picture of the designer's intentions, but it does not give the technical director or carpenters all of the information they need to build the set. This information is contained in a series of mechanical drawings, called designer's plans, that depict every detail of the set as well as providing exact measurements of its components. These plans are prepared by the set designer and consist of a ground plan, front elevations, detail drawings, full-scale drawings, sight-line drawings, and painter's elevations.

Ground Plan   The ground plan (Figure 9.9) is the key drawing on which the remainder of the designer's plans are based. It is a scale mechanical drawing showing the top view of a setting in its proper position on the stage. It clearly shows the form of the set and its relationship to the physical structure of the theatre. The location and measurements are given for all architectural features of the set, onstage and off, such as doors, windows, fireplaces, columns, stairs, and ramps. Additionally, the position and measurements for all **backing, ground rows,** wings, borders, and cycloramas are indicated.

backing: Flats, drops, or draperies on the offstage side of doors and similar openings to prevent the audience from seeing backstage.

ground row: Low, horizontal flats used to mask the base of cycs or drops; frequently painted to resemble rows of buildings, hedges, or similar visual elements.

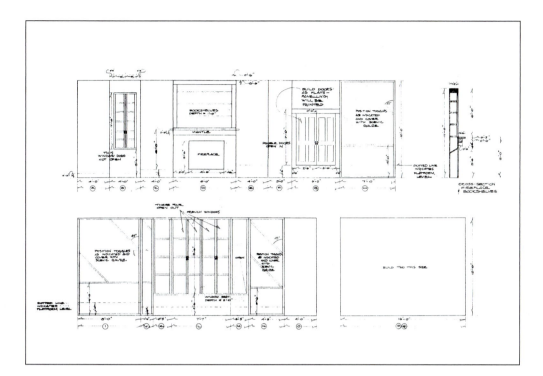

FIGURE 9.10
Front elevations for *Blithe Spirit,* produced at the University of Arizona; scenic design by K. Pistor.

The primary ground plan normally shows only the architectural information about the set as described above. Frequently a second ground plan is created. This one shows how the set "functions." It shows the placement of furniture, rugs, hanging chandeliers, window dressings, and other relevant information. This ground plan is quite useful to the stage manager so he or she will know where the various functional and decorative props will be placed in relationship to the physical structure of the set. Frequently the location/placement of these pieces will be adjusted during the rehearsal process, but this "functional" ground plan provides a good beginning point.

A majority of the work done in planning a production depends on the information provided by the ground plan. During the rehearsal period, the director has the stage manager, using the ground plan as a guide, tape or chalk the outline of the design onto the rehearsal room floor. Then the actors can rehearse and perfect their blocking in a space that corresponds to the actual set.

The lighting designer, when drawing the light plot, uses the ground plan to provide information about the shape and placement of the set within the theatre. This type of information is needed when making decisions about the hanging positions for the various instruments that will light the production.

The technical director uses the ground plan for a wide variety of functions. Together with the **center-line section,** it tells the TD where the set will sit on the stage and where to place the masking. It also indicates a great deal of information about the amount of materials that will be needed to construct the set(s).

Information on how to draw a ground plan, as well as the other drawings that make up the designer's plans, is contained in Chapter 7, "Mechanical Drafting."

center-line section: A sectional drawing whose cutting plane is the center line of the stage and auditorium, showing the height of the various elements of the theatre; usually drawn in the same scale as the ground plan.

Front Elevations   Front elevations (Figure 9.10) show a front view of the set as if it were flattened into a single plane. The main purpose of these scale drawings (normally ½ inch to 1 foot) is to indicate all of the vertical measurements that cannot be shown on the ground plan. These dimensions include the height of walls, doors, and windows as well as the location of any features on the walls such as baseboards, wainscoting, chair rails, cornices, paintings, or other decorative features.

Frequently a second set of front elevations will be drawn to show the location of decorative items such as style of window dressings, suggested shelf/fireplace dressing, pictures, mirrors, and so forth. These details can range from relatively complete pencil drawings that show the style, fabric, and fullness of a window treatment to simple outlines with notes such as a rectangle with a note "landscape painting with moose — gold frame." These detail elevations suggest what the scenic designer envisions for the set dressing and are of great benefit in communicating those ideas to the property designer.

Even if the scenic designer has constructed a functional model of the set, he or she will actually be designing as much when drafting the elevations as when producing the thumbnail sketches, renderings, or models, because what appears on the elevations is actually a proportional reduction of the appearance of the finished set. If the designer wants to change or adjust any element, it is fairly easy to erase and redraw the elevations. A corresponding change needs to be made on the ground plan whenever the changes made on the elevations, such as widening or moving a flat, affect its accuracy.

The primary purpose of the front elevations is to describe the appearance of the set; they don't tell how to build it. For this reason, no attempt is made to indicate the width of the individual flats that will be used to construct the various wall units. This breakdown of the wall segments into manageable units is the responsibility of the technical director or, in the professional theatre, the scene shop foreman. The construction of the flats is made from rear elevations, which are drawings that show the reverse side of the flats depicted in the front elevations. These scale drawings show the framework of the flat, including the placement and dimensions of all its various parts. The structure and nomenclature of flats will be discussed in Chapter 11, "Scenic Production Techniques," and the drawing of rear elevations is taken up in Chapter 7, "Mechanical Drafting."

Detail Drawings   The scale of ½ inch to 1 foot normally used in drawing the front elevations reduces the size of some of the smaller features to the point that it is difficult, if not impossible, to draw all of their details. Detailed pieces, such as an elaborate fireplace or an intricately designed stained-glass panel, need to be drawn in a larger scale (Figure 9.11).

Detail drawings need to be made for properties and stage dressing that must be constructed — furniture, torches, specific hand props, and so forth. These are normally sketched rather than drafted and include notes on size, color, weight, fabric type, finish, and decoration.

Many features of a setting cannot be fully described by drawing them in top and front (or rear) views only. Three-dimensional objects often require a third view to supplement the other two. There are several methods of drafting (orthographic projection, isometric drawing, oblique drawing, and cabinet drawing) that show more than two sides of an object. The techniques of these methods of drafting are discussed in Chapter 7, "Mechanical Drafting."

Full-Scale Drawings   A few of the smallest features of a set should be drawn in full scale, or actual size. If the design is unusually intricate or the object rather small, such as the pattern for a turned bannister or a wallpaper pattern, it is usually both easier and faster to draw it in full scale. It is also easier to construct something from a full-scale drawing than one that has been proportionally reduced.

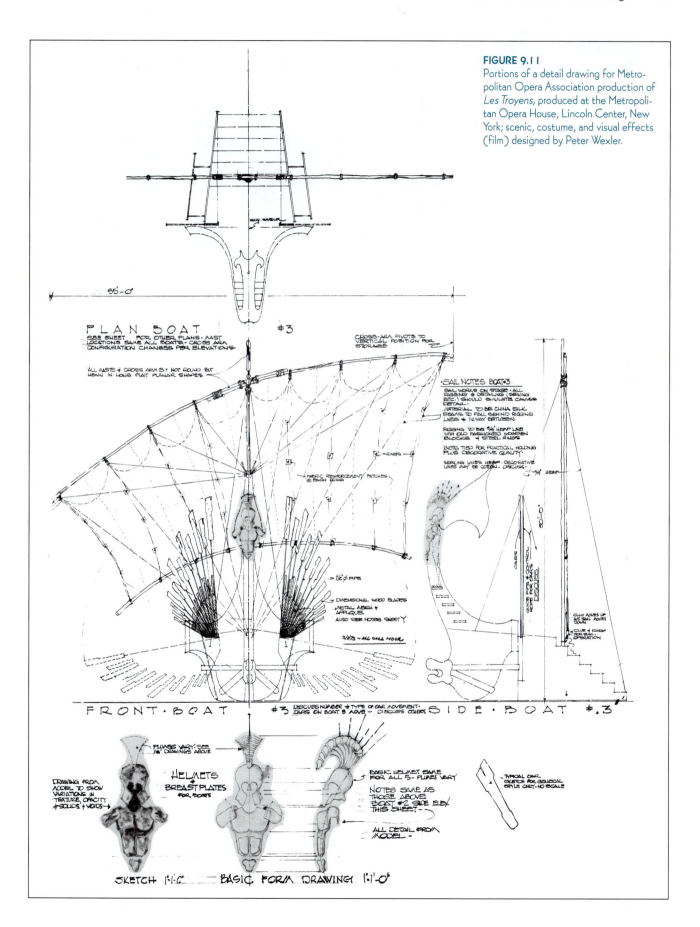

FIGURE 9.11
Portions of a detail drawing for Metropolitan Opera Association production of *Les Troyens,* produced at the Metropolitan Opera House, Lincoln Center, New York; scenic, costume, and visual effects (film) designed by Peter Wexler.

The following discussion is based on and quotes extensively from "Onstage Magic With Water," by Mel Gussow (New York Times, July 28, 1998, pp. E1, E3).

The setting for *Twelfth Night* is an Oriental fantasy of the mind. As far as the eye can see, there is a road winding through water. At the front of the Vivian Beaumont stage, actors are lolling on the stage, surrounded by burning candles and incense. Nearby is a pool for swimming and dunking. Later in the play there will be a rainstorm. In Bob Crowley's scenic design for Nicholas Hytner's production, water is the central motif—more than 10,000 gallons is used at every performance.

"This is literally and metaphorically a waterlogged play," Mr. Crowley said. "It begins with a shipwreck, and the water imagery is in virtually every other scene. There is also the narcissism of the characters, constantly looking at their own reflections. The idea of water being the first mirror, the twinning of things—all that has resonance."

"And," he said, "there is a liquidity about the theatrical floor plan." The set is "all curved."

This is an unusual design for *Twelfth Night*, which is generally presented as

alternating between the Duke's palace and Olivia's home, with Viola disguised as the Duke's male messenger plying a path between the two. Seldom is the play presented completely alfresco as in this Lincoln Center Theatre production.

Mr. Crowley, who was born in Ireland, studied painting and sculpture before

going to drama school and deciding to be a scenic designer.

Mr. Hytner, who has frequently worked with Mr. Crowley in theatre and opera over the last ten years, said about his collaborator: "He always responds poetically to a play. His sets are often painterly. My taste, which is influenced by Bob, is not toward architectural literal-

sight-line drawings: A scale drawing (plan and section views) of sightings that extend from the extreme seats (usually the outside seats on the front and last rows of the auditorium) to any position on the stage; used to determine how much of the stage and backstage will be visible from specific auditorium seats.

Sight-Line Drawings   An improperly or inadequately masked set is a sign of a second-rate production. Most people come to the theatre to be entertained, to escape into the world of the play. When they can see backstage and watch actors waiting for their cues, stagehands lounging around, or any of the backstage paraphernalia, their concentration on the substance of the play is broken. All of these unnecessary distractions can be avoided if the scenic designer takes the time to draft some **sight-line drawings.**

The sight lines of any set can be checked through the use of two drawings, a ground plan and a vertical section of the stage and auditorium, with the set in its proper position on the stage (Figure 9.12). The horizontal section, or plan view, shows the view of the stage, or sight line, of the people sitting in the extreme side seats of the first and last rows of the auditorium. The vertical section shows a side view of the sight line for the same seats.

The little time required to draft sight-line drawings is time well spent. Too often the scenery is built, painted, and assembled on stage before the sight lines

Scenic Design, continued

ism or social realism. The kind of worlds we like to create are worlds of the imagination."

Mr. Crowley specializes in creating magical environments. To the director as to the designer, Shakespeare's Illyria in *Twelfth Night* meant, in Mr. Hytner's words, "not here, not now, somewhere different, a world where romantic impossibilities are made possible — a midsummer madness that can be resolved through the power of the stage."

As usual, Mr. Crowley began his research in a museum. In creating the New England background for *Carousel,* he was inspired by the paintings of Andrew Wyeth and Winslow Homer. With *Twelfth Night,* he drew upon two exhibitions at the Metropolitan Museum of Art: one of Oriental carpets, the other of illustrated pages from an Indian manuscript. Mr. Crowley made clear that he had not tried to reproduce anything in the exhibitions for *Twelfth Night,* but approached them for their atmospheric emanations.

The environment is generically Eastern, stressing the play's fabulistic side. "We talked about the hallucinogenic nature of the piece and the obsessive nature of the people who occupy the place," Mr. Crowley said. The aim was to give "people's desire and dreams — and the language — room to breathe." The approach, as with all his Shakespeare designs, is to keep it "fairly free and abstract" and not to "straitjacket it into a certain time, place, or period."

Another of Mr. Crowley's design inspirations were pictures of the Alhambra gardens in Granada, Spain. He was struck by the way that light filtered through the space so that things were only half visible. Avoiding solid scenery, he wanted the setting to have a translucent quality, so that people could be glimpsed on the wing. Intentionally, the feeling is cinematic, with crosscuts between scenes. As one scene finishes downstage, another begins upstage. "If the characters met," he said, "they would recognize each other and the play would finish. Instead, they take the opposite road like we all do in life, and life goes on."

Mr. Crowley's concept of design may seem somewhat heretical: he does not like scenery. At least not an abundance of it. Whenever possible he chooses the simplest setting. In this production, there are a bench and at one point a wall, both of which pop out of the floor. "I hate moving furniture onstage," he said, "and it is even harder to move it offstage." Only cushions are carried on and off.

"I would rather look at a beautifully lit backstage with a great actor in the middle of it than a great production with fifty-five tons of naturalistic living rooms flying in and out," Mr. Crowley said. In his eyes, an empty stage can be a design choice, and it can be exquisite, if properly lighted. "I'm putting myself out of work, aren't I?" he said with a laugh.

Pointing to Peter Brook's production of *The Cherry Orchard,* in which there were carpets and an absolute minimum of furniture, he said there was no such thing as something not being designed: "As Brook says in *The Empty Space,* the minute an actor walks across the stage and somebody looks at him, that is the beginning of a piece of theatre."

But where does the designer come in? Mr. Crowley responded with questions: "Is the floor wooden or is it a piece of canvas? Is it covered in dirt? Does it need sweeping? What's illuminating the actor? Those are all design decisions."

---

are checked. The sight lines may be perfectly satisfactory, but occasionally some area of the set is out of sight of the audience, the backing flats are too small, or the masking drapes have been hung in the wrong position. Sight-line drawings can reveal any potential problems with masking in sufficient time to correct them.

Painter's Elevations   Painter's elevations are front elevations of the set, but they are drawn on watercolor board and painted to show not only the colors but also the painting techniques that will be used in finishing the set. The painter's elevations (Figure 9.13) are the renderings that the scenic artist and paint crew use when painting the set. The scenic artist mixes the colors to match the palette used on the painter's elevations, and the crew applies the paint using techniques that will duplicate the style illustrated in the painter's elevations. Information on the materials and techniques of scene painting is contained in Chapter 12, "Scene Painting."

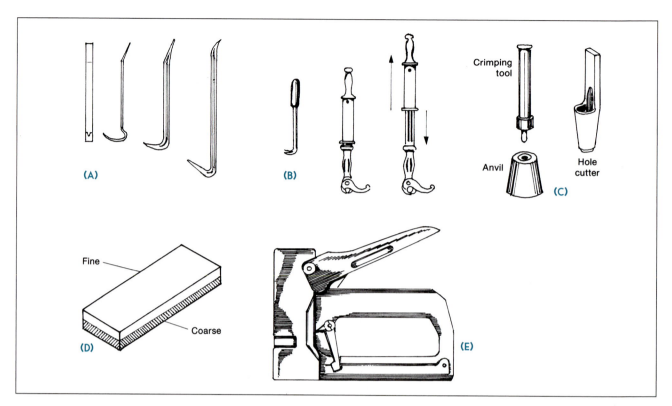

FIGURE 10.14
Miscellaneous hand tools.
(A) Wrecking bars
(B) Nail pullers
(C) Grommet set
(D) Oil stone
(E) Staple gun

Metalworking Hand Tools

Although many of the basic woodworking tools are equally useful when working with metal, there are a few additional tools designed specifically for metalwork.

Anvil　A heavyweight anvil (Figure 10.15A) is an essential tool for bending metal. It is a solid metal device with varying shaped faces. Strap metal and rod can be shaped by bending it around these faces. Sheet metal, rod, and strap can also be formed by holding the material against the anvil and pounding it with a blacksmith's or mechanic's hammer. The metal will take on the shape of the particular facet on which it is being worked.

Conduit Bender　Thin-wall conduit (used in nonscenic construction as a housing for electrical wires) can be bent into curves with a conduit bender (Figure 10.15B). The notch at the end of the curved face of the conduit bender holds the conduit, and the bend is made by pulling on the pipe handle of the conduit bender.

Center Punch　Made of hardened steel, the center punch (Figure 10.15C) is used to make small indentations in metal that can be used as hole starters for drill bits in both metal and wood.

Bolt Cutter　Bolt cutters (Figure 10.15D) are heavy-duty shears that use a great deal of leverage to cut through mild-steel bolts and round stock up to ½ inch in diameter.

Pipe Cutter　A pipe cutter (Figure 10.15E) is used to make clean, right-angle cuts through steel pipe of ½-inch and larger diameters. A smaller version, called a tubing cutter (Figure 10.15F), is designed for cutting ½-inch and smaller tubing.

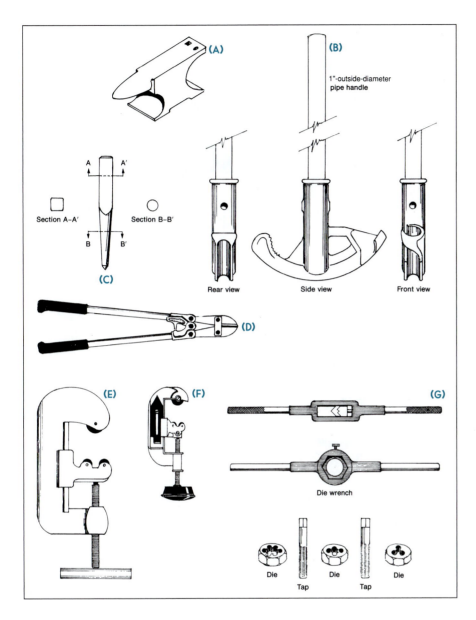

FIGURE 10.15
Metalworking hand tools.
(A) Anvil
(B) Conduit bender
(C) Center punch
(D) Bolt cutter
(E) Pipe cutter
(F) Tubing cutter
(G) Tap and die set

Tap and Dies   Tap and dies (Figure 10.15G) are used to cut threads on pipe and rod stock. The tap is used to cut threads on the inside of pipes (internal threads), and the die is used to cut threads on the outside of pipe and rod stock (external threads). Dies used to cut threads on pipes ¾ inch in diameter and larger are also called pipe threaders.

 ## Power Tools

Power tools by and large perform the same function as hand tools. But they usually do it quicker and with less effort. However, the use of power tools does increase the safety hazards that are present in the shop. Before you work with any power tool, you must be certain that you have received thorough instructions in its safe operation. As a general safety rule, you should remember that any power tool, if improperly used, has the potential to cause severe injury.

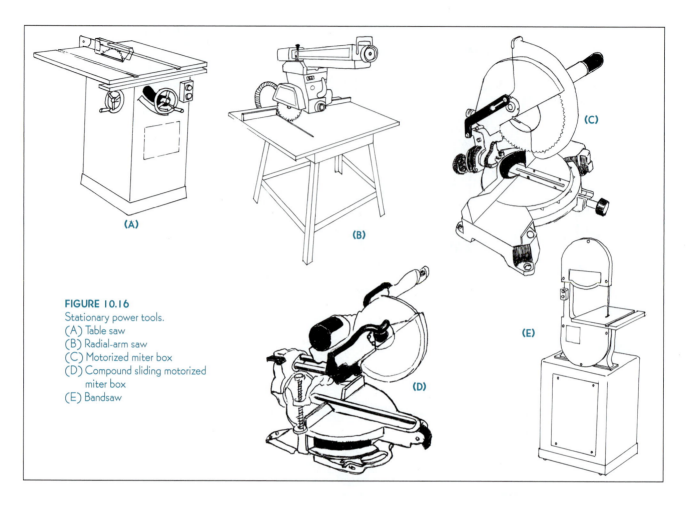

FIGURE 10.16
Stationary power tools.
(A) Table saw
(B) Radial-arm saw
(C) Motorized miter box
(D) Compound sliding motorized
      miter box
(E) Bandsaw

Although almost all power hand tools are commonly available with 120-volt electric motors, many are also made with pneumatic drives (pneumatic tools are discussed later in this chapter), and due to advances in battery technology, most of these power hand tools are now run very efficiently and effectively on rechargeable batteries.

Stationary Power Saws

Stationary power saws are mounted on a stand and are normally located in a fixed position in the shop.

Table Saw   The circular blade of the table saw (Figure 10.16A) projects through a slot in the table of the saw. The height and angle of the saw blade can be adjusted. Primarily used for ripping lumber, the table saw also can be equipped with a **dado head** to cut wide slots (technically, a dado cut runs across the grain of the wood, whereas a groove runs parallel with the grain) or a **molding cutter head** for making a variety of decorative moldings. Blade diameters vary between 7 and 12 inches. Commercial-quality table saws with 10- or 12-inch blades are appropriate for almost all scenic work.

Radial-Arm Saw   The radial-arm, or pullover, saw (Figure 10.16B) is probably the most versatile power tool in the scene shop. The housing containing the circular blade and motor is suspended from an arm above the surface of the work table. The height of the blade is adjusted by raising or lowering this supporting arm. The angle of the cut can be adjusted by swinging the arm or rotating the

dado head: A saw accessory consisting of a set of toothed blades that sandwich a chisel-like chipper; the blades smooth-cut the outside edges of the kerf while the chipper gouges out the wood between the blades; the distance between the blades is variable.

molding cutter head: A heavy cylindrical arbor in which a variety of matched cutter blades or knives can be fit.

Safety Tip

Wood Dust, Wood Dust, and More Wood Dust

Power woodworking tools create copious amounts of sawdust and wood chips. Safe woodworking practice requires keeping as much of this wood dust out of the air as possible. Clean air in the shop environment is also required by Occupational Safety and Health Administration (OSHA) regulation. Every power saw should be fitted with some type of dust-collecting system. Most power woodworking tools manufactured since 1990 have some type of integral dust/chip chute that is connected to either a dust bag or power vacuum. Hand-held power tools, like belt sanders, typically use a bag collector. Larger tools, like table saws, are typically connected to a power vacuum via a flexible hose.

Professional scenic woodworking shops typically have a centralized vacuum system connected to all stationary power tools via ductwork and flexible hoses. Sometimes stationary power tools are mounted on castered benches or platforms so they can be moved around the shop. In these installations, portable shop vacuums—shop vacs—are typically attached to the platforms and connected via flexible hose to the dust chute of the power tool.

Because of the static electricity generated within these shop vacuum systems, and the potential explosiveness of airborne wood dust, great care must be taken to properly install and ground all shop vacuum systems. Be sure to check with appropriate authorities to determine that the system is properly installed and grounded before operating it.

angle of the housing. Although primarily used for cross cutting and angle cutting, the radial-arm saw can also be used for ripping. Commercial-quality saws with blade diameters of 10 or 12 inches are appropriate for theatrical work. Accessories are available for converting this saw for use as a router, planer, or grinder.

Motorized Miter Box   Like the table and radial-arm saw the motorized miter box uses a circular saw blade. The blade and motor housing are attached to the end of an arm that pivots up and down, giving the saw its common name: chop saw. The motor/blade assembly also pivots to allow angled cuts, usually having stops at 30, 45, and 90 degrees. Although light enough to be portable, chop saws should be bolted to some type of supporting stand or table for safety before they are used.

Compound Sliding Motorized Miter Box   The compound sliding motorized miter box combines the best functions of both the chop and radial-arm saws. Like the chop saw the saw/motor housing pivots up and down at the end of an arm and rotates side to side. It also slides back and forth like a radial-arm saw. This allows it to cut wider stock than a "straight" chop saw. The sliding function also allows the saw to be rotated around its horizontal axis so it is capable of making double-angled cuts. Because of its versatility, it is replacing both radial-arm and chop saws in many shops. Too heavy and awkward to be considered truly portable, the compound sliding miter box is normally attached to a shop stand or table.

Bandsaw   Whereas the table saw and radial-arm saw are used to make straight cuts in lumber, the bandsaw (Figure 10.16C) is used to make curvilinear cuts. The narrow, continuous loop (or band) blade passes through a table that supports the work to be cut. If the bandsaw has either mechanical or electronic speed-reduction capability, an appropriate blade can be substituted for the wood-cutting blade, and the bandsaw can be used to cut mild steel, nonferrous metals, and plastic.

Power Handsaws

Some power saws are handheld rather than being mounted on a bench or stand.

Stationary Power Tools

Table and radial-arm saws should be equipped with protective blade guards. Before operating these saws, be sure that the blade guards are in place, are in good operating condition, and do not bind on either the blade or the wood that you are cutting.

Before using any power saw, be sure that the blade is sharp. A dull blade can bind and kick the wood back toward the operator. To avoid kickback when using a table saw, be sure that you feed the wood into the blade without twisting or forcing.

Keep your hands well away from the operating blades. Use a push stick when feeding small pieces into a table saw.

Keep your eyes, and your attention, on the saw and the work. Don't talk to anyone when operating a power tool.

Always maintain your balance when working with a saw. Don't lean toward the saw.

Be sure to wear goggles or a face mask when you are working with any power tool to protect your eyes from flying chips.

When working with any power tool be sure to tie back, pin up, or secure long hair under a cap. Don't wear loose clothing such as baggy shirts or neckties.

Be sure to unplug any power tool before changing the blade or bit.

Use a push stick to keep hands away from the blade of a table saw.

Circular Saw   The portable circular saw (Figure 10.17A) normally has a blade diameter between 7 and 8 inches. The angle and depth of cut can be adjusted, and the saw has a guard that completely covers the blade when it is removed from the work. The portable circular saw is used for straight-line cross cutting and angle cutting as well as ripping of stock lumber, plywood, and composition board.

Saber Saw   The saber saw (Figure 10.17B) uses a reciprocating action with stiff, narrow blades to make curvilinear cuts. With a speed control and appropriate blades, the saber saw can cut metal and plastic as well as wood. It is excellent for cutting curved lines in plywood, composition board, and stock.

(A)

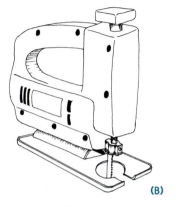
(B)

Power Hand Tools

There are several commonsense safety tips for working with any handheld power tools:

1. Watch what you are doing.

2. Don't talk to anyone or allow yourself to become distracted when operating the tool.

3. Keep long hair tied up or pulled back so that it doesn't get tangled in the tool.

4. Don't operate the tool when you or the electrical cord is in contact with water or something that is very damp.

5. Wear some type of eye protection.

6. Be sure work is properly supported so that the blade or bit won't bind (become stuck).

7. Before cutting be sure the path of the intended cut is clear so that the blade or bit won't cut sawhorses, extension cords, nails, and the like.

Cut Awl   Also used for making curvilinear cuts, the Cut Awl (a registered trade name) combines reciprocating cutting action with a swiveling blade mount (Figure 10.17C). Available with both toothed and knife-edged blades, the Cut Awl can be used to make very intricate, smooth-edged cuts in wood, plywood, and composition board as well as plastic, paper, and cloth.

Reciprocating Saw   Generally known by its trade, and aptly descriptive, name Sawzall,[1] the reciprocating saw is used for very rough cutting of just about anything. The bare blade has no guide so the depth, line, and angle of the cut must be controlled by the operator. The Sawzall will easily cut both wood and thin metal such as nails and wiring. In general construction it is used for demolition jobs—cutting down walls during remodeling projects and the like. In theatre it's used for the same type of work. Generally not used when constructing traditional scenery, it can be very useful for trimming jobs, carving Styrofoam, and during **strike.**

Biscuit Cutter   The biscuit cutter is used to cut a narrow groove in wood. It is typically used when edge-joining two pieces of stock, as when building a tabletop. A thin piece of specialty wood called a biscuit is inserted into the slots of facing pieces to strengthen the resulting joint. The biscuit is made of a wood composite that expands when wet by the glue. The whole unit is then clamped until the glue dries.

Power Drilling Tools

Power drills speed the process of drilling holes.

Drill Press   Mounted on a stand or bench, the drill press (Figure 10.18A) has variable speeds and is very accurate. The chuck usually accepts bit shanks up to $\frac{1}{2}$ inch in diameter as well as a variety of accessories that enable the operator to polish and sand as well as cut mortise and tenon joints for furniture construction.

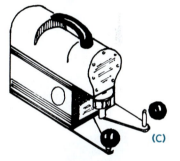
(C)

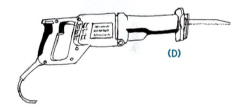
(D)

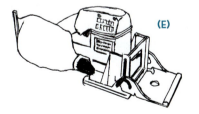
(E)

FIGURE 10.17
Power handsaws.
(A) Circular handsaw
(B) Saber saw
(C) Cut awl
(D) Reciprocating saw
(E) Biscuit cutter

strike Taking down and/or destruction of the set following the conclusion of a play's production run.

---

[1] Trade name of Milwaukee Power Tools.

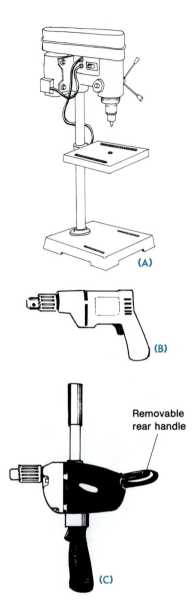

FIGURE 10.18
Power drilling tools.
(A) Drill press
(B) Electric hand drill
(C) Heavy-duty electric drill

Electric Hand Drill   The electric hand drill (Figure 10.18B) is a lightweight, handheld drill that accepts bits up to ¼ or ⅜ inch in diameter. Many electric hand drills have variable speed and reverse controls. The electric drill is generally used for light-duty drilling on lumber 1½ inches thick or less and on light metals.

Heavy-Duty Hand Drill   Heavy-duty handheld drills (Figure 10.18C) generally have more powerful motors and a lower gear ratio (which turns the chuck more slowly). They can accept drill-bit shanks up to ½ inch in diameter. They are used for heavier work such as drilling through multiple layers of wood, ³⁄₁₆-inch and thicker mild steel, and concrete.

Battery-Powered Tools

Advancements in battery technology over the past few years have made life easier for the shop technician. Every type of electrically powered hand tool—drills, screwdrivers, circular saws, sanders, and so forth—is now available with rechargeable batteries. The higher voltages of today's rechargeable batteries—typically 12 to 18 volts and climbing—are much more powerful than those of their predecessors. They also recharge much more quickly. It took several hours, or overnight, to fully recharge a tool's battery with the battery technology of the late 1990s. Currently (no electrical pun intended) batteries can be fully recharged in 30 minutes to 3 hours. The only thing preventing most shops from going completely cordless is budget. Top-of-the-line battery-powered hand tools are still significantly more expensive than their 120-volt counterparts. Even so, most scene shops now use battery-powered handtools—particularly drills and screwdrivers—almost exclusively.

Pneumatic Tools

Pneumatic tools perform the same functions as electrically powered tools, but they are driven by air pressure. To effectively use pneumatic tools, a shop needs to have a large-capacity compressor and air tank as well as an efficiently designed system for distributing the compressed air to convenient locations around the shop and stage. Again, almost every type of electrically powered hand tool is available in pneumatic form.

Pneumatic Stapler   The pneumatic stapler (Figure 10.19A) uses air pressure to drive the staples. The length of the staple legs that can be used with pneumatic staplers varies from about ¼ to 2 inches depending on the manufacturer. Staples are available in a variety of styles: straight-leg staples go straight into the work; coated-leg staples have a heat-activated adhesive; and the legs of divergent-leg staples spread in opposite directions when they enter the wood. The pneumatic stapler is used for the same types of jobs as a hammer and nails. It can be used for assembling flat framing, putting tops on platforms, and performing similar functions.

Pneumatic Nailer   The pneumatic nailer (Figure 10.19B) uses clips of coated nails in much the same manner that the pneumatic stapler uses staples. It can be used for rapid assembly of platforms and similar structures.

Impact Wrench   The pneumatic impact wrench (Figure 10.19C) uses air pressure to tighten or loosen nuts. If you have ever watched someone change a tire in a service station, you have probably seen a pneumatic impact wrench in action. In the scene shop, this device is useful when you are "legging" (bolting legs onto) platforms. The impact wrench is also available in an electrically powered version.

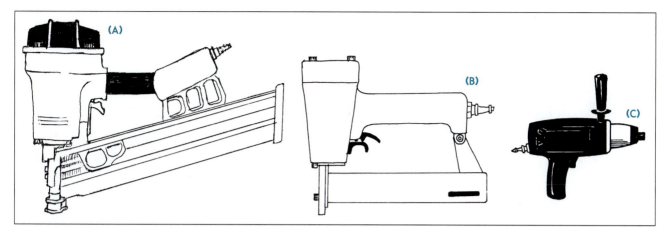

FIGURE 10.19
Pneumatic tools.
(A) Pneumatic stapler
(B) Pneumatic nailer
(C) Pneumatic impact wrench

Other pneumatically driven tools, such as sanders, grinders, and drills, work exactly as their electrically powered counterparts do.

Metalworking Power Tools

Welders   Several types of welders are used for fusing metal in the scene shop.

Oxyacetylene Welder   The oxyacetylene welder (Figure 10.20A) combines oxygen and acetylene to produce a very hot flame (approximately 6000°F) capable of melting most metals. The oxygen and acetylene are stored under pressure in steel tanks. The amount of each gas in the mixture is controlled by pressure regulators attached to the top of each tank. The gas is fed to the torch, where the mixture is again adjusted with the small valves at the end of the torch.

A cutting torch (Figure 10.20B) has an extra lever that introduces more oxygen into the mix, enabling the flame to burn through the metal. (See Chapter 11, "Scenic Production Techniques," for a discussion of using welding equipment.)

Arc Welder   The arc welder (Figure 10.20C) consists of a power housing unit, cables, and a welding handle. It works by creating an electrical arc that melts the metals being welded. There are several power settings, which can be adjusted for the heat range that is appropriate to the composition and thickness of the metal being welded.

MIG Welder   The MIG (metal insert gas) welder (Figure 10.20D) is an arc welder that focuses a flow of inert gas (usually argon) on the welding zone as the weld is being made. The electrode of the MIG welder is a thin piece of wire that is automatically fed through the welding handle from a spool stored in the housing of the power unit. The MIG welder can also be used without the inert gas if a special flux-core wire is used rather than the "regular" wire electrode. The flux effectively provides the same inert-gas environment while the weld is being made.

Soldering Equipment   Soldering provides a low-strength bond between most common metals such as steel, copper, and brass. It is frequently used to bond wires together in an electrical circuit. Aluminum can be soldered, but it requires high heat and a special **flux.**

Various soldering pencils, guns, and irons are used to heat solder to its melting point. Soldering pencils (25 to 40 watts) are used for lightweight projects such as working on the circuitry of electronic equipment (Figure 10.21A). Soldering guns (50 to 200 watts) are trigger-operated, rapid-heating, medium- to heavy-usage devices (Figure 10.21B). Soldering irons (Figure 10.21C) are larger versions

flux: A chemical that reduces surface oxidation, which would prevent the solder or filler rod (welding) and the metal being soldered or welded from flowing together.

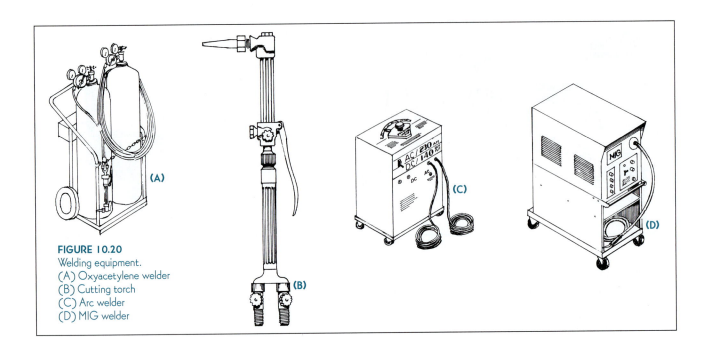

FIGURE 10.20
Welding equipment.
(A) Oxyacetylene welder
(B) Cutting torch
(C) Arc welder
(D) MIG welder

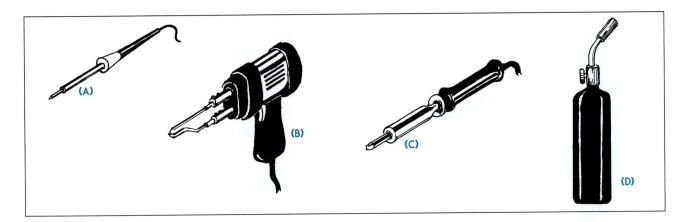

FIGURE 10.21
Soldering equipment.
(A) Soldering pencil
(B) Soldering gun
(C) Soldering iron
(D) Propane torch

of soldering pencils with proportionally higher wattages (80 to 500). They are used for heavy-duty soldering projects in which the iron is required to heat a relatively large mass of metal.

Propane Torch   The propane torch (Figure 10.21D) consists of a small bottle of propane gas and a nozzle with a number of fittings designed to produce different flame shapes. The heat produced by the torch is sufficient for soldering most heavy-duty scenic jobs. It is also useful for heating thin-gauge steel for bending or shaping.

Power Hacksaw   A motorized gear assembly provides the forward and backward movement necessary for the blade of the motorized hacksaw (Figure 10.22A) to cut through various types of metal stock.

Cutoff Saw   Also called a motorized miter box, the cutoff saw (Figure 10.22B), equipped with a wood-cutting blade, can also be equipped with a metal-cutting blade to make either straight or angle cuts through various types of metal stock.

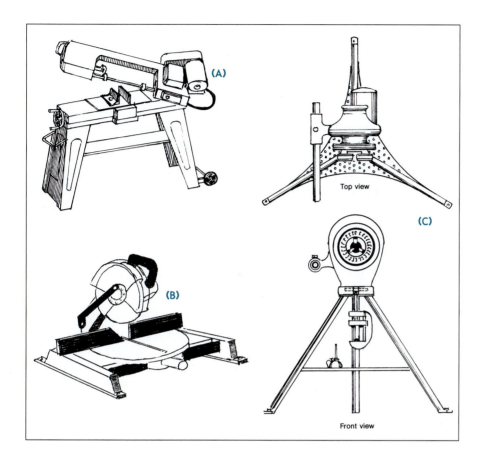

FIGURE 10.22
Metal-cutting power tools.
(A) Power hacksaw
(B) Cutoff saw
(C) Power pipe cutter

Power Pipe Cutter   The power pipe cutter (Figure 10.22C) performs the same functions as the manual pipe cutting tools: cutting and threading metal pipes with diameters from approximately ½ to 2 inches.

Miscellaneous Power Tools

Some additional power tools cannot be neatly placed into any particular category.

Router   A router (Figure 10.23A) is a handheld, motor-driven tool used for shaping wood. The chisel-like rotating bit is driven at extremely high speed (generally 25,000 revolutions per minute) to shape or carve designs from the surface or edge of the piece of wood. It is primarily used for shaping decorative moldings and trim pieces.

Wood Lathe   The wood lathe (Figure 10.23B) is a bench-mounted tool that holds and spins wood rapidly so that it can be shaped by carving. Special wood-turning chisels are used to carve the wood. The speed is variable and is controlled by either mechanical or electronic means. In the scene shop, the lathe is used for turning bannisters, table legs, and the like. The wood lathe can also be modified for use in turning Styrofoam.

Bench Sander   A variety of sanders is available, but the bench sander (Figure 10.23C) is normally mounted and is usually a combination of belt sander and disk sander. It is used to bevel or smooth the surface or edges of wood and some plastics.

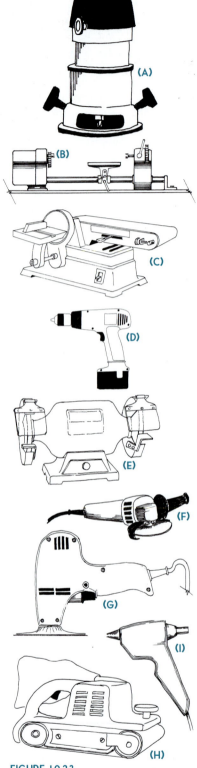

Electric Screwdriver   One very handy tool bears a strong visual resemblance to an electric hand drill, but instead of holding drill bits its special chuck holds the magnetized tip of a Phillips screwdriver. Electric screwdrivers (Figure 10.23D) have variable-speed motors, so the screws can be started slowly, and a clutch that stops the chuck from turning when the screw is fully seated. It is designed for use with case-hardened Phillips screws that work equally well in wood and metal with no starter hole. The electric screwdriver is used for assembling flats and platforms and in similar situations where assembly and the strength of a screw fastener are needed.

Bench Grinder   The bench grinder (Figure 10.23E) is used for grinding and sharpening metal. It is normally equipped with a grinding wheel and a wire brush (for polishing), although a cloth buffing wheel can be used for polishing metal to a high luster.

Hand Power Grinder   A portable version of the bench grinder is the hand power grinder (Figure 10.23F). It is particularly useful for pieces that are too heavy or awkward to be worked on the bench grinder.

Hand Power Sander   Basically a slightly less powerful version of the hand power grinder, the hand power sander (Figure 10.23G) uses a rotating disk of sandpaper to sand wood, metal, and plastic.

Belt Sander   The powerful belt sander (Figure 10.23H) uses belts of sandpaper for rapid sanding of (primarily) wood.

Hot-Melt Glue Gun   One of the most versatile tools in the shop, the hot-melt glue gun (Figure 10.23I) uses sticks of heat-activated adhesive for making rapid-hold glue bonds on and between just about every type of material—wood, plastic, paper, cloth, metal, dirt, sand, and so on.

 Wood

Three categories of wood are used in scenic construction: stock lumber, moldings, and sheet goods.

Stock Lumber

To be appropriate for use in scenic construction, stock lumber must possess the following characteristics. It should be strong, lightweight, free of knots, splinter resistant, easily worked, and fairly inexpensive. White pine, a generic name applicable to a number of separate species of pine grown in the western United States, generally satisfies these requirements. White pine is normally used to build the frames of flats and in similar lightweight construction projects.

Unfortunately for the theatrical technician, white pine isn't always called white pine. The name varies considerably depending on the locale. Because of these regional name variations, it isn't possible to simply call up your friendly lumber store and order "white pine." First, visit the lumberyard and look for the wood that has the required characteristics. Then, find out what it's called.

Another commonly used wood in scenic construction is Douglas fir. This wood is heavier than white pine, is stronger, and generally sells for one-half to one-third the cost of white pine. It is normally used for heavier construction projects such as weight-bearing structures and platform legs.

FIGURE 10.23
Miscellaneous power tools.
(A) Router
(B) Wood lathe
(C) Bench sander
(D) Electric screwdriver
(E) Bench grinder
(F) Hand power grinder
(G) Hand power sander
(H) Belt sander
(I) Hot-melt glue gun

All stock lumber is graded. There are two primary grades of wood, *select* and *common.* Each of these categories is further subdivided.

A Select   "A select" wood is free of all knots, blemishes, erratic graining, and warps.

B Select   Also known as "B or Better," "B select" wood is primarily the same as A select except that the grain can be less uniform and the wood can contain more pitch, which increases its weight.

C Select   "C select" wood can have a few tight knots (that will not fall out) of less than ½ inch in diameter, slightly less uniform graining, and still more pitch.

D Select   "D select" wood can have more tight knots (still only ½ inch in diameter), an occasional pitch pocket, and some warping.

No. 1 Common   No. 1 common lumber can have knots up to 1½ inches in diameter. The knots do not have to be tight; in other words, they may fall out, leaving a knothole in the plank. Warping and twisting are more prevalent in this grade of lumber.

No. 2 Common   The knots in No. 2 common lumber can be greater than 1½ inches in diameter, and the edges can show an occasional strip of bark. The wood will probably be warped and twisted.

The cost of lumber goes down as you move down the scale from A select to No. 2 common. It is difficult to find A select in most lumberyards. When it is available, it is almost always very expensive. Most stage construction can be accomplished by using C select or D select. The occasional knot, split end, or slight warp that will be found in these grades can usually be trimmed to prevent it from interfering with the construction project. The common grades of lumber are not particularly suitable for stage purposes, although they can be used for applications where their appearance and structural weakness would not adversely affect the appearance or safety of the set.

Dimensions of Stock Lumber   The Department of Agriculture determines the standards for the thickness, width, and length of all stock lumber sold in the United States. Since the sizing of lumber is done before the boards are milled to a smooth surface, the actual dimensions of the lumber that we buy are smaller than the indicated size, as shown in Figure 10.24. Slight variations in the actual dimensions of the lumber can be measured on almost any piece of stock because of milling variations and shrinkage. Because of these discrepancies, it is a good practice to measure the width of every piece of lumber before you use it. The typical scenic uses of the various sizes of lumber are described in Table 10.1.

Molding and Trim

In addition to stock lumber, there are a number of standard trims and moldings (Figure 10.25) that can be used in theatrical production. Decorative moldings are normally manufactured from white pine and are used extensively for architectural trim on and around door and window casings as well as to provide visual interest on baseboards, chair rails, cornices, wall panels, and similar locations.

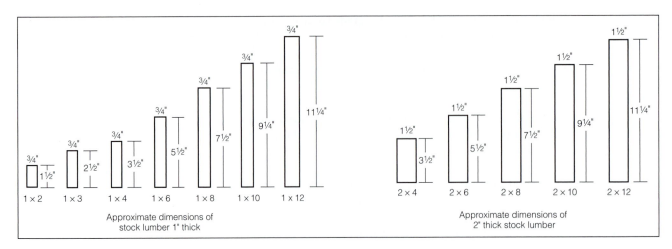

FIGURE 10.24
Standard lumber dimensions.

TABLE 10.1

Standard Uses of Lumber in Scenic Construction

Indicated Size (cross section)	Actual Size	Typical Stage Uses
1 × 2	¾ inch × 1½ inches	small flats; lightweight corner bracing of flats
1 × 3	¾ inch × 2½ inches	standard flat framing (6–14 feet); diagonal bracing of platform legs
1 × 4	¾ inch × 3½ inches	large flat framing (over 14 feet)
1 × 6	¾ inch × 5½ inches	door and window frames and similar architectural trim work; narrow sweeps
1 × 8	¾ inch × 7½ inches	
1 × 10	¾ × 9¼ inches	stair treads, sweeps, profile cutouts, furniture
1 × 12	¾ inch × 11¼ inches	
2 × 4	1½ inches × 3½ inches	platform framing, platform legs, and similar weight-bearing structures
2 × 6	1½ inches × 5½ inches	
2 × 8	1½ inches × 7½ inches	
2 × 10	1½ inches × 9¼ inches	temporary scaffolding; some stair carriages
2 × 12	1½ inches × 11¼ inches	not normally used for stage scenery

Sheet Stock

Various materials fall into the general classification of sheet stock or lumber products that are manufactured in sheet form.

Plywood   Plywood is made by laminating several layers of wood. Most plywood used in the theatre is composed of either three or five layers of wood. The direction of the grain of each successive layer lies at a 90-degree angle to the layers immediately above and below it, as shown in Figure 10.26. Because the strength of wood lies across its grain, plywood is much stronger than solid wood of a similar thickness.

Plywood is manufactured in interior and exterior grades. The only difference between them is that the exterior grade is laminated with a waterproof glue, whereas the interior grade uses a glue that is water soluble.

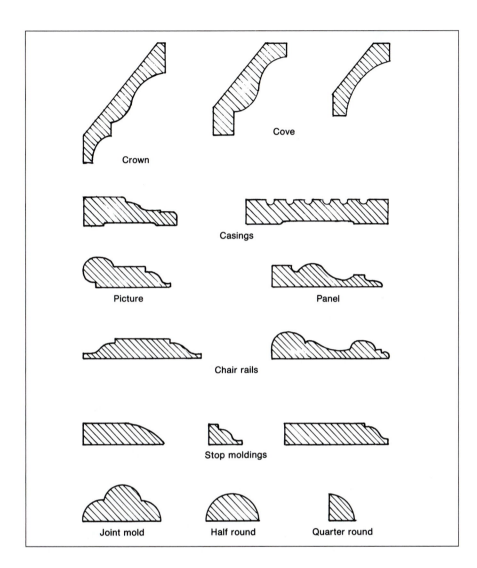

FIGURE 10.25
Specialty-cut lumber and moldings.

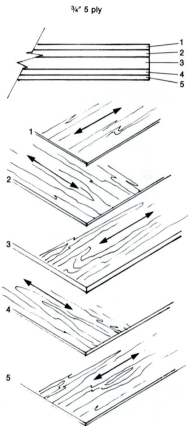

¾" 5 ply

FIGURE 10.26
Plywood laminations.

Plywood is available in most lumberyards in thicknesses of ⅛, ³⁄₁₆, ¼, ⅜, ½, ⅝, and ¾ inch. Almost all plywood, unless precut by the lumberyard, is sold in 4-by-8-foot sheets. Generally, the only exception to this 4-by-8-foot rule involves ⅛-inch **lauan,** or Philippine mahogany, plywood. While lauan plywood is available in 4-by-8-foot and 4-by-10-foot **paper clad** sheets, in both ⅛-inch and ¼-inch thicknesses, it is also sold as "door skin" in which the ⅛-inch-thick sheets are 3-foot-by-6-foot-9-inch or 7-foot.

Plywood is graded according to its surface finish, as shown in Table 10.2. Although there are other grades of plywood, those listed in the table are the most common and are readily available.

AD plywood, despite the fact that it has **plugs,** small knotholes, and grain irregularities on one face, is the standard grade for almost all theatrical construction purposes. BC plywood is available in some areas of the country, is generally less expensive than AD, and can be used in applications like platform decking. The AA grade is rarely used because of its high cost. **Keystones** and **cornerblocks** are made from ¼-inch AD plywood. Sweeps, profile pieces, and other curvilinear forms can be cut from any appropriate thickness of AD plywood. Three-quarter-inch AD plywood (A side up) is often used to make platform tops. CD plywood costs less than AD, and its inherent strength is not reduced by its surface imperfections. As the price of AD plywood has risen, more and more technicians are opting to use ACX as their plywood of choice. ACX plywood has almost the same

lauan: Also known as Philippine mahogany. This ⅛-inch lauan plywood is strong and quite flexible. Commonly used as a flat-covering material and for covering curved-surface forms.

paper clad: Both sides covered with paper.

plug: A wooden insert used to replace a knothole or other imperfection in the surface layer of a sheet of plywood.

keystones and cornerblocks: Pieces of ¼-inch AD plywood used to reinforce joints in the construction of stage flats.

TABLE 10.2

Plywood Grading System

Grade	Surface Appearance
AA	smooth sanded on both sides; both faces free from knots, plugs, or grain irregularities
AD	smooth sanded on both sides; one face (A) is free from imperfections, and the other (D) is not
BC	rough sanded on both sides; one face (B) may have plugged surface imperfections, the other side (C) may have plugs, some open knotholes, and slight grain irregularities. Whole sheet may have slight warp.
CD	rough sanded on both sides; each face may have many surface imperfections, some open knotholes, and grain irregularities; whole sheet may be slightly warped

(A)

(B)

FIGURE 10.27
Closeup views of (A) particle board and (B) oriented strand board (OSB).

characteristics as AD. The D face is upgraded to C, it is made with exterior glue, and it is frequently easier to find than AD. CD or CDX plywood can be used instead of AD or ADX for platform tops if the rough surface is going to be covered with some other material or if it is not going to be seen by the audience.

Furniture-grade plywood is manufactured with higher-quality filler layers. The outer surfaces are usually AA or AD and are made from hardwoods such as mahogany, birch, oak, or walnut. There is also a wide variety of plywoods, usually ³⁄₁₆- or ¼-inch thickness, that have prefinished, painted, or hardwood veneer surfaces. These prefinished panels can be used to cover flats as well as in other applications.

Particle Board   Particle board (Figure 10.27A) is composed of wood chips and sawdust mixed with a glue binder and compressed into 4-by-8-foot sheets. Particle board is usually available in ³⁄₈-, ½-, ⁵⁄₈-, and ¾-inch thicknesses. It is much heavier than plywood of similar thickness and isn't nearly as strong, but it can be used for subflooring, cabinet shelves, and similar structures.

Medium-density fiberboard (MDF) is a finer-grained version of particle board. It is widely used in the furniture and cabinet industries. Like particle board, it isn't as strong as either stock lumber or plywood. In scenic construction it can be used for a variety of non-load-bearing functions—cabinets, shelves, trim—where its finer grain and lower cost make it an acceptable substitute for stock lumber or sheet goods. Because of these qualities the use of MDF has increased in professional scene shops. Most MDF is made using urea-formaldehyde resins. Just sitting uncut in the shop, it emits small amounts of formaldehyde. When cut, the dust particles likewise contain formaldehyde. It can irritate the eyes and respiratory system and can cause severe reactions in people with an extreme sensitivity to formaldehyde. Be sure to wear an appropriately rated particulate screening respirator when working with this material. Two brands of "alternative MDF" are manufactured with resins that emit extremely low levels of formaldehyde. They are Medex and Medite II from the Medite Corporation (www.sierrapine.com).[2]

Oriented Strand Board (OSB)   Similar to particle board but composed of much larger chips, OSB (Figure 10.27B) is actually as strong as plywood and is lighter and cheaper. OSB (also called wafer board) is finished with one smooth face and one that has a slight texture. Because it is more "springy" than plywood of similar thickness, if OSB is used for platform-topping material the number of cross

[2] Duckworth, William, "Is MDF Hazardous?" *Fine Woodworking,* Taunton Press, November/December 2006, p. 98.

supports used in the platform structure needs to be increased. Its other construction uses, such as the web material for manufactured wooden I beams used as joists and rafters, are continually being discovered. Its use in professional scenic studios has increased in the past decade.

Hardboard   Hardboard, frequently called Masonite, a registered trade name, is manufactured from wood pulp that is compressed into 4-by-8 sheets of ⅛-, ¼-, and ⅜-inch thickness. It is available in two degrees of hardness, untempered and tempered. Untempered hardboard, which is light brown, has a soft, easily gouged surface. Tempered Masonite is dark brown and has an extremely hard surface.

Although hardboard is brittle and can be broken easily with a sharp blow, the ⅛-inch board can be used as a facing surface for counters, stair risers, and other vertical surfaces that may receive moderate physical abuse during the production. It is flexible enough to be bent around slightly curved forms. Either ¼- or ⅜-inch tempered Masonite can be used to cover the permanent wooden stage floor, because the hard surface resists the abuse caused by heavy stage equipment and can easily be painted with casein, latex, or acrylic paint.

Upson Board   Upson board is basically paper pulp and binder that have been mixed and compressed into 4-by-8 sheets. It is available in thicknesses of ⅛, ³⁄₁₆, and ¼ inch. The material is fairly flexible and has little inherent strength. Unless the edge of a piece of Upson board is supported by a wooden framework, it can be easily bent, broken, or frayed.

Upson board ⅛-inch thick, also known by the trade name of Easy Curve, is used to cover fairly sharply curved surfaces such as columns or curved walls. The ³⁄₁₆- and ¼-inch Upson board can be used as a hard cover for flats or profile cutouts if they won't be subject to too much physical abuse.

Sonotube

Sonotube is a paper tube used for forming concrete. In the world of theatre it also makes a great column. Sonotube is available in a variety of diameters ranging from 8 to 56 inches, and in lengths up to 18 feet. The wall of the tube is about ¼ inch thick, but since it is strong enough to hold concrete, it should be strong enough for almost any decorative stage use.

Fabrics that are normally used for covering scenery are discussed in Chapter 11, "Scenic Production Techniques," and typical drapery and upholstery materials are dealt with in Chapter 13, "Stage Properties."

Manufactured Wood

An ever-increasing number of woodlike construction materials made from wood by-products (chips, strands, sawdust, and so forth) are finding their way into scenic construction. One significant advantage to these products is their dimensional stability. They are milled to much closer tolerances than stock lumber and generally don't swell or shrink as much as stock lumber. In larger sizes they are also cheaper than stock lumber. Lumberlam (a trade name) is a laminated, engineered material used as a replacement/substitute for stock lumber. Glue-lam beams are laminated beams made from relatively short pieces of stock lumber. They can be used to span openings of up to 18 to 20 feet and still have sufficient load capacity to support platforming on top. Other stock lumber substitutes are molded by subjecting a slurry of sawdust and high-tech adhesives to heat and high pressure.

Theatrical uses for these products will undoubtedly expand as more types and variations are introduced and more technicians try them.

Metal

Metal is being used with increasing frequency in scenic construction. This popularity can be attributed to three specific factors: (1) The increasing cost of wood has eliminated what was once a significant cost difference between wood and steel; (2) metal is inherently stronger than wood; and (3) with proper tools, metal can be worked as easily as wood.

The greater strength of metal allows the construction of frameworks for platforms and large flats that are as strong as or stronger than, but weigh less than, similarly sized wooden units. Additionally, metal's strength encourages its use in the fabrication of delicate or irregular shapes that would be impossible to duplicate in wood.

Although there are literally hundreds of metals and alloys, only two types—mild steel and aluminum—are used extensively in scenic construction. Other metals, most notably bronze, brass, and copper, are occasionally used in prop construction, but their relatively high cost and working characteristics argue against their being used for other than decorative purposes.

Mild Steel

Mild steel, officially known as AISI (American Iron and Steel Institute) C-1020, is the most commonly used type of steel in theatrical construction. It is malleable and is fairly easy to cut, bend, drill, and weld, and its strength is sufficient for most general scenic uses such as flat and platform frameworks.

AISI C-1020 is manufactured in two primary forms: *structural* and *merchant bar.* Structural steel has a uniform chemical composition throughout, complete internal soundness (no air pockets, cracks, nonuniform crystallization formations, or other weaknesses that would affect its strength), and no significant surface flaws. Merchant bar may have internal defects that would affect the material's strength and more apparent surface flaws. Because of its questionable strength, merchant bar shouldn't be used for critical weight-bearing structures. Mild steel is finished at the mill with several different surfaces. The two most common finishes are *plain oxide* and a treatment called *oiled and pickled.* Plain oxide is the most common and least expensive finish. The steel is covered with a gray oxide that naturally forms as the steel cools and has some **scale** and a light coating of rust. For welding, brazing, or painting, the contaminants (oxide, scale, and rust) must be removed, usually by wire-brushing or grinding. An oiled and pickled finish provides a clean surface to the steel. At the mill, the steel receives an acid bath and a neutralizing rinse while it is still hot. It is then coated with oil to prevent the natural formation of oxide as it cools. The oil coat also prevents the formation of rust. Steel that has been *plated* or *painted* is also available from the factory. Generally, it isn't used in scenic construction because of its higher cost. But a galva-

scale: A black scaly coat that forms on iron when it is heated for processing.

Heating Galvanized Coatings

Galvanized finishes—the mottled, silvery finish frequently found on steel water pipes, rigid and thin wall conduit, water/paint buckets, and thin steel sheet colloquially known as "galvanized tin"—emit noxious fumes when the galvanized finish is drilled, welded, or flame-cut. Be sure to work with these materials in well-ventilated areas or outdoors, and wear a proper respirator.

Safety Tip

nized finish has a bright silvery finish that is difficult to duplicate with paint and may be appropriate for some applications.

Mild steel is readily available from steel suppliers in the shapes illustrated in Figure 10.28 as well as in sheets of varying sizes and thicknesses.

Typical scenic-construction uses of the various shapes of steel are listed below.

Square and Rectangular Tubing Square and rectangular tubing are arguably the most used and useful shapes of steel for theatrical construction. Rectangular tubing is frequently used for platform framing and similar weight-bearing structures, whereas square tubing is more typically used for flat framing and other lightweight forms that will be covered with cloth or thin hard coverings (plywood, Upson board, Masonite, and so forth).

Rectangular tubing is available in sizes ranging from slightly under 1 by 2 inches up to 6 by 12 inches with a variety of wall thicknesses ranging from about 0.035 inch up to ½ inch. Square-tubing sizes range in ⅛-inch increments from ⅜ inch to 1¼ inch, with wall thicknesses ranging between 0.035 inch and 0.065 inch. For small- to medium-sized platforms and flats, 1-inch-by-2-inch rectangular and 1-inch square tubing with wall thicknesses of 0.035 to 0.065 are typical.

Tubing or Pipe One of the most common uses of pipe is for electrical conduit. There are two types of conduit, rigid and EMT (electrical metallic tubing). Rigid conduit is sold with internal diameters ranging from ½ inch to 6 inches. EMT, commonly known as thin-wall conduit, is available in sizes ranging from ⅜ inch to 2 inches. Thin-wall conduit can be bent in fairly intricate shapes with a pipe or conduit bender and is primarily used for decorative elements. Before bending thin-wall conduit, be sure to fill the pipe with sand to prevent the walls of the pipe from collapsing. Neither type of conduit is strong enough to be used for weight-bearing structures.

Thicker-walled pipe, such as the "black pipe" used for gas lines, is more typically used for structural purposes such as platform legs and battens.

Channel Channel is most typically used in structures requiring significant strength, such as the framework for large platforms or wagons.

Angle Angle, or angle iron, is frequently used in those situations requiring less strength than rectangular or square tubing provides—lightweight frames, braces, and stiffeners.

Strap Strap is used to strengthen or brace existing wooden structures. Its most apparent use is as the sill iron that spans the bottom of door openings in wooden framed flats.

Proprietary Structural Systems

Several companies manufacture steel structural systems that can be used like giant Erector sets to construct a wide variety of structural and scenic items ranging from lighting grids to stairways, platforms, scaffolds, flat frames, and open frameworks. The advantage of these systems is the speed with which structures can be assembled and the reusability of the materials. The disadvantage lies primarily in the increased cost of the materials and specialized fastening hardware.

Unistrut This system consists of U-shaped channels of differing sizes, as shown in Figure 10.29A. The Unistrut system requires only that the channels be cut to length and bolted together with the specialized hardware (Figure 10.29B).

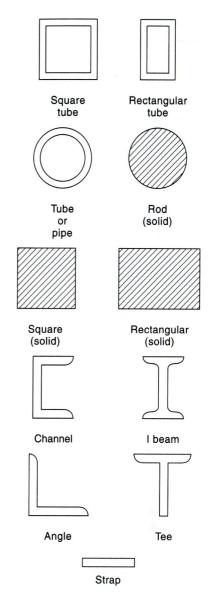

FIGURE 10.28
Basic forms of metal.

Square tube

Rectangular tube

Tube or pipe

Rod (solid)

Square (solid)

Rectangular (solid)

Channel

I beam

Angle

Tee

Strap

(A)

(B)

FIGURE 10.29
(A) Unistrut metal framing. (B) Joining requires special hardware. (Courtesy of Unistrut Corporation.)

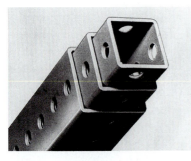

FIGURE 10.30
Telespar is square telescoping tubing. (Courtesy of Unistrut Corporation.)

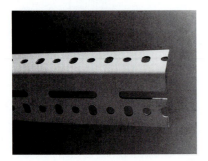

FIGURE 10.31
Slotted angle.

Telespar   Also manufactured by the Unistrut Company, Telespar (Figure 10.30) is a system of telescoping square steel tubing. Tubing with ⅜-inch holes on **1-inch centers** punched into all four faces of each section of tubing is available in sizes ranging between 1½ and 2½ inches. Telescoping plain-tube sizes range between 1 inch and 2½ inches. The telescoping feature allows the length to be adjusted without cutting.

Slotted Angle   Slotted angle (Figure 10.31) is manufactured with a variety of holes and slots punched into both faces of the stock. These holes permit the slotted angle stock to be bolted together without additional drilling. The slotted angle is cut to length and fastened together using standard bolts, washers, and nuts.

This listing of shapes and uses of steel materials is far from exhaustive, but it does provide an introduction to the use of mild steel in theatrical construction. A trip to your local steel distributor can show you the materials available in your area. A trip to your metal scrap junkyard can be equally illuminating.

Aluminum

Aluminum is manufactured in the same shapes as mild steel. Additionally, decorative panels made of aluminum can be purchased in many hardware or lumber stores.

Aluminum is not used as extensively as mild steel, primarily because it is more expensive and is more difficult to weld than steel. It is used mainly for decorative purposes in scenic construction.

Plastics

Various plastics are useful in technical production, but more substantial safety hazards are involved in forming and processing plastics than in dealing with any other common construction material.

Friction between a saw or knife blade and plastic creates heat. This heat liberates gases from the plastic. Some of these fumes simply smell bad; some are noxious, or unhealthy; others are toxic, or poisonous; and still others can be lethal.

Because it is frequently difficult to determine the level of toxicity of these various fumes, it is vital that you work with plastics only in a well-ventilated area. If your workshop isn't equipped with a good fresh-air circulation system, create your own. Set up a cross-ventilation pattern, illustrated in Figure 10.32, between outside windows and doors. Use box fans or similar large-bladed fans set on high speed to move a large volume of air. When you first open the windows or doors, check the natural direction of the airflow and reinforce it with your fans. How-

Urethane Plastics

If at all possible, completely avoid using urethane foams. When the formed foam is heated, either with a saw blade or an open flame, it emits a toxic gas. The same gas is emitted as the pour-in-place foams set up and cure. If you must use this material, be absolutely sure to wear an appropriate respirator and have a high volume of fresh-air ventilation in the workplace. Additionally, all personnel in the area should also wear appropriately rated respirators.

Safety Tip

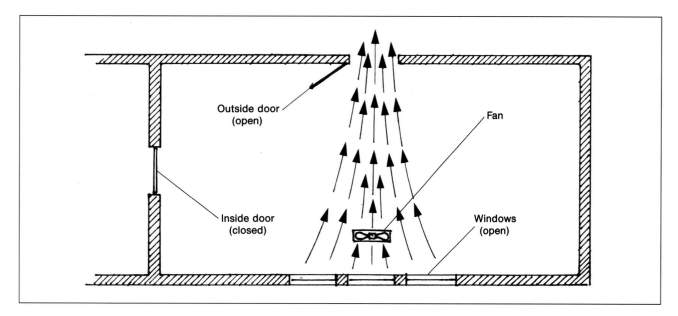

Outside door
(open)

Fan

Inside door
(closed)

Windows
(open)

FIGURE 10.32
Cross-ventilation airflow pattern for
a shop.

ever, be sure that you ventilate the fumes to the outdoors rather than simply blowing them into another part of the building. If your shop doesn't have direct access to outside fresh air, don't work on plastics in the shop. Work on them outdoors, or if that isn't possible, appropriate a room that can be properly ventilated. The necessity for a high volume of air movement cannot be stressed too much. Your physical health, and the health of everyone else in the shop, depends on it.

When working with plastics, be sure to wear a respirator specifically designed for use with the plastic with which you are working. This mask filters the air through appropriate materials that remove the harmful elements from the air. The use of a respirator and an effective fresh-air ventilation system, when combined with the commonsense rules of shop safety, can make working with plastics safe.

Acrylic

Frequently identified by one of its trade names, Plexiglas, acrylic is available in rigid sheets of varying sizes and thicknesses in clear, translucent, textured, and colored finishes. It is also available in rods, tubes, and bars and in a liquid form for use as a **casting resin.** It is commonly used as a glass substitute, and the casting resin can be used to make decorative baubles for costumes, props, and stained glass. The sheets, rods, and tubes can be formed by heating and bending the material to the desired shape.

Epoxy

Epoxies are available in a variety of formulations to suit a number of purposes, but in theatrical construction the most commonly used types are those for adhesives and casting resins. All epoxies are extremely durable and moisture resistant. Depending on the particular formulation, epoxies can be worked with either wood- or metal-cutting tools.

Epoxy adhesive is useful for scenic and property construction projects that require strength or water resistance. Epoxy auto-body putty is useful for molding and sculpting decorative detail on sets and props. The casting resin can be used

1-inch centers: The centers of adjacent elements, such as holes, are spaced 1 inch apart.

casting resin: Any of a number of liquid plastics used for casting forms in molds.

OSHA requires manufacturers to provide a Material Safety Data Sheet (MSDS) for each of their products. MSDSs are available by calling the manufacturer or by accessing the manufacturer's home page on the Internet.

Safety Tip

The MSDS provides all pertinent safety information about the product: hazardous materials the product contains; known health hazards associated with the product; required protective equipment (gloves, type of respirator, and so forth) for working with the product; first-aid procedures to be used when product overexposure occurs; emergency contact phone numbers for information about the product.[1]

Everyone working in any shop should be familiar with the safe handling of any materials to which they will be exposed. The MSDS for each product provides you with that information.

[1] Chris Minik, "Hazardous Chemicals in the Workshop," *Fine Woodworking*, May/June 1999, pp. 117–118.

to make objects that are much stronger than those cast with either acrylic or polyester casting resins.

Fluorocarbons

Teflon is probably the best-known trade name in this family of tough, durable, low-friction, nonstick plastics. Although it is commercially available in a variety of forms, the most useful for theatrical purposes are the sheets and tapes.

Teflon makes an excellent bearing surface because of its extremely slippery qualities. It can be used for turntables or for covering the tracks and runners of **skids.**

skid: A low-profile substitute for a wagon; usually a piece of ¾-inch plywood on which some small scenic element is placed.

Polyesters

There are two types of polyester, saturated and unsaturated. All polyesters have a characteristically smooth surface and great tensile strength.

Saturated Polyesters   Saturated polyesters are used to form the fiber from which polyester fabrics such as Dacron are made. Saturated polyesters are also used to manufacture films such as Mylar.

Polyester fabrics have a variety of uses in both scenic and costume construction, and they can be worked with normal fabric-cutting tools. The film, which is available in a variety of textures, treatments, and colors, has many uses in the scene shop. Aluminized Mylar film is frequently used as a lightweight, unbreakable stage mirror, and Mylar film is used as the base material for several lines of lighting-instrument color media as well as audio and video recording tape.

Unsaturated Polyesters   Unsaturated polyesters can be used in casting or to create the multipurpose material known as fiberglass.

The unsaturated polyester casting resin can be used for the same purposes as the acrylic and epoxy casting resins. Fiberglass, also called glass-fiber plastic, is used in situations where its great strength and flexibility of form are an advantage. A water-based resin, Aqua Resin, manufactured by Sculptural Arts Coatings, is a safer alternative casting resin when working with fiberglass. It has the same general working characteristics as unsaturated polyester resin.

Unsaturated polyesters can be worked with both woodworking and metal-working tools. A basic introduction to working with glass-fiber plastics can be found in Chapter 13, "Stage Properties."

Polyethylene

Polyethylene plastics are available in a variety of formulations, but the forms most commonly used in the theatre are film and foam. All polyethylenes have a characteristically slick, waxy surface.

Polyethylene film, generally available in black, white, and clear, can be used for such things as drop cloths and projection screens. Polyethylene foam, gener-ally known by the trade name Ethafoam, is very flexible and is generally available in sheets and rods. It is frequently used for architectural trim and similar non-structural functions. It rejects every type of paint except acrylic, and even acrylic will chip off if the surface of the foam is flexed. Ethafoam can be painted if, after it is applied to the scenery, it is coated with Sculptural Arts Coatings' Sculpt or Coat or Rosco's Flexcoat or it is covered with several layers of cheesecloth that have been coated with white glue. Sheets of polyethylene foam, sold under the trade name of Bubble Board, make excellent rear-screen projection surfaces.

Polystyrene

As with other plastics, the strength of polystyrene is directly dependent on the density of its molecular structure. High-impact polystyrene has a fairly dense molecular structure and a hard surface and is moderately flexible, fairly strong, and somewhat brittle. It becomes very limp when heated, and it is the primary plastic used in vacuum forming (to be discussed in Chapter 13).

Polystyrene foam, commonly known by the trade name Styrofoam, does not have a dense molecular structure, yet it retains the basic characteristics of all poly-styrenes—a hard surface, moderate flexibility, strength, and brittleness. It is fre-quently used for making decorative trim such as cornices and statuary. Techniques for carving Styrofoam will be discussed in Chapter 13.

Polyvinyl Chloride

Although there are probably more formulations of vinyls than any other family of plastics, arguably the most useful formulations for stage purposes are those members of the polyvinyl chloride group. Characteristically, polyvinyl chlorides (PVCs) are strong, lightweight, and rigid.

PVC pipe has those characteristics. Normally used in lawn sprinkler systems, it can also be used for a variety of decorative scenic purposes. PVC is available in a variety of other forms (sheet, rod, and so forth) that are useful for the the-atre artisan.

PVC pipe, and its other forms, can be formed using heat. Heat forming will be discussed in Chapter 13.

Urethanes

Urethane plastics have a number of uses in technical production. Flexible ure-thane foam is commonly used for cushions and padding in furniture. The rigid foam, which has a tighter cell structure than polystyrene foam, is used as the modeling block in floral displays and has also been used as an insulation mater-ial in building construction. Urethane is also available as a casting resin.

Kits for hand-mixing rigid or flexible foams can be purchased from building-insulation companies and scenic or plastics supply houses. Two types of kits are generally available. The hand-mix, or pour-in-place forms are two-part compounds that are mixed together and poured into molds. Spray-pack foams, such as the Insta-Foam Froth Pak, are also two-part formulations, but they are automatically mixed as they are sprayed. Both molds and casting techniques are discussed in Chapter 13.

Be sure that you don't use any kind of heat—friction-generated heat from saw blades, open flames, or otherwise—when working with urethane foams. Heating the urethane releases a toxic gas. That same gas is emitted during the curing process when using foam-packs or pour-in-place urethane. If at all possible, entirely avoid working with urethane foam. If you must, be sure to adhere to the safety procedures outlined on the MSDS for the specific material with which you are working.

Fasteners

Fasteners in a variety of forms are used in scenic and property construction.

Nails

Nails are the most commonly used mechanical fasteners. They are driven into two or more pieces of wood with a hammer to hold them together. The strength of the fastening depends on the gripping pressure that the wood exerts on the shaft of the nail.

The size of nails is designated by the term *penny,* which is symbolized by the letter *d.* There is a rough equivalency between the length of the shaft, or shank, of a nail and the penny designation: the higher the number, the longer the shaft.

All of the nails, screws, and bolts listed in this section are commonly used in nontheatrical construction and are readily available at lumberyards.

Common Nail   The common nail (Figure 10.33A) has a large head and thick shank. It is used for heavier general construction—platforms, bracing, and the like.

Box Nail   Similar in shape to the common nail, the box nail (Figure 10.33B) has a narrower shaft that reduces the chance of splitting the lumber.

Coated Box Nail   Similar to the box nail but with a slightly narrower shaft, the coated box nail has an adhesive applied to the shaft. The friction generated when the nail is driven activates the adhesive to tightly bond the nail to the wood.

Finish Nail   The finish nail (Figure 10.33C) has a slender shaft and a very narrow, almost nonexistent head. It is designed so that the head can be driven below the surface of the wood and the resultant hole filled with putty or filler. The finish nail is not normally used in general scenic construction but is employed in the building of props or furniture and at any time that it is desirable to hide the nail head.

Wire Nail and Brad   Wire nails and brads (Figure 10.33D) are small (under one inch long) finish or box nails with very slender shafts. They are used in property construction or for attaching delicate decorative moldings or panels to larger scenic elements.

4d
1½"

6d
2"

8d
2½"

(A) Common
nails

10d
3"

16d
3½"

2d
1"

4d
1½"

(B) Box
nails

6d
2"

8d
2½"

2d
1"

4d
1½"

6d
2"

(C) Finish
nails

8d
2½"

10d
3"

½"

¾"

¾"

½"

Wire nails   Brads

(D)

FIGURE 10.33
Standard nails.

Double-Headed Nail Double-headed nails (Figure 10.34A) are also known as scaffolding nails. They are driven into the wood until the lower head is flush with the surface, leaving the upper head exposed so that it can be pulled out easily. As the secondary name implies, these nails are used for scaffolding or any temporary structure that you may want to dismantle quickly.

Screw Nail The screw nail (Figure 10.34B) has a threaded shank that rotates as it is driven into the wood. It has more holding power than a common nail and is used for attaching platform tops and for similar jobs where the greater holding power would be useful.

Clout Nail The specialty nail known as the clout nail (Figure 10.34C), once used in flat construction, is included here primarily as a historical reference as power-driven screws and pneumatic staplers and nailers, which provide equal or greater gripping power with a lot less fuss, muss, and bother, have relegated the clout nail to hardware heaven. Made from soft iron, the wedge-shaped clout nail was about 1¼ inches long and was used to attach cornerblocks and keystones to the framing of a flat. It was driven through the wood onto a steel backing plate, which curled the end of the nail back into the lumber. This process, called clinching, is what gave the nail its strong grip.

Tack Various tacks are used in scenic construction. Carpet tacks (Figure 10.35A) have very wide heads and tapered shafts varying from approximately ⅜ to ¾ inch in length. Carpet, gimp, and thumbtacks (Figure 10.35B) are generally used for attaching fabric to some type of wooden backing—for example, tacking carpeting to the floor, upholstery fabric to furniture frames, and so forth. Decorative tacks have rounded heads and straight shanks, as shown in Figure 10.35C. Although they do hold upholstery fabric to its wooden frame, their primary purpose is simply decoration. They are also very useful to the property master in the decoration, or "glitzing," of various stage props.

Corrugated Fastener Corrugated strips of metal about ⅝ inch tall and 1⅛ inches wide, shown in Figure 10.36, are primarily used to hold lightweight frames together.

Staple Staples are U-shaped fasteners sharpened at both ends. Fence, screen, and poultry staples (Figure 10.37) are driven with a hammer and can be used to attach wire, rope, cording, chicken wire, screening, and similar materials to supporting wooden frameworks.

Spring-powered and electrically powered staple guns use short-legged staples (¼ to ½ inch) to attach fabric to wooden frames. Relatively long-legged staples (¾ to ½ inch), when driven by a pneumatic stapler, are used to fasten various types of wooden structures together.

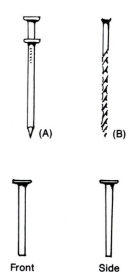

Front　　　Side

Flat side of clout nail
at right angle to wood grain
to prevent splitting

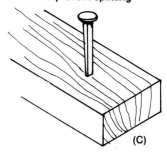

FIGURE 10.34
Specialty nails.
(A) Double-headed nail
(B) Screw nail
(C) Clout nail

FIGURE 10.35
Tacks.
(A) Carpet tacks
(B) Gimp tack (left) and thumbtack (right)
(C) Upholstery tacks

Brass　Patterned　Nickle　Leather

(A)　　　(B)　　　(C)

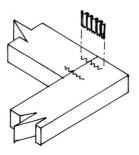

FIGURE 10.36
Corrugated fastener.

Allen wrench: An L-shaped piece of steel rod with a hexagonal cross-sectional shape; used for working with Allen-head screws and bolts.

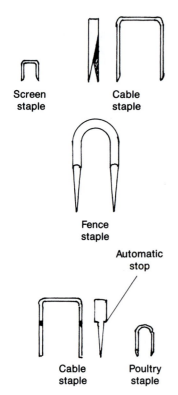

Screen staple

Cable staple

Fence staple

Automatic stop

Cable staple

Poultry staple

FIGURE 10.37
Staples.

Screws

Screws provide a stronger method of joining than nails, because their augerlike thread digs into the material on the sides of the screw hole to mechanically bind them to the material. Various screws are used in scenic construction. The type of screw appropriate for an individual job depends on the type and thickness of the material being worked and the strength needed in the particular joint. Most screws are designed with either a standard or slotted or a Phillips head (Figure 10.38A and B), although some are manufactured for use with an **Allen wrench** (Figure 10.38C) or have a combination slotted hex head or square head (Figure 10.38D and E). Robertson-head screws (Figure 10.38F) are becoming more popular probably because the square, slightly tapered, drive hole seems to hold the screwdriver bit more securely than slotted or Phillips-head screws, particularly important when driving the screws with a powered screwdriver.

Flat-Head Wood Screw   The flat-head wood screw (FHWS), with the possible exception of the drywall screw, is probably the most common type of screw used in the scene shop (Figure 10.39A). It has a flat head that is beveled on the underside to easily dig into the wood. This countersinking action allows the upper face of the head to be flush with the surface of the work. Common uses for the FHWS are attaching hardware (hinges, doorknobs) and joining various wooden elements together. FHWS's range in length from about ½ inch to 3 inches, although the most common sizes used in the shop vary from ¾ to about 1¼ or 1½ inches, with a screw shank diameter of No. 8 or No. 9. (The numerical rating of screw shank sizes is roughly dependent on their diameter: the higher the number, the larger the diameter.)

Round-Head Wood Screw   Identical in most respects with the FHWS, the round-head wood screw (RHWS) has a head with a flat underside and a rounded upper surface (Figure 10.39B). The RHWS is used in those situations in which you do not want to have the top of the screw flush with the surface of the work, such as when you are attaching thin metal or fabric to a wooden frame.

Drywall Screws   Drywall screws are used in general construction to attach gypsum board or drywall to wooden wall and ceiling studs (Figure 10.39C).

The screws are coarse-threaded, Phillips-head, self-starting (which means they don't require a pilot hole) and are designed to be driven with a power screwdriver. Drywall screws have excellent gripping power and can be quickly attached and easily removed. They do, however, have a disconcerting habit of shearing or breaking when being driven into thick or particularly dense wood. The yellow zinc screw has the same shape and characteristics as the dark grey

FIGURE 10.38
Types of screw heads.
(A) Standard or slotted
(B) Phillips
(C) Allen
(D) Slotted h ex
(E) Square
(F) Robertson (square)

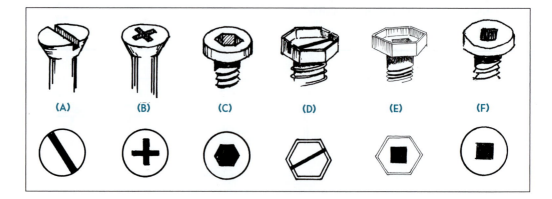

(A)   (B)   (C)   (D)   (E)   (F)

Starter, or Pilot, Holes

Unless you are using a power screwdriver, a screw is much easier to use if you drill a starter, or pilot, hole. Ideally this hole should be the same diameter as the solid shaft of the threaded portion of the screw (not counting the flange of the screw thread).

Specialty drill bits called screw starters, designed for use with electric

drills, can drill starter and countersink holes in the same action. They are available for most common sizes of screws.

The starter hole for a bolt should be the same diameter as the full diameter of the bolt (including the screw flange).

drywall screw, but the brass-colored metal seems to be stronger than the regular drywall screw.

When paired with the latest generation of power screwdrivers that utilize replaceable/rechargeable battery technology, drywall screws are the fastener of choice for many types of wooden scenic construction. One note of caution: The points of drywall screws are extremely sharp. Use caution when picking them up.

Sheet-Metal Screw   As the name implies, sheet-metal screws are used for joining sheets of metal. They are commonly available with either a pan head (Figure 10.39D) or a hex head (Figure 10.39E). Most jobs using sheet-metal screws in the scenic or property shop require shank lengths between ¼ and ¾ inch.

When pieces are to be joined with the use of a hand-driven screw, the metal must be predrilled with a hole slightly narrower than the width of the screw shank. If a power screwdriver is used, it is not necessary to predrill the work.

Lag Screw   Lag screws, also called lag bolts, are very large wood screws with hexagonal or square heads (Figure 10.39F). They are used where the lack of access to both sides of the work prevents the use of bolts, such as when attaching something to a wall or the floor. Shaft diameters generally range from ¼ to ⅝ inch with shaft lengths commonly varying from 1 to 6 inches. A washer should be used under the head of the lag screw to increase the bearing area and prevent the head from biting into the surface of the work.

TEK Screws   In scenic construction TEK, or self-tapping, case-hardened, screws primarily are used to attach plywood coverings to metal frames. Figure 10.39G

FIGURE 10.39

Screws.
(A) Flat-head wood screw
(B) Round-head wood screw
(C) Drywall screw
(D) Pan-head sheet-metal screw
(E) Hex-head sheet-metal screw
(F) Lag screws
(G) TEK screw

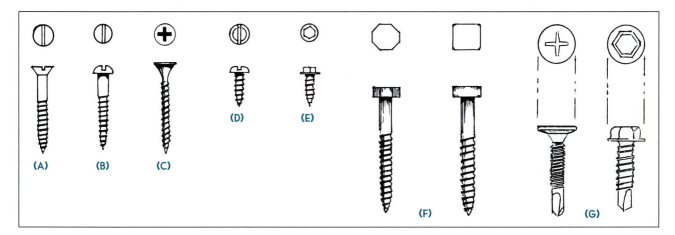

(A)   (B)   (C)   (D)   (E)   (F)   (G)

illustrates two of the more common configurations—a pan, or flat, head and a hex head. A round head is also available. The pan or flat head is more commonly used in scenic construction because the top of the head can be driven **flush** with the face of the covering material. The tip of the screw is hardened and sharpened so, when used with a power screwdriver, it drills a hole and screws itself into the work in the same operation.

flush: Smooth, level, even.

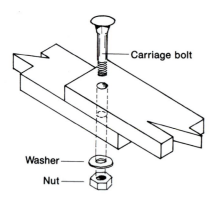

FIGURE 10.40
Bolts are the strongest form of mechanical fastener.

Bolts

Bolts are used when you want the strongest type of mechanical fastening. In using a bolt, a hole is drilled in both members of the work, the appropriate type and size of bolt is inserted into the hole, a washer is slipped onto the bolt shaft, and a nut is threaded onto the bolt shaft and tightened (Figure 10.40).

Carriage Bolt   The upper face of a carriage-bolt head has a rounded surface, and the underside has a slightly tapered square collar a little wider than the diameter of the bolt shaft, as shown in Figure 10.41A. The carriage bolt is used to join either wood to wood or wood to metal. After the bolt has been inserted into the hole, the head is struck with a hammer to make the square collar seat, or bite into, the surface of the wood to prevent it from turning. This type of bolt is commonly used to fasten legs to platform frames and in similar types of work. Carriage bolts range in diameter from ¼ to ¾ inch and in length from 1 to 24 inches.

Machine Bolt   Machine bolts are designed to join metal to metal, although they can be used to join wood to wood if a washer is used under the head of the bolt as well as under the nut. Machine bolts are manufactured with both square and hexagonal heads (Figure 10.41B). The bolt shaft diameters range from ¼ to 1 inch and the lengths from 1 to 6 inches.

Stove Bolt   Stove bolts (Figure 10.41C) are smaller than carriage or machine bolts and have threads on the entire length of the shaft. They have head shapes identical to flat- and round-head wood screws to serve similar purposes. Sizes appropriate for general scenic purposes range from diameters of ⅛ to 5/16 inch, with shaft lengths ranging between 1 and 6 inches. Much smaller stove bolts (shaft diameters less than ⅛ inch and lengths under 1 inch) are available from hobby or electronic stores.

Stove bolts are generally used for attaching stage hardware, hinges, and similar items in situations that might require the extra fastening strength available with the use of bolts instead of screws.

Washers

Washers are flat steel disks with a center hole cut for the bolt shaft. When placed between either the nut or the head of the bolt and the material being joined, a

FIGURE 10.41
Bolts.
(A) Carriage bolt
(B) Machine bolts
(C) Stove bolts

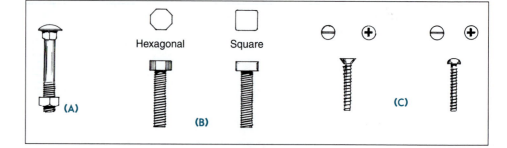

washer (Figure 10.42A) increases the bearing surface of the nut or bolt head and prevents the head from cutting into the surface of the work. Lock washers (Figure 10.42B) are made from spring steel and are cut and slightly spread apart to form a compression tension when the nut is tightened. The purpose of the lock washer is to hold the nut in place after it has been tightened.

Torque washers (Figure 10.42C) are designed to prevent carriage bolts from twisting once they have been seated. The torque washer is slipped onto the shaft of the carriage bolt before it is inserted into the predrilled bolt hole. The square collar on the underside of the bolt head fits into the square hole on the face of the torque washer. When the bolt is seated, the four prongs bite into the surface of the wood. By firmly seating the head of the carriage bolt in the wood, the torque washer allows more torque, or pressure, to be applied when tightening the nut.

Nuts

Nuts are applied to the threaded ends of bolts to close and tighten this type of fastener. Nuts designed to be tightened with wrenches are generally either square (Figure 10.43A) or hexagonally shaped (Figure 10.43B). The wing nut (Figure 10.43C) is designed to be tightened with your fingers. Nuts are available in sizes and metallic compositions identical to the shaft diameters and composition or coating of their corresponding bolts.

The T-nut (Figure 10.43D) is a slightly different kettle of fish. It is basically an internally threaded tube surrounded by a pronged washer. A hole, the same diameter as the tube portion of the T-nut, is drilled into the wood in the proper location. The T-nut is then driven into the hole. Similarly to the torque washer, the prongs prevent the T-nut from turning when the bolt is tightened.

The thread insert (Figure 10.43E) is similar in function to the T-nut, but rather than being held in place with prongs the outside of the tube is threaded. Basically, it is a tube that is threaded on both the inside and outside. It can be used in wood, plastic, or metal. The top of the insert is slotted so it can be twisted into the supporting wood, plastic, or metal with a screwdriver.

 ## Glues and Adhesives

Myriad glues and adhesives are manufactured today, and many of them have applications in theatrical work, particularly in the area of property construction. Although the following list is certainly far from exhaustive, it does introduce you to the glues and adhesives commonly used in scenic and property construction.

There are general guidelines for using all glues and adhesives. Be sure that the faces being glued are clean, dry, and free from oil and dust. Most glues, except contact cement, require some type of clamping. The amount of pressure and the time that it must be maintained depend on heat and humidity as well as the type of glue being used. The working characteristics of each glue and adhesive are discussed in the following sections.

Glues

Glue is made of, or primarily derived from, natural substances.

Animal Glue Animal glue is just what the name implies. A by-product of the meat-packing industry, it is purchased in a dry form (granular or flaked) and must be prepared in the theatre shop before it can be used. The dry glue is poured into an electric glue pot or double boiler, covered with water, and soaked (no heat

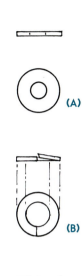

FIGURE 10.42
Washers.
(A) Washer
(B) Lock washer
(C) Torque washer

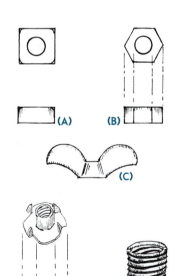

FIGURE 10.43
Nuts.
(A) Square nut
(B) Hex nut
(C) Wing nut
(D) T-nut
(E) Thread insert

added) until it becomes a gelatinous mass (about 6 to 10 hours). It is then heated until it reaches the consistency of syrup, at which time it is ready for use. It is one of the prime ingredients of scenic glue, which is one of the formulas used to glue muslin or canvas to flats and other scenic elements. It is also used as a binder in the mixing of scene paint. These formulas are discussed in the section of Chapter 11, "Scenic Production Techniques," on covering flats.

Animal glue can be used to join most natural substances—wood, paper, cloth. When dry it has a glossy, smooth surface that is stiff and brittle. It is not effective for any project that requires a flexible joint. It can be purchased from scenic paint and supply houses as well as some paint and hardware stores. Animal glue sets when it cools. If it is diluted with water, the drying time varies between one and four hours depending on the heat and humidity. Animal glue used to be used extensively in furniture construction as well as scene painting. In furniture and general construction, animal glue has been replaced by synthetics such as white and carpenter's glue. In scene painting, where it functioned as the binder for dry pigments, it has largely been replaced by clear acrylic/vinyl binders. Its passing should be noted with awe if for no other reason than its use in scene painting can be traced back to the 1500s and possibly earlier.

Flexible Glue   Flexible glue is animal glue with glycerine added. It must be prepared in the same manner as animal glue and can be used for projects requiring flexibility. It is available from scenic supply and paint houses. The drying characteristics of flexible glue are the same as those of animal glue.

Wheat Paste   Wheat paste is made from a mixture of unrefined wheat flour and water. Although it looks like flour, wheat paste shouldn't be used for cooking, because it is usually laced with rat poison to prevent it from being eaten when it is in storage. It is used for hanging wallpaper, as the glue in papier-mâché, and as one of the ingredients in the glue used for attaching **dutchmen** to wall units. After wheat paste has dried, it is reasonably flexible and has a dull, or matte, surface finish. It can be purchased at paint and wallpaper stores, hardware stores, and lumberyards.

Adhesives

Adhesives perform the same functions as glues but are primarily composed of synthetic materials. They have a distinct advantage over natural glues in that they will not spoil, rot, or turn sour, and they generally come in ready-to-use formulations.

Drying and curing times for adhesives vary considerably depending on type and manufacturer. Read the label of the specific product to determine its particular characteristics.

White Glue   White glue (widely known by the trade name of Elmer's Glue-All) is a synthetic glue that is used extensively in scenic construction. It is reasonably fast drying, is slightly flexible, and adheres to wood, paper, cloth, Styrofoam, and some other plastics as well. When dry, it leaves a slightly glossy surface. It can be purchased from almost any lumber, paint, or hardware store. White glue dries in about 1 or 2 hours depending on heat, humidity, and air circulation around the glue joint, but for the joint to develop strength, the glue must be allowed to cure for about 24 hours.

Carpenter's Glue   Carpenter's glue is another readily available synthetic glue extensively used in woodworking. Similar in many respects to white glue, car-

dutchman: A 5- to 6-inch-wide strip of cloth of the same material as the flat covering; applied over joints between flats to give the appearance of a smooth, unbroken wall unit.

penter's glue is yellow when liquid but dries almost clear. It is stronger and generally dries more quickly than white glue.

Latex Cement   A milky-white, flexible cement commercially used in laying carpet, latex cement can be used whenever a very flexible glue joint is required. It adheres to cloth, paper, wood, and many other materials and can be purchased from many carpet shops, some furniture stores, and scenic supply houses.

Contact Cement   Contact cement is an adhesive for bonding nonporous surfaces together. As the name implies, the surfaces being joined are bonded as soon as they come in contact with each other. Each surface to be joined is spread with a light coating of the contact cement and allowed to dry for a few minutes; then the pieces are brought together and are immediately bonded. There are two basic types of contact cement: One has a highly volatile, extremely flammable base, and the other has a water-soluble latex base. The volatile-base contact cement dissolves most foamed products, such as Styrofoam. Additionally, while the adhesion of the volatile-base cement appears to be slightly better, in the interest of safety it is recommended that the latex-base contact cement be used whenever possible.

Polyvinyl Glue   A white liquid adhesive that resembles white glue in appearance, polyvinyl glue is a synthetic with excellent adhesion to porous surfaces and good flexibility. It can be used for a number of jobs, ranging from furniture repair and construction to use as the binder for scene paint.

Cyanoacrylate Cement   Cyanoacrylate cements are very powerful adhesives that will bond almost any porous or nonporous surface to almost anything else. Therein lie their strengths and dangers. Sold under trade names such as Super Glue, Krazy Glue, and so on, these powerful adhesives are too expensive for use in general scenic construction but are excellent for use in property construction. Like contact cement, cyanoacrylate cements bond very rapidly. However, they also bond skin to skin or skin to anything else just as rapidly. When using cyanoacrylate cements, be sure to follow the instructions very carefully.

Epoxy Resin Adhesive   Two-part epoxy resin adhesive is available in a number of formulations that enable the user to do gluing, filling, and painting. The bond created by an epoxy adhesive is extremely strong and waterproof. It is used in the shop in situations where its strength can be an advantage, such as furniture construction and property work.

Almost all of the adhesives discussed in this section can be purchased at any well-stocked hardware store. If you are involved in scenic construction, particularly property construction, it would be to your advantage to spend some time wandering around a hardware store familiarizing yourself with the vast range of adhesives.

Hardware

A great deal of hardware is used in the construction of stage scenery. Most of this hardware is also used in building construction and can be purchased at a lumberyard or hardware store. The specialized hardware designed for specific stage applications is usually not available locally and must be purchased from a scenic supply house.

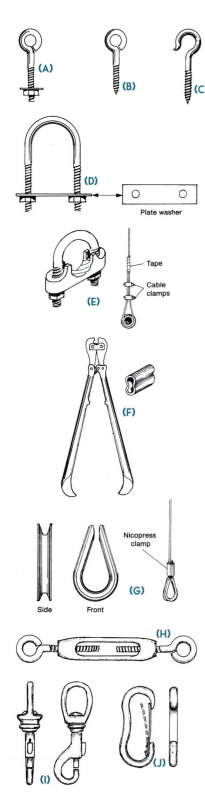

FIGURE 10.44

Common construction hardware.
(A) Eye bolt   (G) Cable thimble
(B) Screw eye   (H) Turnbuckle
(C) Screw hook   (I) Swivel snap
(D) U bolt   (J) Spring snap
(E) Cable clamp
(F) Nicopress and sleeve

Construction Hardware

Eye Bolt   Eye bolts (Figure 10.44A) can be used for almost any situation that requires attaching lines or ropes to an object, such as the pull rope for a stage wagon or a guide for the piano wire or cable on a piece of flying scenery. The diameter of the steel rod used to manufacture the eye bolt varies from approximately $\frac{1}{8}$ to $\frac{3}{8}$ inch. The shaft length varies from about 1 to 6 inches.

Screw Eye   Screw eyes (Figure 10.44B) are similar to eye bolts but are used when the additional strength of the bolt fastener isn't necessary or when the back of the surface to which the screw eye is being attached cannot be reached. Screw eyes are available in a wide range of sizes: Shaft diameters vary from about $\frac{1}{16}$ to $\frac{3}{8}$ inch and lengths from $\frac{1}{2}$ inch to 4 inches.

Screw Hook   Screw hooks (Figure 10.44C) are similar to screw eyes but have a hook instead of an eye so that items hung from the hook can be removed quickly. Size variations are similar to those of screw eyes.

U Bolt   U bolts (Figure 10.44D) are made from metal rod that has been bent in a U shape and threaded on both ends. They are typically used to secure or fasten pipe, tube, or rod to a flat surface.

Cable Clamp   Another type of U bolt, the cable clamp (Figure 10.44E), also known as a cable clip, has a grooved metal clamp that fits over the bolt shafts. The size of the grooves corresponds to the diameter of the wire rope or cable that is used to hang scenery and battens. For safety reasons, cable clamps should always be used in pairs. When attaching wire rope clips always place the saddle—as opposed to the U-bolt portion of the clip—on the live, or free, end of the cable. Doing this will ensure that the saddle bites into the free end of the cable, which makes for a safer and more secure attachment.

Nicopress Tool   Another cable fastener, the Nicopress tool (Figure 10.44F), provides a permanent, nonremovable friction clamp for wire rope or cable. Nicopress sleeves, which are thin, soft metal tubes approximately $\frac{1}{2}$ to $\frac{3}{4}$ inch long, are designed for specific diameters of cable and must be crimped or tightened with a Nicopress tool. Like the sleeves, the Nicopress tools are designed to work with only one diameter of cable. Each Nicopress tool is packaged with a gauge—generically referred to as a "go/no go" tool—that is used to check sleeve compression. When making any Nicopress connection be sure to use these gauges to determine whether the sleeve has been adequately and safely attached to the cable.

Thimble   The thimble (Figure 10.44G) is a narrow, grooved, teardrop-shaped piece of sheet metal used to protect wire rope or cable from sharp bends or kinks when the cable is attached to a ring or similar device.

Turnbuckle   A turnbuckle (Figure 10.44H) has a long, oval body with a threaded eye bolt protruding from either end. When attached as a link in a cable, it can be used to lengthen or shorten that line system. This property makes it an excellent device to place between a flying line and a flown piece of scenery to adjust the trim of the flown unit. When using these in a flying system, be sure to securely twist 12-gauge wire around the threaded ends of both eye bolts so they cannot become uncoupled from the turnbuckle body.

Snaps   There are various types of snaps—some with swivel bases (Figure 10.44I); some designed for use with rope; and others intended for use with cable, chain, and curtains (Figure 10.44J). But they all have the same purpose—they provide a quick means of attaching a line to its associated load.

Hinges A hinge is composed of two joined metal plates that swing around a pivot point. A number of types of hinges have applications in scenic construction.

Strap Hinge Strap hinges (Figure 10.45A) are composed of two tapering leaves that are joined by either a loose or a fixed pin. Strap hinge **leaves** vary in length from 2½ to 8 inches. Each leaf is drilled and countersunk to accept flat-head wood screws or stove bolts. They are commonly used to hinge stage doors by bending one leaf, attaching it to the depth piece of the casing, and attaching the straight leaf to the back of the door.

Butt Hinge Butt hinges (Figure 10.45B) are available in a wide variety of sizes and finishes, but they are all used for the same general purpose—hanging doors. They are composed of rectangular leaves joined by either a fixed or a loose pin. The holes are countersunk to accept flat-head wood screws or stove bolts.

T-Strap Hinge A combination of one leaf from a strap hinge and an elongated leaf from a butt hinge, the T-strap hinge (Figure 10.45C) is used for hanging doors, gates, and box lids.

Loose-Pin Back-Flap Hinge Loose-pin back-flap hinges (Figure 10.45D) have square leaves in sizes ranging from approximately 1¼ to 2½ inches in width. The 1½- and 2-inch sizes are the most commonly used in scenic construction. These hinges can be used as "regular" hinges, but in scenic construction they are primarily used for joining scenery. The individual hinge leaves are attached to the separate pieces of scenery, and the pin is inserted to hold the unit together. The pin can be removed whenever it is necessary to break the unit into its component elements for shifting or storage.

Tight-Pin Back-Flap Hinge The tight-pin back-flap hinge (Figure 10.45E) is primarily used for the same purposes as its loose-pin companion whenever a permanent joining is desired. It is frequently used when two or more flats are joined to form an unbroken expanse of wall. Details of this type of wall construction are covered in Chapter 11, "Scenic Production Techniques."

Piano Hinge The piano hinge is a narrow-leaved, very long, tight-pin hinge made of thinner metal than the other hinges described in this section. It gets its name from its original use—attaching piano lids. If only three or four "regular" hinges were used to attach the lid, its weight would quickly tear the screws out of the wood. Enter the piano hinge; the screw holes are typically spaced an inch or less apart for the entire length of the hinge. These numerous attachment points allow the leaves to be quite narrow—typically less than an inch. Piano hinges are generally 6 feet long but can easily be cut to fit the needed length.

Stage Hardware

Lashing Hardware Lashing, the technique of joining flats together by a process that is closely akin to lacing your shoes, requires some very specific stage hardware. Lashing is done with a lash line, which is a piece of ¼-inch cotton clothesline approximately 18 inches longer than the height of the flats being lashed together. The location of lashing hardware is illustrated in Figure 10.46. For safety purposes, all lashing hardware should be attached to the flats with 1-inch (No. 8 or 9) flat-head wood screws or stove bolts.

Lash-Line Eye The lash-line eye (Figure 10.47A) is used to attach the lash line to the flat. It is placed on the inside edge of the **stile** just beneath the cornerblock.

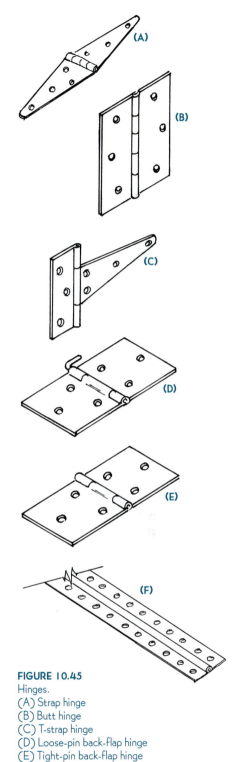

FIGURE 10.45
Hinges.
(A) Strap hinge
(B) Butt hinge
(C) T-strap hinge
(D) Loose-pin back-flap hinge
(E) Tight-pin back-flap hinge
(F) Piano hinge

leaf: The movable flap of a hinge.

stile: A vertical side member of a flat.

FIGURE 10.46
Locations for lashing hardware.

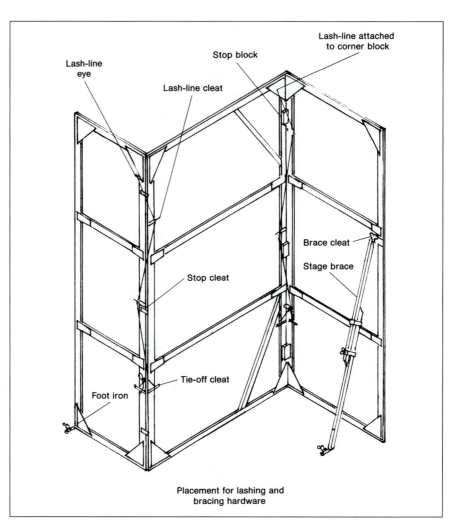

Placement for lashing and
bracing hardware

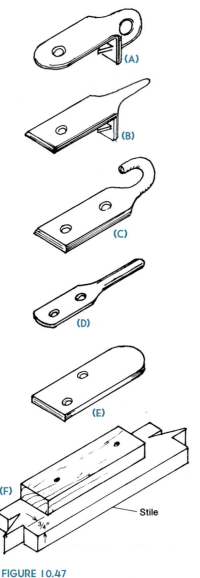

FIGURE 10.47
Lashing hardware.
(A) Lash-line eye
(B) Lash-line cleat
(C) Lash-line hook
(D) Tie-off cleat
(E) Stop cleat
(F) Stop block

Lash-Line Cleat The lash-line cleat (Figure 10.47B) is attached to the flat so that its pointed end projects over the inside edge of the stile. The lash-line cleat is used to hold the rope in place so that the flats can be lashed together.

Lash-Line Hook The lash-line hook (Figure 10.47C) serves the same purpose as the cleat. However, it is used when the construction of the flat prevents the use of a cleat, as when the stile is extra wide or is next to an opening in the flat (window, doorway) or some type of projection. It can also be used in place of a tie-off cleat.

Tie-Off Cleat Tie-off cleats (Figure 10.47D) are used in pairs approximately 30 inches above the stage level to tie off the line after the flats have been lashed together. Regular cleats or hooks can also be used for this purpose.

Stop Cleat Stop cleats (Figure 10.47E) are attached to the back of the flats with their ends projecting ¾ inch past the outside edge of the stiles to prevent the flats from slipping past each other when they are being lashed together in an outside corner configuration.

Stop Block Although it is not an actual piece of lashing hardware, a stop block (Figure 10.47F) is a small piece of scrap wood that is attached to the stile of a flat to prevent flats from slipping past each other when they are being lashed together in an inside corner configuration.

Flying Hardware Several pieces of stage hardware aid in flying scenery and stabilizing flown scenery. For reasons of safety, all flying hardware should be attached with bolts. One bolt and screws can be used if the piece is quite light. Never suspend or fly anything using only screws. Always use at least one bolt. Remember: the safest way to attach flying hardware is with bolts.

Hanger Iron The hanger iron (Figure 10.48A) is a metal strap with a D ring at the top. It is attached to the stile at the top of the flat in a position that keeps the D ring hidden behind the top of the flat. The hanger iron, also called a top hanger iron, is used in conjunction with a bottom hanger iron for flying heavy scenery, but it can be used by itself for flying lightweight pieces.

Bottom Hanger Iron The bottom hanger iron (Figure 10.48B) is a metal strap with a hooked foot at the bottom and a D ring at the top. The bottom hanger iron, also called the hook hanger iron, is attached so the bottom of the flat rests on the hooked foot. The flying line is attached to the D ring so that the flat will, in effect, be picked up from the bottom or lifted under compression.

When rigging a heavy or tall flat for flying, use the bottom hanger iron in conjunction with a hanger iron. The hanger iron is attached to the top of the flat in a line directly above the bottom hanger iron. The flying line is fed through the D ring of the hanger iron and attached to the D ring of the bottom hanger iron. If the flat is very small, a screw eye can be substituted for the top hanger iron.

Ceiling Plate The ceiling plate (Figure 10.48C) is bolted to primary structural members of the ceiling to provide a means of attaching the flying lines to the ceiling.

D Ring and Plate The D ring and plate (Figure 10.48D) is another piece of hanging hardware. It is normally used on vertical pieces that are to be flown such as flats.

Bracing Hardware Most flats need some type of external support to be able to stand up. If the flats don't need support to stand, they will probably need some type of bracing to prevent them from wiggling. The normal positions for placing these pieces of hardware are shown in Figure 10.46.

Stage Brace The stage brace is the mainstay of scenic bracing. It is an adjustable wooden (Figure 10.49A) or aluminum (Figure 10.49B) pole that can be quickly attached to a brace cleat on the back of a flat. The other end of the stage brace is secured to the stage floor by one of the several methods to be described.

Brace Cleat Attached to the stile of a flat with the end projecting past the inside edge of the stile, a brace cleat (Figure 10.49C) provides a point of attachment between the scenery and the stage brace.

Rigid Foot Iron The rigid foot iron (Figure 10.49D) is an L-shaped piece of metal. The long leg is attached to the bottom of the scenery with screws or bolts. The horizontal foot sticks out and is secured to the stage floor with a stage screw inserted through the ring at the end of the foot.

Hinged Foot Iron The hinged foot iron is similar to the rigid foot iron. Its horizontal foot (Figure 10.49E) is hinged to fold out of the way when the scenic unit is being shifted or flown.

Stage Screw The stage screw is a large, coarse-threaded, hand-driven screw used to anchor a foot iron or the foot of a stage brace to the wooden stage floor. Although stage screws (Figure 10.49F) provide an effective means of anchoring stage braces, they leave ragged holes and splinters wherever they are used.

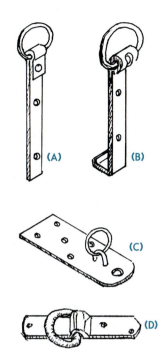

FIGURE 10.48
Flying hardware.
(A) Hanger iron
(B) Bottom hanger iron
(C) Ceiling plate
(D) D ring and plate

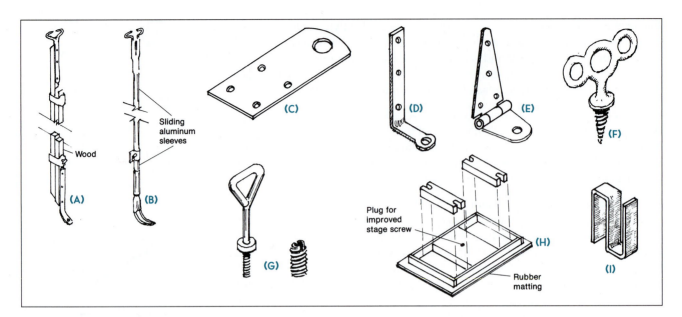

FIGURE 10.49
Bracing hardware.
(A) Extension stage brace
(B) Lightweight stage brace
(C) Brace cleat
(D) Rigid foot iron
(E) Hinged foot iron
(F) Stage screw
(G) Improved stage screw
(H) Floor plate
(I) S hook

Improved Stage Screw   The improved stage screw (Figure 10.49G) doesn't tear up the stage floor nearly so much as its unrefined cousin does. A steel plug, threaded on the outside and inside, is inserted into an appropriately sized hole that has been drilled into the stage floor. The improved stage screw screws into the plug. When the production is over, the plug can be removed from the floor, and the hole patched by gluing a small piece of hardwood **dowel** into the hole.

Floor Plate   It is rather difficult to use either a stage screw or an improved stage screw if your stage floor is concrete or if the building owner or administrator has said, "Thou shalt not put any holes in the stage floor." Fortunately, all is not lost, because a floor plate (Figure 10.49H) can come to the rescue.

The lower end of the stage brace is secured to the floor plate, which is a block of wood with a nonskid material (foam, rubber) attached to the bottom. Sandbags or counterweights are piled on the plate to anchor it to the floor.

S Hook   Also known as a latch keeper, the S hook (Figure 10.49I) is used to hold stiffening battens on the back of wall units that are made up of two or more flats. Normally used on flats that must have the stiffening battens removed for shifting, S hooks can be purchased or made in the shop from ⅛- or ³⁄₃₂-by-1-inch mild-steel strap.

Miscellaneous Hardware   There are several additional pieces of stage hardware that cannot be neatly categorized because their use is not necessarily limited to a single purpose.

Corner Plate   The corner plate (Figure 10.50A) is an L-shaped piece of ¹⁄₁₆-inch galvanized steel, available in a variety of sizes. Each leg is predrilled, or tapped, for use with No. 8 or No. 9 flat-head wood screws. Corner plates are used to reinforce the corners of doors, windows, door or window casings, and picture frames and in similar applications.

Tee Plate   Made of the same galvanized steel as the corner plate, the tee plate (Figure 10.50B) can be used as a substitute for keystones or in similar applications.

Picture Hook and Eye   Picture hooks and eyes (Figure 10.50C) are shop-made pieces (³⁄₃₂-by-¾-inch or 1-inch mild-steel strap) that facilitate the rapid hanging

dowel: A short cylinder of hardwood (usually birch).

and removal of decorative draperies on a set. They are used in sets of two or more. The sockets are attached to the face of the flat with screws or bolts, and the hooks are similarly attached to the drapery rod.

Casket Lock   The casket lock (Figure 10.50D) is a heavy-duty hidden lock that is used to hold platforms together or in similar applications. Its use as a platform lock is detailed in Chapter 11, "Scenic Production Techniques."

Casters   Casters come in a bewildering array of sizes, styles, and load ratings. To be useful for stage purposes, casters should meet a few specific requirements. They should have hard rubber tires, should have a load rating of at least 300 pounds, and should be sturdily constructed. Although stage casters can be purchased from theatrical-equipment supply houses, it is sometimes advantageous to buy your casters at a local building-equipment supply firm.

Swivel casters (Figure 10.51A) are mounted on a bearing plate that allows the wheel to pivot around a vertical axis. To turn easily under a load, the pivot should be supported by ball bearings. For use with stage wagons, the overall height of the caster should be 4 to 5 inches. The tires on a swivel caster should be made of rubber to reduce the rumble that inevitably accompanies the movement of a stage platform. The wheel of the caster should be metal, and it should have some type of bearing (ball, tube) to decrease the friction between the axle and the wheel. The axle should be removable so that a metal strap can be attached to the axle and the platform to lock the swivel caster in a stationary position. Some swivel casters are equipped with built-in pins that can be used to hold the caster stationary.

Rigid casters (Figure 10.51B) are permanently locked in position so that they cannot pivot. The specifications for the swivel caster regarding the structure of the tire, wheel, axle, height, and load rating are applicable to the stationary caster.

Furniture casters do not have the same rigorous specifications as stage casters. They should be sturdily constructed, but because they are often seen by the audience, they need to look as if they belong to the period being depicted in the production. Furniture casters can be purchased at furniture and hardware stores.

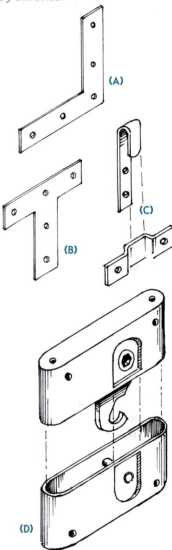

FIGURE 10.50
Miscellaneous stage hardware.
(A) Corner plate
(B) Tee plate
(C) Picture hook and eye
(D) Casket lock

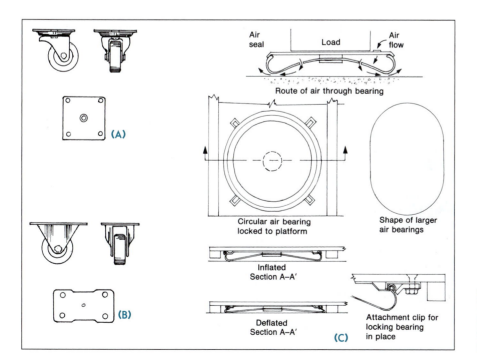

FIGURE 10.51
Types of casters.
(A) Swivel caster
(B) Rigid caster
(C) Air caster

A revolutionary type of compressed-air lifter literally floats heavy objects on a thin cushion of air. The *air caster* or *air bearing* (Figure 10.51C) is an inflatable saucer-shaped disk of rubberized fabric. The air caster works as follows: Compressed air inflates the doughnut-shaped bearing to raise the load; the compressed air continues to flow, creating an air cushion under the bearing. Three or four air casters are needed to raise an object. Although they are available in a variety of diameters ranging from 1 to 4 feet, the 1-foot size, which is load rated at approximately 2,000 pounds, is adequate for almost any theatrical use. Air casters don't work well if the stage floor isn't perfectly smooth. Another drawback to the air caster is the noise of the compressor needed to supply the low-compression, high-volume air. The noise problem can be solved, however, if the compressor (a shop vacuum cleaner works well) is located in an adjacent space (not on stage) and air hoses are run to the casters.

Rope, Cable, and Wire

Several types of ropes are used for a variety of purposes in the theatre.

Synthetic Rope

It used to be that manila rope was the primary type of rope used for raising and suspending loads (scenery, equipment) in the theatre. That is no longer the case. Synthetic ropes such as Multiline II and Stage-Set X, offered by the stage rigging company J. R. Clancy, have replaced manila. The Multiline II handles like manila but weighs less, is stronger, and has better durability. Unlike manila it does not change length with temperature/humidity variations. Because of their superior characteristics synthetic ropes of this type have replaced manila as the operating line in counterweight systems.

It is a common characteristic of most natural-fiber ropes that, when stretched out, they have a tendency to twist. This is because of the way that they are made. Stage-Set X however, has a nonrotating construction. It has a parallel core of polyester fiber that is wrapped in polyester tape and covered by a soft, braided polyester jacket.

Synthetic ropes are available in a variety of compositions and diameters. They have generally replaced all natural-fiber ropes in general theatrical use.

Rope

Regardless of the type of rope being used, there are several general safety rules. Any rope that is suspending a load over the stage should have a breaking strength at least ten times the weight of the load that it is required to bear. Any rope should be carefully inspected before use — at least annually and more frequently if the rope is part of a permanent system (counterweight, rope set and the like) or is in constant use — for signs of abrasion, cuts, gouges, seriously worn or broken fibers, discoloration, kinks, or twists. If any of these conditions is evident, the rope should be replaced. Any rope used as the operating line for a counterweight system should be replaced at least every three years, even if it appears to be in good condition. The strain that has been placed on the rope during those years will have broken down the fibers enough to significantly decrease its effective working strength.

Monofilament Line

Commonly sold in sporting goods stores as fishing line, monofilament line is basically a single-strand plastic string. It is transparent, comes in a variety of breaking strengths ranging from 2 to over 100 pounds, and is used whenever an "invisible" or "trick" line is needed.

Aircraft Cable

Aircraft cable is frequently used in the theatre, because it is very flexible and very strong. One-eighth-inch aircraft cable is often used for flying heavy stage scenery because its breaking strength is approximately one ton.

Wire

Wire is used for a variety of purposes in both scenic and property construction.

Stovepipe Wire Soft-iron stovepipe wire is approximately $\frac{1}{16}$ of an inch in diameter and is generally colored black. It is quite flexible but has very little tensile strength. It is normally used for tying or wiring things together. It shouldn't be used for flying scenery, because it isn't strong enough to support a load. Stovepipe wire of slightly greater diameter is known as baling wire. Soft-iron, or stovepipe, wire is also manufactured with a galvanized finish to prevent rust.

Piano Wire Piano wire is made from spring steel and is frequently used to fly scenery because of its remarkable tensile strength in comparison with its diameter. Care should be taken to avoid making sharp bends in piano wire, because kinking greatly reduces its strength.

Block and Tackle

The term *block and tackle* refers generically to arrangements of pulleys and ropes that provide a mechanical advantage. A pulley has one specific job: It changes the direction of travel of the rope passing through it. An ideal pulley accomplishes this task with no friction and little noise. Unfortunately, this ideal pulley doesn't exist. All pulleys create friction and make noise. But, as in all things, some pulleys are better than others. The small galvanized pulleys found in a hardware store can be used for lightweight applications such as the curtain pull for some decorative set drapes, but they are rather noisy. A better solution can be found in the marine-hardware section of a boat supply shop. These stores usually stock high-quality pulleys that are very quiet and have relatively little friction loss.

For heavy-duty use, the best pulleys are available from scenic supply houses or, sometimes, from well-stocked hardware stores. These pulleys have wooden bodies, have well-matched sheaves (wheels) and axles, and are fairly quiet in operation. Three common tackle rigs are illustrated and explained in Chapter 4.

Safety Equipment

There is a variety of protective equipment for working in the shop. The specific device depends on the materials with which you are working.

dust mask: A device covering the nose and mouth that filters particulate matter from the air.

respirator: A mask covering the nose and mouth that filters out gases as well as particulate matter.

Clear-lensed goggles, safety glasses, and face shields will protect your eyes from flying wood and metal chips as well as from chemical splashes. Specially tinted eye shields such as welding goggles or (preferably) welding masks need to be worn when welding.

A **dust mask** should be worn when working with any material that produces dust. A **respirator,** equipped with an appropriate type of filter, should be worn any time that you are working with materials which produce fumes or vapors.

Proper hand protection is necessary to prevent possible injury: chemically resistant rubberized gloves for working with chemicals; heavy leather gloves for welding; heat-resistant gloves (not asbestos) for handling heated objects; and regular light leather or cotton work gloves for handling manila rope such as that found on the operating lines of the counterweight system.

When working with noise-producing objects, wear hearing protectors such as noise-abatement earmuffs or earplugs. When working with heavy objects such as metal pipe, tubing, or sheet or when moving or building large stage platforms, you should wear steel-toed shoes or steel shoe caps. When there is any danger of something being dropped from above the stage floor, all personnel should wear protective headgear, such as a plastic helmet that meets or exceeds the minimum federal standards.

There are a variety of other safety-related issues that need to be addressed in the shop. Most of the following have specific OSHA guidelines that dictate minimum levels of acceptability. Check with appropriate school or city/county authorities to determine if your shop is in compliance. The air in the shop should be run through some type of recirculating filtering system to meet OSHA guidelines for clean air. As mentioned earlier, every power tool that generates wood dust or chips should have some type of collection system, either a vacuum draw or collector bag. There should be an OSHA-approved eye wash station in the shop area. Fire extinguishers should be placed in strategic locations around both the shop and stage. Make sure that they are *always* accessible and fully charged. First-aid kits should be clearly visible in the shop and stage areas. Their contents should be kept up-to-date and fully stocked. Do not place or lean anything in front of, or on, either fire extinguishers or first-aid kits.

Use common sense in the shop. It is filled with equipment and materials that can injure or kill. But if you are careful and abide by commonsense safety practices and OSHA-prescribed safety regulations, it can be a safe and enjoyable work environment.

This chapter has outlined the tools and materials used in the construction of scenery and properties. Chapter 11, "Scenic Production Techniques," will discuss basic techniques of scenic construction, and Chapter 13, "Stage Properties," will take up some of the more specialized techniques and materials—foams, thermoplastics, and fiberglass—used to make stage properties.

Chapter 11

Scenic Production Techniques

Playwrights have set their plays in almost every imaginable environment. Thousands of plays have been set in ordinary rooms in homes or buildings, and thousands more have been set in representational settings like caves, mountaintops, river beds, lakesides, wheat fields, war zones, and even the gondolas of hot air balloons. Nonrepresentational scenery can be, and frequently is, beautifully imaginative, evocative, and representative of the emotional content of the play. Whether wheat field or moonscape, representational or nonrepresentational, the setting must work as conceived by the scenic designer and director—and it's the technical director's job to see that it does.

Technical production refers to the broad field concerned with the processes and techniques used in taking the design from conception to reality. Specifically, the field encompasses the construction and painting of the scenery and properties, the assembly of the set(s) onstage, the shifting of those sets and props during the production, and the tools that are used to accomplish those tasks. The specific organization and assigned responsibilities vary considerably depending on the type of producing unit.

In the Broadway theatre, personnel are generally hired for a single production. After the producer has approved the construction bids, the designs are constructed and finished by independent professional scenic and property studios. During construction and painting, the scenic designer is in frequent contact with the scene-shop foreman to answer artistic and practical questions about the scenery. When the scenery is completed, it is moved from the studio to the theatre and set up on the stage. This **load-in** is carried out by union stagehands under the supervision of the production's stage manager. The scenic designer and the stage manager work together to choreograph any scene shifts, and the stage manager is responsible for supervising the work of the union crews that will be shifting the scenery.

The Broadway theatre's single-production concept is the exception rather than the rule in the American theatre. Most theatre in the United States is produced on a limited-run, multiple-production basis by colleges, universities, community theatres, and regional professional theatre groups. Almost all of these theatres produce three or more productions a year. They are almost always working on more than one production at any given time. This situation creates a definite need for some very specific organization to keep all of the production activity flowing smoothly. The primary organizer of the technical aspects of production is the technical director. Probably the most important skills that the TD must possess are the ability to effectively organize time and resources and the ability to

technical production: All organizational and procedural aspects of the construction, painting, and operation of scenery and properties.

load-in: The moving of scenery and associated equipment into the theatre and the positioning of them on the stage.

237

PRODUCTION INSIGHTS
The Production Calendar

The production calendar (see Figure 1.8) helps the technical director keep track of progress on the various productions. It specifies pertinent information (tryouts, design due dates, construction and painting schedules, rehearsals, and performances) for every play being produced by the theatre during the season. It also provides a visual reference that shows at a glance the status of each production. The production calendar is usually developed by the technical director in conjunction with the producer or managing and artistic directors with input from the resident directors and designers.

manage people. The technical director is an expediter. He or she needs to know the current status of the work being produced by every member of the production team. This task is compounded because most technical directors are keeping track of two, three, or more productions simultaneously.

The technical director's work on scenic and property construction cannot begin until the designer provides plans (ground plan, front elevations, detail sheets, functional models, painter's elevations) for the production. After studying the plans, the technical director or an assistant draws any necessary rear elevations or construction drawings that will facilitate the building of the scenery and props, then orders the construction materials. At this same time, he or she also creates a construction calendar. This calendar specifies the amount of time scheduled for the construction, painting, and assembling of the individual elements of the sets.

Scenic Construction Techniques

Although the overall construction plan, as well as the specific methods used to build each piece of scenery, should be guided by the basic tenets of the design process (see Chapter 2), some fairly standardized construction techniques are used to fabricate stage scenery.

Woodworking

Wood is used extensively for building two- and three-dimensional scenery. It is relatively inexpensive and can be worked easily with a variety of tools, which were described in Chapter 10.

Various wood joints are used. The following are most common in scenic and property construction.

Butt Joint   The butt joint is made when two pieces of wood are cut square at the end and fitted together, as shown in Figure 11.1A–D. Because the area of contact between the two pieces of wood is relatively small, a butt joint isn't very strong unless some type of reinforcement is applied.

Lap Joint   A lap joint (Figure 11.1E) is probably the simplest of all joints. Two pieces of lumber are joined face to face and fastened together. This type of self-reinforcing joint is used when attaching legs to platforms.

Battened Butt Joint   A battened butt joint (Figure 11.1F) is created when two pieces of stock lumber are butted end to end, and an 18- to 24-inch piece of

irregular flat: A flat having nonsquare corners.

lumber of similar width is attached directly over the joint with glue and screws. Specialized battened butt joints (Figure 11.1G and H) are used in flat construction. Cornerblocks of ¼-inch plywood are used to reinforce the butt joints at the corners of the flats. Keystones, also made from ¼-inch plywood, are used to reinforce the butt joints made for any internal bracing on the flats.

Miter Joint A miter joint (Figure 11.1I) is a type of butt joint. The only difference is that the wood being joined is cut on an angle instead of square. A miter joint is used when making **irregular flats** and picture frames.

Figure 11.1
Standard wood joints.
(A) Butt joint
(B) Butt joint
(C) Butt joint
(D) Butt joint
(E) Lap joint
(F) Battened butt joint
(G) Butt joint reinforced with a cornerblock
(H) Butt joint reinforced with a keystone
(I) Miter joint

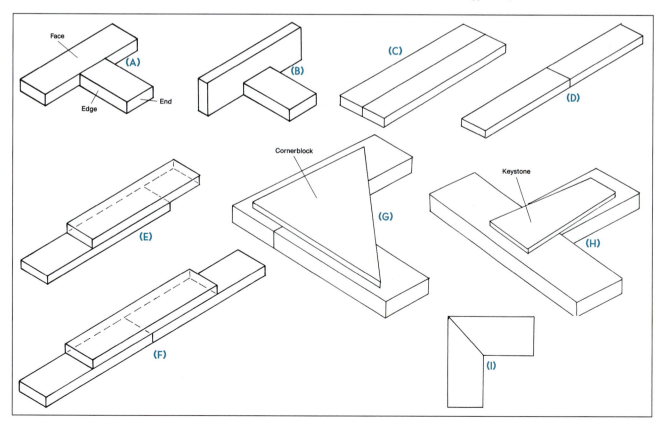

PRODUCTION INSIGHTS
Construction Drawings

Construction drawings or rear elevations are scale mechanical drawings that show the back of the flats depicted on the front elevations. These drawings:

1. show the construction details of the framework of the flats.

2. indicate which flats are to be joined to form wall units.

3. show the unusual construction challenges.

In professional scene shops, the foreman is responsible for drawing any rear elevations. In practice very few are drawn, because the carpenters working in these scenic studios are very knowledgeable about construction methods and techniques.

In educational theatres, however, the construction crews are usually students who are just learning how to build scenery. Rear elevations should be drawn to provide the student carpenters with all of the information needed to build the scenery.

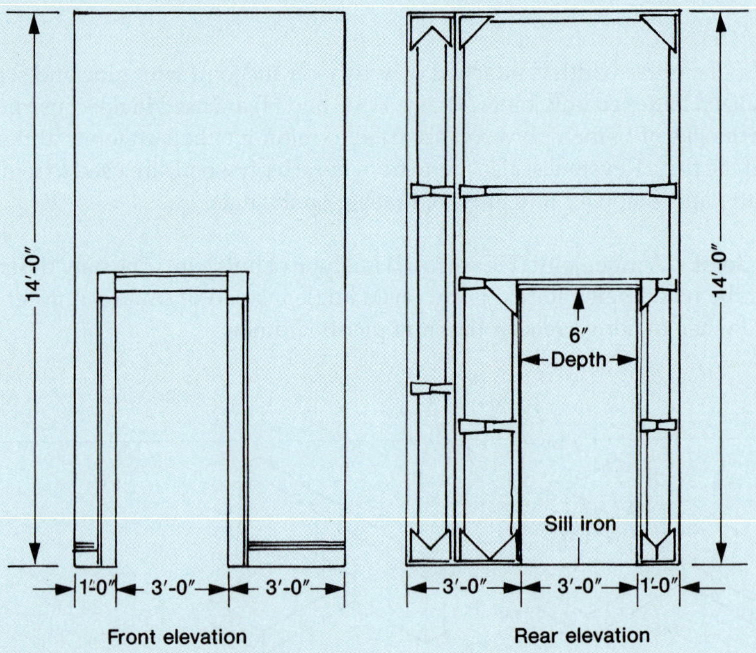

14'-0"

6"
◄—Depth—►

Sill iron

14'-0"

|◄—|1'-0"|◄—| 3'-0" |◄—| 3'-0" |◄—| |◄— 3'-0" —►|◄— 3'-0" —►|1'-0"|◄—|

Front elevation   **Rear elevation**

Rear elevations show the framework of a flat.

Dado Joint   A dado joint (Figure 11.2A) is made by cutting a slot across the face of one piece of lumber to receive the edge of another. The slot is cut only halfway through the depth of the lumber. Fastened with glue and nails, the dado joint is frequently used for shelving and similar applications.

The dado slot can be cut with several passes of a regular blade in a radial-arm saw or with a dado blade. The width of the kerf on the dado blade can be adjusted so that the dado slot can be made in a single pass.

Halved Joint   A halved joint (Figure 11.2B and C), also called a halved lap joint, is made by removing half of the thickness of each piece of lumber from the area to be joined so that the thickness of the finished joint will be no greater than the stock from which it is made. This is a very strong joint when secured with glue and nails, screws, or staples, and it can be cut fairly easily with a dado blade. It is used in making the **muntins** and **mullions** of windows and in similar applications.

muntin: A horizontal crossbar in a window.

mullion: A vertical crossbar in a window.

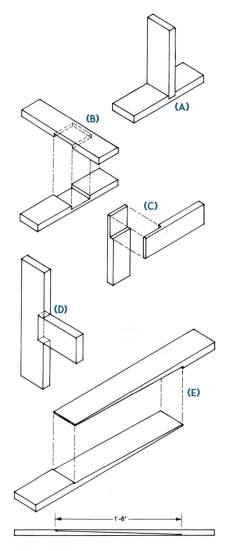

Construction Calendar

The complexity of the construction calendar depends on the complexity of the play. A single-set production will not be so difficult or time consuming as a multiset musical. The following construction calendar shows a reasonable work schedule for a production of a single-set show.

February	27	Receive designer's plans. Begin analysis of the plans. Order any special building materials. Begin drafting working drawings. (This calendar assumes that the theatre shop maintains an inventory of standard building materials in the scene shop at all times. If all building materials are ordered on a per-show basis, additional time will be needed at the beginning of the calendar to allow for their delivery.)
	28	Continue drafting working drawings.
	29	Continue drafting working drawings.
March	1	Begin construction: platforms, properties. Continue drafting working drawings.
	2	Construction: platforms, stairs, properties. Finish drafting working drawings.
	3–4	Weekend (no work)
	5	Construction: platforms, stairs, properties. Hang flying units and masking above area occupied by the set.
	6	Construction: same as preceding day. Hang and circuit lights above set.
	7	Construction: same as preceding day.
	8	Construction: same as preceding day. Erect platforms; begin platform facings.
	9	Construction: platforms, stairs complete. Build facings, railings.
	10–11	Weekend
	12	Construction: same as preceding day. Begin painting offstage. Hang lights.
	13	Construction: same as preceding day.
	14	Construction: same as preceding day.
	15	Construction: major construction complete. Paint floor. Build and paint props.
	16	Construction: same as preceding day.
	17–18	Weekend
	19	Construction: all scenic construction complete. Focus lights. Paint props.
	20	Construction: same as preceding day.
	21	Construction: all set and prop construction and painting complete. Lighting rehearsal.
	22	Touch-up and detail work. Decorate set. Adjust lights. Load in sound.
	23	Detail work. Final property adjustments.
	24	Technical rehearsal: make necessary adjustments.
	25	Sunday (no work)
	26	Dress rehearsal: make necessary adjustments.
	27	Dress rehearsal: make necessary adjustments.
	28	Dress rehearsal: make necessary adjustments.
	29	Opening of play.

Figure 11.2
Specialty wood joints.
(A) Dado joint
(B) Halved joint
(C) Halved joint
(D) Notched joint
(E) Scarf joint

Notched Joint   A notched joint (Figure 11.2D) is created when the edge or face of one board is inserted into a notch cut in another. The size of the notch is determined by the width and thickness of the piece that the notch will receive. The notched joint is used for shelving and similar applications.

Scarf Joint   The scarf joint (Figure 11.2E) is used to make one long board from two short ones with no increase in the thickness of the lumber. The angled surface of the joint should be at least 18 inches long. It can be cut using a band saw (with a wide, newly sharpened blade to rough-cut the diagonal cut). A plane or power sander should be used to smooth the surface of the cut so that the faces of the joint will be flush when joined. Each face is coated with glue, and the unit is clamped together and fastened with screws or bolts and allowed to dry.

Mortise and Tenon Joint   A square hole, the mortise, can be chiseled into one of the pieces to be joined. This is much easier than it sounds if a **mortise drill bit,** which drills square holes, is used. The other piece of wood has the edges cut back to create the tenon. The tenon must snuggly fit into the mortise. The mortise and tenon joint (Figure 11.3A and B) is normally secured only with glue.

An open mortise and tenon joint has the tenon exposed; a closed mortise and tenon joint looks from the outside just like a butt joint. Because of their strength,

mortise drill bit: A drill bit housed inside of a square hollow chisel; used with a drill press to make square holes; available in a variety of diameters.

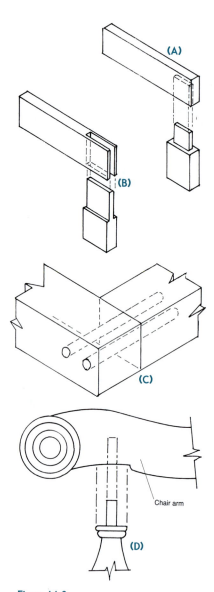

Figure 11.3
Internally supported wood joints.
(A) Closed mortise and tenon joint
(B) Open mortise and tenon joint
(C) Open doweled joint
(D) Closed doweled joint

filler rod: Metal piece, of the same composition as material being welded, used to replace the metal lost during the welding process or to fill a hole or groove in the work.

The Scene Shop

Any workplace that uses electricity, flammable and toxic materials, and tools capable of cutting, gouging, and sawing is an inherently dangerous environment. With a healthy dose of common sense and a few safety rules, however, working in the scene shop can be safe, efficient, and enjoyable.

1. Wear clothing suited to the work: long pants, short- or long-sleeve shirt, and hard-toe, hard-sole shoes (not sandals or sneakers). Clothing should be reasonably close fitting. Don't wear flowing robes — they might get caught in power equipment.

2. Tie back, put under a cap, or otherwise contain long hair so that it won't get caught in a power tool. For the same reasons, don't wear jewelry.

3. Always get instructions before operating any power or hand tool. Be sure you know what you're doing before you do it.

4. Pay attention to what you are doing. Don't operate any tool unless you are giving it your undivided attention. Watch your work area for potential hazards such as wood with protruding nails and potential fire or electrical hazards. Either correct the hazard (if you know how) or report it to your supervisor.

5. Keep your work space clean. If the shop is kept neat, clean, and organized, accidents are reduced and you can find the tools and supplies you need.

6. Know where the first-aid materials are kept. Disinfect all cuts and splinters, and bandage even minor cuts. Report all accidents to your supervisor.

7. When working with materials that emit dust or fumes, make sure that the work area is well ventilated and that you wear an appropriate mask.

both the opened and closed mortise and tenon joints are used extensively in furniture construction.

Doweled Joint   A doweled joint is a butt joint that is reinforced with small pieces of hardwood dowel. An open doweled joint (Figure 11.3C) has the end of the dowel exposed; a closed doweled joint (Figure 11.3D) shows no outside evidence of its existence.

Three additional types of joints — the open dowel joint, the pocket hole joint, and the biscuit joint — are discussed in Chapter 13, "Stage Properties," because these joints are more commonly used in furniture-making and other property-related construction projects than in typical scenic construction. That material can be found on pages 326–328.

Welding

Welding is the process of fusing metal by heating the pieces being joined to their melting temperature and inducing the metal to flow together before it cools. During this high-temperature process, a certain amount of the metal is vaporized or otherwise lost. The **filler rod** is used to replace the lost metal.

Surface Preparation   Before welding, the surface of the metal must be cleaned of all oil, grease, paint, rust, and any other contaminants. This can be done by polishing the welding zone with a wire brush, by sanding, by grinding, or by cleaning with commercial chemical removers.

Welding Techniques   Several welding techniques have been developed to use with the various types of welders (see Chapter 10 for a description of welding equipment).

Guidelines for Welding

According to OSHA guidelines, welders shall be required to wear (1) non-flammable gloves with gauntlets, (2) shoes, boots, or leggings, (3) leather aprons, (4) shirts with sleeves and collars, (5) face shields or helmets suitable for head protection, (6) suitable eye protection, and (7) respiratory protection.

The necessity to protect your body from being burned from the sparks of molten metal generated at the welding zone is obvious. What isn't so obvious is the necessity to protect your eyes and respiratory system.

Gas and arc welding generate differing levels of visible and ultraviolet light. Ultraviolet (UV) light can cause temporary and/or permanent diminution or loss of sight. Be sure to wear the type of protective lens appropriate to the type of welding in which you're engaged. If you aren't sure whether your eye protection is correct for the type of welding you're doing, don't weld.

Various metal compositions and/or finishes, such as the silvery coating used to galvanize steel, emit noxious or toxic gases when heated or burned. High-volume ventilation and the use of an appropriate respirator will eliminate this health risk. OSHA regulations state that there must be a 100-CFM (cubic feet per minute) airflow in a welder's breathing zone or that an appropriate respirator must be worn. Whenever you weld, be sure you have adequate ventilation.

Oxyacetylene Welding   Oxyacetylene welding uses the **two-handed welding** technique. With this method, the welder holds the torch or welding handle in one hand and the copper-clad filler rod in the other. As the flame melts the pieces being joined, the operator feeds the filler rod into the welding zone. The rod melts, flows into the joint, and replaces the lost metal.

In oxyacetylene welding (Figure 11.4), the strength of the weld depends on a chemically neutral flame. This neutral flame is achieved through a proper mix of the oxygen and acetylene gas. After the torch flame has been lit (using acetylene gas only), oxygen is introduced to the mix. When the oxygen is first introduced, a small white cone appears at the base of, and inside, the flame. At first this cone is rather long. Sometimes it is a double cone. As more oxygen is added, the cone gets smaller. A neutral flame is produced when this white cone is short and slightly rounded. An oxidizing flame, which will burn the molten metal, is produced when more oxygen is added to a neutral flame.

A cutting torch (see Chapter 10) is equipped with a lever-actuated valve that introduces additional oxygen to the flame, creating an oxidizing flame. This flame burns the metal, resulting in a cut.

Arc Welding   The arc welder utilizes electricity to generate an **arc** that has a temperature of approximately 13,000°F. This extremely high heat almost instantaneously melts most common types of metal.

To use an arc welder, you attach the ground cable from the welding machine to the work, effectively turning the work into an electrode. When a flux-coated **welding rod,** which is connected to the power side of the welding machine, comes into close proximity with the work, an arc is formed across the gap. The resultant heat melts the metal, and the weld is made. The electrode, which also acts as a filler rod, is consumed in the welding process. Since the welding handle is held with only one hand, the process is called **single-hand welding.**

The MIG (metal inert gas) welder (discussed in Chapter 10) is another single-hand arc welder. It differs from the arc welder in that the welding handle focuses a flow of inert gas on the welding zone (as shown in Figure 11.5) as the weld is

two-handed welding: A technique in which the torch or welding handle is held in one hand and the filler rod in the other.

arc: An electric current that leaps the gap between two closely placed electrodes.

welding rod: A rod, usually covered with flux, that serves as the positive electrode in arc welding.

single-hand welding: A technique in which one hand holds the welding handle and the other hand is not used.

Figure 11.4
Oxyacetylene welding technique. For portability the oxygen (tall) and acetylene tanks are normally secured to a rolling cart (A). To light the welding torch, close the valves on the handle of the torch, then turn on the oxygen (B) to approximately 30–35 pounds and the acetylene (C) to 5–7 pounds. (The pressure settings will vary with the composition and thickness of metals.) Open the acetylene valve on the torch handle and light the torch (D). Adjust the acetylene flame until the base of the flame just touches the tip of the torch (E), then slowly open the oxygen valve on the torch and adjust the flame until the small inner cone at the base of the flame is approximately $1/4$ long (F). Be sure to wear protective clothing and use welding goggles or a welding mask (G) when you weld.

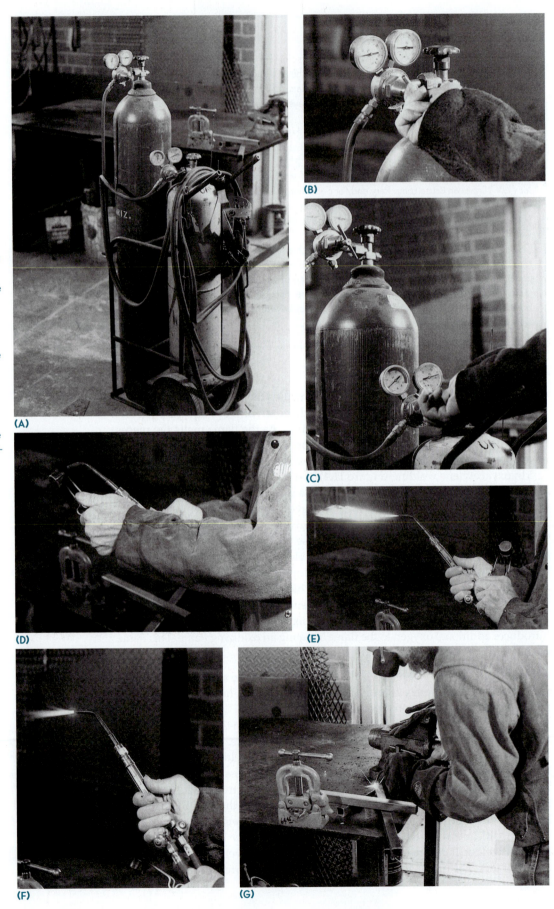

(A)

(B)

(C)

(D)

(E)

(F)

(G)

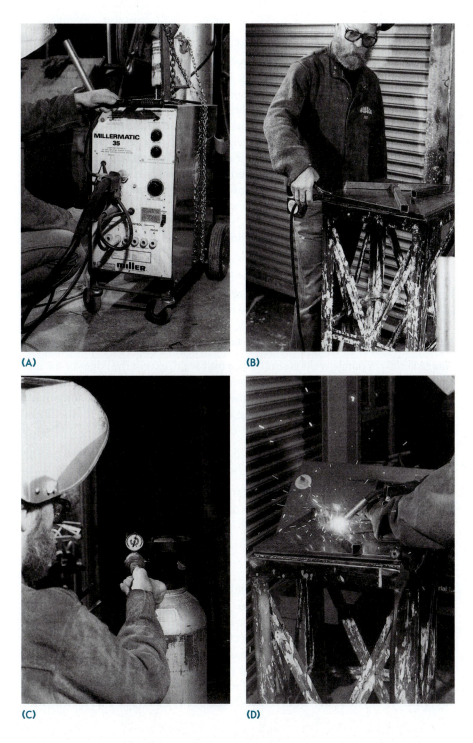

(A)

(B)

(C)

(D)

Figure 11.5
MIG (metal inert gas) welding technique.
(A) Adjust the power setting of the
welder to suit the composition and thickness of the metal being welded (consult
the welding machine's instruction book).
(B) Attach the ground cable to the welding table or the work. (C) Turn on the gas
(carbon dioxide or argon) to 5–9 pounds
(consult the welder's instruction book for
appropriate setting for your specific equipment). (D) Bring the welding wire close to
the welding zone, press the trigger, and
weld. Be sure to wear appropriate protective clothing.

being made, and it has a wire electrode. The inert gas reduces **oxidation,** which
can substantially weaken the weld. The thin wire electrode of the MIG welder is
automatically fed to the handle from a spool in the housing of the power unit. A
flux coating for the wire electrode isn't used because of the oxidation-reducing
properties of the shielding gas. The MIG welder can also be used without the
inert gas if you use a special flux-core wire rather than the "regular" wire electrode. The flux effectively provides the same inert-gas environment while the
weld is being made.

oxidation: A chemical reaction between
the metal and air that forms a very thin,
discolored "skin" over the metal; this skin
effectively prevents heat transfer and
reduces the strength and conductivity of
the joint.

solder: A metal alloy of lead and tin.

When equipped with a steel wire electrode and carbon dioxide or argon gas, the MIG welder does an excellent job of welding steel. It can be used for welding aluminum if aluminum wire and argon gas are used.

Although the single-hand welding technique used with the arc and MIG welder is the same, the MIG welder is easier to use. It is probably the easiest welder on which to learn how to weld, because the electrode is automatically fed to the welding zone, and the shielding gas yields a substantially better weld than does either an arc or an oxyacetylene welder.

The TIG (tungsten inert gas) welder uses a nonconsumable tungsten rod as the electrode and requires a two-handed welding technique. A filler rod of the same composition as the materials being welded is held in the other hand and fed into the welding zone as the weld is being made.

Types of Welds   Common welding joints are described below and illustrated in Figure 11.6.

Butt Weld   The butt weld is probably the most common, and strongest, type. The edges of the materials to be joined are clamped edge to edge with a narrow space ($\frac{1}{16}$ to $\frac{1}{8}$ inch) between them. If the material is between $\frac{3}{16}$ and $\frac{1}{2}$ inch thick, the edges should be ground to form a V, as shown in Figure 11.6A. If the metal is less than $\frac{3}{16}$ inch thick, the V will not be needed.

Flange Weld   A flange weld is similar to a butt weld, except the edges of the material being joined are bent up, as shown in Figure 11.6B, before the sheets are clamped in place. The weld is made by melting the upturned flanges. Although it is necessary to apply flux to the welding zone, the flange weld can frequently be made without the use of a filler rod.

Lap Weld   A lap weld is made when two pieces are overlapped, as shown in Figure 11.6C. Both overlapped edges must be welded.

Fillet Weld   A fillet weld (Figure 11.6D) is made when the edge of one piece is joined to the face of another. Both sides of the angled piece should be welded to create the strongest possible weld.

Soldering

Soldering is the process of heating metal (usually lightweight steel, copper, or brass) until it is hot enough to melt **solder.** The solder flows over the surface of the metal and bonds the pieces together. For an effective soldering bond to be made, there must be a good mechanical connection between the parts being soldered. The parts must be clean and free of grease, oxidation, and other contaminants.

Soldering flux is applied to further clean the metal and prevent oxidation when the joint is heated. Flux is manufactured in solid, powder, paste, and liquid forms. The type of flux used depends on the project. Rosin flux is noncorro-

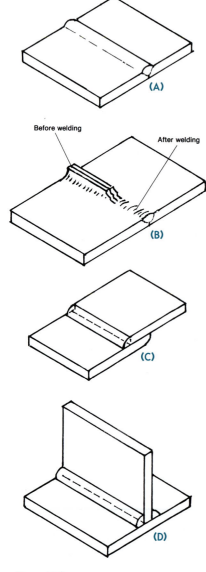

Figure 11.6
Types of welded joints.
(A) Butt weld
(B) Flange weld
(C) Lap weld
(D) Fillet weld

Safety Tip

Strength of Welds

The strength of any weight-bearing welded structure depends on the strength of its welds. Before attempting to construct any metal platforming or other structures on which actors are going to stand, be sure to practice enough so that you are sure you are producing high-quality welds. Have your work checked by an instructor so that you know your welds will be strong.

PRODUCTION INSIGHTS

Making a Good Solder Joint

A good solder joint can be made only if you heat the work to the melting point of the solder. If the work is not heated sufficiently and the solder is melted by touching it to the soldering iron, the solder will just sit on top of the work rather than bonding with its surface. This produces what is known as a "cold" solder joint. A cold solder joint isn't very strong, and it doesn't conduct electricity very well. A cold solder joint can be identified by its appearance. The solder looks dull, whereas a good solder joint will appear bright and shiny. A cold solder joint can generally be fixed by adding a little flux to the joint and reheating the work until it is sufficiently hot to make the solder flow freely.

sive and should be used on all electrical work. Soldering wire with a rosin-flux core can be purchased at almost any hardware store. Acid fluxes are very effective, but the acid is corrosive, so the work must be washed with warm water to prevent corrosion. Be sure to wait for the solder joint to cool before you wash it.

If you aren't using a soldering wire with a flux core, it will be necessary to apply flux to the joint before it is heated. After the joint has been fluxed, heat is applied to the work. The solder should be melted by touching it to the work, not the iron. The melted solder should freely flow over and through the joint where the hot solder bonds with the surface of the metal and fuses the joint together.

Two-Dimensional Scenery

Two-dimensional scenery can be divided into two basic subgroups: hard scenery and soft scenery. Hard scenery generally refers to flats, and soft scenery to unframed units such as drops and draperies.

Flats

Nothing stays the same forever. Flats provide a prime example of this phenomenon. For more than two hundred years fabric-covered wooden-framed flats were the standard construction technique for making scenic walls. In recent years several trends have converged to reduce the dominance, and usefulness, of this type of flat.

Perhaps the most important reason that soft flats have fallen into semi-disfavor is that contemporary scene designs tend to be more sculptural than pictorial. Soft flats worked well when designs attempted to re-create the look of a drawing room interior with its large expanse of walls. When there aren't large expanses of wall on a set, the need for soft flats is reduced. What walls remain in a sculptural scenic design are frequently treated with some type of 3-D coating to simulate stone, brick, or whatever. If applied to fabric-covered flats these coatings, if they adhere at all, will frequently flake off if the scenery is moved or cause the fabric to sag and pull out of shape. Either of these situations generally ruins the desired effect. Sculpturally applied coatings need the base support of a hard, solid surface—hard-covered flats.

The increased use of **show control** and other methods to shift scenery in front of the audience have also added to the fading away of soft-covered flats. If the scenery, which is supposed to be the stone wall of a castle, glides onto the stage and twirls around, the illusion would be totally destroyed if the "stone

show control: The use of computer-controlled, motorized devices to shift scenery, almost always in view of the audience.

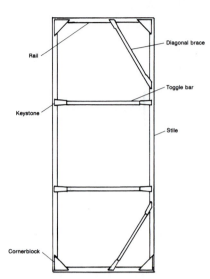

Figure 11.7
The parts of a flat.

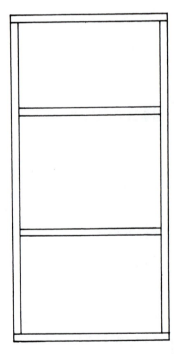

Figure 11.8
Positioning of butt joints on a flat.

rail: A top or bottom framing member of a flat.

stile: A vertical side member of a flat.

toggle bar: An interior horizontal framing member of a flat.

corner brace: A diagonal internal framing member that helps keep a flat square.

jog: A flat less than 2 feet wide.

walls" flapped and wiggled as they moved. Those walls need to be hard-covered simply so they will be firm and solid—so they'll look like what they're supposed to be.

For the above-stated, and several other, reasons most contemporary flats are made for specific applications, are not reused, and are generally hard- rather than fabric-covered. These techniques, as well as wooden-framed construction, will be discussed next.

There are three types or styles of flats: soft, or soft-covered; hard, or hard-covered; and studio, also called Hollywood or face-on-edge flats. Each type has its own general characteristics and will be discussed in the following section.

Regardless of the type or style of flat, the various pieces that make up the framework of a flat have specific names, as shown in Figure 11.7. The top and bottom horizontal members are called **rails,** the outside vertical elements are called **stiles,** and the interior horizontal members are referred to as **toggle bars. Corner braces** are located in the upper and lower corners of the same side of any flat over 3 feet wide.

The toggle bars are used to keep the stiles parallel. On fabric-covered flats if toggle bars were not used, fabric shrinkage (caused when the flat is painted) would cause the stiles to twist and bow in toward each other. Toggles should be spaced approximately 3 to 4 feet from the nearest toggle bar or rail.

Individual flats normally are not constructed wider than 6 feet because anything wider is awkward to handle. Flats less than 2 feet wide are generally referred to as **jogs,** and jogs less than 1 foot wide are normally made from solid stock rather than fabric-covered framework. The solid jog is covered with the same fabric so that when it is included in a wall, which is normally made up of several flats and jogs, all elements of the wall will look the same when they are painted.

Soft Flats   Soft, or soft-covered, flats generally refer to wooden-framed flats covered with some type of fabric. Soft flats can be designed to be almost any size or shape, but the vast majority resemble tall rectangles from 1 to 6 feet wide and 8 to 16 feet high. The wooden framework for a flat up to 14 feet tall is usually made of 1 × 3 white pine ("B or better" or "C select"). Because of the cost, and frequent nonavailability, of "B or better" or "C select" 1 × 3 white pine, many scene shops now use 1 × 4 pine, or its locally available equivalent, even if it has a few tight knots. The significant factor of whether to use 1 × 3 or 1 × 4 is the quality of the wood. Lumber used to build wooden flats needs to be straight, free from warps or twists, relatively lightweight, and it should have few knots. If it has knots, they need to be small enough so that they don't interfere with the strength of the wood. Wooden flats over 14 feet tall are almost always built from 1 × 4. Generally, flat frames over 14 feet tall are built from welded metal tubing rather than wood.

The general structure of a wood-framed flat is illustrated in Figure 11.8. The rails extend the full width of the flat. The stiles are inset inside the rails so their total length equals the full height of the flat minus the combined width of both rails. The toggle bars—which are normally evenly spaced 3 to 5 feet from adjacent toggle bars or rails—are placed inside the stiles so their overall length equals the width of the flat minus the combined widths of both stiles.

The butt joints of a wooden-framed flat are reinforced with cornerblocks and keystones. On fabric-covered flats the cornerblocks—used to reinforce the outside corners of the frame—are inset ¾ inch from the outside edge of the frame as illustrated in Figure 11.9. The keystones, Figure 11.10, are similarly inset from the outside edge of the frame by ¾ inch. The reason that they are inset ¾ inch is so that the ¼-inch thickness of the cornerblock, or keystone, won't interfere with a smooth, or flush, joint between the edges of the flat when they are placed at 90 degrees to each other when forming a wall unit.

PRODUCTION INSIGHTS

Keystones and Cornerblocks

Keystones and cornerblocks are used as reinforcement for the butt joints commonly used in flat construction.

The *cornerblock* is a triangle of ¼-inch AD plywood with 8- to 10-inch legs. To provide effective reinforcement, position the cornerblock so that its grain runs perpendicular to the joint between the rail and the stile.

Also made of ¼-inch AD plywood, the *keystone* is 6 inches long and shaped like a keystone of an arch. The small end is slightly narrower (½ inch) than the width of the toggle bar that it is covering; the wide end is approximately ½ inch wider than the toggle bar.

Some technicians prefer rectangular strips of plywood, called straps, to keystones. These straps should be cut approximately ½ inch narrower than the width of the toggle bar. Both keystones and rectangular straps provide about the same amount of bracing for the joint, but many technicians think that keystones are prettier, so they continue to use them in preference to the plywood straps.

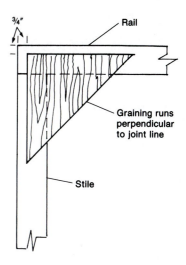

Figure 11.9
The placement of cornerblocks on a flat.

Both keystones and cornerblocks are typically attached using pneumatic glue-coated staples or power-driven screws. A relatively recent improvement in this area is the use of Robertson screws. These square-holed—as opposed to Phillips- or slotted-head—screws seem to be much more efficient. They provide a much firmer grip between the power screwdriver and the screw. This reduces the incidents of the driver "jumping" off the screw and ripping fabric, dinging wood, or injuring the operator.

When the flat is wider than 3 feet, diagonal corner braces made of 1 × 2 are placed in the upper and lower corners of the same side of the flat. These are secured with plywood straps ripped in half and angle cut so they can be inset ¾ inch from the outside of the flat as illustrated in Figure 11.11.

Detailed information on how to build, and cover, a standard soft flat with muslin is contained in Appendix C on page 574.

Hard-covered Flats   Hard-covered flats are simply traditional wooden flat frames covered with a hard material such as plywood, Masonite, or other hard covering material.

Generally the "hard cover" material is ¼ inch thick although other thicknesses can be used as necessity, budget, or availability dictates. Many technicians have discovered that ¼-inch lauan plywood seems to warp less than the more common A-D plywood. The wooden structure of a hard flat is the same as its fabric-covered cousin. The only significant difference is that the keystones and cornerblocks are inset 1 inch to account for the increased thickness of the covering material.

The covering material is generally attached to the frame using pneumatic glue-coated staples or power-driven screws spaced around the outside edge of the frame, and across each toggle bar, on 12- to **18-inch centers.** If the flat cannot be covered with one sheet of material, a toggle bar needs to be centered behind any joints in the covering material so both edges of the covering sheets can be secured to the flat. To ensure a smooth surface for finishing—either paint, fabric, wallpaper, or sculptural coating—many technicians like to fill any joints between covering sheets or indentions caused by the staples or screws with some form of **spackling.**

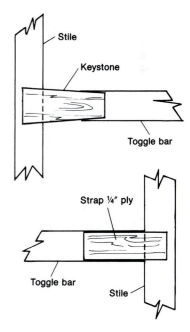

Figure 11.10
The placement of keystones on a flat.

Metal-frame Flats   Many production companies now routinely make their flat frames from metal rather than wood. There are two linked reasons for this: quality and cost. As previously discussed, the quality of wood needed to make traditional

18-inch centers: Spaced 18 inches apart.

spackling: A paste used to fill small holes in walls.

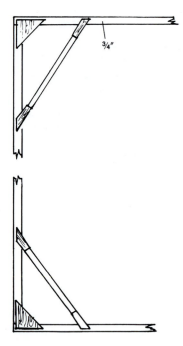

Figure 11.11
The placement of reinforcement for diagonal braces on a flat. Be sure that all cornerblocks, keystones, and straps are placed with their outside edges ¾" from the outside edge of the flat.

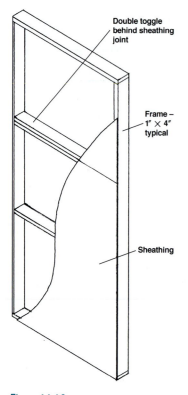

Figure 11.12
Studio flat. Constructed of 1 × 4 placed on edge and covered with hard material such as plywood. See text for details.

flats has become increasingly expensive. In most locations it now simply costs less to make a metal-framed flat than a similarly sized wooden one. Case closed.

Metal-frame flats employ the same structural design as traditional wooden flats. The rails extend to the full width of the flat, the stiles are the full height minus the combined width of the rails, and the toggle bars are inset inside the rails. The use of diagonal braces follows the same general guidelines as wooden flats—anything wider than 3 feet requires the use of diagonal braces.

Typically metal-frame flats will be made from 1 × 1 metal tubing, although the structural needs of the individual flat may dictate the use of some other dimension of tubing or angle iron.

Each tubing butt joint—rails to stiles, stiles to toggle bars, and so forth—should be welded on at least two or three sides. Normally the face of the flat frame is not welded. If, however, a weld is made on the face of the flat, it should be ground flat so the covering material will smoothly mate with the metal surface of the frame.

It is almost impossible to "soft-cover" a metal-frame flat with fabric. Typically metal-frame flats are covered with lauan plywood or "regular" A-D plywood (see the discussion of hard-covering materials above). The covering material is normally attached using **construction adhesive** and/or power-driven flat-head TEK screws—screws that drill their own pilot holes. The screws are typically spaced 12 to 18 inches apart. They are normally driven into the covering material so the top of the screw head is flush with the surface of the covering material. The resulting "ding" is then patched with spackling to create a uniformly smooth surface. The finish covering for metal-framed hard flats follows the guidelines outlined for wood-framed hard flats, which is provided above.

Studio Flats   Studio flats, also called Hollywood-style or "on edge" flats, are wood-framed flats similar in structure to hard flats with one major exception: the framing material, usually 1 × 4, is placed "on edge" rather than flat, as illustrated in Figure 11.12. The studio flat is then covered with hard material such as plywood, **drywall,** or Masonite, typically using 1¼- to 1⅝-inch drywall screws driven flush with the covering surface on 12- to 18-inch centers. Any surface imperfections are normally covered with spackling. If the flat cannot be covered with one sheet of material, a doubled toggle bar or stile—two toggles/stiles, placed on edge and nailed/screwed together—needs to be centered behind any joints in the covering material so both edges of the covering sheets can be secured to the flat.

In a studio flat the wood is placed "on edge" rather than flat for one simple reason: strength. To illustrate: If you pick up the end of a 10- or 12-foot 1 × 4, you'll notice that the board flexes and bounces up and down quite freely because the movement is being countered only by the ¾ inch thickness of the plank. But if you turn the board on edge and wiggle it again it barely flexes up and down. This is because the wood countering the up-and-down movement is now 3½ inches, rather than ¾ inch, thick. For this reason the wooden frame of a soft flat is de-

PRODUCTION INSIGHTS
Flat-Covering Fabrics

A variety of fabrics can be used to cover flats. Remember that they need to be certified flame retardant.

Unbleached Muslin

Heavyweight unbleached muslin is an excellent, low-cost flat-covering material. It is available in a variety of widths—72, 81, 90, and 108 inches and 33 feet. The narrower widths are used for flat covering, and the 33-foot material is usually used for making seamless drops and cycloramas.

This type of muslin, which is available from scenic supply houses, has a high-thread count—128 or 140 threads to the inch—which gives sufficient strength for flat covering and most other scenic uses. Muslin accepts all scenic paints well and has a uniform shrinkage rate.

Although bleached muslin is available in fabric stores, it isn't particularly useful for scenic purposes, because the bleaching process weakens its fibers, it normally isn't available in sizes wider than 48 inches, and it is more expensive.

Linen Canvas

Linen canvas is an excellent flat-covering material, because it is extremely durable and has a coarse weave similar to artist's canvas. The fabric is 69 to 72 inches wide and weighs 12 to 16 ounces per square yard. It accepts paint well and doesn't shrink much. Unfortunately, it is also the most expensive of the flat-covering materials, is not always available, and can be purchased only from scenic or fabric supply houses.

Cotton Canvas

Cotton canvas is an excellent substitute for linen canvas, because it has many of the same properties, is approximately the same weight (9 to 16 ounces), is readily available, and is much less expensive. It is the preferred type of canvas for making platform covers and ground cloths.

Cotton canvas is available in widths up to 72 inches, is sometimes available from tent and awning suppliers, and can also be purchased from scenic or fabric supply houses.

Cotton Duck

Cotton duck is a lighter weight—5- to 8-ounce—cotton canvas. It has the same properties as cotton canvas and is generally available locally, although it may be difficult to find in sizes wide enough for stage purposes (generally 69 inches or wider). It is available from local fabric stores, tent and awning suppliers, and scenic-fabric supply houses.

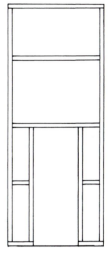

Figure 11.13
Standard door flats.

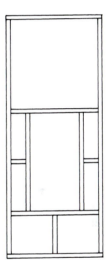

Figure 11.14
Standard window flats.

signed so the 3½-inch width of the lumber counters the inward pull created by the shrinkage of the covering fabric. But the covering material of hard-covered flats doesn't flex in that direction. They only flex perpendicular to the material's thickness. Therefore, the wood in a studio flat frame is placed on edge to counter any flexing of the covering material.

When several studio flats are used to form a wall unit, bolts and nuts normally are used to join them. Holes are drilled approximately one-quarter of the distance down from the top and up from the bottom of the stiles of adjacent flats, then bolts are inserted and nuts are used to snug the units together. Alternatively, the individual studio flats can be clamped together with C-clamps.

Door and Window Flats   All wooden and metal-framed flats can be constructed and covered using the general principles previously listed. The stiles of all flats (regular, irregular, door, window) are always placed inside their respective rails to prevent splintering of the stiles (if wood is used). The sizes of any interior openings in the flats (doors, windows, and so forth) are determined by the position of the toggle bars and door or window stiles, as shown in Figures 11.13 and 11.14.

Door flats have one construction variation. The bottom rail across the door opening of a wooden framed flat is removed and replaced with a **sill iron,** which is a mild-steel strap ³⁄₁₆ or ¼ inch thick and ¾ inch wide, as shown in Figure 11.15. The

construction adhesive: Also called panel adhesive, an adhesive contained in a caulking tube; dispensed with a caulking gun. Available in a number of formulations for use in gluing wall panels to studs (wood to wood), Styrofoam to wood, wood to metal, and so forth.

drywall: Gypsum board typically used to cover interior walls in home construction. Normally ½ inch thick although other thicknesses are available.

sill iron: A strap of mild steel attached to the bottom of a door flat to brace it where the rail has been cut out.

PRODUCTION INSIGHTS
Scenic Canvas and Muslin Glue Formulas

There are several effective methods of gluing covering fabric to flats.

Paint

Probably the easiest method of gluing muslin to a flat frame is with casein, acrylic, or latex paint. When using paint, either select white paint (which is close to the color of muslin) or mix a color that closely approximates the prime coat that you will be using to paint the set. Simply paint the stiles and rails with the paint, apply a very light coat of paint to the underside of the fabric flap, flop the fabric back onto the wood, and smooth it out. The binders in the paint will glue the fabric to the wood. This method works well if the flat is going to be used for a single production, as the binders in the paint are not strong enough to permanently bond the fabric to the flat. If the flat is going to be reused, one of the following glues would be more appropriate.

Animal Glue and Whiting

Animal glue is combined with whiting (a thickening agent made of low-grade chalk) in the ratio of one part prepared animal glue (see Chapter 10 for instructions) to one part whiting paste. To make whiting paste, put the dry whiting in a container and stir in enough water to make a paste the consistency of sour cream. Add the glue to the whiting paste, and use while it is hot. The mixture dries when it cools, but it can be reheated in a double boiler or glue pot to make it workable again.

White Glue and Water

A mixture of two parts of white glue thinned with one part of water makes a good muslin glue. Take care to use a light coat of glue, because if the white glue bleeds through to the surface of the fabric, it can leave a glaze coat that may discolor any subsequent coats of paint.

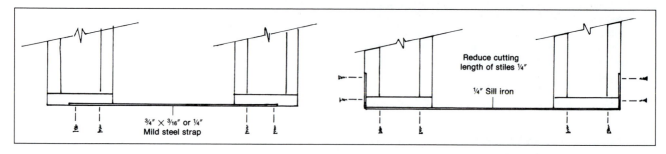

Figure 11.15
A sill iron is used to replace the bottom rail that is cut out when constructing a door flat.

sweep: A wooden curvilinear form, generally used to outline an arch or irregular form in door- and window-flat openings.

sill iron should extend at least 1 foot beyond either side of the doorway. For maximum strength, the sill iron should run to the outer edges of the door flat, bend at right angles, and run up the outside edge of the stiles a minimum of 6 to 8 inches. With either method, a thin strip of wood the thickness of the sill iron needs to be removed from the bottom of the rail and/or the outside edge of the stile to maintain the overall height and width of the flat. The sill iron is attached with 1- or 1¼-inch No. 8 or 9 flat-head screws or yellow zinc drywall screws. On metal-framed door flats, unless the door opening is quite wide, the sill iron isn't needed.

Arches and irregular openings in flats are made by insetting **sweeps** in regular door and window openings, as shown in Figure 11.16. Sweeps can be made from ¾-inch stock or plywood. Stock is preferable, because it will better hold the nails driven into its edge to support the depth pieces, also known as reveals. Sweeps that are used to create arches in either doors or windows should be notched into the door or window stiles approximately ½ to ¾ inch. If they aren't, the end of the sweep will have to be cut to a feather edge, and the chances of breaking that slivered end will be very good.

Standard Door Dimensions

Although the appearance of any door is the province of the scenic designer, certain dimensions and characteristics of doors are fairly standard.

1. Doors that people will pass through need to be at least 2 feet 6 inches wide. Set doors normally vary in width from 2½ to 3½ feet, depending on the height and style of the door. Closet doors are often narrower. Double doors are usually 5 to 7 feet wide.

2. Door heights vary between 6 feet 9 inches and 7 feet 6 inches.

3. Doorknobs are generally placed about 3 feet above the floor, although certain European styles place the doorknob closer to 4 feet.

4. Doors normally swing offstage. They are usually hinged on the upstage side of the doorway unless other needs (stage business, architectural faithfulness) dictate that the door be hung in some other manner.

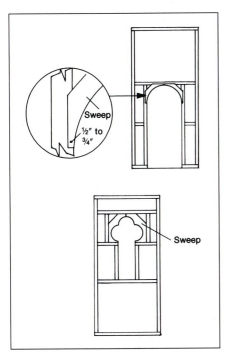

Figure 11.16
Sweeps are used to create irregularly shaped openings in door and window flats.

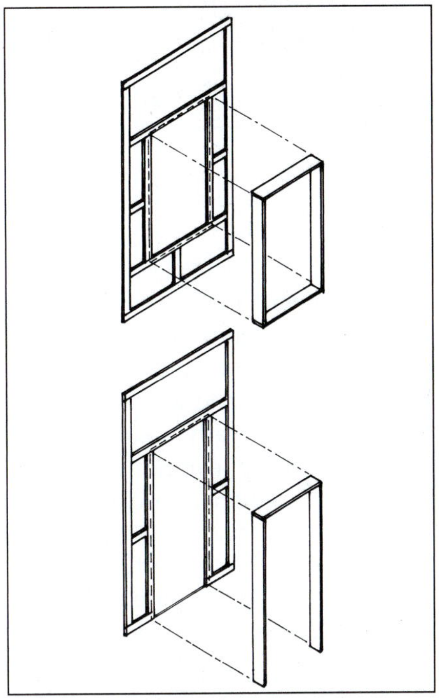

Figure 11.17
Depth pieces, or reveals, help create the illusion of wall thickness.

Trim enhances the realistic appearance of a door or window flat. Depth pieces create the illusion that the flat has actual thickness. Straight-line depth pieces can be made from 1 × 6 stock, ¼-inch Masonite, or similarly rigid material, as shown in Figure 11.17; curved depth pieces can be made from ⅛-inch Easy Curve, 3⁄16-inch Upson board, or ⅛-inch Masonite. The actual depth of the door or window depends entirely on the style and architectural period chosen by the scenic designer. The appearance of the window or door is similarly dependent on its architectural model.

There are two types of stage windows and doors: dependent and independent. The basic difference between the two is that the dependent unit is fixed to

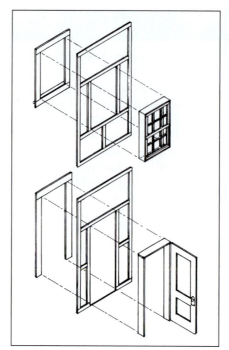

Figure 11.18
Dependent doors and windows.

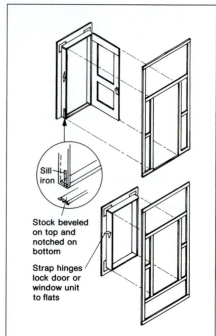

Figure 11.19
Independent doors and windows.

the flat, whereas the independent unit is largely self-contained and can easily be attached to or removed from the flat. Figure 11.18 shows exploded views of dependent doors and windows, and Figure 11.19 shows similar illustrations of independent doors and windows.

There isn't really a single, "correct" way to build either stage doors or windows. The appearance and function of doors and windows are determined by the scenic designer, and their appearance largely determines how they need to be built.

It is fairly standard practice to design doors to pivot on their upstage side and swing offstage (Figure 11.20), because, with this arrangement, they are self-masking. Self-masking doors block the spectators' view of the backstage area, they don't mask the actors' entrances, and they don't cut off the spectators' view of any part of the set. Because doors usually swing offstage, the spectators normally see only one side of them. For this reason, it is fairly common to build them on a base piece of ¼-inch plywood. Decorative trim can be applied to the face of the plywood (Figure 11.21). If both sides of the door are going to be seen, the same type of trim is applied to the back.

Joining Flats   Up to this point, the discussion has been confined to constructing individual flats no more than 6 feet wide. But most designs call for walls that are considerably wider. To construct such a larger wall, you join individual flats. As shown in Figure 11.22, varying styles of door, window, and plain flats can be joined to form a wall unit.

There are two primary methods of joining flats to form wall units: rigid and flexible. The rigid joining method is used when the wall unit doesn't have to be folded for shifting or storage. The flexible method is used when it is necessary to fold the wall.

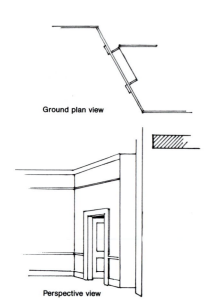

Figure 11.20
Stage doors are usually hinged to swing offstage.

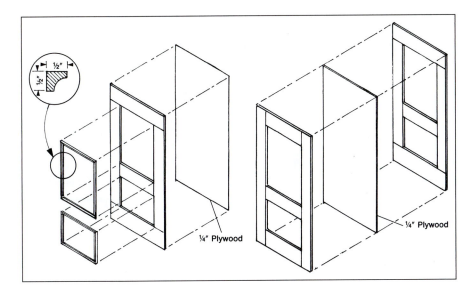

Figure 11.21
Trim is attached to a plywood door to provide appropriate decoration.

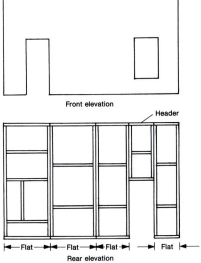

Front elevation

Rear elevation

Figure 11.22
Flats can be joined together to create a wall unit.

Rigid Joining   If the multiflat wall does not need to fold, the flats can be joined to form a rigid unit (Figure 11.23) in the following manner:

1.   Lay the flats face up in their proper order. Where adjacent flats butt together, attach tight-pin hinges to the stiles, as shown in Figure 11.23.

2.   Cover the joint and hinges with a dutchman. Fray ¼ inch of the edges of a 5- to 6-inch-wide strip of cloth (the same material as the flat covering), and attach it to the flat by coating one side of it and the stiles with latex, acrylic, or vinyl paint the same color as the **prime coat.** Apply the dutchman to the joint, smooth out any wrinkles, and allow to dry. (You don't have to put the dutchman on at this time. You can wait until you are doing the other painting.)

3.   Turn the hinged wall unit onto its back, and attach **stiffening battens.** Stiffening battens are 1 × 3s, on edge, that are attached to the back of a multiflat wall as stabilizers. The stiffening battens are held in place with tight-pin hinges. One flap of the hinge is attached to the batten and the other to a stile or toggle bar of the flat. To keep the stiffening batten in the proper position, the hinges are attached alternately to opposite sides of the batten. If the stiffening batten needs to be removed for shifting, the tight-pin hinges should be replaced with loose-pin hinges so the pins can be removed.

prime coat: The first coat of paint applied to the flats, to develop a relatively uniform color and surface to the wall units.

stiffening batten: A length of 1 × 3 attached to a multiflat wall unit to keep it from wiggling.

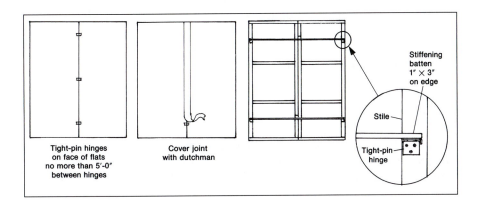

Figure 11.23
Rigid flat-joining techniques.

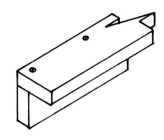

Figure 11.24
An effective stiffening batten can be made from two 1 × 3s.

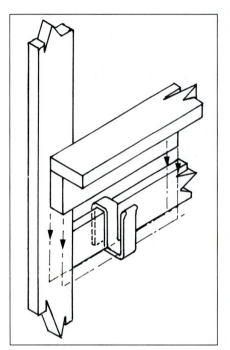

Figure 11.25
S hooks can be used to hold removable stiffening battens.

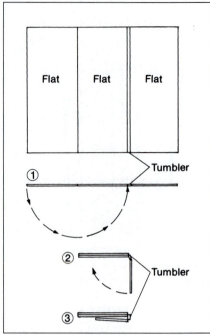

Figure 11.26
A tumbler permits the flats being booked to fold completely.

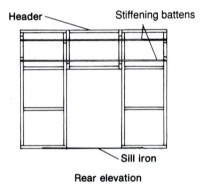

Figure 11.27
A header can be used to create a doorway.

book: To fold hinged flats together (so that they resemble a book).

tumbler: A ¾-inch-thick-by-1-inch-wide (or 1 × 3) piece of stock used as a spacer when three or more flats are going to be booked.

header: A small flat that can be placed between two standard-sized flats to create a doorway or window.

book ceiling: Two large flats about the same width as the proscenium arch, stored in a booked position in the flies; when needed to create a ceiling, they are opened and lowered onto the walls of the set.

Some technicians prefer to lay the stiffening battens on their sides and attach them to the flats with screws. Although this method holds the flats together, it does not provide nearly the stiffening effect that is supplied by the 1 × 3 standing on edge. However, if another 1 × 3 is screwed to the edge of the stiffening batten, as shown in Figure 11.24, the stiffening effect will be regained.

Flexible Joining Flexible joining uses the same principles as rigid joining, with the exception that the stiffening batten is removable. The flats are joined with tight-pin hinges on the faces of the flats, and the joint is covered with a dutchman. To make the stiffening batten removable, attach it with loose-pin hinges. To remove the batten, take the pins out of the hinges. S hooks provide another method of attaching a removable batten, as shown in Figure 11.25.

If more than two flats are going to be **booked,** you will have to use a **tumbler.** A tumbler is basically a miniflat. It is a piece of ¾-inch stock the full height of the flats but only 1 inch wide. A tumbler can also be made from a 1 × 3. It acts as a spacer between two flats and allows the flats to be fully closed, as shown in Figure 11.26. It is attached to the other flats with tight-pin hinges and covered with a dutchman.

When joining flats, you can use **headers** to create doors or archways simply by placing them between two regular-sized flats, as shown in Figure 11.27.

Ceilings Ceilings for sets are primarily used on proscenium stages. They are really large, horizontal flats, but they do provide some special challenges simply because of their size. The **book ceiling** (Figure 11.28) is a permanent piece of stage equipment in many proscenium theatres. It is composed of two large flats approximately the same width as the proscenium arch. The depth of the opened book ceiling is normally about 16 to 20 feet. It can be stored on a single counterweight line.

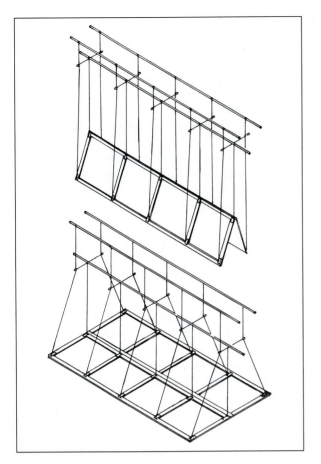

Figure 11.28
A book ceiling.

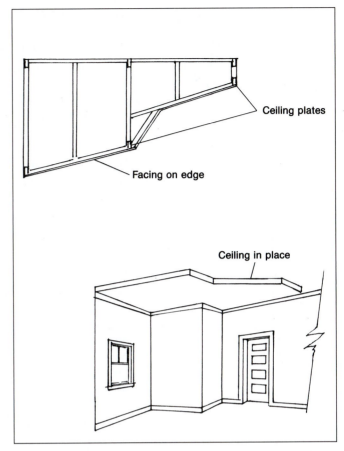

Figure 11.29
An irregular ceiling.

Irregular ceiling pieces (Figure 11.29) that do not completely cover the set can be built just as any other flat is. They are normally built of 1 × 4 stock for additional strength. Spot lines of piano wire can be dropped from the grid or a batten to support the downstage edge of the ceiling.

Soft Scenery

Soft scenery refers to unframed fabric units such as drops and draperies, which are usually suspended from the grid, a batten, or some type of structure capable of supporting their weight.

Drops   Drops are large, flat curtains that have no fullness. There are two primary methods of attaching drops to their respective supporting battens: ties and batten clamps.

Tie-Supported Drops   Probably the easiest way of hanging a drop is to tie it to the batten. Ties (which can be made from strips of scrap muslin, ½-inch heavy cotton tape, 36-inch shoelaces, or similar materials) are attached to the top of the drop and then tied to the batten. Cotton-tape ties can be sewn to the 4-inch jute backing tape at the top hem of the drop, as shown in Figure 11.30. The other kinds of ties are used in conjunction with grommets in the jute-tape backing of the drop.

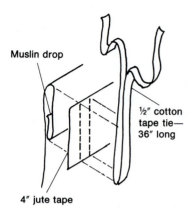

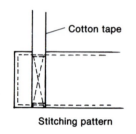

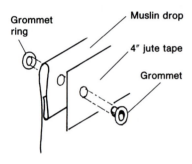

Figure 11.30
Methods of attaching drops to battens.

The grommet-reinforced holes are usually spaced on 1-foot centers across the width of the drop. The ties (ideally 36 to 40 inches long) are looped through the grommet holes and tied to the batten.

Batten-Clamp Drops   Drops are sometimes attached to a counterweight batten with batten clamps. The batten clamp facilitates rapid hanging or removal of a drop from the batten. The top of the drop is sandwiched between two 1 × 3s, as shown in Figure 11.31. The batten clamp is designed to hold the wooden batten "sandwich" without touching the drop.

A variety of effects can be achieved with drops. Drops are generally hung on an upstage batten and provide a background such as a forest, street scene, or the upstage wall of a ballroom. To an extent, the effects the drops create are dependent on the type of material from which the drop is made and the manner in which it is painted and lit.

Opaque Drops   Commonly made of heavyweight muslin, opaque drops are painted with opaque paints (scene paint, casein, latex, acrylic, and so on) and are lit from the front. The audience cannot see through them.

Translucent Drops   Made of heavyweight muslin, translucent drops are painted with dyes or a combination of dye and opaque paint and are lit from both front and back. This makes the areas that have been dyed translucent, increasing the apparent depth of the scene. Since any seams would show when such drops were back-lit, they are frequently made from seamless muslin 33 feet wide. If the translucent area is fairly small, the drop can sometimes be made so that any seams fall in the opaque painted areas.

Scrim Drops   Made from sharkstooth scrim or theatrical gauze, scrim drops have the unique ability to become transparent when the scene behind the drop is lit. The material can be painted with dyes or thinned paint. Be sure that the paint does not fill the large holes in the fabric.

Cutout Drops   Cutout drops have sections or pieces of the drop actually cut out of the material. The sense of depth in a design can be greatly enhanced by the use of a series of cutout drops placed in back of one another. The drops are painted before they are cut to keep the cut edges from curling. Bobbinet or similar loose-weave netting can be glued to the back of the drop to support the cutout areas if necessary.

Draperies   The two types of draperies used in the theatre are discussed elsewhere in this book. Stage draperies are covered in Chapter 4, and the drapes and curtains used to decorate sets will be discussed in Chapter 13, "Stage Properties."

 ## Three-Dimensional Scenery

Although flats and architectural trim actually have three dimensions, the term *three-dimensional scenery* generally refers to the construction of platforms, stairs, and similar objects.

Stage Platforming

Directors love multilevel stage floors, because they make it easy to create interesting blocking pictures. Platforms are used to create these levels. There are several types of platforms and a number of techniques for joining them.

PRODUCTION INSIGHTS
Scenic Specialty Fabrics

A variety of fabrics can be used for special scenic-construction purposes. These fabrics are not normally available in local fabric stores and must be purchased from scenic supply houses.

Sharkstooth Scrim

The 30-foot-wide, seamless cotton material called sharkstooth scrim has a unique property. When lit from the front, the material is opaque. When light is taken off the fabric and objects behind it are lit, the scrim becomes transparent because the material has a very open weave that creates rectangles of open space about $3/16$ inch wide by $3/16$ inch high.

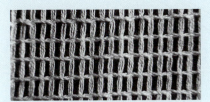

A close-up view of sharkstooth scrim.

It is available from scenic-fabric supply houses in natural (a creamy white), white, and black. It can be painted with dye or paint, although if paint is used, care must be taken to avoid filling the open spaces.

Sharkstooth scrim is used for transparent drops, in illusion effects, and in similar applications. It can also be used as a diffusion drop (a drop that softens light) for cyc lighting. If sharkstooth scrim is hung in front of a muslin cyc, it diffuses and softens the effects of the cyc lighting and creates a greater illusion of depth.

Bobbinet

Another 30-foot-wide, open-weave cotton material is bobbinet. It is lighter in weight than sharkstooth scrim, is more transparent, and has a hexagonal weave. It is also available from scenic supply houses in natural, white, or black. It can be used as a substitute for glass in windows, as a diffusion drop for cyc lighting, as net backing for cutout drops, and in similar applications.

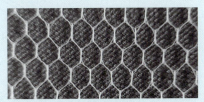

A close-up view of bobbinet.

Theatrical Gauze

Theatrical gauze is a cotton fabric with a fine-mesh weave similar to cheesecloth, but its threads are thicker and the weave is slightly tighter. It is 72 inches wide and can be purchased from scenic-fabric supply houses in natural, black, and a limited range of colors. Its applications are similar to those of sharkstooth scrim with the exception of those situations where the seams every 6 feet would prove objectionable.

A close-up view of theatrical gauze.

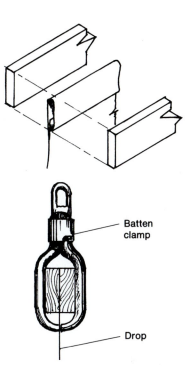

Figure 11.31
A drop that has to be quickly removed from the batten can be supported with batten clamps.

Rigid Wooden Platform   Probably the easiest stage platform to build, the rigid wooden platform, is also the least expensive. An added bonus is that the legs are detachable, so its height can be varied easily.

The framing for a rigid platform is generally made of 2 × 4 although 1 × 6 or 2 × 6 can also be used. The frame is a ladderlike construction with the rungs, or **joists**, spaced no more than two feet apart, as shown in Figure 11.32. Rigid platforms can be easily constructed in almost any irregular shape, but standard rigid platforms that are kept in a theatre's inventory of stock scenery are normally 4 feet wide by 8 feet long. They can be legged using a variety of techniques illustrated a little later in the chapter.

joists: Parallel beams that support flooring.

Figure 11.32
A rigid wooden platform consists of a top and a ladderlike supporting structure.

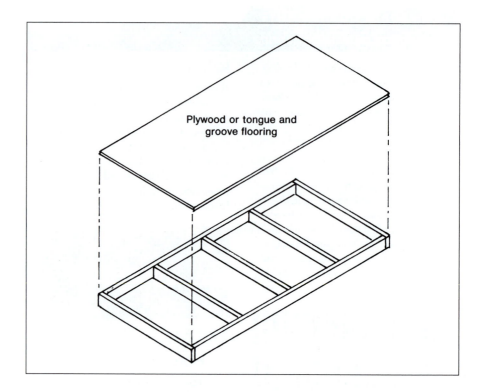

Plywood or tongue and groove flooring

Figure 11.33
Stressed-skin construction principles.

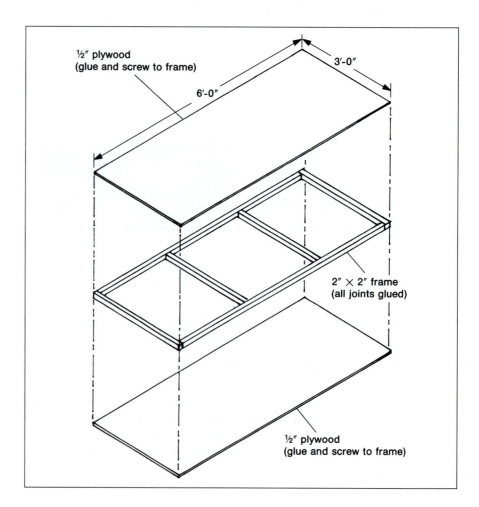

½" plywood
(glue and screw to frame)

6'-0"

3'-0"

2" × 2" frame
(all joints glued)

½" plywood
(glue and screw to frame)

Stressed-Skin Platform   The concept of stressed-skin construction is illustrated in Figure 11.33. A wooden support frame is covered on both the top and bottom surfaces with plywood. The advantages of this deceptively simple structure are many: they're lighter and stiffer (which means they have less give/sag/bounce) than similarly sized rigid platforms; they take less storage space; they have a high strength to weight ratio; and they can carry a heavier load than the typical ¾-inch plywood-covered rigid platform. The primary disadvantage of stressed-skin platforms? They require very precise, time-consuming, construction techniques. That being said, the advantages that stressed-skin construction offers clearly outweigh the disadvantages.

Probably the most common type of stressed-skin platform used in theatre today is the triscuit—probably so-called because the platforms look like giant versions of the little crackers—a design developed at the Yale School of Drama in 1990.[1,2] The triscuit is a 4 foot by 4 foot stressed-skin structure 2½ inches thick, illustrated in Figure 11.34. The frame must be built of specifically dimensioned, knot-free lumber. The top and bottom skins must be glued to the frame, with no gaps or dry spots, and both skins must be screwed to the frame with the screws spaced on **6-inch centers** around the perimeter and along each cross member. Specific plans containing design and construction information for building triscuits can be found on the websites identified in footnotes 1 or 2 at the bottom of this page or by doing an Internet search for "triscuit stressed-skin platforms" and selecting either, or both, site from the resulting list.

Experimentation in the theatrical use of stressed-skin construction has been ongoing for the past thirty years. At Penn State University a 1-inch panel of extruded polystyrene (Styrofoam) has been sandwiched between OSB skins,[3] which results in a platform only 2 inches thick.

Another theatrical use of stressed-skin construction was developed in the late 1970s.[4] This technique involves sandwiching **honeycomb paper** (Figure 11.35) between two ½-inch plywood skins. This process is basically the same way that hollow-core doors are made. To make a hollow-core door, a core of honeycomb paper is sandwiched between two sheets of ⅛-inch plywood. The outer edges of the door are made of wood that is just thick enough to keep the door from flexing. Honeycomb paper fills the interior area bordered by the wooden frame. The inner sides of both plywood skins are covered with glue so they bond to not only the frame but the top and bottom edges—yes, that narrow edge of paper—of the honeycomb paper. This technique results in a very strong door that is remarkably light.

The same process is used to make honeycomb paper platforms. The inside face of one of the outer skins is liberally covered with a strong adhesive such as polyvinyl or white glue, the honeycomb paper is placed, edge down, on the face, then the inside face of the other skin is slathered with glue—using a brush or a short nap paint roller to apply the glue pretty much assures the fast application of an even, thorough coating—and that skin is placed on top of the honeycomb paper. Careful alignment before finally lowering the top skin into place will assure that the honeycomb paper isn't crumpled. The entire surface needs to be

6-inch centers: Spaced 6 inches apart from the center of one item to the center of the next.

honeycomb paper: A manufactured paper product with a hexagonal structure similar to a honeycomb.

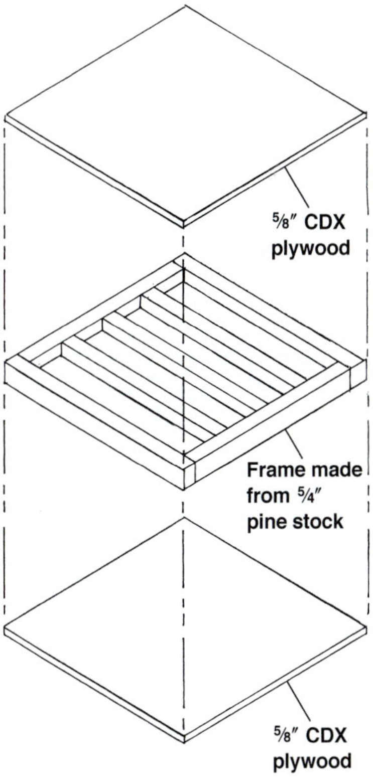

[1] Triscuit information source: http://www.hstech.org/howto/carpentr/plats/mpplats3.htm, pp. 1–4.

[2] Triscuit information source: http://www.google.com/search?q=cache:Q29YiHmUsY4J:ocw.mit .edu/NR/rdonlyres/Music-and-Theater-Arts/21M-735Spring2004/FE368A89-71AF-4573-81D7-AB373C54B593/0/drkp_tn4.pdf+Triscuit+stressed+skin+platforms&hl=en&gl=us&ct=clnk&cd =1, pp. 1–4.

[3] Ibid. p. 4.

[4] Tom Corbett, "Laminating Stage Platforms Using Honeycomb Paper," *Theatre Design and Technology* (Winter 1980): 24–25, 57–58.

⅝" CDX plywood

Frame made from ⅝" pine stock

⅝" CDX plywood

Figure 11.34
A triscuit. See text for details.

laminating: The process of gluing thin pieces of wood together to make a thicker piece.

compound curves: A surface that curves in more than one direction (like a ball) or changes the radius of its curve (like a playground slide.)

Figure 11.35
Honeycomb-laminate platform construction principles.

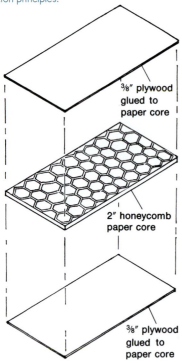

⅜" plywood glued to paper core

2" honeycomb paper core

⅜" plywood glued to paper core

Enlarged view of honeycomb paper

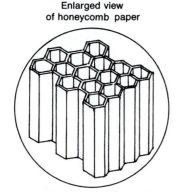

Figure 11.36
Skins for curved-top, honeycomb-paper stressed-skin platforms are made by laminating multiple layers of thin plywood. Be sure to separate the joints on adjacent layers of plywood by at least 1 foot 6 inches.

clamped while the glue cures. Pieces of ¼-inch steel plate or counterweights can be used. Vacuum pressure can be used instead of weights. To vacuum clamp, the assembled platform is covered with heavyweight plastic sheeting, and the plastic is taped to the shop floor with gaffer's tape. (Be sure to thoroughly wipe the area where you're going to tape with a damp rag to take up all the dirt and dust so the tape will adhere to the floor.) Use a vacuum pump to remove the air from under the cover. The "out" or "blow" vent on a shop vacuum will quickly exhaust most of the air, but a genuine vacuum pump may be needed to remove the remainder. The clamping pressure needs to be maintained for the length of time that it takes the adhesive to set—generally 3–4 hours. It's better if you can maintain the clamping pressure overnight. Depending on the type of glue used and the shop heat and humidity, the adhesive should be fully cured in roughly 24 hours. But no weight or stress should be placed on the units for a day or two longer. The edges of the platforms are then filled in with ½-inch stock or MDF.

The honeycomb paper stressed-skin technique can be used to make curved surfaces simply by **laminating** the skins from thinner sheets of plywood. Gentle curves can be made by laminating two ¼-inch sheets of plywood as shown in Figure 11.36. Sharper or **compound curves** can be made by gluing together three or four sheets of ⅛-inch lauan plywood. To make the curves, you have to construct some type of sturdy form or jig that will brace the plywood veneer sheets into the desired arc and allow you to place weights or vacuum clamp the structure as the glue between the sheets cures.

Both the Styrofoam panel- and honeycomb-paper-core stressed-skin platforms have an inherent additional advantage over other types of platforming. Because the Styrofoam or paper core absorbs sound, they're quieter than the wooden triscuit and much quieter than old-style rigid platforming.

All stressed-skin platforms are designed to be legged using a stud-wall legging system that will be discussed later in this chapter.

Rigid Steel-Tubing Platforms   Steel tubing can be used to fabricate rigid platforms. The framework for the platforms can be made from either 16-gauge 1½-inch square tubing, 16-gauge 1 × 2 tubing (with the 2-inch dimension placed vertically), or ⅛-inch by 2-inch by 2-inch angle iron. The general shape of the platform framework is similar to its wooden cousin. The exact number of required cross-sectional pieces, called stringers, is determined by the intended covering material. If the deck is going to be ¾-inch plywood or OSB then the spacing between the stringers is normally 2 feet. If the deck is going to be ⅝-inch OSB then the stringers need to be placed no more than 1 foot 4 inches apart.

Rigid steel platforms can be legged either using the stud-wall legging system or in the traditional manner. Figure 11.37 illustrates a design developed by Stan-

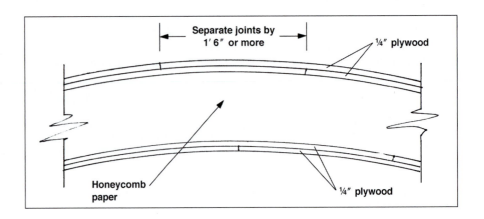

Separate joints by 1' 6" or more

¼" plywood

Honeycomb paper

¼" plywood

cil Campbell.[5] The framework is made from 16-gauge 1 × 2 steel tubing placed on edge, and the top from ¾-inch plywood. **Gussets,** ¼-inch steel plates predrilled in a pattern to accept casters or legs, are inset on the stringers at the corners of the platform. Casket locks are attached to the underside of the platform in a uniform pattern so that the platform can be locked to an adjacent unit.

The deck of steel-tubing platforms is normally made from ¾-inch plywood or ⅝-or ¾-inch OSB.

The Texas Triscuit was developed at Trinity University.[6] Like the triscuit it is a 4-foot by 4-foot platform. But the frame is constructed of 1½-inch square-steel tubing, and the bottom isn't covered with a second skin, so technically it is a "metal-framed rigid platform" and is not a stressed-skin structure. The top is made of ⅝-inch OSB. It is designed to be used with a stud wall legging system, which will be discussed a little later. Complete design and construction details for the Texas Triscuit can be found at the footnoted website.

Platform Tops   Platform tops, also called "decks" or "lids," are typically made from ¾-inch AD plywood or ⅝-inch or ¾-inch OSB. Because ⅝-inch OSB is more "springy" than ¾-inch plywood, when using this covering material space the platform's cross stringers no further apart than 1 foot 4 inches on center. If the deck is ¾-inch plywood or OSB the spacing between stringers normally can be 2 feet on center unless special circumstances dictate otherwise.

The top for a wooden-framed platform can be attached with nails but using screws will help prevent squeaking. If the frame is metal the deck is normally attached using flat-head **ply-metal** TEK screws. Pilot holes normally are not necessary when using these self-tapping screws on 16-gauge metal tubing, but generally will be needed when the framework is made from ⅛-inch angle iron. Whether nails or screws are used you generally want to space them about 9 inches on center around the perimeter of the platform and 1 foot on center on the cross members. Some technicians like to run a bead of **construction adhesive** along the top of all framing members before attaching the lid. This permanent bond also helps prevent squeaking.

Individual platform tops are not usually covered. But rugging is frequently applied to the surface of a finished platform structure for decorative reasons and/or to muffle noise. For safety reasons, the rugging should be of uniform height to prevent the actors from tripping.

Soundproofing of rigid platforming can be achieved using one of two methods: (1) a ⅛-inch thick strip of ethafoam the width of the framing member can be stapled or glued with construction adhesive to the top surface of the entire frame before the lid is attached; (2) a sheet of ½-inch sound board—Celotex or the equivalent—can be nailed or glued to the frame before the top is attached.

Platforms are frequently covered with Masonite to create a smooth, uniform surface that can be painted. See the box, "Stage Floors," on page 55 for a discussion of the use of Masonite as a floor covering.

Rigid Platform Legs   Legs for rigid platforms can be fabricated from a variety of materials, as shown in Figure 11.38. All platform legs over 18 inches tall should be braced, regardless of whether they are wooden or metal, because the sideways forces exerted on the platform by the movement of the actors can easily break either the joint between the leg and the platform or, possibly, the leg itself.

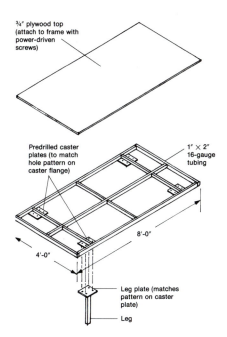

Figure 11.37
Steel tube platforms are similar in appearance to rigid wooden platforms.

gusset: A triangular piece of material used to reinforce a corner joint.

ply-metal: Refers to TEK screws specifically designed to attach plywood to metal. The flat head of the screw is typically driven flush with, or slightly into, the top surface of the plywood.

construction adhesive: Also called panel adhesive; an adhesive contained in a caulking tube; dispensed with a caulking gun. Available in a number of formulations for use in gluing wall panels to studs (wood to wood), Styrofoam to wood, wood to metal, and so forth.

[5] This design is based on the following article: Stancil Campbell, "Steel Framed Stock Platforming," *Theatre Design and Technology* (Summer 1984): 16–20.

[6] Texas triscuit information: http://www.hstech.org/howto/carpentr/plats/mpplats3.htm, pp. 4–6.

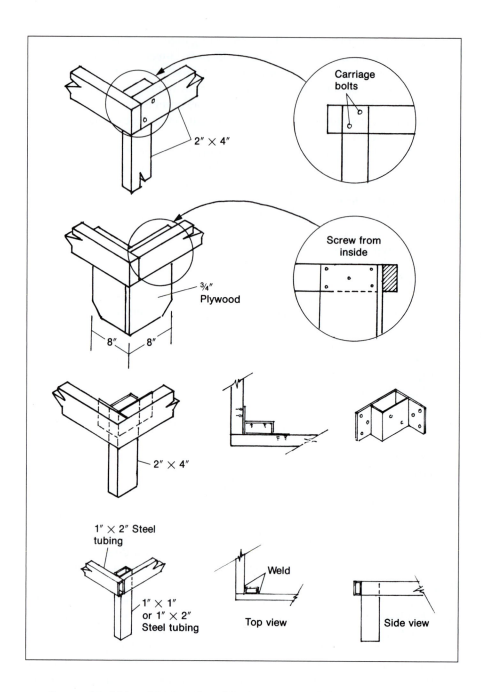

Braces should be placed so that they form a triangle between the leg and the rail to take advantage of the structural strength of the triangular form, as shown in Figure 11.39A. Braces will be effective if placed at any angle between 30 and 60 degrees, as shown in Figure 11.39B, although 45 degrees provides the maximum strength. There should be no more than 4 feet between bracing support points, as shown in Figure 11.39C.

The strength of the rigid wooden platform is primarily based on the depth of the wood used to construct the frame. There are pragmatic limits to the size of a rigid wooden platform that are loosely based on the weight of the assembled platform and the platform storage space available in the theatre. Rigid platforms are generally made no larger than 4 by 8 feet.

Stud Wall Legging System   Stressed-skin platforms, because of their smooth bottom surface, and metal-frame platforms, because of the relatively short height

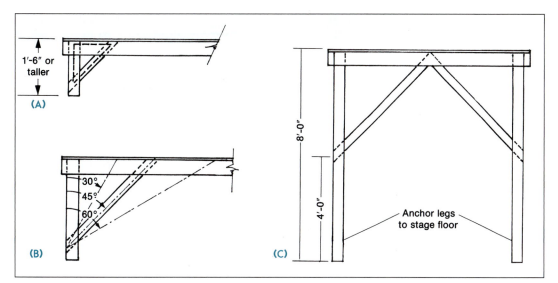

1'-6" or taller

(A)

30°
45°
60°

(B)

8'-0"

4'-0"

Anchor legs to stage floor

(C)

Figure 11.39
Platform-leg bracing techniques.

of their framework, can't be legged using any of the traditional methods used with rigid wooden platforming. Enter the stud wall legging system.

The stud wall legging system is composed of stud walls, which are illustrated in Figure 11.40. The framework—both the vertical elements (studs) and the top and bottom plates—for the stud wall, Figure 11.40A, is constructed of 2 × 4s. The studs are normally spaced 2 feet apart although heavier than normal loads may require closer spacing.

Each stud wall section must be diagonally crossbraced with 1 × 3s or 1 × 4s, as shown in Figure 11.40B, to keep it from turning into a parallelogram. Each piece of diagonal bracing needs to be attached with two nails or screws to each stud that it crosses. The stud wall must also be braced perpendicular to its longitudinal axis, as shown in Figure 11.40C, to keep it standing upright. The bottom plate of the stud wall is nailed or screwed to the stage floor or supporting wagon. Triscuits and other types of platforming are typically attached to the top plate of the stud walls with bolts or lag screws, with the bolt heads inset into the plywood so their tops are flush with its surface.

Like traditional platform legs, stud walls are typically spaced 2 feet apart under the platforms they are supporting. Unlike traditional legging methods the platforms resting on stud walls are supported along their entire length. Figure 11.41 illustrates how the stud wall system is used to support 4 foot by 4 foot triscuits. It is extremely important that triscuits, and other stressed-skin platforms, be placed on the stud walls so the grain of the covering plywood is perpendicular to the axis of the stud wall. This will ensure that the triscuit's internal stringers are supported by the wall if, and this is a very important point, the triscuit has been built according to plans. If this guideline is *not* followed—if the triscuit is placed so its internal stringers are not supported by the stud wall—the load-bearing capacity of the platform will be considerably weakened. The stud walls can be built to any length, although for economy and ease of handling they are generally made in 8- to 12-foot lengths. If a longer run is necessary, several shorter sections can be butted together. The walls can be built to any reasonable height, although 12 to 14 feet is a generally accepted maximum height.

Once the walls are constructed, placed, and braced in their proper positions onstage the triscuits, steel-framed platforms, or traditional rigid wooden platforms can be quickly loaded onto the top of the walls and secured in place.

There are several distinct advantages to the stud wall system when comparing it to traditional legging methods. The finished platform is much stronger and

Studs

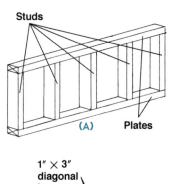

(A) Plates

1" × 3" diagonal braces

(B)

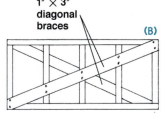

1" × 3" diagonal braces

(C)

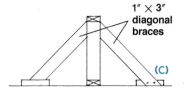

Figure 11.40
A stud wall legging system. (A) The wall sections are made of 2 × 4. Each wall section must be diagonally braced in two directions to keep it upright. The diagonal bracing is generally made of 1 × 3 or 1 × 4 lumber. (B) The 2 × 4 framework is diagonally braced to prevent movement along its longitudinal axis. (C) Diagonal bracing between the wall and floor prevents sideways movement.

kit-cutting To cut *all* the individual pieces needed to make something *before* assembly is started—like a model airplane kit.

carriage: The part of a stair unit that supports the tread and risers.

tread: The horizontal surface of a stair.

riser: The vertical face of a stair unit.

score: To cut partially through.

DESIGN INSPIRATIONS
Scenic Production

The following discussion is based on and quotes from "Hooping It Up," by Si Morse (Stage Directions, March 1999, pp. 9–11).

Design inspiration—the inspiration for any good design solution—is just as important for a technician as it is for a designer.

In the Seattle Children's Theatre production of *The Former One-on-One Basketball Champion* by Israel Horovitz, technical director Si Morse devised an inspired solution to a very real problem. The play tells the story of a junior-high basketball hotshot who encounters a depressed former basketball star at a city playground. The kid challenges the star, and they exchange views on life while playing one-on-one. The action of the play requires the two actors to play basketball—dribbling, jumping, and actually making shots.

The design challenge for the technical director came from the "booming" sound that the platformed court made as the actors dribbled, jumped, and cut.

Morse's first thoughts were to cover the platform with carpet. "But the carpet absorbed not only sound energy," Morse said, "it also absorbed some of the ball's rebound energy. Similarly, any kind of plastic foam (with a layer of plywood on top) absorbed rebound as well as sound energy." Morse thought of using multiple layers of particle board. Experimentation showed that five or six layers of particle board deadened the sound, but the cost exceeded the available budget.

An inspired potential solution presented itself at a building supply store. "I noticed bags of 'cold-patch,' granular asphalt for tamping into pot holes in a driveway," Morse said. He built a 2-foot by 4-foot wooden box and tamped the cold patch into a 2-inch layer on top. "Even with the box propped across 2 × 4s, the ball rebounded normally, and while it 'thwacked' on the asphalt, that was a much shorter and quieter sound—there was no 'boom.'"

Morse "cut a deal" with a neighborhood paving company. The platform-cum-basketball court was paved with 1 ½ inches of asphalt and hand-rolled in about an hour.

"By the next day, all the fans in the building had removed the odor, and the asphalt had cooled so the designer could paint stripes and 'dirt' on it."

Striking the court wasn't a problem. The asphalt was easily pried up with large steel bars, and the same company that "paved the stage" hauled the material away.

The lesson to be learned from this example is *Don't overlook the obvious.* Many of us become focused on "building it theatrically." Sometimes the real thing works even better.

Figure 11.41
Stud wall legs are used to support platforms. (A) Stud walls supporting a triscuit. (B) If properly installed—if the triscuit's internal structure is resting on wall rather than running parallel to it—the edges of two adjacent triscuits can be supported by the top plate of a single 2 × 4 stud wall.

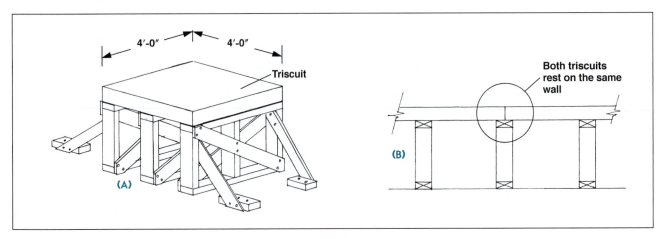

"shake resistant." The height variations between the tops of adjacent platforms are almost nonexistent, particularly if working with stock triscuits. Additionally, it is much easier to build a raked stage by using raked stud walls than legging individual platforms with any of the traditional legging methods. Finally, since most of these walls are put together by **kit-cutting** the materials and using either pneumatic nailers or power screwdrivers, the construction time for assembling the entire platform area is normally reduced, sometimes significantly, when compared with traditional legging methods.

Connecting Platforms When more than one platform is used to create a new floor level, the platforms must be connected to improve the lateral stability of the unit. Fastening them together can be accomplished in a number of ways.

Bolting Wooden platforms can be bolted together by drilling through the framing members of adjacent units and using ⅜-by-4-inch bolts, as shown in Figure 11.42. Two or three bolts per long side and one at each end are usually sufficient.

Clamping If the platforms need to be shifted during the production, C clamps can be substituted for the bolts described in the process above, as illustrated in Figure 11.43.

Casket Locks Casket locks can be inset into the framing members of rigid wooden platforms, as shown in Figure 11.44, to tie the platforms together. Casket locks can also be welded to the bottom of the frame on steel-framed platforms.

 If casket locks are attached to every stock platform in a standard pattern (Figure 11.45), it will be easy and quick to lock any platform to an adjacent unit of the same height. Because platforms equipped with casket locks can be locked or unlocked quickly, they can be used for either permanent or temporary staging.

Stairs

Two basic types of stairs are used in scenic construction: dependent and independent. The dependent units require support from some other element, usually a platform, for support; the independent units are self-supporting, as shown in Figure 11.46. Although the primary difference between independent and dependent staircases is in their method of support, the actual units are built in much the same manner.

 The **carriage** can be built in a variety of ways, as shown in Figure 11.47. Carriages can be cut from 1 × 12 for stair runs of less than 6 feet. For runs over 6 feet or in those instances where the stairs must support an unusual amount of weight, 2 × 12 should be used.

 The **treads** can be made from ¾-inch stock or plywood. They should be cut with the grain running parallel with the long side of the tread (Figure 11.48A) to take advantage of the strength of the wood. For safety reasons, the unsupported span of a tread should never exceed 2 feet 6 inches. **Risers** are usually made from ¼-inch tempered Masonite or plywood. If the riser has to curve, ⅛-inch Masonite or plywood can be used, and the back of the ¼-inch sheet stock can be **scored** so that the wood can be bent more easily. Scoring can be done by adjusting the blade height of the radial-arm saw so that it cuts about halfway through the wood. Depending on the arc of the anticipated bend, cuts are spaced between ⅜ and 1 inch apart.

 Although the size of treads and risers varies considerably, 10 to 12 inches could be considered a fairly normal tread depth, and a riser of 6 to 7 inches would be typical and appropriate.

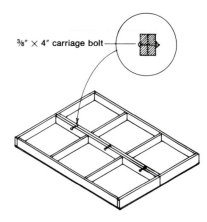

Figure 11.42
Platform modules can be bolted together to create a larger platform.

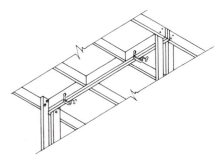

Figure 11.43
Platforms can be temporarily joined together with C clamps.

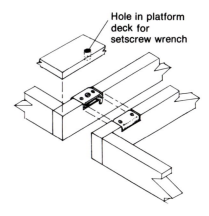

Figure 11.44
Casket locks can be used for permanent or temporary platform locking.

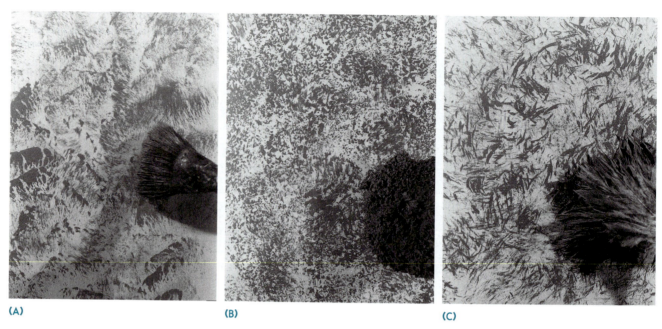

(A)   (B)   (C)

FIGURE 12.10
Stippling with a brush (A), with a sponge (B), and with a feather duster (C). Stippling is frequently used to create the appearance of surface texture.

nozzle, strain the paint through cheesecloth, window screening, or commercially available paint strainers before putting it into the sprayer. Be sure to thoroughly clean the sprayer after each use.

Stippling   Although similar to spattering, stippling applies a heavier texture to the scenery. As shown in Figure 12.10, stippling can be done with the tip of a brush, a sponge, or a feather duster. It can also be done with the frayed end of a rope or the edge of a piece of burlap.

Stippling is accomplished by loading one of these applicators with paint and touching it to the scenery. To avoid making an obvious pattern, you need to constantly change the position of the applicator and the pressure with which you apply it to the scenery.

Dry Brushing   Dry brushing is painting with a brush that holds very little paint. Just the tip of the brush is dipped in the paint. Any paint that has been picked up by the bristles is scraped off on the lip of the bucket. The brush is then lightly drawn across the surface to deposit a linear, irregular pattern of paint (see Figure 12.11).

Dry brushing is very effective in creating the appearance of wood. If the dry-brushing paint(s) is fairly close in hue and value to the color of the base coat, the result will look like smooth wood. If the contrast between the hue and value of the base and dry-brush paints is greater, the result will look more rough hewn.

FIGURE 12.11
Dry brushing is often used to create the appearance of wood grain. The tip of the brush is dipped in paint, scraped across the lip of the bucket (to remove excess paint), and lightly dragged across the surface of the work.

Lining   Lining involves painting narrow, straight lines of varying width. The lines are painted with lining or angle sash brushes, which were illustrated in Figure 12.1, with larger brushes creating wider lines. A straightedge is used in conjunction with the lining brush, as shown in Figure 12.12A.

Lining can be used to create the appearance of depth, as shown in Figure 12.12B and C. The illusion is primarily achieved through the use of highlight, shade, and shadow lines. The effect of the **source light** on an object will determine where the highlight and shadow lines need to be painted. On the bricks, notice the highlight at the top edge and the shadows below. On the paneling, see how the placement of the highlight, shade, and shadow lines creates the illusion of

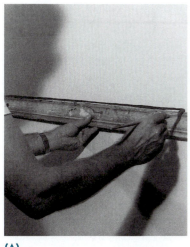

(A)

(B)

(C)

(D)

(E)

FIGURE 12.12
Lining is accomplished with a straightedge and a lining brush (A). It is frequently used to create the illusion of highlight and shadow, as shown in B, C, and D. E shows how lining is done when painting "down"—painting on the floor or mat. (Photos D and E courtesy of Kimb Williamson.)

depth. Both of these examples are effective because the highlights and shadows look as if they were created by some specific source light. The location of the source light should appear to be some specific source within the design—either a practical onstage lamp or a specific position and angle (agreed on by the scenic and lighting designers) for an offstage, unseen source such as the sun. It is important that you do not put a gloss or shiny topcoat or glaze over these carefully created highlight/shadow illusions. To do so will destroy the effect.

Applications of Painting Techniques

Figure 12.13 shows a potpourri of fairly standard applications of the various painting techniques that have been discussed in this section. Careful study of the individual pictures can be helpful in understanding how the images were created.

Specialized Finishing Techniques

The following techniques are not used so frequently as the previously discussed methods of painting, but when the design opportunity presents itself, they can provide dazzling and effective results.

source light: The apparent source of light that is illuminating a scene or an object.

(A)

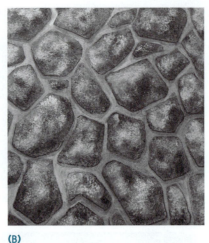

(B)

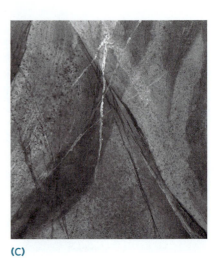

(C)

(D)

FIGURE 12.13
Scene-painting techniques can be combined to create a variety of realistic forms. Wood grain (A) is primarily accomplished with successive layers of dry brushing in (generally) two or three tones of paint and an overcoat of glaze(s) in one or more tints. Stone (B) is usually created by scumbling two or three tones of a similar hue with a light, uneven overlay of stippled or spattered highlight and shadow to provide a slightly rougher texture. Marble (C) is created by wet-blending (scumbling with a lot of paint) several tones or related hues in a loose, vaguely linear pattern and over-spattering with large drops of the same paint. Foliage (D) uses a combination of all techniques; the tree trunk and branches are created by scumbling and dry-brushing, the foliage and grass with scumbling, stippling, and spattering, and the distant bushes with stippling and a light spatter. Scene painting and photos for B, C, and D courtesy of Kimb Williamson.

Texturing   Texturing refers to the use of materials that create a three-dimensional relief on an otherwise flat surface. With the ready availability of manufactured texturing products, as well as a number of recipes for shop-mixed coatings, many illusions can be created that range from rough wood to brick, stone to tree bark, as well as stucco, ice, and snow. The number of textures that can be created is only limited by the scene painter's imagination.

These texturing products generally need to be applied to a solid surface so they won't crack or flake off if the scenery is moved. There are several products available that can be used as a coating over flexible foams such as polystyrene (Styrofoam) or ethafoam. General practice is that if a texture coating is going to be applied to flats those flats are hard-covered, usually with minimally ³⁄₁₆-inch plywood or hardboard. Because texture coats are heavier than paint and because each particular mixture or recipe has its own working characteristics it is highly advisable to make a test patch. Apply some of the texturing mix to a sample piece of the actual material that's covering the scenery to determine if it will adhere and how it's going to behave after you've applied it.

There are many commercial texturing products available from scenic or builder's suppliers that can be applied directly from the can and troweled, rolled, brushed, and otherwise annoyed, until they create the desired effect. Sculpt or Coat from Sculptural Arts Coatings (http://www.sculpturalarts.com) is an excellent smooth water-based plastic texture coating that will stick to just about anything—wood, metal, and most plastics. It is not particularly flexible when cured. It will stick to polystyrene (Styrofoam) but if the foam is flexed the Sculpt or Coat may crack. It is thick enough to be built up into three-dimensional shapes such as stucco, bricks, bark, adobe, and so forth. FoamCoat, CrystalGel, and FlexCoat are several coating products offered by Rosco (www.rosco.com). FoamCoat is a water-based hard protective coating for use on foam plastics such as polystyrene. CrystalGel is a water-based material used to create a clear coating on just about any surface. FlexCoat is a water-based coating designed to preserve and protect the flexible surface of most foam plastics—polyurethane, polystyrene, ethafoam, among others. Jaxsan 600 (by Plastic Coatings, Inc.) is a water-based roofing product that dries to a flexible, rubbery finish. It is good for coating polystyrene and other foam plastics as well as wood and metal. Joint compound—the premixed plaster used with drywall in home construction—is a good, if heavy, coating that is quite brittle when dry. In thin coats it will adhere to just about anything. Paint and/or commercial colorants can be added to any of the above-listed texturing products to color the basic texturing coat. They can also be supplemented with a wide variety of what are euphemistically referred to as additives—common materials such as sand, sawdust, *clean* kitty litter, newspaper, tissue—that can be added to texturing base to create a variety of useful textures.

Texturing coats with additives and colorants that are mixed in the shop are appropriately referred to as "goop." There is no limit to the variety of texturing coats that can be created as long as attention is paid to the compatibility of the products. Because most texturing products are water-based, compatibility usually won't be an issue, but it is important to check the labels and read the MSDS sheets for the products you'll be using before you mix them together. When creating your own batch of goop, consider not only the texture that you're trying to create but the surface upon which it's going to be applied. Is it going to be walked on? Are the actors wearing costumes that might be snagged by a highly textured surface? Is it going to be handled repeatedly? All of these considerations are used to determine the type of mixture that you should use. A semi-universal general recipe for an effective non-commercial, non-flexible texture coating would be a base of joint compound, thinned and supplemented with either Flexbond, white glue, or flexible glue until it is a good working thickness. Mix in any appropriate additives, paint, or colorants to create the desired look, then apply.

There are a delightfully wide variety of tools that can be used to apply texture coats. Basically the only rule about which applicator to use is that you want to use something that will get the material on the object being textured with as little mess as possible, while creating the desired texture. If an old piece of 1 × 3 works, that's great. Trowels, spackle knives, brooms, and large synthetic sponges can be used to quickly apply almost any mixture of goop. Rollers are generally more useful than brushes for smoothing it out. The ultimate texturing treatment depends entirely on the effect desired. The secret to creating a realistic texture is to carefully study an example of the actual thing that you're trying to copy and then duplicate its general shape, surface quality, and color.

Stenciling   Stencils are large cut patterns that facilitate the creation of repetitive, intricate designs such as wallpaper patterns. The stencil can be cut from **stencil paper,** a commercial product made of heavy, stiff paper impregnated or coated with oils that make the paper water-resistant. Stencil paper can be made in the shop by painting thin illustration board with a water-resisting coating such as shellac, lacquer, or spray varnish. Be sure to coat the paper *after* you have cut the design. The high-impact polystyrene plastic used for **vacuforming** is completely waterproof and is excellent for use as stencil material.

After the stencil is cut, it is normally framed with 1 × 2 stock to hold it flat and make it easier to handle. The paint can be applied with a brush, **stencil brush,** roller, paint sprayer, or sponge, as shown in Figure 12.14. Generally, spraying works best, simply because it is gentler on the stencil. Regardless of the application tool used, the stencil will have to be cleaned frequently to remove any excess paint that could be accidentally transferred to the scenery.

Translucency   An incredible depth can be created when you paint, and light, both the front and back of muslin-covered scenery. Although this technique, also called translucent painting, is normally used with drops, equally effective results can be achieved on flats and other framed scenery.

Imagine you are painting a landscape on a small drop that will be hung upstage of a window of an interior set. The normal tendency is to paint the entire scene with paint and light in from the front. However, if you paint the solid objects (ground and trees) with paint and the translucent or transparent items (sky

stencil paper: Stiff, water-resistant paper used for making stencils.

vacuforming: The process of shaping heated plastic, usually high-impact polystyrene, around a mold through the use of vacuum pressure.

stencil brush: A short, squat brush with a circular pattern of short, stiff bristles; the bristles are pressed onto, rather than stroked across, the work, to prevent the paint from bleeding under the edges of the stencil.

FIGURE 12.14
Stencils are often used to apply repetitive patterns, such as for wallpaper.

and clouds) with dye, you can light the drop from both the front and the back. The apparent depth that is created with this technique is really amazing.

The technique is particularly effective if the scene involves a sunset effect. If the front lights are dimmed and the back lights are up, the painted areas will appear in silhouette. If, after looking at the drop with the back lights turned on, the silhouetted areas still allow light to bleed through, the challenge can be solved by **backpainting.** On the back, or reverse, side of the scenery or drop simply paint the silhouetted area—only the silhouetted area—with a light coat of opaque paint, preferably black or dark brown to reduce reflection. Apply a relatively light coat—but thick enough to be opaque—when backpainting to prevent any paint from bleeding through the material and ruining the finished paint job on the front of the drop or scenery. The hue of the backlights, and projections, can be used to create spectacular sunset or night-sky effects.

Translucent painting can also be used to create stained-glass windows and similar effects. Be sure to work with the paint before the dye, because the paint will act as a "dam" to prevent the dye from creeping into other areas of the fabric.

Glazing and Glossing   The difference between glaze and gloss coats is simple. A glaze has a matte finish while a gloss coat is shiny—generally either satin or gloss. Both are applied over existing dry paint jobs. A glaze is a thin, translucent layer of very thin paint made by adding water to acrylic, vinyl, or casein paint. The one caveat is that the glaze must be translucent, not opaque. Its purpose is to tone the underlying paint job, not cover it. The purposes of glaze coats are varied: they can be tinted to tone down the brilliance or slightly change the hue of the paint job over which they are being applied; they are frequently used to add shadow details to the set. Glaze coats are normally applied by spattering or by applying a uniform coat with a brush or sea sponge or synthetic sponge. However, there aren't any laws that dictate the particular uses of glaze coats. Use the type of glaze that is appropriate to the specific design need.

Gloss coats, which impart a shine to whatever they're painted on, are generally used on furniture and natural woods. Thinned white glue, clear vinyl acrylic paint, lacquer, shellac, and polyurethane varnish are all frequently used to create gloss coats. The choice of which material to use is predicated on the use that the particular piece will receive. Finishes that are more water- and scratch-resistant (shellac, clear vinyl acrylic, polyurethane varnish) should be used for those objects that may be subjected to water or abrasive physical treatment.

Metallic Finishes   The types of material that can be used to create metallic finishes have been discussed in various other sections of this chapter. Briefly, bronzing powders, which are powdered metal (available from scenic supply houses or well-stocked art stores), are mixed with a vehicle and applied to the work. High-gloss materials such as shellac, clear vinyl acrylic, varnish, and polyester resin all work very well as vehicles for the bronzing powders. Bronzing powders are highly toxic. The standard safety caveat applies: Read, and follow, the information contained in the MSDSs for the products with which you are working.

The secret to a good metallic finish is the undercoat. The wood, plastic, or fabric to which you are applying your alchemy must be filled until there is absolutely no evidence of any wood grain or other texture. The best undercoat is polyester resin or Aqua resin. Generally, one coat of resin will fill any but the roughest surface.

After the undercoat has dried or cured, the bronzing powders or colorants are mixed with vehicle and applied to the work. For small areas, metallic spray paints create a nice metallic appearance if they are used on top of a smooth undercoat.

backpainting: Literally to paint on the back. You paint the back, or reverse, side of the scenery or drop.

There are healthier alternatives to bronzing powders. Mica powders, which come in a wide variety of colors, when mixed with **polyvinyl alcohol** (PVA) or clear vinyl acrylic base produce a highly reflective, metallic-like surface. An aluminum finish can be created by mixing silver mica powder with PVA and applying it over a matte gray-blue base color. Gold-tone mica powder applied over a muted dark yellow base coat produces a similarly convincing gold finish. The secret to this technique is that the colored base coat must have a matte finish. Experimenting with different colored mica powders and base coats will produce an amazing array of metallic finishes. A number of sources for mica powders can be found by doing a Web search for "mica powders." Additionally, many scenic and art paint manufacturers, such as Nova Color, Rosco, and Sculptural Arts Coatings, now sell a wide variety of water-based metallic paints that produce very convincing results when correctly applied over a base coat of similar color. Visit their websites for more information.

Wallpapering

As an alternative to painting, particularly in theatres where the audience is sitting very close to the stage, real wallpaper can be used. For the best appearance wallpaper should be applied to flats covered with some type of hard surface—⅛-inch luan plywood, Masonite, or ³⁄₁₆- or ¼-inch plywood. The wallpaper is applied with vinyl acrylic wallpaper paste, which is available in wallpaper stores as well as paint stores and home improvement centers. When using wallpaper on the stage particular attention needs to be paid to the size of any images in the wallpaper. The scale of the image on many manufactured wallpapers is too small for use on stage. The distances at which the audience sits from the set will, in many cases, make the use of small, delicate patterns impractical. That small pattern that you think is absolutely perfect will, many times, simply be a blur when viewed from 25 to 50 feet. It's best to take a sample roll from the store and view it as the audience will see it. Unroll it vertically—drape it down the side of a step-ladder placed on the stage or in the shop—and look at it at a typical "audience distance." If the pattern "works" from that distance—if it is clearly visible and supports the designer's intent—then you have a winner.

Drop Painting Techniques

Drops need to be stretched and framed in some manner before they can be painted. The stretching not only produces a smooth surface on which to paint but also minimizes shrinkage. The drop can be stretched on a vertical paint frame by

1. Nailing a framework of boards the same width and height as the drop to the paint frame. It is imperative that these boards be squared—all corners at 90 degrees—so that the drop will remain square.
2. Attaching the drop to the framework. Staples with ½-inch legs, spaced 3 to 4 inches apart, normally secure any muslin drop to the framework. If the drop is going to be saturated with dyes or paint (which causes it to shrink a great deal), it will be better to secure it with staples spaced 1 to 2 inches apart.

Some painting techniques are more easily executed with the drop in a horizontal position. In these cases, the drop will need to be stretched and secured on a wooden floor with staples spaced on 3- to 4-inch centers. (Partially seating the staples will make them easier to remove.) Again, if the drop is going to be heavily saturated, space the staples 1 to 2 inches apart to prevent scalloped edges on the drop. Be sure to put a layer of **bogus paper** under the drop to absorb the dye or

polyvinyl alcohol (PVA): A water-soluble synthetic thickener/adhesive.

bogus paper: A heavy, soft, absorbent paper. Similar to blotter paper.

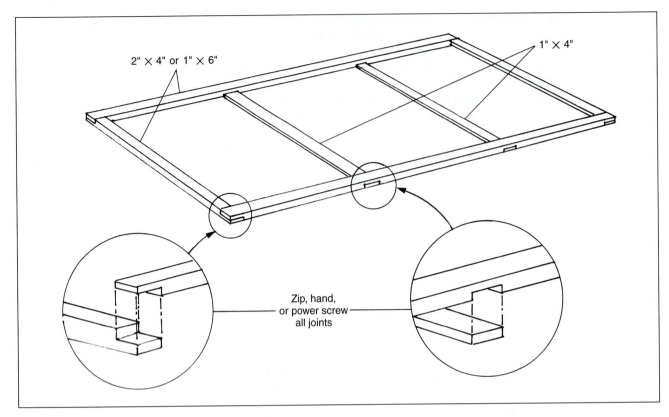

FIGURE 12.15
Temporary drop stretcher.

paint. Place a layer of Kraft or butcher paper underneath the bogus paper. (If the bogus/butcher paper backing isn't used, the paints or dyes may stain the floor or the drop may pick up some staining from old paint or dye already on the floor.)

If you do not have a wooden floor large enough to accommodate the size of the drop, you will need to build a temporary frame large enough to stretch the drop. The frame can be made of notched 2 × 4 or 1 × 6 so that it will hold its shape against the strong force created when the fabric shrinks. As shown in Figure 12.15, the toggle bars of this oversized frame are made of 1 × 4s. Be certain that the drop frame is square. After painting, the drop will shrink to the shape of the frame. If the frame is out of square, the drop will also be out of square and may be impossible to hang or trim properly. Finally, before you stretch the drop and staple it to the framework, don't forget to cover the area under the drop with the aforementioned layers of bogus and butcher paper.

In the final analysis, the quality of any scenic paint job depends on the talent and ingenuity of the scenic artist. The materials and techniques suggested in this chapter provide only a beginning point for the scene-painting artist. Although each of the materials has specific properties, there aren't any artistic "rules" to which the painter must adhere. Experimentation, trial and error, and learning from your happy accidents are the only guidelines that need to be followed as you work to develop your skill in the challenging field of scene painting.

Chapter 13

Stage Properties

(This chapter has been extensively updated thanks to the input of Sandra J. Strawn, professional property director and educator. The author wishes to publicly thank her for her extensive knowledge and expertise on this subject and contributions to this chapter.)

In the proscenium theatre, the stage properties are the icing on the scenic designer's cake. Although the set usually creates the dominant visual motif, the properties are coequal design elements. They are generally the primary design tool used to provide clues about the personality and socioeconomic status of the inhabitants of the set. Figure 13.1 demonstrates these principles. Figure 13.1 is a rather nondescript living room that is furnished in three different ways. In Figure 13.1A, it is furnished with utilitarian props that don't say much about the nature and character of the inhabitants or the period of the play. Figure 13.1B illustrates how changing the style of the properties to late Victorian changes our perception of the social class and characteristics of the room's inhabitants. Additionally, it suggests a fairly clear idea of the period of the play. These visual clues are again demonstrated in Figure 13.1C, where the absence of any furnishings other than the stacked boxes, broom, and a crumpled newspaper suggests that the room's inhabitants are either moving in or moving out.

The visual importance of stage properties increases significantly when the play is produced in either a thrust or arena theatre or any of the other configurations that preclude or restrict the use of vertical scenic elements such as flats and drops. In these intimate theatre spaces where the audience is usually sitting close to the stage, the furniture and decorative props are frequently the major visual elements of the scenic design.

Although the duties and responsibilities of the members of the prop department were covered in Chapter 1, it bears repeating that the property master needs to have a detailed working knowledge of every craft area in theatre; woodworking, metalworking, electrical wiring and electronics, mold making, ceramics, sewing, upholstery, furniture construction, weaponry, special effects, and scene painting are but a few of the craft areas in which a true property master will be competent. A good props person also has a solid knowledge of a variety of computer programs ranging from word processing to spread sheets to drawing and drafting.

When you understand the impact of properties on the appearance of a design and the scope of knowledge that a prop master or director must possess, it becomes obvious that a full discussion of how to construct stage properties cannot be contained in this chapter. Probably more than in any other single craft area in theatre production, someone who is interested in property design and construction needs to know it all—the history of fashion, architecture, furniture, and decoration; design theory and practice; and craft construction techniques.

FIGURE 13.1
Stage properties can be used to provide information about the character and period of the set.

FIGURE 13.1
Stage properties can be used to provide information about the character and period of the set.

(A)

(B)

(C)

What Is a Prop?

Stage properties have traditionally been divided into three categories: (1) set props, (2) hand props, and (3) decorative props or set dressing.

Set Props

Set props are generally defined as larger movable items, not built into the set, that are used in some way by the actors. This group would include such things as furniture, floor lamps, rugs, stoves, tree stumps, swings, and so forth.

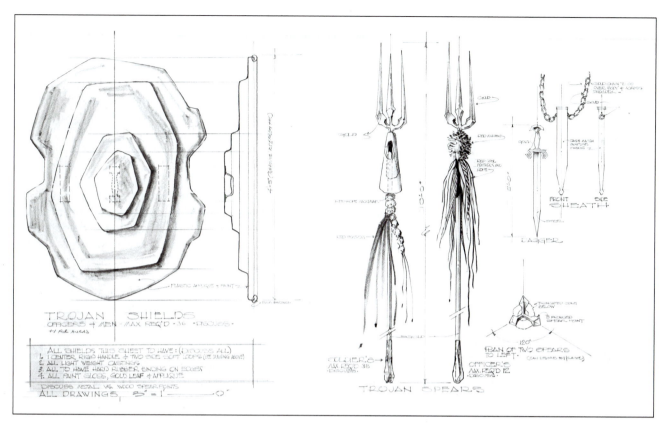

FIGURE 13.2
Property designs for the Metropolitan Opera Association's production of *Les Troyens*, produced at the Metropolitan Opera House, Lincoln Center, New York. Scenery, costumes, and visual effects (film) designed by Peter Wexler.

Hand Props

Hand props refer to small items that are handled or carried by the actors. This group includes plates, cups, letters, books, fans, lanterns, and similar items.

Decorative Props

Into the category of decorative props, also known as set dressing, fall all the things that are used to enhance the setting visually but are not specifically touched by the actors. Such items as window curtains, pictures, doilies, table lamps, bric-a-brac, and the books in a bookcase are typical of decorative, or dress, props.

 ## Property Design

As discussed in Chapter 1, "Production Organization and Management," the credit for property design is evolving into a collaborative effort between the scenic and property directors/designers in both commercial and educational theatres. In the design illustrated in Figure 13.2 the initial property sketches were made by the scenic designer. Not all prop sketches are that ideal or precise. Some harried scenic designers will simply give the property director a collection of printed or photocopied material from books, websites, or magazines showing pictures of similar items with notes jotted in the margins. But these lists work. In whatever form the initial visual information is received from the scenic designer, in current practice the property designer, who is frequently the property director, takes those images and, after doing appropriate period and style research, makes sketches, working drawings, detail drawings, and construction/acquisition decisions. During this phase the scenic and property designers are normally in frequent communication, either face-to-face or by e-mail (with attachments), as the designs evolve from the original material. When all parties—designers, director, and production manager (the person usually in charge of budgetary decisions)—are satisfied with the designs, the property director gets down to the actual work of making and collecting all the props for the production.

Real or Fake?

If an actor is going to touch or pick up a prop, it should feel real. For example, assuming that you are trying to project a realistic or naturalistic appearance, a book should look and feel like a real book and, if it is going to be opened, it should have pages. The scenic designer and the property master may want to alter the appearance of the book by painting or staining the cover, covering it with cloth or leather, or hot-gluing jewels or appliqués to it.

Props can be faked if they aren't going to be used by the actors. If the decorated prop book just discussed isn't going to be touched by an actor, and if you were adverse to the idea of "defacing" a real book, it could simply be a cigar box or piece of wood that is painted and decorated to look like a book. Frequently, the books in a bookshelf are the spines of books that have been attached to a frame. Other types of props can be treated in the same way.

Property Organization

What does the property designer/director actually do and how are the props for a production actually acquired? This section explains the duties of the property director and the organization of a prop shop. Obviously, not every producing organization has the funding available to have a property director and/or a separate prop shop with its own staff of artisans and equipment, but the duties and procedures outlined below provide a good understanding of the practices and procedures used in a typical regional professional theatre organization to build, collect, and run the stage props for a production and, as such, provides an excellent how-to guide. If a producing organization has only one faculty/staff member/graduate student assigned as property director and a few students and/or volunteers to make, assemble, and run the props for a show, it should be obvious that the property design cannot be as complex as for a theatre with a complete, fully staffed prop shop. But the procedures and processes outlined below should work for them as well.

Property Director   The property director is ultimately responsible for all props used during the production. His or her number one job is to assure the timely production of appropriately designed props for each play produced by the organization. Property directors assign the prop shop artisans to specific buying/building/collecting projects and then supervise the actual work. The property director determines which props will be pulled from the theatre's property storage and which will be built, bought, rented, and/or borrowed. She or he is responsible for managing both the time and fiscal construction-phase budgets. Property directors need to determine how many hours it will take to build/buy/acquire all the props so they can plan for an adequately sized crew. To determine the budget needed to cover a show, they need to know the cost of buying/renting any props as well as the cost of the materials needed for prop construction.

It is standard practice when estimating a prop budget to build in a contingency of 10 to 20 percent of the total prop budget to cover the inevitable changes that will occur during the rehearsal process. This seems to be an appropriate point to offer another axiom/caveat: in theatre production there's never enough time or money—sort of like life, eh? Striking a happy balance between what the budgets—time and fiscal—will allow you to do, and what is wanted, is a constant battle not only for props, but in the scenic, costume, lighting, and sound departments as well. However, it can be done with patience, energy, collaboration, compromise, and integrity. Maybe that's one of the things that makes this business so interesting.

Like other members of the production design team, the properties director attends all necessary production meetings and technical rehearsals. If the property director has not already done period and style research as the property designer, he or she familiarizes him- or herself with the period and style of the production. This information is used to keep all relevant personnel "on track" regarding the appearance and function of the props. The property director must be aware of the status and progress of all projects and must keep all the property artisans on schedule so the props can be completed on time. He or she is also the conduit through which notes about any prop changes reach the property artisans. The property director also oversees the maintenance of the prop shop's tool, equipment, and supplies inventories. She or he also needs to be computer savvy and minimally be conversant with word processing, spreadsheets, graphics, and drawing/drafting/painting software.

Property Acquisition

To create an aura of authenticity, property masters frequently try to find actual objects appropriate to the period of the play to use as props. For a contemporary production, props can usually be purchased or borrowed from local stores. For a play set twenty or thirty years ago, it is fairly easy to find most props in junk shops or used-furniture stores. However, when producing a period play such as *Amadeus,* which moves in time between 1780 and 1820 and is set in Vienna, it is very difficult to find actual furniture or decorative props of that period. Even if you could find them, you wouldn't want to put them on the stage for fear that they might be damaged. In these situations, the property director frequently builds the props or acquires reproductions. When acquiring props for a show, property directors use what some of them frequently refer to as "The 3Bs and a P"—Build, Buy, Borrow, and Pull.

Building Props   Every production has some props that must be built or altered. It might be a nonstock item like the warrior's shield shown in Figure 13.2 that is stipulated by the designer. It might be a piece of period furniture or a 1920s-era gramophone that won't be played. It might be a period newspaper or magazine, or a food-stained tablecloth, 1940s-era Venetian blinds, or a colorful vase that sits on the mantle. It is the property artisan's job to build whatever it is.

Let's look at that gramophone. While doing research the designer finds a picture of the gramophone and indications of its general size. The prop artisan's challenge is to build it. With specifications and dimensions provided by the property designer, the box and lid could be made of oak-faced plywood, stained mahogany, and varnished or shellacked to a suitable satin or gloss finish. A plywood disk topped with dark felt and edged with metal tape could be used for the record platen, while a bent metal rod with a wooden bead glued to the end could serve as the winding crank. The gramophone's signature playing arm and horn could be fashioned from tin, aluminum, or plastic sheet goods and finished with a mica-powder metallic silver treatment and black paint to match the look of the period piece.

Furniture frequently requires special attention. If an actor is supposed to dance on a sofa while it twirls about the stage, the prop artisan will probably start with a stock sofa and build a complete metal undercarriage with heavy-duty castors to guarantee its strength and ease of movement, and underpin the stock upholstery on the seat and arms with plywood supports and extra-firm padding so the sofa will provide a firm, nonwiggly base for the actor.

Many props require "toning" or "distressing" to fit the look of the scenic design. The clever use of spray paint/dyes on the fabric and tinted shellac, bronzing/mica powders, and paints on woodwork can frequently make a new piece seem appropriately ancient and decrepit.

If a newspaper from the 1930s is required it is frequently possible to download an actual front page from the Web, import it into Photoshop, add or change the required headline, then print it on newsprint or similar thin paper on a plotter. Paper goods of all types can be similarly created. Because the audience is frequently only a few feet from the stage it is essential that paper items such as menus, newspapers, match books, and the like be period and accurate. This level of accuracy also helps the actors stay in the moment. Besides, doing this sort of thing is fun.

As you can see, the range of construction work that the prop artisans do is amazing and endless. A prop item can be found, built, or purchased. It can be altered, aged, strengthened, painted, or re-covered to fit the look of the show. A solid understanding of the materials and processes used to construct props from wood, metal, fabric, plastic, and so forth, provides the prop artisan an arsenal of problem-solving and innovative techniques with which to build props.

Buying Props   Buying props that cannot be built, borrowed, or pulled from stock often falls to the props director and/or the artisan designated as the props buyer.

Any show has a given amount of shopping if only for consumables—food that will be eaten onstage or materials (lumber, fabric, paper, and so forth.). Having good money management skills and a willingness to bargain makes a good props shopper.

The Internet has revolutionized the props shopper's job. It used to be that he or she had a thick Rolodex of numbers, numerous catalogues, and a keenly honed sense of where-to-buy-what. Those skills are still helpful, but now online auction sites such as e-Bay allow props shoppers to find the frequently arcane items that props people need to get quickly and cheaply. With express mail, purchases can be delivered to the theatre in relatively short order. Traditional sources and supply houses, with online catalogues, are still equally useful.

One of the specific challenges that props people face is the need to find an item that has a very specific look but must be altered—either to survive or have the appropriately worn look—to work on stage. Furniture pieces with that "correct" look are frequently purchased from retail stores, stripped back to the frame, the understructure rebuilt to make the pieces more **stage worthy,** and covered in a different fabric and trim—frequently aged or distressed—that more accurately matches the look of the production.

Many props that are purchased are retained after the show closes and are added to the theatre's prop stock. Items that are inexpensive and/or can be easily replaced are usually not stored if storage space is at a premium.

Borrowing or Renting Props   Some special challenges need to be considered when borrowing props. Any type of prop used in the theatre is subject to unusual

stage worthy: Strong enough to withstand the use inflicted on them when used on the stage, for example, sofas/chairs that are stood and/or danced on; tables that break apart during fights, and so forth.

stresses and wear. Furniture, which is designed to sit in one location in a room in someone's house and occasionally be moved for cleaning, when used in the theatre will be moved around the stage as the scenery is shifted. Even if it isn't moved, the director may block someone to stand on it, flop on it, run across it, or spill a drink on it. It should be obvious that if any of these things are going to take place, the furniture involved shouldn't be borrowed or rented.

It should also be obvious that borrowed items should not be altered in any way without the expressed written permission of the owners. Even then it's an "iffy" proposition. Some theatre organizations form alliances with other theatre groups to facilitate a borrowing/sharing system between members of the group. Generally, other theatre organizations are more amenable to allowing some modifications to the borrowed pieces than are most stores and production rental houses. But even if you've borrowed something from another theatre be sure to get permission, in writing, before performing any modifications to the piece.

Many retail rental companies stock a variety of items used for weddings and parties that can be rented for the length of the run. Some retail furniture companies also rent furniture. But you'll frequently find that the rental costs are equal to, if not more than, the cost of buying the same item. Cultivating the relationships that allow for prop rental or borrowing generally take a long time to establish and are maintained only through taking diligent care of the borrower's goods. Just one careless "oops" has doomed many of these relationships.

If you are borrowing furniture from a person or company, you should be able to assure the lending party that it will be returned intact. Lenders are frequently more at ease if a lending agreement (Figure 13.3A) is executed. This agreement stipulates the use of the item, that the object will be returned in good condition, and that the borrower will be responsible for any necessary repairs resulting from accidental damage. If the borrowed prop is expensive or rare, the borrowing organization should investigate the cost of insurance to cover any possible repairs or replacement. Finally, if the producing organization cannot afford to replace the prop, it should not be borrowed in the first place.

Many producing organizations loan or rent properties. Figure 13.3B shows a sample form typical of a prop lending agreement used when organizations/individuals borrow props from a theatre organization. Unfortunately, all too frequently borrowed props are damaged or "modified" in some manner. That is why much of what is contained in this form relates to costs associated with repair/replacement if a prop is damaged or lost. It lets the borrower know the potential costs associated with the act of borrowing.

Pulling Props   Almost every theatre organization has a "prop room." This is a storage space in which props that were built or bought for previous productions are stored. This reservoir of often fascinating furniture and knick-knacks forms the basis of most theatres' property production work and offers valuable savings as pieces can be altered, reupholstered, used for parts, or "freshened up" for use in a current production.

Furniture pieces with classic designs that have been in vogue for decades can be easily altered by changing the upholstery, adding different pillows or cushions, or trimming with ruffles, new braid, or decorative nails. A stock piece can be altered by using different legs to better match a particular period or stained darker to match a newly acquired piece to make a nicely matching set of furniture. Designers often use existing prop furniture as a pattern or guide for designing/building new pieces of furniture.

Hand props such as kitchen dressing—pots, pans, silverware, plates, glasses, and so forth—can be used without alteration on a variety of shows.

FIGURE 13.3
Forms used when borrowing and lending
props. (A) Sample forms used when borrowing a prop from others. (B) Sample
form used when lending props to others.

LENDING AGREEMENT FORM

1. Old Time Productions agrees to return the below listed borrowed items in the same condition in which they were borrowed.

2. If any item is damaged while in the possession of the theatre, Old Time Productions will be responsible for its repair.

3. The items will be borrowed on _____ and returned no later than _____ .

4. The prop will be used in the following manner: _____
_____ .

ITEMS

_____

For Old Time Productions: _____   Date: _____

Lender: _____   Date: _____

(A)

Paper props, such as the previously mentioned 1930's newspaper, can be saved and reused as set dressing for every subsequent 1930s-era show.

Stock items can also be used during rehearsal until the actual prop is built. Obviously, the wear and tear on the stock item must be balanced against having the rehearsal needs met. Sometimes it is more appropriate for the prop artisans to simply rough out an approximation of the finished prop for rehearsal use rather than using something from stock.

Many theatres now have the furniture stock—notice that this is the *furniture* stock, not *all* props—on a computerized inventory system. Data management files can be created for each piece. Each file typically includes photo(s) of the item, its dimensions, as well as alteration information—dates for upholstery/trim changes, and so forth—and other pertinent data such as shows/dates in which the piece was used and so forth. These programs can be used to search all stock items by category—"Victorian," "settee," and so forth—which can significantly speed up the design/communication process between the prop director and the scenic/property designers. Obviously, maintaining the currency of the computerized inventory by updating the material on each item every time it is used/altered is absolutely essential.

Organizing Props for a Production

The process used when assembling the props for a production is similar to the design/construction process used for the scenery, costumes, lighting, and

Theatre Prop Borrowing Form

LOANED TO: _____ ADDRESS: _____

PHONE: _____ PICKED UP: ___/___/___ TO BE RETURNED: ___/___/___

CONTACT: _____ PRODUCTION: _____

The Theatre Properties Department is loaning the following items for use in your production/workshop/class as listed above. You *personally,* and for your organization (when applicable), by accepting these items and signing this loan form, agree to the following conditions:

1. Appointments must be made with the Props Manager to: (1) look thru props storage; (2) for PICK-UP and RETURN of props. If an appointment is missed by more than 15 minutes, it must be rescheduled at the convenience of the prop shop.

2. All borrowed items will be kept in a safe and secure location at all times.

3. All items will be returned in the same condition as they left prop storage, excluding **normal** wear and tear.

4. If modifications are desired, permission must be obtained from the Prop Manager in advance. Any "modifications" made without prior permission will be viewed as damage to the specific item, and repair charges will be accessed.

5. All repairs to damaged items must be completed by the Theatre prop shop (based on an hourly fee plus materials) unless other arrangements are made with the Properties Manager *in advance* of any actual repairs being started. REPEAT: Repairs done without permission will be considered "damage".

6. The borrowing organization is responsible for the stated value of any item that is lost, stolen, or damaged beyond reasonable repairs. Damaged items remain the property of Theatre even when total replacement cost is accessed.

7. The Theatre Properties Manager must be notified A.S.A.P. after any item is damaged. Please do not wait until the end of your rental to let us know.

8. All items are to be returned *on or before the date specified* on this form. Props must be checked in by the Properties Manager at the time of their return. REPEAT: If an appointment is missed by more than 15 minutes, it must be rescheduled at the discretion of the prop shop.

9. Renter is responsible for all shipping fees, moving and pick up arrangements. Items must be insured for stated value if returned by shipment

THEATRE: _____

Prop Master, phone number, e-mail

CONTACT _____

Returned: Donation due: ☐

Notes: paid: ☐

Item	Description	Value	Fee

RENTAL CHARGE:		

CHECKS SHOULD BE MADE OUT TO: THEATRE COMPANY

(B)

sound. There is preproduction planning and organization followed by the construction and adjustments, then running of the props during the technical/dress rehearsals and performance, and finally the strike or taking-down-and-putting-away phase.

Preproduction Planning

The first thing that the property director does when working on a new show is create the prop list. The prop list, illustrated in Figure 13.4, is a complete listing of all the props needed for the show including set props, hand props, decorative props, consumables, special effects, weaponry, and any "crossover" props such as

FIGURE 13.4

A prop list from McCarter Theatre production of *Gem of the Ocean.* This is the first page of a four-page list. Courtesy of Sandra J. Strawn, property director.

Gem of the Ocean

Prop List

McCarter Theatre ◆ 91 University Place ◆ Princeton, NJ 08540
Prop Shop ✱ 609-258-6580 ✱ props@mccarter.org

#	Pg	Prop	Description/ Movement	Character/ Placement	Status/ Questions
F00			**Furniture**		
F10		Kitchen Table	6' x 2'6", splayed leg, country table	DSL	Built by McCarter
F14		4 Kitchen chairs	Simple, country, some turning, not necessarily matching	Around table	McCarter Stock
F18		Aunt Ester's Chair	Large arm chair with heart carving on top	DSR	McCarter Stock
F19		Aunt Ester's Side table	Short, square table w/ shelf & drawer, scalloped skirt; has a strike pad on it; has doily bottom shelf	SR of AE's chair	McCarter Stock
F20		Side Chair	Windsor back chair w/ rush seat	SL of AE's chair	Empire Antiques
F22		Tall side table	Round table w/barley twist pedestal & pom poms; has round doily on top	DS of stiars	McCarter Stock
F26		Square side table	Fluted legs, bottom shelf & a drawer; green; has embroidered runner on top.	US of stairs	Wal-Mart
F30		Counter		US	Built by McCarter
F34		Long Side table	Black w/ drawer & bottom shelf; has embroidered runner on top	SR of counter	American Country
F38		Sink	Metal basin, big blue legs	SL or counter	Built by McCarter
F42		Stove	2.5' - 3.5' wide, wood burning, black cast iron	Against back wall	Anything But Costumes
F46		Coat rack	Turned post, Victorian hooks	SL of front door	McCarter Stock
F50		Cupboard	Painted green milk paint	In SR corner	Built by McCarter
F54		Half Moon Table	Dark brown, turned legs; has oblong doily on top	US of Ester's door	E-bay
F58		Half Moon Table	Orangy finish, swirly detail	In Ester's room	E-bay
D00			**Dressing**		
D10		2 Sconces	Antique copper, amber shade	SL & SR sides of column	Rejuvenation
D14		Shelf dressing	Bowls, crocks containers, cracked blue glaze		Bought/McCarter Stock
D18		Large Rug	9' x 5'-6", braided, browns, reds	DSR	E-bay
D26		Pantry Door Curtain	Dark red calico, on rings, never moves	Pantry Door	Built by McCarter
D34		Door Shade	Hempish looking roll shade	On porch door	Lowe's
D38		Cupboard Dressing	Dishes, pans, pitchers, bowls, etc	In Cupboard	Bought/McCarter Stock
D42		Kitchen Dressing	Utensils, pans, garlic, peppers		Bought/McCarter Stock
D46		Coal Shuttle	Galvanized metal w/ red handle; has logs inside	SL of stove	McCarter Stock
D48		Large Stoneware Jar	Off white, tall	SR of Stove	Bought
D50		Little Shelf	Wooden, green, cups hung underneath, bottles on top	On wall SL of Stove	Built by McCarter
D51		Curio Shelf	Dark brown, 3 shelves	US of Ester's door	Built by McCarter
D52		Oil Lamp	Large, brass, frosted chimney, electrified	On half moon table #F54	McCarter Stock
D53		Round box	Small, bronze colored, decorative	On shelf on Aunt Ester's Table #F19	McCarter Stock
D54		Reed Basket	Dark brown, side handles, red & off white fabric inside	On shelf on square side table #f26	McCarter Stock
D56		2 African Baskets	Round, woven, red fabric in one	On shelf on long side table #F34	Bought
D58		Vegetable basket	Small woven basket filled w/ fake vegetables	On DS end of counter	McCarter Stock

Director: Ruben Santiago-Hudson   Set Designer: Michael Carnahan

wallet dressing or flying electrical units such as chandeliers. Normally the process of making the prop list begins when the property director reads the script and studies the scenic design. He or she will make note of any props specifically called for in the script or design as well as any props that she or he feels might help establish the mood and flavor of the play. It is important to understand that this is just a beginning, and this preliminary props list will be added to and adjusted, probably many times, as the process continues.

After the prop list has been started the prop director normally will make the preproduction budget estimate from that list. This is an estimate of the cost and time that it will take to assemble and/or build the props for the production.

The preliminary prop list is distributed to the scenic and property designers, the director, and the stage manager for their study and input. A prop meeting is held, usually during one of the regular production staff meetings, to discuss the preliminary designs, color, fabric choices, research, and so forth. It is normal for the original prop list to be modified at this time as new props are discussed and added by the director and other members of the production design team.

During one of the preliminary production meetings there is frequently a "renegotiating" of the production budget—taking a little from here, giving a little there—so that the various departments can stay within the overall budget for the production. If the props department needs more money for an essential prop, then it normally has to come from somewhere else within the overall production budget—scenery, costume, lights, and sound. This type of negotiation is normal for all areas of production and should be expected. Remember, theatre production is a collaborative process.

Properties Production   After the prop budget and designs have been approved the fun begins. Normally, the property director and/or the prop shopper, fabric swatches in hand, go shopping for any needed furniture and/or upholstery materials. The prop director also starts pulling props from storage and acquiring any needed supplies. The basic tools, construction techniques, and processes used in building and modifying props are similar to those used in scenic production. Those subjects are covered in Chapter 10, "Tools and Materials," Chapter 11, "Scenic Production Techniques," and Chapter 12, "Scene Painting." Some additional techniques more specific to property construction will be discussed later in this chapter.

Properties production requires clear and constant communication between the director/stage managers and the property department during the rehearsal process. During rehearsals it is normal for props to be added or cut or the use of a specific prop to be changed. Remember: this is normal. Getting information about those changes from the rehearsal hall to the prop shop on a daily basis is vital and essential. The stage manager normally generates that information in the daily rehearsal report. The daily rehearsal report is delivered, frequently by e-mail, to all technical production departments on, surprise(!), a daily basis. That report includes a variety of information. Of importance to the prop department are the notes about any changes to the props: additions, cuts, changes in use, maintenance issues, and general information/questions affecting props. Similar update information is provided to the other technical departments. The property director updates the prop list from the rehearsal report then goes through the collaborative communication/design process with the scenic and property designer for any new props, and discusses any changes with the artisans working on the affected props. This constant back-and-forth communication, both e-mail and verbal, goes on daily as well as during the weekly production meetings.

As the communication flows and props are added, deleted, and changed it is absolutely essential that the prop list be updated by the property director every time a change is made. Without this level of organization it is very easy to forget to make or buy some essential prop. So keep the prop list up to date!

It is very common for there to be overlap between technical departments in relation to stage props. For example, table lamps belong to both the props and lighting departments. The prop department will normally design and fabricate the lamp, but there must be coordination with the lighting department regarding the circuit into which the lamp will be plugged, as well as who is going to plug/unplug it and who is going to move it during a scene shift. Similarly, many "costume properties" fall into both camps. While there is a general rule that, "if you carry it, it's a prop," every producing organization works out its own guidelines in this area. Irrespective of whether it's a costume or a prop, there needs to be strong coordination/communication between the prop and costume departments regarding the design and function of items such as parasols, umbrellas, purses, flower bouquets, and so forth. Similarly, there needs to be strong coordination between the prop and scenic departments. In many small theatre operations the props are painted by the scenic artists. But even if the prop shop is lucky enough to have its own painters, there still needs to be strong consultation between the departments when it comes to the selection of upholstery fabric, as well as the painting and finishing of furniture, picture frames, and so forth, so that the finished props work well with the look and palette of the scenic design.

Rehearsal Props   Every prop that will be handled by an actor should be duplicated in some fashion during rehearsals. Because of the potential for loss or damage "performance props" are generally not used during the rehearsal period, although they may be rotated into the rehearsal period for a few days so the actors can adjust to the real item. The only exception to that general rule regards specialty items. If there is a sword or pistol fight the weapons that will be used during the performances may be used during rehearsals so the actors will feel comfortable and confident in their use. For props such as paper goods and books, items of similar size and weight can be substituted until technical rehearsals begin. Furniture of similar size and shape is normally used during rehearsals instead of the performance furniture. The key to all these substitutions is that they provide a reasonable match in terms of size, weight, and design to the items that are going to be used during the production. Perishable props, which include items like cigarettes, matches, letters that will be written, food that will be eaten on stage, and so forth, are often requested early in the rehearsal process to allow the use of the props to be integrated with the dialogue and other stage action. A sufficient supply of these items for the rehearsal period is usually supplied by the prop department or stage management.

Load-in and Technical Rehearsals   Property directors generally try to attend one rehearsal prior to the load-in to the theatre or, if the play is rehearsing in the theatre, prior to the first technical rehearsal, to work out running crew concerns and finalize the prop set-up and load-in logistics with the stage manager.

Prior to the first technical rehearsal it is helpful if the furniture props, and ideally any window dressings, can be placed onstage for at least some of the sessions when the lighting designer is initially setting the light levels, simply because those props—their colors, textures, and shadows—will affect, sometimes significantly, the appearance of the stage picture.

The running of props during the technical and dress rehearsals as well as during performances is under the supervision of the stage manager. During the technical and dress rehearsals either the property director, or a designated assistant, should be in attendance to go over all the props, show the actors and, if the props are particularly complex, the director and stage manager as well, how the props work. They will also discuss any special needs with the appropriate personnel and take notes on any changes. The furniture props are placed onstage in collaboration with stage management. Set dressing is often placed in coordination with the scenic designer. Hand props are turned over to the run crew who place them in the prop storage cabinets.

The run crew, under the supervision of the stage manager, is responsible for placing the hand props on the props tables as well as monitoring their whereabouts during all technical/dress rehearsals and performances.

The property director advises the stage manager and scenic designer regarding any special treatment that the props might need during any scene shifts.

All set dressing, hand props, and furniture will need to be onstage for the first technical rehearsal. Set dressing can usually start as soon as the finished set is in place.

Because there are many notes generated during a technical rehearsal there is frequently a mini-production meeting following each tech rehearsal. These meetings are normally attended by the director, stage manager, all designers, and department heads. The meeting is used to go over those notes and discuss/resolve changes and challenges. The prop director, and other department heads, then prioritize that information and work the next day to resolve as many of the challenges as possible. This process normally continues throughout the technical and dress rehearsal period and may even extend through previews to the actual opening of the show.

Running Props

If properties are going to be an effective addition to a production, they must be consistently placed in their proper locations on or around the set. If a floor lamp that is supposed to be placed next to a specific chair is misplaced, the concentration of the actor who is supposed to turn it on at a crucial moment in the play will undoubtedly be broken. Similarly, if an actor is supposed to pick up a book from a stack of books on an end table, the specific book must always be placed in the same position and location in or on the stack so that the actor can pick it up without having to look for it. A little thought, preparation, and organization will smoothly integrate the use of properties into the flow of the production.

The person designated as the property director together with the property running crew head, in coordination with the stage manager, will carefully organize and orchestrate the storage, placement, and use of all properties.

Hand props and small set props, such as lamps, pictures, radios, and so forth, should be locked in storage cabinets adjacent to the stage area between rehearsals and performances. Many theatres have lockable storage bins in the wings for this purpose. Other organizations use small lockable storage rooms. Valuable and borrowed props should always be stored in a secure area. Ideally, all props will be stored under lock and key. However, some pieces may be too large and/or cumbersome to move into the locked storage area. These items should be moved off the set, if possible, and covered with muslin dust covers and marked with a sign stating: "Theatrical Property. Do Not Use or Remove."

A written list, including a ground plan or location indicator, detailing the onstage placement of all set props *must* be created by the appropriate person in charge of running the properties. This list should also indicate where each item is stored between rehearsals and performances. The exact placement of the set props will be determined by the scenic designer, and any electrical connections will be coordinated with the master electrician. During rehearsals and performances the property running crew, under the guidance of the crew head and the stage manager, will place the set props in their appropriate locations. Depending on the union rules, if any, affecting the producing organization, any electrical connections will be made by either electricians or members of the prop running crew.

The organization of hand props must be equally exact. The prop running crew head and the stage manager create a precise, written master list of what props are handled by the actors during each scene. This list includes the secure location where these items will be stored between rehearsals and performances. If the show is complex or multiscene, a separate list should be compiled for each scene in the play.

A hand-prop list normally includes the identity of all handled props; the location of each prop at the beginning of the scene, and whether that location is different from the preceding scene (thus necessitating re-placement by the prop

prop table: A table, normally located in the wings, on which hand props are stored when not in use onstage.

blackout: When the stage is completely dark. The stage lights are out and no other lights are on.

crew); the condition of the prop if it is functional (wine glasses full or empty, book opened or closed, and so forth); where the prop is to be left by the actor (on- or offstage location); and any other pertinent information.

A **prop table,** on which all hand props are placed, is normally set up in the wings adjacent to the stage. To aid in organizing the props, this large table is frequently covered with brown butcher paper and "mapped" with names of specific props, such as "Act I, Scene 2, tray/4 glasses" for the silver tray and four stemmed glasses that the butler carries onto the set during Act I, Scene 2. The tray and glasses are placed just above or below the caption. If there are a lot of props, or if the actors make entrances and exits from a variety of directions, it may be helpful to have more than one prop table.

Because it is so easy to misplace small hand props such as eyeglasses, snuff boxes, and the like, it is essential that the location of all props be carefully tracked and that prop running crew members be responsible for placing all props in their appropriate locations and for retrieving them from the actors when they leave the stage, if the actor does not have time to return the item to the prop table.

Sometimes, as during productions that do not use an act curtain, the prop running crew will move the props as the audience watches. At other times, the crew may be required to shift the props during a **blackout.** Frequently, the prop running crew accomplishes its work with the act curtain down and the stage worklights on. Regardless of the circumstances under which the crew works, it is essential that the prop running crew head hold specific rehearsals to train the crew in the coordinated, speedy, and accurate placement of all props (both set and hand) in their appropriate locations about the stage.

Opening   Following the opening the actual running of the props during the show is in the hands of the stage manager. Daily performance reports, similar to daily rehearsal reports, are sent to all departments. Sometimes during the course of the production a prop may be damaged or consumable supplies run low. The prop artisans fix those challenges that can't be resolved by the prop running crew.

Strike   All props and set dressing need to be removed from the set immediately following the final performance to facilitate other departments' strikes and to guarantee the safety of the props. Following strike all rentals and borrowed items need to be returned and all stock items cleaned and/or laundered and returned to their proper storage location. If a prop inventory list is maintained, it should be updated to reflect the most recent additions and alterations.

 ## Craft Techniques

Properties construction utilizes a wide variety of skills and processes that overlap with many other areas of production. Many props can be built using the tools and techniques discussed in the various chapters covering scenery, lighting, and costuming. A number of additional construction techniques primarily used in building stage properties are discussed in the rest of this chapter.

Furniture

Prop furniture is always seemingly in need of restoration, alteration, or change. Stock and newly purchased furniture—frequently acquired from second-hand stores—is subject to an abnormal amount of wear and stress just in the course of being moved from props storage or store to the shop, shop to stage, and then the normal shifting/movement that occurs in almost every play. This abuse is in addition to anything that is inflicted upon it during the action of the play. So it is not at all unusual for furniture props to be in need of repair—glue joints tightened/reglued, broken parts mended/remade/replaced, or strengthened—to withstand the sometimes amazingly physical action of the play. It is also normal for the appearance of stock furniture to be altered—the style of leg changed, wood trim replaced with a different style, the whole piece reupholstered, and so forth. To handle all of this, props people need to know how to disassemble, clean, repair, replace, and generally resurrect and reconstruct all types of wooden and upholstered furniture.

The ability of the property director or artisan to be able to see beyond the basic form of a piece of furniture to "what-it-could-become" is an invaluable tool. It's very helpful to have the vision—and knowledge of period furniture design— to know that a common kneehole desk can be changed into an appropriate period piece by adding a rolltop or cubby-hole topper. Similarly, the period appearance of a chair or sofa can be altered by replacing its legs with ones of a different style/design. Being able to see the form in the furniture and to know how it can be altered by the addition of more detail, moldings, or structural changes allows the prop shop to save money and resources by the creative alteration of stock and/or inexpensively found items.

Carpenter-style furniture (Figure 13.5) can be built using ordinary woodworking tools and techniques. The illustrated table will be very strong if it is assembled with open doweled joints. Because of its strength and ease of fabrication,

FIGURE 13.5
Exploded view of a carpenter-style table and the finished product.

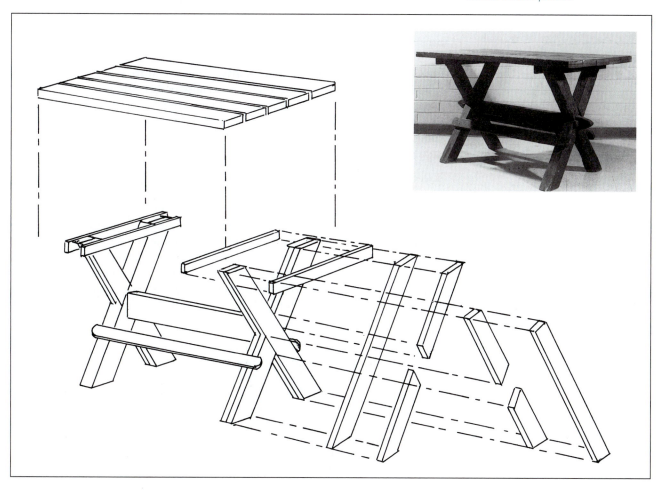

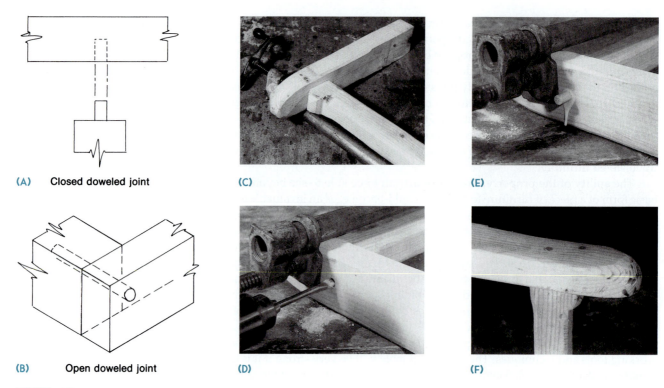

(A)   Closed doweled joint

(B)   Open doweled joint

(C)

(D)

(E)

(F)

FIGURE 13.6

Open doweled construction technique. (A) Closed doweled joint. (B) Open doweled joint. Clamp together the parts to be joined (C), and drill a hole through the top piece and approximately 1 to 1 ½ inches into the second piece (D). Squirt glue into the hole and insert a dowel the same diameter as the hole (E). The finished open dowel joint (F) creates a very strong joint.

jig: A device used hold pieces together in proper positional relationship.

the open doweled joint can be used for reinforcing almost any joint in furniture construction.

Prop and Furniture Construction Joints   There are three types of what appear to be semi-complicated wood joints that, because of their strength, are frequently used in property construction. Actually, they're not complicated and they're all easy to make. They are the open doweled joint, the pocket hole joint, and the biscuit joint.

Open Doweled Joint   The extremely strong doweled joint, which was introduced in Chapter 11, is used extensively in the furniture industry. The closed doweled (Figure 13.6A) is preferred for assembling fine furniture because the dowel is hidden inside the wood. The open doweled joint (Figure 13.6B) is just as strong and is very easily made. The basic technique for making this joint is detailed in Figure 16.5C–F. The open doweled joint can be used for making many furniture joints and has many other uses in prop construction. Even if the joint is on exposed wood that will be seen by the audience the dowels will rarely be noticed, even in arena productions, because the spectators won't be close enough to see the exposed dowel, particularly if the joint has been sanded, filled with wood putty, stained, grained, and varnished.

Pocket Hole Joint   The pocket hole joint is a very strong joint that is held together with specially designed screws. It has the advantage over doweled joints that, if the pieces are not glued together when the joint is made, it can be taken apart without damaging the wood. The pocket hole joint is used extensively in the commercial furniture and cabinet industries and is extremely useful in a variety of applications in property construction.

To construct a pocket hole joint a commercially available **jig** and specialty drill bit are used to drill a pocket hole at a shallow angle into the face of one of the pieces to be joined. Examples of the jigs, clamps, drill bits, and long-shafted

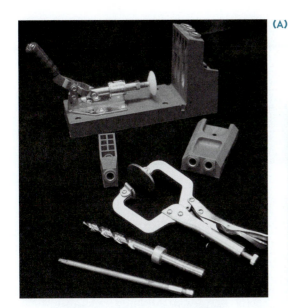

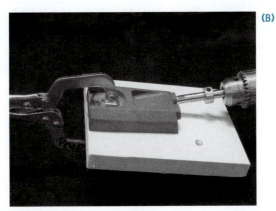

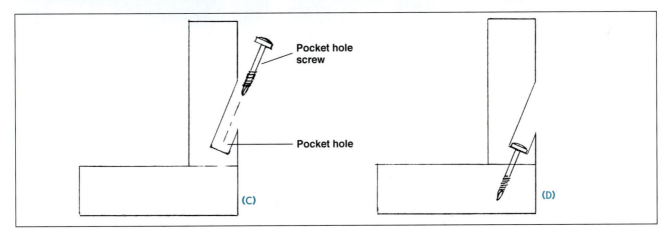

FIGURE 13.7
A pocket hole joint. (A) Jigs, clamps, drill bit, and screw-driver bit used in pocket hole joint construction. (B) A pocket hole being drilled. (C) A pocket hole screw is used to hold the joint together. (D) Completed pocket hole joint. Photos courtesy of Blaird Wade.

square-headed screwdriver bits typically used to construct these joints are shown in Figure 13.7A. Figure 13.7B illustrates the jig being used to drill the shallow-angled pocket hole. After the pocket hole is drilled the pieces to be joined are clamped together, and the screw is placed in the pocket hole and power-screwed into the second piece of wood as shown in Figures 13.7C and D. These specially designed, **self-tapping** screws have a wide flat head that bears against, rather than biting into, the wood at the bottom of the pocket hole. The unique design of the screw head works like a mini-clamp and is what gives the joint its strength. Information about the types and styles of jigs, clamps, and supplies as well as how-to information can be accessed by doing an Internet search for "pocket hole screws."

Biscuit Joint   The biscuit joint, Figure 13.8, is frequently used to edge-join pieces of wood. It can also used to make edge-to-face joints. A typical application would be when making a table and several planks need to be joined edge to edge to make the table top. The biscuit joint is also used to make the edge-to-face joints typically found in cabinet **carcasses.**

To make a biscuit joint, a machine called a biscuit cutter is used to cut crescent-shaped holes in the two pieces of wood that are to be joined. Glue is applied to the two faces of the joint and a "biscuit," a flat oval-shaped disk made

self-tapping: Screws that drill their own pilot holes as they are power-screwed into wood or metal. The screws have an auger-like tip that drills a smaller diameter hole than the screw threads.

carcass: The foundation structure of something, for example, the framework of a cabinet.

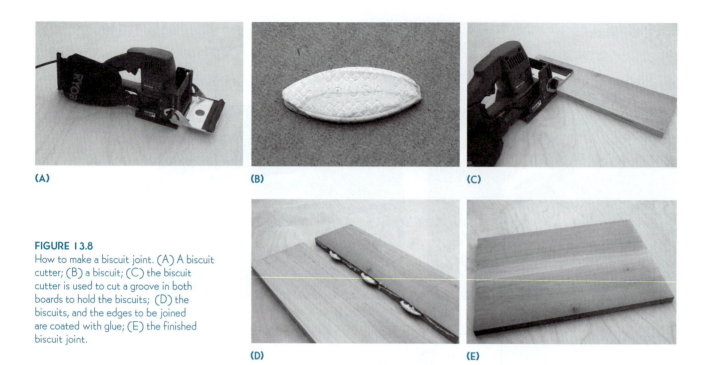

(A)   (B)   (C)

(D)   (E)

FIGURE 13.8
How to make a biscuit joint. (A) A biscuit cutter; (B) a biscuit; (C) the biscuit cutter is used to cut a groove in both boards to hold the biscuits; (D) the biscuits, and the edges to be joined are coated with glue; (E) the finished biscuit joint.

of compressed wood chips, is inserted into the facing oval slots and the joint is then clamped together. The glue causes the biscuit to swell and tighten. Once the glue has cured, the biscuit joint is incredibly strong as well as invisible.

Wood Turning

Wood turning is done on a lathe. Various prop and scenic items such as furniture legs, decorative poles, banisters, and newels are frequently turned on a lathe.

Because hardwoods such as walnut, oak, mahogany, and cherry have a fairly dense structure, they are usually considered the best candidates for turning, although carefully selected, knot-free, tight-grained pine or fir can be used. To turn wood securely, mount it in the lathe, and as the lathe spins the stock, carve it using special chisels called turning tools.

Foam can be turned on a wood lathe by using a slow speed and using sandpaper rather than cutting tools. It can also be shaped with a hot-wire cutter. Urethane foam shouldn't be turned because of the toxic gas it emits when heated. Styrofoam sheets will probably have to be laminated to provide stock of sufficient thickness. Since Styrofoam is not very dense, pieces of ¼-inch plywood of the same size as the ends of the work will need to be securely glued to the ends so that the lathe's **spindle chucks** will have something to bite into to hold the work in the lathe. If the foam turnings are to be very narrow, a wooden armature (a ⅜-inch or ½-inch dowel or ¾-by-¾-inch white-pine stock) may need to be sandwiched into the foam laminate to provide sufficient strength for the unit to be turned. Be sure that the wooden armature is absolutely straight.

spindle chuck: A device used to hold wood in a lathe.

Upholstery

Many times the apparent age or period of a fabric-covered piece can be altered simply by changing the upholstery fabric. For example, the relatively square silhouette of the tuxedo-style sofa (Figure 13.9) has been in continuous fashion since the 1920s. Although the dust ruffle has been in and out of vogue and floral prints

The Wood Lathe

All stationary power tools are inherently dangerous. But they can be operated safely. To do so requires a knowledge of safe work practices and an understanding of how the machine operates. The following precautions should be followed when working with a wood lathe.

1. Never wear loose clothing. It might get caught in the spinning wood.

2. Wear goggles or a face shield.

3. Be sure the wood doesn't have any defects (knots, weak spots) that might cause it to break while spinning.

4. Be sure that all glue joints on stock that is going to be turned are very carefully and thoroughly made and that the glue is completely dry before turning.

5. Center the work, and be sure that it is securely mounted between the spindles.

6. Keep the tool rest as close to the stock as possible. Before starting the motor, rotate the stock by hand to make sure it doesn't hit the tool rest. Adjust the position of the tool rest to keep it close to the stock as the turning progresses.

7. Turn stock over 6 inches in diameter at a slow speed, that from 3 to 6 inches at medium speed, and that under 3 inches a little faster.

8. Don't make any adjustments to the tool rest or other mechanical elements of the lathe while the motor is running.

9. Run all stock at the slowest possible speed until it is rounded.

10. Hold tools firmly with both hands.

11. Remove the tool rest before sanding or polishing the work. If you don't, your fingers may become caught between the stock and the tool rest.

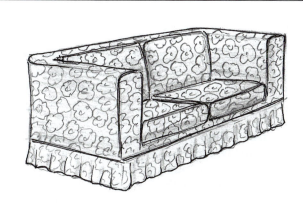 

FIGURE 13.9

Changing the upholstery can change the apparent period of a furniture piece.

have come and gone, the basic style and shape of the sofa have remained basically unchanged. The fabric covering for **stock furniture** is normally altered in two ways: by slipcovers or reupholstery.

Slipcovers   A slipcover is upholstery fabric that is tailored to fit a particular piece or type of furniture and is applied over existing upholstery. Slipcovers are normally used on fully upholstered furniture rather than on pieces that have exposed wood. They should be used only if the underlying fabric, padding, and frame are in good condition. Slipcovers can be used on borrowed furniture, since the existing upholstery material is left in place.

stock furniture: Items owned by the producing organization and held in storage until they are needed for a production.

FIGURE 13.10
Basic reupholstery technique. (A) A chair in need of reupholstery. (B) Carefully remove and save the old fabric and torn elements of padding. (C) Apply new padding. (D) Use the old fabric as a pattern. (E) Cover the padding with muslin to hold the padding in place and to provide a smooth surface over which the covering fabric can slip. (F) Attach the new fabric with staples or decorative tacks. (G) The finished chair.

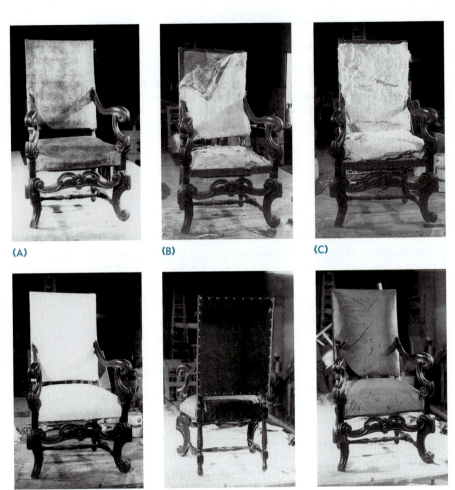

Reupholstery   Reupholstery involves removing the existing fabric covering and making the item stage ready by making any necessary repairs and strengthening the piece, restructuring the padding, and replacing the outer covering and decoration. The existing fabric should be carefully removed, as shown in Figure 13.10, so it can be used as a pattern for cutting the new covering material. Once the old fabric is removed, the padding, springs, and webbing should be examined and repaired as necessary. Depending on the age of the piece, the old padding may be urethane foam, cotton batting, or horsehair. Any damaged or compressed padding should be replaced with the same type of material.

When upholstering stage furniture the sofa or chair springs are frequently removed and replaced with plywood. The plywood not only provides a solid base for the padding, it helps strengthen the chair frame and provides some of the extra durability needed for most stage business. A base of urethane foam—urethane foam is available in a variety of densities from most upholstery supply houses—is cut to size and covered with polyester or cotton batting to create the appropriate period shape and feel.

Before applying the new upholstery fabric, the padding/batting should be covered with muslin. The muslin holds the padding and batting in place, allows the upholstery fabric to move freely without snagging the padding, and serves as a base for any future reupholstery jobs.

Upholstery **gimp,** fringe, or trims are often glued or tacked onto the piece to cover the raw edges of upholstery fabric that have been stapled to the frame. The

gimp: An ornamental flat braid or round cord used as trimming.

FIGURE 13.11
Several styles of curtains.

judicious use of glue and/or upholstery tacks will make it easier to remove them when the time comes to, once again, reupholster that piece.

Decorative Curtains and Draperies

Decorative curtains are used by the scenic designer to help **dress** the set. The type and style of drapery or curtain selected should be dictated by the period that is being represented in the design. Background research is done by looking at paintings, drawings, or photographs that show drapery styles of the period being represented. Figure 13.11 illustrates several typical styles of curtains.

A variety of materials are used in making draperies. The specific type of material is dictated by where it is used in the drape. The **valance, drapes** (also called overdrapes), and **sheers** are the primary elements of any window-curtain arrangement. The valance is generally made from heavy drapery material, although it can be made of wood painted or covered with fabric. A wooden valance is called a valance box. Heavy, soft drapery materials like those used for stage drapes (velour, velveteen, corduroy, commando) are generally used for the drapes, and lightweight, translucent materials such as chiffon and netting (see Chapter 18, "Costume Design") are used for making sheers.

Papier-Mâché

Papier-mâché is one of the oldest craft techniques used in the theatre. It is also one of the cheapest. It is used to make, or cover, a wide variety of shapes and objects that range from logs to statues, clubs, and various types of fake food.

Papier-mâché is made by building up a form with successive layers of paper that are bound together with a wheat-paste binder. The normal method of working with it is to tear newspaper into strips about 1 inch wide, dip them in the wheat-paste mixture, and form them over the mold. Between three and six layers of paper are usually applied to the form. After the object has dried (usually 24 to 48 hours), it can be painted with any of the paints used in the shop.

Craft stores frequently sell a prepared mixture of very finely shredded paper and wheat paste. You only need to add water to this papier-mâché mix to create a pastelike substance that can be used for sculpture or as a smooth finish coat over rough objects. It can also be formed in molds.

The disadvantages of papier-mâché have resulted in it rarely being used in the theatre today. It's fragile, so things made out of papier-mâché don't stand up very well to anything other than very limited-run productions. It takes a fairly long time to dry. It's native finish is pretty crude unless you coat it with something like **paperclay,** which then allows you to apply a number of different

dress: To place decorative props such as curtains, doilies, knickknacks, or magazines on the set to help make the environment look lived-in and provide clues to the personality of the set's inhabitants.

valance: A horizontal element at the top of a drapery arrangement that covers the curtain rod.

drape: A vertical element of heavy fabric that frames the sides of a window or archway; can usually be pulled across the opening.

sheer: A thin gauze curtain that hangs across the opening of a window to soften the "sunlight" and obscure the view into a room.

paperclay: A nontoxic modeling material that can be sculpted, molded or shaped, and air dries to a hard finish that can be carved or sanded.

PRODUCTION INSIGHTS
Drapery and Upholstery Materials

All materials used for stage draperies have roughly the same characteristics. They generally have a soft, nonreflective surface and are available in a variety of colors. Upholstery and decorative drapery materials are not nearly so limited. They are available in a variety of finishes and a panoply of colors.

Factory flame-retardant treatment for stage drapery and flat-covering materials is required by law. When you purchase stage drapes, or material from which to make stage drapes, be certain that the supplier provides a certificate of flame-retardant treatment and keep it on file as it is a distinct possibility that a fire marshal may ask to see it. If the materials aren't flameproofed when you buy them, they will have to be treated by hand, and most flameproofing solutions, if applied by hand, will darken the fabric in an uneven pattern.

Velour

Velour is a cotton-backed material with a deep surface pile generally made from cotton, rayon, or nylon. It is available in a variety of weights ranging from 12 to 25 ounces per square yard and widths from 45 to 54 inches. The material is available in a wide variety of colors, has a rich, lustrous appearance, and absorbs light well. It is generally the preferred material for stage drapes as well as rich, heavy decorative curtains and some upholstery applications. Crushed velour, in which the nap is compressed to create an irregular textural pattern, is a common upholstery material.

Velveteen

Velveteen possesses the same general characteristics as velour does, but it is much lighter—6 to 8 ounces. It has a lustrous pile finish and is generally available in 45- to 48-inch widths from local fabric stores. It is normally used for decorative curtains and upholstery. The material, which wrinkles easily, is not durable enough to be used for stage drapes.

Plush

The pile of plush is softer and longer than that of velveteen but has the same characteristically silklike sheen. Available in a variety of colors and widths from 45 to 54 inches, plush can be purchased from local fabric and upholstery shops. It is used as an upholstery or drapery material.

Commando

Commando cloth, also known as duvetyn, is a lightweight cotton fabric with a very short, feltlike, almost matted pile. It is available in two widths and weights: 36-inch (lightweight) and 48-inch (heavy-weight). The heavy-weight material is good for stage drapes but is a little stiff to be used for decorative drapes. The lightweight is suitable for decorative drapes but is a little too delicate for the rugged treatment that most stage drapes receive. Neither type is particularly appropriate for upholstery applications. Commando cloth is available in a variety of colors and can be purchased from scenic-fabric supply houses.

Cotton Rep

Cotton rep is a tough cotton fabric with a ribbed finish that is similar to a very-narrow-wale corduroy. It reflects light more than other drapery materials do. Rep is available in a wide range of colors from scenic-fabric supply houses. It can be used for stage or decorative drapes.

Damask

Damask achieves its rich appearance from the raised patterns of high-luster yarn that are normally woven into the matte finish of the background cloth. The heavy material is available from local fabric houses in a wide range of colors and in widths ranging between 45 and 54 inches. It is primarily used for decorative drapes and upholstery.

Brocade

Brocade is similar to damask but lighter in weight. The pattern, which can be either raised or flat, is generally created through the use of high-luster yarn that contrasts with the matte finish of the background. 45 to 54 inches wide, brocade is available in a wide range of colors and patterns in fabric and drapery shops. It is primarily used for decorative drapes and upholstery.

Satin

Satin is a heavy, stiff fabric with a smooth, shiny finish on the front and a dull finish on the back. If it is patterned, the design is generally printed on, rather than woven into, the fabric. Available in a wide range of colors and pattern designs, it is normally between 45 and 54 inches wide and can be purchased at local fabric and drapery shops. It is used for decorative drapes and upholstery.

Corduroy

Corduroy is a cotton material whose pile ridges, called wales, alternate with a low-luster backing. The width of the wale varies from only $1/32$ to approximately $3/16$ inch. The weight of the material also varies considerably, with the lighter-weight versions suitable for costumes and the heavier weights more appropriate for upholstery. Corduroy is available in a wide selection of colors and in fabric widths from 45 to 54 inches. It can be purchased from local fabric and upholstery shops. Waleless corduroy (similar to a very-short-nap velour) or very-narrow-wale corduroy can be used as a substitute for velvet in draperies, costumes, and upholstery; the wide-wale fabrics are primarily used for upholstery purposes.

paints/coatings with finish reflectivities ranging from matte to gloss. Even with these disadvantages, if you have the time to work with it, and you're looking for a formable material that is very inexpensive, papier-mâché may be just what you're looking for.

Vacuum Forming

Vacuum forming, or vacuforming, is the process of shaping plastics through the application of heat and vacuum pressure. Shapes can be formed with a vacuforming table of the type shown in Figure 13.12.

The vacuum-forming machine consists of a heating oven, a forming table, and a pump to evacuate air from a tank to create a vacuum reservoir. A sheet of plastic is heated by the oven until it becomes limber. While it is still hot, it is placed over a mold on the forming table, and the valve to the vacuum reservoir is released. The pressure of the outside air trying to reach the vacuum reservoir forms the plastic around the mold. When the thermoplastic cools (in a few seconds), it retains the shape of the mold.

This very flexible system can be used to form decorative items for both properties and scenery. Small decorative relief panels glued onto basic frames or box forms can be used to create very realistic looking items like decorative screens, stoves, and desks. Appropriately designed vacuum-formed panels can also be used to create scenic items like wall panels and cornices. Generally speaking, the vacuum form machine is used in those situations where one basic form has to be repeated a gazillion times and that form either can't be purchased or is simply too expensive to purchase in quantity.

High-impact polystyrene 0.020 inch thick is the most commonly used material in vacuum forming, because it is thick enough to be reasonably strong after it has been stretched over the mold during forming. The material can be painted with acrylic vinyl, casein, and most oil- or lacquer-base paints. Other types of plastic that can be vacuum formed include thin sheets (0.010 to 0.025 inch thick) of acrylic, vinyl, and cellulose acetate butyrate (CAB). (See Chapter 10 for a discussion of the various types of plastics.) Plans for vacuum-forming machines are available at several online sites. Just search for "vacuum-forming machines."

Molds

In property, costume, and scenic production, molds can be used to create multiple copies of a wide variety of objects ranging from fake loaves of bread to costume jewels and decorative panels. But a word of caution seems advisable. Making molds and casting objects in those molds generally subscribes to Murphy's Law: if something can go wrong it will. If only a few copies of something are needed it's usually faster, cheaper, and easier to simply buy whatever it is. But, at the

FIGURE 13.12
A vacuforming table. Photo courtesy of Jim Guy.

Safety Tip

MSDSs — A Reminder

It's axiomatic that in technical theatre we're almost always working in a hurry. There's so much to do and, usually, not enough time to do it. But just because you're in a hurry, don't try to take a shortcut when it comes to safety issues.

The materials typically used in property construction—exotic combinations of adhesives, paints, resins, coatings, and so forth—create what is potentially the most hazardous working environment that you'll encounter anywhere in theatre. Be sure the area in which you're using any of these materials is ventilated according to MSDS and OSHA standards. Also be sure that you read the MSDSs for any material you're working with and follow the safety instructions therein. If the data sheet for the material with which you're working recommends wearing a mask or respirator with a specific type of filter, be sure that you wear it! 'Tis better to be safe than sorry.

FIGURE 13.13
Rigid (top) and flexible (bottom) molds.

same time, mold-making and casting provides the property artisan with a technique can be used to create multiple copies of intricately detailed small articles.

Molds can be divided into two categories — open and closed. The only significant difference between the two is that the open mold has an open top or port, whereas the closed mold is enclosed on all sides and has one or more ports into which the casting material is poured.

Molds can further be subdivided into rigid and flexible. Rigid molds (Figure 13.13 top) are generally made from such materials as wood, plaster of paris, fiberglass, or rigid urethane foam. Flexible molds (Figure 13.13 bottom) can be made from a variety of synthetic materials such as room-temperature-vulcanizing (RTV) silicone rubber. RTV silicone rubber and other mold-making materials can usually be found at local craft or art supply shops.

In order to remove the cast object from the mold, the inside of the mold must have been treated with a release agent before being filled with the casting material. The release agent needs to be compatible with the type of material being cast. A silicone release agent, commercially available in spray cans, will work well for polyester, acrylic, and epoxy resins, but the heat generated by the urethane casting resins requires that a urethane mold release be used with both pour-in-place and spray foams. Both types of release agent are generally available at craft or hobby shops.

Many molding and casting products release gas or fumes during the mixing or curing process. When working with any of these materials it is important that all recommended safety procedures are followed carefully. Information for the safe use of each product is normally printed on the container labels. It is also available on the MSDS sheets that can be obtained from the dealer or online. Good ventilation is necessary for all of them. Most of these materials necessitate the wearing of disposable latex or vinyl gloves. Face shields, respirators, and protective clothing should be worn when working with the more hazardous products. But again, the specific safety equipment required, and its specifications, are detailed on the relevant container labels and MSDS sheets.

Making a Mold   Rigid molds of objects that don't have a great deal of detail can be made fairly quickly by coating the **model** with a urethane release agent and then covering it with either pour-in-place or spray urethane foam (rigid formulation), as shown in Figure 13.14. This type of mold works well for objects that are free from **undercuts,** such as bricks and planks. Rigid molds can also be made in the same manner from plaster of paris or fiberglass.

If there are undercuts on the object being cast, a flexible mold is needed. This type of mold can be made with RTV silicone rubber, as shown in Figure 13.15.

A flexible mold that reveals a great deal of detail of the object being cast can be made by coating the model with silicone release, followed by several layers of liquid latex. Three to five coats are generally required. After the latex has dried, the inside of the box is coated with urethane release agent or lined with polyethylene film (urethane won't adhere to polyethylene), and flexible urethane foam is poured into the mold box. The flexible urethane foam will bond with, and provide a strong backing for, the latex mold.

Casting Molded Objects   It is fairly easy to cast objects from molds. The inside of the mold is coated with an appropriate release agent, and the molding material is poured into the mold and allowed to dry or set. After the material has cured (the time required varies depending on the material, heat, and humidity), the cast object is taken out of the mold. Depending on the complexity of the mold and the material being cast, some finishing details such as sanding or trimming may be required.

model: An object that is being used as the subject of a mold casting.

undercut: An indentation in a form that leaves an overhang or concave profile — for example, the nostrils in a mask of a face.

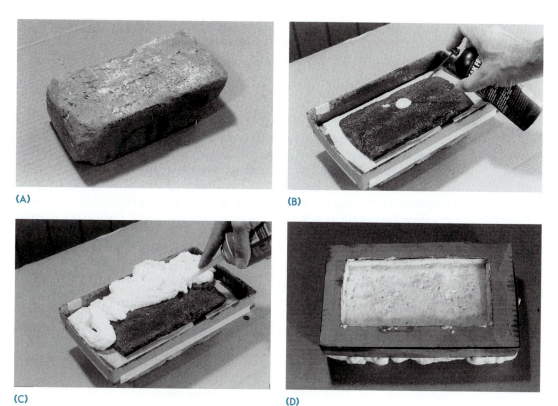

(A)

(B)

(C)

(D)

FIGURE 13.14
Rigid mold-making technique. (A) The object being cast: a brick. (B) Attach a collar to create a box for the mold, and coat the brick and box with a silicone release agent. (C) Coat the brick and box with spray urethane foam (rigid formula). (D) The finished mold. Be sure to read, and follow, all safety directions on the labels and MSDSs for the materials with which you're working.

(A)

(B)

(C)

(D)

FIGURE 13.15
Flexible mold-making technique. (A) The object being cast: a brooch. (B) Place the brooch in a cardboard box, and spray both with a silicone release agent. (C) Pour RTV rubber into the box until it covers the top of the brooch to a depth of about $1/8$ inch. (D) The finished mold and the brooch.

In order to paint the cast object, you will generally need to remove all traces of the release agent. Read the label on the release agent's container to determine the type of cleaner that will be needed.

Heat Forming

Heat forming generally refers to warming plastic until it becomes flexible enough to bend. Sheet and rod acrylic or PVC can be heated and formed without any preparatory work. Tubes should be filled with sand before they are heated, to prevent them from crimping or collapsing as they are being bent.

If the pieces of acrylic or PVC are small enough, it will be possible to heat the plastic in the oven of a kitchen stove. Remove any paper or protective covering from the plastic, and put the plastic on a cookie sheet. Preheat the oven to 300°F, and heat the plastic for a couple of minutes, or until it is limber enough to bend. The plastic can be formed over a mold or clamped in position until it has cooled. Be sure to wear heavy gloves when heat-forming plastics.

Fiberglass

Fiberglass is formed by coating glass-fiber reinforcement with polyester or epoxy resin, as illustrated in Figure 13.16. Polyester resin is normally used, because it is less expensive. The most common types of glass reinforcement are (1) a woven glass-fiber cloth in either sheet or tape form and (2) a glass mat that closely resembles felt cloth. The great strength of fiberglass results from the tensile strength of the glass reinforcement being locked into place by the resin.

Because of safety issues involved in the use of catalyzed polyester resin (see the box "Catalyzed Polyester Resin" on page 337) most theatrical fiberglass projects now use Aqua Resin rather than polyester or epoxy resin. Aqua Resin is a water-based material that poses none of the health or safety risks of the other resins. It has the same properties and is used in exactly the same manner as polyester resin. The only exception involves large structures where strength becomes an issue. Aqua Resin is not as strong as either polyester or epoxy resin. A tech sheet detailing the specifications and working characteristics of Aqua Resin can be found at: http://www.sculpt.com/technotes/Tech_Sheets/TECH_SHEET_AR_L_S.pdf.

For most applications in property construction, the cloth or mat is draped over an **armature** and held in place with clothespins, wire, or tape. It is also possible to form the fiberglass by using molds.

When the glass-fiber cloth is formed, it is saturated with a coating of resin. A second layer of cloth or mat can be added for additional strength after the resin

armature: A basic skeletal form that holds the covering materials in the desired shape or alignment.

FIGURE 13.16
Fiberglass construction techniques.
(A) "Flesh out" a wooden skeleton with newspaper to create the basic form.
(B) Cover the armature with aluminum foil, and (C) drape fiberglass cloth over it to create the line of the sculpture, and coat it with catalyzed resin. (D) The finished form. It can be reinforced with additional coats of glass cloth or mat as necessary and painted or finished as desired.

(A)

(B)

(C)

(D)

Catalyzed Polyester Resin

Polyester resin does not dry the way paint or varnish does. It will remain in its liquid state until a catalyzing agent, methylethylketone (MEK), is added and thoroughly stirred into the resin. The catalyst initiates a change in the molecular structure of the resin from liquid to solid. MEK is highly toxic. Be sure to read, and follow, the MSDS regarding appropriate safety equipment, working procedures, and shop ventilation when working with this chemical.

When the resin "kicks off" (begins to change its physical state), heat is released. If you carefully follow the suggested recipe that is printed on the resin container, you should have between 10 and 20 minutes to work with the catalyzed resin. When the resin kicks off, it turns to a jellylike consistency very quickly. From this point, it will take 12 to 24 hours for it to fully cure.

Disposable paper cups make excellent mixing containers for resin, since you can throw them away after the resin has kicked off. Apply the resin with natural-bristle brushes, because it will dissolve synthetic bristles. Thoroughly clean any application equipment with acetone before the catalyzed resin gels; you won't be able to clean it after the resin has begun to cure.

has cured for 12 to 24 hours. Be sure to lightly sand the surface between coats. Generally, two to three coats will be strong enough for most scenic or property applications. Another advantage of the use of Aqua Resin is that most water-based paints will adhere to its cured surface. If polyester resin is used, it generally has to be first painted with a lacquer-based primer before most stage paints can be applied.

The design and construction of stage properties is a genuinely fascinating field. If your interest in this field has been piqued, you should undertake further study of the almost innumerable design and craft areas such as painting, furniture construction, upholstery, electricity, metalworking, ceramics, and sewing that are part of this theatrical specialty.

Chapter 14

Lighting Design

Any dramatic production, unless it is performed outdoors in the daytime, needs some kind of artificial light. On the other hand, if illumination were the only function of stage lighting, you could hang a bank of fluorescent lights over the stage and forget about all the dimmers, control boards, cables, instruments, and other complicated paraphernalia of stage lighting.

Obviously, there is something more to stage lighting than simply bathing the stage with light. Effective stage lighting not only lets the spectators see the action of the play but also ties together all the visual elements of the production and helps create an appropriate mood and atmosphere that heighten the audience's understanding and enjoyment of the play.

Controllable Qualities of Light

Tharon Musser, a prominent professional lighting designer, has said, "If you ask most people who walk in and tell you they want to be lighting designers, what kind of weather we are having—what's it like outside?—half of them won't know how to describe it, if they remember it at all. They simply don't know how to see."[1] Learning how to see—to understand how light shapes and modifies people and objects—is absolutely essential in learning to understand lighting design.

A lighting designer can "see" how the lighting should look for a production only if he or she has an understanding of the controllable qualities of the medium. The qualities of light that the lighting designer can control are divided into four categories: distribution, intensity, movement, and color.

Light and Perception

Before you can design with light you need to understand how light influences human perceptions and understanding. We all know what light does—it makes things visible. But to know "how lighting design works" it is essential to fully comprehend the following concept: our impressions and understanding of what we're looking at are determined, to a great extent, by the way that object is illuminated. The angle of the light, its intensity, color, and sharpness or diffusion all affect our perceptions. Almost everyone has heard of the phrase "the ever-changing face of the mountains." But, if you stop to think about it, unless there is some cataclysmic disaster, the features of any particular mountain or mountain range

---

[1] "Tharon Musser," *Lighting Dimensions* 1(1977):16.

change very little over hundreds or thousands of years. But the light striking those mountains changes significantly over the course of a day. The play of highlight and shadow shift continuously as the sun moves across the sky. Clouds or fog soften or obscure part of the range. A hillside that is in full sun in the morning may be in deep shadows in the afternoon. At sunset the whole mountain can be bathed in a beautifully soft peach twilight. The manner in which the sun illuminates the mountain controls not only what we see but, to a great extent, how we feel about what we're seeing.

Intellectually everyone understands that the physical structure of the mountains hasn't changed. But our individual perception, our personal reaction to those mountains, is based on a complex process involving both our intellectual recognition and emotional reaction to what we're seeing.

Our emotional reaction to anything is controlled by two primary elements: instinct and learned behavior. An example may help explain the process. Imagine it's a pleasant sunny day. You're walking on a sidewalk next to a small park. A low stone wall is between you and the park. The park is visually pleasant—a thick carpet of grass under a canopy of large shade trees. A young couple sits on a blanket quietly talking. Across the street are several stores—a bookshop, a clothing store, a bank, and a drugstore on the corner. Now, imagine that you're on the same sidewalk at 2:00 A.M., on a moonless night. It's really dark. The only light comes from the window of the all-night drugstore across the street at the far end of the park. As you walk beside the stone wall you hear a noise coming from the park. You peer into the darkness. A little starlight filters through the leaves. You see something move. You get scared and quicken your pace as you cross the street then almost break into a run as you rush into the drugstore.

As mentioned earlier, our emotional reaction to anything we see is controlled by two primary elements: instinct and learned response. Instinctively, most people are afraid of the dark. This response was genetically programmed into our ancestors hundreds of thousands of years ago when our progenitors were roaming the plains and woodlands looking for food. Our primary defense against being eaten by something larger, faster, and stronger was to be able to see it. If we couldn't see it, it might "get" us. Humans don't see well in the dark, so those of our ancestors who avoided dark places generally had a better chance of surviving to pass on their gene pool than those who indiscriminately wandered off into the dark. With each succeeding generation this healthy act of self-preservation became more and more reinforced in our genetic makeup.

The second contributor to our reaction to what we see is learned response. From the time we're infants we are busy learning. Almost all of that early learning is experiential—learning by experience. That information is stored in the brain. What we learn experientially is a major contributor to how we will react in any given circumstance. On a cloudy summer day I've occasionally looked outside and absently thought, "It looks like it going to snow." Logically, I know that it can't snow, but there was something about the "look" of the clouds—their shape, color, movement—that reminded me of the way it looks before a snowstorm. Our subconscious mind is constantly comparing incoming information —what we're currently seeing—with memories of what we've experienced in the past in its ongoing struggle to help our conscious minds make sense of our surroundings.

An interesting example of this learned response took place during the University of Arizona production of *Terra Nova*, which is primarily set in Antarctica and chronicles Scott's ill-fated trip to the South Pole. (See Figures 6.14 through 6.21.) The director wanted the light for the Antarctica scenes to be "white and painfully bright." At first I left the lights uncolored, but the white light seemed warm rather than color. Before the next rehearsal I put a light blue **color media** into

color media: Colored plastic, gel, or glass filters used to modify the color of light.

all the lights. At rehearsal that night almost all the people in the audience, including myself, complained of being chilly or cold. The thermostat in the theatre hadn't been changed from the previous day. The only difference was the light blue color in the lights. My assumption was that our subconscious minds saw the pale blue light, compared it with memories of "the color of cold," and convinced our conscious minds into thinking that the theatre actually was cold. After opening night we had numerous complaints from the paying audience that the theatre was "too cold." We raised the thermostat a few degrees even though the production occurred in late September in Tucson when the average temperature was in the high nineties. Such is the power of the mind.

The reasons that we design the lighting for an event or place are to influence the audience's perception and understanding of what they're seeing. That is the reason that lighting is thoughtfully designed for theatre, films, and television as well as for rock concerts, theme parks, and retail stores. Lighting influences our perceptions and understanding. Machiavellian, isn't it?

Distribution

Distribution is a catchall term that refers to several elements: (1) the direction from which the light approaches an area, actor, or object; (2) the shape and size of the area that the light is covering; and (3) the quality of the light—its diffusion or clarity.

Intensity

Intensity is the actual amount, or level of brightness, of light that strikes the stage or actor. Intensity can range from total darkness to painfully brilliant white light.

Movement

Movement can be divided into three general categories: (1) the timed duration of the light cues; (2) the movement of onstage lights, such as a lantern or candle that an actress carries across the stage; and (3) the movement of an offstage light source, such as a followspot or kinetic/moving lights.

Color

Color, which was discussed at length in Chapter 6, is an extremely powerful tool of the designer. The judicious use of appropriately tinted light can greatly assist the audience's understanding of, and reaction to, the play.

Functions of Stage Light

To increase the audience's understanding and appreciation of a play, stage lighting needs to perform several basic functions.

Visibility

A reasonably accurate adage in the theatre holds that "if you can't see 'em, you can't hear 'em." Stage lighting needs to make everything on stage—the actors, costumes, and setting—clearly visible to the spectators. At the same time, how-

FIGURE 14.1
Selective focus with light. Notice how your attention moves from person to person in the photo on the left, whereas your attention is directed to the highlighted actress in the photo on the right.

ever, the concept of "designed," or controlled, visibility dictates that those actors and objects be seen only in the manner that the designer and director intend. One of the real challenges of lighting design is to create a selective visibility that subtly directs the spectators' attention. The number of lighting instruments and other sources used to light a scene, the color of those lights, and their direction and intensity all affect visibility.

Selective Focus

Selective focus means directing the spectators' attention to a specific place. The lighting designer can selectively focus attention in a number of ways, but the primary method is by manipulating our instinctive response to light. Everybody has a strong instinct to look at an area of brightness or movement in an otherwise neutral scene. By simply making one part of the stage brighter than the rest of the set, the lighting designer forces the spectators to look there (Figure 14.1). This technique of emphatic focus is amply demonstrated, for example, whenever a followspot is used in a musical number.

Modeling

Modeling is the revealing of the form of an object through the pattern of highlight and shadow that is reflected from that object to the eye. The distribution and intensity of the light will, to a great extent, determine our visual understanding of that object. If you have ever yelped, "But that doesn't look like me!" when confronted by a flash snapshot of yourself, you have had a demonstration of this effect. The light from a camera-mounted flashbulb or strobe approaches us from a very unnatural angle—straight from the front and parallel with the floor. Light coming from this direction fills in the areas where we normally expect to see shadows—under the eyebrows, cheekbones, nose, and jaw line. It also puts highlights in rather unexpected places. Because of this redirection of the expected pattern of highlight and shadow, the picture doesn't look like the face that we remember.

Direction is the primary element used in modeling, although intensity, movement, and color all affect modeling to a lesser degree. A change in any or all of these variables will inevitably result in an apparent change of form and feeling of the object being lit.

Mood

Creating a mood with light is one of the easiest and, at the same time, most difficult aspects of stage lighting. It is relatively easy to create a spectacular sunset effect or a sinister feeling of lurking terror; the difficulty comes in integrating these impressive effects with the other elements of the production. Effective stage lighting is subtle and rarely noticed. Although it is fun to create a sunset or similar breathtaking visual display, the opportunity to do so legitimately does not present itself in many plays. Within the parameters of the production concept, stage lighting is usually designed to enhance the mood of the play as unobtrusively as possible.

Designing with Light

Before you can create with light, you have to *see* the light. Let's explore (with visual aids) the effects that can be achieved by manipulating the first two controllable qualities of light—distribution and intensity—to affect the four functions of light: visibility, selective focus, modeling, and mood.

The series of photographs in Figure 14.2 illustrates how varying the direction of light affects the face of an actress. Each photograph is accompanied by a drawing that shows the relative **plan angle** of the light. The **sectional angle** of the light is 45 degrees and shows the angle of the light relative to the actor's face.

Surrounding an actor with a number of light sources provides the potential for modeling with light. In Figure 14.3 the direction of the light varies, but the intensity remains the same. A front light (Figure 14.3A) by itself is unflattering; it tends to flatten and compress facial and bodily features. Both side lights (Figure 14.3B) and top lights (Figure 14.3C) create highlights along the edges of the head and body but cause deep shadows across the face and front of the body. A combination of side and top lights (Figure 14.3D), together with a front light that fills in the shadows created by the side and top lights, reveals the form of the model by surrounding her with light.

When lit from the side-front at about 45 degrees in both plan and section (Figure 14.3E), the model is smoothly illuminated, but her facial and bodily features are slightly compressed. If a top light or back light is added to the side-front light (Figure 14.3F), the resultant rim or edge light creates a highlight that adds depth to the face and body. As you can see, the greatest potential for modeling is achieved when the model is surrounded with light.

Key and Fill

The terms *key light* and *fill light* (borrowed from film and television) are frequently used to describe the relationship between the direction and relative intensity of light striking an object. The key light is the brightest light on the scene, and the fill light is used to fill the shadows created by the key light.

Psychological Effects of Light

In lighting design, just as in literature, the concepts of good and evil are often associated with light and darkness. When a scene is lit with dark and murky shad-

plan angle: The ground-plan view of an object.

sectional angle: The angle of intersection between the axis of the cone of light emitted by an instrument and the working height—usually the height of an average actor's face (about 5 feet 6 inches)—of the lighting area.

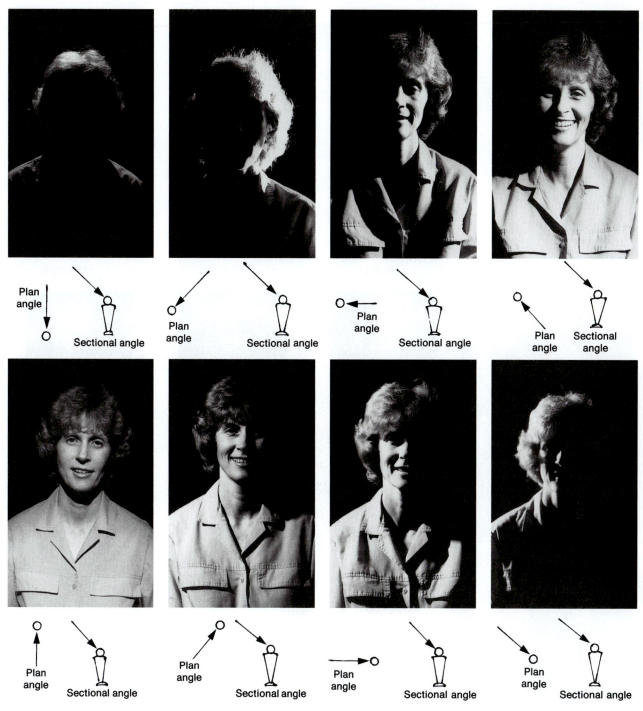

FIGURE 14.2
Effects of varying the direction of light.

ows, most people instinctively react with a sense of foreboding. The suspicion that something could be lurking unseen in the shadows is almost universal. When a scene is brightly lit, we instinctively relax, because we realize that nothing can sneak up on us unseen.

The direction from which light strikes an object has a direct effect on our perception of that object. Light striking a face from a low angle (Figure 14.4A) effectively creates a "monster" light, because such light does not occur in nature. Any light that places the face in heavy shadow, such as the back light shown in

FIGURE 14.3
Surrounding an actor with light creates the most potential for modeling.

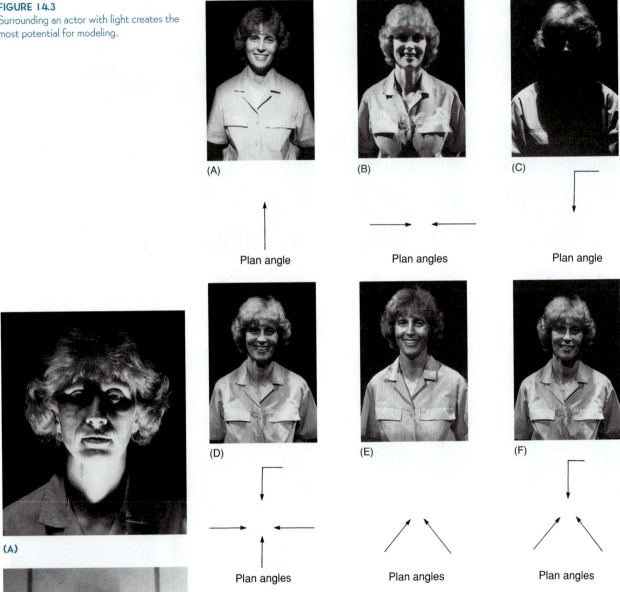

Plan angle   Plan angles   Plan angle

Plan angles   Plan angles   Plan angles

(A)

(B)

FIGURE 14.4
Psychological effects of varying the angle of light.

Figure 14.4B, will create an uneasy reaction in viewers, because they cannot see the facial expression of the person in the shadows and so cannot read his or her intentions.

Those who are interested in learning more about lighting design should become more fully aware of these instinctive, and learned, responses. More information on the psychology of color can be found in Chapter 6, "Color."

The Light Plot and Related Paperwork

Because the product of lighting design—light—is probably the most intangible and abstract of all the theatrical design elements, some specialized paperwork is needed to help in carrying out the design.

The following discussion is based on and quotes extensively from "Thomas Lynch: Far East Marks This Designer's Latest Scenic Transformation," by Arnold Wengrow (Entertainment Design, March 1999, pp. 38–41).

Thomas Lynch, scenic designer of the 1998 revival of *Ah, Wilderness!* produced by Lincoln Center Theatre at the Mitzi Newhouse Theatre in New York City, says, "I'm interested in storytelling, and I'm interested in kinetic scenery, moving the scenery through an evening in a way that helps tell the story, which is different from just putting a drawing room onstage."

For *Ah, Wilderness!*, Lynch and director Daniel Sullivan stripped the gingerbread—and the walls—from the play's turn-of-the-century rooms. Lynch let his interiors breathe against horizontal swathes suggesting forest, ocean, and sky. The setting's visual purity was like sherbet against the sweetness of Eugene O'Neill's sentimental comedy.

Even pared to basics, the rooms exposed on the Newhouse's open stage had to change without impeding the dramatic flow. Lynch also believed that the play's progression demanded specificity. "You have to go to all those places, you can't just skip them. The porch is not the beach. Really you're on the porch. Really you're in the bar. Then, really, you're inside. And then, really, you're at the beach. It's hard to imagine the play, given the language, being simplified all the way down to a unit set. On the other hand, it seems to me that the play is often overburdened with scenic description. You just want to take a machete to it all."

"The transformation into the beach," Lynch said, "was kind of cool. The black band across the bottom at the back was made out of slanted veins covered in Merlin cloth that is 10 times as black as black velour. So actors could come in and out of a seemingly complete blackness. The platform, with its furniture from the porch, could track and swivel, the boat flipped out of the deck downstage right. As that occurred, there was a trade of drops. The green drop rose out of the way, and the ocean drop with the moon was there."

To divert the audience's attention, Lynch and Sullivan sent the story's young protagonist riding on a bicycle in the front of the black strip, as if going to the beach. Lighting completed the illusion. "At the moment of getting to the beach, a feeling of sand was created on the carpeted floor with some blacklight highlights, and the boat was picked up very subtly with blacklight. And then we were just there. It was in seconds, in this big space, so you felt you were looking at everything, but you didn't know how it was being done."

The design included a large, deceptively simple green drop that was actually quite complex. "The big green drop looks like a simple thing. It was not," Lynch said. "It was a very, very complicated thing. It could be frontlit, it could be backlit, and it had opaque painting on the back. Peter Kaczarowski [lighting designer for the production] could do many things on that drop and on this whole set that could give a lusciousness that isn't totally apparent in the bare bones of the scenery pieces. Boy, was I counting on Peter."

To get the painterly density that he wanted on the drop, Lynch specified filled scrim for its lush, velvety weave. But it did not take backlighting well. Kaczarowski suggested backing the drop with rear-projection material. "We needed an RP material which would allow a good deal of transmission and color acceptance," Kaczarowski said. "We were using a lot of patterns—trees and leaves and quite a lot of fireworks effects—and all of that had to go onto a material that would maintain the integrity of the image, rather than diffusing it into one blobby, blurry thing. It had to have clarity and yet prevent us from seeing the lights that did it." After experimenting at Lincoln Center with various materials, they decided on Review, manufactured by Gerriets. In addition to the scrim, the floor and costumes became a canvas for Kaczarowski's light. Colors and patterns were layered onto the neutral floor around the set's central platform.

"There were shadows that had colors in them," said Kaczarowski, "and there was a great variance of color within the shadows. We did a daytime into sunset where the folds in the costumes and the shadows on the floor filled in starting with medium reds and yellows and oranges, going into deeper versions. Then it segued into cool colors for the evening. There was this always-changing, layered picture.

"Tom [Lynch] is interested in oddities," Kaczarowski said, "things that have an effect that you don't generally see on the stage, even if it's only momentary, like the blacklight in *Ah, Wilderness!*. It wasn't something that could stay onstage for very long, but it was a brief moment of great beauty. It was surprising."

Director Dan Sullivan recalls another moment of Lynchian surprise in *Ah, Wilderness!*: "When we got into tech and went to the beach scene, the dark space which had always been there below, butted against the black silhouette of the land above. That negative space itself turned into water, which was fascinating. Looking at the model, I hadn't known that was going to happen." Did the designer know it was going to happen? Sullivan laughs. "I asked Tom if he did, and he said of course he did."

The Light Plot

The light plot is a scale mechanical drawing—a "road map"—that indicates where the lighting instruments should be placed (Figure 14.5). More specifically, it is a "horizontal offset section in which the cutting plane intersects the theatre at whatever level gives the most descriptive view of the instrumentation in the stage

FIGURE 14.5
The light plot for the Canadian Opera Company Hummingbird Centre production of *Il Trovatore*. Lighting design by Joan Sullivan-Genthe. Associate lighting designer: Michael McNamara. Drafting by Joshua Windhausen.

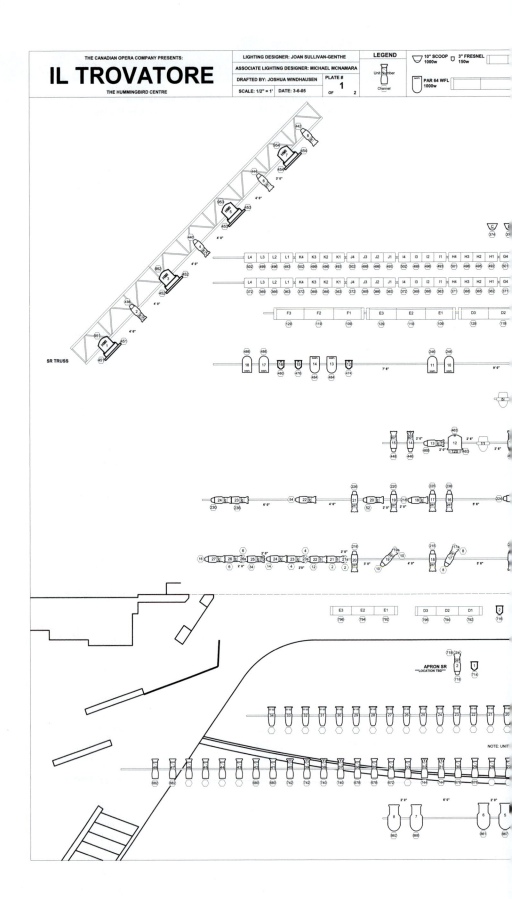

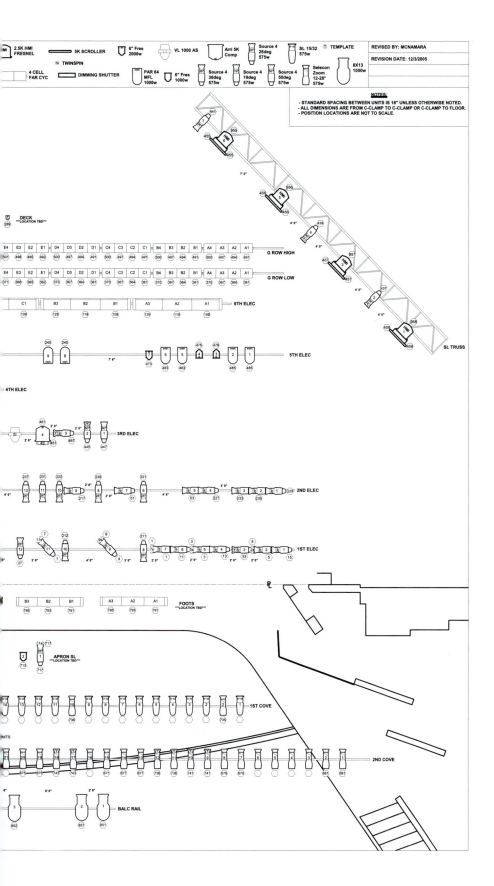

Legend (top):
2.5K HMI FRESNEL · 5K SCROLLER · 6" Fres 2000w · VL 1000 AS · Arri 5K Comp · Source 4 26deg 575w · SL 15/32 575w · TEMPLATE
TWINSPIN · DIMMING SHUTTER · PAR 64 MFL 1000w · 6" Fres 1000w · Source 4 36deg 575w · Source 4 19deg 575w · Source 4 50deg 575w · Selecon Zoom 12-28" 575w · 8X13 1000w
4 CELL FAR CYC

REVISED BY: MCNAMARA
REVISION DATE: 12/3/2005

NOTES:
- STANDARD SPACING BETWEEN UNITS IS 18" UNLESS OTHERWISE NOTED.
- ALL DIMENSIONS ARE FROM C-CLAMP TO C-CLAMP OR C-CLAMP TO FLOOR.
- POSITION LOCATIONS ARE NOT TO SCALE.

Position labels:
DECK ***LOCATION TBD***
G ROW HIGH
G ROW LOW
6TH ELEC
5TH ELEC
4TH ELEC
3RD ELEC
2ND ELEC
1ST ELEC
FOOTS ***LOCATION TBD***
APRON SL ***LOCATION TBD***
1ST COVE
2ND COVE
BALC RAIL
SL TRUSS

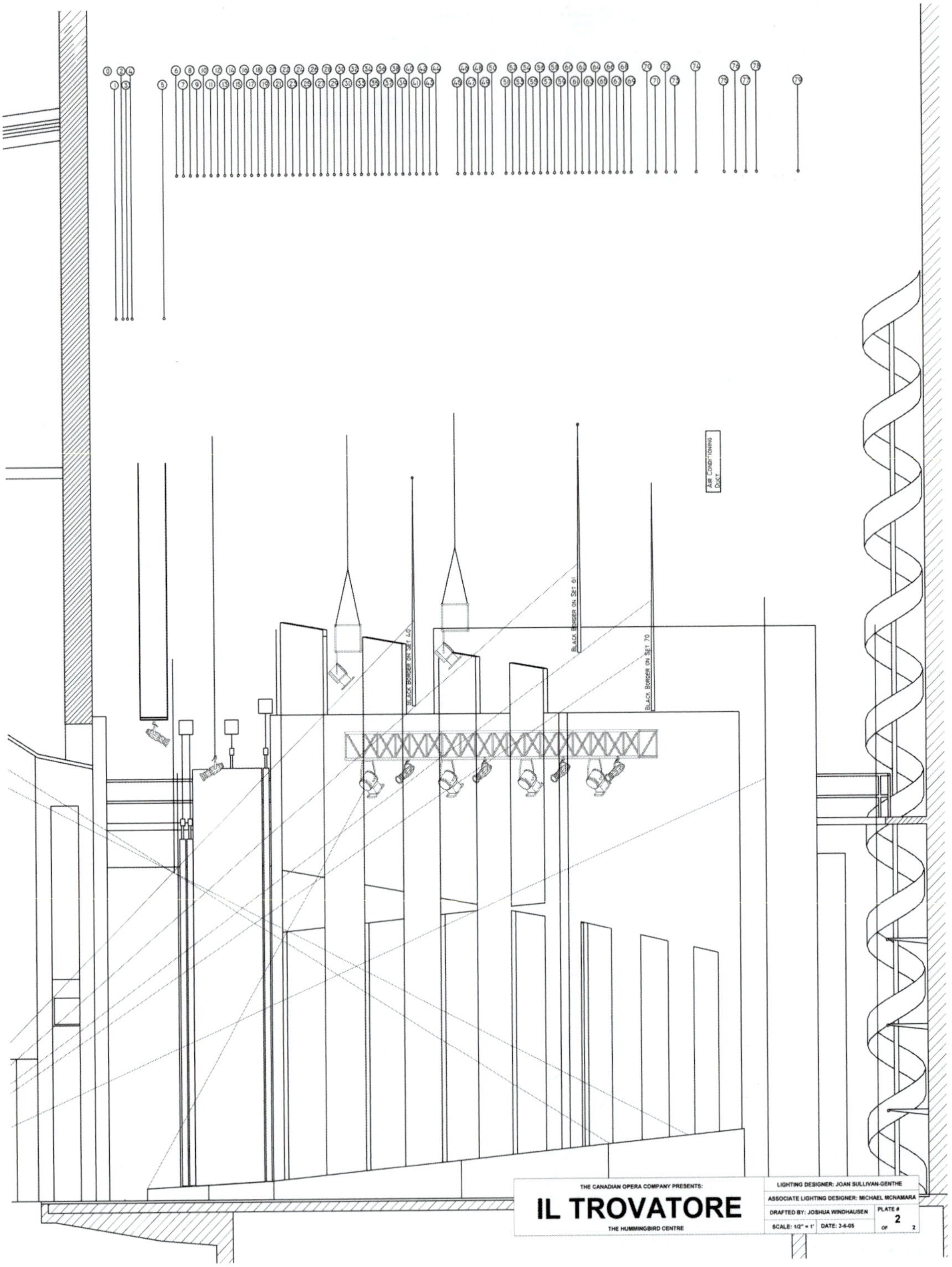

FIGURE 14.6
The lighting section for the Canadian Opera Company Hummingbird Centre production of *Il Trovatore*. Lighting design by Joan Sullivan-Genthe. Associate lighting designer: Michael McNamara. Drafting by Joshua Windhausen.

IL TROVATORE

configuration,"[2] according to the 1991 United States Institute for Theatre Technology's (USITT) graphic standards for stage lighting. The USITT standard for lighting design graphic language is in a constant state of revision. The latest version of the revised standard, which has not officially been adopted by the USITT,

[2] Gill, Patrick, et al., "Revised Standard Graphic Language for Lighting Design," *Theatrical Design and Technology*, Fall 1991, p. 61.

but nevertheless serves as a clear example of the types and styles of standard graphic language that are being recommended for lighting design, is included as Appendix A. The following discussion of lighting design graphics is based, to a large extent, on the recommendations contained in the USITT standard.

Although there is no universally accepted style of drafting light plots, some general information must always be included. Depicting the location of all lighting instruments being used in the production is the primary purpose of the light plot. The lighting designer specifies, to scale (usually ½ or ¼ inch to 1 foot), where the instruments should be placed. The master electrician uses this scale drawing as a guide in hanging and circuiting the plot.

The Lighting Section

The lighting section is a scale drawing, normally in the same scale as the light plot, that isn't really a sectional drawing at all. It is a composite side-view drawing (if the set is basically symmetrical) that shows the position of lighting equipment in relation to the set and the physical structure of the theatre (Figure 14.6). If the set is significantly asymmetrical, then two sections will normally be drawn, one looking stage right from the **centerline,** the other looking stage left. This drawing, used primarily by the lighting designer, has several purposes: to check sight lines of the lighting instruments, to assist in determining the appropriate trim height for horizontal masking, and to ensure that the lighting equipment won't interfere with any scenic elements or vice versa.

The Legend

A legend, or instrument key (Figure 14.7), provides complete identification information about each instrument used on the plot. In addition to identifying the particular type or style of instrument that is denoted by each symbol, the legend should also contain an explanation of the peripheral information (Figure 14.8) that is associated with each instrument symbol. The types of peripheral information that can be used with each lighting instrument symbol are explained below.

Focus Area   The focus area for each instrument is identified by a letter placed in front of the lens housing of the symbol for that instrument. This letter corresponds to the same letter that identifies a specific lighting area on the light plot.

Color   The color number refers to the specific color media that will be used in that particular instrument.

Beam Designation   This symbol provides an indication of an ellipsoidal reflector spotlight's (ERS), or other appropriate instrument type's, focal length or beam angle. This symbol generally isn't used with fresnels.

Gate Accessory   Used to indicate if an ERS has an accessory, such as a gobo or other device, placed in the instrument's gate accessory slot.

Instrument Number   Each instrument needs to be assigned an identification number so that it can be cross-referenced with the **instrument schedule,** or hookup sheet. Figure 14.9 shows how lighting instruments are numbered on the light plot. The specific number recorded for each lighting instrument on the instrument schedule is determined by two factors: (1) its hanging location and (2) its position relative to the other instruments on that **pipe.** The first segment of the number is an abbreviation of its hanging location. The number "1E," illustrated

centerline: A leader line that runs perpendicular to the set line from the midpoint or center of the opening of the proscenium.

instrument schedule: A form used to record all of the technical data about each instrument used in the production; also known as a hookup sheet.

pipe: A counterweighted batten or fixed metal pipe that holds lighting instruments.

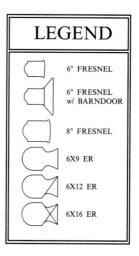

FIGURE 14.7
A sample legend.

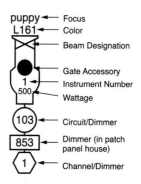

FIGURE 14.8
Recommended instrument notation style.

PRODUCTION INSIGHTS
Drafting for Lighting Design

As we have seen, the lighting designer uses two principal mechanical drawings to record the information that is needed to hang, circuit, and focus the lighting design: the light plot and the lighting section. The purpose of these drawings is to guide the master electrician and crew. The amount and kind of information shown on the paperwork associated with a lighting design vary greatly from production to production and designer to designer. But a set of basic criteria pertains to the drawings associated with any lighting design. The following information is based on the 1991 USITT "Revised Standard Graphic Language for Lighting Design." A newer, proposed USITT standard is included in its entirety as Appendix A at the end of this book.

1. The light plot and lighting section should be drawn to scale.

2. The light plot should show the location of the lighting instruments in relation to the set and the physical structure of the theatre. Instrument symbols should be scale representations of the size of the actual instruments they represent to precisely detail the amount of space they will occupy. They should also be drawn in the same scale as the rest of the drawing.

3. All drawings should adhere to the tenets of good mechanical-drafting techniques (see Chapter 7, "Mechanical Drafting").

4. The darkest lines on the plot should represent instrument symbols and related information, architectural lines should be of medium darkness, and set lines should be the lightest.

5. The instrument key or legend should be used to explain all symbols used on the plot. It should minimally contain

   • Symbol identification for all instruments and devices shown on the plot and controlled by the lighting console, including the instrument manufacturer and wattage.

   • A representation of the typical instrument notation method used.

   • A drawing of the technique used to represent "two-fers."

6. The instrument symbol should include

   • An instrument number as an aid to location.

   • A symbol for attached hardware (such as templates, irises, color scrollers, top hats, barn doors, and so forth).

   • The channel, the circuit and/or dimmer number, and the color notation.

   • A symbol for lamp axis alignment on PAR cans.

   • The method used to illustrate "two-fers."

7. The designation and numbering of hanging positions and instruments in proscenium configurations include the following conventions:

   • Onstage pipes should be numbered from downstage to upstage.

   • Onstage booms should be numbered from downstage to upstage.

   • Box-boom or torm positions should be numbered consistently within each plot.

   • All lighting positions should be designated by stage directions.

   • Front of house (FOH) ceiling positions should be numbered from the apron to the rear of the house as should FOH boom positions, side coves, ladders, or ports.

   • Balcony rails should be numbered from the floor to the ceiling.

   • Pipe grids in "black box" type theatres should be numbered on the x or y axis of the grid and lettered on the opposing axis.

   • Nonconventional black box lighting positions should be identified by compass directions.

   • Trim heights should be indicated from the stage floor or the deck to the pipe with a note on the plot to verify that the measurement is from the "stage floor" or "deck."

   • Instruments on stage electric pipes should be numbered from stage left to stage right.

   • Instruments on booms should be numbered from top to bottom.

   • Strip lights should be labeled (using numbers or letters) from stage left to stage right.

8. Acceptable locations for title blocks are in the lower right-hand or left-hand corners or centered on the bottom of the plate.

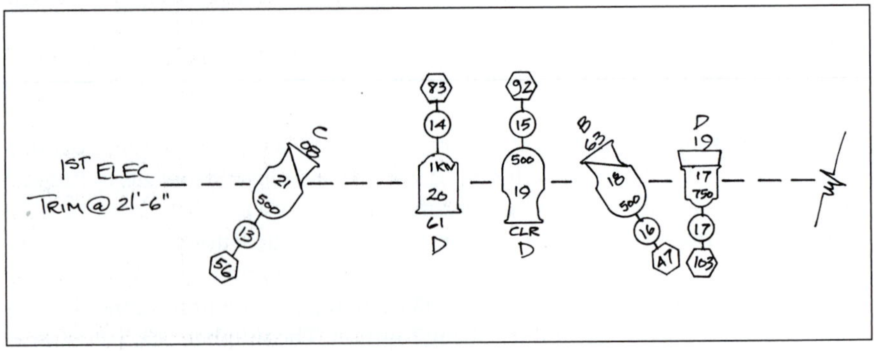

FIGURE 14.9
Instruments are numbered according to two factors: the pipe on which they are hanging and their position relative to other instruments on the pipe.

in Figure 14.10, indicates that the instrument is hanging on the **first electric.** The second part of the number indicates the instrument's sequential position on the pipe. In a proscenium theatre, the numbering of any **electric** starts at the left end of the pipe when viewed as if you were standing with your back against the upstage wall of the stage house. The box "Drafting for Lighting Design" on page 350 explains the USITT-recommended method for numbering instruments for all of the hanging locations in the theatre.

Wattage   This number refers to the wattage of the lamp used in that fixture.

Circuit and/or Dimmer Number   This identifies the stage circuit into which the instrument should be plugged. The appropriate circuit or **dimmer** number can be assigned in this space by the lighting designer, or the space can be left blank to be filled in by the electrician when he or she hangs and circuits the instrument.

Dimmer   This identifies the specific dimmer that will control this instrument. If the theatre is equipped with a patch panel, the circuit number is usually assigned to the circuit/dimmer space (see above), and this space is used for the assignment of the specific dimmer used with this instrument. Again, the dimmer number can be assigned by the lighting designer but is frequently left to the discretion of the master electrician.

Channel/Dimmer   If the theatre has a computer board, this space is normally used for the assignment of the control channel related to this specific instrument.

The above-referenced stipulations should be thought of as guidelines and not as rules that must be slavishly followed. The only *real* criteria pertaining to what information is located in which position, and inside of what type of circular/square/hexagonal space, is that there be consistency, and that that visual logic be applied to all symbols throughout all the drawings for a single design. Realistically, there are so many variables possible for each lighting design—a theatre's in-house equipment (preset or computer control system, dimmer per circuit or dimmers and patch panel circuiting, and so forth) as well as the instrument inventory available (in-house only, or in-house and rental, or all rental) for any particular design, that it is just about impossible to create a standard that can realistically be applied to all design possibilities.

The Instrument Schedule

The instrument schedule, also known as the hookup sheet, is a specification sheet that contains everything you might want or need to know about every instrument that is used on the production (Figure 14.11). It identifies each instrument by its instrument number and specifies its type, hanging location, focus area, circuit, dimmer, lamp wattage, and color. A section for special remarks is used to note anything else that might be appropriate, such as focusing notes, auxiliary equipment that needs to be attached to the instrument, and so forth.

All of the paperwork required in connection with a lighting design can be generated with computer programs. CAD programs can be used to draw the light plot and sectional. Database programs such as Lightwright 4 can be used to compile the instrument schedule or hookup sheet, or you can use a generic database or spreadsheet program such as Lotus or Excel to create your own instrument schedule. If a software program has been specifically developed for lighting design, it may link these two elements. With a linked program, such as Vectorworks Spotlight or LD Assistant, if you change anything—instrument location, color, channel, circuit number, and so forth—on either the plot or hookup sheet,

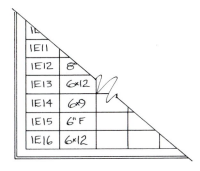

FIGURE 14.10
Details of instrument-notation technique.

first electric: The onstage pipe for lighting instruments that is closest to the proscenium arch.

electric: Any pipe that is used to hold lighting instruments.

dimmer: An electrical device that controls the intensity of a light source connected to it.

FIGURE 14.11
The instrument schedule contains all the technical data about each instrument used in the production.

IL TROVATORE **CHANNEL HOOKUP** Page 1
03 Dec 2005

Canadian Opera Company
Production: Stephen Lawless
LD: Joan Sullivan-Genthe & Michael McNamara

Hummingbird Centre
ALD: Wendy Greenwood
ALD: Heidi Lingren

Channel	Dim Position	Unit	Type & Accessories & Watts	Purpose	Color & Tmp
(1)	1st ELEC	7	ETC S4 19° 575w	X FAR W	
	1st ELEC	7s	Wybron C-Ram II S4 Scroller	1E #7 Scroller	SCROLL 1
(2)	1st ELEC	21	ETC S4 19° 575w	X FAR W	
	1st ELEC	21s	Wybron C-Ram II S4 Scroller	1E #21 Scroller	SCROLL 1
(3)	1st ELEC	5	ETC S4 26° 575w	X CEN W	
	1st ELEC	5s	Wybron C-Ram II S4 Scroller	1E #5 Scroller	SCROLL 1
(4)	1st ELEC	23	ETC S4 26° 575w	X CEN W	
	1st ELEC	23s	Wybron C-Ram II S4 Scroller	1E #23 Scroller	SCROLL 1
(5)	1st ELEC	2	ETC S4 26° 575w	X NR W	
	1st ELEC	2s	Wybron C-Ram II S4 Scroller	1E #2 Scroller	SCROLL 1
(6)	1st ELEC	26	ETC S4 26° 575w	X NR W	
	1st ELEC	26s	Wybron C-Ram II S4 Scroller	1E #26 Scroller	SCROLL 1
(7)	1st ELEC	11	ETC S4 26° 575w	P2 FAR W	
	1st ELEC	11s	Wybron C-Ram II S4 Scroller	1E #11 Scroller	SCROLL 1
(8)	1st ELEC	17	ETC S4 26° 575w	P2 FAR W	
	1st ELEC	17s	Wybron C-Ram II S4 Scroller	1E #17 Scroller	SCROLL 1
(9)	1st ELEC	9	ETC S4 26° 575w	P2 CEN W	
	1st ELEC	9s	Wybron C-Ram II S4 Scroller	1E #9 Scroller	SCROLL 1
(10)	1st ELEC	19	ETC S4 26° 575w	P2 CEN W	
	1st ELEC	19s	Wybron C-Ram II S4 Scroller	1E #19 Scroller	SCROLL 1
(11)	1st ELEC	6	ETC S4 19° 575w	X FAR C	L161
(12)	1st ELEC	22	ETC S4 19° 575w	X FAR C	L161
(13)	1st ELEC	4	ETC S4 26° 575w	X CEN C	L161
(14)	1st ELEC	24	ETC S4 26° 575w	X CEN C	L161
(15)	1st ELEC	1	ETC S4 26° 575w	X NR C (Slash Slider)	L161
(16)	1st ELEC	27	ETC S4 26° 575w	X NR C (Slash Slider)	L161
(21)	1st ELEC	15	ETC S4 26° 575w	XO RIGHT	
	1st ELEC	15s	Wybron C-Ram II S4 Scroller	1E #15 Scroller	SCROLL 1
(22)	1st ELEC	14	ETC S4 26° 575w	XO LEFT	
	1st ELEC	14s	Wybron C-Ram II S4 Scroller	1E #14 Scroller	SCROLL 1
(27)	1st ELEC	12	ETC S4 26° 575w	42 Cell	L161
(33)	1st ELEC	3	ETC S4 26° 575w	Temp X Mid Cen	R99+R99, T: R7806
(34)	1st ELEC	25	ETC S4 26° 575w	Temp X Mid Cen	R99+R99, T: R7806
(51)	2nd ELEC	7	ETC S4 26° 575w	X FAR IN 2	G841
(52)	2nd ELEC	20	ETC S4 26° 575w	X FAR IN 2	G841
(53)	2nd ELEC	5	ETC S4 26° 575w	X CEN IN 2	G841
(54)	2nd ELEC	22	ETC S4 26° 575w	X CEN IN 2	G841

the program will automatically change the same data on the other. The data contained on the instrument schedule can also be used to generate a wealth of other information such as **cut lists, hanging cards,** and so forth.

More information on light plot drafting can be found in Chapter 7, "Mechanical Drafting."

The Image of Light

The image of light is a picture or concept of what the light should look like for a production. The following discussion makes reference to the image of light as a pictorial vision. For the majority of lighting designers these images are pictorial, but they can also be auditory or emotional. It is essential that you develop some type of core image. The mental manifestation of that concept isn't nearly so important.

The analysis of the image of light for its distribution and intensity is probably the prime creative factor in determining the hanging positions for the lighting instruments. To analyze the image of light for its distribution and intensity, you have to see the image of light and then analyze its appearance to determine the angles and relative intensities of the various sources that are illuminating that

cut list: A listing of the colors to be used in the show. Normally listed by gel frame size, for example, 20–6" Roscolux 09, and so forth.

hanging cards: Pieces of the light plot, by position, glued to card stock. Used by electricians when hanging the plot.

PRODUCTION INSIGHTS

Lighting Symbols

Because so much data must be included on a light plot or vertical lighting section, the United States Institute for Theatre Technology has developed a system of symbols for use on these drawings. The following information on lighting symbols is based on those recommendations. The full lighting graphic standard can be found in Appendix A.

Instrument Notation

The normal procedure in drawing a light plot is to use symbols to represent the various types of lighting instrument being used. The USITT-recommended symbols are illustrated in the accompanying figure. A great deal of information is usually associated with each lighting symbol.

Lighting Templates

Lighting templates are used to help in drawing the various symbols for the stage lighting instruments and practical lamps used in most productions. The accompanying photo shows examples of both plan and sectional lighting templates.

Templates are readily available in scales of ¼ inch to 1 foot and ½ inch to 1 foot (which are the most commonly used scales for drafting light plots).

Lettering

The lettering used on the drawings associated with lighting design needs to follow the same criteria of clarity and uniformity outlined in Chapter 7, "Mechanical Drafting."

Lighting templates.

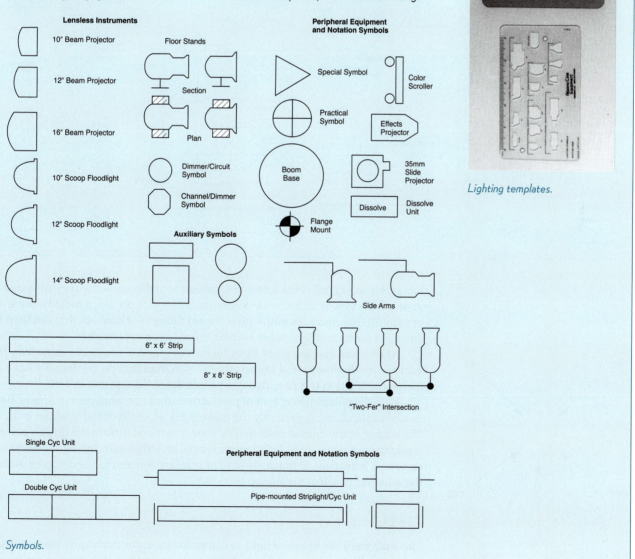

Symbols.

(continued)

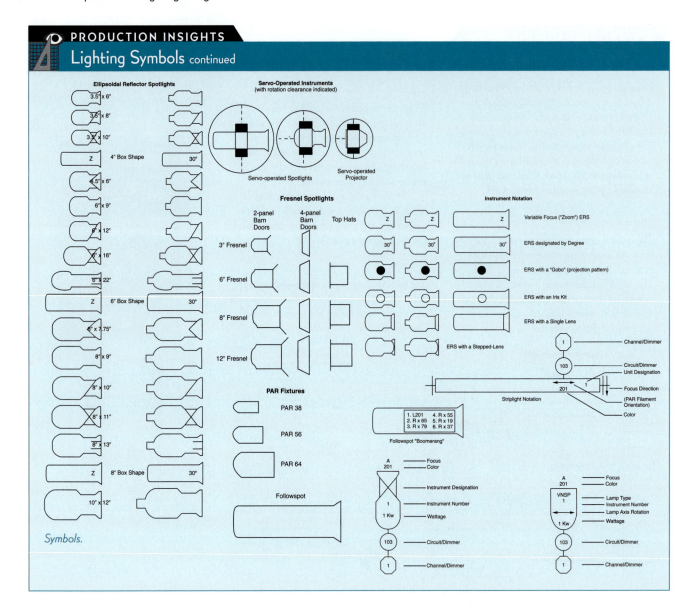

Symbols.

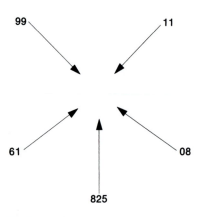

FIGURE 14.12
A lighting key.

image. However, all is not lost if you cannot actually see some type of image in your mind's eye. You can create a nonvisual image (a phrase, a melody, some set of stimuli) that provides you with a central thought or concept that can then be analyzed for its quality (mood, texture, color, intensity) of light.

Analysis of the image of light for its component colors is easier than the analysis for distribution, if for no other reason than that people usually have an emotional reaction to a play that can be translated into specific colors.

With the notable exception of productions that use intelligent or kinetic light fixtures, movement is probably the most easily adjusted of the qualities of light. The timing of the cues is customarily conceptualized during the design period, implemented during the lighting rehearsal, and adjusted during the technical and dress rehearsals. It normally isn't of primary concern to the designer during the selection phase of the design process.

The Lighting Key

The analysis of the image of light to determine its controllable qualities is not just an idle intellectual exercise. The lighting designer codifies that information to create a very pragmatic tool called the lighting key. The lighting key (Figure 14.12) is a drawing that indicates the plan angle and color of the various sources that illuminate the image of light. The lighting key is used by the designer as the primary guide for locating the hanging positions of the lighting instruments.

Acting and Lighting Areas   To fully understand the purpose and function of a lighting key, it will be necessary to digress momentarily and discuss acting areas and lighting areas. Acting areas are those spaces on the stage where specific scenes, or parts of scenes, are played. The shape and size of an acting area (Figure 14.13A), although roughly determined by the shape of the setting, are specifically determined by the blocking patterns used by the actors. A lighting area (Figure 14.13B) is a cylindrical space approximately 8 to 12 feet in diameter and 7 feet tall.

To achieve a smooth wash of light throughout an acting area, it is necessary to overlap individual lighting areas by approximately one-third, as shown in Figure 14.14. This overlapping of adjacent areas takes advantage of the optical properties of the **beam angle** and **field angle** of the stage-lighting instruments to create a smooth wash of light throughout the acting area.

Creating the Lighting Key   The process of converting the image of light into a lighting key is best explained through example. To illustrate this process, we will create a lighting key for *The Playboy of the Western World* by John Millington Synge.

Let's assume that the image of light for this production could be stated as "a bright, twinkling Irish morning." Our analysis of this statement leads us to the conclusion that to achieve the concept of a bright, twinkling Irish morning on the stage it will be necessary to create the following: (1) a light and cheery atmosphere, (2) no shadows, and (3) thin tints of springlike colors.

If an actor in our play were surrounded with light, as shown in Figure 14.15, we would have achieved one of our stated objectives — no shadows. If we adjusted the dimmers that control those lights to a fairly bright setting, we would achieve another of our objectives — a bright atmosphere. By selecting happy, springtime, pastel colors, we would also meet the third objective — a cheery springlike atmosphere.

With this brief analysis of the image of light, we have already determined a great deal of the information that is needed for completing the basic lighting key for our production. Specifically, we have determined the distribution for the basic lighting of each lighting area (four diagonal cross lights) and the basic range of the color palette (pastel tints). Let me hasten to add that this particular solution is not the "correct" analysis of the image of light. There are myriad other possibilities, all of them equally "correct." You could have light from more or fewer

FIGURE 14.13
Acting and lighting areas.

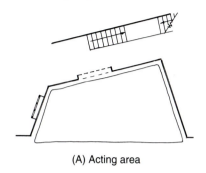

(A) Acting area

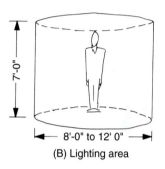

7'-0"

8'-0" to 12' 0"

(B) Lighting area

beam angle: That point in the cone of light emitted by an instrument where the light is diminished by 50 percent when compared with the output of the center of the beam.

field angle: That point in the cone of light where the output diminishes to 10 percent of the output of the center of the beam.

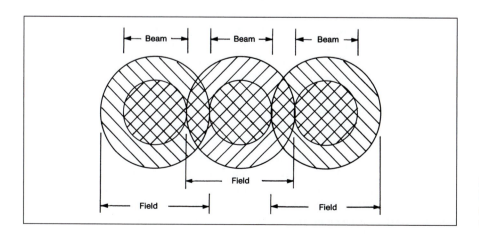

FIGURE 14.14
Lighting areas are overlapped in an acting area to facilitate the creation of a smooth wash of light.

FIGURE 14.15
Four-source lighting key for *The Playboy of the Western World.*

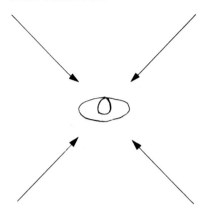

FIGURE 14.16
Six- and three-source lighting keys for *The Playboy of the Western World.*

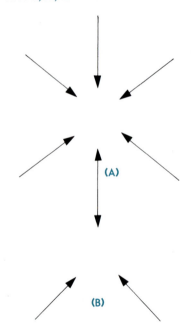

(A)

(B)

FIGURE 14.17
Five-source lighting key for *The Playboy of the Western World.*

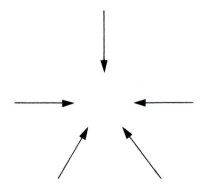

directions (Figure 14.16A and B). You could also interpret the concept of "springtime pastel colors" to mean thin tints of cool colors as opposed to warm — it just depends on your personal understanding of the idea of a springtime atmosphere.

With the foregoing proviso firmly in mind, we make the conscious decision that our lighting key is going to be based on a five-sided distribution pattern (Figure 14.17). We made this decision because this pattern will provide a smooth, shadowless light that will support our interpretation of the image of light. Additionally, the top or back light (the arrow at the top of the pentagon) will provide a nice rim or halo light around the head and shoulders of the actors to prevent them from blending into the set.

Before selecting specific colors for the lighting instruments, you must study the color palettes of the scenic and costume designers. This "color study" normally occurs during the various production conferences as each designer (scenic, costume, lighting) presents his or her design and color concepts. The reason that the lighting designer must know what colors the other designers are using is fairly simple. Colored light can drastically alter the apparent color of the sets and costumes, and it isn't in the interests of a unified production concept (or the lighting designer's physical well-being) to change the other designers' work without their knowledge and consent.

During the initial conferences of our hypothetical *Playboy* production, the design team decided that the play would be produced in a realistic style. Based on this concept, the lighting designer will want the set to appear as though it were being lit by the source lights that are located on the set. To determine the nature of these sources, and their locations, it will be necessary to look at a scenic rendering or model of the set. The scenic sketch (Figure 14.18) shows that there are oil lamps on the counter and each table, there is a peat fire glowing in the fireplace, and the window and door are open. Each of these sources would provide light of differing hues. The sunlight, according to our analysis of the image of light, is cool-white, bright, and cheerful. The fireplace is warmer and redder than the sunlight, and the oil lamps give off a soft, amber glow.

Using this analysis and information as a guide, Roscolux 61, Mist Blue, is selected to represent the bright, clean sunlight. Roscolux 02, Bastard Amber, is chosen for the firelight, and Roscolux 09, Pale Amber Gold, is selected to represent the color emitted by the oil lamps. (Roscolux colors, a common brand of theatrical lighting-instrument media, are being used to identify the specific hues selected for this exercise. These colors are identified by the manufacturer with a name and number.)

Now that the colors have been selected to represent the various sources, they need to be applied to the lighting key. The application of color to the basic distribution pattern of the lighting key should support the thesis that the source lights are providing the light for the environment of the play. To achieve this goal, the lighting designer should color the light from stage left to represent the fireplace color, Bastard Amber, because the fireplace is on the stage-left side of the set. The oil-lamp color (Pale Amber Gold) is used from a direction (stage right) that supports the visual impression that the oil lamps are primarily on the downstage-right part of the set. The light approaching the stage from an upstage direction should represent the sunlight (Mist Blue), because the window and doorway are on the upstage wall of the set.

Figure 14.19 on page 317 shows the colors assigned to the specific distribution pattern that we had previously determined from our analysis of the image of light. The stage-left side light is assigned Bastard Amber, to support the concept that the fireplace is lighting the room from this direction. The top-back light is colored with Roscolux 61, Mist Blue, because this supports the idea that any light approaching the stage from this direction would be sunlight coming through the window or door. The stage-right side light and the stage-right front light are col-

Beam and Field Angles

The field angle for an ellipsoidal reflector spotlight (the most commonly used stage lighting instrument) is approximately twice the beam angle for any given design or make of instrument. In practical terms, this relationship between the beam and field angles means that when the lighting areas are overlapped by one-third, the beam angle of each instrument lights the central, or "un-overlapped," portion of each lighting area, and the field angles of adjacent lighting areas overlap. The result is an additive effect that brings up the intensity level of the overlapped areas to approximately that of the area covered by the beam angle.

FIGURE 14.18
The set design for *The Playboy of the Western World*.

ored with Pale Amber Gold, to support the notion that the primary source light for this side of the stage comes from the oil lamps.

This leaves the stage-left front light as the only uncolored instrument. Since there is no specific source light coming from this direction, it will be necessary to refer back to the image of light to determine the appropriate color for this instrument. The image of light specifies that the atmosphere should resemble a "twinkling spring morning." Roscolux 51, Surprise Pink, is selected for use from this direction, because this bright, cheerful color will blend with the Pale Amber Gold (used in the other front light) to produce a warm white light that supports the concept of a cheery morning that is dictated by the image of light.

Using the Lighting Key to Draw the Light Plot

The lighting key is the primary tool in drawing the light plot. The shape of the acting areas determines the number and arrangement of the lighting areas. In our hypothetical production of *The Playboy of the Western World*, the whole set is a

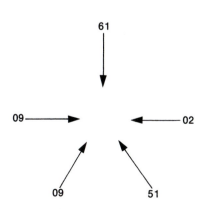

FIGURE 14.19
Five-source lighting key, with color, for *The Playboy of the Western World*.

single acting area. In order to draw the light plot, it will be necessary to subdivide that acting area into lighting areas, as shown in Figure 14.20.

To create a smooth wash of light over the entire acting area, the lighting designer needs to replicate the lighting key in each of the lighting areas. This process of duplication is demonstrated for a single lighting area in Figure 14.21, page 359.

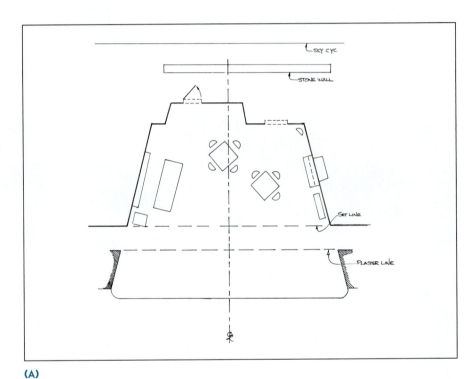

(A)

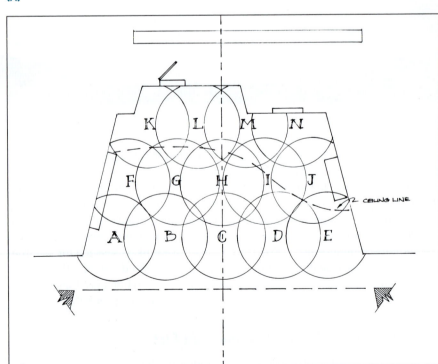

(B)

FIGURE 14.20
Acting (top) and lighting areas for
The Playboy of the Western World.

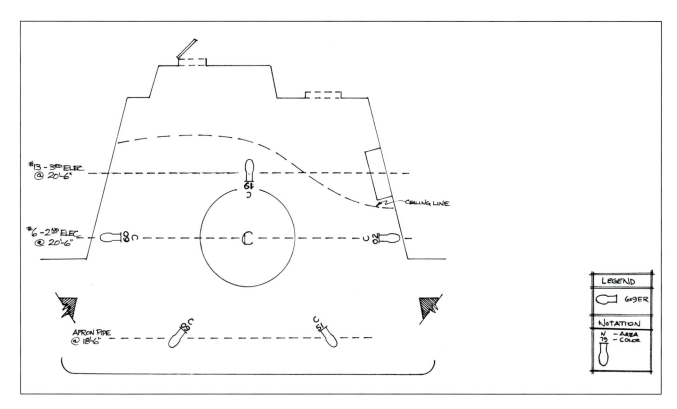

FIGURE 14.21
Replication of the lighting key in a lighting area for *The Playboy of the Western World.*

Unfortunately, it isn't always possible to achieve an exact duplication of the lighting key in every lighting area, because the walls of the set prevent the use of side light in the lighting areas that are adjacent to the walls, and the ceiling interferes with a great deal of the top and back light. More challenges are imposed by the physical limitations of the auditorium, which generally inhibit some of the front-of-house hanging positions.

When a situation occurs that makes it difficult to place an instrument exactly where it is needed, the lighting designer must make a design decision. If the light can't be placed in a position where it will replicate the angle specified in the lighting key, the compromise solution should be guided by the principles outlined in the lighting key and the designer's interpretation of the image of light. For example, it isn't possible to use direct stage-left side light for Area J (see Figure 14.22 on page 000), because the wall gets in the way. Two possible compromise solutions to this challenge might be (1) Put an instrument on the stage-left end of the first electric, as shown in Figure 14.22. (2) Eliminate the instrument. The choice of which solution to use should be guided by your interpretation of the image of light and the lighting key.

To complete the basic, or first, layer of the lighting design, it will be necessary to duplicate, as closely as possible, the lighting key in every lighting area. This process of replication results in a basic light plot that creates the atmosphere and look dictated by the image of light.

Layering

A lighting design exists in time as well as space. It ebbs and flows as the mood of the play changes. Creating a temporal development in the lighting design requires that some method of creating that time-based element be designed into the light plot.

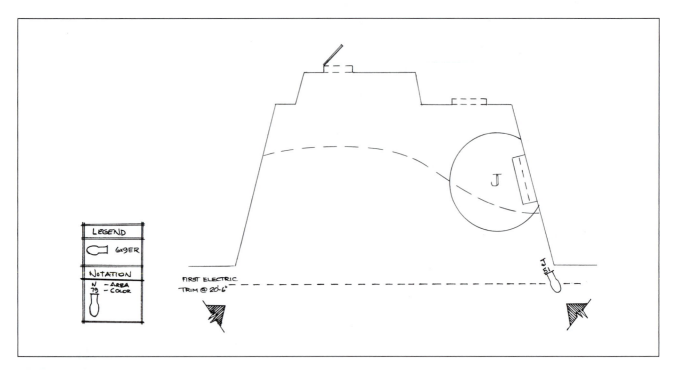

FIGURE 14.22
Replication of the lighting key for *The Playboy of the Western World* in a lighting area that is difficult to light.

Layering is primarily an organizational tool of the lighting designer. It refers specifically to the process of designing layers of light.

The first layer of light for our hypothetical production of *Playboy* was created when we implemented our interpretation of the image of light—"a bright, twinkling Irish morning." This image works well for Acts II and III, which take place in the morning and afternoon, respectively. However, Act I takes place in the early evening. The "twinkling morning" look simply doesn't translate as night. To create an appropriate look of early evening for Act I, it will be necessary to do one of two things: (1) Create a completely separate lighting key and design for Act I, or (2) create some supplemental "early evening" lighting that can be used in conjunction with the basic "twinkling Irish morning" lights.

From an aesthetic standpoint, a completely separate plot for Act I would be the preferred solution, but a separate design would necessitate a very large instrument inventory.

The supplemental lighting solution would achieve relatively similar results with a considerably smaller number of instruments. The instruments used to create this second layer of light need to be positioned and colored to create the look of "indoor evening" in the pub, where the principal sources of light are oil lamps and the peat fire. Any light coming in the window and door should have the appearance of "night light" rather than daylight.

Since this second layer of light needs to be integrated with the "twinkling Irish morning" lights to achieve the look of "early evening," it will be necessary to select angles and colors that work to support the premise that the pub is actually lit by the oil lamps and the peat fire.

A wash of "night" colors (Roscolux 79, Bright Blue) could be used to flood the stage from the front-of-house positions, as shown in Figure 14.23A on page 361. By balancing the intensities of these night colors with those of the basic lighting key, we can ensure that the blue lights won't override the basic hues that were selected for the lighting key. They will, however, provide a blue wash over the

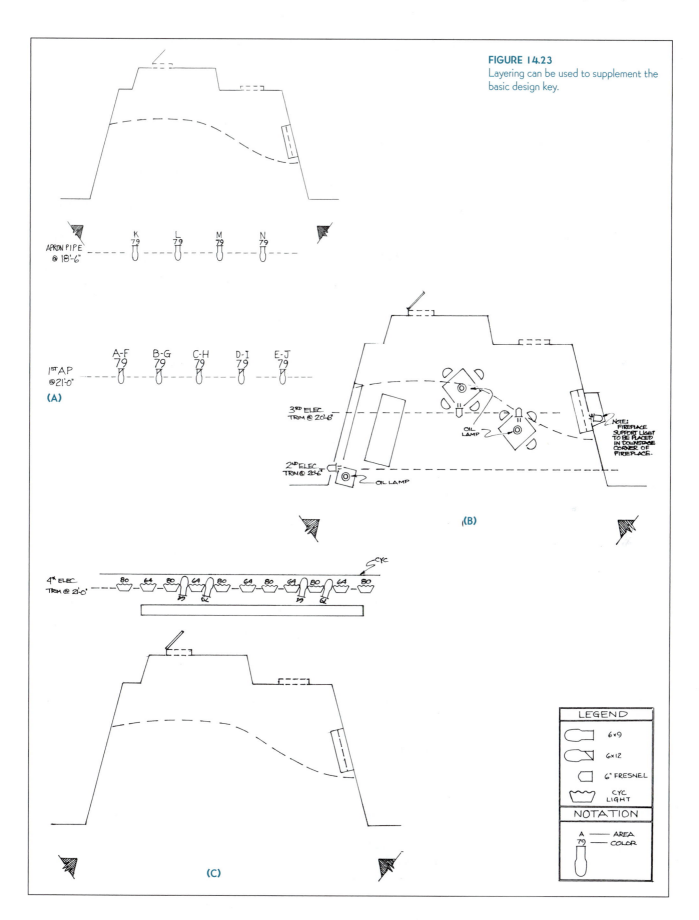

FIGURE 14.23
Layering can be used to supplement the basic design key.

whole acting area that will fill any shadow or underlit areas with a blue light to help create the illusion of nighttime.

Additional instruments could be hung to augment the color selected to re-inforce the source lights—the oil lamps and peat fire—in the first layer of the plot. These instruments, as shown in Figure 14.23B, should be colored in more fully saturated hues than their "first layer" counterparts, and they should be hung in positions that will support the effects of the source lights.

Additional layers of light can be used for a variety of purposes. Figure 14.23C shows the location of those instruments that are used to create the "daylight" and "night light" that come through the window and door.

As indicated at the beginning of this discussion, layering is primarily an organizational tool of the lighting designer. It isn't necessary to divide your thinking about the design into segments, but many designers find that this compartmentalization of the design into specific segments, or layers, makes it easier to concentrate on solving the challenges imposed by the individual elements of the design. Figure 14.24 shows the finished light plot for *The Playboy of the Western World*.

Designing Lights for Thrust and Arena Stages

Designing lights for an arena or thrust stage is not significantly different from designing for a proscenium theatre. The only substantive difference is the location of the audience. In the thrust configuration, as you will recall, the audience sits on three sides of the stage, and in an arena theatre it surrounds the stage. It is the lighting designer's responsibility to light the stage so that all spectators, regardless of where they are sitting, are able to see the production equally well.

We can use our hypothetical production of *The Playboy of the Western World* to demonstrate the relative lack of difference between designing lighting for the three modes of stages. Figure 14.25 on page 364 shows a sketch of the modified scenic design that would work for a thrust production of our play. Note that the side walls have been removed so that the spectators sitting on the sides of the thrust stage can see all of the action. Also notice that because the walls are gone, the ceiling has been eliminated.

The image of light remains the same as before, simply because the concept of how we are going to produce the play hasn't changed. The distribution of the design key has been slightly modified because of the position of the audience relative to the stage. We are still surrounding the actors with light to re-create our "bright, twinkling Irish morning" as shown in Figure 14.26A on page 364. The color of the design key also remains relatively unchanged, although we will lower the saturation of the "warm" color because of the proximity of the audience, as shown in Figure 14.26B.

The second layer for our thrust production could concentrate on enhancing the source lights—oil lamps, fireplace, window, and door (Figure 14.27A, page 365). The third layer (Figure 14.27B) would concentrate on creating the "night" wash.

The lighting design for an arena production of our play would be very similar to the thrust design. The set for the arena production is shown in Figure 14.28 on page 365. Notice how all of the walls that might in any way interfere with the spectators' sight lines have been removed. The scenic design has been essentially reduced to a furniture arrangement, with just enough set left to provide a hint of what the cottage or pub actually looks like. The set has been shifted to a diagonal angle so that the entrances are lined up with the auditorium entryways.

The distribution of the lighting key for the arena production is slightly different from the other two configurations (Figure 14.29A, page 366). The color portion

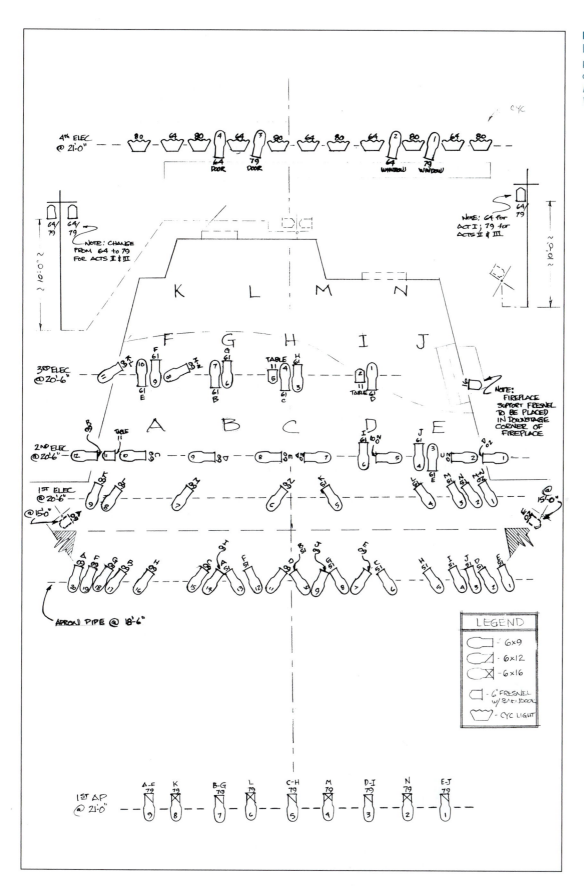

FIGURE 14.24
Light plot for a proscenium production of *The Playboy of the Western World*.

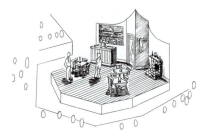

FIGURE 14.25
Scenic design for a thrust production of
The Playboy of the Western World.

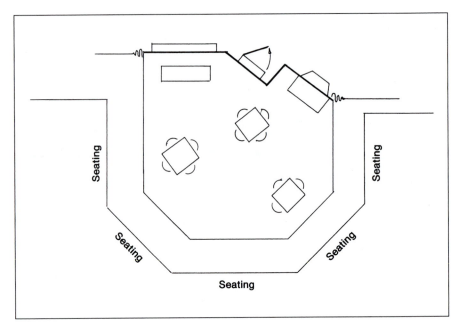

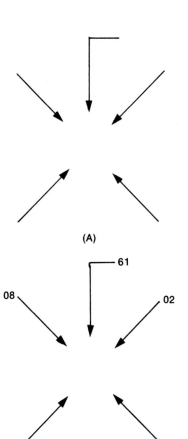

FIGURE 14.26
Lighting key for thrust production of
The Playboy of the Western World.

of the design key is also different, but only because we want everyone looking at the play to get the same feeling. For the proscenium and thrust productions, we were able to have the light coming from the direction of the door and window gelled with colors that would support the "outdoors" look of the light coming through the window and door. Because we now have the audience surrounding the stage, however, we need to create the same feeling of "interior" lighting from all angles. These changes are shown in the color selection for the design key illustrated in Figure 14.29B.

Similarly, the "night" layers must place lights in positions that will enhance the idea of "night" for all of the viewing audience, as shown in Figure 14.30A on page 366. In this particular design, the third layer of light is used to support both the internal and external source lights. These lights need to be reasonably directional, as shown in Figure 14.30B, because the apparent source lights that they are reinforcing (sunlight, moonlight, peat fire) are also directional. The instruments that are reinforcing the oil lamps are placed over the general area of the lamps, simply because the light from the oil lamps illuminates everything around it.

The only other type of design modification that needs to be made when working in an arena theatre is that the instruments are probably hung considerably closer to the actors than in either a thrust or proscenium configuration. Because of this you will want to use less-saturated color media, as the closer the instrument is to the actor, the stronger the effect of any color that is used with that instrument.

Other than these relatively minor adjustments required by the positioning and proximity of the audience, there really aren't any significant changes in philosophy, practice, or techniques when designing for thrust or arena theatres.

Drawing the Light Plot and Lighting Section

The lighting designer needs to acquire several specific drawings or computer files from other members of the production design team before he or she can start to draw the light plot. In addition to sketches, models, or photos of the scenic models, the lighting designer will need

1. the ground plan(s) of the scenic design

2. the sectional(s) of the scenic design

3. a scale ground plan of the stage and auditorium

4. a sectional of the stage and auditorium

5. a layout of, and specifications for, the stage lighting system(s) of the theatre

6. an accurate inventory of the theatre's lighting equipment and/or a lighting rental budget.

The ground plans of the theatre and set are traced, using a thin line, onto the light plot. The layout of the stage lighting system provides information about the location of the various stage circuits (connecting strips, floor and wall sockets, and so on). The sectionals of the set and the stage and auditorium are traced to create the basic visual information necessary for the lighting section. See the box "Drafting for Lighting Design" on page 350 for specific drafting conventions and information.

Information regarding the lighting key, beam and field angles, and lighting areas was presented earlier in this chapter. However, some additional technical information may prove helpful when you start to draw the light plot.

Determining the Sectional Angle

The lighting key codifies the plan angle and color for each instrument, but it doesn't provide any information about the sectional angle for each instrument. Although the sectional angle should be determined from an analysis of the desired appearance of the light, in fact the sectional angles of most lighting instruments used in the theatre will usually be somewhere between 30 and 60 degrees. The reason for this apparently arbitrarily selected angle is that people living in

FIGURE 14.27
Additional layers for lighting key for thrust production of *The Playboy of the Western World.*

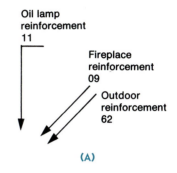

Oil lamp reinforcement 11

Fireplace reinforcement 09

Outdoor reinforcement 62

(A)

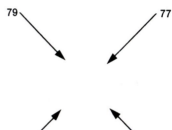

79   77

83   **(B)**   79

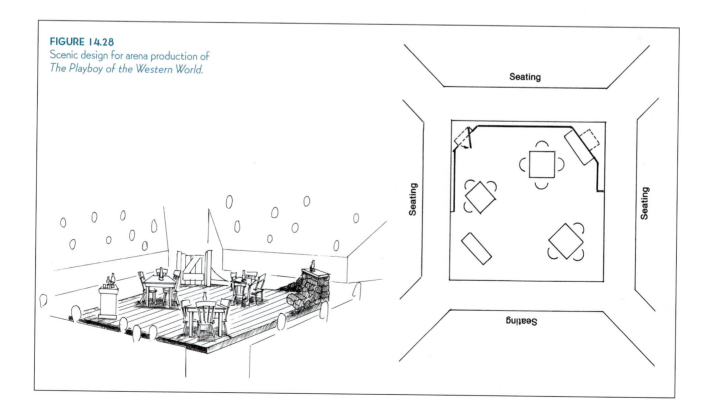

FIGURE 14.28
Scenic design for arena production of *The Playboy of the Western World.*

Seating

Seating

Seating

Seating

FIGURE 14.29
Lighting key for arena production of *The Playboy of the Western World.*

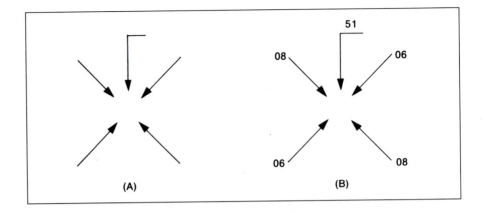

FIGURE 14.30
Additional layers for lighting key for arena production of *The Playboy of the Western World.*

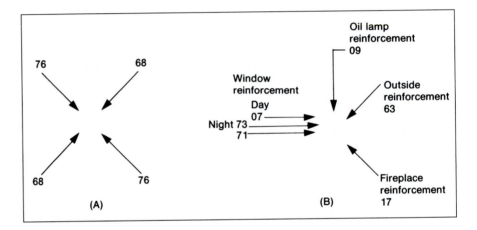

temperate climates are used to seeing objects illuminated by the sun within this angle range, so we perceive of this angle range as being natural, normal, and appropriate.

Dance and other applications in which the revelation of form is more important than the visibility of the face are notable exceptions to this generalization about the sectional angle. Dance lighting normally makes very effective use of side lighting with an angle of approach parallel with the stage floor.

Figure 14.31A shows the plan view of a single lighting instrument. Figure 14.31B shows a sectional view taken at right angles to the axis of that same instrument. Since the lighting instruments are usually hidden from the spectators' view, the lighting designer will set a specific trim height (height above the stage floor) for the instrument. Since any point along the axial line will produce the "correct" sectional angle, the sectional line can be extended until it reaches the predetermined trim height (x). At that point, a vertical line can be dropped to the stage floor, and the distance from that point to the center of the lighting area can be measured (y). This information is recorded on the light plot by placing the symbol for the instrument at the measured floor distance from the center of the lighting area, as shown in Figure 14.31C. The trim height for the pipe is noted, at the end of the pipe, on the plot.

Selecting Instrument Size

At the same time that the sectional angle is being determined, the lighting designer can also determine the appropriate size of instrument to use. From the beam and field angle information (see page 355), or from the manufacturer's specification sheets for specific lighting instruments, templates of the beam and field angles can be constructed for each instrument. These are simple triangular, scale, acetate, or cardboard templates that contain the **throw distance** and the beam and field angles of the light emitted by each instrument. The photometric data required to construct these templates is also available on computer programs such as Rosco Light Shop.

Figure 14.32 shows how to use the beam and field angle template. After the **working sectional** for the instrument has been drawn, the apex of the template is placed at the specified trim height for the instrument. The appropriately sized instrument will have a field angle that slightly overlaps the lighting area and a maximum throw distance that is longer than the required throw distance.

This method of instrument selection is suggested only as a general guide. In the final analysis, the designer needs to make instrument selections based on what is aesthetically appropriate for the particular situation.

Rehearsal and Performance Procedures

It has been said that any lighting design is only as good as its paperwork. The light plot, lighting section, and instrument schedule are only about half of that paperwork. The rest of it is associated with the recording of the dimmer intensity levels and other data that are used when running the lights for a production.

This section will present a series of rehearsal and performance procedures, forms, and practices that can be used to assist in the running of the lighting for any production. Every action involving the adjustment of one or more lighting instruments needs to be recorded to ensure that the intensity settings for those dimmers and the timing of each **lighting cue** remain the same from rehearsal to rehearsal and performance to performance.

The forms and practices suggested in this section are not sacrosanct; they are just one of many methods that can be used to record the information that is needed to run the lighting for a production. Any well-organized system that works for the lighting designer and electrician can be used. The important point

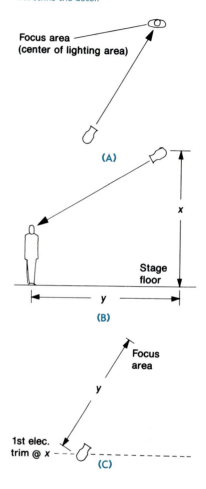

Focus area
(center of lighting area)

(A)

x

Stage floor

y

(B)

Focus area

y

1st elec.
trim @ x

(C)

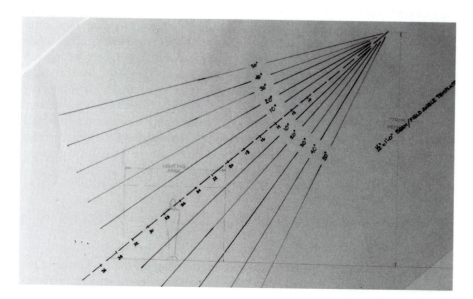

FIGURE 14.32
How to use a beam and field angle template.

throw distance: How far light from an instrument travels from its hanging position to the center of its focus area.

working sectional: A drawing showing the sectional angle for a lighting instrument; used to determine its trim height; not to be confused with the lighting section.

lighting cue: A command to take some type of action involving lighting, usually, to raise or lower the intensity of one or more instruments.

PRODUCTION INSIGHTS
Lighting Instrument Specification Sheets

It is extremely useful for a lighting designer to assemble a collection of data sheets that specify the photometric data (beam, field angle, light output at specific throw distances, and the like) for the instruments of the various manufacturers (see example). The maximum throw distance is the farthest distance at which the instrument can effectively be used. At this distance, the light emitted by the instrument measures 50 foot-candles, which is used as the industry standard and is considered to be the lowest effective illumination level for stage use.

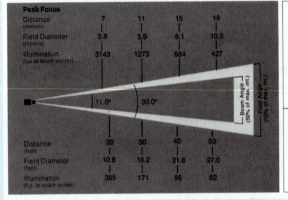

A portion of an instrument specification sheet for the Colortran 30-degree ellipsoidal reflector spotlight.

is the necessity of having a clearly written, systematic method of recording the necessary information.

Electrician's Cue Sheet

board operator: An electrician who runs the lighting control console during rehearsals and performances.

The electrician's cue sheet is the **board operator's** bible. It contains the primary operating instructions (cue number, what specific action the board operator takes, the timing of the cue, and so forth) for every lighting cue, as shown in Figure 14.33. It is also important to note what information the electrician's cue sheet does not contain. It doesn't give the specific dimmer intensity level settings (commonly referred to as dimmer settings) for major shifts in the lighting. That information is stored in computer memory or written on the preset sheet, which will be discussed a little later in this section. But the electrician's cue sheet is often used to record the dimmer levels for minor shifts of intensity that involve only one or two dimmers.

If you carefully study the information written on the electrician's cue sheet shown in Figure 14.33, you will be able to follow the progress of the lighting from the lowering of the house lights through the end of the first scene of the play.

Recording Dimmer Intensity Levels

There are actually two methods of recording lighting cues: electronically and in writing.

Electronic Cue Storage   Electronic cue storage is a significant advantage of the computer board. Although the capabilities of computer boards vary from manu-

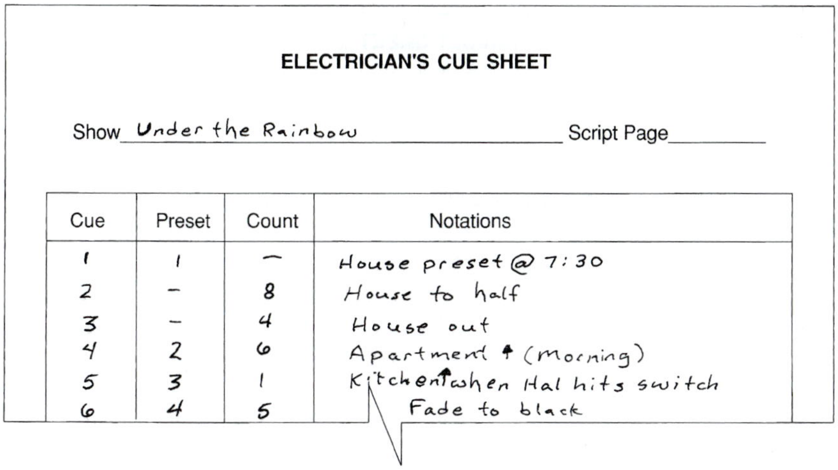

ELECTRICIAN'S CUE SHEET

Show *Under the Rainbow* Script Page ________

Cue	Preset	Count	Notations
1	1	—	House preset @ 7:30
2	–	8	House to half
3	–	4	House out
4	2	6	Apartment (morning)
5	3	1	Kitchen when Hal hits switch
6	4	5	Fade to black

FIGURE 14.33
An electrician's cue sheet.

facturer to manufacturer, they all provide a basic level of computer memory that allows them to electronically store the intensity levels of each dimmer that is used in each cue and the time associated with each cue. If a production company doesn't have a computer board to electronically record and store the data associated with each cue, that information will have to be recorded manually.

Preset Sheet If a manual or preset control board is used, a preset sheet (Figure 14.34) is used to record the intensity levels for each dimmer during major shifts in lighting. The layout and content of the preset sheet are dependent on the type of control system used for the production. But regardless of the exact form of the sheet, it will have an open space adjacent to each dimmer or channel number for recording the intensity level of that particular dimmer for that particular cue.

Each time a shift in the lighting involves more than two or three dimmers, a preset sheet is completed for that cue. The sheet provides the board operators with the information necessary to accurately adjust the dimmers.

Preset sheets are used in conjunction with electrician's cue sheets. The electrician's cue sheets tell the board operator what action is necessary for any particular cue, and the preset sheets are inserted between the cue sheets where they are needed. To keep everything tidy, the cue sheets and preset sheets are usually kept in a three-ring binder.

If the company has a computer board, it is advisable not only to make a backup disk of the show, but to make printout hard copies of each cue as well.

Designer's Cue Sheet

After the designer has a general idea of the intensity levels for each cue, the levels are recorded on a designer's cue sheet similar to the one illustrated in Figure 14.35. The designer's cue sheet, also known as the cheat sheet, is a form that identifies the function (color, direction) of the light(s) associated with each channel or dimmer and provides a space for recording its intensity level. The cheat sheet allows the designer to record the rough intensity levels and timing of each cue in a systematic manner. Using one page per cue, the designer records the intensity level for each channel or dimmer used in a cue so that he or she will have a clear idea of what changes are being made to each dimmer for every cue. Notations can be made on the sheets to indicate the purpose, function, or effect of that particular cue. Designer's cue sheets should be kept in a loose-leaf binder

FIGURE 14.34
A preset sheet.

PRESET SHEET

Production:_____

Preset Bank:_____ Cue:_____

1		16	
2		17	
3		18	
4		19	
5		20	
6		21	
7		22	
8		23	
9		24	
10		25	
11		26	
12		27	
13		28	
14		29	
15		30	

so that cues can be easily added or deleted by inserting or removing sheets from the binder. As with other paperwork, copies should be made of the designer's cue sheets.

It is also possible to program a digitizing tablet to create a designer's cue sheet that interacts with the light board[3] Part of the tablet's surface is programmed to emulate the various control features of the light board. The remaining space is programmed with needed information such as lighting areas, washes, and so forth. The programmed tablet allows you to remotely make adjustments to instrument intensity and cue timing, as well as control projectors, moving light fixtures, and so forth.

An article, "Cupped in the Hand," in the February 2004 edition of *Stage Directions* provides information about how to program a Palm Pilot or PDA to wirelessly run a light board controlled by a Windows operating system.[4] We can only expect more and more or these time- and labor-saving developments in the future. Isn't technology grand and amazing?

It is essential that the lighting designer and master electrician devise some type of organized system which will ensure that the lighting designer's concepts

[3] This idea supplied by Dr. Richard Gamble, Florida Atlantic University.
[4] Marc Beth, "Cupped in the Hand," *Stage Directions*, February 2004, pp. 22–23, 25.

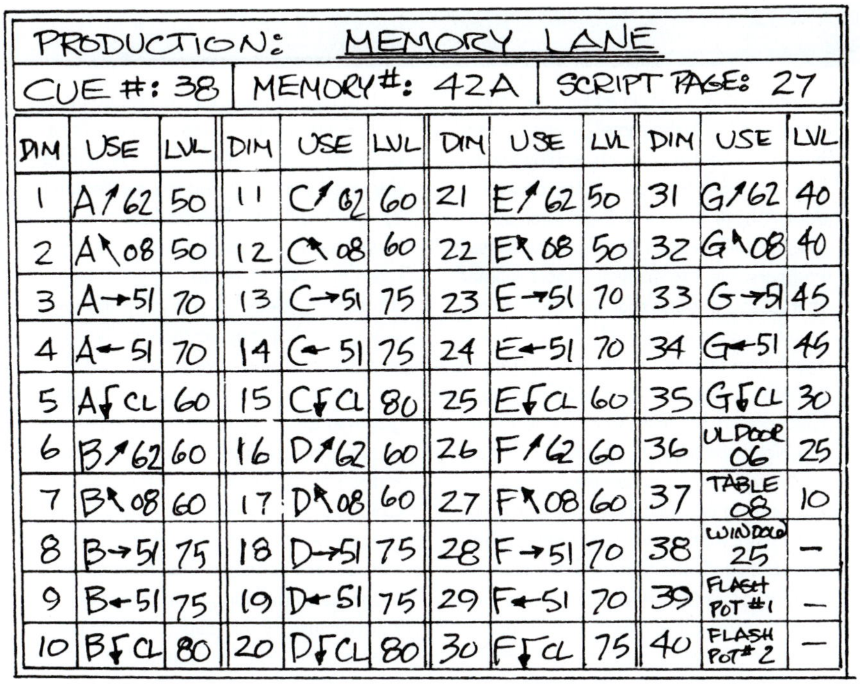

PRODUCTION: MEMORY LANE

CUE #: 38 | MEMORY #: 42A | SCRIPT PAGE: 27

DIM	USE	LVL	DIM	USE	LVL	DIM	USE	LVL	DIM	USE	LVL
1	A↗62	50	11	C↗62	60	21	E↗62	50	31	G↗62	40
2	A↖08	50	12	C↖08	60	22	E↖08	50	32	G↖08	40
3	A→51	70	13	C→51	75	23	E→51	70	33	G→51	45
4	A←51	70	14	C←51	75	24	E←51	70	34	G←51	45
5	A↓CL	60	15	C↓CL	80	25	E↓CL	60	35	G↓CL	30
6	B↗62	60	16	D↗62	60	26	F↗62	60	36	UL DOOR 06	25
7	B↖08	60	17	D↖08	60	27	F↖08	60	37	TABLE 08	10
8	B→51	75	18	D→51	75	28	F→51	70	38	WINDOW 25	—
9	B←51	75	19	D←51	75	29	F←51	70	39	FLASH POT #1	—
10	B↓CL	80	20	D↓CL	80	30	F↓CL	75	40	FLASH POT #2	—

FIGURE 14.35
A designer's cue sheet, also known as a cheat sheet.

are accurately recorded and reproduced during each rehearsal and performance of the production. It is of the utmost importance that the various cue and preset sheets be clear and current; any changes in the timing, intensity, or location of any cue must be recorded so that they can be duplicated during the next rehearsal or performance.

Lighting Rehearsal

The lighting rehearsal is a period devoted to setting the intensity levels and timing for each lighting cue. The lighting designer, the electrician (board operator), the stage manager, an assistant lighting designer or assistant stage manager to **walk the cues,** a small crew to shift the scenery (if necessary), and the director are the only members of the production team who need be present for this rehearsal.

Before the lighting rehearsal, the lighting designer will have noted the position of any motivated or unmotivated lighting cues that he or she may want to use in the production. (Motivated cues are those prompted by an internal action of the play—for example, a sunset, a character's turning on a light, and the like. Unmotivated cues are prompted by an action external to the play—for example, changing the intensity of an instrument to shift the focus of action or change the mood or tempo of the scene.) The designer will have discussed these cues with the director during one of the production conferences. The extent of this discussion varies greatly. Some directors want to know the exact location, purpose, and function of every cue, whereas other directors will leave the matter entirely up to the lighting designer. The lighting designer and board operator will have "roughed in" the intensity settings for each cue before the lighting rehearsal.

There are two primary reasons for holding a lighting rehearsal: (1) It provides the director and the lighting designer with a specific time to discuss the effect, purpose, and content of each cue when they are relatively unencumbered by other elements of the production. Additionally, it gives them an opportunity to discuss any additions, deletions, or other changes that they feel should be made

walk the cues: To move about the stage as the cues are being run in order to show what the light looks like shining on a person rather than on the bare stage.

DESIGN INSPIRATIONS
Lighting Design

The following discussion is based on "Nothing In Excess," by Ann Anderson (Stage Directions, November 2003, pp. 51–53) and is reprinted by permission of Stage Directions.

If you can, does that mean you should? Following this introduction you'll read some thoughts from three lighting designers on the topic of restraint. This discussion is included to provide support for the idea that "lighting is lighting" and it doesn't matter whether you're designing for theatre, rock concerts, or auto shows: the same basic concepts seem to apply to the many venues or lighting design.

John Featherstone has lit everything from museums to rock concerts. "There's a great line in *Jurassic Park*. Jeff Goldblum's character says, 'You spent so long trying to figure out if you could, you didn't even think about whether you should.' Just because you have a moving light with a feature doesn't mean you have to use it!" says Featherstone. With the increased availability of moving lights, there has been a sense that the kids have been in the crayon drawer. [Good lighting design] is often more about the cues you don't do than the ones you do."

"The key to a truly inspired design is whether it's appropriate," says Featherstone. He allows that it's difficult to go over the top when lighting a group like KISS, but one wouldn't light Norah Jones the same way. Citing another example, he says, "A design for a new, hip car by Pontiac would be inappropriate for the reveal of a Cadillac."

A designer has to see a bigger picture. The question, according to Featherstone, is "What is the client trying to communicate?" Musicians want to connect with the audience emotionally, and corporate clients

have a key message. In either case, the designer's job is the same—to understand what the client is trying to achieve and to help him reach that goal. If the designer doesn't have a grasp of the overall objective, he will fail both the client and himself. Featherstone, like many designers, learned that lesson through trial and error. He remembers an instance early in his career in which he was asked to design a system for a charity event that featured a number of Chicago artists. "Instead of focusing on the bigger picture," he recalls, "I leaned on the vendor to provide the biggest, flashiest rig possible. Not only was it entirely inappropriate for the event, it took ages to install, and [ran up] labor costs. At the end, I didn't have any time to program—it was a big mess!" From that experience Featherstone says, "I definitely learned to walk with style rather than trying to run and fall on my face."

"Ask questions," Featherstone counsels young designers. "Try to understand what your client is really trying to say. Get them to talk about their feelings and think about how you respond emotionally to light—especially natural light. Make big boards of images from any source that 'speak' to you and use them for inspiration. Use the same boards to find points of connection with your clients. See every kind of event. Don't be a snob; you can learn something from every genre. Most importantly, spend as much time thinking about the cues you can cut from a show as the ones you leave in."

Rob Bell is a designer and programmer who says, "Using something because you can is the mark of an amateur. It's a much more mature approach to refrain." His rule of thumb is "If the narrative doesn't justify it, don't use it." Additionally, Bell

maintains that ideas can always be modified. He remembers creating a cue for a production of *Starlight Express* that he designed that "engulfed the auditorium in open white light." The producers thought it was too much, so Bell added a saturated blue, which made everyone happy. "Presenting ideas," Bell says, "is always a selling job. You may be technically correct, but first you have to build trust."

Lighting director, designer, and programmer Benny Kirkham has lit industrial shows and such musically diverse groups as the Pat Metheny Group, the Dixie Chicks, and Aerosmith. He thinks that there is definitely a point of 'too much,' even in rock concerts. "You have to appropriate to the song. Don't show off just because of the [capabilities of the] console," he says. He's noticed that whatever is newest is what's overused. "For a while, all the gobos had to rotate. Then there was cross-fading colors into a rainbow chase. I can't wait to see what they do with the new video stuff," he noted ruefully.

Kirkham developed his own aesthetic by working with more experienced designers. Kirkham, who describes his own style as "very dynamic without being tacky," says that lights shouldn't be moved without motivation. "Don't move a light unless you have a reason."

Kirkham doesn't make a big distinction between corporate and music clients. "Everyone wants a good show," he says. "You won't light Nine Inch Nails like a Century 21 show. But [realtors] go to concerts, too." Kirkham, who built his reputation on lively designs, says that the key is to care about what you're doing. "It makes all the difference in the world to the client."

in the location or duration of the cues or anything else affecting the lighting design. (2) It provides the designer, director, stage manager, and board operator with an opportunity to make sure that the paperwork affecting the lighting design is correct. Since the stage manager will be calling all of the cues, he or she can use the lighting rehearsal to make sure that the lighting cues have been noted in their appropriate positions in the prompt script. It also gives the board operator a chance to check the accuracy of the electrician's cue sheets and preset sheets.

DIMMER/INSTRUMENT CHECK SHEET			
Dimmer	Number of Instruments	Instrument Location(s)/Color(s)	Area of Focus

FIGURE 14.36
A dimmer/instrument check sheet.

Technical and Dress Rehearsals

Changes and adjustments to the timing, content, and positioning of lighting cues are normal during the technical and dress rehearsals. Although this can be a very frustrating time, it is essential that the lighting crew understand that the majority of the lighting cues will probably have to be adjusted; intensities and timing will be changed, entire cues will probably need to be added or deleted, instrument focus may need to be shifted, and the color in various instruments may also have to be changed. These adjustments should be considered as normal, rather than extraordinary, because it is part of the lighting designer's responsibility to develop the lighting design to work with the production concept that has evolved during the rehearsal period.

Instrument and Dimmer Check

Several routine equipment checks should be conducted before each technical or dress rehearsal and each performance. All dimmers and instruments need to be checked to determine that they are functioning properly. With the aid of a check sheet (Figure 14.36), two crew members can test all the instruments and dimmers in a short time. As the board operator turns on each dimmer, the other electrician checks to see that all of the instruments assigned to that dimmer are functioning properly. At the same time, the person checking the instruments can see if any of the color media are bleached out, torn, or otherwise in need of replacement. Each instrument should also be tested to determine if it is focused into its respective area.

The dimmer and instrument check is normally made about an hour and a half before curtain time to allow any necessary repairs, replacements, or adjustments to be made.

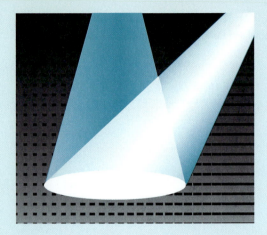

Chapter 15

Electrical Theory and Practice

As theatre (and everything else) enters the new millennium, it has become a pragmatic reality that students of technical theatre have to comprehend the function of electricity and electronics. The discussion that follows differentiates between the terms; electricity generally pertains to the use of the electromotive force to perform work—make lamps glow, motors run, and so on; electronics generally refers to the low-voltage circuits and devices used to control the flow of electricity.

Electricity — What Is It?

The study of electricity has to begin with a brief excursion into the not so mysterious realm of basic atomic theory. This is because some fundamental laws of electricity are based on the laws of atomic structure. For this reason we need to know a little bit about the **atom.**

The atom is the smallest complete building block in nature. But an atom is composed of even smaller particles: **protons, neutrons,** and **electrons.** These subatomic particles possess specific electrical properties. The proton has a positive charge, the neutron a neutral charge, and the electron a negative charge. The physical structure of any atom is similar to the configuration of our solar system. In the same manner that the earth rotates around the sun (Figure 15.1A), electrons follow a slightly elliptical orbit as they whirl around the **nucleus** of an atom (Figure 15.1B).

In a stable atom, the number of electrons in orbit around the nucleus is equaled by the number of protons in the nucleus. Hydrogen, the lightest and least complex atom, is a perfect example of this principle. Figure 15.2 shows the single electron of the hydrogen atom in orbit around the nucleus, which is composed of a single proton. Since the orbiting electron has a negative charge and the proton in the nucleus has a positive charge, an electrical attraction exists between them. The electron is prevented from being pulled into the nucleus by the **centrifugal force** of its orbital movement. At the same time, the electron is restrained from breaking out of orbit and flying away by the attraction. This attraction is an important underlying principle of electricity and is the basis for the first important law of electricity, the Law of Charges: *Like charges repel, and unlike charges attract.*

If it were physically possible to isolate two protons, they would defy all attempts to bring them together. The same results would occur if attempts were made to push two electrons together. But if an electron and a proton were placed

atom: The smallest particle of a chemical element that retains the structural properties of that element.

proton: A fundamental particle in the structure of the nucleus of an atom; possesses a positive charge.

neutron: A fundamental particle in the structure of the nucleus of an atom; possesses a neutral charge.

electron: A negatively charged fundamental particle that orbits around the nucleus of an atom.

nucleus: The central part of an atom; composed of protons and neutrons.

centrifugal force: Force that moves away from the center; for example, the circular motion of electrons spinning around a nucleus generates centrifugal force.

374

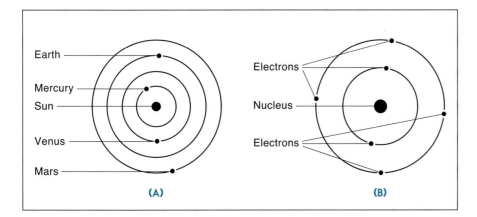

FIGURE 15.1
The structure of an atom is similar to the structure of the solar system.

in proximity, they would zip toward each other until they met. The Law of Charges is the "electrical glue" that holds the atom together.

In atoms that are more complex than hydrogen, such as oxygen (Figure 15.3), additional electrons orbit in several planes around the nucleus. These electrons are counterbalanced by an equal number of protons in the nucleus, so the atom remains in an electrically balanced, or stable, condition. These additional orbiting electrons occupy orderly spherical shells at specific distances from the nucleus. Each of these shells can hold only a certain number of electrons. When each shell is filled with its quota of electrons, a tight bonding takes place, and no additional electrons can be added. Although it is possible to dislodge an electron from one of these filled shells, it takes a relatively large amount of energy to do so.

As the structure and weight of the atom grow, the number of protons in the nucleus increases, as does the corresponding number of electrons orbiting around it. Since the electrons cannot force their way into the already filled shells, they must orbit at a greater distance. The increased distance between the orbiting electron and its counterbalancing proton in the nucleus decreases the attractive force that holds the electron in orbit.

An atom of copper has twenty-nine electrons in orbit around its nucleus. Because of copper's particular atomic structure, only a very weak force holds its outer electrons in orbit, and only a very weak force is needed to dislodge them from the outer shell, or **valence shell,** of the copper atom.

A strand of copper wire is composed of billions upon billions of copper atoms, all having the same characteristically weak valence electron. The atoms in the wire are in such close proximity to one another (most of them are intertwined with their neighbors) that the nuclei of adjacent atoms can actually exert the same or more attractive force on their neighbors' valence electrons than they do on their own. Consequently, many of the valence electrons break away from their "home" atoms, momentarily attach themselves to other atoms, or simply float freely within the confines of the wire.

If this cloud of **free electrons** meandering in the wire could be organized to move in the same direction, an **electrical current** would be generated, simply because an electrical current is defined as the flow of electrons from one point to another. The unit of measurement for this electron flow is the **ampere.**

How can free electrons be motivated to move from one point to another? The answer lies in a practical application of the Law of Charges (like charges repel, and unlike charges attract). Since the electrons have a negative charge, they are attracted to a body that has a positive charge. However, it isn't possible to create a positive charge by itself. A negative charge must be created simultaneously with

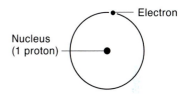

FIGURE 15.2
A hydrogen atom.

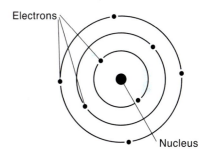

FIGURE 15.3
An oxygen atom.

valence shell: The outermost plane of orbiting electrons in the structure of an atom.

free electron: An electron that has broken away from its "home" atom to float free.

electrical current: The flow or movement of electrons through a conductor.

ampere: The unit of measurement of electrical current.

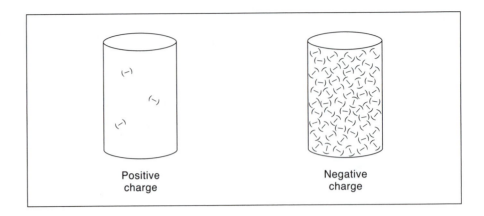

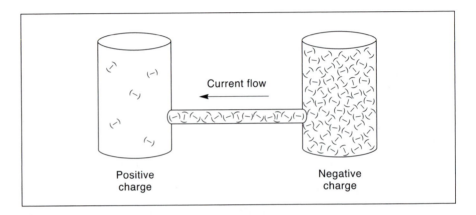

the creation of a positive charge, because electrical charges are produced by the transfer of electrons from one point to another. (In the process, electrons are neither created nor destroyed but simply transferred.) Figure 15.4 simplistically illustrates the principle that the positive charge is created by the removal of electrons and the negative charge is the result of an accumulation of electrons.

If two bodies of opposite charge are created, an electrical current could be generated if a conductor, such as a copper wire, were connected between them. Free electrons would flow from the negatively charged body to the positively charged body, as shown in Figure 15.5. The flow, or current, would continue as long as there was a difference in charge between the two bodies. This difference in the electrical charge between the bodies is called **potential** and is measured in **volts.**

The amount of voltage, or potential strength of the electrical system, is directly related to the difference in potential between the charged bodies. The greater the difference in potential between the charges, the greater that system's capacity to do work. A system with a rating of 220 volts has a greater potential capacity to do work than a 117-volt system.

potential: The difference in electrical charge between two bodies; measured in volts.

volt: The unit of measurement of electrical potential.

source: The origin of electrical potential, such as a battery or 120-volt wall outlet.

load: A device that converts electrical energy into another form of energy: A lamp converts electrical energy to light and heat; an electrical motor converts electricity to mechanical energy.

Electricity at Work

Every electrical system must have three parts: a **source,** a **load,** and a circuit. The source is a mechanism that provides a difference in potential, or voltage. The load is a device that uses the electricity to perform some function. The circuit is a pathway that the current follows as it flows from the negative to the positive terminal of the source. (A negative terminal is created by an excess of electrons; a positive terminal, by a dearth of electrons. In batteries this electron transfer happens through a chemical reaction.)

A practical demonstration of the interrelationship between the three elements of any electrical system is provided by the example of a very simple battery and lamp, as shown in Figure 15.6. The source of this system is an ordinary flashlight battery. The load is a small incandescent lamp. The circuit is composed of copper wire. When the wires are attached to the lamp and the terminals of the battery, electrons flow from the negative to the positive terminal of the battery. As the electrons pass through the filament of the lamp, resistance to their flow causes the filament to heat up and incandesce, or give off light. The current will continue as long as the circuit is intact and there is enough voltage left in the battery to overcome the resistance within the circuit and lamp filament. When the voltage is reduced to the point that it cannot overcome the circuit resistance, the current will stop, and the lamp will no longer glow.

Ohm's Law

Although it's interesting to know that electrons flow within a circuit, unless there is some way of determining how the various parts of the circuit affect one another, there is no way to understand and predict what will happen in any electrical circuit. Fortunately, a German physicist, Georg Simon Ohm, discovered in the nineteenth century that some very basic rules apply to the functioning of electricity in a circuit. These relationships have been formalized as Ohm's Law, and they are the primary mathematical expressions used in determining electron action within a circuit. Ohm's Law states: *As voltage increases, current increases; as resistance increases, current decreases.*

The diagrams in Figures 15.7 and 15.8 will help illustrate these relationships. They show simple schematic diagrams or drawings that substitute symbols for the various parts of the circuit. The $\frac{\perp}{\top}$ symbol represents a battery, and the -\/\/\- symbol represents a **resistance,** or load, within the circuit. Figure 15.7 illustrates the first portion of Ohm's Law. The voltage of the battery in Figure 15.7A is 10 volts. With this voltage, the 1-ohm resistance allows a current flow of 10 amperes. If the voltage is doubled to 20 volts, as shown in Figure 15.7B, and the resistance is not changed, the current will also double, to 20 amperes.

Figure 15.8 illustrates the second element of Ohm's Law. Figure 15.8A is a 10-volt system with a resistance, or load, of 1 ohm. This configuration allows a current flow of 10 amperes. In Figure 15.8B, the voltage remains constant at 10 volts, but the resistance has been doubled to 2 ohms, which results in a reduction of the current to 5 amperes.

In both cases, it is important to remember that the speed of the electron flow is constant. The increase or decrease in current flow is the result of an increase or decrease in the number of electrons flowing in the circuit.

Another way of looking at the relationships stated in Ohm's Law may help in understanding them. The voltage can be compared to the electrical pressure that causes the electrons to flow within the circuit. If more pressure (voltage) is applied, it would be logical for more electrons to flow. Since resistance is defined as opposition to the flow of electrons, any increase in the resistance would naturally cause the electron flow to decrease.

The relationships of Ohm's Law can be mathematically expressed as

$$I = \frac{E}{R}$$

where I = current in amperes, E = voltage in volts, and R = resistance in ohms. This basic formula can be rearranged into two other forms. Each of these can be used to find the value of the other components of the relationship:

FIGURE 15.6
A lamp will incandesce when current flows through it.

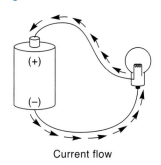

Current flow

resistance: The opposition to electron flow within a conductor, measured in ohms; the amount of the resistance is dependent on the chemical makeup of the material through which the electricity is flowing.

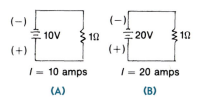

I = 10 amps I = 20 amps

(A)   **(B)**

FIGURE 15.7
As voltage increases, current increases.

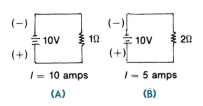

I = 10 amps I = 5 amps

(A)   **(B)**

FIGURE 15.8
As resistance increases, current decreases.

PRODUCTION INSIGHTS
Conductors, Insulators, Grounding, and Shorts

An electrical conductor is any material with an abundance of free electrons. Copper, aluminum, gold, and silver are excellent conductors. Water is also a very good conductor. Conversely, an insulator is a material with few free electrons. The lack of free electrons effectively prevents the flow of electricity through an insulator. Air, glass, paper, rubber, and most plastics are good insulators. In electrical wire, the conductor (usually copper) is surrounded with an insulator (normally rubber or plastic) to keep the electrical flow confined to the conductor and to prevent the conductor from making contact with anything else.

Safety dictates that all electrical equipment be grounded. This involves making a direct mechanical connection between the conductive housing of an electrical device and the earth. This connection is made through the ground pin on the electrical cord of the equipment. (The ground pin protrudes farther than the circuit connectors on all late-model plugs.) The ground pin makes contact with the ground wire, which, if you followed it back to the point where it enters the house or building, would be clamped to a metal rod driven five or more feet into the ground or to a metal water pipe. The purpose of the ground wire is to provide a low-resistance path for the electricity to follow in case of a short circuit between the power circuit and the device's metallic housing.

The difference between an overloaded circuit and a short circuit is really just a matter of degree. An overload occurs when the current flowing through a circuit is greater than the maximum current for which the system was designed. A short circuit is created when a very large surge of current in an overloaded circuit causes a portion of the wire, insulation, and anything else at the point of the short to melt very rapidly—basically explode.

An overload is created when a too heavy load is placed on a circuit—as when a 3,000-watt load is placed on a circuit that was designed to safely carry a load of only 2,400 watts. A short circuit, or short, happens when a very-low-resistance alternative to the primary circuit is created. These alternate paths form when a wire breaks or comes loose from its terminal or when the insulation is worn away from the conductor, allowing it to touch another conductor or come into contact with the unit's metal housing.

If a short occurs in a grounded circuit, the very-low-resistance path between the circuit and the earth invites the surge of current to follow the ground-circuit path. The high current flow activates a fuse or circuit breaker to shut off the electricity to the shorted equipment. If the circuit isn't grounded or the ground circuit doesn't function (perhaps because someone clipped off the ground pin from the plug), and you picked up the shorted device, you would be severely shocked, and possibly killed, because your body would act as the ground circuit to provide the path of least resistance between the shorted circuit and the earth.

You may find that some electrical hand tools do not have a grounding pin on the plug. The information plate attached to the tool's casing will probably carry the words *double insulated.* These tools don't need grounding, because the casing that you hold is actually a second, or outer, casing. These two layers of plastic insulators (casings) effectively isolate you from harm from any potential short.

$$E = IR$$

$$R = \frac{E}{I}$$

These mathematical expressions of Ohm's Law are extremely valuable when working with low-voltage electronic systems such as those found in microphone and low-power speaker hookups as well as the control portion of electronic dimmers.

The Power Formula

Another formula, which is a derivation of Ohm's Law, is much more useful when dealing with higher-voltage electricity. It is called the power formula. This formula is used when it is necessary to determine how much power will be consumed by an electrical circuit.

Household light bulbs, toasters, stage lamps, and electrical motors all convert electrical energy into mechanical energy, light, or heat in accomplishing their tasks. The amount of electrical energy converted, or consumed, is measured in watts. Usually the wattage figure is written on a label located somewhere on the device. Almost all household lamps have both the voltage and wattage printed on the top of the bulb. Toasters, electrical motors, and similar devices usually have a tag or label fixed on the bottom or back of the unit. The label states both the voltage and wattage of the unit. Stage-lighting lamps have this information printed on either the metal lamp base or the top of the lamp.

The power formula is usually referred to colloquially as either the "pie" or the "West Virginia" formula:

$$P = IE \qquad\qquad\qquad W = VA$$

where   where

P = Power in watts W = power in watts

I = current in amperes V = voltage in volts

E = voltage in volts A = current in amperes

Both the power formula and Ohm's Law can be rearranged into the following expressions:

$$P = IE \qquad\qquad\qquad W = VA$$

$$E = \frac{P}{I} \qquad\qquad\qquad A = \frac{W}{V}$$

$$I = \frac{P}{E} \qquad\qquad\qquad V = \frac{W}{A}$$

With these three expressions of the power formula, it is possible to find the unknown quantity in an electrical circuit if the other two factors are known.

An everyday example will help illustrate the point. You want to put a desk lamp on a table, but the power cord connected to the lamp won't reach from the table to the wall outlet. You go to the hardware store to buy an extension cord, and the only information attached to the power cord indicates that it will safely carry 6 amperes of current. You know that the voltage in your apartment is 117 volts (standard household voltage in the United States). The lamp you plan to use is rated at 150 watts. To determine if the extension cord is safe to use, you will need to find out how many amperes of current the 150-watt lamp will create. To find the answer, just plug the known information ($V = 117$, $W = 150$) into the appropriate variation of the power formula—the variation that has the unknown variable (in this case, A) located on the left side of the equal sign:

$$A = \frac{W}{V}$$

$$A = \frac{150}{117}$$

$$A = 1.28 \text{ amps}$$

> ## PRODUCTION INSIGHTS
> ### Output and Input Voltage
>
> Input voltage is the voltage that is fed into a device (amplifier, dimmer). The output voltage is the voltage that comes out of the same device. In stage-lighting systems, input voltage refers to the voltage that is fed to the dimmer pack (used with portable dimming systems) or rack (used with permanently installed systems). The input voltage (usually 208–240 volts) is broken down (reduced) inside the dimmer pack so that it can be used by the individual dimmers, which are designed to work at an output voltage of 117–120 VAC.
>
> Electronic dimmers have two voltage systems: a low-voltage control circuit and a high-voltage load circuit. The low-voltage control circuit (which varies between 8 and 28 VAC depending on the manufacturer) is used to regulate the output of the high-voltage (117–120 VAC) load circuit. This means that the intensity of the lighting instruments, which are connected to the load circuit, is controlled by the low-voltage control circuit.

The lamp creates a current of 1.28 amperes, so the extension cord, which can carry 6 amperes, will be safe to use.

Practical Information The output-load voltage of dimming systems in the United States is 117–120 volts alternating current (VAC). The input voltage for most portable dimming systems is 220 VAC. The input voltage for most permanently mounted dimming systems is either 220 or 440 VAC. (The figure 220 VAC is a generic term used to describe voltage in the 208–240 range. The specific voltage is important for calculating purposes and varies from community to community. The figure 440 VAC is a similarly generic term.) The voltage figure that you will use in calculating the safe loading capacity for dimmers is the output voltage—117–120 VAC.

Electrical wires and cables are designed to carry specific current loads, as shown in Table 15.1.

Any electrical system is designed to work within certain limits. If those safe limits are exceeded, the system will do one of two things: (1) If adequate protective devices (**fuses, circuit breakers**) have been placed in the circuit, those units will break the continuity of the circuit and stop the flow of electricity. (2) If there are no fuses or circuit breakers in the circuit, the various elements within the system will heat up. If the overload is sufficiently large, the elements within the system (dimmers, cables, plugs, and so on) will heat up to the point where they will either melt or burn up. If combustible material is in the immediate proximity of the overheated elements, it is very possible that a fire will be started.

The following problems illustrate how the power formula can be used to calculate the safe electrical-load limits of typical stage-lighting situations.

fuse: A device to protect a circuit from an overload; has a soft metal strip that melts, breaking circuit continuity.

circuit breaker: A device to protect a circuit from an overload; has a magnetic device that trips open, breaking circuit continuity.

TABLE 15.1

American Wire Gauge Current-Capacity Chart

Gauge of wire	10	12	14	16	18
Capacity in amps	25	20	15	6	3

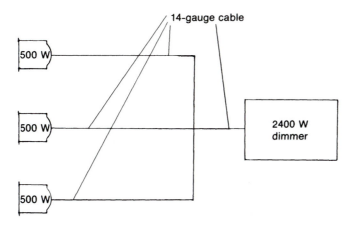

FIGURE 15.9
Problem number 2.

Problem No. 1   The output voltage of a dimmer is 120 VAC. The dimmer can handle 20 amperes of current. What is the maximum safe load that can be placed on this dimmer?

$$\text{watts} = \text{volts times amperes } (W = VA)$$

$$W = 120 \times 20$$

$$W = 2{,}400 \text{ watts}$$

The dimmer can safely carry any load up to, but not exceeding, 2,400 watts.

Problem No. 2   The system voltage is 120 VAC. The dimmer can carry 2,400 watts (2.4 kilowatts, or KW). The 14-gauge cable connecting the dimmer to the lighting instruments can carry 15 amperes (see Table 15.1). How many 500-watt lighting instruments can be safely loaded onto the dimmer (Figure 15.9)?

We already know that the dimmer can handle 2.4 KW, but we need to determine the load that can be safely carried by the cable.

$$W = VA$$

$$W = 120 \times 15$$

$$W = 1{,}800 \text{ watts}$$

The cable can carry a maximum load of 1,800 watts. To determine the number of 500-watt lighting instruments that can be carried by the cable, divide 500 into 1,800:

$$\frac{3.6}{500)\overline{1{,}800}}$$

Theoretically, the cable can safely carry 3.6 instruments. Pragmatically, it can safely carry 3 instruments. Even though the dimmer can safely carry 4 instruments, the single cable connecting the dimmer to the instruments can handle only the current flow generated by three 500-watt stage lighting instruments.

Electrical Circuits

Two primary types of circuits, series and parallel, are used to distribute electricity. A third type, known as a combination circuit, combines the principles of the two.

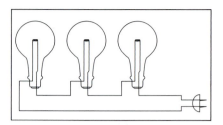

FIGURE 15.10
A series circuit.

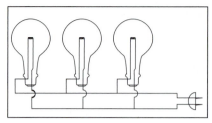

FIGURE 15.11
A parallel circuit.

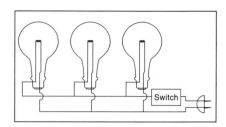

FIGURE 15.12
A combination circuit.

Series Circuit   In a series circuit, all of the electricity flows through every element of the circuit, as shown in Figure 15.10. In a series circuit, if any of the lamps burn out, the circuit will be broken, the electricity won't flow, and the remaining lamps will go out.

Parallel Circuit   In a parallel circuit, only a portion of the electricity flows through each of the branches of the circuit. If one of the lamps shown in Figure 15.11 burns out, electricity will continue to flow in the rest of the circuit, and the other lamps will continue to glow.

Combination Circuit   Any electrical circuit that uses a switch to control a light is a working example of a combination circuit. In a typical application of a combination circuit in stage lighting, a control device (switch, dimmer, fuse, circuit breaker) is used in series with the lamp load, and the lamps are wired in parallel, as shown in Figure 15.12. The series arrangement allows the switch or dimmer to exert control over the whole circuit, and the parallel wiring of the lamp outlets allows individual lamps to be inserted in or removed from the circuit without affecting its operation.

Electrical Current

There are two types of electrical current: direct and alternating.

Direct Current   In direct current (DC), the electron flow is in one direction only. The battery demonstration discussed in a previous section is an example of direct current. The flow of the current is always from the negative terminal of a battery to its positive terminal. All batteries are examples of direct-current sources.

Alternating Current   The overwhelming majority of electrical power generated by power stations throughout the world is alternating current (AC). The electron flow in AC is the same as in DC with one exception: The current flow periodically changes polarity, which causes the electron flow to change direction. In the United States, alternating current changes polarity at the rate of 60 cycles per second (60 Hz). This means that the electricity changes polarity (direction) every 1/120th of a second, as shown in Figure 15.13.

   An example may help to explain this phenomenon. If the wires connected to the terminals of a battery, as shown in Figure 15.14A, were reversed (Figure 15.14B), the lamp would still emit light, but the current flow would have changed directions. Alternating current works like this example, except that the direction of current flow changes direction every 1/120th of a second.

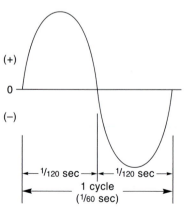

FIGURE 15.13
An alternating current (AC) cycle.

PRODUCTION INSIGHTS
Electrical Wiring

Before beginning this discussion of electric-power service, remember: These high-voltage distribution systems can kill; if you don't fully understand how the systems work, call a supervisor or licensed electrician.

A number of wiring configurations are used to distribute AC power. Figure A illustrates a typical 120-VAC service system. According to National Electrical Code (NEC) practice, in the United States the insulation of one wire is normally colored black; it is called the "hot" wire. The insulation on the other wire is white, and it is called the "neutral."

The ground wire is not included in any of these illustrations, because it should not be used as part of the electrical distribution system. However, it needs to be included in the wiring of the system, and according to code, its color should be green.

Figure B illustrates a three-wire single-phase 120/240-VAC system. The voltage between either of the two hot wires (normally black or red) and the neutral (white) will be 120 VAC. The voltage between the two hot wires will be 220–240 VAC. Electrical service is delivered to most houses with this three-wire system. At the main service box (fuse box or circuit-breaker panel), the 120 VAC is distributed to the various lamp and wall outlets, and the 240 VAC service is usually routed only to the electric range and clothes dryer.

Figure C shows a four-wire three-phase 120/208-VAC service system. The voltage between the neutral (white) and any of the three hot lines (black) will be 120 VAC. Although the input voltage measured between any of the hot lines and ground will be 240 VAC, the voltage measured between any two of the hot lines (phases) will be 208 VAC.

High-voltage distribution systems.

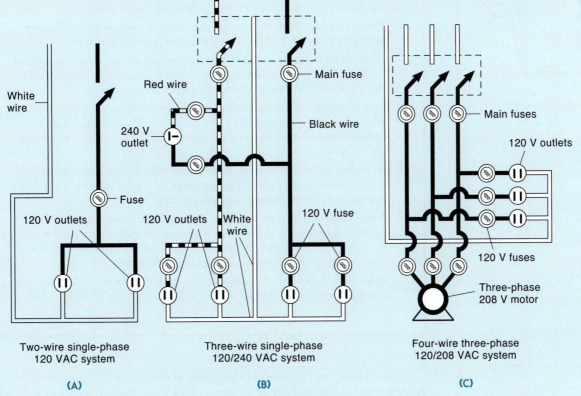

Two-wire single-phase 120 VAC system

(A)

Three-wire single-phase 120/240 VAC system

(B)

Four-wire three-phase 120/208 VAC system

(C)

The principal advantages of AC over DC are that AC is easier and cheaper to generate and that there is less voltage loss when the electricity is transmitted over a great distance.

FIGURE 15.14
Current flow reverses direction when the circuit wires connected to the battery are reversed.

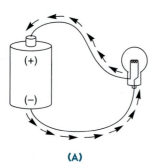

(A)

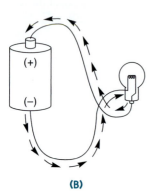

(B)

Safety Tip

Electrical Hazards

Electricity is extremely dangerous. It can burn, maim, and kill. Any piece of equipment that is connected to an electrical outlet should always be handled with caution and common sense. If you follow the safety procedures and work habits outlined below, your work with electricity can be safe and productive.

1. If you don't know what you're doing, don't do it. Ask your supervisor, or consult a trained electrician.

2. Use tools that are covered with plastic or rubber insulation when working with electricity.

3. Use wooden or fiberglass ladders when working on elevated electrical jobs. Electricity will always take the path of least resistance, and a metal ladder (and your body) provides a very-low-resistance path. If metal ladders must be used, insulate them with high-quality rubber foot pads. Movable metal scaffolds or adjustable ladders should have lockable rubber casters.

4. Disconnect any device (lighting instrument, motor, amplifier) from the circuit before you work on it. Unplug any lighting instrument before changing the lamp.

5. Use common sense: Don't touch any bare wires. Don't work in damp locations or put a drink where it could spill on an electrical or electronic component. Don't intentionally overload a circuit. Don't try to bypass fuses or circuit breakers.

6. Maintain the integrity of all ground circuits. Don't clip the ground plug off any extension cord or power cord. When necessary, use ground-plug adapters.

7. Check cables and connectors periodically, and replace any items that show signs of cracking, chipping, or other deterioration. Cracks in the insulation of cables and connectors increase the chances of receiving a shock from the device.

8. Keep the cables and connectors clean. Remove any corrosion, paint, grease, dust, or other accumulations as soon as they become evident. These substances can act as insulation between the contacts of the connector, and if flammable they can pose a fire hazard.

9. When stage or microphone cables are not in use, coil them and hang them up. A cable will stay neatly coiled if the connectors are plugged together or if it is tied with light rope or fastened with a Velcro loop.

10. Always disconnect a plug by pulling on the body of the connector, not the cable. Pulling on the cable puts an unnecessary strain on the cable clamp and will eventually defeat the clamp. When the cable clamp no longer functions, pulling on the cable places the strain directly on the electrical connections.

11. Be sure that all elements of a cable are of the same electrical rating: 12-gauge cable (capable of carrying 20 amperes of current) should have only 20-ampere-rated connectors.

This chapter has provided a brief glance at the nature and uses of electricity. Anyone who is thinking about a career in any area of theatrical design or production would be wise to take a course or two in practical electronics as well as making an intensive study of standard electrical-wiring practice.

Chapter 16

Lighting Production

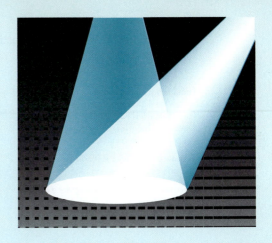

You might dream up the most imaginative lighting design ever conceived, but unless you know how to execute that design, you won't get far as a lighting designer. In this chapter, we explore the tools and technology that lighting designers use.

It is very easy to become enamored of the various tools (some would call them toys) of lighting design. The lighting instruments and dimmers as well as the control and distribution systems are not ends in themselves, however; they are simply the metaphorical mallet and chisels that lighting designers use to create their sculptures in light.

Not so long ago it wasn't necessary for a practitioner of scenic or lighting design or technical production to have a thorough knowledge of electricity and electronics. Today that simply isn't true. Each of these technical areas uses a plethora of electronically controlled devices, and anyone who works in these areas needs to have a *thorough* working knowledge of both electricity and electronics. To help you prepare, the previous chapter presented a comprehensive discussion of the fundamentals of electricity and electronics.

Lenses

The angle of the beam of light emitted by the most frequently used stage lighting instruments is controlled by the optical properties of the lenses used with those instruments. Lenses refract light, which means that they redirect, or deflect, light from its normally straight path. The amount of deflection depends on the angle of intersection between the light ray and the surface of the lens, as well as the density of the medium through which the light is passing.

When a light ray passes from one medium into another of greater density—for example, from air into glass—it bends away from its original direction of travel. When the light ray passes out the other side of the glass and back into the air, it bends back toward its original line of travel. The angle or amount of this deflection depends on the angle of intersection between the light ray and the glass. If the glass has parallel sides, as illustrated in Figure 16.1, the light ray will be deflected in one direction when it enters the glass, then back the same amount in the opposite direction when it emerges from the glass on the other side. However, typical lenses do not have parallel sides. Figure 16.2 illustrates two plano-convex lenses. Unlike window glass, which redirects light passing through it in a direction parallel to its original line of travel, a curved-face lens causes light passing through it to be deflected away from its original direction of travel. The greater the curvature of the lens face, the greater the dispersion of any beam of light passing through it.

FIGURE 16.1
Light rays are deflected when they pass through a lens.

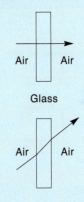

FIGURE 16.2
The greater the curvature of the convex face of a lens, the greater the angle of deflection, and vice versa.

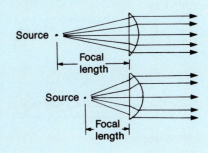

focal length: The distance from the lens at which the light rays converge into a point; for lenses used in stage-lighting instruments the focal length is most frequently measured in even inches.

plano-convex lens: A lens with one flat and one outward-curving face.

diffuse: To soften the appearance of light by using a translucent filtering element to scatter the rays.

The distance between the convergence point of a plano-convex lens—labeled "Source" in Figure 16.2—and the plano, or flat, face of the lens is referred to as the **focal length** of the lens.

The focal length of a lens affects the angle of the beam of light emitted by that lens. When considered in relation to the diameter of the lens, the shorter the focal length, the wider the beam of light it produces. A standard stage lighting instrument—the ellipsoidal reflector spotlight (ERS)—can be used to demonstrate this principle. If it is equipped with a lens 6 inches in diameter that has a focal length of 9 inches (known as a 6 × 9), it will produce a wider beam of light than an instrument equipped with a 6 × 12 lens. Similarly, a 6 × 12 ERS produces a wider beam of light than a 6 × 16 ERS. The lens trains on almost all of the newer ERSs are designated by a number which is a close approximation of the angle of beam spread in degrees (20, 30, 50, and so forth) for that instrument. For these instruments, the higher the number, the greater the beam spread.

The focal length of a **plano-convex lens** is determined by the curvature of the convex face of the lens. The greater the curvature, the shorter the focal length.

Three primary types of lens systems are used with theatrical lighting instruments: the double plano-convex lens train, the step lens, and the Fresnel lens.

Double Plano-Convex Lens Train

The double plano-convex lens train consists of two plano-convex lenses placed with their convex surfaces toward each other, as shown in Figure 16.3. This double configuration provides the same optical properties as a single lens of greater thickness and curvature, and the total thickness of the two lenses is less than the thickness of the optically comparable single lens. The single lens with short focal length is not used in lighting instruments, because its thickness makes it susceptible to heat fracture. The thicker single lens also transmits less light than its thinner optical equivalent in the double plano-convex lens system.

FIGURE 16.3
Double plano-convex lens train.

Step Lens

A step lens retains the optical characteristics and shape of a plano-convex lens, but the glass on the flat side is cut away in steps, as shown in Figure 16.4. The stepping process gives the lens the optical properties of a thick, short-focal-length, plano-convex lens while eliminating its negative characteristics.

An inherent property of step lenses is the prismatic effect caused by the steps themselves. Light passing through the steps at a shallow angle tends to create a spectral flare in the same manner that a prism breaks white light into a rainbow. Finishing the edges of the steps with a flat-black ceramic coating eliminates the spectral breakdown in most step lenses and does not interfere with the light passing through the rest of the lens (Figure 16.5).

FIGURE 16.4
A step lens.

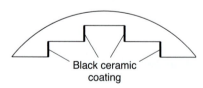

Black ceramic coating

FIGURE 16.5
A black ceramic coating prevents spectral breakdown.

Fresnel Lens

The Fresnel lens is a type of step lens with the glass cut away from the convex face of the lens instead of its plano side, as shown in Figure 16.6. The advantages of the Fresnel lens are the same as for the step lens; reduction of the thickness of the lens allows more light transmission and lessens the chances of heat fracture.

Fresnel lenses are primarily used in Fresnel spotlights. Occasionally you may encounter an older ERS with a Fresnel-type lens. You'll be able to identify it by the black ceramic coating applied to the vertical faces of the steps to eliminate spectral flare. Lenses for use in Fresnel spotlights don't have this coating, and the plano side of the lens is finished with a surface treatment to **diffuse** light. The

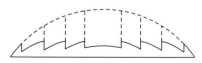

FIGURE 16.6
A Fresnel lens.

diffusing treatment generally makes the plano side of the lens appear as though it has been sandblasted or dimpled, or it may be finished with a series of small rectangular indentations. Regardless of the appearance of the treatment, its purpose is to soften the light to create the characteristically soft, luminescent light of the Fresnel spotlight.

filament: The light-producing element of a lamp; usually made of tungsten wire.

bulb: The Pyrex glass or synthetic quartz container for a lamp filament and gaseous environment. Synonymous with envelope.

 ## Lamps

Each stage-lighting instrument requires some type of lamp to produce light. The three primary sources used for stage lighting are the standard incandescent lamp, the tungsten-halogen lamp, and the encapsulated arc.

Incandescent Lamp

The standard incandescent lamp contains a tungsten **filament** that is placed in an inert gas environment inside the lamp **bulb,** as shown in Figure 16.7. The inert gas within the bulb is not pure and contains some oxygen. As an electrical current passes through the filament, heating it to incandescence, particles of tungsten are released. These particles are deposited to form the dark coating frequently found on the inside of older bulbs or envelopes. Eventually, the filament weakens sufficiently to cause it to break. The average life expectancy of a regular incandescent lamp designed for use in stage-lighting instruments ranges anywhere from 50 to approximately 200 hours. The life rating for a lamp does not mean that the light will burn out in the rated time. It means that the original output of the lamp will be reduced by 40 percent by the tungsten buildup on the inside of the bulb. Most lamps continue to burn long after their rated life, but at a significantly reduced output.

Tungsten-Halogen Lamp

Although it looks rather different than its cousin, the tungsten-halogen (T-H) lamp (Figure 16.8) is primarily the same as the standard incandescent lamp in all respects but one. That principal difference is that the atmosphere inside the bulb of the T-H lamp is a halogen, or chemically active, gas instead of an inert gas. As the particles of tungsten are released from the filament, they unite with the halogen gas to form a compound that is attracted back to the filament. The particles of tungsten reunite with the filament, and the halogen gas is released to repeat this chemical action. Because of the halogen cycle, the tungsten particles are not deposited on the inside of the bulb, and the filament of the T-H lamp is constantly being replenished. This results in a significantly longer life expectancy for the T-H lamp. Many T-H lamps designed for stage-lighting instruments are rated from 150 to 2,000 hours, as shown in Figure 16.9.

The halogen cycle becomes active only in a high-temperature environment. To achieve this goal, the T-H filament is encased within a small, highly heat-resistant synthetic quartz envelope. The heat generated by the filament is confined within the small space, and the resultant temperatures are much higher than if a larger bulb were used.

Arc Sources

An electric arc that produces a brilliantly blue white light is created when an electric current jumps the air gap between two electrodes. An arc is used as the source on some followspots.

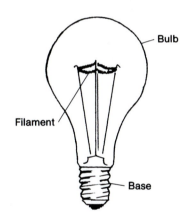

FIGURE 16.7
A standard incandescent lamp.

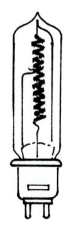

FIGURE 16.8
A tungsten-halogen incandescent lamp.

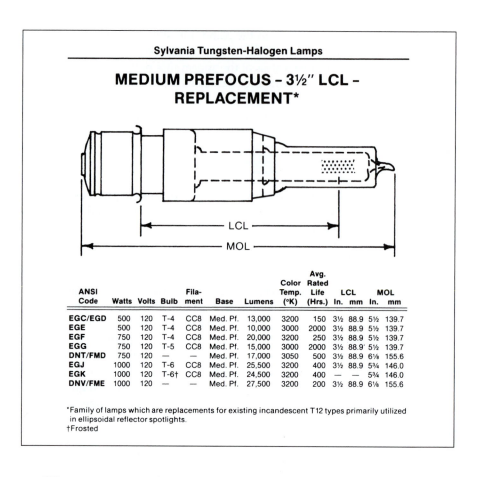

Sylvania Tungsten-Halogen Lamps

MEDIUM PREFOCUS – 3½″ LCL – REPLACEMENT*

ANSI Code	Watts	Volts	Bulb	Filament	Base	Lumens	Color Temp. (°K)	Avg. Rated Life (Hrs.)	LCL In.	mm	MOL In.	mm
EGC/EGD	500	120	T-4	CC8	Med. Pf.	13,000	3200	150	3½	88.9	5½	139.7
EGE	500	120	T-4	CC8	Med. Pf.	10,000	3000	2000	3½	88.9	5½	139.7
EGF	750	120	T-4	CC8	Med. Pf.	20,000	3200	250	3½	88.9	5½	139.7
EGG	750	120	T-5	CC8	Med. Pf.	15,000	3000	2000	3½	88.9'	5½	139.7
DNT/FMD	750	120	—	—	Med. Pf.	17,000	3050	500	3½	88.9	6⅛	155.6
EGJ	1000	120	T-6	CC8	Med. Pf.	25,500	3200	400	3½	88.9	5¾	146.0
EGK	1000	120	T-6†	CC8	Med. Pf.	24,500	3200	400	—	—	5¾	146.0
DNV/FME	1000	120	—	—	Med. Pf.	27,500	3200	200	3½	88.9	6⅛	155.6

*Family of lamps which are replacements for existing incandescent T12 types primarily utilized in ellipsoidal reflector spotlights.
†Frosted

When an arc is struck in an oxygen-rich environment such as air, the electrodes are consumed in the same way that a welding rod deteriorates during arc welding. If the arc is encapsulated in a noncorrosive atmosphere, however, the electrodes deteriorate extremely slowly. Encapsulated arcs such as the xenon and HMI (metal halide) lamps are frequently used in followspots and kinetic or moving light fixtures. Neither arc nor encapsulated arc sources can be dimmed, so they are not used in "regular" stage lighting instruments. However, encapsulated arcs such as the xenon and halide metal incandescent (HMI) lamps are frequently used in followspots and moving light fixtures where internally mounted mechanical dimmers allow the light to be dimmed.

Light-Emitting Diodes (LED)

High-output light-emitting diodes (LED) have recently been introduced as sources for some stage lighting fixtures. The first practical LED, which emitted red light, was developed in 1962 by Nick Holonyak, Jr.[1] LEDs are now available in a wide variety of colors and output levels, from the relatively low-output LEDs that you see everyday in devices such as the red/yellow/green status lights on electronic equipment to high-output applications for outdoor video displays, traffic lights, and now stage lights.

A precise explanation of how an LED emits light requires knowledge of electrical engineering beyond the intent of this introductory textbook.[2] Fortunately, it

[1] http://web.mit.edu/invent/a-winners/a-holonyak.html, p.1.
[2] For those technically minded readers who want to know exactly how an LED emits light, a good explanation is offered at: http://electronics.howstuffworks.com/led.htm.

isn't necessary to understand *how* an LED emits light to understand how it works. An LED is a special type of semiconducting diode that emits light. The color of the light is determined by the chemical composition of the material from which the LED is made. The amount of light emitted by the LED is directly proportional to the amount of electrical power (wattage) needed to make it produce light. Status light LEDs typically operate in the 30–60 **microwatt** range. High-output LEDs operate in the 1 to 5-watt range. Ongoing research indicates that significantly brighter LEDs, with brightness levels equivalent to 50-watt household light bulbs, should be commercially available by the time you read this or in the near future.[3]

Light-emitting diodes have numerous advantages over incandescent sources: They can produce colored light of a specific wavelength without the use of filters; the shape of the transparent LED case can be designed to focus light to a specific beam width; they have an expected life of 100,000 hours; they dim over time rather than burning out abruptly; they provide more light output per watt; their operational temperature is cooler than incandescent lamps.

Three primary, but solvable, technological challenges stand in the way of the adoption of LEDs as a primary light source for several classes of stage lighting instruments: The relatively low brightness of individual LEDs (when compared to other sources); the destructive effects of heat on LEDs; LEDs' need for DC, not AC, power. But these challenges may very well be overcome within the next decade.

More information about the current use of LED sources in stage lighting instruments is covered later in this chapter in the discussion of intelligent or kinetic fixtures.

Color Temperature

All the standard light sources appear to be white. They are actually a variety of colors, however, and these colors can be identified by using the color-temperature scale.

The color-temperature scale was originally determined by heating a device known as a blackbody radiator. As the blackbody was heated, its color was read at specific temperatures by a **spectrometer.** The color-temperature scale, measured in degrees Kelvin (K), was the result of this experiment. Table 16.1 shows the color temperatures of a number of standard sources.

There is a loose, but fairly constant, correlation among color temperature, light output, and lamp life. Generally speaking, the higher the light output of a lamp (which is measured in lumens), the higher its color temperature and the shorter its rated life. A comparison of the specifications for similar lamps such as the EGC/EGD and the EGE (the American National Standards Institute codes for two commonly used theatrical lamps) illustrates this relationship (Figure 16.9).

Although it isn't essential that the color temperatures of all lamps used to light a production be the same, the instruments that are going to be **gelled** with color media of a specific hue are generally equipped with lamps of the same color temperature so that the color of the resultant light will be uniform.

Lamp Structure

All lamps, regardless of shape or type, are composed of three basic parts: bulb, base, and filament, as shown in Figure 16.10.

---

[3] http://compoundsemiconductor.net/articles/news/9/9/1/1, p. 1.

microwatt: One millionth of a watt.

spectrometer: A device for measuring specific wavelengths of light.

gelled: To put a color filter into a color frame and place it in the color-frame holder of a lighting instrument.

FIGURE 16.10
Lamp structure.

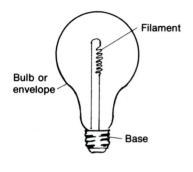

TABLE 16.1

Color Temperature of Some Common Sources

Color Tempertaure	Light Source
6,500	Xenon
6,000	
5,500	HMI (halide metal incandescent)
5,000	
4,500	Fluorescent (cool white)
4,000	
3,500	
3,000	Theatrical Incandescent
2,500	(standard and tungsten-halogen)
2,000	

Sunshine

FIGURE 16.11
Common incandescent lamp shapes.

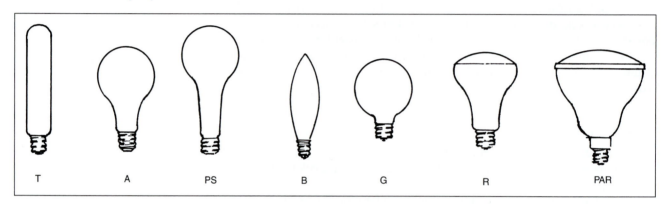

| T | A | PS | B | G | R | PAR |

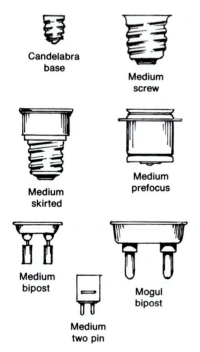

Candelabra base

Medium screw

Medium skirted

Medium prefocus

Medium bipost

Mogul bipost

Medium two pin

FIGURE 16.12
Typical lamp bases.

Bulb   The bulb is the Pyrex or synthetic quartz envelope that encases the filament and acts as a container for the gas-filled atmosphere of the lamp. The shape and size of the bulb are determined by the position and shape of the filament, the burning position of the lamp within the lighting instrument, and the heat-dissipation requirements of the lamp. Figure 16.11 illustrates common incandescent bulb shapes. Bulb sizes vary depending on individual lamp requirements.

The diameter of the bulb is indicated by a figure representing eighths of an inch. Thus the T-4 bulbs listed under the "Bulb" heading in Figure 16.9 are T-shaped and have a diameter of ⅘—or ½—inch, and the MR16 lamp illustrated in Figure 16.14 has a diameter of roughly 2 inches.

Base   The lamp base secures the lamp in the socket and provides the electrical contact points between the socket and the filament. There are several styles of lamp bases, as illustrated in Figure 16.12. Generally, large, high-wattage incandescent lamps have the larger bases. Figure 16.12 shows not only the different bases but also the relative size relationship that each base has to the others. The candelabra base is approximately ½ inch in diameter, the medium-size bases are approximately 1 inch in diameter, and the mogul bases are about 1½ inches across.

The prefocus, bipost, and two-pin bases are used for instruments that need the filament in a specific location in relation to the reflector—such as the ERS or Fresnel spotlight.

Lamp Maintenance

Although it is a good idea to keep all lamps clean and free from dirt and grease, it is particularly important to handle tungsten-halogen lamps with extreme care. The bulb of the T-H lamp must be kept free of all fingerprints, grease, or any other foreign substance that could cause a change in the heat-dissipation characteristics of the bulb. Because a T-H lamp reaches a high temperature, any change in its heat-dissipation characteristics could cause the lamp to break or explode.

When installing lamps, grasp the lamp by the base rather than the bulb. If this is not practical, a soft cloth or glove should be used to handle the glass envelope. This practice will protect both your hands and the lamp bulb.

Although it is not as important to keep a regular incandescent lamp as scrupulously clean as a T-H bulb, it is good practice to wipe the bulb with a soft cloth after handling.

Lamp bases should be kept free of any corrosive buildup or insulating deposits that could interfere with the electrical contact between the socket and base.

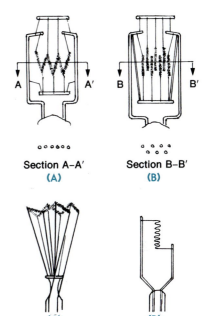

FIGURE 16.13
Filament styles.

Filament   Various lamp filaments are available, each designed to perform a particular function. All filaments for stage-lighting lamps are made of tungsten wire, usually tightly coiled, and strung in one of the general configurations shown in Figure 16.13.

MR16 Lamps

These small-diameter (approximately 2 inches), low-voltage, low-wattage lamps integrate a small, coiled-filament tungsten-halogen lamp into a focusing mirrored reflector (hence the designation MR16). The lamp, shown in Figure 16.14, is available in a variety of voltages and wattages as well as several beam-angle widths from very narrow to flood. The small size of the lamps allows fixtures to be created that are small in size and weight with light output characteristics similar, and in some cases superior, to the output of their larger-lamped counterparts. Each low-voltage fixture contains a transformer that reduces the input voltage from the dimmer to match the specific voltage of the lamp.

Light Output of Lamps

The output of an incandescent lamp, while related to the lamp wattage, is primarily a function of the size and composition of the filament. This output is measured in lumens. Generally speaking, if two lamps have the same wattage but one has a smaller filament, the smaller-filament lamp will have a higher lumen output but a shorter life expectancy, as shown in Table 16.2.

Color Media

Three transparent color media are used to color the light output of stage-lighting instruments. Each medium has its own particular characteristics and advantages.

Plastic   The majority of filters used in theatrical lighting are generally made of either Mylar or polyester because of the rugged, long-lasting, heat-resistant qualities of these plastics. They are available in a wide and ever-increasing variety of colors. Light, heat, and ultraviolet radiation from T-H lamps tend to bleach the color out of plastic **gels.** Low-saturation tints bleach out relatively slowly, while heavily saturated colors such as dark blues can bleach out within a few hours.

FIGURE 16.14
An MR16 lamp.

gel: Generic term referring to flexible (gelatin or plastic) color media.

TABLE 16.2

Comparison of Same Wattage/Different Output Lamps

Watts	Sylvania Ordering Abbreviation	Other Designation	NAED Code	Standard Case Quantity	Volts	Color Temperature (°K)	Nominal Lumens	Average Rated Life (hr)	Filament Class	Fused Silica Bulb Finish	Lighted Length (in.)
1,000	DXN	—	53993	12	120	3,400	33,500	30	CC-8	Clear	11/16
1,000	DXW	—	53997	12	120	3,200	28,000	150	CC-8	Clear	13/16
1,000	FBY	Frosted DXW	53996	12	120	3,200	26,000	150	CC-8	Frosted	—
1,000	FBZ	Frosted DXN	53999	12	120	3,400	31,500	30	CC-8	Frosted	—
1,000	BRH	—	54563	12	120	3,350	30,000	75	CC-8	Clear	—

Source: OSRAM SYLVANIA INC.

roundel: A glass color medium for use with striplights; frequently has diffusing properties.

Glass   Glass filters are used infrequently because they are heavy and expensive, and they shatter if dropped. The most prominent use of glass is in **roundels,** the glass filters used with striplights. Roundels are generally available in red, blue, green, amber, and clear. Roundels normally have a slight diffusing treatment to help spread the light more evenly.

Dichroic   Dichroic filters are a relatively new addition to theatrical color media. Dichroic filters do not work in the same way as other color media. Plastic and glass filters allow their own color to pass through the filter while *absorbing* the undesired colors. Dichroic filters *reflect* the unwanted colors. To produce a particular color, you use a dichroic filter to remove its complementary. To illustrate, if you want to produce the color red from a beam of white light, you use a dichroic filter that reflects the complementary of red (cyan). Removing the cyan from white light produces red light.

There are tangible advantages to this system of filtration. For one, the output of the resultant light is measurably greater (light input/light output) than that produced with traditional plastic and glass filters. Another advantage of dichroics is the property of reflecting rather than absorbing unwanted wavelengths of electromagnetic radiation (remember that light is just a small segment of the electromagnetic spectrum). Cold mirrors are dichroic filters that are coated to reflect the visible spectrum and allow infrared radiation (heat) to pass. A reflector made with a cold-mirror finish vents heat *through* the reflector, which makes the reflected light considerably cooler. Hot mirrors, as you would expect, are just the reverse. They reflect infrared radiation and allow the visible spectrum to pass. Hot mirrors are used as heat filters in projectors as well as several of the kinetic instruments discussed in another section of this chapter.

Further advantages of dichroic filters are that the filters, if made of glass, are extremely heat-resistant and that color fade is all but nonexistent. The range of colors currently available in dichroic filters for theatrical instruments is relatively limited, but it is anticipated that there will be more colors available as the use of these filters increases.

The primary disadvantage of dichroics is their cost. However, in professional situations where replacing the color in a lamp frequently requires bringing in a crew on a four-hour call, it may be cost-effective to use dichroic filters when you consider that heavily saturated plastic filters need to be replaced after two to three hours of use.

Lighting Instruments

A variety of lighting instruments are used in the theatre, but the ellipsoidal reflector spotlight and the Fresnel spotlight are the real workhorses for the lighting designer.

Ellipsoidal Reflector Spotlight

The light produced by an ellipsoidal reflector spotlight (ERS) has a narrow beam width and is capable of traveling long distances. The quality of the light produced by this instrument, also generically known by the trade name Leko, can be characterized as generally hard edged with little diffusion. The shape of the beam is controlled by internally mounted shutters. The spill light from an ERS—that is, any light that escapes past the edge of the beam—is minimal. Because of all these characteristics, ERSs are the primary lighting tool of the designer. Several manufacturers' versions of the ERS, and an exploded view showing the main parts of the ellipsoidal reflector spotlight, are shown in Figure 16.15.

General Operating Principles   The reflector of an ERS is a truncated conical ellipse, which has properties that are uniquely suited to focusing light. The conical elliptical reflector shown in Figure 16.16A has two focal points, F1 and F2. Light emitted by a light source at F1 will reflect off the walls of the conical ellipse and pass through F2. If half of the elliptical reflector were removed (Figure 16.16B), light emitted from the source at F1 would again pass through F2, although some of the light would pass out of the open end of the reflector and be lost.

The ERS operates on this basic principle of gathering light from one focal point (F1) and focusing it on the second focal point (F2). Some ERSs have a kickback reflector placed at the open end of the conical ellipse to redirect any spill light back into the reflector, as shown in Figure 16.16C. The shutters, made of stainless steel or some other highly heat-resistant metal, are located in a plane close to the second focal point to shape the light.

FIGURE 16.15
Ellipsoidal reflector spotlights. (A) Source Four courtesy of Electronic Theatre Controls (ETC); (B) Pacific courtesy of Selecon Performance Lighting; (C) Exploded view of ERS courtesy of Lee Colortran.

(A)   (B)   (C)

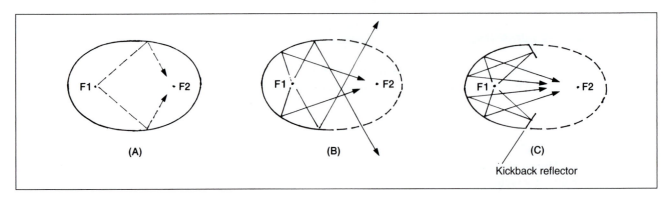

FIGURE 16.16
Optical properties of a conical ellipse reflector.

Figure 16.17 shows a cross section of an axial-mount ERS, so called because the lamp is placed on the optical, or centerline, axis of the instrument. This configuration, now standard for almost all ERSs designed since approximately 1985, was made possible by the development of the tungsten-halogen lamp. Compare the position of the lamp in the axial-mount instrument (Figure 16.17) with the instrument shown in Figure 16.18, an ERS designed for the larger incandescent T-shaped lamp, which predates the T-H lamp. Note how the lamp filament is still located at the focal point of the ellipsoidal reflector even though the lamp is mounted in a different position.

The lens is placed at a point in front of the shutters to focus the light into the desired field angle, as shown in Figures 16.17 and 16.18. ERSs are equipped with one of three lens systems: a double plano-convex lens train, a step lens, or, on a few older models, a Fresnel lens without the diffusing treatment on the plano face. Although there may be slight differences in light output and quality, the three types generally work equally well.

FIGURE 16.17
Cutaway view of an axial-mount ellipsoidal reflector spotlight.

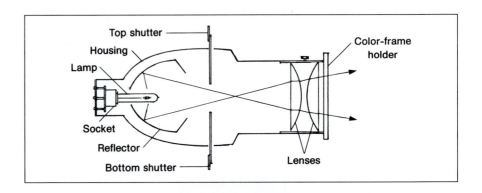

FIGURE 16.18
Cutaway view of an ellipsoidal reflector spotlight designed for a standard incandescent lamp.

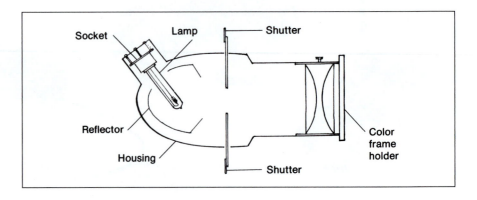

FIGURE 16.19
A continuously variable-focal-length ellipsoidal reflector spotlight. (Courtesy of Altman Stage Lighting.)

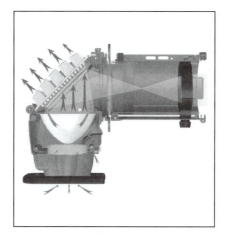

FIGURE 16.20
Light is bounced off a cold mirror reflector in the Selecon Pacific ERS. (Courtesy of Selecon.)

The **zoom ellipse,** more officially known as the variable-focal-length ERS (Figure 16.19), is an extremely versatile instrument. This variation of the standard ERS has lenses that can slide forward or backward to change the focal length of the instrument. Changing the focal length affects the beam and field angles of the instrument, with those angles widening as the focal length becomes shorter. The field angle of most zoom ellipses can be varied between approximately 20 and 45 degrees.

Recent additions to the ERS family, the ETC Source Four, the Source Four Jr., and the Altman Shakespeare 600 series, use an excellent innovation in theatrical instrument design—cold mirror reflectors. These reflectors, which are made of heavy Pyrex glass, have an applied dichroic coating that reflects visible light while transmitting infrared (heat) wavelengths. This means that the majority of the heat generated by the lamp *passes through* the reflector and is vented out the rear of the instrument rather than being reflected with the rest of the light. The result is less heat deterioration of the shutters, iris, and gobos, as well as longer color media life.

More innovative ERS design is evident in the Pacific family of fixtures by Selecon. This instrument has a unique shape because it is designed to reflect light off of a dichroic cold mirror before the light strikes the gate as shown in Figure 16.20. The cold mirror reflects visible light but passes infrared (heat) and ultraviolet light through the mirror. A heat sink vents the infrared heat outside of the housing. The net effect is a much cooler beam of light which, in turn, results in longer shutter and color media life. Additionally, the lens tube rotates 360 degrees, which allows the shutters to be positioned to make the most appropriate **shutter cut.**

Table 16.3 lists the beam and field angles in degrees of arc for several varieties of 6-inch ERSs. As mentioned in Chapter 14, the beam angle (Figure 16.21) is that point where the intensity of the cone of light emitted by the instrument diminishes to 50 percent of its intensity as compared with the center of the beam. The field angle is that point where the light diminishes to 10 percent of the output of the center of the beam.

Accessories   The most basic accessory designed for use with an ERS is the **color frame** (Figure 16.22), a lightweight metal or heat-resistant fiber holder for plastic

zoom ellipse: An ellipsoidal reflector spotlight with movable lenses that allow the focal length to be changed.

shutter cut: The shadow line created by the edge of the shutter when it is inserted into the beam of light emitted by an ERS.

color frame: A lightweight metal holder for color media that fits in a holder at the front of a lighting instrument.

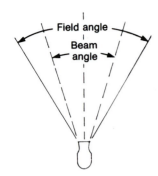

FIGURE 16.21
Beam and field angles.

TABLE 16.3

Beam/Field Angles for Typical ERSs*

Instrument Type	Beam Angle	Field Angle	Maximum Effective Range†
6 × 9	16°	37°	35 feet
6 × 12	11°	26°	50 feet
6 × 16	9°	18°	60 feet
20°	10°	20°	70 feet
30°	12°	30°	60 feet
40°	15°	40°	55 feet

*All data are approximate but typical. Specific data vary with manufacturer.
†Determined by point at which output diminishes to 50 foot-candles.

FIGURE 16.22
A color frame.

colored media. The color frame is inserted into the holder on the front of the ERS to color the light.

The **gobo** (Figure 16.23), also known as a pattern, template, or cookie, is a lightweight metal cutout that turns the ERS into a pattern projector. Most ERSs are equipped with a built-in pattern slot located adjacent to the shutter plane. A wide variety of commercially designed gobos, usually made of stainless steel, are available from scenic and lighting supply houses. Gobos can be constructed from metal offset printing sheets or from heavy-weight disposable aluminum cookware (roasting pans, pie plates), as shown in Figure 16.24. Offset printing sheets are thin, flexible aluminum sheets, which can usually be obtained from local newspaper publishers at low cost. They can withstand the heat generated by an ERS, are stiff enough to prevent flexing or buckling, and can be worked easily with scissors, chisels, or a **Dremel tool.** The disposable aluminum pie plates are satisfactory for making cloud gobos and similar patterns that have little intricate detail. The aluminum used in these products is about one-third as thick as the offset printing sheets and will vaporize under the high heat generated by the instrument lamp if the pattern is too detailed. It is much better to make intricately designed gobos from offset printing sheets or from stainless steel because they

gobo: A thin metal template inserted into an ellipsoidal reflector spotlight to project a shadow pattern of light.

Dremel tool: A hand-held router similar to a dentist's drill, which can be equipped with a number of bits for grinding, cutting, or carving of wood, plastic, and metal.

FIGURE 16.23
(A) A gobo and (B) the pattern that the gobo projects.

(A)

(B)

Lamp Comparison Chart

Although the specific lamp that is used with any instrument depends on the design of the instrument, some fairly standard wattages are used with various families of instruments.

Instrument	Standard Lamp-Wattage Range
4-inch ERS	250-600
6-inch ERS	500-1,000
8-inch ERS	1,000-2,000
6-inch Fresnel	250-750
8-inch Fresnel	750-1,000
Scoop	350-1,500
Striplight	150-500
Followspot (incandescent)	1,000-2,000

iris: A device with movable overlapping metal plates, used with an ellipsoidal reflector spotlight to change the size of the circular pattern of light.

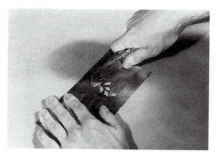

FIGURE 16.24
Gobos can be built in the shop by cutting the pattern out of disposable aluminum cookware.

stand up to the heat generated by the tungsten-halogen lamps much better than do their aluminum counterparts.

Custom gobo designs can be created by using scanned photos, drawings, or designs created with a software program such as Photoshop. The custom divisions of American Market and Rosco, among others, can produce these self-designed patterns. Additionally, colored glass patterns—using dichroic filters to create color—are commercially available from the aforementioned manufacturers, among others. Do an online search or check the trade publications for current manufacturers.

Another useful accessory for an ERS is the **iris** (Figure 16.25). The iris varies the size of the circular pattern produced by an ERS. It is mounted in the shutter plane, and the size of the aperture is controlled by an external handle.

Fresnel Spotlight

The Fresnel spotlight produces a soft, diffused, luminescent light. Some Fresnel spotlights are shown in Figure 16.26. When the instrument is focused on narrow beam, or spot, as shown in Figure 16.27A, it produces a beam with a central hot spot that rapidly loses intensity toward the edge. When the instrument is focused on wide beam, or flood (Figure 16.27B), it produces a smooth wash of light.

The standard Fresnel spotlight is equipped with a Fresnel lens producing a circular beam of light. The oval-beam Fresnel lens (Figure 16.28) has the same luminescent and optical qualities as its round-beam counterpart but produces an oval, instead of round, beam of light.

General Operating Principles The Fresnel spotlight is simple. The instrument housing holds the lens and provides a mounting platform for the socket, lamp,

FIGURE 16.25
An ellipsoidal reflector spotlight equipped with an iris.

FIGURE 16.26
Fresnel spotlights. (Courtesy of Altman Stage Lighting and Strand Lighting.)

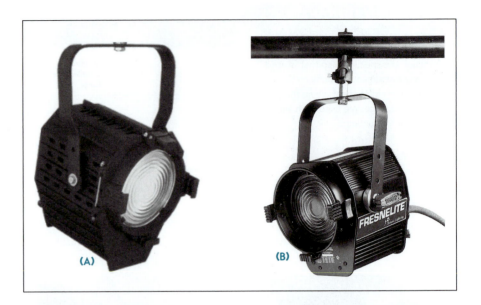

(A)   (B)

FIGURE 16.27
The Fresnel spotlight can be focused on spot (A) or flood (B).

(A)   (B)

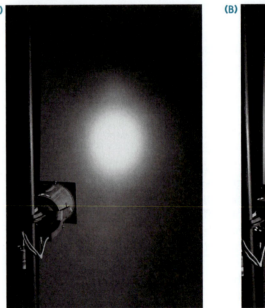
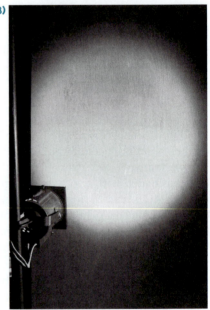

FIGURE 16.28
An oval-beam lens for a Fresnel spotlight.

and reflector assembly, which are mounted on a small sled that moves closer to or farther from the lens during focusing, as shown in Figure 16.29. Figure 16.30A shows the instrument on spot focus with the socket and reflector assembly moved toward the back of the instrument housing. In this position, most of the light is concentrated into a hot spot in the center of the beam. Figure 16.30B shows the instrument on flood focus, with the socket and reflector assembly moved all the way forward. This creates a smooth wash of light from edge to edge, with only a small, almost undetectable, hot spot in the center of the beam.

Accessories   The primary, and almost indispensable, accessory for the Fresnel spotlight is the **barn door** (Figure 16.31). Its flippers are movable and can be swung into the beam of light until they cut off as much light as desired.

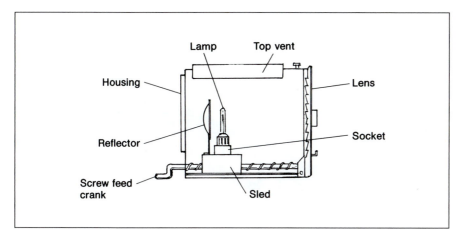

FIGURE 16.29
A cutaway view of a Fresnel spotlight.

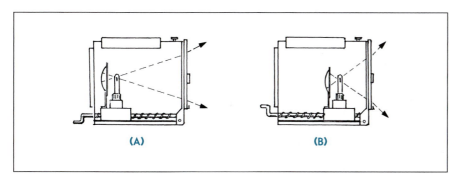

FIGURE 16.30
The sled holding the lamp/reflector assembly is (A) moved backward to produce a hot spot in the middle of the beam or (B) moved forward to produce a smooth wash of light.

barn door: An accessory for a Fresnel spotlight whose movable flippers are swung into the beam to control it.

funnel: An accessory for a Fresnel spotlight that masks the beam to create a circular pattern; also called a snoot or a top hat.

FIGURE 16.31
A four-flipper barn door.

FIGURE 16.32
Funnels are used to create small circular patterns of light with a Fresnel spotlight.

Another accessory is the **funnel** (Figure 16.32). The funnel, like the barn door, fits into the color-frame slot on the front of the instrument. The circular pattern of light that it creates is dependent on the diameter of the funnel's cone.

Striplight

The striplight is used to create a smooth wash of light. It resembles a long trough with a series of lamps inside, as shown in Figure 16.33. Striplights are available in a variety of lengths and configurations, but they are most often between 4 and 10 feet in length.

The individual lights within the instrument are wired in parallel to form three or four circuits, as shown in the block diagram of Figure 16.34. This type of configuration provides designers with the opportunity to mix and blend color if they gel all the lamps of each circuit with a separate color. By placing each circuit of the striplight on a separate dimmer, designers can manipulate the intensities of the individual colors to mix the desired resultant hue. To create the maximum potential for color mixing, designers frequently color the individual circuits of a three-circuit striplight with the primary colors in light (red, blue, and green). If a four-circuit striplight is used, the fourth circuit is frequently gelled with amber. It

FIGURE 16.33
Striplights. (A) A standard striplight. (Courtesy of Altman Stage Lighting.) (B) A "mini" striplight. The lamps are low-voltage MR16 lamps allowing the fixture to be relatively small—6 feet long, 3½ inches wide, and 7 inches deep. (Courtesy of Strand Lighting.)

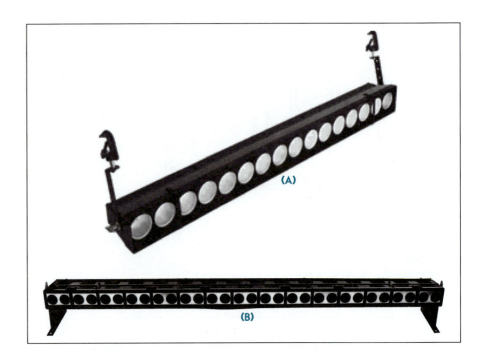

FIGURE 16.34
Circuiting pattern for striplights.

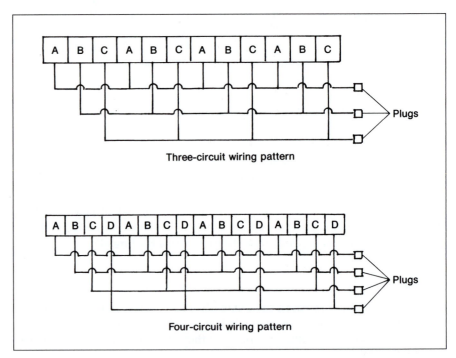

FIGURE 16.35
Roundels are glass filters used with striplights.

is not mandatory that striplights be colored with red, blue, and green; if the designer knows that he or she will be working in a narrow color spectrum, it is usually preferable to color the individual circuits in the appropriate hues.

Striplights are primarily used to light background drops and cycloramas, although they can be used in any position wherever a diffused, general wash of light is desired. Striplights are equipped to hold plastic color media as well as roundels (Figure 16.35), which are glass color media that have diffusing properties to help blend the light. Roundels are available in the primary colors as well as amber, frosted, and clear.

Cyc Light

The cyc light is superior to the striplight for creating a smooth wash of light over the expanse of a cyc or drop. This fairly new type of fixture uses an eccentric reflector to create such a wash from only 7 or 8 feet away. The cyc light emits a much smoother light than does the striplight, and it is equipped with a color-frame holder so that the light can be colored as desired.

There are two types of cyc lights. One, such as the Hui Flood from Selecon (Figure 16.36) has a symmetrical reflector which produces a smooth, evenly distributed output of light. They are typically used for producing color washes on the acting areas of the stage. The other type of cyc light, illustrated by the Selecon Aurora illustrated in Figure 16.37A, has an asymmetrical reflector that produces an uneven wash of light perfectly suited for cyc lighting. Several of the individual fixtures can be bolted together, as shown in Figure 16.37B, and hung from a batten to create a top-down, smooth, multicolor wash of light on the cyc. A variation with rubber feet—illustrated by the Aurora Groundrow (Figure 16.37C)—can be placed on the stage floor to light the cyc from the bottom up.

Ellipsoidal Reflector Floodlight

The ellipsoidal reflector floodlight (Figure 16.38), also known as the scoop, is primarily used to light drops and cycloramas. It is a lensless instrument that has the light-focusing characteristics of a conical ellipsoidal reflector, which provides a wide, smooth wash of light. It is equipped with a large color-frame holder that, in many cases, has wire restraining lines crisscrossed over the circular opening to prevent the color medium from falling out. The scoop is available in a variety of sizes, but in the theatre the 14-, 16-, and 18-inch diameters are most commonly used.

FIGURE 16.36
The Hui Flood has a symmetrical reflector. (Courtesy of Selecon.)

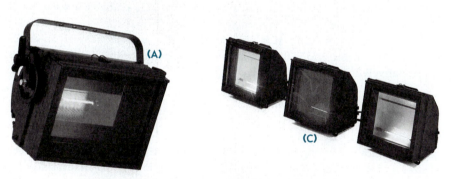
(A)
(C)

(B)

FIGURE 16.37
The Aurora Cyc (A) has an asymmetrical reflector. Several units can be used together to create a hanging multicolor fixture (B) or a groundrow (C). (Courtesy of Selecon.)

FIGURE 16.38
Ellipsoidal reflector floodlight, also known as a "scoop." (Courtesy of Altman Stage Lighting.)

(A)   (B)

FIGURE 16.39
(A) A PAR 64 can. (Courtesy of Altman Stage Lighting.) (B) A Source Four PAR. (Courtesy of ETC.)

PAR Can

The parabolic aluminized reflector, or PAR, is a sealed-beam lamp similar to the headlight of an automobile. The lamp housing, known as a PAR can (Figure 16.39), performs no function other than safely holding the lamp and its color media.

The most widely used size of PAR can is designed to hold the PAR 64, a 1000-watt lamp about 8 inches in diameter. The PAR 64 lamp is available in a variety of beam and field angles, as shown in Table 16.4. The PAR 64 produces a powerfully intense oval punch of light, yet it has a soft edge. It is used extensively in dance and concert lighting and is finding increased usage in theatre lighting because of its relatively low cost, portability, durability, and light weight.

Followspot

The followspot is used when a high-intensity, hard-edged beam of light is required to follow a moving performer. Followspots are manufactured in a variety of sizes and styles (see Figure 16.40). The smallest followspot is an incandescent

TABLE 16.4

Beam and Field Angles for Various PAR 64 Configurations

PAR 64 Lamp	Beam Angle (in degrees) (height × width)	Field Angle (in degrees) (height × width)
Very Narrow	6 × 12	10 × 24
Narrow	7 × 14	14 × 26
Medium	12 × 28	21 × 44
Wide	24 × 48	45 × 71

FIGURE 16.40
Followspots. (Courtesy of Strong International.)

model capable of a useful light throw of about 35 feet. The larger models use high-intensity xenon, HMI, or unencapsulated arc-lamp sources and have a useful light throw of up to 300 to 400 feet.

All followspots function on the same general principles, illustrated in Figure 16.41. They have an illumination source—incandescent, tungsten-halogen, HMI, xenon, or arc. Many have a forced-air cooling system that helps to dissipate the heat generated by the light source.

The iris and **shutter** are internal control devices used to shape the beam of light. By manipulating them simultaneously, the operator can create a variety of beam-edge patterns.

All followspots have some type of lens or reflecting system to gather and shape the light. Portions of the system can be adjusted to focus the light and adjust the crispness of the edge of the beam.

Some followspots are equipped with a mechanical dimming device called a **douser.** Since the intensity of some of the light sources used in followspots (arc, encapsulated arc, xenon, HMI) cannot be adjusted, the douser provides the only way of smoothly dimming those sources. The douser can also be used to achieve

shutter: A lever-actuated device used to control the height of the top and bottom edges of a followspot beam; also called a chopper.

douser: A mechanical dimming device used in followspots.

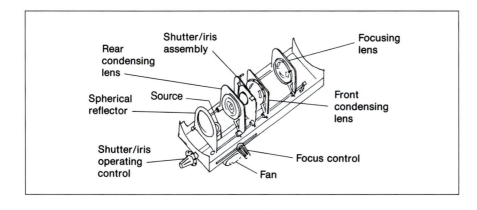

FIGURE 16.41
Cutaway drawing of a followspot.

transformer: A device that changes the voltage in an electrical system; the output voltage of a step-down transformer is less than its source; a step-up transformer increases it.

legitimate theatre: Refers to plays that rely on the spoken word to convey the message. Does not include musicals, reviews, dance, opera, or concerts.

concert: In this context, primarily refers to touring rock and country western shows.

club: In this context, refers to night clubs in which high-energy music (live or recorded) is the prime attraction.

a slow fade-in or fade-out of the light. Followspots are also equipped with a color boomerang, which holds five or six color filters that can be easily inserted into the beam of light to control its color.

Specialty Instruments

Several lighting instruments do not fall conveniently into other categories.

Low-Voltage Sources   A number of specialty lamps use a voltage lower than the 120 output volts of most stage dimmers. The output of these low-voltage lamps is frequently as high as that of their 120-volt cousins. Aircraft landing lights (ACLs) have a very high output and high color temperature, and the parabolic reflector provides a very narrow beam spread. Automobile headlights provide another narrow-beam, low-voltage source.

A primary advantage of lower-voltage lamps is that their filaments can be much smaller than their higher-voltage counterparts. The smaller filament can be used effectively in some types of scenic projectors discussed in Chapter 17, "Projections."

These low-voltage lamps require a **transformer** to decrease the 120-volt source voltage before it reaches the lamp, as shown in Figure 16.42. A step-down transformer of appropriate voltage and capacity to match almost any lamp can be purchased at any electrical supply store. For 12-volt lamps, a heavy-duty automotive battery charger can be used as long as the current created by the wattage of the lamp does not exceed the rated capacity of the battery charger or its leads.

A number of lighting instruments and projectors have been designed to take advantage of the properties (small filament size, low heat output) of low-voltage lamps. These instruments normally have the required step-down transformer mounted inside of the instrument housing.

Intelligent or Kinetic Instruments   One of the primary functions of an effective lighting design is the establishment of a mood that supports the production concept. To creatively, and effectively, light a **legitimate theatre** production, the lighting designer generally uses the basic tools just discussed—ERSs, Fresnels, PARs, cyc lights, and so forth. With this equipment he or she can create the normally subtle lighting that supports the production concept and covertly affects the audience's understanding of the play.

In the application of its basic principles, lighting design for **concerts** and **clubs** is no different than lighting design for legitimate theatre. However, there are two substantial differences: the nature of the production concept and the impact of the lighting on the audience. Production concepts for legitimate theatre productions are almost always intellectual, cerebral, and metaphorically introspective. The production concept for rock concerts and clubs is almost always visceral, bold, and extroverted. The atmosphere at a rock concert or club is about as far removed as you can get from a production of Shakespeare, Williams, or Stoppard. The music is fast, hard, and loud. The atmosphere is high energy. So is the lighting. It is overt and spectacular, and the way it affects meaning and mood is anything but subtle. Basic area lighting is normally done with multiple washes of heavily saturated color from PAR 64s. Moving light fixtures provide punch, emphasis, and focus. As more designers have had a chance to learn the capabilities of these versatile fixtures, they have learned that these instruments don't always need to be used to spectacular effect. They can also be very effective if used subtly. Consequently, when budgets permit, we are seeing more use of this fascinating class of instrument in legitimate theatre.

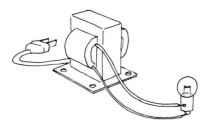

FIGURE 16.42
A low-voltage lamp and transformer.

Safety Tip

Instrument Maintenance

To function effectively, the various instruments discussed in this chapter must be maintained in good working order, and as with any delicate piece of equipment, they must be handled with care.

The position of the lamp filament and the reflector must be kept in alignment, particularly in an ellipsoidal reflector spotlight. If this relationship is disturbed, the light output from the instrument will be greatly reduced, and the hot spot will be moved from the center of the beam. One of the significant advantages of the PAR 64 is that the filament and reflector are permanently aligned during the manufacturing process, so when the lamp in a PAR can is changed, there is no need to check the relationship.

The lenses and reflectors need to be kept clean and free from dust and fingerprints, and all nuts and bolts on the housing, yoke, and pipe clamp should be maintained so that the instrument can be locked securely into place.

When not in use, instruments should be hung on pipes or on rolling racks so that they won't be knocked over. If the theatre does not have an instrument storage cage, the instruments can be stored on a counterweight batten above the stage.

Ellipsoidal reflector spotlights should be stored with the shutters pushed all the way in to prevent them from being accidentally bent. When the instruments are in storage, care should be taken that the electrical pigtails are not pinched between the yoke and the instrument housing. The electrical plug and pigtail must be kept in good working order.

Followspots are mounted on a yoke and swivel-stand base that must move smoothly to follow the action of a performer. The base and yoke need to be properly lubricated, usually with graphite rather than oil or grease, and all nuts and bolts must be properly tightened.

The kinetic fixtures and associated digital control equipment that constitute this exciting class of instruments provide the lighting designer with the capability to create the in-your-face lighting (both literally and figuratively) that supports the production concept and mood of many concert productions.

The common feature of kinetic fixtures is movement: Light beams **pan** the stage, zoom in and out, change shape, change color, diffuse, and sharpen; gobos materialize, spin around, change pattern, then disappear. This is an exciting and active class of instrument.

There are a plethora of moving light fixtures available, as shown in Figure 16.43. Obviously, they don't all function in the same way, nor do they all have the same features. But generally they all use the same principles of operation. Almost all functions—pan, **tilt,** mechanical dimming, color changing, gobo movement and changing, beam spread, beam diffusion, and so forth—of these instruments are controlled by very precise electric **step motors.** Some of these instruments contain up to twenty separate motors to control the various functions.

Control of these step motors would be almost impossible without the development of USITT DMX512, a digital control protocol employed by a majority of the kinetic lighting and control manufacturers, as well as the manufacturers of "regular" stage lighting systems. (See the box "USITT DMX512" on page 410.) Digital control allows control signals for all functions of these instruments to be fed to the fixture through one low-voltage control cable. A separate 120 or 208/220 VAC power line is required to power the lamp and control motors.

Tungsten-halogen and encapsulated arc lamps are most commonly used with these instruments. T-H lamps can be dimmed, but encapsulated arc lamps, which are used because of their very high output, cannot be dimmed. They re-

pan: To rotate an object, such as an ERS, about its vertical axis.

tilt: To rotate an object about its horizontal axis; to pan vertically. The instrument is suspended from a yoke, which allows the fixture to both pan and tilt.

step motor: An electric motor whose movement consists of discrete, angular steps rather than continuous rotation. Precise movement is achieved by programming the motor to run, in either direction, for a specific number of steps.

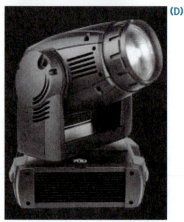

FIGURE 16.43
Types of moving light fixtures. (A) High End Cyberlight. (B) Martin RoboScan Pro 918. (C) VL 500 Wash Luminaire by Vari-Lite. (D) MAC 700 Wash by Martin. (Courtesy of High End, Martin, Vari-Lite.)

quire mechanical dimming or dousers. The dousers are very precisely regulated with digitally controlled step motors.

Many kinetic instruments have internally mounted gobos and gobo changers. In some fixtures the gobos can be made to spin either forward or backward. Again, the functions of inserting, changing, and spinning the gobos are controlled by step motors.

Almost all of these instruments move the beam of light around the stage. Generally this is done in one of two ways: (1) a mirror is used to direct the beam of light, or (2) the entire fixture pans and tilts. The advantage of the mirror system is that you don't have to rotate the entire instrument. Moving light fixtures are heavy—weighing anywhere from 30 to more than 100 pounds. The mirror is lightweight, and its movements can be controlled with less powerful motors than would be required to rotate the whole fixture. An added bonus is that the smaller motors and associated hardware generally make less noise. More optically complex fixtures such as the High End Cyberlight (Figure 16.43A) and the Martin's RoboScan Pro 918 (Figure 16.43B) normally use mirrors for directional control of light. Lighter-weight, less optically complex instruments such as the Vari-Lite VL 500 Wash Luminaire (Figure 16.43C) and the Martin MAC 700 Wash (Figure 16.43D) generally use whole-fixture pan/tilt movement.

The Cyberlight is a complex fixture that uses almost every available feature. Weighing just over 100 pounds, it has an encapsulated arc source, mechanical dimmer, mirror directional control, variable diffusion, motorized zoom and focus, three separate internally mounted diachronic color systems, and both moving and static gobos that can be used independently or in conjunction with the fixtures of other systems.

The Varilite VL 500 Wash Luminare (Figure 16.43C) can be equipped with either a tungsten-halogen or arc source. The T-H models use the theatre's dimming system or they can be equipped with an internal dimmer. Arc-equipped models have an internal mechanical douser. Both units have a dichroic color changer, interchangeable front lenses for beam control, and an internal diffuser mechanism on some models. Directional control is achieved by panning and tilting the whole fixture.

The Martin MAC 700 Wash (Figure 16.43D) has an arc source, mechanical dimming, motorized zoom and focus, dichroic color mixing, gobo wheel and gobo animation, and strobe effects. Directional control is also achieved by panning and tilting the entire fixture.

The technological wizardry and aesthetic uses of this class of instrument are just beginning to be explored. While their use in most plays is generally limited by both budgets and aesthetic need, kinetic fixtures have already become a staple fixture in the equipment inventory of big-budget Broadway musicals. Their use in dance and concert lighting as well as in clubs is very exciting and will continue to evolve.

LED-sourced Fixtures   High-output LEDs currently are being used in several types of theatrical lighting instruments. The advantages/disadvantages of LEDs over incandescent lamps were discussed earlier in this chapter. But there are several characteristics that make this source very intriguing to those in the lighting industry.

Because of their small physical size, a number of individual LEDs can be clustered together to effectively create a single lamp of sufficient output to be useful for stage lighting. These clusters have already been used to create PAR and striplight-type lamps. Further development in this area is challenged by one of the by-products of LED clustering—heat. Individual LEDs don't generate much heat, but, when clustered together, heat can build to destructive levels, particularly for those units in the center of the cluster. Current fixture design removes this heat with **heat sinks.** Effective heat dissipation will continue to be a primary, but solvable, design challenge as higher wattage, brighter LEDs, which generate even more heat, are developed.

LEDs require DC power. Stage lighting systems use AC power. This requires that separate rectifier/transformers are needed to provide DC electricity to the LED units. LEDs can run on AC electricity, but because LEDs only conduct when exposed to a positive electrical charge, and because AC changes polarity 60 times a second, an LED powered with AC electricity produces a noticeable 60-cycle per second flicker. Unless an economically viable AC-powered LED is developed, which isn't too likely, the need for a separate DC supply to power these fixtures will probably continue. This challenge is currently met by either mounting rectifier/transformer devices in the fixtures that convert AC to DC and reduce the voltage to the appropriate level for the lamps or by using a separate AC/DC power supply such as the LED 300 illustrated in Figure 16.44. This unit distributes 24-volt DC power to the LED-lamped fixtures and acts as a router through which control data from the light board is sent to those same fixtures.

Because LEDs can be designed to produce light in a very narrow color range it is possible, by using separately controlled red, blue, and green LEDs in the same housing, to produce over 16 million different colors. The SpectraPAR fixture, from Altman, is one of the first lighting instruments available in the United States to employ this color-mixing capability.

The high-output, color-mixing capabilities of LED sources, as well as their inherent lower electrical consumption, are primary reasons that many people in the lighting industry, not only those in theatre, but media and architectural lighting as well, are excited about the developments in this area. There don't appear to be any insurmountable impediments in the way of the continued development of LEDs for use in stage lighting instruments. It will be exciting to watch what happens in this arena in the next few years.

Color Changers   Color changing is accomplished with either a color scroller or a dichroic color changer. The color scroller, Figure 16.45A, normally is used with an ERS, a Fresnel, a PAR, or any other instrument that doesn't have internal color-changing capability. It fits in the color-media holder on the front of the instrument and contains a roll of plastic color media that, if stretched out, would look like a series of different-colored gels taped together. A dichroic color changer generally uses three dichroic filters—normally the secondary colors—to change the color of the light. The individual filters can be partially or fully inserted into the fixture's beam of light. The degree of insertion determines the color and level of saturation of the resulting hue. The three filters are used in combination to produce virtually any possible hue. The ColorFader M dichroic color changer (Figure 16.45B) is designed to fit in the color media slot at the front of the lighting fixture. The

heat sink: A metal devide that absorbs heat from an operating unit and dissipates it into the air.

FIGURE 16.44
The LED 300 power supply is used to distribute control data and 24-volt DC power to LED-lamped fixtures. (Courtesy of Doug Fleener Design.)

FIGURE 16.45
Color changers utilize two different types of systems to change the color of the light output. Color scrollers, such as the Chroma-Q Universal by A.C. Lighting, Inc. (A), use a scroll of colored plastic media. The ColorFader M by Morpheus Lights, Inc. (B) and the ColorMerge by High End (C) utilize dichroic filters. (Photos courtesy of manufacturers.)

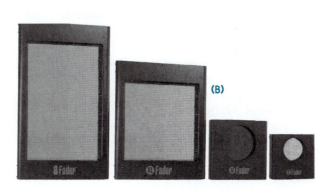

(B)

(C)

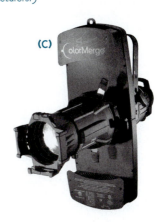

(A)

ColorMerge module (Figure 16.45C) fits just in back of the shutter plane in the ETC Source Four fixture. The operation of the color-changing function for all these devices is controlled by DMX.

 ## Dimmers

In the relatively brief history of electrical stage lighting, many different kinds of dimmers have been used to control the intensity of instruments. The older dimmers, such as the salt water, saturable core, thyratron tube, resistance, and auto transformer dimmers, have dropped by the wayside. The only types still in regular use are electronic dimmers.

Electronic Dimmer Control

When you move a controller to increase or decrease the intensity of lights connected to an electronic dimmer, you are using a low-voltage control circuit to manipulate the high-voltage output of that dimmer. Until recently, analog control systems were the only method available for controlling SCR dimmers. Now digital control has become the new standard.

To appreciate why "digital is better," you first need to understand how both analog and digital systems work and the basic differences between them.

Analog systems work on the following principle: Output varies as a continuous function of input. For example, increasing or decreasing the output of the control circuit causes a corresponding increase or decrease in the output of the dimmer. This control signal is sent from the light board over a control **line** to the dimmer. Because the analog system requires a continuous signal, every dimmer in the system must be connected to the light board by its own control line.

Digital systems work on a different principle: Output varies in discrete steps. At first glance the difference in operating principles between analog and digital systems appears relatively inconsequential. But the differences are significant. To understand why, we first need to understand how digital information differs from analog. As stated earlier, analog information is continuous. Digital information isn't. Digital information is **discrete.** It is neither continuous nor variable. Digital information exists as binary code—a series of on-off pulses.

The finite nature of the digital signal is very important. It enables digital information to be made up into discrete information or instructional packages. These "packages" can contain any information that we want them to. Further, they can be sent to specific locations. Figure 16.46 shows a light board and three dimmers using digital control. The light board continuously sends information—instructional packages—to all three dimmers. However, the dimmers "read" only those instructions that are addressed to them. For example, dimmer 1 reads only instructional packages addressed to itself. It pays no attention to the instructions for any other dimmer. Dimmers 2 and 3 react the same way, reading only that information addressed to them. Because each instructional package is read only by the dimmer to which it is addressed, different information can be sent to each dimmer.

The process of sending two or more messages simultaneously on the same channel is called **multiplexing** and is the primary advantage of digital over analog control systems.[4] Figure 16.47 shows the two types of control systems. Fig-

line: The wires in low-voltage control systems are frequently called "lines" rather than "wires."

discrete: Separate and complete; in this case, pertaining to information represented by binary code.

multiplex: (1) To transmit two or more messages simultaneously on a single channel. (2) To carry out several functions simultaneously in an independent but related manner.

---

[4] Analog signals can also be multiplexed, but the quantity of signals that can be multiplexed and the quality of the individual signals are lower than with digital.

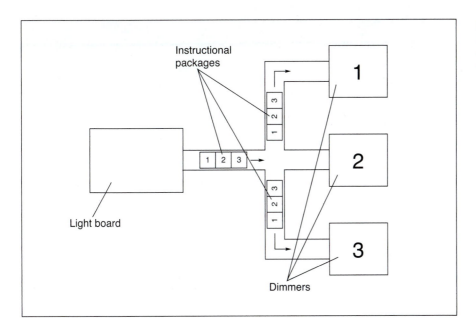

FIGURE 16.46
Digital instructional packages are continuously sent to all dimmers. The dimmers read only those instructions addressed to them.

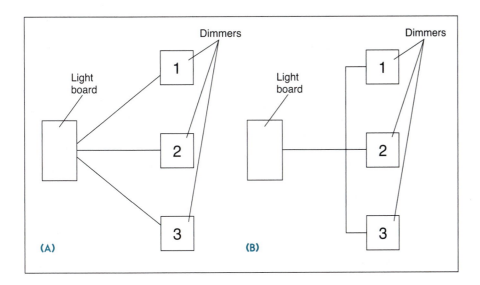

FIGURE 16.47
Schematic drawing of lighting control systems: (A) analog and (B) digital.

ure 16.47A is an analog system. It requires that each dimmer be connected to the light board by its own control line. Figure 16.47B is a digital system. Notice that there is only one control line connecting all three dimmers to the light board. This is because the multiplexed instructional packages are sent to all dimmers but are read by only those dimmers to which they are addressed.

Saving on costs in the wiring of control circuits isn't the only advantage that digital control offers. Multiplexing offers another distinct advantage with digital control. Some of the intelligent or moving light fixtures require up to twenty control channels to function as designed. Digital control requires only one control line to provide instructions to all twenty functions. An analog system would require that twenty separate control lines be connected to the instrument. The final advantage that digital offers over analog is precision of control. Digital instructional packages are finite. Once encoded, they don't change. While analog signals can be remarkably accurate, they aren't as accurate as the unchanging digital

PRODUCTION INSIGHTS
USITT DMX512

USITT DMX512 is not the title of a bad science fiction movie. It is a standard created by the United States Institute for Theatre Technology (USITT) "as a means to control dimmers from lighting consoles via a standard interface."[1] Basically, DMX512 is a recommended practice that allows the various pieces of a digitally controlled lighting system—computer boards, dimmers, and peripherals—to "talk" to each other. Prior to the adoption of this standard in 1990, each manufacturer had its own proprietary method of control, which made it difficult, if not impossible, for the customer to use a light board from one manufacturer to control dimmers, or any other equipment, made by another manufacturer. DMX512 resolved that issue. Now almost all digitally controlled equipment manufactured for the entertainment industry uses the DMX512 protocol.

To understand DMX512, you first need to understand how digital control works. (In the example explaining the process, dimmers are used as the controlled device. However, it is important to understand that digital control isn't used solely to control dimmer output. It also can be used to manipulate the functions of any type of electrical equipment, such as the stop/start functions and speed of the electrical motors found in moving light fixtures.)

The signal of most controllers—for example, the slide pots on a light board—is analog. When a controller is set to a specific level, it generates a signal that is an electronic indication of that setting. An analog-to-digital converter reads the controller's signal. Each time the converter reads the signal, it translates that information into binary code, adds the address of the dimmer or equipment associated with that particular command, and sends this "instructional package" to all the dimmers and equipment in the system. Each dimmer and piece of equipment receives all the instructional packages, but responds only to those addressed to it. This send/receive process occurs 44,000 times per second—the rate at which the analog-to-digital converter reads the original signal.[2]

DMX512 is simply a technical standard that specifies how much information is sent out on each of the 44,000 cycles that occur every second. DMX512 specifies that the signal shall contain 512 instructional packages and each package will have 256 discrete steps. This protocol has been adopted by the majority of equipment manufacturers and has significantly increased the compatibility of equipment used in the entertainment industry.

[1] Bennette, Adam, "Recommended Practice for DMX512: A Guide for Users and Installers," PLASA/USITT, 1994, p. 7.

[2] Some systems create the control signal digitally, which eliminates the need for the analog to digital conversion. These signals also are scanned and distributed 44,000 times a second.

---

code. For all of these reasons, digital is now the mode of choice in almost all dimmer control applications.

Silicon-Controlled Rectifier Dimmer

Until the development of the insulated gate bipolar transistor (IGBT) and sine wave dimmers, which will be explained a little later in this section, the silicon-controlled rectifier (SCR) dimmer, Figure 16.48, was considered the most reliable and efficient unit used for stage lighting. It still remains the workhorse of the industry. But the operational advantages offered by IGBT and sine wave dimming suggest that they, or something even more advanced, will ultimately replace the SCR as the dimmer technology of choice. The SCR dimmer operates on a gating principle, which is simply a rapid switching on and off of the power. That principle is explained in the box "Gating Principle" on page 414.

FIGURE 16.48
(A) An SCR dimmer. (Courtesy of Strand Lighting.) (B) A portable dimmer pack containing six SCR dimmers. (Courtesy of Electronics Diversified.)

(A)

(B)

The SCR is a solid-state power transistor, which means that it has no moving parts and no filaments to burn out. The electronic circuitry necessary to switch the SCR to a conducting state is also fairly simple. These properties result in a dimmer that is rugged, long lived, compact, relatively lightweight, moderate in cost, and reasonably quiet in operation.

With the rapid advancements being made in the electronics industry, discoveries will undoubtedly lead to even more efficient dimmers. At present, however, the SCR dimmer is recognized as the best solution.

Safety Tip

Dimmer Maintenance

The greatest enemy of an electronic dimmer such as the SCR is heat. To dissipate the heat, some dimmers are equipped with large heat sinks. Heat sinks are metal — usually aluminum — structures that absorb the heat generated by an SCR and radiate it to the atmosphere. Other dimmer packs are equipped with fans.

It is vital for the longevity of dimmers that they have plenty of air circulating around them. Don't pile anything on top of a dimmer. If you are working with portable dimmers, be sure that the dimmer pack is raised off the ground so that air can circulate under, as well as over, the case.

If your dimmer system is equipped with fans, be sure that they are running smoothly. The dimmers will frequently function for several hours even if the fan isn't working, but the heat buildup will cause a rapid deterioration of the electronic equipment that will usually lead to premature dimmer failure.

Almost all SCR dimmers need to be adjusted periodically so that they will smoothly increase or decrease their lamp loads. The specific methods vary from manufacturer to manufacturer, but they all involve an adjustment of the low, midpoint, and high-output voltage of the dimmer. These adjustments should be made by a qualified electrician at least annually.

PRODUCTION INSIGHTS
Gating Principle

If, in a given period of time, you turn a lamp on, then off, then on, off, on, and off, you effectively control the amount of light it puts out for that specific amount of time. If the lamp is turned on, and left on, for one second, it burns at full intensity for that one-second period. If you turn the lamp on for half a second and turn it off for half a second, it burns at half intensity for the one-second span. If you turn the lamp on for three-quarters of a second and off for one-quarter of a second, it burns at three-quarters intensity for the one-second span. In each of these cases, you will obviously see the lamp being switched on and off. But if the time span for the on-off cycle is reduced to ¹/₁₂₀th of a second, you perceive the on-off sequence as being a continuous level of illumination—an average of the on-off cycle ratio.

The SCR dimmer operates on this principle. The SCR is actually an electronic switch. The switch, or gate, opens and allows current to pass through the SCR when it receives the proper electronic command. The gate stays open until the power to the SCR is turned off. Sixty-cycle alternating current (AC), the standard current in the United States, alternates its polarity 120 times a second, or twice in each cycle, as illustrated in Figure A. Each time that it alternates its polarity, or crosses the zero point on the graph, there is no voltage. The effective result of this "no voltage" situation is that the electricity is turned off. If a command is fed to the SCR to start conduction at the beginning of the cycle, point A in Figure B, the SCR will conduct for the full half cycle, or until the electricity is shut off when it changes polarity at point B. Similarly, if the command specifies that the SCR is to begin conducting halfway through the cycle (Figure C), the transistor conducts for only half the cycle, or half as long.

By varying the time that the SCR is able to conduct electricity, you vary the intensity of any lamp load connected to it. This means that if the SCR conducts for a full half cycle, the lamp will glow at full intensity for the duration of that half cycle. If it conducts for only half of the half cycle, the lamp will be perceived to be glowing at half intensity. Similarly, a quarter-cycle electrical conduction means the lamp will appear to be glowing only one-fourth as brightly. Since each SCR conducts for only half a cycle, two SCRs, one for each half cycle, are necessary to make an effective dimmer. The IGBT dimmer operates on this same gating principle, but rather than beginning conduction, or "turning on," at a specific point during the AC cycle—as the SCR does—the IGBT stops conducting, or "turns off," at a specific point during the AC cycle.

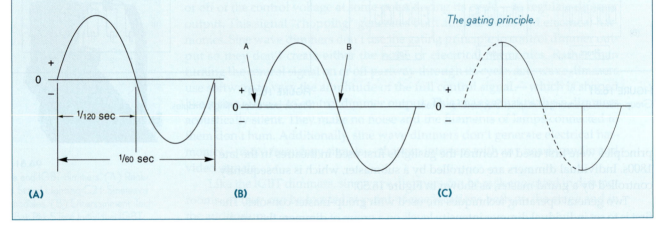

The gating principle.

(A)   (B)   (C)

---

this one, all boards with preset function work on the same basic principles being discussed here.

The controls for dimmers 1 through 6 are repeated three times in the blocks of dimmer controls labeled Preset Scenes I, II, and III. In this simplistic example, we will assume that the intensity levels of the lighting for the first cue will be preset on Preset Scene I, the second cue will be assigned to Preset Scene II, and the third cue will be set on Preset Scene III. After the board operator sets the appropriate intensity levels for each dimmer on the three preset scenes, he or she assigns control of Preset Scene I to **fader** A by pushing the button marked I next to fader A. When the cue is called by the stage manager, the operator brings up fader A, which automatically raises the intensity of the lights to the levels that had been preset on the dimmer controls of Preset Scene I. The second cue, preset on Scene II, is assigned to fader B. When the cue is called, the operator simulta-

fader: A device, usually electronic, that effects a gradual changeover from one circuit to another; in lighting it gradually changes the intensity of one or more dimmer circuits; in sound it changes audio circuits or channels.

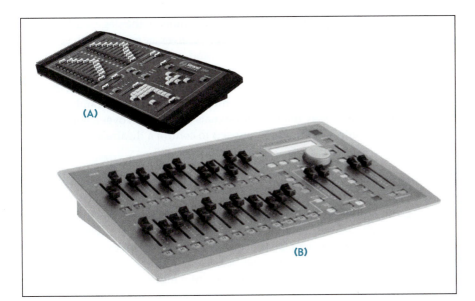

FIGURE 16.53
Combination boards. (A) The 200 Series
12/24 Channel lighting console from
Strand Lighting. (B) The SmartFade
12/48. (Courtesy of Strand Lighting and
Electronic Theatre Controls.)

neously moves fader B up and fader A down, which results in a cross-fade between the lights preset on Preset Scenes I and II. Similarly, before the third cue being called, the operator assigns control of Preset Scene III to fader A. When the cue is called, the operator cross-fades between faders B and A, which results in activation of the dimmer intensity levels associated with Preset Scene III.

To preset the intensity levels for the fourth cue, the operator presets the appropriate intensity levels on Preset Scene I as soon as he or she has cross-faded into the second cue. To run the remaining cues in the show, the operator repeats the process of presetting intensity levels on open, or nonactive, preset scenes as often as necessary. Many preset control consoles have mechanically or electronically interlocked faders, so when either fader A or B fades up, the other fader automatically dims down.

A fusion of the principles of preset and group-master control provides an extremely flexible lighting-control system. The relatively simple consoles shown in Figure 16.53 combine the principles of preset and group master control without too many additional bells and whistles. The advanced computer boards that will be discussed a little later use not only preset and group master principles but have a plethora of other features as well.

Wireless Dimmer Control

The dimming control techniques discussed up to this point all require that a control cable—over which the control signals are sent—be connected from the control console to the dimmer. Wireless dimmers don't require this control cable because the digital control information is sent to the dimmer by radio.

Wireless dimming systems are generally self-contained, battery-powered, component units small enough to be placed inside portable props or, in some cases, hidden in costumes. They are used in special situations such as portable torches or similar situations where a power cord trailing from the prop or costume as it moves around the stage would create physical and/or aesthetic hazards.

The wireless dimmer's control signal typically originates at the theatre's "regular" lighting console. The signal is sent from that console to a wireless transmitter. Because the transmission distance between most of these wireless transmitters and their receivers is quite limited the transmitter is generally hidden

glitch: A computer/electronic term meaning a system malfunction or error, usually of a short-term nature.

volatility: Nonpermanence; in computers, a volatile memory will be lost if the computer loses its power supply.

hard drive: A computer storage device. A spinning magnetic or optical disk on which data are stored and from which data can be retrieved.

floppy disk: A thin plastic disk coated with metal oxide, used to record the information stored in a computer's memory.

crash: In reference to hard drives, to become inoperative. Data normally cannot be retrieved from a hard drive that has "crashed."

writable CD: A compact disc on which data can be recorded, and read, by the user.

cassette tape: Audio recorder tape, used in computer storage.

microcassette tape: Audio recorder tape for use in small cassettes; used in computer storage.

either onstage or placed in the wings in close proximity to the stage. Each battery-powered wireless dimmer has a miniaturized receiver associated with it. The receiver gets the "radioed" control information and uses that to control the dimmer output. The dimmer then operates whatever device is connected to it.

Although the latest generation of wireless control systems seems to be relatively **glitch**-free, it is a reality that transmitted signals can be scrambled by interference much more easily than control signals that are sent over a wire. For this reason wireless control is almost never used to control a theatre's main lighting system.

Computer Memory   All contemporary light boards—computer boards—function in fundamentally the same way: a computer electronically stores the intensity levels of all dimmers for each cue. Even the most basic computer boards have a minimum of about 300 memories for cue storage. More expensive boards (Figure 16.54) may have sufficient storage capacity for up to five thousand or more cues. The latest generation of computer boards frequently can be used to control automated lighting fixtures in addition to nonmoving stage lights. However, in shows where there are numerous moving lights it is not uncommon for the production to use two separate light boards—one for the "regular" nonmoving stage lights and one for the automated fixtures. In those circumstances each console typically is run by a separate operator or crew independent of the other board. Rosco Labs offer a Windows-based lighting control software program that is used with *your* PC. You use your own PC with Rosco's software and output control devices to control most existing electronic dimmers.

Because computers lose their memory when the power is turned off, these systems have an internal battery backup that provides enough power so that the system can retain its memory for a reasonable length of time. This period varies from several hours to several weeks, depending on the model and manufacturer.

Because of **volatility** almost all computer boards have some method of storing the cuing and programming information. Higher-end boards frequently store this information on a **hard drive** while lower-end systems typically store information on **floppy disks.** While even the smallest-capacity hard disk will store all the data for just about any show, it is very important to back up the hard disk with some type of library storage in the event that the hard disk **crashes.** The most common methods used for library storage are 3½-inch floppy disks, **writable CDs, cassette** and **microcassette tapes.**

FIGURE 16.54
Computer boards. (A) The Congo by ETC. (B) grandMA from Electronics Diversified.

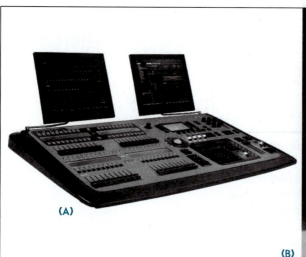

(A)

(B)

It is also essential to make backup copies of the show disks if your computer board uses floppy disks, or some other form of removable storage, as its storage method. Some designers prefer to record every change on both disks as those changes occur, while others feel that running the backup at the end of every rehearsal or board session is adequate.

Computer Board Control Capabilities All computer boards have control capabilities that duplicate those of preset systems. But what makes computer control so dynamic is that these boards have numerous capabilities that simply cannot be duplicated by preset or any other extant control systems.

As previously explained, analog control systems require that a pair of wires be connected directly from each dimmer to a potentiometer, or "pot," on the control console. In these systems increasing or decreasing the level of a specific dimmer's control pot determines the intensity of any instruments connected to that dimmer. In a digitally controlled system, a single pair of control wires runs between the control board and all of the dimmers. The control circuit of each dimmer is wired in parallel with every other dimmer, and that single pair of control wires runs from the dimmer racks to the digital control board. Information about intensity levels and so forth is distributed to all dimmers simultaneously, with the individual dimmers reacting only to information that is addressed specifically to them.

The digital control method just described allows much greater control flexibility than previous systems. To facilitate this flexibility, almost all computer boards employ an electronic patching system, generally referred to as **channel control.** To set the level of a dimmer, you assign it to a control channel, or channel, then adjust the channel level to the desired setting. Channel control allows you to assign any number of dimmers—from one to all the dimmers in your system—to one particular channel. In practical application there are two primary techniques used with channel control—one dimmer per channel and ganged dimmers per channel. The one-dimmer-per-channel approach lets you adjust each dimmer, and the instruments connected to it, individually. The ganged-dimmers-per-channel approach involves assigning the dimmers—for example, the six dimmers controlling the blue lights on the cyc—to a single control channel. Another way of controlling the blue cyc lights would be to assign the channels controlling each of the "blue light dimmers" to a **group** controller. The intensity levels of the lights assigned to the individual dimmer channels can be adjusted so the blue wash can be balanced as desired, and then the group controller is used to raise or lower the intensity of the lights without changing the balance.

All computer boards have some type of timer or time-function capability. The timer is used to assign a fade time to a cue. For example, you could assign a time of 5 seconds to a cue so it takes 5 seconds to execute that particular cue, whether it is a **fade-in** or **fade-out.** Most boards facilitate **split time fades** that allow you to, in one action, fade out one cue in a given time while fading in the next cue either faster or slower. When executing a split time fade you frequently want to **delay** the start of the following action. With this capability the designer can with one board action—pressing the "execute" or "go" button—execute a 15-second fade-out on a scene and, after an 8-second delay, begin a fade-up of another cue with a completely different fade rate.

The capabilities outlined above provide the basic building blocks of creative lighting control for the designer. Many computer boards have additional capabilities that enhance the designer's ability to control and manipulate light. It is important to become familiar with the specific capabilities and functions of as many computer boards as possible, because an understanding of those capabilities of the equipment will inform the designer's approach to **cueing** the show.

channel control: An electronic patching system in which one or more dimmers can be assigned to a control channel, which in turn controls the intensity level of those dimmers.

group: The grouping of two or more dimmers/channels under one controller.

fade-in: A gradual increase; in lighting, usually from darkness to a predetermined level of brightness. Synonymous with fade-up.

fade-out: A gradual decrease; in lighting, usually from a set level of brightness to darkness.

split time fade: A fade-in which the fade-up and fade-out are accomplished at different rates or speeds.

delay: Refers to the time interval that the second part of a split time fade follows the first.

cueing: Designing the light cues. Manipulating, and recording, the distribution intensity, movement, and color of the lights for each cue to create the appropriate look for that moment in the play.

Smaller Systems

1. memory for up to several hundred cues

2. capability of controlling 100–150 dimmers

3. maximum of one video screen for displaying various system functions

4. a timed fader

5. some type of group or submaster control

6. control of dimmer intensity by individual sliders

7. keypad for addressing memory and functions

8. limited backup system in case of main-computer malfunction

These smaller, less expensive systems work well in theatres that have modest production demands.

Larger Systems

1. memory for approximately 1,000 cues

2. control of 1,000 or more dimmers

3. expanded functions

   A. two or more video screens to display more functions simultaneously

   B. advanced backup systems

   C. sophisticated group or submastering

   D. more control functions to permit simultaneous cues at different fade rates

4. dimmer and other functions addressed through a keypad

5. remote keypad

6. hard-copy printer for printing data about the lighting design

7. self-diagnostic program to identify malfunctioning component in case of breakdown

These larger and more expensive systems work well in facilities that have extensive production programs.

Cables and Connectors

A flexible system of distributing electricity to lighting instruments is necessary, because the hanging position of the lights will be changed for each production. This section discusses the types of cables and connectors that make up this flexible distribution system, as well as several methods of circuiting, or connecting, the lighting instruments to the dimmers.

Electrical Cable for Stage Use

The National Electrical Code (NEC) stipulates that the only electrical cables approved for temporary stage wiring are types S, SO, ST, and STO. These cables have stranded copper conductors and are insulated with rubber (S and SO, shown in Figure 16.55) or thermoplastic (ST and STO). S and SO cables are more commonly used than ST and STO, because their thick rubber jacket can withstand more physical abuse than the thin, heat-resistant thermoplastic insulation of the ST and STO cable. Type S cable is generally used for stage lighting, because SO costs more and its only advantage is that it is impervious to oil and gasoline.

Wire Gauge

The American Wire Gauge (AWG) system rates wire according to the amount of current that a conductor of a particular size and composition can safely carry. The rated current capacity for any given gauge should never be exceeded. Most cables have the gauge and wire type imprinted every foot or so on the insulating jacket.

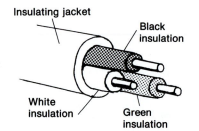

Insulating jacket

Black insulation

White insulation

Green insulation

FIGURE 16.55
An electrical wire.

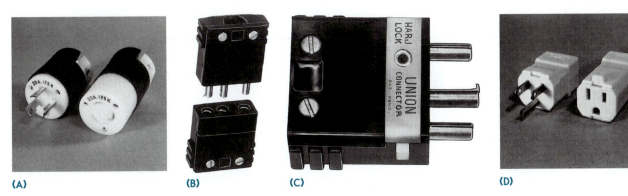

(A)   (B)   (C)   (D)

FIGURE 16.56
(A) A twist-lock; (B) grounded pin connector; (C) locking grounded pin connector; (D) grounded parallel blade (Edison) connector. ([B] and [C] Courtesy of Union Connector Co.)

The amount of current that can be safely carried varies greatly, as we saw in Table 15.1. There is no standard size of cable for theatre use, because load requirements differ from one theatre to another. However, the NEC stipulates that receptacles used to supply incandescent lamps on stage must be rated at not less than 20 amperes and must be supplied by wires of not less than 12 gauge. Practical or decorative lamps are the only exception to this rule. These lamps may be wired with cable of smaller capacity as long as the lamp load doesn't exceed the rated capacity of the cable. This means that you can use 18-gauge wire (also known as lamp or zip cord) as long as the lamp load doesn't exceed 360 watts (assuming the system voltage is 120 volts: $W = VA; 360 = 120 \times 3$).

Connecting Devices

Several different styles of connectors are used in stage lighting, as shown in Figure 16.56. Twist-lock connectors (Figure 16.56A) are considered by many people to be the best type of stage connector. The male portion, or plug, fits into the female portion, or receptacle, and is twisted to lock the two halves together. This locking action prevents most accidental disconnections of the circuit.

Pin connectors are probably more widely used than twist-lock connectors, primarily because they have been in existence longer. Older models of pin connectors (Figure 16.56B) have three distinct disadvantages: (1) They can be easily disconnected by accident; (2) the pins of the plug do not always make a good electrical connection with the receptacle; and (3) if the cable is connected to a live power source, it is very easy to be shocked, because the metal conductors in the receptacle are not deeply recessed.

Newer models of the grounded pin connector (Figure 16.56C) overcome the previously mentioned disadvantages. The new designs, which also meet the NEC guidelines, have an excellent locking device that prevents accidental disconnections, and the metal contacts within the receptacle are recessed quite deeply into the insulating body of the connector.

The Edison, or parallel blade, plug (Figure 16.56D), should be used only on decorative lamps or devices that carry a similarly small load.

All connectors, regardless of style, are designed to carry a specific amount of current. The maximum load is usually printed somewhere on the plug, and that limit should be strictly obeyed.

The NEC stipulates that each plug should be equipped with an effective cable-clamping device (see Figure 16.57). The purpose of the cable clamp is to secure the connector to the jacket of the cable. This clamping action transfers any physical strain from the plug casing directly to the cable jacket, which effectively eliminates any strain on the electrical connections inside of the plug.

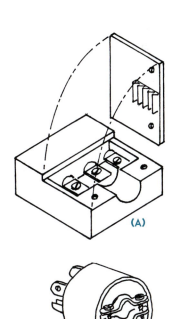

(A)

(B)

FIGURE 16.57
(A) Internal and (B) external cable clamps.

Control-System Maintenance

The operating voltage for most electronic lighting-control systems is relatively low—normally, between 8 and 24 volts. Because of the low voltage and the miniaturization of the electronic components, the systems need to be kept scrupulously clean and free from dust, dirt, and grease. For this reason, smoking and eating should not be permitted in the lighting control booth. The tar from tobacco smoke can settle on the printed circuit boards and actually change the resistance within the electronic circuits. Even a small change in resistance can cause some elements of the system to malfunction. The obviously disastrous results of spilling a soft drink on a computer or control board don't need further elaboration.

The floppy disks that are used for library storage in many computer systems need to be handled carefully. They should be stored vertically in a dust-free environment away from power lines and electric motors. (The power lines and motors generate magnetic fields that can scramble or erase the information stored on a disk.) Use only a soft-tip marker to write on the floppy-disk label. Pencils and ballpoint pens can dent the recording surface of the disk, and the graphite and ink can interfere with the reading head.

FIGURE 16.58
A "Y," or two-fer.

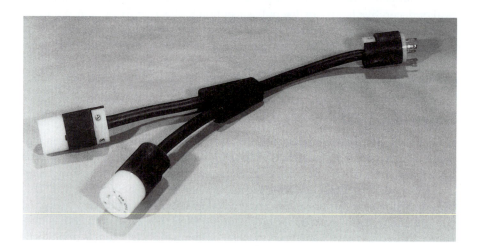

Extension Cables

Extension cables can be purchased, or made in the theatre's electrical shop, in any reasonable length. As previously noted, they are generally made of type S cable, although types SO, ST, or STO can also be used. Different theatres present differing requirements, but in general, if a theatre has a permanent lighting system, an inventory of cables 5, 10, and 20 feet long should meet the needs of most operations.

A **two-fer** is used to connect two instruments to the same circuit. When using two-fers (Figure 16.58) or any other device that can increase the electrical load on a circuit, take particular care not to exceed the maximum current rating of any element (cable, plug, dimmer, and so on) in that circuit.

two-fer: An electrical Y that has female receptacles at the top of the Y and a male plug at the bottom leg of the Y; used to connect two instruments to the same circuit.

Circuiting

The distribution of electricity from dimmers to lighting instruments creates a complex system. Any complex system is built on compromise, simply because the maximum amount of efficiency that can be built into any system is finite. The compromises on which stage-lighting systems are predicated are speed and ease of hanging and circuiting versus flexibility of hanging position. The following methods of stage circuiting demonstrate the effects of tinkering with the variables of this complex equation.

Permanent Wiring

The simplest method of circuiting is to permanently wire the instruments to the dimmers. In this system, a few ellipsoidal reflector spotlights are usually hung somewhere on the ceiling of the auditorium, and some striplights or **work lights** over the stage. These instruments are permanently wired to specific dimmers. To operate the system, you just turn on the dimmers. The only possible changes or adjustments within the system are changing the color or area of focus for each instrument.

Although this method is certainly the easiest to operate, it provides little flexibility and just about eliminates any chance for creatively designing with light. Permanently wired lighting systems appear with great frequency in high school auditoriums, music halls, and other facilities where the lighting installation has been guided by criteria other than the needs and requirements of the creative use of designed light.

Spidering

Spidering, also known as direct cabling, involves running a cable from each lighting instrument directly to the dimmer to which it is assigned. It gets its name from the tangled web of cables created by circuiting a production in this manner.

Spidering is used extensively in Broadway theatres and on touring shows. It provides the greatest flexibility, because it allows the designer to put an instrument wherever it is needed. On the negative side, spidering requires an extensive inventory of electrical cable, and this method takes a long time to hang unless the hanging crew is very experienced and the designer or master electrician has carefully planned the cabling requirements for the production.

Connecting Strips and Patch Panels

An electrical distribution system that utilizes connecting strips and a patch panel provides two advantages in a theatre that has an extensive production program: (1) The light plot can be hung and circuited quite rapidly, and (2) the system provides a great deal of flexibility by enabling you to patch any circuit into any dimmer.

Two principal parts make up this system: the stage circuits and a patch panel. Most of the stage circuits are contained in connecting strips, which are sections of wireway, or electrical gutter, that contain a number of circuits (Figure 16.59).

The connecting strips are hung in a variety of positions about the stage and auditorium—counterweighted battens over the stage; various front-of-house positions (ante-proscenium cuts or slots, beamports, coves, boxes); and various locations on the walls of the stage house. Each circuit terminates in a receptacle that is usually mounted at the end of a 2- to 3-foot pigtail, although the receptacles are sometimes mounted flush on the gutter itself.

Additional stage circuit outlets are often contained in **drop boxes, floor pockets,** and **wall pockets** (Figure 16.60). Drop boxes are small connecting strips fed by cables that are attached to the grid above the stage. They usually contain four to eight circuits and are equipped with one or two pipe clamps so that they can be easily attached to pipes or booms. Floor and wall pockets are recessed into the floor or wall and usually contain three to six circuits.

work light: A lighting fixture, frequently a scoop, PAR, or other wide-field-angle instrument, hung over the stage to facilitate work; generally not used to light a production.

drop box: A small connecting strip, containing four to eight circuits, that can be clamped to a pipe or boom.

floor pocket: A connecting box, usually containing three to six circuits, the top of which is mounted flush with the stage floor.

wall pocket: A connecting box similar to a floor pocket but mounted on the wall.

FIGURE 16.59
A connecting strip.

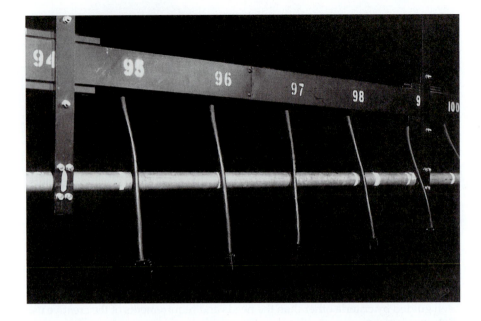

FIGURE 16.60
(A) Drop box; (B) floor pocket; (C) wall pocket.

(A)

(B)

(C)

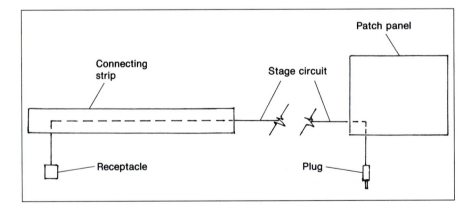

FIGURE 16.61
In a patch-panel system, the stage circuit runs from the female receptacle on the stage outlet to a male plug at the patch panel.

All of the circuits contained in connecting strips, drop boxes, and floor or wall pockets have certain properties in common. Each circuit is a rather long extension cable that, at the stage end, terminates in a female receptacle. Some connecting strips are designed to provide two receptacles for each circuit. In the patch-panel system, the other end of the circuit terminates at the patch panel in a male plug, as shown in Figure 16.61.

Why Not Hang Dimmers on the Connecting Strip?

Entertainment Technology, among several other manufacturers, has developed a connecting strip that has integral dimmers. One of the chief advantages of this type of system, which they market as Intelligent Raceway, is the elimination of the need for separate dimmer racks to hold the dimmers and all attendant wiring.

This system takes advantage of the IGBT dimmer technology discussed ear-lier in this chapter. IGBT dimmers are generally lighter and quieter in operation than SCR dimmers, which makes them appropriate for use in locations—onstage electrics, house electrics—where they might be heard by the audience. More information about the various applications of this technology can be found at the Entertainment Technology website www.etdimming.com.

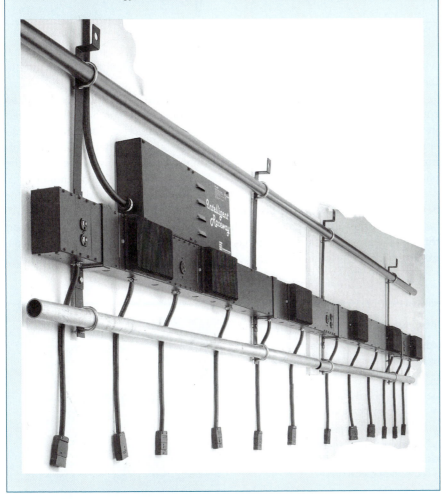

The second part of the distribution system is the patch panel, or patch bay. It is an interconnecting device that provides the system with the capability of connecting, or patching, any stage circuit into any dimmer. Patch panels (Figure 16.62) are manufactured in a variety of styles and configurations.

Figure 16.63 illustrates the basic operational design of a patch panel. The lighting instrument is connected into a stage circuit, which terminates at the patch panel in a male plug. The dimmer, which is usually located in another part of the theatre, is permanently wired to a receptacle on the face of the patch panel. To enable the electricity to flow from the dimmer to the lighting instrument, it

FIGURE 16.62
Patch panel. (Courtesy of Colortran.)

FIGURE 16.63
The patch panel allows you to plug more than one circuit into a single dimmer.

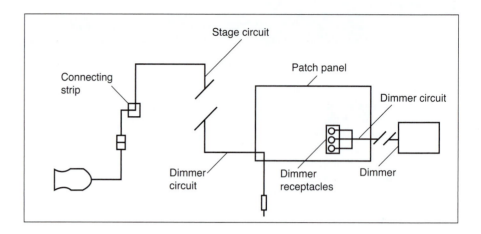

FIGURE 16.63
The patch panel allows you to plug more than one circuit into a single dimmer.

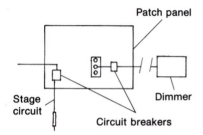

FIGURE 16.64
Circuit breakers provide overload protection for both the stage circuits and the dimmer circuits.

will be necessary to complete the circuit. This is done by patching the circuit into the appropriate receptacle for the dimmer.

The patch panel is actually very simple to operate. What makes it seem so complex is that it contains many more than the one circuit and one dimmer cited in this example. In fact, a patch panel usually contains between sixty and several hundred stage circuits and from forty to several hundred dimmers. In addition, each dimmer is usually provided with several receptacles on the face of the patch panel so that more than one circuit can be patched into each dimmer.

Patch panels usually have some type of electrical-overload protection for both the stage circuit and the dimmer circuit. The circuit breaker automatically breaks the continuity of the circuit when an unsafe amount of current is passed through the line. Each stage circuit has a circuit breaker, as shown in Figure 16.64, that provides overload protection. Another circuit breaker is usually located

Cable and Connector Maintenance

The following steps are suggested to keep cables and connectors in good operating condition and in compliance with NEC and federal regulations.

1. When a cable is not in use, coil it and hang it on the wall of the lighting storage room. The cable will stay neatly coiled if the connectors are plugged together or if it is tied with heavy twine or narrow rope.

2. Check cables and connectors periodically, and replace any items that show signs of cracking, chipping, or other deterioration. Cracks in the insulation of cables and connectors increase the chances of someone's receiving a shock from the device. Also, dust can accumulate in the crack and may cause an electrical fire.

3. Always disconnect a plug by pulling on the body of the connector, not the cable. Pulling on the cable puts an unnecessary strain on the cable clamp and will eventually defeat the clamp. When the cable clamp no longer functions, pulling on the cable places the strain directly on the electrical connections.

4. Keep the connectors clean. Remove any corrosion, paint, grease, or other accumulations as soon as they become evident. These substances can act as insulation between the contacts of the connector and, if flammable, pose a fire hazard.

5. All elements of a cable should be of the same electrical rating; for example, 12-gauge (AWG) cable (capable of carrying 20 amperes of current) should have only 20-ampere-rated connectors, and so forth.

Cable storage.

either in the line connecting the patch panel to the dimmer or in the dimmer itself. This circuit breaker protects the dimmer circuit and dimmer from an overload.

Dimmer per Circuit

The dimmer-per-circuit configuration combines the efficiency in hanging and circuiting of the connecting strip with the ease of operation of the permanently wired system.

Dimmer-per-circuit systems eliminate the patch panel, so the electrical flow runs straight from the dimmers to the individual stage circuit outlets. The onstage end of each circuit terminates in an outlet on a connecting strip, floor pocket, or similar location. The other end of the circuit is directly wired to a dimmer.

Before the introduction of computer boards, it required a very large and unwieldy control system and three to six—or more—electricians to run all the dimmers required by this type of system. But the computer board makes control of the large number of dimmers associated with this type of system a fairly simple task for one person. The dimmer-per-circuit configuration, when combined with a computer board, provides what is possibly the most flexible system available at this time.

Chapter 17

Projections

Projections enhance the visual texture of a design immeasurably. They can provide the stage with seemingly unlimited depth or create an aura of surrealism as one image dissolves into another. They can be used to replace or complement other visual elements of the setting, or as an accent.

However, projections aren't a universal panacea. They are simply another tool for the designer to use in the never-ending quest for an evocative visual expression of the production concept.

While digital projection is clearly becoming the new standard for image projection, and will be discussed later in the chapter, there are some older technologies that are still effective. The lenseless projectors are inexpensive devices that can be shop-built, frequently with scrap materials. The various slide projector technologies discussed still project effective images. There's no question that digital projection will ultimately make these older methods obsolete, but these "older technologies" still work, are still effective, and will probably remain so for the foreseeable future. Besides, many theatres have both lenseless and various types of slide projectors in their equipment stock, so the need to know about how they work continues.

Two basic systems of projections are used in the theatre: lens and lensless.

 ## Lensless Projectors

If you've ever made shadow pictures by holding your hands in the beam of a slide or movie projector, you understand the principle of lensless projection. As shown in Figure 17.1, a shadow image can be projected when an opaque object is placed in the path of a light source. If the object casting the shadow is colored and transparent rather than opaque, a colored image is projected instead of a shadow.

Several factors determine the sharpness of the projected image, but the primary one is the size of the projection source. Although an arc or encapsulated arc provides a very small point source, it isn't particularly practical in this application because its intensity can't be varied through the use of a dimmer. There are two practical lamp sources for lensless projectors:

1. For large-scale projections, a 500-, 750-, or 1,000-watt, 120-volt, tungsten-halogen lamp normally used in an ellipsoidal reflector spotlight works well. When selecting a specific lamp, remember that the smaller the filament, the sharper the image.

2. For small-scale projections—under 6 feet wide—a single-filament, 12-volt lamp (used for automotive brake and turning lights) can provide a high-intensity, small-filament source. For the lamp to provide enough output, it

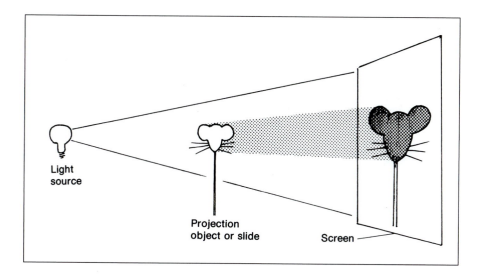

FIGURE 17.1
Principles of lensless projection.

must be run at about 15 volts. This voltage is supplied to the lamp through a 15-volt step-down transformer, as shown in Figure 17.2. The transformer may not work properly, however, and the intensity of the 12-volt lamp will probably flutter if you try to dim the unit with an SCR dimmer. The flicker occurs because the filaments of these 12-volt lamps usually don't have sufficient mass to retain the heat necessary to give off light during the SCR's "off" cycles, particularly at low-intensity readings. (The operational principles of an SCR dimmer were discussed in the previous chapter.) A smooth fade can be achieved only if the transformer is dimmed with an autotransformer or a resistance dimmer.

Another important factor in determining image sharpness with a lensless projector is the distance between the slide and the projection surface. The closer the slide is to the screen, the sharper the image. Having the slide closer to the screen does not necessarily mean that the projector is closer to the screen. A fairly long, somewhat skinny projector, as shown in Figure 17.3A, can be built in the shop. If the ratio of the distance between the projection surface and the slide and the distance between the slide and the lamp of this somewhat bizarre projector can be kept at approximately 1:1, an acceptably sharp image can be produced. The multiplane lensless projector (Figure 17.3B) is a natural adaptation of this development. As slides are placed closer to the lamp, the image they project becomes less focused. This phenomenon can be used to good advantage to create **aerial perspective.** In the projection of a landscape, the clouds and distant objects could be painted on one slide and placed relatively close to the lamp to create a soft-edged image. Middle-distance objects, such as hills and a forest, might be painted on a second slide and placed farther from the lamp, so the image they project is more clearly defined. A third slide, with perhaps a fence row and the branch from an overhanging tree, could be painted on a third slide and placed farther away from the lamp, so its image is the sharpest of the three.

Although the multiplane projector might seem to be an ideal solution, there is one very basic problem: slide size. You will remember that for a slide to project a sharp image it needs to be approximately the same distance from the screen as it is from the lamp. If you wanted to project an image 20 feet wide, the sharp-image slide would have to be 10 feet wide! However, if you are only trying to project on a small area (5 feet wide or less), the multiplane projector can provide you with a realistic aerial perspective effect.

FIGURE 17.2
A low-voltage lamp can provide a high-intensity, small-sized source for a lensless projector.

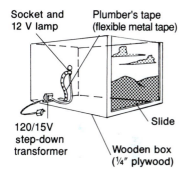

aerial perspective: An optical phenomenon in which objects that are farther away appear less sharply in focus and less fully saturated in color.

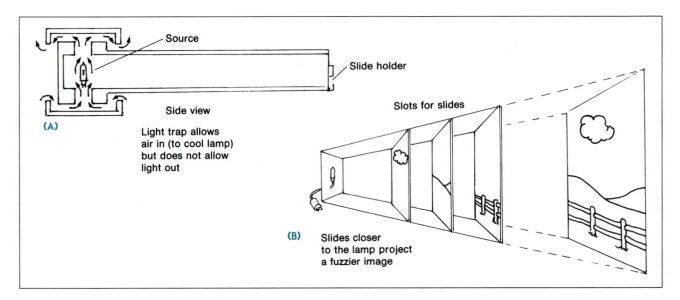

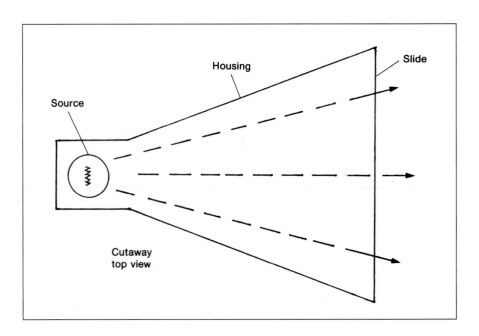

FIGURE 17.3
(A) Sharp-image and (B) multiplane-image lensless projectors.

A multiplane projector can be built in the shop using the techniques described in the next section for making Linnebach projectors. A 750- or 1,000-watt tungsten-halogen lamp from an ellipsoidal reflector spotlight will usually provide a more than adequate light for projections less than 5 feet wide, and the slides can be painted on ⅛-inch Plexiglas with transparent acetate inks.

Linnebach Projector

The primary lensless projector used in the theatre was developed by Adolph Linnebach. All lensless projectors are based on its principles of operation, which are illustrated in Figure 17.4. The metal housing holds the lamp at a fixed distance from the open front of the projector, which is designed to securely hold a removable glass slide. The design is painted on the slide with transparent acetate inks.

FIGURE 17.4
Principles of operation of a Linnebach projector.

Projectors that work on the Linnebach principles can easily be made in the theatre shop using galvanized tin and a **pop riveter.** They can also be fabricated using plywood (Figure 17.5), but the inside of the back and top sides of the plywood box must be lined with tin or some other heat-reflecting or -absorbing material.

Linnebach projectors for use with curved cycs can also be shop-built, as shown in Figure 17.6. These projectors, while using only a 1,000-watt **FEL lamp,** can project a patterned wash of pastel color over a full semicircular cyc. Slides for the curved-front Linnebach are made from 20-mil acetate. (1 mil = $\frac{1}{1000}$ inch. For example, 20 mils = $\frac{20}{1000}$ inch, or 0.02 inch.) These slides are fitted to the curved edge of the projector, and the image is painted on the slide using transparent acetate inks. Dr. Martin's Watercolors, when supplemented with a commercial additive that allows the paint to adhere to plastic, work extremely well for this purpose.

Other Lensless Projectors

Small lensless projectors can be made by removing the lens from Fresnel or plano-convex spotlights and inserting a slide (painted or photographic transparency) in

pop riveter: A tool used to secure rivets in thin metal.

FEL lamp: Lamps made in the United States are designated with a three-letter code that specifies all design criteria such as wattage, voltage, filament and base type, color-temperature-rated life, and so forth. FEL specifies a very specific 1,000-watt lamp.

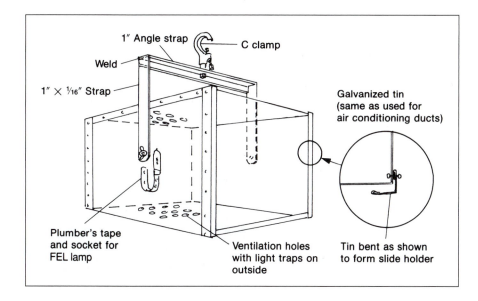

FIGURE 17.5
Shop-built Linnebach projector.

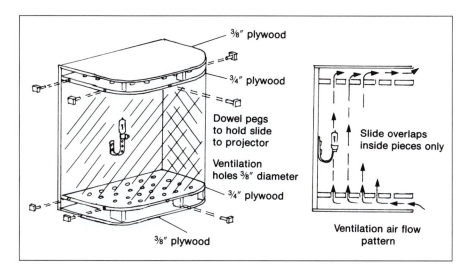

FIGURE 17.6
Curved-image Linnebach projector.

scenic projector: A high-wattage instrument used for projecting large-format slides or moving images.

slide projector: A reasonably high-output instrument capable of projecting standard 35 mm slides.

the instrument's color-frame holder. Although these makeshift projectors won't cover a large surface, they are handy for making soft projections on small surfaces.

Lens Projectors

The second basic type of projector uses a lens to control the focus and size of the image on the projection surface. Three primary types of lens projectors are used in the theatre: the **scenic projector,** the **slide projector,** and the digital projector.

Scenic Projector

The scenic projector is composed of three basic parts: the lamp housing, the optical train, and the slide, as shown in Figure 17.7A.

Lamp Housing   A lamp of high intensity is a prime requisite of a good scenic projector. Incandescent lamps of 1,000 to 2,000 watts are fairly typical, and some top-of-the-line scenic projectors use xenon or HMI lamps and mechanical dimming systems. The housings are frequently equipped with blowers that help dissipate the rather substantial heat that these powerful sources generate. Unfortunately, the fans on many scenic projectors are less than whisper quiet, so the scenic projector should be placed in a location that will mask the fan noise.

Optical Train   The optical train, shown in Figure 17.8, is composed of several parts that perform specific functions. The reflector (usually ellipsoidal or spheri-

FIGURE 17.7
(A) A scenic projector is composed of the lamp housing, the optical train, and the slide. (Courtesy of Pani.) (B) Scenic projector. (Courtesy of Pigi.) (C) Slide projector. (Courtesy of George R. Snell Associates.)

(A)

(B)

(C)

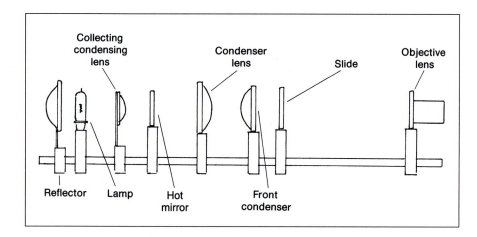

FIGURE 17.8
A typical scenic-projector optical train.

cal) and collector lens gather and concentrate the light. Some scenic projectors utilize a **hot mirror,** which is a clear dichroic filter that reflects a substantial portion of the infrared (heat) segment of the electromagnetic spectrum emitted by the lamp. The **condensing lenses** focus the light onto the **slide-plane aperture,** which is the point where the slide or moving projection effect is placed. The **objective lens** is used to focus the material in the aperture onto the projection surface.

The reflector, lamp, collector lens, and aperture are normally mounted in fixed positions within the lamp housing unit. In contrast, the relative positions of the condensing lens and objective lens are variable on some models of scenic projectors to allow the size of the projected image to be changed. Other scenic projectors are available with several **heads,** which hold the condensing and objective lenses in fixed positions to control the image size.

Slide   Glass slides are frequently used with scenic projectors to project still images. The image can be painted, with transparent inks, on a single glass slide, or a photographic transparency can be sandwiched between two glass slides. The longevity of a painted or photographic image on the slide can be increased if a dichroic hot mirror is placed between the collector lens and the slide.

A variety of moving effects can be created through the use of **effects heads.** These motorized devices are attached to the lamp housing in place of the slide holder. Effects heads move images in front of the aperture gate to create abstract or relatively realistic moving images, such as the lighted windows of a passing train, on the projection surface. The speed of the control motor is usually variable, so the speed of the projected effect can be adjusted to suit the design need. Depending on the specific model, effects heads use either rotating disks or bands to create the specific effect desired. Most scenic-effects projectors are equipped to use either Plexiglas or metal disks or plastic bands.

hot mirror: A glass dichroic filter that reflects the infrared spectrum while allowing visible light to pass.

condensing lens: A device that condenses the direct and reflected light from a source and concentrates it on the slide-plane aperture of a projector.

slide-plane aperture: The point in a projection system where a slide or other effect is placed.

objective lens: A device to focus a projected image on a screen or other surface.

head: A housing that holds scenic-projector lenses in fixed positions to project images of a specific size.

effects head: A motor-driven unit capable of producing crude moving images with a scenic projector.

PRODUCTION INSIGHTS
Keystoning

Unless the projector is placed on a perpendicular axis to the projection screen, some linear distortion will be introduced to the projected image. This phenomenon is known as keystoning, because the distortion generally resembles the shape of a keystone.

Keystoning results when the light from one side of the projected image (slide) has to travel farther than the light from the other side of the slide, as illustrated in the Figure (A).

Keystoning can be corrected in one of two ways: (1) The screen can be tilted so that the projection axis is perpendicular to the screen (C), or (2) a distortion can be introduced to the slide that counteracts the effects of the projection distortion. To do this, determine the angle of intersection between the projection axis and the screen. To introduce the counterdistortion to the slide, place the camera at the same angle, but on the opposite side, when you are taking the picture of the slide material (D).

Another advantage of computer projections is that many of the software programs used to create and/or manipulate the images offer keystone correction as part of the package.

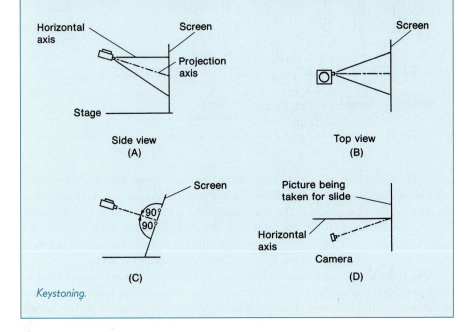

Keystoning.

Slide Projector

Projectors using 35 mm (2-by-2-inch) slides provide another excellent system for producing scenic projections. The challenge of using these projectors, which are designed for audiovisual, not theatrical, purposes, is that the lamp output is frequently not as bright as that of a scenic projector. If you work within the limitations that the lower lamp output imposes, however, the slide projector can be an extremely useful tool.

The Kodak Carousel equipped with a 300-watt lamp provides sufficient light to create a readable image if the slide is of normal contrast and the maximum dimension of the projected image is kept at about 6 to 8 feet.

Adaptations of the basic audiovisual (Ektagraphic) line of Kodak Carousel projectors, Figure 17.7C, provide higher-wattage lamps and a number of other interesting features. Although the 300-watt lamp available on the basic models will work adequately, by all means acquire the higher-output models if your budget can afford them. The image can be significantly brighter.

1. Use the slide tray that holds 80 slides rather than its larger-capacity (140-slide) cousin, because the greater space allocated to each slide in the 80-count tray significantly reduces the chances of the slides becoming stuck in the tray.

2. Mount the slides in plastic, rather than pasteboard, slide holders. The plastic holders are slicker and slightly heavier, which makes it easier for them to be fed into the projector.

3. For the best image, use the highest-wattage lamp designed for the specific model with which you are working.

4. Select a lens that will permit you to place the projector as close to the projection surface as possible.

Other types of 35 mm slide projectors can be used, but the carousel types generally offer specific qualities that make them preferable for theatrical projection work: dependable and versatile slide-feeding capabilities, adequate light output, and interchangeable lenses.

Digital Projectors

Digital projections, also called computer projections, are rapidly becoming the standard theatrical projection technique. While the image brightness, sharpness, and color clarity of many first- and second-generation digital projectors was not sufficient for stage use, the latest iterations of many of these machines provide brilliant images appropriate for any stage environment.

Digital projections are truly an exciting addition to the designer's toolbox and will probably, in time, replace all other forms of theatrical projection. Why? Because not only can digital projection systems duplicate, or exceed, the image quality of all lensless and lensed and film-based still projections, they can project video as well.

One of the distinct advantages of digital projection is simply that the images are digital files. Digital files of visual images—digital photos—are now commonplace. The images are stored on a computer, and they can be manipulated using one of the many available photo modification programs, which makes digital projections ideal for theatrical use. It's axiomatic that an image intended for theatrical projection can't be used without some kind of modification. Even if that image is a simple snapshot of someone or something or a captured image from another source,[1] the image will normally need to be changed to fit the specific design needs—look, feel, palette—of the production. That's where the digital file is a huge boon to the projection designer. It's much easier to manipulate these images than it is to change a "regular" photograph or slide.

The Digital Projection website—http://www.digitalprojection.com/—has information about their line of digital projectors, almost all of which are suitable for theatrical use. (An Internet search for "Digital Projection" will also provide a plethora of other sites.) The Digital Projection site also provides a link—http://www.digitalprojection.com/content/view/149/57/—to the company's

---

[1] When taking a photo of an existing object—person, picture, place, or thing—that you intend to use in public performance, you must get legal permission from the owner of that property to do so. If you don't, you're potentially inviting a lawsuit for copyright or ownership rights infringement. Consult your producing organization's attorney regarding necessary "permissions" before using any photographed images onstage.

"Screen Brightness Calculator." This program can be used to determine the brightness that a screen image of a specific size will have when provided by a projector with a specific output brightness. The screen dimensions and projector output brightness are both "operator variable." It's a very handy program that can be used to determine two things: (1) the specific output requirements necessary for a projector to function effectively in a particular theatrical venue; (2) determining whether the brightness level of an image projected onto a screen of a specific size by a given projector will be bright enough for stage use.

The sources for images—both still and moving—to project are almost limitless. And therein lies a potential trap. Projected images, whether digital or otherwise, have an enormous visual impact that makes it very easy for the projections to upstage the actors. That is a basic no-no. Ideally, the visuals will be integrated into the production concept to *enhance* the overall mood and feeling of the production, not steal focus. Sometimes discretion is the better part of valor.

Gobo

An ellipsoidal reflector spotlight can be converted into a pattern projector through the use of a gobo. A full discussion of gobos and how to make them can be found in Chapter 16.

Projection Screens

Actors' bodies, painted scenery, dust motes, smoke, and fog have all been used as projection surfaces. However, they don't work nearly so well as scenic elements that have been specifically designed as projection screens. There are two basic types of screen materials: front and rear.

Front-Screen Material

Front-screen projection materials are those surfaces that are designed to reflect light. The best front-projection materials are slide or movie screens. They are white and highly reflective, and the surface is often designed to focus the reflected light in a specific angular pattern. Unless you want a large, glaringly white screen sitting in the middle of the stage, however, it is essential that the screen be lit with either a projection or color wash at all times.

A smooth, white, painted surface (muslin, Masonite, and the like) provides a low-cost alternative to the commercial projection screen. Although the reflected image won't be so crisp as that from the projection screen, it will be more than adequate for most theatrical purposes. When the projections or color washes are turned off, however, the challenge of what to do with the "great white blob" continues.

Unless you are planning on using continuous projections or removing the screen from the set, it is frequently desirable to have the projection screen blend into the surrounding scenic elements until it is time to use it. In these cases, the vertical or horizontal surfaces of the set itself can be used instead of a projection screen. When you are projecting on scenery, the sharpness and brightness of the reflected image will be directly related to the hue, value, and texture of the paint job used on the scenery. Surfaces with low saturation, high value, and little texture provide the best reflective surfaces for projected images.

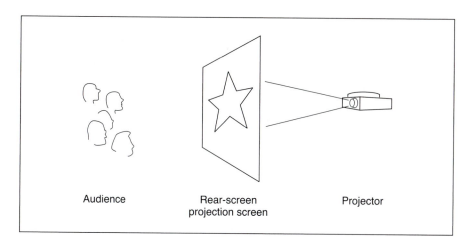

FIGURE 17.9
A typical rear-screen projection setup.

Audience

Rear-screen
projection screen

Projector

Rear-Screen Material

A major challenge of front-screen projection—actor shadows on the projection surface—is eliminated through the use of rear-screen projection. In this technique, illustrated in Figure 17.9, the projector is placed behind the screen, and the image is transmitted through the screen to the audience.

A significant challenge of rear-screen projection is created by the **hot spot.** If the projector is located within the audience's sight line, as illustrated in Figure 17.10, a small, intensely bright circle of light will appear on the screen. This bright circle is caused by seeing the actual lens of the projector through the screen material. The hot spot can be eliminated in one of two ways. You can position the projector so that the hot spot is out of the audience's sight line, or you can use a screen material that eliminates the hot spot.

Commercial rear-screen materials transmit clear, crisp images while diffusing or eliminating the hot spot. Rosco Labs produces several types of reasonably priced flexible plastic rear-screen materials in rolls 55 inches wide. Wider screens, with invisible seams, can be made by butting strips of the material edge to edge and taping the joints with No. 200 Scotch transparent plastic tape. Unless the atmosphere is of low humidity, however, the tape seams are only a temporary solution. **Heat welding** of the seams will provide a permanent bond.

If the projector can be placed in a position that will eliminate the hot spot, a variety of translucent materials can be used to receive the projected image. Scenic muslin and other fabrics of similar weight and weave transmit light quite well. The muslin (which will present a crisper image if it is primed with a starch solution—one cup of starch per gallon of hot water) can be painted with dye if it is necessary or desirable for the screen to blend into the set. When using this technique, be sure to use dye, not paint. Dye is transparent and won't interrupt the transmission of the image.

Nylon tricot, which is sold in 108-inch widths, also provides a quality rear-screen material. The nylon can be stretched tight to eliminate any wrinkles; and, if is painted with a few coats of diluted white glue, the surface provides a good projection surface that transmits more light, and therefore a more "readable" image, than muslin.[2]

FIGURE 17.10
A hot spot, caused by seeing the lens of the projector through the screen, will result unless special rear-screen projection material is used.

hot spot: An intense circle of light created when a projector lens is seen through a rear screen.

heat welding: The use of a heat gun (a high-temperature air gun, visually similar to a hand-held hair dryer) to fuse two pieces of plastic.

---

[2] Suggested by Professor Richard Gamble at Florida Atlantic University.

Plain white shower curtains provide another effective, low-cost rear-screen material. The plastic transmits light well, the larger-sized shower curtains are big enough for many scenic uses, and some of the plastics diffuse the hot spot.

White (not clear) polyethylene plastic sheeting, sold as plastic drop cloths in paint stores, is also an effective rear-screen material.

 ## Slide Preparation

Slides for the various types of commercial and shop-built Linnebachs are generally made from ⅛-inch clear Plexiglas. Slides for the curved-image Linnebach can be made from 0.020-inch acetate. Although still quite flexible, the 0.020 thickness provides enough stiffness so that these slides don't bend or flop when secured to the projector.

The slide image can be painted on the acetate with a variety of materials. Transparent acetate inks, which are available in a wide range of colors, are a standard type of slide paint. If an additive, which makes the water-base dyes adhere to the plastic, is used, Dr. Martin's Watercolors are an excellent choice. As a last resort, the bottles of Magic Marker refill inks can also be used. Although the Magic Marker inks remain slightly tacky, they don't smear easily, but they do attract a great deal of dust.

Scenic projectors can use both photographic and painted slides. To be used in a scenic projector, photographic transparencies should be sandwiched between sheets of projection-grade glass. This type of glass is usually available from photography stores. This "sandwich" accomplishes two things: It keeps the heat of the lamp from crinkling or melting the slide, and it keeps the slide in a vertical plane. Painted scenic-projector slides are also usually sandwiched for heat protection. The image is painted on a glass slide, and either that slide is sandwiched between two other clear slides or the painted surface is simply covered with a second slide. The transparent inks mentioned previously will also work on glass. Additionally, silhouettes can be created by using opaque acetate inks. However, you must take care when using opaque inks, simply because they absorb more heat than do transparent ones. The additional heat may crack the glass or cause a deterioration of the other inks.

Thirty-five-millimeter slides shouldn't be used in the cardboard mounts in which they are placed by the film processors. These mounts don't really have enough weight to drop the slide into the projector if the projector is mounted at anything other than a perfectly horizontal angle. At a minimum, the slides should be remounted in plastic slide mounts, and ideally you will sandwich them between two layers of slide glass. (The plastic mounts and 35 mm glass mounts are available at photography stores.)

 ## Other Projectors

A wide variety of other projectors can be used for special situations in the theatre. However, two of them, the overhead projector (Figure 17.11) and the opaque projector, are arguably the most useful.

A large transparent slide (most overhead projectors will accept slides up to 11 by 14 inches) is placed on the light table of the overhead projector. A high-output lamp shines through the slide, and the image is redirected and focused on the screen by a mirror mounted in an optical head located a short distance above the

FIGURE 17.11
An overhead projector. (Courtesy of George R. Snell Associates.)

light table. The luminance level of this projector is fairly low, but it can work well in short-throw, low-light situations.

The opaque projector works in generally the same fashion, except that the slide is opaque and the lamp is located above the slide so that the light can be reflected, rather than directly transmitted, to the mirror and optical head. The output of the opaque projector is generally less than that of the overhead projector, because some of the lamp output is lost to absorption and scattering during the reflection process. Although this projector is effective on stage only for specific low-light applications, it is very helpful in the scene shop, where it can be used to project detail from painters' elevations and other drawings or photos onto scenic elements during the scene-painting process.

General Projection Techniques and Hints

It is prudent to test the characteristics of any projection system, technique, or material (commercial or noncommercial) under actual stage conditions before you launch into a design concept that depends on projections. You will frequently discover that your vision of how the projections should look is at odds with the physical reality of how they actually appear on stage. Some general hints and guidelines may help you in working with projections:

1. To prevent the projected images from being washed out, keep ambient light off of the screen. Be sure that the stage lights for the acting areas in the vicinity of the screen(s) are placed at angles that minimize their effect (direct and reflected) on the screen.

2. To reduce the effects of ambient light and to keep the actors from blocking the spectators' view of the projected image, try to place the screen so that its bottom edge will be no lower than 5 to 7 feet above the stage floor.

3. To maximize the brightness of the image when working with an audio-visual slide projector:

   A. Keep the size of the projection as small as possible.

   B. Use a lens with a low f-stop (3.5 or less).

   C. Use a short-focal-length lens, and place the projector as close to the screen as possible.

4. Rear-screen projection is affected by ambient light less than front-screen projection is, so whenever possible try to work with rear-screen techniques.

5. Become thoroughly familiar with the equipment that you will be using well before technical rehearsals begin. Shoot your slides early so that you will have time to shoot and process additional slides if it becomes necessary.

Chapter 18

Costume Design

This chapter has been updated thanks to the input of Patrick Holt, professional costume designer and educator. The author wishes to publicly thank him for his extensive knowledge and expertise on this subject and for his contributions to not only this chapter, but his work on Chapter 19, Costume Production, and Chapter 20, Makeup, as well.

There may be some truth to the adage that "clothes make the man." A study, summarized in the book *The Four Minute Sell*, by Janet Elsea, indicates that during the first four minutes of contact with a stranger our understanding of that person's nature and personality will be based on three primary, but unequal, factors: appearance, 55 percent; tone of voice, 38 percent; and what the person is saying, 7 percent.

Costume designers are aware of these factors, either intuitively or from training. They know that when an actor walks onto the stage for the first time, the audience's feelings about the character will be based, to a great extent, on the information that guides all first impressions.

What is a costume? According to Barbara and Cletus Anderson in their text *Costume Design*, "Anything worn onstage is a costume, whether it be layers of clothing or nothing at all."[1] More specifically, this definition includes all clothing, underclothing, hairdressing, makeup, and accessories such as hats, scarves, fans, canes, umbrellas, and jewelry, worn or carried by each character in a production. The design and appearance of all these costume elements is the province of the costume designer.

Most people agree that the costume worn by an actor profoundly affects the audience's perceptions of the character being created by that actor. If that assumption is correct, then it would logically follow that the costume designer's job entails the manipulation of the design of each character's clothing to project some specific personal information about that character and, if appropriate, to affect the physicality of the actor by inhibiting or limiting, in a manner appropriate to the characterization, the way an actor moves, speaks, stands, or sits on the stage. How the costume designer does that is the subject of this chapter.

The Nature of Costume Design

In fashion design, primary attention is given to creating a striking visual design that gives little, if any, thought to the character or personality quirks of the individual person who ultimately will wear the clothes. While fashion designers generally break their collections into two categories—haute couture and

[1] Barbara and Cletus Anderson, *Costume Design* (New York: Holt, Rinehart, Winston, 1984), p. 20.

This discussion is a capsulization of the specific applications of the design process to costume design. A review of Chapter 2 may be appropriate if you are hazy on the fundamentals of this problem-solving technique.

Commitment

In order to accomplish your best work, you have to promise yourself that you will perform the task to the best of your ability.

Analysis

The type of information that is needed to clarify and refine the challenge can be gathered by reading the script and asking questions of the other members of the production design team. Typical questions that relate specifically to costume design include:

1. What is the costume budget?
2. What is the production concept?
3. Are we going to be producing the play in the period in which it is written? What is that period?
4. When is the first dress rehearsal?
5. Does the director want a costume parade?
6. What does the set design look like? What is its color palette?
7. What is the lighting designer's color palette?

Some questions will be answered when you study the script. Others will be discussed and answered during the production conferences, in which the director and all designers freely exchange ideas and information.

The second phase of analysis involves discovering areas and subjects that will require further research. Note these areas so that you can investigate them during the next phase of the design process.

Research

Research is divided into two separate areas: background research and conceptual research. The primary function of background research is to answer the questions generated during the analysis phase. The vast majority of costume designs are based on a fairly realistic interpretation of the style of clothing worn during some particular period of history. For this reason it is particularly important in costume design to consult primary research materials whenever possible.

Primary research items include clothing and accessories actually made during the period under investigation. The reason for primary research is to obtain the most accurate information about the period silhouette, the type and nature of the fabrics used, and construction techniques. Nothing tells you more about the design and construction of a dress of the 1890s than examining a dress made in the 1890s.

If primary resources are not available for examination, then the costume designer's research naturally expands to include examining photographs of actual garments of the period, museum displays of actual clothing and accessories, paintings appropriate to the time and locale of the intended production, and texts on the history of clothing and costumes.

The further back one goes in history, the greater will be the variations in the style of clothing from region to region and country to country. Before 1800 land transportation was by foot, horse, carriage, or cart. Travel between continents was by sailing ship. With the development of steamships, railroads, and the telegraph, the time that it took for information to travel from one place to another shrank from months and years to merely minutes and days. Consequently, the readily identifiable regional variations in the style of clothing began to diminish as the interchange of ideas, goods, and services became easier.

Even in our own age of information, regional differences in dress are still alive and well. But the current variations in clothing between regions and countries are generally more subtle today than they were even one hundred years ago.

During conceptual research, you need to visualize as many potential solutions to the design challenge as possible. Sketch a lot of ideas. Gather fabric samples that might be appropriate for material from which to construct the various costumes, and attach them to the sketches.

Incubation

Rest. Relax. Get away from the project. Work on something else. Go for a walk. Go to the library. Go see a play or movie. Do anything but work on or think about the project.

Selection

After you have selected the appropriate overall costume concept for the production, you will also need to select the appropriate design idea that will be used for each individual costume in the production.

Implementation

The implementation phase in costume design involves the drawing and painting of costume renderings, the selection of the appropriate fabrics for each design, and sometimes the supervision of the construction of each garment. (To be technically correct, the costume designer is responsible for the appearance, not the construction, of the finished costume. It is the costumer, not the costume designer, who is responsible for the supervision of the actual making of the costumes. In some production companies, these lines of responsibility become fuzzy.)

Evaluation

Finally, take an objective look at the communication process that has taken place between you and the other members of the production design team and your own use of the design process. The purpose of this evaluation is to discern ways in which you could improve your communication with other members of the production design team as well as your use of the design process.

ready-to-wear—with each carefully designed for a particular season of the year as well as the social/economic level of clientele, the purpose of costume design for the theatre is somewhat different. Its needs are more specific. Each costume that an actor wears in a play is generally designed to visually reinforce the emotional, mental, and physical traits of a unique character at a particular time in a specific play. That costume also needs to be designed to fit, and work with, the body of one individual actor. To be effective, the costume designs for a production need to (1) reflect the production design team's agreed-upon interpretation of the production concept (discussed in Chapter 1); (2) exhibit a unity of style among all the costume designs for that production; (3) provide a visual reflection of the personality and nature of each character at a given time in the play; and (4) provide visual information about the world of the play including locale, period, season, time of day, culture, as well as the play's socioeconomic, religious, and political environment.

After the production design team agrees on the style of the production concept—the compositional characteristics that will be used as the unifying elements in each designer's work—the costume designer uses those compositional

FIGURE 18.1
Costume design by Peggy Kellner for Mrs. Mullin in *Carousel.*

principles as guides in creating the costume designs for the production. The particular style selected might be based on the line and color palette used in a specific painting by a particular artist that was discovered while doing background research. Or it might be synthesized from the works of several artists, filmmakers, or composers. It could even be a subjective reaction to seemingly random thoughts, textures, and colors. The actual elements used in its creation aren't important. What is important is that the production design team agrees on, and understands the meaning of, the stylistic guide called the production concept.

Costume Design for the Theatre

All costumes for a production need to be thought of as equally important. Whether they are designed for the lead (Figure 18.1) or an **extra,** (Figure 18.2), or whether the costumes are to be built "from scratch" or pulled from a theatre's stock and altered, all costumes are equally important.

extra: A nonspeaking part. A person who provides "visual dressing" for the scene.

3 BEAUTIES from EUROPE
CAROUSEL

FIGURE 18.2
Costume design by Peggy Kellner for extras in *Carousel.*

In terms of design parameters, costume design is identical to the other design areas in the theatre. The two primary sources of information about a production—how this particular performance is going to be interpreted and performed—are the script and the production concept. The script contains general information about the play—the historical period of the play, the socioeconomic status and occupations of the characters, the season and climate. Specific information about the characters—personality traits, character quirks—is frequently revealed in the script by what the characters say about themselves and what others say about them. All of this information can be, and frequently is, modified, sometimes extensively, by the production concept adopted for that specific production. The production concept, generally initially voiced by the producer or director, evolves during conversation in the meetings of the production design team until it becomes a unified thought that is the focus point—the "this-is-the-way-that-we're-going-to-do-it" image—used by all members of the production design team as they go about their individual tasks.

The designs for all costumes for any given production need to be guided by the designer's interpretation of the script and the production concept. Doing so helps assure that those designs will visually reinforce the agreed-upon production concept as well as assisting the audience to understand the nature and personality of each character in the production.

The Psychological Meaning of Clothes

What a person wears, and how it is worn, says a great deal about that person and the society in which he or she lives. In contemporary Western countries, corporate businesspersons traditionally wear conservatively cut, somber-colored suits and ties. A man or a woman who wants to fit into that environment would buy only those clothes appropriate to the fashion and wear them as prescribed by the style.

A certain type of clothing can be worn to conform to or rebel against a certain segment of society. During World War II, American pilots demonstrated their collective individualism by wearing their hats at jaunty angles rather than the "hat bill level and two fingers above the bridge of the nose" prescribed by the military dress-code manual. A visit to a contemporary American high school would reveal numerous distinctive styles of dress—"mod," "preppie," "stoners," "skaters," and "jocks"—that visibly demonstrate the peer groups to which the various students belong.

Clothes can also be visible clues to the wearer's emotional state. An introvert would probably wear something that would make him blend into the crowd, whereas an extrovert might wear something that would make her stand out and be noticed. Similarly, someone who is gloomy might wear something dark and dreary to reinforce and visually announce that mood, whereas a cheerful, happy individual might dress in bright and cheerful colors.

Objective Information Provided by Clothes

In addition to providing psychological clues, clothing can provide a variety of objective information about a person.

Historical Period   The shape or silhouette of garments can provide clear indications of their historical period. Theatrical costumes may be faithful to their historical period, or the costume designer may choose to use history as a reference point from which to create a design that is more meaningful to the production concept for a particular play. Either way, the historical silhouette can be a primary indicator of the historical period of the play, as shown in Figure 18.3.

DESIGN INSPIRATIONS
Costume Design

The following discussion is based on "Designing Woman," by Ginia Bellafante (Time, February 22, 1999, pp. 82–83).

How often can articles of clothing be credited with having performance-enhancing power? It happened, it seems, during the shooting of Todd Hanes' *Velvet Goldmine,* an homage to the David Bowie '70s and the world of men in makeup. According to Toni Collette, who played a rock-star's wife, all the leopard print and lamé she wore in the film coaxed the hidden extrovert right out of her. "The clothes made me want to show off," she said, "which is just what the character had to do."

The pen—and mind—behind that transformative wear is Sandy Powell, winner of the 1999 Oscar for costume design for *Shakespeare in Love* and perhaps the movies' most celebrated costume designer since the heyday of Edith Head, a 35-time Oscar winner.

Powell briefly attended London's venerable Central Saint Martin's College of Art and Design before dropping out to work as an assistant designer in the theatre. Her movie career was launched in the mid '80s when she met director Derek Jarman, with whom she collaborated on *Caravaggio.*

She has since developed a working method that involves little initial sketching. Powell first researches the era she's dealing with by visiting museums and galleries and studying paintings and photographs. "Unless of course the film requires it, I'm not interested in an exact replica of the period. I look at the period, how it should be, how it *could* be, and then I do my own version," she says. Next, she scours London for splendid fabrics. "I rarely start with a drawing," says Powell. "I start with a fabric I like and base the design on how that fabric behaves."

"Sandy comes with strong responses to the material," noted John Madden, director of *Shakespeare in Love,* which speculates fancifully about the Bard's inspiration for *Romeo and Juliet.* "She comes armed with instinct." Among Madden's favorite creations for the film were the costumes she made for the staged production of *Romeo and Juliet.* He loved the way in which the lavishness of the players' dress contrasted with the shabby browns worn by the commoners in the audience. "At first we thought it looked bizarre," said Madden, "but what was so brilliant was how she captured in costume how extraordinarily intoxicating that play must have been to the grubby creatures down in the pit watching."

Shakespeare [in Love] also showcased Powell's obsession with detail. In the film, the dressing gown worn by Gwyneth Paltrow appears to be festooned with iridescent jewels—but they are actually dried beetle wings, intended to replicate Elizabethan materials. When Paltrow's character pretends to be a boy, she wears a top with embroidery delicate enough to remind us that she is female. But Powell also put birdseed pouches in the crotch of Paltrow's breeches so the actress would remember to walk like a boy.

Despite her obvious talent for the splashy, one could argue that Powell's gift best manifests itself in smaller, brocade-free dramas such as the film *Hilary and Jackie.* Powell's mod clothes never overwhelm the tale of the relationship between the impassioned cellist Jacqueline Du Pré and her sister, but instead lend a keen visual intensity to the women's profound differences. As Jackie becomes increasingly famous—and depressed—her knits seem to get more blindingly pink and blue; Hilary, meanwhile, recedes into neutrals. The look stays with you. Powell's work, it seems, never fades to black.

Age   In any period the color, style, and fit of clothes provide a great deal of information about the age of the wearer. While the clothing of each period has its own characteristics that differentiate between youth and age, one generalization holds true for almost all periods: Young people tend to reveal more of their bodies than do their elders. Two theories suggest the reasons: Young people generally are more interested in attracting romantic partners than are their elders, and exposed skin attracts notice; young bodies with smooth skin and superior muscle tone are generally more attractive to look at than the skin and muscles of their elders, on whom time and gravity have taken their toll. For example, miniskirts, short-shorts, halter tops, and muscle shirts are all clothes of youth. Put these clothes on an out-of-shape middle-aged body and the almost universal viewer response will be that that person is trying to recapture, or doesn't want to let go of, his or her youth.

Gender   Throughout history, with a few exceptions, clothes have almost always clearly indicated the gender of the wearer. When specifying gender differentiation, fashion design has almost always provided a visual reflection of the society from which it sprang. For example, during the Victorian and Edwardian periods, women were fully covered from neck to foot, but there was visual emphasis on

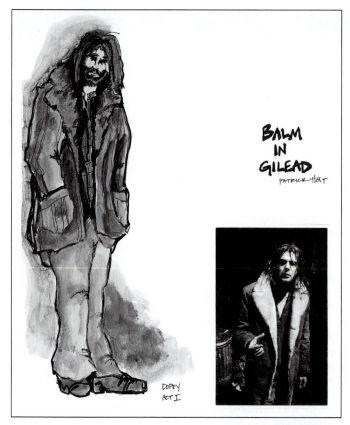

(A)

(B)

FIGURE 18.3
The silhouette of a costume can provide visual clues about character and historical period. Costume designs by Patrick Holt for (A) Dopey in Act I in the North Carolina School of the Arts production of *Balm in Gilead* and (B) Warlock in *Faust*. (C) Asolo State Theatre's (Sarasota, Florida) production of *Charley's Aunt*. Costume design by Catherine King, scene design by Gordon Miconis; photo by Gary W. Sweetman. (D) Jeri Leer, Candy Buckley, Linda Gehringer (left to right) and Michael O'Hara (background) in Dallas Theatre Center's production of *The Three Sisters*. Designed by Leo Akira Yoshimura; photo by Linda Blase.

(C)

(D)

the hair, bust, and bustle, providing a visual reflection of the Victorian ideal of woman as wife and mother. The 1920s saw a revolt against the strict Victorian codes and the bold (for the time) assertion that women were individuals who could possibly have a life outside the traditional roles of wife and mother. A primary fashion statement of the 1920s, the flapper style, reflected the societal reevaluation of the role of women with its boyish look of short hair, flat bosom, and slender hips.

Socioeconomic Status   Social status has always been indicated with clothes. Someone dressed in shabby, ill-kempt clothes of rough homespun materials would rarely be mistaken for a member of the upper class. A woman dressed in beautifully fashioned linens, silks, and satins would rarely be mistaken for a servant. Prior to about 1930, the cut and fit of many upper-class clothing styles actually precluded the possibility of manual labor. The upper classes didn't work, so their clothes were designed to reflect and enforce their lives of leisure. Generally, servants' clothes have always been similar to those of their masters, but the designs have been simpler, the cloth plainer, and the colors more drab.

Occupation   Similar to the clues that clothing provides about a character's socioeconomic status, clothes can also tell us about a person's job. Uniforms are obvious indicators of occupation. Police officers, military personnel, chefs, maids, workers in franchised businesses such as McDonald's and Pizza Hut are all readily identifiable. Sometimes the identification is not so clear. But we would probably identify a man in a flannel shirt, jeans, and heavy boots, with a tool pouch hanging from his belt, as some kind of workman, not a corporate lawyer. If he *were* a corporate lawyer, then we probably would instantly label him as eccentric.

Climate and Season   If we see someone bundled up in a heavy fur coat, we assume that the weather is cold. Dark hues, heavy fabrics, and multiple layers are also strong indicators of cold climate. Light colors, lightweight fabrics, and fewer clothes provide good indications that the weather is warm. Interesting inferences can be made about the personality of a character who dresses "out of season," such as the Reverend Hale, who, in James Michener's novel *Hawaii,* wears long underwear and a woolen frock coat while living in the tropical heat and humidity of the Hawaiian islands.

 ## General Considerations for Costume Design

A variety of diverse considerations and sources of information affect the work of the costume designer.

Analyzing the Script

The costume designer reads the script to gather various kinds of information about the play and the characters in it.

The script provides specific factual information about the historical period in which the play is set: the time of day, season, climate, and time span covered by the play; the sex, age, socioeconomic status, occupation of each character; and so forth. In addition to discovering this historical data, the costume designer gleans the emotional quality of the play and learns about the interrelationships existing between the various characters in the play from reading the script.

The analysis of the script expands beyond the printed page to include the views and interpretations of the producer, the director, and the other designers. Any or all of these other members of the production design team may see the relationships between the characters differently than you do. Their opinions must be acknowledged and evaluated.

All of this information provides the essential background material that the costume designer uses to create designs which effectively reflect the personality and characteristics of each role in the play.

Chapter 2, "The Design Process," contains a specific script-analysis discussion and suggests a procedure that can be used to create effective costume designs.

Other Conceptual Considerations

While an analysis of the script provides a substantial beginning point in the conceptualization of each costume design, several other considerations must be addressed by the costume designer during the design process.

Stereotypical Costuming   The actor, not the costume, is the primary vehicle for conveying a character's nature and personality. For this reason, costume designers normally avoid stereotypical designs that clearly proclaim who or what a character is—a gangster in dark pinstripe suit, black shirt, and white tie or a prostitute in a tight, bust- and thigh-revealing red dress. The obvious exception to this principle involves those vehicles or production concepts which are based on flat, two-dimensional cartoonish characters, as in musicals such as *Li'l Abner* or *Guys and Dolls.* The use of design features that hint, rather than scream, at the true nature of the character allows the actor to develop the character with the aid of the costume, rather than being upstaged by it. But it shouldn't be assumed that designers never use stereotypes as the basis for a design. Sometimes stereotypes are used to quickly define a character or to deceive the audience into making incorrect assumptions about a character. In reality stereotypical design, and the decision of when and how often to use it, is simply another tool in the designer's arsenal or bag o' tricks.

Character Evolution   Costumes need to match the growth and change that characters experience during the course of the production. In Carson McCullers's *The Member of the Wedding,* the character of Frankie matures and changes from a child into a young adult over the course of the play. The costumes that she wears should reflect this maturation process. Similarly, costumes worn by characters who experience emotional or intellectual growth should reflect those changes. A young woman who evolves from a flirt into a serious businesswoman might start out dressed in light-colored, ruffled tea dresses and finish the play costumed in dark-hued business suits.

Costume Stylization   The type and degree of stylization dictated by the script and production concept must be recognized by the costume designer. Stylization is a complex subject perhaps best described by example. What follows is a sampling of some of the types of stylization that can be used. None of them should be thought of as "right" or "correct." They simply show some of the myriad styles that can be created. Obviously, any particular style that is adopted should be a reflection of the production concept for that particular production. Some plays set in contemporary America are populated by ordinary characters using vernacular language. These slice-of-life dramas may be appropriately costumed with clothes purchased or faithfully copied from fashions available at JCPenney, Saks Fifth Avenue, or a local Salvation Army store. These costumes should reflect the everyday world of the play. Verse dramas, on the other hand, are populated by people who speak in heightened language. The thoughts, speech, and actions of Shakespearean characters, for example, are frequently more lofty, or at least more exaggerated, than ours. If produced in a straight period style, faithful to an author's original setting and intent, the characters' costumes should mirror their eloquence and grand thoughts. Similarly, plays in which the protagonist struggles against the gods or the cosmos are not "ordinary" or "normal" in their scope. The costume design for such a production can reflect the "supernormal" world of

DESIGN INSPIRATIONS
Costume Design

The following discussion is based on "Designing Women," by Amy Reiter (Entertainment Design, May 1999). Photo by Stan Barouh.

Claire Booth Luce's *The Women* may not be 100% politically correct—its portrayal of the so-called gentle gender is far more tart than sweet—but the early 1999 production of the 1936 play, which took place in the Fichandler Theatre of Washington D.C.'s Arena Stage, seduced even the most PC audiences, like a dazzlingly beautiful, tough-talking, wisecracking femme fatale.

In many ways the production was as much about clothes as it was about power: the power of clothes, clothing as power. "How glamorous these women look is of paramount importance," director Kyle Donnelly said. Costume designer Paul Tazewell's costumes didn't just suit the characters; the costumes helped to define the characters and traced their trajectories through the play.

Although director Donnelly cast all women, "there was an element of the drag idea that interested her," Tazewell recalled. "It was this idea of facade, which synthesized itself down to being kind of a Hollywood facade, where many American women got their sense of glamour and style in that period." The world of *The Women* mirrored that Hollywood facade in that the characters in the play are beautiful but backstabbing, outwardly friendly but inwardly false.

Once the Hollywood concept was established, said Tazewell, "the door was open for it to be as out there as possible and not feel that I had to stick to a natural or realistic scale in either choices of color or silhouette."

Tazewell and scenic designer Thomas Lynch decided to art direct the play as they might have a film. Because capturing the black-and-white look of the films of the period in which the play takes place was not feasible—"You can't really get to the subtlety of everything, even the skin tones being some shade of gray," Tazewell pointed out—the designers decided to color-coordinate each scene. They found inspiration in the vivid Technicolor movies of the 1950s.

"We identified the pervading color that spoke of each scene," Tazewell said. They then integrated that color into all the design elements. For the play's opening scene, which takes place in the living room of the lead character, Mary, the designers chose Wedgwood blue, which evokes upper-crust coolness and polish, but also has a warm undercurrent. Tazewell dressed the women in chic, somewhat true-to-period suits in blues and grays. Black and yellow accents—in hats and other accessories—provided highlights and shading.

Other scenes were similarly constructed around color themes. The final scene centers on an evening gown–clad cat fight in a casino. The dresses in this scene were sumptuous—beaded bodices, feathers, and shimmering metallic fabrics.

The play "is structured that way," Tazewell said. "You start off in day clothes and go into evening. Once you're

in Mary's boudoir (the penultimate scene), you think the story is done. She's in her nightgown. She's in bed. And then she gets more information—and here we go into this casino room, with all these women in glamorous dresses, and then Mary enters in her red dress. It really hits the height you hope it will. You feel like it's never-ending, like there's all this abundance. That feels good for me."

Costume designer Paul Tazewell concluded, "I didn't worry so much about trying to make it the late '30s. It has the flavor of the '30s and then a lot of Paul in it."

---

the play. Many contemporary productions of Shakespeare and other classical works are performed quite effectively in modern dress. The production concept adopted for that particular production should dictate the design style. For example, the costume design for a Brechtian play presented in minimalist style could be reflected in the simplicity of the designs regardless of whether the costumes were period or contemporary.

Interpretation of Period   Costumes make a statement that visually unifies the historical period, the style of the script, and the production concept. However, any historical period, regardless of whether it is one or forty years long, has a plethora of design styles, and each of those styles has an overwhelming number of subtle variations. If the costume designer were to randomly select costume elements from the entirety of the period, the result would be a visual hodge-podge.

detailing: Trim, appliqués, buttons, ribbons, braid, and so forth attached to a garment to enhance its appearance.

Therefore, the costume designer needs to distill that mound of information into a few typical lines, colors, textures, and details that represent the essence of the period. Once that visual theme is established, then variations can be created within it to reflect the traits of the individual characters in the play. This distilled line is frequently an interpretation of the historical data. Character traits, or merely the importance of a character within a scene, sometimes require a departure from historical accuracy of the costume. Sometimes historical accuracy itself can cause visual problems. The **detailing** on gowns of Elizabethan nobility was incredibly ornate. If accurately reproduced for the stage, it could result in a visual "war" between the various trim designs. Simplification of the trim could increase the significance of what is selected and, depending on the production concept, perhaps create a design more appropriate to the production.

Interpretation of Color and Fabric   Historical research will acquaint the costume designer with the color and types of fabrics used in a particular historical period. This information needs to be manipulated in the design process. While historically accurate data may form the root of the design, the colors and fabrics selected must be appropriate to the production concept and the individual characterizations. Typically, the designer will select a range of colors, textures, and fabrics appropriate to the period and production concept and then develop variations within those themes for individual characters.

Practical Considerations

In addition to historical, analytical, and conceptual considerations, the costume designer must be aware of a number of practical matters before the designs can be finalized.

Needs of the Actor   The actor's needs can be divided into two categories — physical and psychological. The physical needs are fairly simple: The costume should fit, it should be reasonably comfortable, and it shouldn't inhibit any necessary and appropriate motion. Because people today are not used to the physical constraints imposed by many fashion modes of the past, the costume designer needs to adapt the costume design to accommodate the actors, while still retaining the historical silhouette and line of the costume. The circumference of the hem of the hobble skirt (shown in Figure 18.4) was so small that women wearing them could take only very tiny steps; it was all but impossible to move up or down stairs. For stage use hobble skirts, and similar movement-inhibiting clothes, are usually designed with authentic lines but with slight modifications to allow for a little more freedom of movement.

It has been said that "Clothes make the man." In the theatre that's true. Because a costume is designed to provide a visual statement about the character's personality and station in life, the simple act of putting it on psychologically helps the actor become the character. And it works. Just ask any actor.

Production Venue   Costume design is also influenced by the production venue. The small, delicately tinted pastel embroidered flowers on a peasant blouse, detail totally appropriate to the character and clearly visible in a production staged in an intimate arena theatre seating 125 people, would be completely lost in a large proscenium theatre seating 3,000 or 4,000.

Budget   Obviously, the amount of money in the costume budget, and the time and staff available to design and construct the costumes, have a direct effect on design choices.

FIGURE 18.4
A hobble skirt. Costume design by Peggy Kellner for *Hotel Paradiso*, Old Globe Theatre, San Diego, California.

Construction Demands of the Design   Construction demands in costume design are generally predicated on the number of costumes in the production, the complexity of the individual designs, the budget, and the expertise of available personnel. Costumes for professional productions are constructed under contract by a costume production house or the resident costume crew, although contemporary tailored clothes such as men's suits are frequently purchased. Because of time, fiscal, or other constraints, some of the costumes for educational and regional professional company productions may be rented or **pulled** from stock and modified. When a production uses a combination of rented, pulled, and constructed costumes, the designer needs to pay extra attention to creating a unified overall design and a visual blending of the costumes acquired from these disparate sources.

Renting Costumes   Carefully tailored, period-specific items such as military uniforms and expensive men's suits are frequently rented. An advantage of renting uniforms is that the costume houses often have the appropriate accessories, such as swords, decorations, headgear, and footwear.

Buying Costumes   When producing a contemporary production, costume designers frequently buy clothes "off the rack" and modify them as necessary to fit the production concept and the specific actor. For productions that are set in the past twenty to thirty years, costume designers can browse through used-clothing stores and pick up many appropriate garments.

Modifying Stock Costumes   Educational and regional professional companies frequently have a stock of costumes that have been used in previous productions. Costumes can be pulled from stock and modified by dyeing and/or the addition or deletion of trim and accessories. Significant variations in the appearance, and apparent period, of a costume can be made by something as simple as creating a lace **overlay** for the **bodice** of a gown. Similar changes can be effected by changing from lace to fur trim or vice versa.

pull: To remove a costume from storage for use in a production.

overlay: A garment, usually made of lace or a similar lightweight, semitransparent fabric, designed to lie on top of another garment.

bodice: The upper part of a woman's dress.

 ## Organizational Paperwork

Since there are frequently between twenty and one hundred costumes per production, the costume designer must use a variety of organizational paperwork to keep track of the myriad details during all phases of production.

The costume designer must keep track of amazing amounts of detail regarding every costume in the production, so it is essential that he or she make copious and complete notes. An ever-increasing number of software programs aid the costume designer and the costume shop personnel in keeping track of all these details. Reviews and content of some of these products may be found on the Web site of the USITT—www.usitt.org.

In Chapter 2, it was suggested that designers carry a notebook for jotting down ideas. In addition to using a notebook, costume designers often jot notes in the margins of the script because of the frequent references to specific items worn by the characters.

Most costume shops have an organizational tool that is frequently referred to as the "costume bible."[2] This book holds all the information regarding the planning

[2] Information extracted from Rosemary Ingham and Liz Covey, *The Costume Designer's Handbook,* 2nd ed. (Portsmouth, N.H.: Heinemann, 1992), p. 157; Rebecca Cunningham, *The Magic Garment: Principles of Costume Design* (Prospect Heights, Ill.: Waveland Press, 1994), p. 229.

and construction of a particular show. If the production company or construction shop is working on more than one show at a time, each show normally will have its own "bible." While the specific information contained in the "costume bible" obviously varies from company to company, it will normally include the following:

cast list and production contact sheets
measurement sheets
calendars and deadlines
costume plots and lists
budget sheets, including an area to keep a running total of costs
rental contracts and pull lists
copies of renderings
swatches and dyeing instructions
production notes from the stage manager

Many of the items listed will be discussed a little later in this chapter.

Costume Chart

The costume chart (Figure 18.5), also known as the actor's scene chart, is used to visually plot what each character (or actor if he or she is playing multiple roles) wears in each scene in the play. Generally, two versions of the costume chart are created. For early discussion and budget purposes, a preliminary costume chart can be created early in the design process to help organize the designer's ideas and thoughts while analyzing the script and noting the needs of the production.

FIGURE 18.5
A sample costume chart. (Courtesy of Dianne J. Holly.)

Romeo & Juliet	I:1	I:2	I:3	I:4	I:5	II:1	II:2	II:3	II
Romeo	Cream sweater Beige silk slacks Beige shoes, socks & belt	Same		White linen suit Black knit shirt Black belt & shoes	Add mask and cape	Same	Same	Same	S
Juliet			Peach kimono Beige slip		White dress White petticoat White shoes Nylons Mask		Kimono Slip		
Nurse			Day dress Nylons Shoes Necklace		Eve. dress Shoes same Jewelry Mask?		Voice only		
Capulet	2 pc. gray silk suit Gray striped shirt Rose tie & handkerchief Black shoes	Same			D. breasted tux Cummerbund Tux shirt Black bow tie, socks, & shoes Wht. handkerchief Cufflinks, studs				
Lady Capulet	Blue knit dress, belt & shoes Slip, nylons Necklace Earrings, purse Bracelet, fur		Same		Black velvet gown Earrings Bracelet Black shoes Mask				
Mercutio	White tux shirt Black leather pants Black boots			Same Add blue cape Baldric sword	Same Add mask	Same			
Time of Day	Sunday about noon	Sunday, minutes later	Sunday late afternoon, early evening	Sunday late afternoon, pre-party	Sunday night, party, visual climax	Sunday night, late post-party			

Another chart is based on the final designs and is a helpful aid to those running the show and stage management.

There are numerous ways to make a costume chart. It can be hand-drawn by gridding off squares on relatively large sheets of paper, or the information can be entered into a computer database and printed either as a large chart or as individual sheets that can be organized in a three-ring binder. In either case the character's names are listed on the left side, and each act (or each scene if the acts are subdivided into scenes) is noted across the top of the page. All costume items, including accessories, are noted in the scene in which they are first worn. Subsequent costume changes are noted in the appropriate scene.

As an organizational device, some costume designers attach color samples to each listing so that they can see the development of the overall color scheme of the production, as well as trace the color progression of individual characters at a glance. Wardrobe personnel use the costume chart as a guide when dressing the actors, and directors and actors use it to help keep the costumes organized in their minds.

Costume List

Frequently created simultaneously with the costume chart, the costume list (Figure 18.6) specifies every element, including accessories, of each costume worn

PRINCIPAL MEN

Romeo
1. Cream sweater, beige silk slacks, beige shoes, beige socks, beige belt
2. White linen suit, black knit shirt, black belt, black socks and shoes
3. Mask, cape MEDIUM QUICK CHANGE

Capulet
4. Two-piece gray silk suit, gray/white striped shirt, rose tie and handkerchief, black socks/shoes
5. Double breasted tux, cummerbund, tux shirt, black bow tie, black socks/shoes, white handkerchief, cufflinks and studs (gold)
6. Pajamas, robe, slippers

Mercutio
7. White tux shirt, black tux trousers, dinner jacket, black boots
8. Blue cape, baldric sword

Extra Men
18. Guard I — dark gray suit, black shoes, black shirt, black tie
19. Guard II — dark gray suit, black shoes, black shirt, black tie
20. Servant I — black dress pants, white shirt, black bow tie

PRINCIPAL WOMEN

Juliet
9. Pink kimono, beige slip
10. White dress, white petticoat, white shoes, nylons mask
11. Cream skirt, yellow sweater, cream nylons/shoes, straw hat

Nurse
12. Day dress, nylons, shoes, necklace
13. Evening dress, matching shoes, jewelry, mask
14. Shawl

Lady Capulet
15. Blue silk dress, matching belt, slip, nylons, blue shoes, necklace, earrings, bracelet, fur
16. Black velvet gown, earrings, bracelet, black shoes, mask
17. Pink nightgown, blue robe, blue slippers

Extra Women
21. Servant I — black maid's uniform, black shoes, nylons
22. Servant II — black maid's uniform, black shoes, nylons

FIGURE 18.6
A sample costume list.

DESIGN INSPIRATIONS
Costume Design

*The following discussion is based on, and quotes from, the article, "Designer Sketch-book: 'Prince of Attire' " by David Johnson (*Entertainment Design, *July 2003, p. 32). Permission granted by* Entertainment Design.

John Pennoyer looked to the Far East for inspiration in designing costumes for the Stratford Festival's production of Shakespeare's *Pericles* in 2003. "It's very *A Thousand and One Nights,* very *Scheherazade,*" says Pennoyer. "The play is a travel adventure placed around the Aegean Sea originally, as that would have been the extent of Shakespeare's geographic knowledge. We give him air miles and take it to North Africa, with a strong Bedouin accent, and go on to Greece, India, Japan, Thailand, and Bali." This Far Eastern landscape gave Pennoyer a wide palette of fabrics and colors as well as traditional costume designs based on Eastern ritual and ceremony. "I went to Thailand for two weeks to do research, and to villages near the Mekong River where silk is made," he explains. "I found fabulous silks at reasonable prices as well as garments and silver jewelry."

The costumes range from a chiton, or simple draped men's garment from Greece, that Pennoyer has re-created in a rayon that drapes nicely, to interpreta-tions of traditional Samurai ornamental costumes. "I looked at Kurosawa's films, especially *Ran,*" says the designer, who created five different warrior costumes using silks and Italian leathers. He also bought a traditional Japanese wedding kimono on eBay. "Even at $500 apiece they are a bargain," he says, describing the rich embroidered and painted silks with gold threads.

The goddesses in the Temple of Diana, placed in Bali, wear costumes in-spired by the Bard's reference to silver livery. "He meant white, but I mixed white and silver," says Pennoyer, who created headdresses with silver feathers on springs and silk sarongs with metal threads for his vestal virgins. Other cos-tumes illustrate the splendor of India, including long embroidered coats called jams. "There is an Indian neighborhood in Toronto that is a treasure trove for great fabrics," Pennoyer adds. "We bought sheer gold saris with spiral thread embroi-dery that they only do in India, and used the fabric for costumes."

Pennoyer also designed the set for *Pericles,* giving the production a neutral look with a white floor that provided the perfect background for the colorful costumes.

---

by every actor. Broken into two sections, men and women, in larger productions it is further subdivided into Principal Men, Chorus Men, Extra Men, Principal Women, Chorus Women, and Extra Women as necessary. Each costume is numbered so that the total number of costumes in the production is readily apparent. Other information, such as any necessary quick changes, is also noted.

This list is extremely useful to the designer when estimating costs or when dealing with a costume house that may build the costumes or with a business from which certain costumes may be rented. The costume list is also used by the dressers/wardrobe maintenance crew as a checklist to verify that all elements of each costume are together and that each costume is placed in its proper location prior to each performance.

Character–Actor Dressing List

dressers: Costume-crew personnel who assist actors in putting on their costumes.

This list is used by the actors and **dressers** during dress rehearsals and performances. Primarily posted in the actor's dressing room, it can also be located wherever the actor makes a costume change (dressing-room locker, makeup mirror, offstage costume-change enclosure). It details everything, including accessories, that the actor wears in each scene, as shown in Figure 18.7.

```
                    DRESSING LIST

    PLAY: ___Romeo & Juliet_____

    ROLE: __Capulet_____

    ACTOR: _Carl Douglas_____

    DRESSER: _Ted Freeman_____


    I: i — 2-piece gray suit
            Gray/white striped shirt
            Rose tie & hankerchief
            Black shoes
            Black socks

    I: ii — Same

    I: iv — Double-breasted tux
            Black cummerbund
            Tux shirt (ruffled front)
            Black bow tie
            White handkerchief
            Gold cufflinks & studs
            Black patent leather shoes
            Black socks

    III: i — Same as I:i

    III: iv — Same as I:i

    III: v — Pajamas
             Robe
             Slippers (no socks)
```

FIGURE 18.7
A sample character–actor dressing list.

Costume Calendar

The costume calendar (Figure 18.8) helps the costume designer budget time and provides a visualization of how much time is to be devoted to each phase of the costume design and construction process. To be effective it must include all facets of the process: readings/conferences, research, design, fabric shopping, construction, and rehearsals leading up to the opening performance.

The forms listed above are almost indispensable to the costume designer, but they can also trap the unwary. It is sometimes easy to lose sight of the fact that any theatrical production is always a work in progress. In even the best-planned production, designs are rarely finalized in the preliminary stages. Adjustments to the costume chart and costume list are frequently made during dress rehearsals. Accessories that were agreed on by both the director and costume designer during

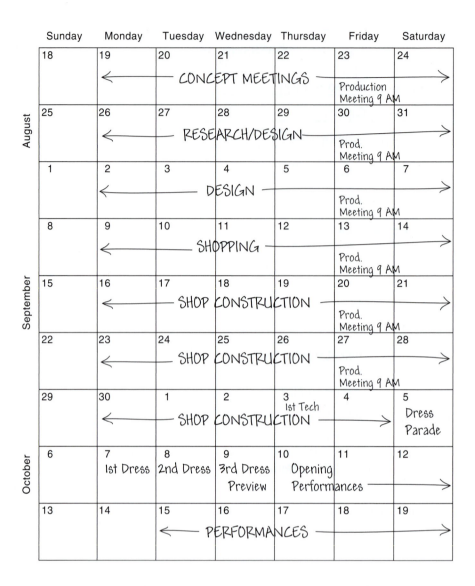

FIGURE 18.8
A sample costume calendar.

the design phase may need to be changed once they're seen onstage during dress rehearsals. Whole costumes may need to be replaced. If the director is truly prepared, and if the agreed-on production concept is fully understood by all concerned, then these adjustments should be minimal and not overly disruptive. Experienced costume designers know and understand these needs, plan for them, and adapt as necessary.

 ## Visual Presentation of the Costume Design

At some point, costume designers need to begin to codify their thoughts about the costume designs. This is when they need to start drawing. Costume designers create several types of drawings: preliminary sketches, the costume layout, and the final costume sketch or rendering.

A vital element in all costume drawings is that the sketches should do two things: show the nature and personality of the character at the time in the play when the illustrated costume is being worn; evoke the mood and spirit of the play. Obviously, these demands require that costume designers be able to draw the human body and clothes with ease and confidence. Chapter 22, "Drawing and Rendering," provides an introduction to the subject of figure drawing, but students who are truly interested in pursuing costume design are strongly encouraged to take courses in figure drawing and painting in the appropriate departments of their colleges or universities.

Preliminary Sketches

Frequently the most exciting time in the creation of costume designs, the preliminary-sketch phase, is that time when the first visible results of the creative process appear on paper. These sketches, often rapidly drawn in pen or pencil on the pages of a sketch pad or notebook, are the first tangible results of the synthesis of the costume designer's thoughts, ideas, impressions, and research. Normally not fully completed drawings, they are rough sketches, equivalent to the thumbnail sketches of the scenic designer, showing the silhouette and perhaps a little detail of the costume, as shown in Figure 18.9. Frequently, costume designers will cover one or more pages of the sketch pad with numerous variations of the same design as they try out different ideas and concepts in search of an appropriate and meaningful design.

As these first sketches are distilled toward their final form, the costume designer will show them to the director and other members of the production design team so that they all can be assured that their work is progressing toward the same goal. During these production conferences, it is typical for adjustments to be made to the design concepts and also quite normal for the sketches to be revised. Some designers make multiple photocopies of the pencil sketches so that they can present a variety of color schemes by coloring the photocopies with markers or watercolor pens. The sketch can be scanned into a computer and modified in line, color, or texture as was discussed in Chapter 9. Sometimes a solution is not readily apparent, in which case the designer goes "back to the drawing board" and continues making new design choices and sketches based on the input from the production design team.

Computer drawing and painting programs, as described in Chapter 22, "Drawing and Rendering," can also be used for making costume sketches.

Costume Layout

The costume layout (Figure 18.10) is a group of small figures, simply and clearly drawn, that illustrate the costume designs for a number of characters. Normally sketched in pencil or ink, the costumes may be fully or partially colored with pencils, markers, dyes, or pigment (see Figures 6.24 and 6.25, p. 111, for costume layouts in color). If the cast for the play is small and the costume changes are few, one layout may suffice, but more frequently several layouts will be necessary. Characters are normally grouped in some logical sequence. For a musical, all dancers might be on one layout, while the leads may be grouped on another, and the secondary characters and extras are on yet another. Alternatively, a series of individual rough sketches for each design can be drawn and checked, as a group, by the designer to see if there are any misfits or irregularities. These preliminary sketches, frequently with color swatches from the paint department of a local home improvement center attached, are shown at an early production meeting so the director and other designers can see the direction the costume designer is thinking in terms of both color and style.

Regardless of the method used, the purpose of the costume layout drawings is to provide an overall view of the costume concept for the entire production and to give an indication of how the various costumes will look, or work, together.

FIGURE 18.9 *(continued)*
(C) Hastings in the Colorado Shakespeare
Festival's production of *Richard III*.
Designed by Patrick Holt.

Costume Sketch

Created by the costume designer, the costume sketch or plate is a full-color drawing that should give a strong indication of character, and the costume should look like it is being worn by the specific character for whom it was designed. Drawn with a single character per plate, as shown in Figure 18.11, the sketch should be large and clear enough to provide accurate information about the line and detail of the garment, yet not look cramped on the plate. Generally, a figure between 10 and 15 inches tall will satisfy those demands, although larger or smaller figures can be used as necessary. Swatches of the fabrics to be used in the construction of the costume frequently will be attached to the drawing. Notes about the costume are often penciled into the margins of the plate. If the design is complex, pencil sketches showing other views of the garment may be drawn on the plate or provided on additional sheets. Research materials that indicate construction details frequently provide more accurate information for the cutter/draper than any pencil sketches. If available, photocopies of these research materials are frequently

FIGURE 18.10
(A) Costume layouts for the finale in the American Southwest Theatre Company's production of *Barnum,* designed by Kathi Perkowski Mills. (B) Costume layouts for Crystal, Chiffon, and Ronnette from the Arizona Repertory Theatre's production of *Little Shop of Horrors.* Costume design by Patrick Holt.

FIGURE 18.11
Costume sketch. Esmerelda in the North
Carolina School of the Arts production of
Camino Real. Designed by Patrick Holt.

provided with the costume rendering. Basically, any information that will help construct the costume as the designer envisions it can, and should, be provided with the costume sketch or rendering. Finally, each plate should identify the play, the name of the character, and the scene(s) in which the costume is worn.

The costume sketch or plate is a working drawing that must communicate in a variety of ways with a number of production staff. The costume sketch conveys the designer's design concepts to the director and producer for approval of the design. It is used by the scenic and lighting designers to provide information about the costume color palette and fabrics, and by the costumer and shop staff as the master construction guide.

Specific information on the pragmatic aspects of designing, drawing, and coloring costume designs is given in other chapters. Figure drawing and rendering techniques are covered in Chapter 22, "Drawing and Rendering," while design elements and color are discussed in Chapter 5, "Style, Composition, and Design," and Chapter 6, "Color."

Costume design is a challenging and rewarding craft. To be able to design effectively, you must be imaginative, be able to draw and paint with ease and authority, and have a thorough understanding of fabrics and their characteristics, as well as an encyclopedic knowledge of the history of clothing. While the acquisition of this required body of knowledge may seem daunting, your reward comes from watching the costumes you've designed help actors create beautifully drawn characters in a well-produced production.

The following discussion is adapted from "I Want My Mummy," by David Barbour (Entertainment Design, February 1999, pp. 5–6). Photo by Anita and Steve Shevett.

The Mystery of Irma Vep is a wonderful little mystery in which the entire cast—the tormented heroine Lady Enid Hillcrest, her equally tormented husband Lord Edgar Hillcrest, the manservant (and sometimes werewolf) Nicodemus Underwood, the sinister Cockney maid Jane Twisden, the shadowy Egyptian guide Alcazar, the mummy Pev Amri, and the mysterious Intruder—are all played by two male actors.

The late Charles Ludlam's so-called "penny dreadful" is made up of bits and pieces of *Jane Eyre, Rebecca,* the novels of Wilkie Collins, and the entire output of Universal Studios from 1930 to 1945. The revival opened off-Broadway in 1998 at the Westside Theatre in New York City.

As the convoluted plot of this over-the-top melodrama unfolds, both actors constantly switch characters, costumes, and genders at a moment's notice. Every costume change was a quick change—some of them ultra-quick.

There was another no less daunting challenge for the costume designer, William Ivey Long. Designing the costumes "was a humbling experience," Long said, "because my director (Everett Quinton) was the original costume designer—and he won the coveted Maharam Award for it."

Costume designer Long indicated, "Our intention was to make very beautiful 1895 dresses for rather stocky ladies. The proportions change, but you fit them beautifully."

The period of the show is "1895," Long said, "because that's the most exaggerated moment—the huge leg-of-mutton sleeves and the tiny, tiny little waist—absolutely ignoring the body underneath. It's a very clever choice, because you can disguise masculine shoulders. I got out books of late 19th-century fashion, and Everett and I went through them, page by page. Every time he oohed over a picture, I put a yellow Post-It note on it. When he did an extra ooh-ooh, I put two Post-Its on it. Then I noticed that every

double Post-It was a striped dress; Everett adores vertical stripes."

But where to find the suitably lavish materials on a budget? Fortunately, Long had a binful of drapery and upholstery fabrics from Scalamandre (the Manhattan fabric house) saved up for the ongoing decoration of his Chelsea home, which became the basic stuff of the *Irma Vep* design. For Lady Enid's striped dressing gown, the designer had a moment of invention worthy of Scarlett O'Hara: "There was this curtain in my garden room in my country house in the Berkshires. It's the widest stripe ever known to God and man—I think it's 10 inches wide. I took it down, dusted it off, and there was just enough material for two costumes—we have doubles."

Other costumes required other flights of invention. Jane's maid uniform is, says Long, "a Chanel suit fabric. It's 100% silk, because Stephen DeRosa (one of the actors) is allergic to wool. For Jane, plaid and checks were the words—even the fabric for her apron, which actually was an old curtain that I got at the Haddassah Thrift Store in New Haven. I've had it for 18 years. I thought I was going to make a curtain out of it, but it was just too fabulous."

One of the costumes is "based on three of Charles James' dresses, from the book, *The Genius of Charles James,*" says Long, invoking the name of the famous couture designer.

In the construction of the costumes, Long said, "Everything is flatlined; before you make the pattern, you lay down a layer of cotton twill and then stitch them

together. It stiffens it and makes it sturdier. The sleeves are extra wide, for stuffing your hands through. The peignoirs, made out of nice linen curtains, are unlined, because I wanted them to flow—so they're beautifully finished off on the inside. The costumes were made by Werner Kulovitz at EuroCo, with his associate, Janet Bloor. Jennifer Love made Jane's costumes and Lord Edgar's fabulous herringbone suit."

Topping off Long's costumes are the wigs designed by Zsamira Sol Ronquillo, who also designed the show's makeup. Ronquillo says her biggest challenge is creating wigs that go on and off in seconds. Thus, "They're not secured," she says. "They're made to fit the actors' heads. They have elastic inside and, after a while, they mold themselves. I make my wigs on a 24 head block, which is the biggest available, and, once I'm through with them, they stretch themselves. When they come off the block, they're already molded, so it's much easier to put one on a head. Each one fits like a skullcap underneath the wig."

Ronquillo adds that the wigs are "all nylon. I don't use hairsprays made for human hair." The spray that was used is "made to bond with the nylon fibers, so each wig keeps. Normally, a wig takes one to two days, because of the mixture of hairsprays that I use, to keep the wig rubbery and bouncy. The hairspray takes two hours to dry. After it sets, I add another coat. I build it up in layers, like lasagna."

Chapter 19

Costume Construction

The realization of a costume design—the process of creating a costume that brings to life the visual and evocative intentions contained in the costume designer's sketch—is the responsibility of the costume shop personnel. The specific job responsibilities of the various costume shop positions are detailed in Chapter 1, "Production Organization and Management."

Building a costume isn't simply a matter of going down to the fabric store, buying a pattern and some fabric, and then going home and making a dress. The process of constructing a costume is much more complex. While there are many obvious similarities between costume construction and home sewing, the differences are considerable. The needs of a costume are different and unique. For example, costumes need to be more durable than street clothes. Drama deals with heightened emotions. While maintaining a period silhouette, costumes also must accommodate the range of motion and rigors imposed by the physicalization of those heightened emotions—running, jumping, leaping, falling, rolling, fighting, dancing, and any number of other activities. Street clothes simply aren't intended for that kind of abuse. At its best costume design helps explain the play's characters to the audience by providing visual clues to each character's emotional state, social rank, and financial status. The line, color, and fabric of street clothes more typically reflect prevalent fashion trends. Costume construction is concerned with the processes, materials, and techniques used in making costumes and costume accessories. Specifically, the field requires knowledge of the **hand** of fabrics used in theatrical costumes; techniques of making and adjusting patterns; sewing; fabric painting, dyeing, and distressing; as well as such specialty skills as jewelry-, shoe / boot-, wig-, and armor-making techniques.

 ## Organization of Costume Shops

In the Broadway theatre, all of the technical personnel are hired for a single production. After the producer has approved the designs and the costume construction bids, the costumes are built by a professional costume house. During construction the costume designer is in frequent contact with the shop supervisor to answer any artistic and practical questions about the costumes. When dress rehearsals begin, the costumes are moved into the theatre dressing rooms or costume storage area; their use and maintenance is coordinated by the wardrobe supervisor (also known as the wardrobe master or mistress) and the dressers or **wardrobe crew or staff.** In the professional theatre, the costume running crew personnel belong to a different union than do the construction crew personnel.

The organization of the costume shops of regional professional theatres, university theatre arts departments, and community theatre groups is not significantly

hand: The quality and characteristics of a fabric that can be evaluated or defined by a sense of touch (Anderson 1984, p. 222).

wardrobe crew or staff: Those crew members such as dressers and wardrobe-repair personnel who work during the dress rehearsals and performances.

different from the organization of a professional costume house because both are frequently working on more than one production at the same time.

 ## The Costume Shop

Because of the wide variety of materials used in the construction of costumes, many types of tools and basic equipment are necessary in any well-equipped costume shop.

Basic Equipment

While costume shops come in a variety of shapes and sizes, all must be equipped with certain basic equipment.

Cutting Tables   Used for laying out patterns and fabrics, cutting tables should be 42 to 50 inches wide (to accommodate all but the widest fabrics), about 36 inches high (so people of average height won't have to bend over while working on the table), and 6 to 8 feet long. The tabletop should be covered with cork or a muslin-covered composition board such as Homosote or Upson board. The cork or composition board make it easy to push pins into the surface (to hold patterns and fabrics in place), and both the cork and muslin surface effectively make the surface skid-resistant (so slick material won't slide off). The considerable area under the table can be used for storage.

Dress Forms   Dress forms, also known as dressmaker's dummies, are extremely useful in the costume shop. These rigid forms, which are padded so that material can be pinned directly to them, are used for draping as well as pinning and adjusting cut pattern pieces. Available in standard men's and women's sizes, a well-equipped shop will have a variety of sizes (Figure 19.1). Foam mannequins should be used only if commercial dress forms cannot be afforded. Adjustable home sewing dummies usually are more trouble than they are worth but can be used if other forms are not available.

 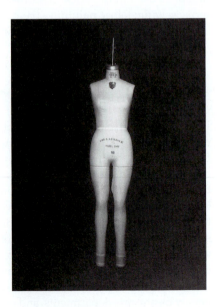

FIGURE 19.1
Two types of dress forms, or dressmaker's dummies. They are available in a variety of sizes for both men and women.

Fabric Storage   Large pieces of scrap fabric should be stored for future use in bins or drawers identified as to fabric type and color. Additional bin/drawer storage should also be available for such accessories as jewelry, millinery, parasols, and so forth. Shelf storage should be available for bolts of fabric such as muslin and rolls of brown paper (both regularly used in pattern-making) and for special-purchase items such as close-out specials and remnants.

Washing Machine and Dryer   Used for cleaning washable costume elements during dress rehearsals and performances, and for dyeing fabrics, large-capacity, heavy-duty machines with a variety of settings are best. It is preferable to have one set for washing and one for dyeing. However, if one set is used for both dyeing and cleaning, both the washer and the dryer must be kept scrupulously clean, including the drain hoses, so that leftover dye won't spot, stain, or discolor clothes that are being washed and dried. Again, it is infinitely preferable to have two sets of machines: one for dyeing and one for washing.

FIGURE 19.2
A jacketed steam kettle, normally used in restaurant kitchens, works very well as a dye vat.

Dye Vat   Commercial dye vats are expensive, but commercial soup kettles, shown in Figure 19.2, cost less and work almost as well. The dye vat should be able to minimally heat 20 to 40 gallons of water to boiling. Budget permitting, it is always advisable to use a commercial dye vat because they are obviously safer than the soup kettle/hot plate arrangement and they will do a better job. Steam-jacketed dye vats are preferable because the heat surrounds the vat rather than just coming from the bottom. The surrounding heat generally results in more uniform dyeing of the fabric.

Hot Plate   A hot plate useful for boiling water for dyeing when the amount of fabric to be dyed does not warrant the use of the dye vat.

FIGURE 19.3
A heavy-duty steam iron. (Courtesy of Sussman.)

Stove   A residential-type stove can be used in place of a hot plate for boiling water. Additionally, the oven can be used for heating certain types of plastics and craft materials frequently used in the construction of costume ornamentation and accessories.

Irons   Heavy-duty industrial steam and dry irons with a multigallon water capacity, as illustrated in Figure 19.3, are preferred because the steam is more concentrated and the irons last longer than those designed for home use. Each iron should be equipped with a metallic or heat-resistant iron rest on which the iron can be placed when heated but not in use. Distilled water should always be used to avoid mineral buildup in the iron and the possibility of inadvertently staining the costumes.

Ironing Boards   Large, heavy-duty industrial ironing boards with sturdy tip-resistant bases are desired. Smaller specialty boards, such as sleeve boards, and needle boards for pressing velours and velvets are highly desirable.

Steamer   Portable steamers (Figure 19.4) generate a stream of steam that is useful for taking wrinkles out of materials that cannot be ironed easily such as velvets, velours, and corduroys. Portable steamers are also useful in millinery for shaping felt.

FIGURE 19.4
Portable steamer. (Courtesy of Sussman.)

Sink   A sink with cold and hot water is essential for cleaning equipment and providing water for a variety of costume shop activities.

FIGURE 19.5
A movable clothes rack.

(A)

(B)

FIGURE 19.6
Sewing machines: (A) heavy-duty machine (courtesy of Husqvarna Sewing Machine Co.),
(B) power machine (courtesy of Chandler Sewing Machine Co.).

Mirror   A full-length three-way mirror is extremely useful during fittings. It allows the costume designer, crew members, and the actor to see the costume from all directions and aids checking fit and finish while the costume is being worn.

Racks   Large-castered, sturdy, movable clothes racks (Figure 19.5) can be moved to convenient locations and used to hang clothes under construction, in storage, or in production.

Tables and Chairs   These are extremely useful for doing hand sewing and other detail work. Stitchers, who frequently sit in these chairs doing handwork for, literally, hours at a time, will be very happy campers if some thought, and funding, is given to providing them with comfortable, ergonomically designed, chairs.

Sewing Machines   A variety of sewing machines are used in the costume shop. Every shop will need at least three or four straight-stitch machines and one zigzag machine. Commercial-grade zigzag machines are normally capable of straight stitching as well, so they can be used for both purposes. The more exotic specialized machines can be added to the shop's inventory as finances permit.

Straight-Stitch Sewing Machines   Heavy-duty, commercial grade (not light-duty homemaker models) straight-stitch machines are used for the majority of the machine sewing in the costume shop.

Zigzag Sewing Machines   There is also a need for one or more heavy-duty machines capable of making zigzag, buttonhole, and similar specialty stitches. These machines, shown in Figure 19.6A, can be used for straight stitching as well.

Walking-Foot Machine   Also called power machines (Figure 19.6B), these high-speed, straight-stitch machines have the power to stitch any fabric from chiffon to leather with equal ease.

Serger   The serger, also called a merrow machine, or overlock (Figure 19.7), sews a seam, cuts both pieces of fabric about one-quarter inch from the seam, and makes an overcast stitch on the edge of both pieces of fabric to prevent it from raveling—all in one operation. Again, as with all shop machines, the heavy-duty, industrial grade models are preferred.

Blind-Stitch Machine   This is a specialty sewing machine used to make hems quickly with an easily removable stitch. The blind stitch is now available on most straight-stitch and zigzag machines.

FIGURE 19.7
A merrow machine.

Sewing Equipment

The following is a nonexhaustive list of basic sewing supplies commonly used in costume construction. Many of these items are illustrated in Figures 19.8 and 19.9. To save money, staple items such as needles, pins, and fasteners should be bought in bulk.

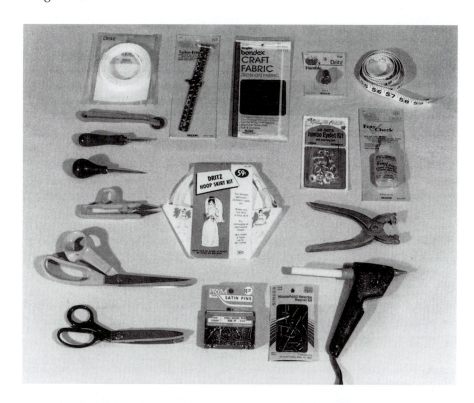

FIGURE 19.8
Hand tools commonly used in costuming.

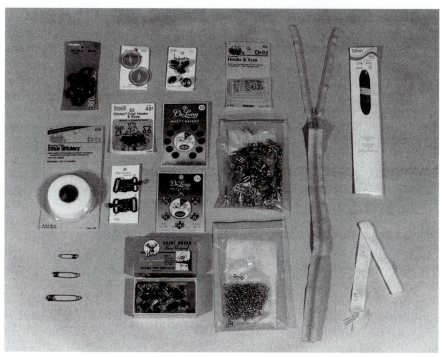

FIGURE 19.9
Fasteners used in costuming.

Measuring Devices   Accurately inscribed 60-inch, plastic tape measures are used for the majority of measuring in the costume shop. Aluminum rules, 48 to 72 inches long, are helpful for laying out large garments such as skirts and capes.

Hand Needles   Long-eyed needles are used because they are the easiest to thread. Sizes 5 to 10 are the most commonly used. Heavy materials require heavy-duty needle types such as carpet and darning, as well as straight and curved upholstery needles.

Machine Needles   Medium-sized universal-pointed needles are used for the bulk of the sewing in the costume shop, although lightweight and heavy needles are used for sheer and heavy-weight fabrics. Ball-pointed needles are used on knit and polyester fabrics, while sharp-pointed universal needles are used on the rest.

Thread   To save money, many costume shops prefer to match the value of thread to costume rather than match color. These shops use only black, white, and gray thread. However, if the audience is particularly close to the stage, they may match the color of the topstitch thread to the fabric. Heavy-duty carpet and button threads are also used for special applications.

Thimbles   A plastic or metal cap for the end of the finger, thimbles are used to protect the finger when pushing a needle through the fabric. Thimbles in a variety of sizes are normally stocked in the costume shop.

Straight Pins   Rustproof pins of medium size are used to pin fabric together and pin patterns to most fabrics. Silk pins are available for use with sheer fabrics. Larger pins are useful when working with heavier fabrics.

Safety Pins   Large sizes are most frequently used, although there is a need for all sizes.

Tracing Wheels   These are toothed wheels used with tracing paper for transferring markings from a pattern to fabric. Available with several "tooth" designs, the regular V-toothed wheel works well in most applications, although the very sharp stiletto-toothed wheel works better with heavy fabrics.

Tracing Paper   A heavy paper with transferable color, it is used with the tracing wheel to transfer markings from patterns to fabric. Several colors are normally stocked so a hue that contrasts with the color of the fabric on which the markings are going to be made can be used.

Tailor's Chalk   Manufactured in chalk and wax bases, it is available in white and colors. It is used for transferring pattern lines and for marking fabric during fittings.

Shears and Scissors   The cost of fabric-cutting shears is directly related to their quality. Buy the best you can afford—as the more expensive ones generally stay sharp longer—and use them for fabric cutting only, as cutting other materials dulls the blades. Bent-handle shears with 8-, 10-, or 12-inch blades are best for fabric cutting. Less-expensive shears and scissors in a variety of sizes should be kept on hand for cutting other things.

Seam Rippers   The small ones seem easiest to use, although this is usually a matter of personal preference.

Single-Edged Razor Blades   These are sometimes unadvisedly used as a substitute for a seam ripper. Murphy's Law would indicate that when so used, the fabric will be cut more often than the thread.

Snaps   All sizes from tiny to huge, in both black and silver, should be kept in stock in the costume shop.

Hooks and Eyes   Again, all sizes from small to large, in both black and silver, should be kept on hand, although the larger sizes — 3 through 5 — seem to be used most often.

Zippers   Although zippers will frequently be bought for a specific costume, a stock of metal dress zippers in both black and white, from 7 to 22 inches long, should be kept on hand. White zippers can be dyed to match the color of the costume.

Velcro   This is used as a substitute for snaps, hooks and eyes, zippers, and buttons, particularly when a very quick change is called for in the play. It is manufactured in 12-yard rolls, and many shops maintain a supply of both black and white Velcro. Although the white doesn't dye particularly well, it can be tinted to approximate the hue of the costume fabric.

Hot Glue Gun   This electrically heated pistol-shaped device melts sticks of glue and dispenses the glue in a narrow line. Arguably the most versatile tool in the costume shop, it can be used as a substitute for sewing in some projects and is almost indispensable in jewelry and ornamentation making, parasol repair, and so forth.

Seam-Binding Tape   This includes any of the twill and/or bias tapes that are sewn to the cut edges of fabric to prevent seams from raveling. It is useful in ¼-, ½-, and 1-inch widths. Finishing seams with seam-binding tape is not necessary if a serger is used.

Fabrics

Fabric is the basic material from which costumes are made, so it is imperative that the costume designer understand fabric materials. Each type and weight of fabric has its own intrinsic characteristics. Some fabrics are crisp and stiff, and when draped they fall in stiff, angular lines. Other fabrics are soft and limp, and when draped they flow into smooth, sensuous curves. The costume designer must select the specific fabric or material that will most appropriately re-create the visual impression conveyed by the costume sketch.

The hand of a fabric — its characteristics that can be determined by a sense of touch — is of prime importance in determining the suitability of a fabric for a particular costume. The hand of any fabric is determined by the type of fiber used in its construction; the weave or structure of the fabric; how, and with what, the fabric is treated; and how it is finished.

Fabric Fibers

Two general types of textile fibers are used in the manufacture of cloth: natural and synthetic. Each type of fiber has its own distinctive characteristics.

breathes: A term that defines a material's ability to transmit heat, air, and water vapor.

blend: A combination of more than one type of fiber, blends are created to take advantage of the best properties of all fibers in the blend.

hang out: In this instance, hang out means that most wrinkles will disappear from the fabric if it is hung up.

hang tag: The small label usually attached to the cardboard core of a bolt of fabric that indicates the percentages of various component fibers.

Natural Fibers

Cotton   Cotton—the white fiber contained in the seed pod, or boll, of the cotton plant—has been used in making cloth for more than 3,000 years. Cotton **breathes** well, readily accepts dyes, and wrinkles easily unless treated. Cotton thread is characterized by ribbonlike twists. Available in a huge number of weaves and **blends,** the varieties of weights, textures, and finishes of cotton fabrics are truly amazing. Mercerization is a caustic soda treatment applied to cotton that causes the fibers to swell and straighten out slightly. Mercerized cotton is more lustrous and dyes better than unmercerized cotton.

Linen   The oldest textile fiber known, linen, derived from the flax plant, is stronger than cotton, has a silky luster, is a good conductor of heat, is lint-free, but does not dye well because of the hardness of the fiber. It washes easily, is hard to stain; shrinks and creases easily.

Silk   Silk is the natural substance from which silkworms spin their cocoons. Silk is expensive, strong, lightweight, pliable; has good elasticity; is lustrous; holds heat; and takes dye extremely well. There are two basic forms of silk filament: cultivated and wild. Wild silk filament is brown and has a rough texture. Cultivated silk filament is smoother, more lustrous, and grayish-yellow. There are two ways of collecting the filament from the cocoon—reeling and spinning—and each method affects the appearance of the silk. Reeling yields longer filaments with less twisting than spinning does, resulting in a stronger, more lustrous filament.

Wool   One of the oldest fibers used in textiles, wool is made from the fleece of sheep. There are two primary types of woolen yarns: woolen and worsted. Woolen yarns are loosely twisted, soft, and weak with a fuzzy, textured surface. Worsteds are more tightly twisted and stronger and have a smoother surface. Worsteds tend to breathe well, whereas the softer surface of woolen yarn traps air, making it a good insulator. Wool readily absorbs moisture and dyes. However, the boiling water used with most dyes can cause substantial shrinkage as well as texture changes. Woolen and worsted fabrics don't readily wrinkle, and most wrinkles **hang out** easily. Wool fabrics can be shaped with steam, which makes them ideal for making form-tailored garments.

Synthetic Fibers   Synthetic fibers are chemical compounds that are changed into hardened filaments by a variety of patented processes. Unless treated further, these fibers have a tendency to be slick, smooth, and dense. In general, synthetic fibers do not absorb moisture or breathe as well as natural fibers, so they tend to trap body heat inside the costume. On the positive side, most synthetic fabrics have an inherent resistance to wrinkling and are quite durable.

Two or more synthetic and/or natural fibers are often blended to form a fabric that will take advantage of the best attributes of each while deemphasizing their negative aspects. These blended fabrics are usually wrinkle-resistant and durable.

The care of any fabric, as well as its fiber content, must by law be indicated on the **hang tag** of the bolt of fabric. Synthetic fabrics that have approximately 40 to 50 percent natural-fiber content (cotton, linen, wool, and so forth) generally breathe well. Fabrics that are 100 percent synthetic generally do not breathe well. The costume designer and the costumer should be acquainted with the care of any fabric used in a stage costume, since those garments will normally need to be cleaned or washed and pressed frequently during the run of the production.

Acrylic   Acrylics are made from compounds based on coal, petroleum, and other materials. The acrylic fiber is soft and lightweight. Commercially, acrylics are frequently made into sweaters, blankets, and socks. Factory dyes are colorfast, but the material does not dye well in the costume shop. It is wrinkle-resistant, holds its shape well, and needs little if any ironing. Common trade names include Acrilan, Orlon, and Creslan.

Nylon   A slurry of air, water, and coal is heated and extruded through spinnerettes to produce the continuous-filament fiber known as nylon. Nylon is light, strong, extremely elastic, and resistant to abrasion. Wrinkles easily fall out of fabrics made from nylon. Nylon fiber doesn't conduct heat well or absorb moisture, so the fabric's heat-transmission characteristics depend on the weave: Smooth, tight weaves trap heat; loose, open weaves do not. Some nylon fabrics dye well, others do not. Common trade names include Antron, Capriolan, and Qiana.

Polyester   Another petroleum-based product, polyester fibers are highly resistant to wrinkling, are very strong, are commercially colorfast and reasonably stain-resistant, but they do not dye well in the costume shop. Polyester fibers are made into many types of light-, medium-, and heavyweight fabrics and, blended with cotton, create a fabric with excellent wash and wear characteristics and breathability. Trade names include Dacron, Kodel, and Quintess.

Rayon   Rayon was one of the first synthetic fabrics. It is made from regenerated cellulose, a viscous solution of **cotton linters** and wood pulp that is extruded through spinnerettes to form a continuous fiber. Rayon dyes easily, has excellent colorfastness, works well when blended with other fibers, and is very absorbent. Similar in many characteristics and weaves to silk, rayon can frequently be used as a low-cost alternative to silk. Common trade names include Avril, Celanese, Fibro, and Zantrel.

cotton linters: The short hairs covering the cotton seed.

Acetate   Similarly to rayon, chemicals are added to the regenerated cellulose solution to create cellulose acetate before the fibers are extruded. Acetates have little strength, must be ironed with low heat, don't hold a crease well, but have good draping characteristics and wrinkle resistance. Triacetates solve the heat-toleration and crease-retention problems associated with acetates while retaining their better qualities.

Weaves

Numerous types of weaves are used in making fabrics, and each type produces specific textural and visual effects. The fiber content of the threads woven into the fabric greatly affect the appearance and hand of the resultant material.

The threads running the length of the fabric are called the warp, and the threads running the width of the fabric are called the woof, fill, or weft. Some common ways that those threads are configured are shown in the weave patterns illustrated in Figure 19.10. Each pattern produces fabric with specific characteristics.

Plain Weave   In the plain weave, the fill passes over one warp thread and under the next. In the next row this pattern is alternated, as illustrated in Figure 19.10A. The visual effect of a plain weave is a simple, uncomplicated fabric. Variations of the plain weave include the ribbed weave, in which the fill yarn is much bulkier than the warp.

Basket Weave   In the basket weave, a variation of the plain weave, two or more fill yarns are passed over an equal number of warp yarns, as shown in Figure 19.10B. Oxford cloth is an example of a basket weave. Variations of the basket weave are numerous.

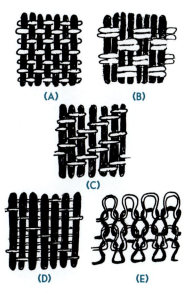

FIGURE 19.10
Types of weave patterns: (A) plain weave, (B) basket weave, (C) twill weave, (D) satin weave, and (E) plain knit.

wale: Visible, usually narrow, ridges in the surface of a fabric caused by a variation in the weaving pattern.

Twill Weave   The most durable of all weaves, twill is created when the fill yarn is interlaced with the warp to create diagonal ridges in the fabric, as shown in Figure 19.10C. Depending on the design of the weave, the **wales** may run diagonally from left to right, right to left, or both ways. Herringbone, in which the direction of the diagonal wales changes directions every few rows, is a common variation of the twill weave.

Satin Weave   The satin weave produces a smooth, very rich-looking fabric. This lustrous look is achieved by passing warp threads over a specific number of fill yarns, passing under one, then repeating the pattern (Figure 19.10D). The number of skipped threads, or floats, varies between four and twelve but remains constant for any particular piece of fabric. The lustrous sheen of satin has a definite direction, and patterns need to be cut keeping the direction of the fabric in mind.

Pile Weave   Lustrous velvets and velours have a plush texture and appearance that is extremely rich. The fabric is created by weaving an extra warp or fill yarn between the warp or fill of the base material. This extra yarn is looped higher than the base material and may, or may not, be cut. Velvets, velours, terrys, plush, velveteens, and corduroys are all variations of the pile weave, and they all have directional characteristics (like satin), so care must be taken to match the direction when cutting the fabric.

Plain Knit   Technically not a woven fabric, knits are constructed from a series of interlocking loops, and each row of loops is dependent for its support on the rows of loops below and above it, as shown in Figure 19.10E. There are many types of knits, and they are all very elastic and porous.

Fabrics and Nonfabric Materials Used in Costume Construction

Fabrics

A number of fabrics are used in the construction of stage costumes (and street clothes, for that matter). This list is not exhaustive, but it does provide examples of the types of fabrics typically used in costume construction.

Brocade   Available in light, medium, and heavy weights, brocade has a slightly raised pattern and is made from high-luster yarn that is woven into the matte finish of the background cloth. These patterns are reversed on the back side of the fabric. Usually made from rayon or silk, the fabric normally has a rich, reflective, multitextured surface.

Buckram   An open-weave material, buckram is a stiff fabric that has been sized with a heavy glue. Available in light, medium, and heavy weights, buckram is used as a foundation for millinery and other costume elements needing stiffness. Buckram can be shaped and molded because it becomes limp when dampened but regains its stiffness when dry.

Canvas   Normally a cotton or cotton-synthetic blend, canvas is a heavy, plain-weave fabric used as lining material or other applications where its semistiff, extremely durable characteristics might prove helpful. Duck and sailcloth are lighter-weight versions.

PRODUCTION INSIGHTS

Fabric Finishes

Irrespective of the type or fiber content of a fabric, most textiles are treated with either a functional or a decorative finish or with both.

Functional Finishes

Functional finishes are normally applied to the fabrics before they leave the mill:

1. Permanent-press processes enable permanent creases to be put into trousers and other garments while all but eliminating wrinkles from the finished fabric and clothes.

2. Mercerization is a chemical process that adds strength and shine to cotton thread.

3. Flameproofing is a chemical treatment of cloth that prevents it from supporting flames. It does not, however, prevent the cloth from charring and smoldering.

4. Preshrunken cloth, particularly cotton, has been bathed in water.

5. Cloth can be impregnated with antibacterial agents to reduce the severity of stains from perspiration and other natural substances.

Decorative Finishes

Decorative finishes alter the appearance of the fabric. These treatments include bleaching, dyeing, printing, and texturing. Although the vast majority of these treatments are applied to fabrics before they leave the mill, some decorative treatments, such as dyeing and fabric painting, are frequently performed in the costume shop.

Chiffon Chiffon is a sheer, usually translucent, cloth frequently made from rayon or silk with soft, diaphanous draping qualities.

Corduroy A medium to heavy material, most frequently made from cotton or cotton-synthetic blends, corduroy has raised ridges (wales). The material is fairly stiff and doesn't drape well. Waleless and pinwale (very narrow) corduroy can be used as low-cost substitutes for velvet and velour although they don't have the softer draping qualities of those fabrics.

Crepe This is a thin, crinkle-finished fabric with a low luster and soft draping qualities. Rayon, silk, and fine cotton crepes are most frequently used for lingerie, blouses, and flowing gowns.

Crinoline This tight-weave material has permanent sizing to provide stiffness.

Denim A fairly coarse twill weave of cotton or cotton-synthetic blend, this slightly stiff fabric is primarily used for blue jeans and similar working-class clothes.

Drill Similar to denim but of smoother surface and more luster, drill is a twill weave of cotton or cotton-synthetic blends.

Felt Felt is a woolen, cotton, or rayon material made from fibers that have been matted or pressed together under pressure. Shaping is best accomplished with wool felt. When steamed it becomes limp and can be shaped and formed. It will retain the molded shape when dry. Felt is primarily used for hats and trimmings.

Flannel A lightweight material woven with soft-finish threads of wool, wool blend, or cotton, flannel is normally used for men's and women's suits, trousers, and shirts.

Gabardine   This is a light-, medium-, or heavy-weight, hard-surfaced twill-weave material made from wool, cotton, synthetics, or blends. It is used for inexpensive suits and outerwear.

Jersey   A knit fabric with excellent draping qualities, jersey is manufactured in a variety of fibers—wool, cotton, rayon, and blends—in a full range of weights.

Linen   Its irregular yarns of linen and linen-synthetic blends give the fabric a nubby, soft-luster surface. It is primarily used for tropical suits and sportswear.

Muslin   A plain-weave durable cotton with moderate sizing, unbleached muslin is commonly used as a lining material. It is also used for making patterns.

Net   Net is a stiff, very-open-weave material commonly made from cotton, rayon, or nylon. Nylon net is the most stiff and is used where light, airy stiffening—ballet skirts, stiff veils—is desired.

Pellon   This is the brand name of a nonwoven stiffening material. Similar to felt in manufacturing method, Pellon is used as a stiffening interfacing material and in petticoats. Pellon does not soften when dampened and will retain its stiffness through many cleanings.

Sateen   A satin-weave cotton fabric of low luster, sateen is primarily used as a lining material.

Satin   This high-luster, satin-weave fabric is made from silk, rayon, and other synthetics. Available in a variety of weights and subcategories, satin is used for a variety of purposes from evening wear to draperies.

Taffeta   This plain-weave, smooth-surfaced, high-luster fabric is normally made of rayon but is occasionally available in silk. *Moire taffeta* has a nonrepetitive pattern pressed into the surface of the cloth that creates an interesting surface treatment. It is used extensively in eighteenth- and nineteenth-century clothes.

Velour   A pile-weave fabric normally made of cotton or cotton–nylon blends, velour has a soft, reflective quality. Heavyweight velour is normally used for upholstery and drapes, while lightweight velour is used for sportswear.

Velvet   Velvet is a pile-weave fabric normally made of rayon or nylon, also available in silk. It drapes sensuously and has rich, light-reflective characteristics. Available in a variety of weights, the heavier are used for capes, drapes, and upholstery, while the lighter weights are typically used for evening wear.

Nonfabric Materials

A variety of materials other than cloth are used in costume construction. Some of these materials are substituted for fabric, and others are used to bind various costume materials together. This list is neither exhaustive nor exclusive. Almost any material can be, and has been, used to make costumes. In addition to the cloth and fabric materials that form the basis of most costumes, any number of decorative materials can be appliquéd to the fabric to enhance its appearance. The only limitations on appropriateness are commonsense rules of safety for the actors and those around them, and the suitability of the material to the design concept for that particular costume.

Leather   Leather is often used for hats, shoes, and certain period pieces such as vests, armor, and belts. In the United States most leather is treated cowhide, although leather can be made from the hide of almost any animal. Leather has a smooth side and a rough side. The side that is used by the costumer is solely dependent on the particular look that is wanted. Most leather can be dyed with special leather dyes and sprays. It can be machine-stitched using a heavy-duty sewing machine equipped with a leather needle. It can also be hand-stitched. The surface of the leather can be tooled, and a variety of tools (awls, leather punches) can be used to punch holes in the material.

Leather can be formed into curves for such items as helmets and breastplates by steaming it and forming it to an appropriately shaped mold. Leather can be rather heavy, is extremely durable, and holds heat well. Complete costumes constructed of leather can become very warm and uncomfortable.

Plastic Coatings   Sculptural Arts Coatings of Greensboro, North Carolina, produces a line of water-base, low-emissivity craft products, paints, and finishes that can be used for myriad projects in the costume as well as scenic and prop shops.

Helmets can be made with Sculptor Coat by coating a head form with a release agent (Vaseline), then forming a felt foundation over the head form. The felt is coated with a mixture of Sculptor Coat, plaster, and water. When the surface is dry, it can be sanded or worked with power tools (angle grinder, sander) and finished to a high metallic sheen using acrylic paint and plastic varnish as shown in Figure 19.11A. Figure 19.11B shows millinery that has been glued together using Sculptor Coat. Forms for other objects can be made from just about anything—Styrofoam, Ethafoam, foam rubber, metal, wood, hard plastics. A cheesecloth covering, applied with a layer of Sculptor Coat, will increase the strength of the form. Filling the texture of the underlying fabric will probably take an additional coating or two of Sculptor Coat. Textural additives such as white paper towels, sand, dirt—anything that will help you achieve the surface look you envision—can be built up on the form by applying the material after wetting it with Sculptor Coat, by working it into the still-wet surface, or by mixing it with the Sculptor Coat before applying it. Basically, any type of material—rigid or flexible—can be bonded together and finished with the products in this line and still retain the structural qualities of the original material. Similar materials are produced by other manufacturers such as Rosco. See the discussion of "texturing" in Chapter 12, "Scenic Painting."

Plaster Bandage   Plaster-impregnated gauze can be used to make built-up forms such as masks and small armor pieces. Available from surgical supply houses and some drugstores, it is the material that doctors use to make casts. It is water-soluble, creates no toxic or noxious fumes, and can be formed easily. After the material has dried, it can be sanded and painted with both water- and oil- or lacquer-base paints.

Thermoplastics   These are stiff plastics that soften in hot water and can be molded before they cool and stiffen. They are available in pellet, mesh, and fabric forms. They can be molded on the face and body for masks and armor, and finished with most paints.

Fiberglass   As we have seen, fiberglass is an extremely strong material formed of two parts: glass fibers in the form of mat or woven cloth and a resin coat that cures into a hard plastic. It is used for constructing armor and helmets, while the resin can be used by itself in the production of jewelry. More information about fiberglass can be found in Chapter 13. Rose Brand Fabric has introduced

FIGURE 19.11
Uses of Sculptor Coat. (A) Helmet construction. See text for details. (B) Sculptor Coat was used as an adhesive to glue the elements of this hat together.

(A)

(B)

FIGURE 19.12
Metal is frequently used in the fabrication of decorative items such as appliqués and buckles.

Aqua-Resin, a water-base, two-part resin that can be substituted for the polyester or epoxy resin normally used in fiberglass construction.

Metal   Aluminum, copper, and brass appliqués and jewelry are often used in the construction of various accessories for gowns, armor, buckles, and similar applications. Metal appliqués (Figure 19.12) can usually be found in fabric stores, while thin sheet metal can be found in craft shops. The sheet metal can be formed using standard woodworking tools, and the copper and brass sheets can be soldered. All three metals can be fastened with pop rivets or glued with appropriate cyanoacrylate cements such as Super Glue or Krazy Glue. (See Chapter 10 for more information on adhesives.)

 Garment Construction

While there are certainly many similarities between clothing construction in the fashion industry and costuming, there is one substantial difference. The goal in garment industry is to make multiple copies, in a number of different sizes, of a single design. That single design is also intended to fit a variety of body types. The goal in costume construction is much more specific—to make one-of-a-kind garments for one specific body. Additionally, the design of the costume must help reveal the personality of the character for whom it was created.

Patterns

Arguably, the most important step in the realization of a costume is the creation of the pattern from which the costume will be constructed. "The three main goals of drafting and/or draping a costume pattern are (1) to manipulate a flat piece of cloth by cutting and shaping so it conforms to a specific three-dimensional body, while (2), at the same time, accurately translating a sketch prepared by a costume designer into reality, and (3) creating a costume that serves all the various needs of the script, the actor, and the production."[1]

There are two main methods of patterning: flat patterning (drafting) and draping. This section will provide a brief explanation of both. Neither flat patterning nor draping should be considered as a preferred method of patterning. Both have advantages, and both should be learned. Some shapes are more easily constructed by draping than flat patterning. Tailored or form-fitting garments, such as men's suits and uniforms, are generally better suited to flat-pattern methods. But it is possible to create tailored garments by draping. The patterning method used in any particular situation is determined by the working preferences of the cutter/draper.

Flat Patterning   One of the primary jobs of the cutter is to create the flat patterns from which costumes are frequently made. Pattern making is both an art and a craft. So it is reasonable to assume that there is really no single "correct way" to make a pattern. Every cutter develops personal methods and techniques of working. But there is a general process that most cutters follow when creating a flat pattern, and that process will be explained here. But remember that this method is neither "right" nor "correct." It is simply one way of going about the process of making a flat pattern.

Since a flat pattern is created for one particular actor, we need to get a set of very specific measurements for that actor. Those measurements are detailed in the measurement chart shown in Figure 19.13. From those measurements the cutter develops a basic pattern. The basic pattern, also called a body block or block, is laid out on wide brown wrapping or butcher paper. This isn't the final pattern for the costume because it doesn't provide any period details. It is simply a generic pattern designed to fit cloth to a particular actor's body. After the block is drawn on paper, it is transferred to medium-weight muslin, cut out, and stitched together. The actor then comes into the costume shop for a fitting (Figure 19.14); or, if the actor is unavailable, the muslin mockup is fit to a tailor's dummy with measurements that very nearly approximate those of the actor, and any necessary adjustments are made. These adjustments are normally transferred back to the paper pattern. This provides a finished basic pattern that fits the actor's body. This is the pattern from which the costume pattern is developed.

The costume pattern is developed by modifying the block to exhibit the design characteristics of a particular style or period as interpreted by the costume designer. For example, the sleeve block provides the pattern for a basic sleeve that fits the actor and allows full range of arm motion. But it doesn't say anything about period or style. By studying the costume designer's sketch, and from conversations with the designer, the cutter will know what the sleeve, and the rest of the costume is supposed to look like, including its period and style. There are many excellent books that contain historical costume patterns. As indicated in Chapter 18, "Costume Design," there are also numerous other sources that the costume designer consults to develop an understanding of the look of clothes from a given period and place. The cutter gleans information from these sources as well. But the cutter's research focuses more on how to construct the costume than on its design. Using information from all of these sources, the cutter modifies the sleeve block to create a pattern that both fits the actor and realizes the

---

[1] Rosemary Ingham and Liz Covey, *The Costume Technician's Handbook,* 3rd ed. (Portsmouth, N.H.: Heinemann, 2003), p. 97.

FIGURE 19.13
Costume-measurement chart.

MEASUREMENT CHART

Name: _____ Height: _____ Weight: _____

Bra Size: _____ Dress Size: _____ Tights/Pantyhose: _____ Leotard: _____

Men's Shirt: _____ Trousers: _____ Men's Suit: _____ Shoe: _____

Chest/Bust	Ribcage (Underbust)	Head (Circ)	Head (Temple to temple, around back of head)	Head (Forehead to nape)	Head (Ear to ear; over head)
CF Neck to waist	F Shoulder to waist	Center of shoulder to bust point	Bust point to bust point	Underbust to waist	Neck at base Neck at midpoint
F Chest width (armseye to armseye)	X Both shoulders (Front)	CB Neck to waist	B Shoulder to waist	B Chest width (X shoulder blades)	X Both shoulders (Back)
Arm length to wrist	Arm length to elbow	Men's sleeve (CB neck to wrist)	Left shoulder	Right shoulder	
Armseye	Bicep	Elbow	Wrist	Overhand	
Waist	Hips	Thigh	Knee	Below knee	Calf
Waist to hip (on side)	Waist to above knee	Waist to below knee	Waist to ankle	Waist to floor	Outseam
CB Neck to floor	CF Neck to floor	Side neck to floor	CB Waist to floor	CF Waist to floor	Inseam
Crotch depth (Seated)	Crotch or 1/2 girth	Full girth (for leotards)			
Glasses?	Contacts?	Pierced ears?	Tattoos?	Other Notes	

designer's intent. This process is repeated until the cutter has a complete pattern for the entire costume.

Using the initial costume pattern, the costume technicians normally make a muslin mockup of the costume and fit it to the actor. Any modifications to the mockup are transferred to the paper pattern. While it is possible to use the adjusted muslin mockup as a pattern for cutting the final costume material, this normally isn't done because the muslin can be stretched or pulled out of shape. Because the paper doesn't distort, it provides a much more accurate pattern.

Draping Draping is the process of pinning fabric directly to a tailor's form and creating pattern pieces or a garment by manipulating the fabric until the desired look is achieved. Draping requires that you have a tailor's form whose dimensions closely match those of the actor for whom the costume is being made. While draping can be used to create tailored clothes, it is more frequently used to create untailored, three-dimensional elements such as bustles.

Depending on the particular production circumstances, drapers will either make a pattern of the object, or they will skip the pattern step and simply use

FIGURE 19.14
A costume fitting.

the costume material to create the draped design. The choice isn't always made to save time. The way a particular fabric drapes is dependent on its physical characteristics—the type of weave, its tightness or looseness, the weight and stiffness of the fabric, and so forth. If the draper is going to make a pattern, the pattern material needs to closely approximate the physical characteristics of the "final" material so that it will hang and drape like the final material. You don't want to use a lightweight, soft material to drape a pattern that's going to be finalized in a heavy brocade simply because the two fabrics don't hang or drape the same way.

Pattern-Drafting Software   There are numerous programs available for flat pattern drafting, but none, as of this writing, that are useful for draping. The advantages of these flat-pattern programs over hand-drafting are similar to those listed for other drafting programs—faster layout, greater accuracy, much faster revisions, and data transfer. The primary disadvantage is also the same—a very steep initial learning curve. To be useful to a cutter/draper, a pattern-drafting program must allow the operator to either modify the program's existing patterns and/or create original patterns. One program, Custom Pattern Maker, allows the operator to draft original patterns on a body block using the same processes that were described above. It also allows the operator to alter the measurements of any existing pattern. Because of their relatively large size, patterns are normally printed out using a plotter.

 ## Special-Effects Treatment of Fabrics

Fabric Dyeing

Before beginning the discussion on dyes and dyeing it really is necessary to consider the safety issues surrounding this subject. Dyes are inherently dangerous. Powdered dyes can be inhaled. So can the vapors from dyes that are in solution.

setting: To help lock the dye into the fiber of the fabric; to reduce or prevent the dye from being rubbed off the fabric.

unified aniline dye: A coal-tar–derivative dye formulated to work on both animal- and plant-derivative fibers.

Companies that manufacture dyes, or import them for sale in the United States, are required to have MSDSs for each color of every dye they make or sell. That may seem excessive. It isn't. Why? Different chemical compounds are used to create different dye colors. And the level of toxicity of a specific dye depends entirely on the chemicals used to make it. Unfortunately, companies who buy in bulk and then repackage dyes into smaller quantities for sale to the general public, and costume shops, aren't required to provide the buyer with the MSDSs for these materials. But be persistent. Find out who the bulk manufacturer was. Contact the company. Try an online search. The bottom line in the safety issue is you. Be smart with your own safety. Don't use dyes that you don't know how to handle safely. Some of them are benign, some are mildly hazardous, and some are carcinogenic. And you can't tell which is which without the safety material.

Fabric must be washed and rinsed before it is dyed. If the material was heavily sized, it should be soaked in a light soda ash solution before it is washed. Dyes go into solution best when initially mixed with boiling water. The working temperature of the dye solution depends on the type of dye and material being dyed. Tightly woven fabrics do not dye as well as those with looser weaves. The colorfast characteristics of any dyed fabric are enhanced if the material is thoroughly rinsed after it has been dyed. (Please review the Safety Tip below.)

Types of Dyes There are a large number of fabric dyes that can be used in the costume shop. Since no single dye works equally well on all types of fabrics, this section will discuss the characteristics of several common dyes. The description of the effects and characteristics of these dyes is necessarily vague simply because the exact impact that a particular dye will have on a specific fabric depends on many variables — the saturation and heat of the dye solution; the amount of time the material is left in the dye vat; the type and amount of **setting** agent in the dye; the type, blend, and finish of the fabric; and so forth.

Union Dyes Union dyes contain several types of dyes and are designed to be moderately effective on many fabric types. Union dyes are exemplified by household dyes such as Rit or Tintex that are available in most fabric stores. If used with boiling water, union dyes will work well on most natural-fiber fabrics and rayon if you are trying to achieve a tint or medium shade. Slightly more intense colors can be achieved by using more dye than is called for in the instructions, but it is almost impossible to achieve a deep shade of full saturation using union dyes. When dyeing cotton or linen, you can enhance the setting of the dye by adding salt to the solution. When dyeing wool or silk, add vinegar to the dye. Union dyes are not particularly effective on synthetic materials other than rayon. To maintain color intensity, wash union-dyed materials in cold water or have them dry cleaned.

Aniline Dyes All-purpose or **unified aniline dyes,** also known as acid dyes, create strong colors of light to full saturation on natural-fiber fabrics and a few syn-

Safety Tip Most of the dyes used in the costume shop recommend heating the dye anywhere from 100°F to boiling. Heated dye solutions give off vapors that are hazardous to some degree. In addition to reading the directions of the dye containers, also read the MSDSs for the specific dyes that are being used. Be sure to follow the recommendations for safe handling of wet and dry dyes, protective clothing and eyewear, respirators, ventilation, and related safety issues.

thetics. Either salt or vinegar (½ cup per teaspoon of dry dye) is used in the dye solution as a setting agent. A little alcohol is added to the dry dye to form a paste, then boiling water is added to the paste. In general, 1 teaspoon of dry dye will make 1 quart of full-strength dye, although the ratio of the mixture can be varied.

Disperse Dyes   Designed for use with synthetics like acetate, nylon, and polyester, disperse dyes have intense color and are quite colorfast if the dye solution is almost boiling when the fabric is dyed. A little liquid detergent in the dye solution helps the dye penetrate the fabric fibers.

Fiber-Reactive Dyes   These dyes are arguably the most useful for fabric painting of natural-fiber fabrics because they produce intense, colorfast colors when the temperature of the dye bath is lukewarm or cool. Salt is used as the setting agent.

Safety Tip

Spray Painting

Any type of spray painting—aerosol spray cans, air brushes, air or airless spray guns—releases atomized paint or dye into the air. This constitutes a potentially serious health hazard.

Always spray paint in an environment where the paint or dye mist is being controlled. An exhaust ventilation system—a location where the spray mist is being evacuated and replaced with clean air—offers the best spray mist control. A paint booth—a walk-in, enclosed environment that exhausts contaminated air, filters it before releasing it into the environment, and replaces the contaminated air with fresh air—provides the most effective protection. A paint station is basically a desktop version of a paint booth with one wall removed. A typical paint station is enclosed on top, bottom, and three sides, with a powered exhaust vent usually located in the top. Fresh air is drawn into the unit from the open side, which is also where you stand to work. The final type of exhaust ventilation system is location with an exhaust hood above a designated workspace. Because this system is entirely open it is critical that the fan be powerful enough to not only suck in the contaminated air, but also prevent any overspray from escaping the updraft.

A dilution ventilation system, rather than exhausting contaminated air, mixes fresh air with the contaminated air to dilute the level of contaminants to acceptable levels. Less effective than the exhaust ventilation system, this type of system should be used only for diluting the vapors of nontoxic materials. Again, consult the MSDS for the material you're working with to see if a dilution ventilation system is even recommended. If it isn't, don't use the material in that environment.

Weather permitting, you can also take the work outside. There are two dangers inherent to working outside: (1) you may pollute the environment; (2) if there's no breeze, the spray may simply hang in the air as it would indoors with no ventilation. To counter that challenge, just set up a fan to blow across the work area. If a breeze is blowing, stand on the "up wind" side of the work so the spray isn't blown onto you.

Regardless of the type of ventilation system you use, be sure to wear the appropriate type of respirator for the materials with which you're working. Respirators filter out a substantial level of contaminants. But not every respirator filters out every type of contaminant. Filters are "contaminant specific." Consult the MSDSs for the dyes or paints you're working with and wear the recommended respirator, with the recommended filter, and wear the recommended safety apparel. If an appropriate respirator or filter can't be found, *do not do the work until one is found.*

As with so much in safety-related issues, be sure to apply a heavy dose of common sense when working with any hazardous materials. If you're spraying *anything,* you don't want to inhale it, and you don't want the spray to land on your skin. So wear recommended type of respirator/filter and protective clothing, and work only in an environment that has a recommended, and functioning, ventilation system.

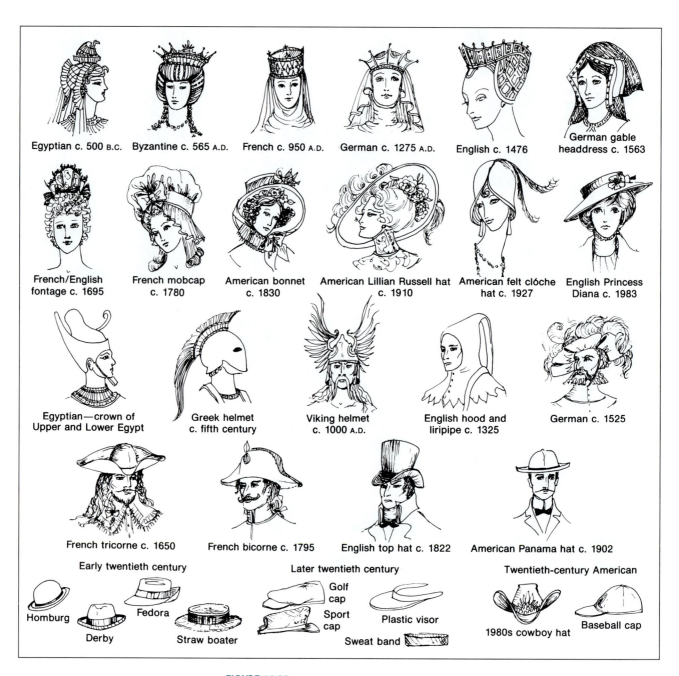

Egyptian c. 500 B.C.   Byzantine c. 565 A.D.   French c. 950 A.D.   German c. 1275 A.D.   English c. 1476   German gable headdress c. 1563

French/English fontage c. 1695   French mobcap c. 1780   American bonnet c. 1830   American Lillian Russell hat c. 1910   American felt clóche hat c. 1927   English Princess Diana c. 1983

Egyptian—crown of Upper and Lower Egypt   Greek helmet c. fifth century   Viking helmet c. 1000 A.D.   English hood and liripipe c. 1325   German c. 1525

French tricorne c. 1650   French bicorne c. 1795   English top hat c. 1822   American Panama hat c. 1902

Early twentieth century   Later twentieth century   Twentieth-century American

Homburg   Fedora   Golf cap   Sport cap   Plastic visor   1980s cowboy hat   Baseball cap

Derby   Straw boater   Sweat band

FIGURE 19.22
A progression of styles in hats, headdresses, and crowns. Drawings by Peggy Kellner.

FIGURE 19.23
A hat mold.

There are endless possibilities for what can be placed on an actor's head. The range is from a simple leather-thong headband to an amazingly complex Las Vegas showgirl headdress complete with flashing lights. When creating large and/or outlandish hats and headdresses a great deal of consideration must be given to its structural stability, centering, and support.

A number of excellent source books, including books that provide patterns for various period headdresses, are listed in the Selected References. Almost any period hat can be constructed using these patterns and the materials available from a well-supplied fabric shop, mail-order millinery store, or Internet supplier.

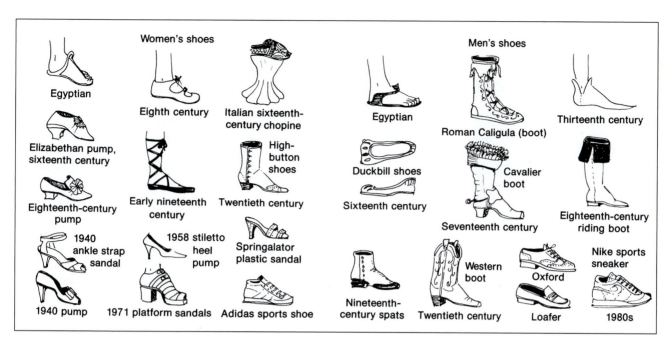

FIGURE 19.24
A progression of period shoe styles.
Drawings by Peggy Kellner.

Footwear

Just as many costumes would not be complete without a wig or a hat, no costume is complete without the appropriate footwear. Examples of shoes from various periods are shown in Figure 19.24.

Although the ideal solution to this challenge is to contract with a cobbler or a shoe company to custom-build footwear of an appropriate style and design, this prohibitively expensive solution is beyond the fiscal means of the vast majority of production companies. Instead, many producing organizations adapt modern shoes by adding elements more appropriate to the desired period. When adapting a modern shoe to a period look, select one in which the toe and heel shape most closely resemble the appearance of the intended style.

Soft- and hard-soled house slippers, in both cloth and leather, with and without heels, are standard items in many costume shops. By dyeing the leather or fabric and adding appropriate accessories such as buckles or bows, you can turn the ubiquitous house slipper into footwear appropriate for many male and female fashion periods. Period-specific boots can frequently be made by sewing a leather boot top to a leather slipper.

Jewelry

A variety of techniques can be used to create jewelry and ornamentation such as buckles, crowns, brooches, and so forth. When making these objects, it is important to adhere to the shape, size, and materials of historical antecedents, but how it will look from the back of the house is more important. "Simplicity and the right amount of exaggeration are the key to good stage jewelry and ornament."[2]

The basic shape of the object to be created can be formed out of wood, metal, Celastic,[3] thermoplastic, or any other material appropriate to the object being built.

[2] Douglas A. Russell, *Stage Costume Design,* 2nd ed. (Englewood Cliffs, N.J.: Prentice-Hall, 1985), p. 157.

[3] The solvents for Celastic are acetone and methyl ethyl ketone. Both are potentially dangerous. Before working with Celastic, be sure to read the MSDS (which can be found online), and work in a properly ventilated area with proper safety gloves, clothing, and respirator.

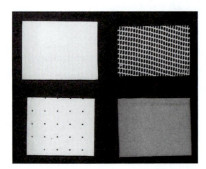

Bits of cording, lace, or other objects can be glued on to add texture. The object is painted flat black, brown, or deep blue, and the raised areas dry-brushed with metallic paints such as silver or gold to add luster and highlights. If a deep, high-sheen surface is required, catalyzed fiberglass resin can be used for the dark base coat. The resin can be colored with dry scenic pigments, aniline dyes, and bronzing powders. Rhinestones or colored glass "jewels" can be hot-glued onto the finished form. (Chapter 13, "Stage Properties," discusses a number of craft processes that are useful in the construction of jewelry and other costume accessories.)

Every costume shop should have a collection of "junk jewelry." These rings, brooches, necklaces, and similar pieces, which almost always look fake and gaudy up close, project a rich, elegant look from the stage.

Armor

Body armor such as breastplates and helmets are frequently made from Fabric Form, fiberglass, or several types of thermoplastics. (See Chapters 10 and 13 for discussions of fiberglass, thermoplastics, and vacuum-forming techniques.)

Fiberglass armor is frequently formed by building up the basic shape on a clay-covered armature, covering the mold with aluminum foil, and applying the material to the form to create the basic rigid shell. Decoration is then applied by hand. When casting items that are fairly detailed and need to be uniform in appearance—military helmets, breastplates, leg shields, and so on—a rigid plaster-of-paris mold of the clay-covered armature is frequently cast. The mold will

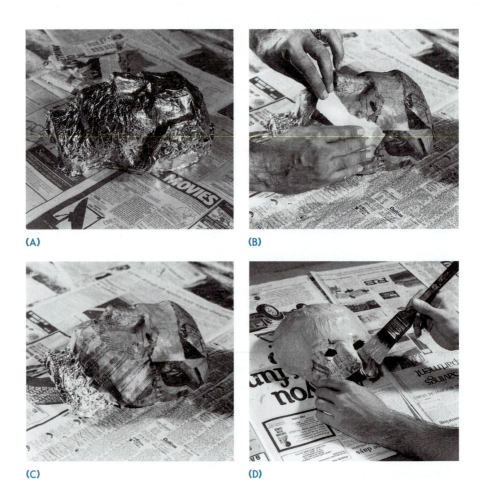

(A)

(B)

(C)

(D)

FIGURE 19.26
Papier-mâché mask construction technique. Cover the armature, a life mask (A), with aluminum foil. Apply several layers of glue-soaked strips of newspaper to the armature (B). Allow the finished mask to dry (24–48 hours) on the armature, and finish it as desired (D).

reveal all the detail on the clay original, particularly if fiberglass construction is used to create the object. After the release agent is applied to the mold, a gel coat of appropriately colored, catalyzed fiberglass resin is applied to capture the detail. After the gel resin has set, glass mat or cloth is applied to the gel coat, while it is still in the mold, to build up the strength of the piece.

Armor can also be formed from thermoplastic materials such as those illustrated in Figure 19.25. These thermoplastics, available from medical supply houses under such trade names as Vara-form, Polyfoam, and Hexcelite, become limp and formable when heated in 160-degree water for approximately 30 seconds. They can also be heated with handheld hair dryers. The nontoxic (unless burned) material can be worked, formed, and fused for approximately 2 to 4 minutes before it must be reheated. Although expensive, these materials are very durable and cost-effective, as any waste scraps can be heated and fused together to form workable-sized pieces. As with Fabric Form fiberglass, these thermoplastics can be formed on or in a mold. If care is taken to insulate the actor—a sweatshirt or cloth of similar thickness is usually enough—the warm thermoplastic can be formed directly on the actor's body.

Masks

Masks are made from a wide range of materials and fabrics, but like armor the base layer of most masks is constructed on a clay or plaster mold. Masks used to be built on a mold using papier-mâché, as shown in Figure 19.26, but now plaster bandage, Fabric Form, fiberglass, and thermoplastics are more commonly used to form rigid shells, while synthetic latex, netting, and various foams are used to create flexible elements, as shown in Figure 19.27. Rather than using a generic face mold, you can make an exact fit for a specific actor if the thermoplastic or plaster-bandage material is formed directly on the actor's face or from a life mask. Again, the painting, texturing, aging, and appliqué techniques discussed in the jewelry- and armor-making sections, and elsewhere in this and other chapters of the text, are equally applicable to the construction of masks.

FIGURE 19.27
A mask made from plastic furnace filter foam hot glued onto a latex/gauze/Celastic base.

Chapter 20

Makeup

Makeup is a vital element in creating the total appearance of the actor. To a great extent, the makeup design gives the audience its primary clue to the age, health, and vitality of the character. Although the overall appearance of the actor is the costume designer's domain, the makeup designer, working with the costume designer, is frequently responsible for the design and execution of the makeup.

Stage makeup enhances the illusion that the actor has become the character. In almost every production some of the actors, for one reason or another, do not facially resemble the characters they are playing. Makeup can help solve this challenge by providing actors with the means to change their appearance. Through the skillful application of the various techniques of makeup, young faces can be made to look older, older faces younger, pretty faces less attractive, blemished skin clear, and rather plain faces ravishingly attractive. On a more mundane level, bright stage lights tend to lighten skin tones, so makeup is also used to put color back in the cheeks of the actor. By thoughtful design, that color can be made more appropriate to the character than are the actor's natural skin tones.

A great deal of the communication process that transfers information from the actor to the audience takes place visually. To fully understand what the actors are saying (actually, what they are meaning), the audience must be able to read the actors' facial expressions. But makeup does more than simply exaggerate the facial features of the actor. Effective makeup will both exaggerate or minimize the actor's natural features as well as project the character (not the actor) to the audience.

In the past twenty or so years makeup design, as well as the technology of makeup, has changed. Prior to roughly the mid-1980s, actors generally covered their entire faces and necks with a foundation of either greasepaint or pancake makeup. This was, at best, uncomfortable. In many cases it caused skin problems. As street makeup—makeup worn by the "average woman on the street"—evolved into products that were healthier for the skin so did theatrical makeup. Simultaneously, the style basis for general theatrical makeup design has become more natural looking. There are exceptions, such as specific character makeup, but the general makeup design trend is toward a more naturalistic style.

 ## Designing the Makeup

It is the responsibility of the makeup designer to create a design that will help transform the actor into the character. In order to accomplish this goal, the makeup designer must understand what the character should look like. As well as looking at the costume sketches and analyzing the script for information about the appearance of the character, the makeup designer uses additional information

PRODUCTION INSIGHTS
The Design Process in Makeup Design

This discussion applies the features of the design process to makeup design. Another tour of Chapter 2 would be appropriate if you think that you don't fully understand the fundamentals of this problem-solving technique.

Commitment

To do your best work, you must promise yourself that you will perform the work to the best of your ability.

Analysis

The first phase of the analysis step involves clarifying and refining the challenge, "What should the makeup look like for this show?" Answers to this question are found by reading the script and asking questions about the characters, costume designs, budgets, schedules, and so forth. Some of these questions will be answered when you study the script. Others will be answered during the production conferences, in which the director and designers freely exchange ideas and information.

The second phase of analysis involves discovering areas and subjects about the appearance of the character(s) that will require further research. You will investigate these areas during the research phase of the design process.

Research

Research is divided into two areas: background research and conceptual research. Background research involves finding answers to the questions raised during your analysis of the challenge. In makeup design, the primary research sources are the designer's analysis of the script and conversations with the costume designer. During the background-research phase, you need to analyze each character in terms of those elements that affect their appearance.

Conceptual research is the process of putting together as many potential solutions to the design challenge as possible. This is the time that the makeup designer begins to draw the preliminary makeup sketches. The best designs are normally achieved when the designer creates several variations of each design during this preliminary design stage.

Incubation

After doing the preliminary sketches, you should move on to some other project or activity. This will give your subconscious mind a chance to sort through the material and synthesize the best design choice.

Selection

After a period of incubation, focus on the project again and consciously make your final design choices.

Implementation

Since the implementation phase of the design process involves the actual production of the design, you are implementing the design when you are producing the sketches for the makeup design *and* when you are creating the makeup design on the actor.

Evaluation

Evaluation involves objectively studying your application of the design process to the creation of the makeup design. Honestly analyze your work. Did you do enough background research? Did you spend enough time analyzing the challenge? The answer to these and similar questions should tell you ways in which you could improve your communication with other members of the design team as well as your own use of the design process.

to help determine the physical appearance of the character. Richard Corson, in his excellent text, *Stage Makeup,* suggests that *genetics, environment, health, disfigurements, fashion, age,* and *personality* are the main influences that affect physical appearance.[1] Genetics is the prime determinant of anyone's physical appearance.

[1] Richard Corson, *Stage Makeup,* 8th ed. (Englewood Cliffs, N.J.: Prentice-Hall, 1990), p. 19.

PRODUCTION INSIGHTS
You Really Can't Do Too Much Research

It's axiomatic that you really can't do too much research for makeup design. One of the best ways to do this is to create a morgue which, in this case, is a collection of a wide variety of images. The morgue shouldn't just be of pretty faces. It should include as many categories as you can think of: young, old, happy, sad, frumpy, grumpy faces; faces with cuts and bruises; animal and fantasy faces. It should include anything that you think might inspire you as you go through the process of trying to conjure up a design. Maybe even pictures of trees, flowers, or rocks. Whatever works for you. These images can be collected from online sources as well as photos from magazines and books. Just be sure to *copy* the images from books and magazines instead of tearing out the pages. With this morgue you'll have a wide variety of visual images at your disposal when it comes time to create a makeup design.

If, when doing research for a makeup design, you discover that makeup was not worn by people from the socioeconomic strata of that particular character the design challenge will be to create and execute a makeup design that makes it appear that the actor is not made up at all.

Genetics determines height, skeletal structure, and hair and eye colors, while basic skin color is determined by genetics and shaped by environment as well.

Exposure to the elements—sun, wind, water, temperature—affects the color and texture of skin, so whether a character spends the majority of time indoors or outdoors, and the climate in which he or she lives, will definitely help shape his or her appearance.

Disfigurements may be genetically or accidentally caused. Richard III's disfigurements are noted in the script of *Richard III* by Shakespeare. Obviously, those deformities must be created in the costume and makeup. But a broken nose or a scar, uncalled for in the script, may aid in projecting the nature of a particular character to the audience.

Research will tell the makeup designer the particular makeup fashions of the period in which the play is set. Unless it is desired to have the character seem eccentric, out of fashion, or weird, the makeup should generally adhere to the fashion of that period.

A character's appearance also reveals something about his or her age and general health. Young, healthy skin usually has good color and a firm, smooth texture, whereas older skin or that of an ill person tends to be pallid, wrinkled, and less firm.

Personality is also revealed by facial appearance. Although we may do it subconsciously, almost everyone monitors the faces of people with whom they're talking to determine that person's mood. An arched eyebrow, eyes that suddenly narrow, a smile that turns into a frown communicate specific meanings. In the same manner, the shape of the face at rest communicates information about the personality of the character. If the mouth is set in a perpetual frown, we tend to assume that the person is serious and/or grumpy. If there are "smile lines" at the edges of the eyes and mouth, we tend to think of the person as happy. Makeup designers use these visual clues to help the actor reveal the character of the roles he or she is playing.

The process of creating makeup designs is similar to that followed by other designers. The script is read; production meetings are attended; individual conferences are held with the director, costume designer, and actors; research is done; sketches of the designs are created; and finally, the makeup is applied to the actors. The specific steps that the makeup designer follows are outlined in the box "The Design Process in Makeup Design" on page 491.

Makeup Drawings

There are several types of drawings that the makeup designer uses. Preliminary sketches are quick sketches (Figure 20.1) drawn in any medium, that show what the makeup should look like. If the makeup artist is inexperienced in sketching, worksheets with predrawn frontal and profile views can be used, as shown in Figure 20.2.

When the design is finalized, it should be adapted to the actor. This can be accomplished by placing tracing paper over a photo of the actor, tracing his or her natural features onto the paper, and then adapting the makeup to the actor's face, as shown in Figure 20.3. This process can also be accomplished by scanning the two images into a software program such as PhotoShop and printing a composite image.

Working drawings in makeup are similar to working drawings in other design areas. They detail information that shows the actor or makeup artist how to apply the makeup. The working drawing in Figure 20.4 shows frontal and profile views of the makeup design and contains written notes specifying techniques and materials to be used to re-create the design on the actor's face. Whether drawn in black and white or color, the most important point is that these drawings fully explain how and what makeup should be applied.

FIGURE 20.1
Preliminary makeup sketches show the idealized design of what the makeup should look like.

ALDONSO   ACT III

BEARD MUCH WHITER THAN ACT I

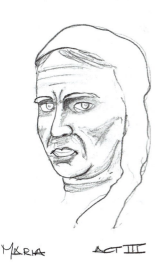

MARIA   ACT III

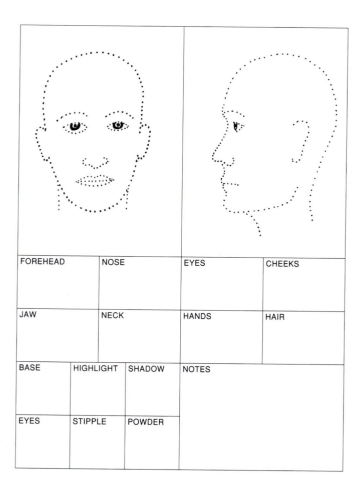

FOREHEAD	NOSE		EYES	CHEEKS
JAW	NECK		HANDS	HAIR
BASE	HIGHLIGHT	SHADOW	NOTES	
EYES	STIPPLE	POWDER		

FIGURE 20.2
Predrawn makeup worksheet.

(A)

(B)

(C)

(D)

FIGURE 20.3 ▲
The makeup design is adapted to the actor's face by (A) transferring the outline of the actor's face to tracing paper from a photo and (B–D) redrawing the idealized design on the representation of the actor's face.

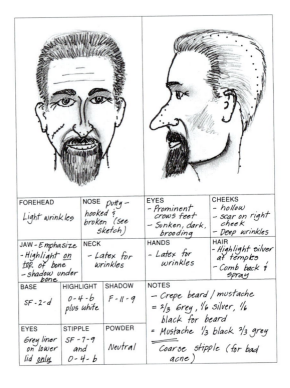

FOREHEAD	NOSE *putty-hooked & broken (see sketch)*	EYES	CHEEKS
Light wrinkles		- Prominent crows feet - Sunken, dark, brooding	- hollow - scar on right cheek - Deep wrinkles

JAW - Emphasize	NECK	HANDS	HAIR
- Highlight *on top* of bone - shadow under bone	- Latex for wrinkles	- Latex for wrinkles	- Highlight silver at temples - Comb back & spray

BASE	HIGHLIGHT	SHADOW	NOTES
SF-2-d	0-4-b plus white	F-11-9	- Crepe beard / mustache = 2/3 Grey, 1/6 silver, 1/6 black for beard

EYES	STIPPLE	POWDER	
Grey liner on lower lid *only*	SF-7-9 and 0-4-b	Neutral	= Mustache 1/3 black 2/3 grey Coarse stipple (for bad acne)

FIGURE 20.4
Makeup working drawing.

Types of Makeup

Various materials are used for makeup base, liners, beards, mustaches, and prosthetic devices, as shown in Figure 20.5.

Cake Makeup

Cake makeup—both dry and moist—is pigmented material compressed into cake form. A variety of bases as well as highlight and shadow colors are available. Natural silk sponges are normally used to apply cake-foundation colors, whereas flat, pointed, and eyeliner brushes are used for detail work.

To apply cake makeup, you dampen the applicator and draw it across the cake, as shown in Figure 20.6. If the applicator is too dry, the makeup won't easily transfer to the face. If it is too wet, the makeup will seem thin and may streak. Best results are achieved if the face is cleaned of any other makeup and moisturizers before application of the cake makeup. Normally, the entire face is covered with a smooth, translucent foundation color, and highlights and shadows are applied over the foundation. However, highlights and shadows can be applied *under* the foundation to achieve muted effects or to cover a heavy beard or pigmentation abnormality. If a heavy, opaque quality is desired, it is normally built up with several light applications rather than a single heavy one. Blending between colors once they're on the face is normally achieved by brushing lightly with a clean, slightly dampened brush. Cake makeup does not require powdering. Kryolan Aquacolor is a brand of cake makeup in common use today. It is heavily pigmented, so not much has to be used, and it blends easily, is available in a wide variety of colors, and doesn't **sweat off.**

Creme Makeup

This moist, nongreasy foundation makeup is applied with a sponge, a brush, or the fingers, as shown in Figure 20.7. It is compatible with cake makeup but does require powdering to be **set.** Creme makeup is also available in stick form that is generally referred to as crayons.

FIGURE 20.5
A well-equipped makeup table. All makeup shown here and in the following illustrations was generously provided courtesy of Kryolan Corporation.

sweat off: When an actor's face perspires, some makeups will run. These makeups are said to "sweat off."

set: To prevent smearing or smudging. Once a greasepaint makeup design is finished, it is locked in place with a coating of powder.

(A)

FIGURE 20.6
Application of cake makeup. (A) A damp sponge is drawn across the cake. (B and C) A smooth translucent foundation color is applied to the face and neck. Makeup by Amy Lederman, professional makeup artist.

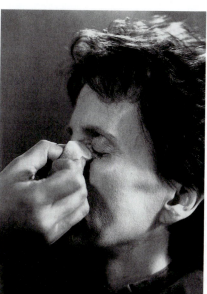

(B)

(C)

(A)

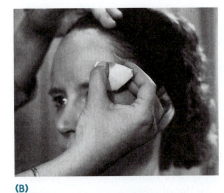

(B)

(C)

FIGURE 20.7
Application of creme makeup. The creme (A) is softened and blended before application (B) with a sponge or fingers. Various color powders are blended (C and D) to match the foundation before it is patted or rolled onto the face (E) with a powder puff. Makeup by Amy Lederman, professional makeup artist.

(D)

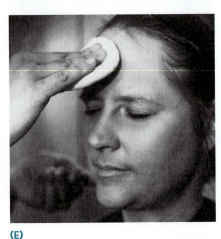

(E)

Liquid Makeup

Liquid makeup manufactured for theatrical purposes is pretty much limited to body makeup. However, a variety of liquid bases formulated for street wear work perfectly well for the stage. The only problem with the use of liquid bases is that they dry quickly, which makes them difficult to blend if more than one color of base is being used.

Dry Makeup

This category includes all makeup that is dry when applied to the skin. Dry makeups, such as face powders and pressed powder rouge, are normally used to supplement other types of makeup such as cake and greasepaint.

Face powder is primarily used to set creme and greasepaint makeup or to reduce shine, although it can be used by itself as a "quick" foundation. It is applied by pressing on the face with a powder puff. Any excess powder is removed by gently brushing with a soft powder brush or clean rouge sponge.

Dry rouge is a pressed cake form of face powder. It is normally applied with a rouge brush, cotton ball, or powder puff.

Greasepaint

Until the development of quality creme and cake makeup, greasepaint was the most commonly used type of theatrical makeup. Opaque and cream based, it is available in jars, tubes, sticks, and tins in a wide variety of colors.

After the skin has been cleansed, soft greasepaint from tubes or jars is applied to the face and neck in little dots, then blended with the finger tips to

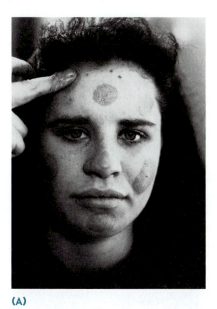

(A)

(B)

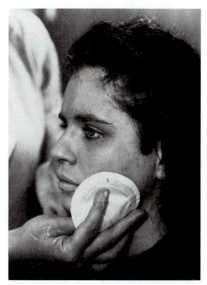

(C)

FIGURE 20.8
Application of greasepaint. The grease-paint is applied in dots (A), then blended to form a smooth foundation (B) and set with powder (C). Makeup by Amy Leder-man, professional makeup artist.

create a smooth translucent foundation, as shown in Figure 20.8. Greasepaint creates a greasy, shiny base that does not take highlights and shadows well and requires a coating of powder to set the makeup. If successive layers are to be built up, as when **stippling,** each layer needs to be set with powder. Another drawback to greasepaint is that it clogs the pores, which promotes facial per-spiration. Because of the ease of application of crème, cake, liquid, and powder foundations, and the fact that they are much easier on the skin, greasepaint is rarely used any more.

Rubber-Mask Greasepaint

This specialty greasepaint, made with a castor-oil base, is primarily used to cover latex. Unlike regular greasepaint, it is applied by gently patting or stippling with a sponge, and it must be thoroughly powdered before any additional makeup can be applied. Like greasepaint rubber-mask greasepaint is now rarely used because foam latex—as opposed to "regular" or "unfoamed" latex—is the current "ma-terial of choice" for the construction of makeup prosthetics. Foam latex can be made up using regular crème or powder-based makeup.

Makeup Removers

Makeup removers such as Kryolan's Makeup Remover and Mehron's Liquefying Cream are sold by the individual manufacturers for use with their products. All-purpose makeup removers such as Ben Nye's Quick 'n Clean Makeup Remover take off both makeup and spirit gum. Spirit gum can also be removed with spirit-gum remover. Cleansing creams, cold cream, and baby oils sold in drugstores remove most makeups but may be slightly harsher on the skin than are the more specific commercial products.

Application Techniques

stippling: A texturing technique in which makeup is applied by touching the skin with a textured surface, usually a stippling sponge. Similar to stippling in scenic painting.

Several application techniques can be used with all types of makeup.

Highlights and Shadows

To a great extent, humans perceive the three-dimensional quality of objects by "reading" the patterns of highlight and shadow created by light falling on the object. Ever since birth we've subconsciously studied the patterns that light creates on faces. We've all learned experientially that highlights are reflected from protruding structures such as the bridge of the nose, cheekbones, and the eyebrow ridge. Therefore, when looking at a face we *expect* to see highlights in those areas. Similarly, we *expect* to see shadows in areas shaded from the light such as eye sockets and under the jaw.

Makeup artists, by painting artificial, two-dimensional highlights and shadows on an actor's face, manipulate the audience's perception of that face. For example, the eye socket is a natural shadow area. By painting the eye socket with a color that is lighter than the foundation color, the makeup artist decreases the apparent depth of that eye socket, as shown in Figure 20.9A and B. Darkening the

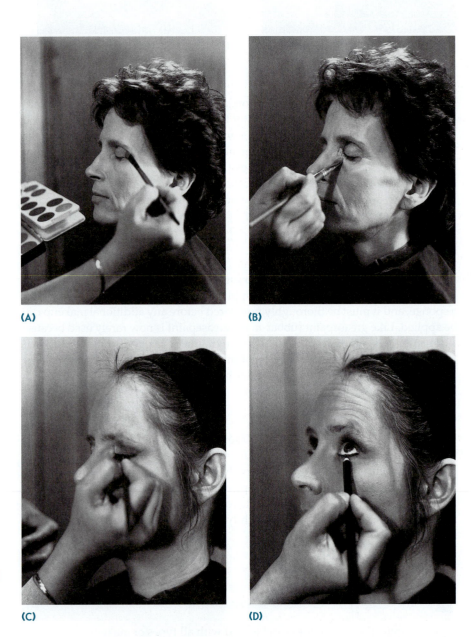

(A)

(B)

(C)

(D)

FIGURE 20.9
Application of highlight and shadow. (A and B) Use of highlight to decrease natural shadows. (C and D) Use of shadow and liner to emphasize eyes. Makeup by Amy Lederman, professional makeup artist.

eye-socket color and the use of eye liner will increase its apparent depth. Darkening the eye-socket color also increases its contrast with the white of the eye, which focuses more attention on the eye, as shown in Figure 20.9C and D. A straight nose can be made to appear crooked by painting the bridge with a crooked highlight, and a crooked nose can be made to appear straight by painting a straight highlight line.

Because there are few harsh angles, such as creases or deep wrinkles, on most faces, almost all junctures between highlight, base, and shadow are soft edged. A soft edge is created by blending—stroking with a brush from the lighter color to the darker, as shown in Figure 20.10. If a hard-edged line is needed, simply brush the shadow color into place with the edge of a small flat brush and don't blend it, as illustrated in Figure 20.11.

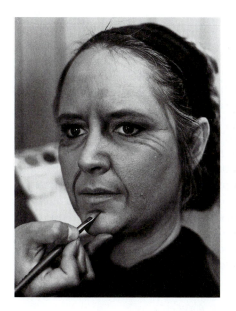

FIGURE 20.10
A soft edge is created by blending the shadow color with the base. Makeup by Amy Lederman, professional makeup artist.

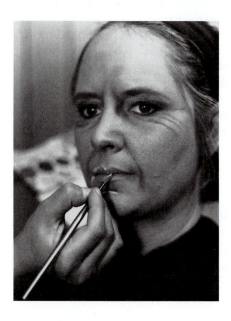

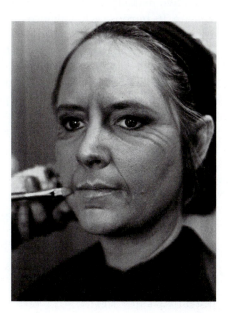

FIGURE 20.11
A hard edge is created by not blending the highlight color. Makeup by Amy Lederman, professional makeup artist.

FIGURE 20.12
Stippling made with contrasting highlight and shadow colors gives the appearance of rough skin texture. Makeup by Amy Lederman, professional makeup artist.

Highlight and Shadow Colors

Facial highlights are simply those areas that reflect more light than the surrounding skin reflects, whereas shadows are those areas that reflect less. Therefore, the highlight color is simply a lighter version of the foundation, whereas shadow color is darker. The amount of difference between the foundation color and its highlight and shadow hues is dependent on a number of variables—principally whether the foundation color is light or dark, skin condition, and age. For normal effects on Caucasian skin, highlights and shadows will be just a bit lighter and darker, respectively, than the foundation. As the value—relative lightness or darkness—of the skin tone decreases—becomes darker—the contrast between the highlight/shadow colors needs to increase in order to project a realistic effect. Increasing the contrast between the highlight/shadow colors and the foundation will increase the apparent age of the skin.

Stippling

Stippling is a method of applying makeup by daubing or patting rather than stroking. Normally accomplished with a sponge, and occasionally with a brush, stippling roughens the apparent skin texture, as shown in Figure 20.12. The roughness of that texture depends on two elements: the surface texture of the applicator and the contrast between the stipple color and the foundation. Generally, the larger the pores of the applicator, and the more contrast between the stipple color and the base, the rougher the apparent texture.

Black stipple sponges, red rubber sponges, natural sponges, and household sponges can be used for stippling. The stipple color is applied to the sponge, then pressed onto the face. The use of two or more stipple colors (rather than one) will create a more natural look. Large textural elements such as freckles are normally applied with a small, flat makeup brush.

Shadow or highlight areas that are too dark, bright, or intense can be toned down by stippling them with the base color.

Corrective Makeup

Corrective makeup is similar in purpose and design to everyday, or street, makeup. Its purpose is to enhance the natural appearance of the actor. Corrective makeup normally begins with a foundation color of one or more colors that are specified on the makeup worksheet.

After the foundation has been applied, the face's natural structure is either emphasized or de-emphasized through the application of highlights and shadows. The highlights are normally applied where highlights would naturally occur, such as the bridge of the nose, the cheekbones, and the top of the eyebrows. Shadow colors are applied to natural shadow areas, such as wrinkle lines, eye sockets, and cheeks.

 ## Three-Dimensional Makeup

Three-dimensional makeup involves the use of various materials to alter the shape of the actor's face, neck, or hands. A variety of materials and processes can be used to achieve these effects.

Nose Putty

Nose putty can be used to alter the shape of the nose, chin, and other nonflexible areas of skin, as illustrated in Figure 20.13. When working with nose putty, be sure the application site is free from all makeup and grease. Apply just enough K-Y jelly or cleansing cream (not petroleum jelly) to your fingers to prevent the putty from sticking to them, and knead the putty until it is soft. Press the putty onto the skin to firmly attach it, then shape it and smooth it into the surrounding skin. Adhesion will be increased if a coat of spirit gum is applied to the skin and allowed to dry until it is very tacky before the nose putty is applied. When it is properly shaped, stipple the putty to give it skin texture, then apply makeup

(A)

FIGURE 20.13
Application of nose putty. (A) The nose putty is kneaded until soft and pliable. (B) Spirit gum is applied to the nose and allowed to dry until tacky. (C) The nose putty is applied and shaped. (D) The nose putty is patted with a black stipple sponge to give it texture. (E) Foundation makeup is applied. Makeup by Amy Lederman, professional makeup artist.

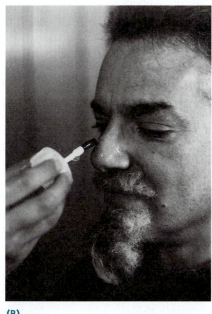

(B)

(C)

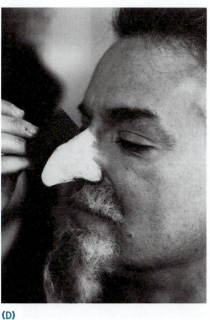

(D)

(E)

to match the actor's natural skin tone, powder if necessary, *then* apply the foundation color and any appropriate highlight or shadow colors.

To remove nose putty, pull or scrape it off and gently massage makeup remover onto the area until the remaining putty is softened enough to be removed with tissues.

Derma Wax

Derma wax is softer than, but does not adhere as well as, nose putty. It is used for similar modifications of hard structures such as noses and chins. The application of derma wax follows the same procedure as nose putty except that the coating of spirit gum is required to firmly attach the derma wax. Increased adhesion will result if cotton fibers are embedded in the spirit-gum layer. When the spirit gum is very tacky, press a cotton ball into it. When the spirit gum is dry, pull the ball off. Some cotton fibers will remain. Work a small amount of derma wax into the cotton fibers, then apply the remaining wax and build up the desired shape.

Derma-wax structures can be pulled off and the residue removed with an all-purpose makeup remover or with spirit-gum remover and makeup remover.

Gelatin

Gelatin, such as unflavored Knox gelatin available in grocery stores, when mixed with hot water to form a thick paste that solidifies when cool, can be used to form three-dimensional shapes such as warts, moles, and scars. If mixed with cool water, the gelatin will have a more grainy texture. Gelatin adheres to thoroughly grease-free skin and is more flexible than either nose putty or derma wax, so it can be used on fleshy, flexible skin such as cheeks.

A working paste is formed by mixing the gelatin one to one with very hot tap water. The paste must be applied when warm and shaped quickly with an orange stick, modeling tool, or similar applicator before it cools. Successive layers can be built up until the desired shape is achieved, as shown in Figure 20.14. If the edges start to peel, they can be glued down with spirit gum. Shapes can also be

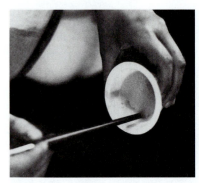

(A)

FIGURE 20.14
Application of gelatin. (A) Gelatin is mixed with water and (B) applied to grease-free skin. (C) The gelatin mole is colored and stippled with a brush. Makeup by Amy Lederman, professional makeup artist.

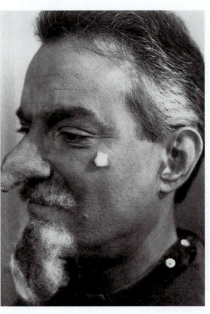

(B)

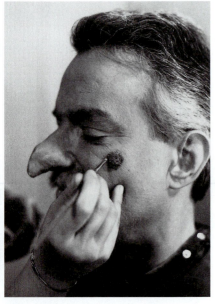

(C)

preformed either in a mold or on a flat glass surface and attached to the skin with spirit gum, which improves adhesion. The gelatin forms can be covered with any type of makeup.

The disadvantages of gelatin forms are that they can melt when heated and perspiration loosens them, although the perspiration problem can be overcome with spirit gum.

Latex

Several types of latex systems are used for a variety of purposes such as forming prosthetic pieces, creating wrinkles, and applying crepe hair. Liquid latex is available in clear and flesh-colored formulations. Foam latex is a soft, flexible expanding foam that is poured into molds to form prosthetic pieces. It is made by mixing liquid latex with foaming, gelling, and curing agents. The mixture is poured into a cast and baked in a low-temperature oven. Specific instructions come with foam-latex kits, which are available from theatrical supply houses that handle makeup.

Liquid latexes specifically designed for forming in molds should not be applied directly to the skin as they may cause irritation or burning. Liquid Plastic Film, manufactured by Kryolan, is a clear liquid plastic, available in two formulations, that is used in the same way as liquid latex. Glatzan L is used for making **bald caps, eyebrow masks,** eye pouches, and so forth. It should not be applied directly to the skin. A variety of manufactured latex pieces (noses, chins, pouches, warts, and so forth) are available from makeup manufacturers or distributors such as Paramount, Bob Kelly, and Kryolan.

Liquid latex is frequently used to create wrinkles. The skin to be aged is pulled tight, and clear latex (white when liquid, clear when dry) is stippled onto the skin with a sponge or fingers, as shown in Figure 20.15. When the stretched skin is released, wrinkles magically appear. Additional coats of latex on the stretched skin will deepen the wrinkles. Kryolan's Old Skin Plast can be used as a substitute for liquid latex. An age makeup can be applied either under or over the latex. If the makeup is under the latex, apply the latex carefully to avoid smearing. If makeup is being applied over the latex, you can tint the latex with appropriate hues of food coloring to approximate the actor's natural skin tone.

A cautionary note when using liquid latex: Before you apply latex to any hairy parts such as the backs of hands, beards, stubble, eyebrows, or soft, downy facial hair, you need to understand that when you pull off the latex, most of the hair will come with it. To avoid this problem, either **block out** or shave off the hair before applying the latex.

If deep wrinkles are desired, torn (not cut) facial tissue can be applied to the stretched skin of the face with either latex or spirit gum. When the tissue has dried on the stretched skin, a coat of latex is applied over the tissue. The use of a hair dryer will speed the drying process. Work a small area at a time, and be sure that the skin is stretched until the latex is dry. If even deeper wrinkles are desired, soft paper toweling can be substituted for the tissue. After the whole face is covered with the tissue (or paper towels) and latex, a rubber-mask greasepaint or greasepaint foundation with appropriate highlights and shadows is applied over the latex. Additional skin texture can be created by stippling with latex or a honey-thick mixture of latex and gelatin.

Prosthetics

Prosthetic devices—latex noses, chins, bald caps, eyebrow blocks, and so forth—can be purchased or made in the shop. If purchased, generic shapes such as bald

bald cap: A latex cap that covers a person's hair.

eyebrow mask: A thin piece of plastic film or latex glued over the eyebrow. Also known as an eyebrow block.

block out: To cover with soap, spirit gum, wax, material, or preformed plastic film so that no hair is evident.

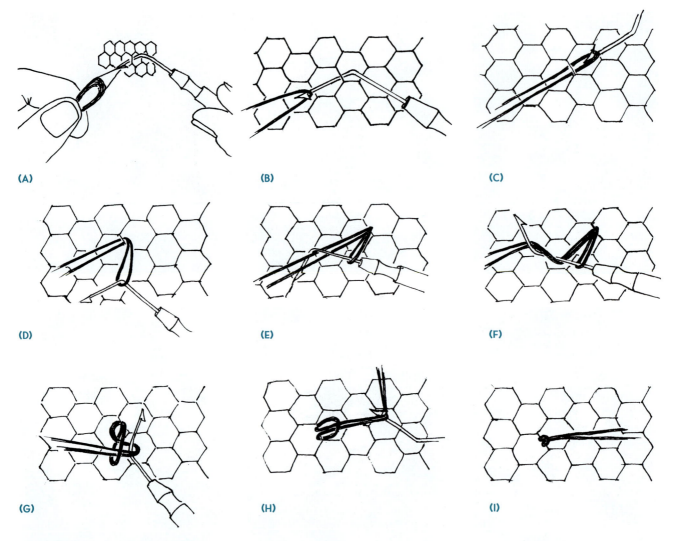

(A)   (B)   (C)

(D)   (E)   (F)

(G)   (H)   (I)

FIGURE 20.23
The ventilating process. A few hairs are caught with the tip of the ventilating hook (A) and pulled through the lace backing (B) to form a loop (C). The hook is then rotated around the strands (D–F) and pulled through the loop (G–H) to form a knot (I). This process is repeated with additional strands to tie the hair to the lace backing. While tedious and time consuming, ventilating does create the most realistic beards, mustaches, and wigs.

Ventilated pieces are normally attached with spirit gum. Generally the spirit gum is applied to clean skin and allowed to dry until tacky, and the gauze or lace netting is pressed into it using a clean, slightly moistened cloth. Any hairs that are glued down can be lifted using a pointed, stiff object such as an orange stick or eyebrow brush. As the netting is delicate and can easily tear, removal of the piece requires the copious use of spirit-gum remover and patience.

Chapter 21

Sound Design and Technology

Not so many years ago, sound in the theatre was fairly simple. If the director wanted some preshow music, you got some records that approximated the mood and spirit of the play and played them over the auditorium public-address system for about ten minutes before the curtain went up. You might get daring and play them again during the intermission.

If the script called for specific sound effects such as a doorbell or a telephone ringing, you either made the sounds live or consulted your sound-effects library, composed of low-fidelity 78-RPM records. If you used library effects, you either recorded them on your wire or tape recorder, or you cued the records up and played them just the way a disc jockey would.

Sound in the theatre has changed substantially since the bad old days. Instead of being an afterthought, sound is now frequently an integral part of the production concept. Increasing numbers of productions are giving credit to sound design as well as to the more traditional scenic, costume, and lighting design. An indication of the professional stature now accorded this field is the fact that sound design was recognized as a credited design position by the United Scenic Artists (USA) a few years ago.

Arguably the most important reason for the increased use of sound is the improvement in sound equipment. A second reason stems from the tastes and expectations of the audience and of theatre craftspeople. Almost every member of the contemporary theatregoing public, as well as those of us who work in the theatre, have seen a lot more television and motion pictures than theatre. Our aesthetic expectations have been strongly influenced by what we have seen and heard in these media. For years both television and motion pictures have made very effective use of music and sound effects to focus the audience's attention and reinforce the dominant emotional theme of the material being presented. High-quality digital home and auto stereo systems have raised our sound expectations too. It seems only natural, then, that we have come to expect carefully designed sound and music in the theatre.

 ## Functions of Sound in the Theatre

Theatre sound can be subdivided into three categories: music, effects, and reinforcement.

constructed sound: Any sound effects created by editing, manipulating, or changing previously recorded sounds.

synthesizer: A musical instrument that creates sounds electronically; can be used to create a close facsimile of instrumental, natural, or vocal tones.

Music

The use of music in a nonmusical production has historically been limited to preshow, intermission, and postshow instrumentals that create an aural atmosphere selected to put the audience in the proper mood for the play. Comedies have been, and frequently continue to be, accompanied by light and sprightly music, while full orchestrations of somber or ominous music have traditionally been associated with Shakespearean tragedies and plays of equally heavy subject matter. Plays that fall between these dramatic extremes are accompanied by music appropriate to their particular mood and subject matter.

Although this musical accompaniment has certainly been functional and effective, the contemporary use of music in the theatre has expanded in a variety of directions. Nonspecific musical effects, such as musical themes for specific characters or scenes, are now used to create or reinforce a particular psychological mood or feeling. Preshow selections have expanded to include almost any type of music or **constructed sound.** Lyrics, which used to be taboo, are now used whenever the production design team decides that their use would be appropriate. Furthermore, sections of many productions are now scored with music, the way motion pictures are, to reinforce the psychological content of particular moments in the script.

Effects

The creation of specific sound effects such as barking dogs, telephones, doorbells, and train whistles is still an important element of the sound designer's work, but it is no longer the sole element. Many production concepts now call for the creation of an effects track to provide an aural backdrop of appropriate sound for the environment of the play. For example, in the University of Arizona's production of Ted Tally's *Terra Nova*, which is set in Antarctica, the director wanted to create an effect that would emphasize the bitter cold and lonely emptiness of that hostile environment. Sound designers Mark Ruch and David Coffman, using a **synthesizer** (Figure 21.1), created a very effective sound effect of wind sweeping across the empty frozen wastes. This sound effect, together with original music composed by Mark Ruch, was played, at varying levels of loudness, throughout all of the Antarctic scenes. When the sound was combined with the impact of an all-white set, the "cold" colors of the lights, and the cold-weather gear worn by the actors, the audience felt so chilly that it was necessary to turn the air conditioning to an above-average setting during the run of the production.

This type of fully scored effects design, which was extremely rare prior to 1980, is not that unusual anymore. Arena, thrust, and black box productions frequently use specific sound effects, such as waves lapping a beach or "jungle noises," to provide aural images of specific locations.

FIGURE 21.1
Yamaha Motif ES synthesizer. (Courtesy of Yamaha.)

Reinforcement

Reinforcement is used whenever there is a need to boost the loudness level of the actors' voices, as when the **acoustics** of the auditorium are not good or during musicals when the singers can't be heard over the orchestra. In the not-too-distant past, actors projected loudly enough to be heard by every member of the audience in all but the largest theatres without the need for electronic reinforcement. Today most actors can still project loudly enough to be heard, but the growth in the use of background and effects sound has introduced a new challenge to theatrical production.

The audience wants and deserves to hear balanced sound. It shouldn't have to strain to hear the actors, nor should it be overwhelmed by the music or noise of a sound effect. The answer to these specific challenges has been to mike the actors' voices, then mix and **balance** the sound with the effects and background music before all three sources are amplified and sent into the auditorium.

Reinforced sound needs to be balanced. The various elements of the sound design, with obvious exceptions, should not call attention to themselves. The loudness level of any music or sound effect should not overwhelm the voices of the actors, nor should the content of the sound, either music or effects, be so vibrant or strident as to draw attention from the central focus of the scene.

The Nature of Sound

To develop a working knowledge of how sound systems operate, you'll need to understand the nature of sound. Sound is a pressure wave that moves, in air and at sea level, at about 1,130 feet per second. The pressure wave is instigated by a source such as the drum in Figure 21.2. The drum compresses the air immediately adjacent to the drumhead when the head is struck with the drumstick. This compression wave travels through the air until it strikes a receptor—in this case, the ear. The ear converts the mechanical force of the pressure wave into a neurological impulse that is sent to the brain, where the stimulus is interpreted as a drumbeat of a particular tone and quality.

Frequency

Frequency is the rate, measured in cycles per second (hertz, or Hz), at which an object vibrates. At one time or another, most of us have strung a rubber band between our fingers and strummed it. The rubber band vibrated and made a sound. As we stretched the rubber band tighter, the vibrations of the rubber band seemed to get smaller, and the **pitch** of the sound increased. This was a demonstration of the direct relationship between frequency and pitch; as frequency increases, pitch increases.

To better understand the concept of frequency and its effect on pitch, let's assume that when the drumhead discussed above was struck with the drumstick, it took one second to complete 20 full vibrations, or cycles, as shown in Figure 21.3. We would hear this 20-cycle vibration as a very low sound. If we were able to tighten the drumhead so that it vibrated at a frequency of 200 cycles per second (200 Hz), we would hear this sound as a much higher pitched sound. Figure 21.4 illustrates the relationship between the frequency of a sound and its pitch.

The average human being can hear sounds that have a frequency range from 20 to 17,000 Hz, although people with very acute hearing can discern sounds

acoustics: The sound-transmission characteristics of a room, space, or material; also, the science that studies these qualities.

balance: To adjust the loudness and equalization levels of individual signals while mixing, to achieve an appropriate blend.

pitch: The characteristic tone produced by a vibrating body; the higher the frequency of vibration, the higher the pitch.

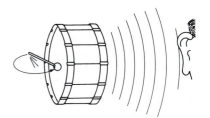

FIGURE 21.2
The transmission of sound in the air.

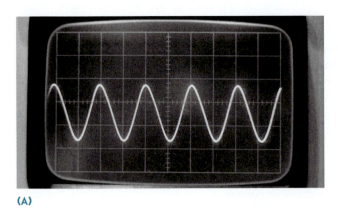

(A)

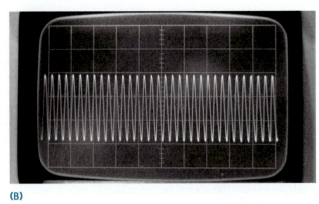

(B)

FIGURE 21.3
The higher the frequency, the higher the pitch. (A) A 20-cycle (Hz) sound; (B) a 200-cycle (Hz) sound.

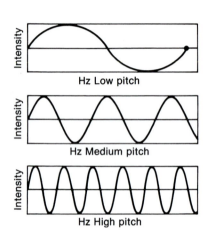

FIGURE 21.4
As frequency increases, pitch increases.

from approximately 15 to 22,000 Hz. Figure 21.5 may help to clarify the relationship that exists between frequency and some readily identifiable sound sources.

Intensity

The intensity of a sound is synonymous with its loudness. Figure 21.6 is a demonstration of the fact that the intensity of a sound can change without affecting the pitch.

The intensity, or loudness, of sound is measured in **decibels** (dB). Figure 21.7 illustrates the relative loudness levels of a variety of sounds.

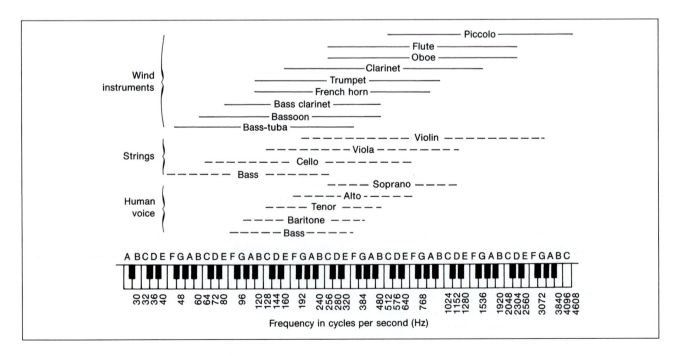

FIGURE 21.5
A sound-spectrum comparison chart.

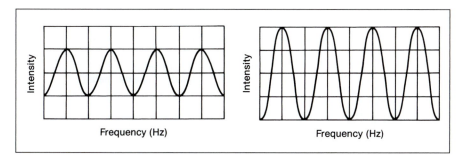

FIGURE 21.6
Intensity can change without affecting pitch.

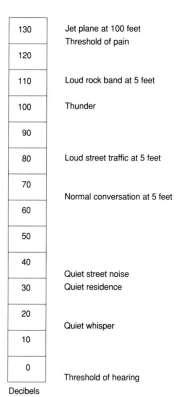

FIGURE 21.7
Relative loudness of some common sounds.

Timbre

Timbre refers to the distinctive quality of a sound that makes one voice sound different from another or a trumpet sound different from a violin. This qualitative difference is based on the **harmonics** of the sound-producing body.

Pure sounds, as shown in Figure 21.8A, rarely occur in nature. Most natural sound sources (voices, violins, pianos, surf noises) produce a variety of overtones, or harmonics, as shown in Figure 21.8B. These harmonic frequencies are based on the pitch of the fundamental, or base, frequency (Figure 21.9).

The amplitude, or loudness, of each harmonic will be less than the loudness of the fundamental frequency, and the amount of each harmonic in the final tone will be determined by the physical structure of the source. The reason that no two voices or instruments sound exactly alike is that each voice or instrument structure has minor, but significant, physical variations that affect the amplitude of the various harmonics it produces.

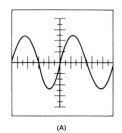

(A)

(B)

FIGURE 21.8
(A) A pure tone and (B) its harmonics.

 Basic Acoustics

Acoustics is the science that studies the absorption and reflection of sound. In the theatre, acoustics is concerned with the study of those qualities of the stage and auditorium space that affect the audience's hearing and understanding of the sound (language and music) of the play.

A theatre with good acoustics will allow every member of the audience to hear, and understand, the words being spoken by an actor standing anywhere on the stage. An almost limitless number of factors determine the acoustics of an auditorium. The room's shape vitally affects the reflection of sound. If the walls are parallel, the sound will **reverberate,** or bounce back and forth between them, reducing the intelligibility of the spoken word. Severe reverberation in an auditorium can so garble the sound that the audience cannot understand anything that the actor is saying. To reduce the reflection of sound waves, many architects slightly curve the auditorium walls so that no wall will be parallel with any other.

The materials used to finish the walls, ceiling, and floor of the auditorium also have a great impact on the reflection of the sound. In general, hard-surface materials (wood, metal, plaster, and the like) reflect sound, and soft- or open-surface materials (cloth, foamed or loosely spun insulation, and the like) absorb sound, as shown in Figure 21.10.

Acoustically balancing a theatre for music creates a problem. Music sounds better when the sounds of the various instruments blend. Sound blending is

decibel: A unit for expressing the intensity of sounds; an increase or decrease of one decibel is just about the smallest change in loudness that the human ear can detect.

harmonics: Frequencies that are exact multiples of a fundamental pitch or frequency.

reverberate: To reflect in a series of echoes.

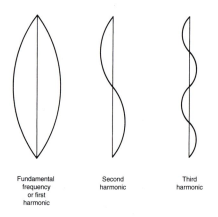

FIGURE 21.9
The loudness of a harmonic will be less than its fundamental frequency.

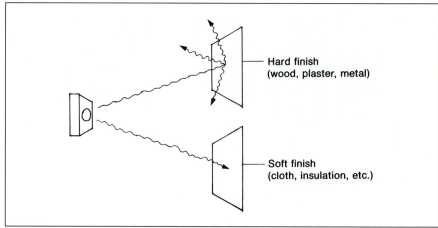

FIGURE 21.10
Sound reflection and absorption are dependent on the type and finish of the reflecting/absorbing surface.

dependent on the reverberation, or multiple reflection, of the sound among several of the reflecting surfaces in the auditorium.

Designing a theatre that is acoustically balanced for both speech and music is a very great, if not impossible, challenge. Speech requires a short reverberation time, whereas music sounds better with a longer period of reverberation. No totally satisfactory solution to this problem exists, but many modern architects and acousticians have tried to solve it by designing acoustically adjustable auditoriums and stages (see the box "Acoustic Balancing" on page 517).

Another not overly satisfactory solution that is frequently tried in an attempt to overcome the challenges posed by poor acoustic design of an auditorium is the use of a complicated and sophisticated sound system. Although the installation of very carefully engineered sound systems may alleviate the problems associated with poor acoustical design, a sound system has not been invented that will completely eliminate the need to have the shape and finish of an auditorium designed with extreme care and expertise.

 ## Sound Production

As with every other area of theatre production, computers are facilitating significant improvements in the field of sound production. Recording tape was the technology of choice for recording and playback of music and sound effects from approximately 1960 to the early 1990s. The development of CD technology in the early 1980s, with its digital signal, offered significantly improved sound quality. The advent, and continuing evolution, of inexpensive and highly effective computer-based sound editing programs provided sound designers with digital recording, editing, and playback capabilities. Together they signaled the end of the **tape deck's** reign. However, not everyone has jumped on the digital bandwagon. Tape is still a viable technology for theatrical sound production. Some sound designers prefer what they refer to as the "softer" sound produced by tape. Some like the "hands on" editing style that is required by recording tape. Some producing organizations simply haven't had the money required to "make the switch." For whatever reasons, tape is still used in many theatres.

tape deck: A magnetic-tape transport mechanism used to record an electrical signal on magnetic tape; also used to play back that signal; does not contain a playback amplifier and speaker.

Acoustic Balancing

An auditorium that is well balanced for understanding the spoken word will have a decay time (the period it takes a sound to quit reverberating and become inaudible) of ¼ to ¾ second. An auditorium with a good balance for music will have a decay time between ¾ second and 1½ seconds.

Since it is not possible to create a theatre that can be equally effective for both speech and music, some type of compromise needs to be made. In any situation where nonmusical plays are going to be presented, the compromise should lean toward balancing the auditorium for the spoken word. This rationale is based on the premise that the audience needs to discern the spoken language in order to

understand what is being said, while the music can be heard with the shorter reverberation time even though it won't sound as good to a trained musician.

A reasonable solution to this very realistic problem has been the development of acoustically adjustable auditoriums and stages. These multipurpose theatres are frequently equipped with adjustable acoustical baffles mounted in various positions on and over the stage as well as in the walls and on the ceiling of the auditorium. These panels can be adjusted to "tune" the auditorium for the appropriate degree of reverberation for the type of group (nonmusical theatre, musical theatre, opera, orchestra) performing on the stage.

The carpeting on the wall and the alternating vertical wood strips and cloth effectively reduce reverberation in the Constans Theatre, University of Florida.

In spite of what seems to be a bewildering array of equipment used to record and play back sound in the theatre (Figure 21.11), a logical, fairly straightforward set of principles guides the design of any sound system.

Basic Sound-System Configuration

Every sound system works on the principles illustrated in Figure 21.12. Sound is picked up by a **transducer** such as a **microphone** which converts the sound from mechanical energy (the pressure waves generated by the sound source) into electrical energy (a very small electrical signal), as shown in Figure 21.12A. The transducer sends the signal to a storage device (computer, recordable CD, or tape recorder) where it is recorded and stored.

To produce an audible recorded sound, the electrical signal is sent from the storage device to an **amplifier,** as illustrated in Figure 21.12B. The amplifier increases

transducer: A device that converts energy from one state into another—for example, a microphone or loudspeaker.

microphone: A transducer used to convert sound waves into electrical energy.

amplifier: A device used to boost the signal received from a transducer to a level that will drive a loudspeaker.

PRODUCTION INSIGHTS
The Design Process in Sound Design

Commitment

If you don't fully accept the challenge and promise yourself that you will do your best work, you will end up with a mediocre product.

Analysis

In defining and refining the challenge of sound design, you will need to read and analyze the script according to the guidelines suggested in Chapter 2. You will also need to ask questions of the other members of the production design team, such as

1. What is the budget for sound?
2. What equipment does the theatre own? What is its status?
3. Are there any local shops where I can rent equipment?
4. Will the actors' voices need to be reinforced?
5. What are the director's thoughts regarding the use of nonspecific background sound?
6. What is the rehearsal schedule for sound? When will the director want the effects tape? When will he or she want the microphones working for the reinforced sound?

Questions regarding the design, use, and scheduling of any live or recorded sound must be asked so that the sound designer will have a thorough understanding of the nature and scope of the design challenge.

Research

Background research for sound design needs to be conducted into both the music and the sound effects for the production. It normally requires that the sound designer become familiar with the music of the particular period in which the production concept is set. Whether the music comes from a specific period is secondary to the dictum that any music used must reflect the mood and spirit of the production. Any preshow, intermission, and post-show music should support the psychological mood dictated by the script and the production concept. Any incidental music that is selected for use during the production should enhance the audience's feelings and understanding about that particular moment in the play.

Research into sound effects is a little more arcane than research in music, because recorded sound doesn't always sound as you would expect. The recorded sound of water rushing down the rocky course of a mountain stream, when played back, may sound exactly like someone crumpling up a piece of cellophane, water running from a spigot, or a flushing toilet. The sound designer needs to be aware of this phenomenon and prepared to deal with it.

It is vital that the sound designer understand the psychological purpose and desired impact of each sound effect as well as the nature of that particular effect. Specifically, if the script calls for a horn honking, the sound designer needs to create a whole little scenario about that effect. He or she needs to know a great deal of specific information about the horn. Is it attached to a vehicle? What kind, type, and year of vehicle is it? Is the driver casually honking, or is he (or she) really mad and insistent? Is the vehicle nearby or far away? Is it moving or standing still? These and similar questions need to be answered by the director before the sound designer can begin to produce a genuinely useful and original sound effect.

The sound designer will need to have access to a good library of sound effects. There are several commercially available collections of effects that should be part of any production company's sound equipment. The *BBC Sound Effects Library* and the *CBS Sound Effects Library* are two excellent collections. Other effects CDs are generally available through any well-stocked music store.

It is rare that any of these prerecorded effects can be used without editing. A usual practice involves the editing and mixing of two or three separate effects to create a new effect that is appropriate for a specific cue.

Conceptual research in sound design means creating, either mentally or by recording, as many potential solutions to each sound cue as possible. For the preshow music, select from the work of a number of composers. With sound effects, let your ideas flow, even if some of them seem to be strange, bizarre, and nonworkable. Do not judge them at this point.

Incubation

Let the ideas sit unattended for a while. Do something else.

Selection

Choose the specific music and sound effects that you intend to use for each particular cue.

Implementation

Stop talking and start recording. Since all sound cues (except those that are going to be produced live such as doorbells, telephones, and similar sounds that demand specific location and presence) need to be stored on tape or disk, you will have to record and edit any and all music and sound effects that you intend to use. Specific instructions on making edited show tapes or disks are provided later in this chapter.

Evaluation

Review your use of the design process on this particular project as well as your communication with the other members of the design team. This review will provide you with a mechanism to improve your use of the process as well as your communication on your next production assignment.

---

loudspeaker: A transducer used to convert an electrical signal into mechanical energy (the movement of a vibrating membrane); converts a signal from an amplifier into audible sound.

(amplifies) the power of the electrical signal so that it can drive the **loudspeaker.** From the amplifier the electrical signal is sent to the loudspeaker, which converts the electrical energy back into mechanical energy. The mechanical energy (sound-pressure waves) reaches our ear.

(A)

(B)

FIGURE 21.11
An open theatrical sound booth located in the house (A) and an enclosed booth (B). The open booth is preferred because the operator can hear the sound balance coming from the stage and adjust it as necessary.

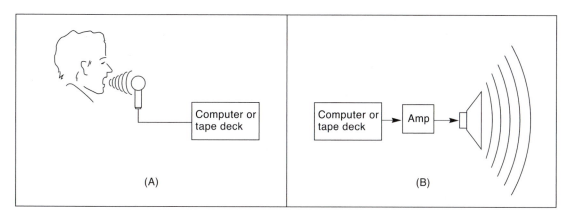

FIGURE 21.12
Block diagram of a monaural sound system.

FIGURE 21.13
Block diagrams of (A) equalizers in a recording system and (B) a playback system.

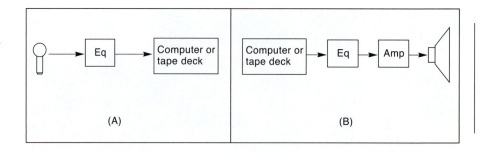

(A)   (B)

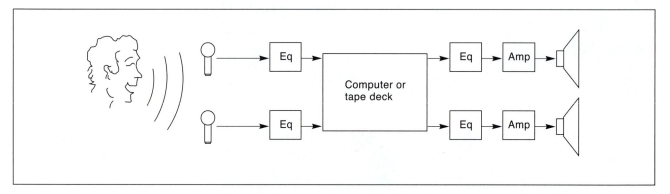

FIGURE 21.14
Block diagram of a stereo system.

tone: A generic term referring to the intensity of the component frequencies contained in any particular sound.

equalizer: An electronic device that selectively boosts or attenuates specific frequencies or ranges of frequencies.

playback system: Devices used to play recorded sound; usually composed of some combination of a turntable, a tape deck, a CD player, or a computer; an equalizer; an amplifier; and a speaker.

preamplifier: A device that boosts the level of a signal, without alteration or reshaping, to the requisite input signal level of the next piece of equipment in a sound system.

graphic equalizer: An equalizer with individual slide controls affecting specific, usually narrow, segments of the sound spectrum; so called because the position of the individual controls graphically displays a picture of the equalization of the full sound spectrum.

Every sound system works on these principles, but the electrical signal needs to be manipulated to control the **tone** (bass through treble frequencies) of the sound. To accomplish this function, an **equalizer** (a device that manipulates and modifies the signal) is placed in the system, as shown in Figure 21.13. Figure 21.13A shows the placement of an equalizer between the microphone and the computer or tape recorder. The purpose of this equalizer is to modify the signal coming from the microphone to enhance the tonal quality of the sound before it is recorded.

Figure 21.13B shows another equalizer inserted into the **playback system** between the computer or tape deck and the amplifier. The purpose of this equalizer is to modify the signal being fed to the amplifier, which will ultimately change the tonal quality of the sound being produced by the loudspeaker.

The basic sound systems illustrated in Figures 21.12 and 21.13 are monaural, or single-channel, systems. They mix all of the sound produced by the various sources (voices, noise, music, synthesizers, and so on) into one channel. Figure 21.14 illustrates a stereo, or two-channel, sound system. A stereo sound system is actually a paired monaural system. There are two electronically discrete (separated) sources, **preamplifiers,** tape decks or computers, amplifiers, and speakers. What makes this rather confusing is that in home systems, where we first learned about "stereos," these separate elements are usually contained in the same housing. Figure 21.15 shows a **graphic equalizer.** Notice that it has a complete set of controls for the two separate channels.

Most theatrical sound systems are stereophonic or multichannel (more than two channels), simply because such systems can produce a more lifelike quality of sound than a monaural system can produce.

Sound-System Equipment

Each piece of equipment in a sound system has a specific function, as we have seen. The functions of those elements of a sound system are described in more detail in this section.

FIGURE 21.15

Stereo equipment has separate controls for each channel as visually demonstrated by the graphic equalizer. The slide pots left of the centerline control one channel while the pots right of center control the other channel.

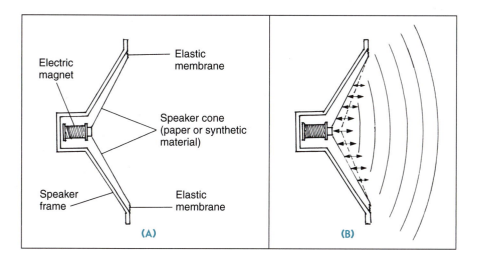

FIGURE 21.16

How a loudspeaker converts electrical energy to mechanical energy. (A) The structure of a typical loudspeaker. (B) The cone is moved forward and backward by the magnet to produce sound.

Loudspeakers and Speaker Systems   The loudspeaker is a transducer that converts the electrical energy of the signal to a mechanical energy that we can hear. Figure 21.16 illustrates this principle and shows the primary parts of the speaker. The signal activates an electromagnet attached to the loudspeaker frame. The electromagnet generates a magnetic field that corresponds in intensity to the frequency and loudness of the electrical signal emitted by the amplifier. The variation in this magnetic field causes a voice coil, which is attached to the rear of a flexible cone, to move the cone forward and backward in a pattern that mimics the frequency and loudness dictated by the electrical signal.

Generally speaking, the quality of a cone-type loudspeaker is directly related to the power of its electromagnet, the rigidity of the speaker frame, and the flexibility of its cone. The power of an electromagnet is roughly determined by its weight—the heavier the magnet, the greater the power.

Speakers work most effectively and efficiently when they are designed for a relatively narrow frequency range. Speakers are generally classified as low-frequency (**woofers**), middle-frequency (**mid-range**), and high-frequency (**tweeters**).

Almost all woofers are cone-type loudspeakers. Mid-range speakers and tweeters are also made using cones, but they are also manufactured using a **pressure driver** and **horn.** The pressure driver (also known simply as a driver), illustrated in Figure 21.17, creates sound in the same way as a cone speaker (a signal drives an electromagnetic voice coil, which is attached to a diaphragm that compresses air to create sound waves). The primary difference between the two is that the diaphragm in the pressure driver is made from very thin metal instead of paper or synthetic material. The metal is stiffer and more resilient and is capable of producing mid- and high-frequency sounds with greater intensity and clarity than a cone.

woofer: A low-frequency speaker, with a frequency range from 20 to approximately 150–250 Hz.

mid-range speaker: A speaker designed to reproduce the middle range of audible frequencies—roughly 200–1,000 Hz.

tweeter: A high-frequency speaker, generally designed to reproduce from approximately 1,000 to 20,000 Hz.

pressure driver: A unit housing a large magnet that vibrates a very thin metallic diaphragm to create mid-range and high-frequency sounds.

horn: A dispersion device attached to the front of a pressure driver to direct the sound emitted by the driver into a specific pattern.

FIGURE 21.17
How a pressure driver works. (See text for details.)

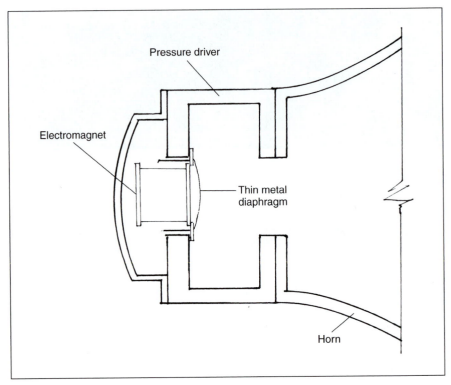

FIGURE 21.17
How a pressure driver works. (See text
for details.)

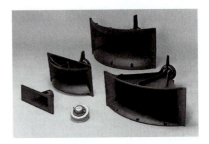

FIGURE 21.18
Acoustical horns. (Courtesy of Peavey Electronics Corp.)

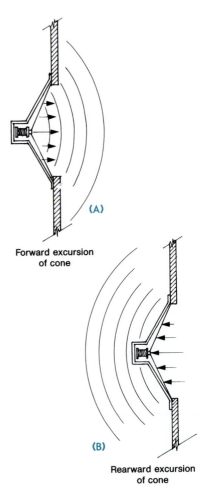

FIGURE 21.19
A loudspeaker compresses air on (A) its forward excursion and (B) its rearward excursion.

The pressure-driver unit is used in conjunction with a horn. The horn is used to direct the sound from the driver in a particular direction and pattern. As shown in Figure 21.18, there are a number of different models of acoustical horns. The differing shapes cause the sound to be focused in specific horizontal patterns. The 60-, 90-, and 120-degree horizontal dispersion patterns are fairly standard.

Speaker Cabinets   Speaker cabinets do more than protect the delicate speaker cones from damage. They form an inextricable part of the speaker mechanism, because the sound produced by any cone-type speaker is greatly affected by the shape and volume of the enclosure in which it is housed.

The design of speaker enclosures is very complex, depending on the number of interrelated variables such as the frequency range of the speaker and the volume of the cabinet. However, the operation of all speaker cabinets is based on certain common properties.

Low-, middle-, and high-frequency sounds have differing characteristics. Low-frequency sounds are fairly nondirectional and require more power to produce than do mid- or high-frequency sounds. The mid-range and high-frequency sounds are more directional. Because of these characteristics, most speaker cabinets are designed to enhance the reproduction of the low-frequency sound spectrum.

When the cone of a woofer moves forward, as shown in Figure 21.19A, it compresses air, which produces sound waves. When the cone moves backward, as shown in Figure 21.19B, it compresses the same amount of air and produces the same amount of sound waves. If the woofer were mounted in a hole in a wall between two rooms, it would produce the same frequency, quality, and intensity of sound in both rooms. Any speaker cabinet is designed to do one of two things: either absorb the sound radiating from the back of the speaker into the "room" in back of the woofer or redirect the sound radiating from the back of the woofer to reinforce the sound coming from the front of the speaker.

PRODUCTION INSIGHTS

Planning a Theatre Sound System

The end product of any theatrical sound system is to produce sound that will support and enhance the mood and feeling of the production. Although it might seem appropriate to begin the planning of such a system from the point of origin of the sound (the microphone, CD player, computer, and so forth), actually the opposite is true. You should begin planning your system with the selection of a speaker system capable of producing the best-quality sound for the money.

Once an appropriate speaker system is selected, you will need to choose an amplifier that can drive those speakers efficiently and effectively. Working backward, you will next need to select equalizers and a mixer that can modify the tonal quality of the separate channels of the playback sources and can route the signal from any source to any of the amplifiers.

For planning purposes, the recording system can be thought of as being separate from the playback system. In actual practice, the average production company or theatre usually doesn't have the budget to purchase two separate systems, so the same equipment is usually used for both purposes.

The heart of the recording system is the recording device—usually a computer. A computer needs to have a multichannel sound recording/editing program. If tape decks are being used, the deck (preferably two or more decks so that you can dub, or transfer, sound from one deck to the other) should be stereophonic and commercial quality—the best deck that you can afford. A quality equalizer will provide the capability of modifying the tonal qualities of the signals before they are recorded. You will also need a CD player for transferring sound effects and music to computer—it can either be a stand-alone unit or the computer's on-board CD player/recorder— or tape, and you will need at least two microphones to record live sounds and music.

Sound reinforcement is also an active part of many theatrical sound systems. In this case, the source for the system is a microphone. Regardless of the number and type of microphones used on the production, the signal from each microphone is fed to a sound-mixing console or mixer, where the signals are equalized, balanced, and distributed to the proper amplifiers and speakers.

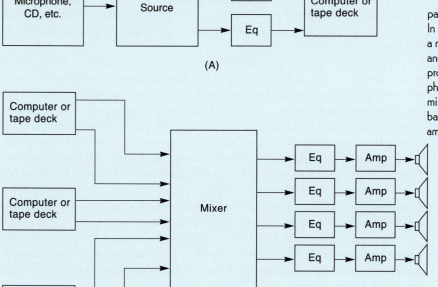

Block diagram of typical theatre sound systems:
(A) record,
(B) playback,
(C) reinforcement.

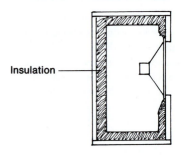

Insulation

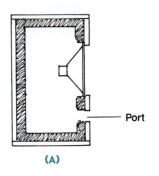

(A)

Port

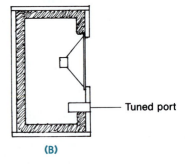

Tuned port

(B)

Finite Baffle   The cabinet design that absorbs sound waves produced by the rearward excursion of the speaker cone is called a finite baffle. It is basically an airtight box heavily lined with sound-absorbing fiberglass batts, as shown in Figure 21.20. The fiberglass helps reduce sound reflections inside the cabinet. In practical terms, it is rather inefficient, because it doesn't let the speaker work freely, and it requires a high-powered amplifier to achieve a satisfactory level of sound.

Bass-Reflex Enclosure   A bass-reflex enclosure is a cabinet with a carefully de-signed hole or port in the front. This port, shown in Figure 21.21A, is designed so that the sound produced by the rearward excursion of the speaker cone comes out synchronized, or in phase, with the sound being produced by the forward ex-cursion of the cone.

    The bass-reflex enclosure is also lined with sound-absorbing material to help reduce sound reflections inside the cabinet. Otherwise, it is distinctly possible that the bass frequencies could overwhelm the mid-range and high-frequency sounds being produced by the other elements of the speaker system.

Ducted Port   Ducted-port speaker cabinets are variations of the bass-reflex de-sign. Instead of an open port, as in the bass-reflex design, they have a tube of a specific length and diameter that projects into the cabinet from the face of the speaker board (the board on which the speaker is mounted). The length of this tube is "tuned" to a specific frequency range to reinforce a particular portion of the bass spectrum (Figure 21.21B).

    Speaker cabinets tend to help reinforce the low frequencies of the woofers and generally smooth out the quality of the bass response. Low-frequency sounds are omnidirectional, and unless they are focused, they spread in every direction from their source, as shown in Figure 21.22. Even though speaker cabinets are rel-atively transparent to low-frequency sounds, they do provide some help in fo-cusing the direction of the bass response. Greater focusing help is provided by solid reflecting surfaces such as floors, ceilings, and walls. Mid-range and high-frequency sound waves tend to radiate more directionally from the front of the speaker. In general, mid-range sound waves radiate approximately 180 degrees from the face of the speaker, and the angle of radiation for high-frequency sound waves becomes narrower as the frequency increases.

    The backs of most high-quality, cone-type, mid-range speakers and tweet-ers are sealed with a thin covering of metal to avoid any possibility of resonant in-terference from the vibrations of the woofer(s) when the smaller speakers are mounted in the cabinet.

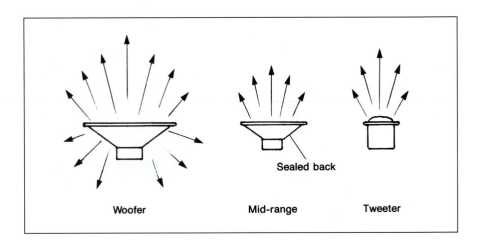

Sealed back

Woofer   Mid-range   Tweeter

PRODUCTION INSIGHTS

More On Amplifiers

A power amplifier does not have the capability of shaping or modifying sound. This is confusing to many people who have home stereo units. Their "amplifiers" almost always have controls that can boost or attenuate the bass and treble spectrum in addition to controls that adjust the volume or loudness of the music.

These home stereo units are more properly called "integrated amplifiers," because they integrate the functions of the preamplifier and equalizer (the shaping of the sound spectrum — bass and treble control) and those of the power amplifier (volume or loudness) into the same piece of equipment.

In professional-quality sound systems, such as those used for theatre sound, it is more usual to provide separate pieces of equipment (preamplifiers, equalizers, and amplifiers) rather than integrated amplifiers in order to increase quality, flexibility, and usefulness.

FIGURE 21.23
A power amplifier. (Courtesy of Crown International.)

Crossover Network   Optimum sound is achieved from a speaker when it is designed for a narrow frequency range. For those speakers to work most efficiently, however, they must receive only the specific frequency range for which they were designed. A crossover network, an electronic device normally mounted inside the speaker cabinet, splits the signal from the amplifier into the frequency ranges most appropriate for use by the speakers being used in the system. The woofer receives the low frequencies (approximately 20–300 Hz), the mid-range speaker is sent the middle frequencies (roughly 200–1,000 Hz), and the high frequencies (approximately 800 Hz up to inaudibility) are sent to the tweeter. There is a little overlap between the branches of the crossover network to smooth the transition of the sound as it moves from one speaker to the next within the system.

Crossovers are also designed for two-speaker systems (with a woofer and a combination mid-range and tweeter) as well as speaker systems that use more than three speakers.

Power Amplifier   The power amplifier is a relatively simple beast. Its sole reason for existence is to boost the low-voltage input signal that it receives from the input source — computer, mini-disk, CD player, tape deck, and so forth — to a higher-voltage output signal capable of efficiently driving the loudspeakers.

There are usually only two controls associated with an amplifier: an on-off power switch and a loudness control. The amplifier pictured in Figure 21.23 has two loudness controls because there are two separate amplifiers mounted on the same chassis.

Appropriately, the power rating of the power amplifier is its most important statistic. The **RMS wattage rating** of the amplifier should match the power-loading

RMS wattage rating: A system (root-mean-square) providing an accurate picture of the energy-dissipation characteristics of sound equipment.

FIGURE 21.24
An equalizer.

capabilities of the speaker with which it will be used. If the speaker system can handle 50 watts of steady power, the amplifier should be rated at no more than 50 watts RMS.

It isn't uncommon to find amplifiers rated at 200 or 400 watts RMS in the theatre. Rock bands routinely use 500- or higher-watt amplifiers to amplify each instrument and microphone in the group.

People frequently wonder why it is necessary to use amplifiers capable of generating so much power. The answer is clarity and quality of sound. A hypothetical, but realistic, example will illustrate the point. An average-sized auditorium may require 20 watts of power to play a musical selection at a reasonable listening level. If there is a momentary peak in the music that is twice as loud, it will take ten times the power from the amplifier to accomplish the task. The amplifier must be capable of putting out 200 watts of power to make the music seem twice as loud. If the amplifier cannot achieve this peak, the music will become distorted and will sound fuzzy and muddy rather than clear and crisp.

attenuate: To decrease or lessen.

Equalizer   An equalizer, as we have seen, boosts or **attenuates** portions of the signal to affect the loudness of specific segments of the sound spectrum. The tone controls for bass and treble on a home stereo integrated amplifier are "broadband" equalizers that affect a wide range of the bass and treble spectrums.

The analog equalizer pictured in Figure 21.24 has controls for boosting or attenuating a wide range of the bass and treble portions of the sound spectrum. It also has progressive filtering controls. These two controls, which can be used as a rumble filter (bass) and a scratch filter (treble), progressively filter out more and more of the bass and treble spectrums. Although this style of equalizer can still be used in both recording and playback, it has, to a great extent, been replaced by the graphic and parametric equalizers.

Graphic Equalizer   The equalizer pictured in Figure 21.25 is called a graphic equalizer because it graphically displays the equalization of the full sound spec-

FIGURE 21.25
A graphic equalizer GQX-3102 Stereo 31-band. (Courtesy of Ashly.)

FIGURE 21.26
A parametric equalizer. PEQ 55 dual channel. (Courtesy of Rane.)

trum. A specific portion of the sound spectrum is assigned to each slide control. When these controls are raised above the center position, they are boosting the specific portion of the sound spectrum that they control. When they are placed below the central position, they are attenuating the same element of the sound spectrum. When they are placed in the center of their movement range, they are not affecting the sound at all.

The graphic equalizer can be used during recording to help mask any scratch, rumble, or unwanted frequencies as well as enhance or shape the sound as envisioned by the sound designer. It is also used during playback of the sound into the auditorium to help balance the sound to the acoustics of the auditorium.

Parametric Equalizer   The parametric equalizer (Figure 21.26) is similar in function to the graphic equalizer in that it boosts or attenuates specific frequencies within the sound spectrum. The primary difference is that individual frequencies or very selective custom-designed bands of frequencies can be programmed for enhancing or attenuation with this equalizer. Although it can be used very effectively during recording, the parametric equalizer is primarily used for balancing the sound during playback into the auditorium.

Preamplifier   A preamplifier, or preamp, is an electronic device that raises the output of a low-level signal so that it can be read and processed, without distortion, by the next piece of equipment in the sound system.

Line level is the standard input voltage for mixers and equalizers. If a preamplifier can only boost the full spectrum of a low-level signal to line level—if it doesn't have the capability to boost or attenuate selected portions of the spectrum —it is generally referred to as a black-box preamp. The black-box preamp shown in Figure 21.27A is used to boost the weak signal of some microphones to line level. Figure 21.27B shows a preamp that boots the signal of a turntable's magnetic cartridge to line level. Figure 21.27C shows how a black-box preamp is

line level: A signal voltage range of approximately 0.75 to 1 volt; specified as a range rather than one particular voltage because the voltage and current of the signal vary with the intensity and frequency of the sound.

(A)

(B)

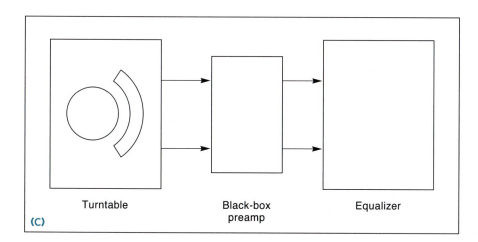

Turntable   Black-box preamp   Equalizer

(C)

FIGURE 21.27
Preamps. (A) ARTcessories MicroMIX. (B) ARTcessories DeeJayPre. (Courtesy of ARTcessories.) (C) Block diagram of the use of a black-box preamp with a turntable.

FIGURE 21.28
Focusrite MH441 4-channel microphone
preamp. (Courtesy of Focusrite.)

FIGURE 21.29
Mixers. (A) Digital Yamaha LS9-16. (B) Analog
Yamaha MG16/6FX. (Courtesy of Yamaha.)

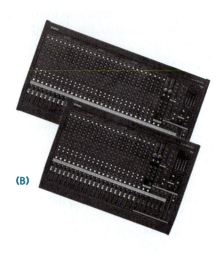

(B)

(A)

inserted into the circuit after the turntable and before the next piece of equipment
in line.

Not every preamp is a black box. Some have additional signal modification
capabilities such as equalization, filtering, and so forth as shown in Figure 21.28.
Many of these capabilities are included in the features of audio mixers, which will
be discussed next.

Mixers   The mixer (see Figure 21.29) is aptly named. It is a device that is used
to mix the output from a variety of sources and route the blended signal on to
other devices. With the increased use of complex sound designs, a mixer has become an indispensable part of the permanent sound-equipment inventory of a
producing theatre group.

Almost all mixers have inputs for microphones as well as line-level equipment (preamps, computers, tape decks, and so on). These inputs are usually permanently wired to a specific control channel or **assignable** to any of the control
channels on the mixer. In most mixers, each of these channels can control not only
the loudness but also the equalization of the signal sent to it. The output from
each control channel is either hard-wired to a specific submaster or master fader,
or it is assignable to any of the mixer's submasters or masters.

Figure 21.30, a schematic drawing of a similar **4-in/2-out** mixer, is provided
to show how a mixer works. The signal from any of the four inputs can be routed
to either of the two outputs. Any mixer, regardless of how many inputs and outputs it has, uses these principals.

assignable: In this case, the property of
being able to be assigned; e.g., an assignable input may be connected to any output
or any number of outputs.

4-in/2-out: A mixer device with four
inputs and two outputs.

Audio Master and Submaster Faders

The submaster and master faders that you'll find on most audio mixers utilize the group master control principles found on many lighting boards. Group master control was discussed in Chapter 16, "Lighting Production." Basically, those principles mean that an individual control channel is controlled by a submaster which, in turn, is controlled by a master fader.

For example, if you are doing sound reinforcement for a musical and you have four lead singers, you might want wireless mics on each singer. Each of those four mics would be assigned to an individual control channel on the mixer so you could balance the loudness and equalization for each singer. Once you have set the appropriate levels for each singer, those four inputs could be assigned to a submaster to provide collective control over the four leads. Assume you also have six mics in

various positions around the stage to pick up the chorus. Once the loudness levels for those mics have been balanced, they could be assigned to another submaster, the mics for the orchestra to a third submaster, and any effects to a fourth submaster. The master fader would then control all four submasters.

Having the various elements—leads, chorus, orchestra, effects—controlled in this manner allows you to balance the loudness and equalization within each group, then balance the groups against each other to provide the blend that best suits the needs of the production.

As you can see from this example, how the show is miked, and how those microphones are controlled, plays a significant role in the creation of an effective sound design.

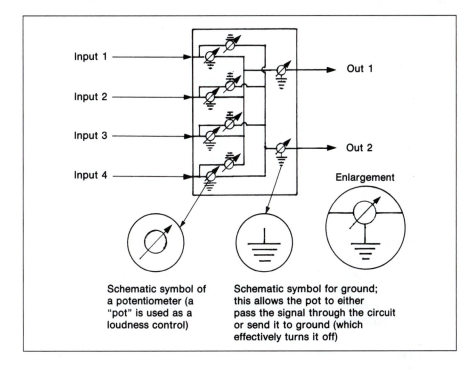

FIGURE 21.30
A block diagram of mixer operation.

In operation, if the mixer has submasters, the equalized signal from one or more control channels is sent through a submaster to a master fader and on to whatever equipment is connected to the output for that master. If the mixer doesn't have submasters, the equalized signal is sent directly to the master fader and on to the next equipment in line. This electronic capability allows the operator to create a designed mix, or blend, of any number of sources. When the mixer is used for recording, the blended signal is sent to whatever analog or digital recording device is being used—computer, CD, mini-disk, tape deck, digital cartridge machine, and so on. When the mixer is being used for playback during a performance, the signal is sent to an amplifier and speaker or headphones in the appropriate location—the auditorium, onstage, and wherever any cast or crew members need to listen to the show.

Current mixers generally have preset capability that works exactly like scene, or cue, memories in lighting. The sound designer creates specific **soundscapes** for those moments in the play when sound is being used and stores that information—relevant equipment, levels, fade times and so forth—in either the mixer's computer or a "stand-alone" computer or hard drive. When the cue is called by the stage manager, the sound operator activates the cue and the sound plays at the prerecorded levels. Presets can be used to store all relevant information—which amp/speakers are being used, loudness levels and equalization for effects, prerecorded music, as well as reinforcement microphones and so forth. The use of cue memories in sound dispenses with much of the "on the fly" mixing that used to be required during musicals and other multisource shows.

In practice, the mixer is used for both recording sound and playing it back. To illustrate how the mixer can be used in recording, let's assume that the production requires a recording of a small band. The sound designer mikes the singer and the individual instruments in the band, as shown in Figure 21.31. Each microphone is connected to an input on the mixer. During rehearsal the sound designer sets the loudness and equalization for each of the input sources. Appropriate loudness levels of these individual sources are then sent to two master controls (so that the song can be recorded in stereo), where those signals are blended. The outputs of these two masters are connected to the inputs of a computer or stereo tape deck for recording.

The mixer can also be very useful when you need to blend a number of sources during playback. Musical comedies present interesting challenges to the sound designer, who may be asked to blend the voice of one or more lead singers, the chorus, the band or orchestra, and perhaps one or more sound effects. This type of balancing act would be all but impossible without the aid of a mixer.

The lead singers are usually fitted with wireless (radio transmitter) microphones, the chorus voices are picked up with some general area microphones, the band is either miked or perhaps prerecorded, and the effects are in a computer file or on tape. Each one of these sources is assigned to a control channel of the mixer, as shown in Figure 21.32. As in the previous example, the sound designer determines appropriate levels for each of these sources, and they are blended on the master control(s). In this situation, the output signal of the master control(s) is sent to one or more amplifiers and loudspeakers. The box "Audio Master and Submaster Faders" shows how this type of mix can be facilitated with submasters. It is the sound designer's responsibility to ensure that the final mix of these various sources is what is needed to support the mood and feeling of the production.

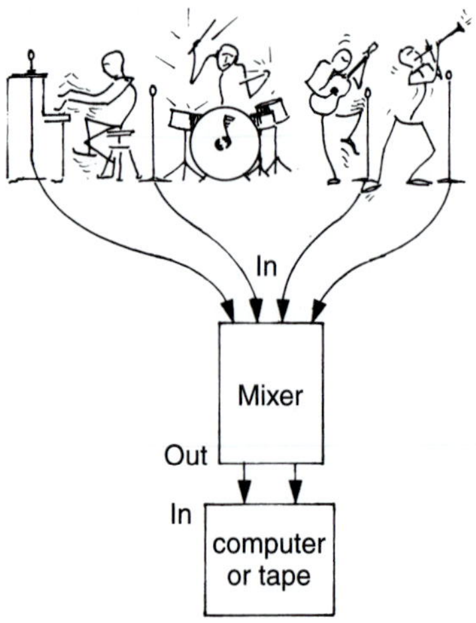

Patch Bay   A sound patch bay (Figure 21.33) is similar in purpose and construction to the patch panel used in lighting. The sound patch bay is used to cross-connect between the various pieces of equipment (CD player, tape deck, computer, equalizers, amplifiers, speakers, and so on). The outputs and inputs for each piece of equipment are connected to corresponding receptacles on the patch panel. A patch cord is used to connect the output of one piece of equipment to the input of another.

soundscape: The sound environment. The sound effects, music, and reinforcement being used at any particular moment in a play.

FIGURE 21.31
A block diagram of how a mixer is used in recording.

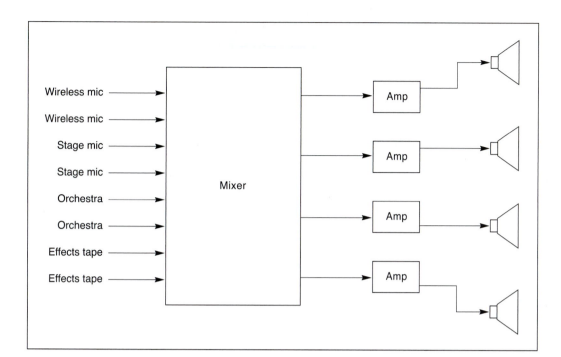

FIGURE 21.32
A block diagram of a mixer used in playback and reinforcement.

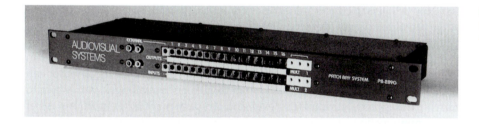

FIGURE 21.33
A sound patch bay. (Courtesy of Audiovisual Systems.)

Recording and Playback Equipment

Several types of equipment are used to record and playback sound in the theatre. While a great deal of analog equipment is still used in theatre sound, digital technology has, to a great extent, replaced analog in the recording and playback arena. Digital technology also enabled one crucial development—**show control**—that simply did not exist in the analog world. And show control would not have been possible without MIDI.

show control: Enabled by the MIDI Show Control protocol, show control generally refers to the process of using computers to precisely control the various equipment—sound playback, lighting, stage rigging, and so forth—used in a theatrical event.

MIDI   MIDI, or Musical Instrument Digital Interface, was developed in the early 1980s to allow synthesizers to communicate with each other. Technically speaking, MIDI is a standard digital protocol for the transmission of data. Just as DMX512 is the language that allows the various pieces of digitally controlled stage-lighting equipment to work together, MIDI is the communication language used between the various types of digital equipment used in theatre sound.

Originally, MIDI was developed so one musician could play multiple synthesizers simultaneously. In the original MIDI demonstration in 1983, two synthesizers were connected with cables—MIDI cables—that carried digital instructions between the devices. When a note was played on one instrument, a corresponding note simultaneously played on the other.

Digital recording is an important advance in the recording industry. The principle behind it is fairly simple. In a nondigital, or analog, recorder, the continuously varying voltage of the signal is converted into a magnetic field by the recorder head. The strength of that field varies according to the frequency, intensity, and timbre of the sound. This continuous signal is recorded onto the tape or disk.

In a digital recorder, the signal is converted into a series of individual, or discrete, numbers rather than a continuously varying magnetic field. The signal is read by an analog-to-digital converter 44,000 times a second. Each time the converter analyzes the signal, it translates that information into a binary number—a series of on-off pulses. It is this binary information that is stored on the tape or disk.

When a digital recording is played back, the process is simply reversed. The playback head reads the stored binary information. A digital-to-analog converter translates each binary number into a signal of a specific voltage and amplitude. The resulting output signal is essentially continuous, because the digital-to-analog conversion happens so frequently.

The advantages of digital recording are a significant increase in the accuracy or fidelity of the recording and a reduction in background noise—tape hiss. The price of professional-quality digital tape and disk recorders is now within the range of most production companies, and they are being used with increasing frequency.

Now MIDI is used to let all sorts of equipment communicate. Computers are at the top of the digital food chain in theatre sound. They are used to record and edit music and sound effects. They are also used to store sound presets, either in their internal hard drive or some type of external storage device. Finally, they can be used for show control. Via the MIDI Show Control protocol, a computer can tell any MIDI-equipped peripheral when to turn on, how long to run, when to turn off, the appropriate loudness level, and any number of other functions. All of this communication, and control, would not be possible without MIDI and, more particularly, MIDI Show Control.

Computer   As indicated above, the computer is now the heart of most theatre sound systems. It is used in every function—recording, editing, storage, playback, and show control.

Sound, whether effects or music, is gathered from a variety of sources—live recordings, CDs, the Internet, and so forth. Once the sound—music and effects—has been recorded or gathered, it will normally be downloaded to a computer's internal hard drive, or an external hard drive or server, and then edited using one of the many available sound editing software programs. The purpose of sound-editing software is to prepare the sound for playback. Specifically, the software is used to (1) edit—mix, process, and equalize—the individual cues; (2) assemble the **show file**—a master file that contains all the individual cues in the sequential order in which they'll be played during the production; (3) set appropriate **line level setting** and **fade rate** for the individual cues. One of the more popular sound-editing programs is Digidesign's Pro Tools. Used in every spectrum of the entertainment industry—theatre, music, film, and television—it is available in a variety of configurations that range from complete workstations to software and hardware plug-ins that can be added to an existing desktop or laptop computer. For more information about Pro Tools consult Digidesign's website at http://www.digidesign.com/.

A separate software package is used for playback. Playback software, such as the relatively low-priced SFX Machine RT, is used to program each sound cue in

show file: A digital file containing all the music and effects cues, in sequence, for an entire production; variously called show tape, sound file, production show tape, production sound file.

line level setting: The electronic equivalent of a loudness setting for the line level signal. An optimum line level signal would be loud enough to be distinctly heard by the next equipment in line—the power amplifier—but not so loud as to introduce distortion.

fade rate: The amount of time it takes for a fade—either fade-up or fade-down—to be completed.

PRODUCTION INSIGHTS
Sound Software Can Be Hypnotizing

The wonderful automation that is offered by the various sound editing/playback packages can be mesmerizing. And that can be a dangerous thing. When working on sound for a production it's both easy and convenient to think that after you've copied an effect from a sound library, tweaked it to create a signal at optimal line level with good equalization, then programmed the cue with speaker assignments, fade times, and loudness levels, that the job is finished. Artistically speaking, it would be better to think of that as the starting point in the development of that particular cue.

After you've created a cue you need to critically listen to it as it is played back in context, in the performance space, during a rehearsal. Does it create the desired effect? Does it sound "right"? Would adjusting any of "the adjustables" — equalization, loudness, fade rates, speaker assignment, or speaker location — enhance the cue's effect? Would an altogether different sound create a better effect — one that is closer to the original intent? It is axiomatic that no cue is ever perfect. Almost all of them can be improved if only a little bit. It is the job of the sound designer to keep listening, and adjusting those adjustables, until the show is as good as she or he can get it, and it is "locked in" during the tech/dress rehearsal period.

the production show file for playback in the performance space. The information assigned to each cue includes its specific speaker routing—which speaker the sound is assigned to—as well as its appropriate loudness level. When running a show with playback software, about the only thing that the sound operator needs to do when a cue is called by the stage manager is make sure the appropriate cue is on standby and ready to be activated, and then push the "GO" button. Information about everything else—equalization, fade rates, loudness, and speaker routing—is programmed into each cue. A demonstration of the SFX software's capabilities can be found at http://www.sfxmachine.com/simulator/index.html. Higher end playback and show control software packages, such as those offered by LCS Audio, are also available. These packages, which are based on their flagship programming and show control system Matrix3, are currently in wide use in a variety of venues ranging from Cirque du Soleil spectaculars in Las Vegas to Broadway musicals, cruise ships, churches, and other production facilities. More information about their products can be found at http://www.lcsaudio.com. It should be noted that there are other reputable manufacturers of excellent playback and show control software and software/hardware packages. A quick search of the Internet will reveal a number of excellent additional manufacturers.

The use of the laptop both as a supplement to, and replacement for, desktop computers is increasing in the area of sound design. Laptops installed with sound-editing software facilitate the designer's ability to edit cues whenever time and circumstances allow. They also allow on-the-fly adjustments to be made to existing cues during sound and tech rehearsals. As smaller more powerful computers come on the market, they will increasingly be adopted for a variety of innovative tasks in sound design as well as in other areas within the broad field of theatrical production.

Digital Audio Tape (DAT)   Digital audio tape (DAT) recorders are cassette tape–based recorders (Figure 21.34). They use a rotary head to lay down information in a diagonal track across the tape, utilizing the same technology as a videocassette recorder. Not coincidentally, the first DAT recorders were simply modified videocassette recorders. Interestingly, some DAT recorders have further

FIGURE 21.34
A DAT recorder. (Courtesy of Tascam.)

FIGURE 21.34
A DAT recorder. (Courtesy of Tascam.)

been modified to replace the cassette tape storage device with Flash Memory cards similar to those used in digital cameras or the widely available USB flash memory devices used for portable memory with computers.

With a DAT recorder the head of each recorded track can be identified by a marker so the operator can quickly search for the lead of the various tracks on a tape. Tapes are available in lengths from a few minutes to two hours although the two-hour tape is somewhat fragile. DATs are generally used for live recording; but because of their somewhat temperamental nature, they are not normally used for playback during a production.

Compact Disc The compact disc (CD) is the standard storage device in the recording industry. The process of digitization is explained in the box "Digital Recording" on page 532. Like digital tapes, CDs have audio information stored on them in binary code. The information is stored on the disc as a series of reflective and nonreflective surfaces. To read the information, the CD player directs a laser on the surface of the spinning disc. The light from the laser is reflected from the shiny surface and absorbed by the nonreflective (black) surface. A light-sensitive reader interprets this information as binary code, which is subsequently sent to the next piece of equipment in line.

For two reasons—cost and quality—CDs are now the storage medium of choice for many sound designers. The cost of recording sound on CDs is extremely low. Most computers now come equipped with CD burners, or they can be purchased aftermarket. The cost of the discs is very low, the quality of the recorded sound is extremely high, and the time required to **burn** the discs is almost negligible.

burn: To record on a CD.

There are two types of CDs used for recording. CD-R discs can be recorded on once. CD-RW discs can be re-recorded. Depending on the recording software and equipment used, it is frequently possible to attach a label to each marker. This labeling system can be used to identify tracks either by name, or cue number, or both. It will appear on a display on the recorder, on the show control computer, or on both.

At this writing there doesn't seem to be any consensus as to how best to use the two "writable" formats or whether one is "better" than the other. But experimentation does, as it always will, continue.

FIGURE 21.35
A MiniDisc recorder. (Courtesy of HHB.)

MiniDisc Sony's MiniDisc (Figure 21.35) is another consumer product that has found its way into the theatre. Sound is recorded in this digital two-track system on a small optical-magnetic, plastic-encased disc. "A laser heats up the surface of the disc to a point where it is easily magnetized, and a coil produces a magnetic field that varies in relation to the current produced in the coil by a digital data-stream."[1] As the rotating disc cools, the magnetized information becomes stable until the recording process begins again. Because the manner in which the information is recorded, it is advisable to keep MiniDiscs away from both heat and strong magnetic fields.

The head of each track on a MiniDisc is identified with a marker that can be labeled. Because you can record and erase either the whole disc or individual tracks on a MiniDisc, the tracks can be reordered, and new tracks can be added or removed. While these qualities would seem to make the MiniDisc an ideal option for recording and playback, in production playback it has a history of both the discs and decks malfunctioning at the most inopportune times. In production, the recommendation is to use a professional-grade deck that is serviced on a regular basis and to use discs that have not been previously recorded.

Digital Cartridge Machines   These machines are digital versions of the NAB analog cartridge machines that were developed for the broadcast industry but found a happy home in the theatre. The advantages of digital cart machines are similar to those of the digital disc and tape media discussed above: The machines are compact and silent; they start instantly, and the head of each track can be marked and labeled. They also offer the distinct advantage that they automatically re-cue themselves. About the only disadvantage is that you need one cartridge per cue. If a show has a large number of sound effects, you could end up with a whole stack of cartridges sitting on the sound desk just waiting to be knocked over.

As if computers weren't taking over everything else, there is now a software program, WaveCart, that replaces the digital cart machine. Instead of a stand-alone machine and all those cartridges, the software provides the instant start/automatic re-cueing features that made cart machines the favorite of many sound designers. WaveCart can be controlled by your computer mouse, keyboard, or mixer.

Tape Deck   Analog reel-to-reel tape decks were, for many years, the standard recording and playback equipment in theatre sound. While some theatres and producing organizations still use this equipment, when it wears out it is generally replaced by some combination of the digital equipment described above. But because there are still a reasonably large number of tape decks out there in theatre land, and knowing how they work is important to some, the information on analog tape decks and constructing a show tape is still included in this text. It has been moved to Appendix B at the back of the book.

Microphones   As noted, microphones convert mechanical sound waves into an electrical signal. Although the ideal microphone would make this conversion without altering the frequency, timbre, or dynamic range (loudness variations) of the mechanically produced sound, such a microphone, unfortunately, does not exist. There are five basic types of microphones, each making the conversion of sound waves into electrical signals with slightly different techniques and with considerable differences in quality.

Carbon Microphone   When the vibrations of sound waves strike the diaphragm of a carbon microphone, as shown in Figure 21.36, they exert minute pressure

[1] John A. Leonard, *Theatre Sound* (New York: Theatre Arts / Routledge, 2001), p. 60.

piezoelectricity: Voltage produced when pressure is placed on certain crystals.

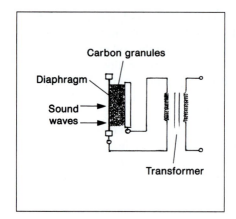

FIGURE 21.36
A carbon microphone.

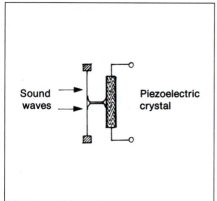

FIGURE 21.37
A crystal microphone.

changes on the granules of carbon. These pressure changes cause a change in the electrical resistance of the granules. The change in resistance causes corresponding changes in a low-voltage current that is applied to the variable resistance of the carbon granules.

The carbon microphone is widely used in the mouthpiece of telephones. It is extremely rugged and has a very narrow frequency response. Carbon mics are not really suitable for recording theatre sound unless you are trying to duplicate the sound of someone talking over a telephone.

Crystal Microphone   Crystal microphones take advantage of the **piezoelectric** properties of certain crystalline minerals. In a crystal microphone, piezoelectric crystals are sandwiched between two pieces of metal, as shown in Figure 21.37. Sound waves striking the diaphragm exert pressure on the crystals, and they produce a signal whose voltage variations mimic the pressure changes caused by the sound source.

Crystal mics have a little better frequency response than carbon ones have, and they are also extremely rugged. They are often sold with less expensive tape recorders. They are not of high enough quality to be used for recording sound that will be used in the theatre.

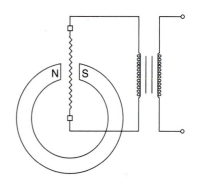

FIGURE 21.38
A ribbon microphone.

Ribbon Microphone   Ribbon microphones are made of a corrugated strip of very thin metal that is suspended between the poles of a magnet, as shown in Figure 21.38. When someone speaks into the microphone, the sound waves strike the ribbon of metal, moving it back and forth within the field of the magnet. This movement induces a small voltage between the two ends of the ribbon. The pattern of this varying voltage is an electrical duplication of mechanical pressure changes produced by the voice of the person speaking into the mic.

The ribbon microphone has a very good frequency response, but it is quite delicate. The ribbon can be easily broken just by blowing on it. High-quality ribbon mics are frequently used in radio broadcasting, but their delicacy makes them a little too fragile to stand up to the sometimes abusive treatment they receive in the theatre.

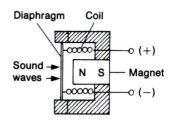

FIGURE 21.39
A dynamic microphone.

Dynamic Microphone   Dynamic microphones create their signals by inducing a small current in a coil that is firmly attached to the diaphragm of the microphone. The coil is surrounded by a magnetic yoke, as illustrated in Figure 21.39. Pressure changes caused by the sound waves striking the diaphragm move the coil up and down within the magnetic field generated by the yoke, with the result

Condenser is actually an obsolete word for a capacitor. A capacitor is a device that has two conductive surfaces separated by some type of insulating material, such as air. The capacitor acts as an electrical reservoir and floodgate. It will store a certain amount of electrical energy. When it reaches its capacity, it allows an alternating current to pass through it as long as the current does not reduce its "full" state. If the distance between the two conducting plates is changed, the "capacity" (more properly known as capacitance) of the capacitor is similarly changed. A greater distance between the plates increases the capacitance; less distance decreases it.

capacitance: The electrical capacity of a condenser, or capacitor.

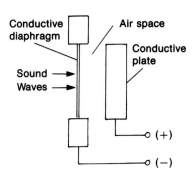

FIGURE 21.40
A condenser microphone.

that a current is induced in the coil. The strength of the induced current mimics the frequency and intensity of the sound source. Dynamic microphones have very good frequency response, are rugged, and are suitable for recording of theatre sound.

Condenser Microphone   The condenser mic is the most electrically complex type of microphone. The diaphragm, which is made of thin conductive material, forms one plate of a condenser, or capacitor. The other plate is placed very close to it, as shown in Figure 21.40. A constant voltage is applied across these plates. When a sound wave strikes the diaphragm, the pressure changes the space between the two plates. This causes a change in the **capacitance** of the condenser, which results in a change in the voltage applied between the two plates. The resultant variations in the voltage are an electrical reproduction of the mechanical pressure changes originated by the sound source.

The condenser microphone is probably the highest-quality one used for recording sound in the theatre. It has excellent frequency response and dynamic range (sensitivity to changes in loudness). It needs a power supply, but in most cases a small battery supplies the necessary power. As with any precision instrument, the condenser microphone needs to be handled with care, but it is reasonably rugged and can stand up to the type of abuse that it will receive in theatrical work.

Microphone Pickup Patterns   Microphones do not discriminate in what they hear. They will pick up, and convert into an electrical signal, any sound within their pickup range. Several distinct pickup patterns have been developed to assist in making microphones somewhat discriminating.

An *omnidirectional* microphone pattern extends in a spherical pattern around the mic head, as shown in Figure 21.41A. Wireless microphones (see box on page 537) frequently have omnidirectional patterns. For stage use, the microphone is usually small enough to be hidden somewhere in the actor's costume. The microphone is connected to a small battery-powered transmitter that is also hidden within the costume.

Stage monitor systems, which pick up the actors' voices and send them to various remote locations around the theatre (lighting and sound booths, dressing rooms, and so on) generally use a microphone with an omnidirectional pattern so that the voices and noises of the production can be picked up regardless of their location on stage.

The *bidirectional* configuration, commonly referred to as the Figure 8 pattern (Figure 21.41B), easily picks up sounds in front of and behind the microphone but does not readily "hear" sounds to its side. Because of their structure, ribbon microphones, which were described in the previous section, inherently possess this

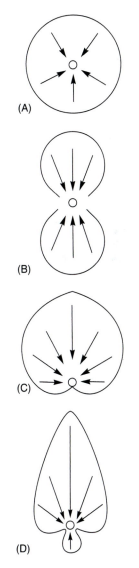

FIGURE 21.41
Microphone pickup patterns.

A wireless microphone has a significant advantage over its wired counterpart. It does not need a mic cable to connect it to the mixer. Instead, the signal is broadcast by a low-power FM radio transmitter to a receiver and subsequently fed into the mixer.

At first glance, the wireless microphone may seem the answer to the sound designer's dreams. However, it does have some significant drawbacks. The batteries that power the microphone transmitter must be checked, and usually changed, for every performance. Since the signal is broadcast, the receiver is also subject to receiving other broadcast signals, as well as other types of interference. In moderate to large cities, it is not unusual for wireless microphone receivers to pick up local radio stations as well as the microphones. If more than one wireless microphone is to be used, they need to transmit on different frequencies so that the sound operator can monitor the individual performers. Typically, a production requires three to five leading characters to be equipped with wireless microphones. Finally, the systems are expensive. A good-quality wireless microphone, which will transmit and receive within a very narrow frequency range, costs between $1,000 and $3,000.

But even with all of these drawbacks, the wireless microphone provides an excellent method of miking a show. If the challenges outlined above can be surmounted (and they can), the wireless microphone provides probably the finest method of reinforcing the voice in the theatre. The presence attained by having the microphone placed close to the actor's mouth can be matched only with a handheld microphone; no other theatrical reinforcement system comes close.

(A)

(B)

(C)

FIGURE 21.42
Microphones. (A) Handheld microphones can be held by performers or mounted on stands. (Courtesy of Electro-Voice.) (B) Wireless microphones use a small radio transmitter and receiver to send the signal to the mixer. (Courtesy of Electro-Voice.) (C) Pressure-zone microphones (PZM) are very small omnidirectional condenser microphones that pick up, with great clarity and presence, sounds up to 10 or 15 feet away. (Courtesy of Crown International.)

bidirectional property. They can, however, be designed to have other pickup patterns. This type of microphone pattern is very good for conducting interviews, for recording two instruments when the musicians are facing each other, and for similar situations.

Directional microphone patterns use two primary configurations, cardioid and hypercardioid. The *cardioid* pattern, shown in Figure 21.41C, is somewhat heart shaped. It has excellent pickup characteristics directly to the front of the microphone, and the sensitivity falls off as you move to the sides. Once you move past the sides of the microphone, there is almost no pickup from the rear. The cardioid pattern is probably most useful for general theatrical applications. It is very good for recording and reinforcement, because of its characteristic rejection of noise from the side and back.

The *hypercardioid,* or supercardioid, pattern is simply a more directional adaptation of the cardioid pattern, as shown in Figure 21.41D. Although it has a stronger rejection of lateral sounds, it does have an increased sensitivity to the rear.

Any type of microphone (carbon, crystal, ribbon, dynamic, or condenser) can be designed with any pickup pattern. For theatrical purposes, high-quality dynamic or condenser microphones with cardioid pickup patterns are the most useful.

As with almost every other type of equipment, a wide variety of microphones are available. A few of the more common types used in the theatre are illustrated in Figure 21.42.

It is all but impossible to determine the pickup pattern of a microphone simply by looking at it. However, every quality microphone will have the manufacturer's name and the model number indicated somewhere on the case of the microphone. When this information is known, the type and pattern of the microphone can be found by referring to the appropriate manufacturer's catalog or website.

PRODUCTION INSIGHTS

Sound Equipment Maintenance

Despite the rugged appearance of some pieces, all sound equipment is delicate. The proper functioning of speakers, microphones, and tape decks relies on the maintenance of physical tolerances measured in thousandths of an inch. All electronic equipment is adversely affected by dust, moisture, and smoke. For these reasons, the following procedures should be followed:

1. Never smoke, eat, or drink in the sound booth or around sound (or other electronic) equipment.

2. Cover all tape decks, amplifiers, and other equipment with cloth dustcovers when they are not in use. While plastic dustcovers will protect the equipment from dust, the static electricity charges that can be generated with some types of plastics can adversely affect the equipment.

3. Store microphones on some type of padded surface in a cabinet.

4. Coil all microphone and speaker cable and hang on a peg board when not in use.

5. Inspect the connectors for all microphone and speaker cables before and after each use. Make sure that there are no loose or frayed wires and that the strain reliefs (where applicable) are in place.

6. Never blow into a microphone when trying to determine if it is "on" or "live." Blowing can damage or get moisture on the internal parts. Don't thump the mike. Speak into the microphone in a normal voice, or gently snap your fingers.

The Sound Booth

The sound booth is designed to facilitate both the recording of cues and the playback of sound effects during the production. The specific layout, or placement, of the equipment in the booth is a matter of individual taste, but the operator should have a view of the stage when playing the sound during the production. The layout should be both logical and efficient (Figure 21.43).

If extensive reinforcement or balancing of a variety of sources has been dictated by the sound design, the sound operator needs to be located in the auditorium rather than the sound booth (see Figure 21.11 on page 519). This configuration is required because the operator needs to hear what the audience is hearing to

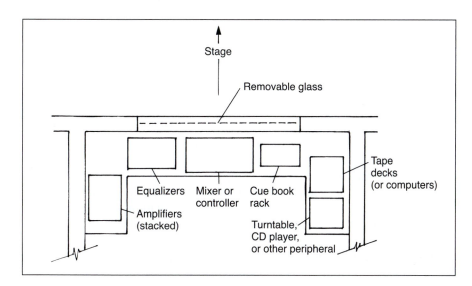

FIGURE 21.43
A typical sound booth layout.

The following discussion is based on, and quotes from, the article, "On Sound: The Art, the Technology, and the Facilitator," by Abe Jacob (Eddy Theatre Product Guide, A Special Supplement to ENTERTAINMENT DESIGN Magazine, Spring 2003, p. 1). Permission to publish granted by Entertainment Design.

In recent years, the implementation of two inventions, the reversible conversions of analog information to digital signals and the computer, have revolutionized sound design almost as much as the introduction of controllable gas lighting at the Paris Opera House in 1920 forever revolutionized established theatrical production values. With today's new methods of managing sound—recording, synthesizing, manipulating, improving, and changing the way sound is perceived—the possibilities for real artistry are boundless. Of the five human senses, hearing and sight are considered the primary instruments for human interaction. Sound design is associated with the knowledge to provide the means for entertainment and communication using the sense of hearing as the medium.

The ability to manipulate sound using digital signals and the computer has done wonders for the artistry of sound. All of the controls needed to operate and mix a Broadway show can be contained within a centralized self-contained digital mixing system and rack containing a computer and a power supply. When engineered and implemented with care, this means far less time for the designer "getting to know" all the different pieces of equipment (because they no longer exist) and more time focusing on the art of sound design.

All that being said, however, for the future, I believe that Mies van der Rohe's dictum "less is more" is still correct. I have come to the conclusion, after all these years, that the theatre's best sound design must be acoustically and physically invisible and transparent. The audience should not think about the sound of the show, merely enjoy it.

I urge all designers to take every advantage of the new technology and science that makes this challenge even easier. But remember, to do our job properly even with the aid of technology, it is the individual designer and the designer's sense of hearing that is the final arbiter of what we do and how well we do it. Use the tools but rely on your ears to do the job properly. With that effort, sound will continue to be a vital part of the entertainment world.

create a properly balanced mix of the various sources. Although this arrangement may bother some theatre patrons, the improvement in the balance and focus of the sound mix more than compensates for the slight aesthetic annoyance of having the sound operator and his or her equipment perched in the middle of the audience space.

Rehearsal and Performance Procedures   For a very good reason, the rehearsal and performance procedures for sound are almost identical to those for lights. Both media are intangible, so you must have clear, concise instructions that tell you at what level to set each piece of equipment (preamps, mixers, equalizers, and amplifiers) for every cue in the production. In this way, the loudness level of the sound will be the same from each rehearsal or performance to the next. A sample cue sheet is shown in Figure 21.44.

The sound cue sheet provides the sound operator with an organized method of recording not only the level of each piece of equipment but also notations on whether the cue is to fade in or start at a specific level. There is also space to make notes regarding anything of importance pertaining to the cue.

Playback Layout Pattern

Sound cues are similar in many ways to lighting cues. They are most noticeable when a mistake is made. Comedians have developed entire comedy routines around sound cues that either don't happen or happen too early or too late—gunshots that come three seconds after the trigger is pulled, explosions that don't go off, clocks tolling the wrong time, and so on. Many of these glitches can be prevented by careful preparation of the playback files.

Sound cues can be played back from computer files or tape. Computer-recorded cues are relatively straightforward and dependent on the capabilities and requirements of the computer program used. Each cue is recorded as a separate file and the file name correlated with a specific cue: for example, "Sound Q3—

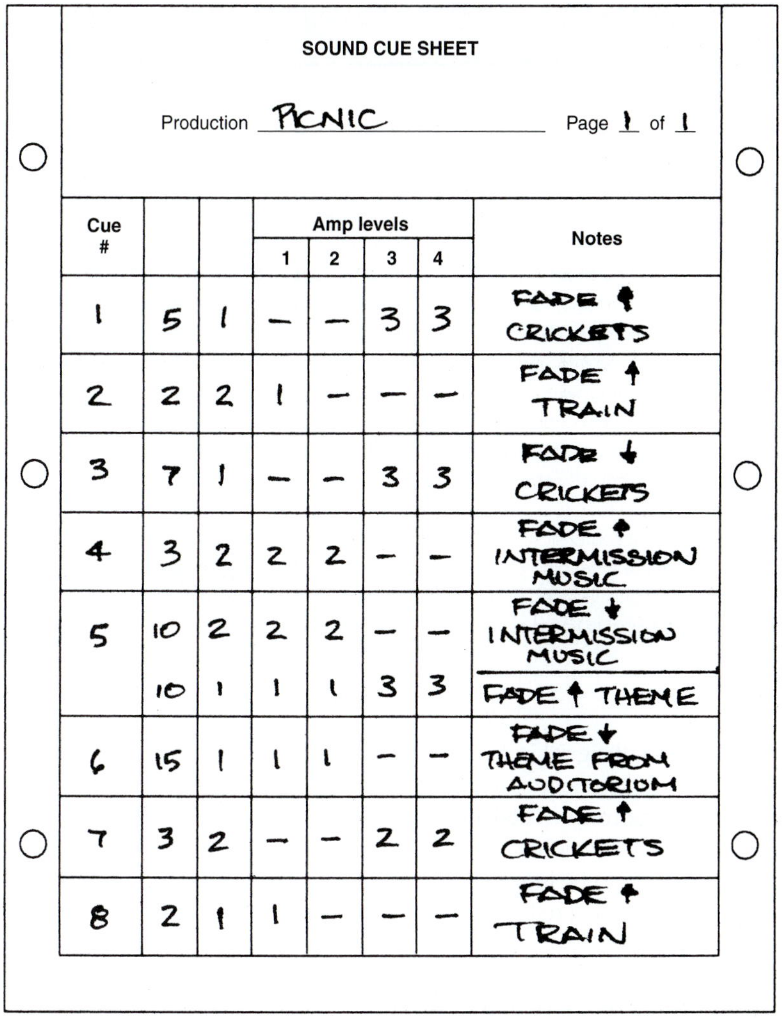

SOUND CUE SHEET

Production **PICNIC**   Page **1** of **1**

Cue #			Amp levels				Notes
			1	2	3	4	
1	5	1	—	—	3	3	FADE ↑ CRICKETS
2	2	2	1	—	—	—	FADE ↑ TRAIN
3	7	1	—	—	3	3	FADE ↓ CRICKETS
4	3	2	2	2	—	—	FADE ↑ INTERMISSION MUSIC
5	10	2	2	2	—	—	FADE ↓ INTERMISSION MUSIC
	10	1	1	1	3	3	FADE ↑ THEME
6	15	1	1	1	—	—	FADE ↓ THEME FROM AUDITORIUM
7	3	2	—	—	2	2	FADE ↑ CRICKETS
8	2	1	1	—	—	—	FADE ↓ TRAIN

FIGURE 21.44
A sample sound cue sheet.

Distant Dog Howl." The cues are stored in sequential order—the order in which they will be played in the production—in a show directory. If a cue is added, it is a relatively simple matter to insert the cue in its appropriate location in the show directory. Cues that are dropped from the production are easily deleted from the show directory. (Note: *Always* run a backup disk after *any* change to the sound cues. It's better to be safe than sorry.)

 ## Practical Considerations

Every time you hook up a modular sound system (one in which each component of the system is a separate unit), you need to be aware of the input and output levels of the various elements. Otherwise, you could damage or destroy one or more of the pieces of equipment.

Preamp and Power-Amp Output

The electronic signal that is created by an analog sound source (microphone, turntable, and the like) is a low-voltage AC signal. Generally, this signal ranges from about 1 to 750 millivolts, depending on the intensity and frequency of the

PRODUCTION INSIGHTS
Magnetic Fields and Inductance

A magnetic field is generated around any electrical wire that has current flowing through it. This includes the permanent wiring running through the walls of a theatre, an electric motor, a table lamp, or an extension cord. To minimize the effects of interference caused by these magnetic fields, you need to understand how they are generated. The field takes the form of a cylinder of varying density and size around the current-carrying wire. The size and strength of the field are dependent on the amount of current passing through the wire: the more current, the stronger and bigger it is.

If a cable carrying a sound signal is placed parallel with the offending electrical wire, a strong signal is induced in the cable. This induced signal is heard as a hum or hiss. If the cable is placed perpendicular to the wire that is generating the field, however, almost no signal is induced in the cable.

The effects of induced interference (known as inductance) can also be lessened by removing the sound cable from the vicinity of the power wire. This solution doesn't always work, because when you move the cable away from one power line, you are probably moving it closer to another.

If you have ever been in a recording studio, you may have noticed that the microphone cables look rather messy, zigzagging across the floor. This frequently changing, apparently random pattern is created to reduce the effects of inductance from nearby power lines.

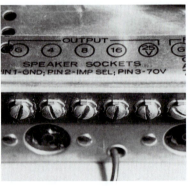

(A)

(B)

FIGURE 21.45
(A) Output terminal board; (B) 8-ohm speaker hookup.

impedance: Resistance in an AC circuit; the only difference between impedance and resistance is that impedance is defined as resistance to the flow of an *alternating* current.

sound. This very small signal is susceptible to interference from almost any device in the vicinity that generates a magnetic field around it. The interference creates noises that range from clicks and hisses to a steady hum, depending on its strength and nature. If the voltage of the signal were greater, however, the effects of the interference would be lessened. Consequently, as soon as the signal is generated by the source, it is usually boosted to line level by a preamp.

Line level is the dynamic voltage range of the signal that is used between the various pieces of equipment of a typical sound system. Because the input and output signal is the same strength (line level) for the various pieces of equipment that make up the major part of any theatrical sound system, it is possible to configure the equipment in any way that suits your needs (mic to preamp to equalizer to tape deck; tape deck to mixer to equalizer to power amp; and so on).

The output of a power amplifier has a much higher voltage so that it will be capable of driving its associated speaker system. Depending on the loudness of the sound, a typical power amp output signal can range between 1 and 35 volts. Because of the power amp's relatively high voltage output, its output terminal should never be patched into the input of anything other than a speaker. If you were to do so, you would probably destroy the equipment that the power amp was patched into and severely damage the amplifier as well.

Speaker Hookup Methods

A wide variety of wiring practices can be used to connect a speaker to a power amplifier. Most of these methods can be conveniently categorized as either low- or high-voltage systems.

Low-Voltage Systems   Most power amps have a variety of output options, as shown in Figure 21.45A. To ensure the best quality sound from the system (and to avoid damaging the amplifier), you should always match the **impedance** of the speaker (normally 4, 8, or 16 ohms) with the output impedance of the amplifier. The most expedient method of matching impedances is to connect a speaker system of a specific impedance to the power-amp speaker output of the same im-

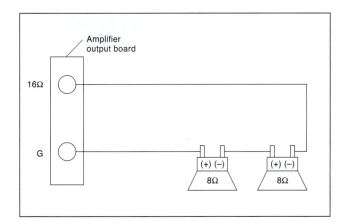

FIGURE 21.46
Series wiring of speakers.

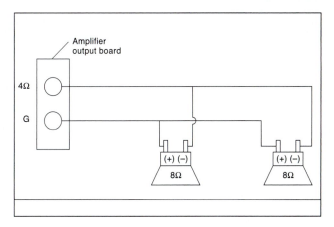

FIGURE 21.47
Parallel wiring of speakers.

pedance, as shown in Figure 21.45B. However, it is frequently necessary or desirable to drive more than one speaker with a single amplifier. This can be accomplished by wiring the speakers in a series, a parallel, or a combination circuit before attaching them to the output terminal of the amplifier.

Figure 21.46 illustrates how to wire speakers in series. To determine the total load for a series circuit, you simply add the impedances of all speakers in the circuit. In the illustrated example, the two speakers each have an impedance of 8 ohms. Adding them yields 16 ohms, which is the total load for the speaker circuit. To achieve distortion-free sound, you would connect this circuit to the 16-ohm connection on the speaker terminal board of the amplifier.

Loudspeakers or speaker systems can also be wired in parallel, as shown in Figure 21.47. The load for a parallel circuit is determined by the formula

$$\text{Circuit impedance} = \frac{\dfrac{S+S+S}{N}}{N}$$

where S equals the impedance of each speaker in the circuit and N equals the number of speakers in the circuit. In Figure 21.47, each of the two speakers in the circuit has an impedance of 8 ohms. Inserting those figures in the formula provides the answer to the circuit impedance:

$$\frac{\dfrac{S+S=8+8=16}{N}}{N} = \frac{\dfrac{2}{2}}{2} = \frac{\dfrac{2}{2}}{2} = \frac{8}{2} = 4 \text{ ohms}$$

This circuit should be connected to the 4-ohm outlet by attaching one wire to the 4-ohm and the other to the ground or neutral outlet on the speaker terminal board of the amplifier.

In order to balance the impedance of the speakers to the impedance of the amplifier output, it may become necessary to use a combination circuit, as illustrated in Figure 21.48. The combination circuit combines the effects of both series and parallel circuitry. To calculate the total impedance of the circuit, first calculate the impedance of the parallel portions of the circuit. Then, treating each parallel portion of the circuit as though it were just one speaker in a series circuit, add the impedances of the individual speakers to determine the impedance of the whole circuit.

In general, speakers wired in parallel have a cleaner sound than speakers wired in series. Series-wired speakers suffer a slight loss of quality, and the sound may seem somewhat muddy.

PRODUCTION INSIGHTS

Unbalanced and Balanced Lines

Two systems are used for distributing the electronic signal between the various pieces of a modular sound system: unbalanced line and balanced line.

Unbalanced Line

The unbalanced-line method of circuiting, shown in Figure A, utilizes one insulated conductor wrapped in a braided or foil shield. This shield is protected by an outer covering of insulation. The single conductor carries the signal, and the shield is used as a combined neutral and ground connection.

Balanced Line

The balanced line is identical to the unbalanced line, except that it has two conductors wrapped in the shield. One of the conductors carries the signal, and the other acts as the neutral. The shield is used as a ground connection. The balanced line requires the use of two small line transformers, so called because they are connected into the line or cable. One, a step-up transformer, is used at the source; a step-down transformer is attached at the other end of the cable. The balanced line creates a circuit that is immune to the effects of magnetically induced interference.

There are two primary differences between the two types of lines. The balanced line (two conductors) costs more and greatly reduces magnetically induced interference.

Balanced lines are frequently employed with microphones used to reinforce actors' voices during a production. In these cases, it is almost always necessary to run the microphone cables for a long distance before they are fed into a mixer. Using a balanced line for these long cable runs keeps induced interference to a minimum.

Unbalanced lines are normally used to hook up the various pieces of equipment in the sound booth. In this type of situation, the cable runs are usually short, which keeps the effects of magnetically induced interference to a minimal level.

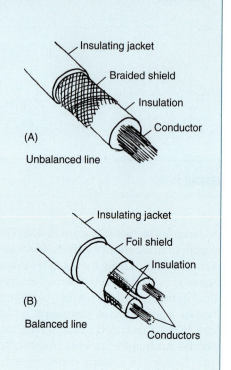

(A)
Unbalanced line

Insulating jacket
Braided shield
Insulation
Conductor

(B)
Balanced line

Insulating jacket
Foil shield
Insulation
Conductors

Most quality amplifiers are capable of driving speakers or speaker systems whose impedance is from one-half to double the rated output impedance of the amplifier. There will be some loss of quality, but most amplifiers are capable of driving these mismatched loads without suffering major damage. However, it is infinitely preferable to exactly match the impedance of the load with the impedance of the speaker. This solution will produce the best possible sound and will also minimize the chances of damaging the amplifier. The ideal solution to all of these challenges is to have each speaker driven by its own matched amplifier.

To avoid any loss of signal due to resistance in the wire that is used to connect the speaker to the amplifier, all connections where the speaker is less than 50 feet from the amplifier (or wall-mounted speaker outlet terminal) can usually be made with 18-gauge electrical wire. When the speaker is between 50 and 150 feet away from the amplifier (or wall-mounted speaker outlet), 16-gauge electrical wire can be used. Lamp cord (also known as zip cord) provides a perfectly adequate, reasonably low-cost alternative to the more expensive speaker hookup wire sold in sound shops.

High-Voltage Speaker Systems   As previously shown in Figure 21.45A, there are often additional speaker-output terminals besides the traditional low-voltage 4-, 8-, and 16-ohm outputs. In the United States, these high-voltage outputs have been standardized at 25 and 70 volts.

High-voltage outputs have three primary advantages: (1) They provide an effective alternative solution when it is necessary to have a number of speakers on the same system, (2) they transmit the signal over a long cable run with less loss

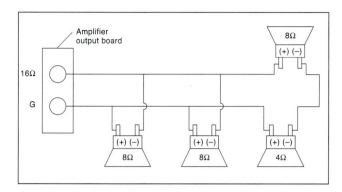

FIGURE 21.48
Combination wiring in a speaker circuit.

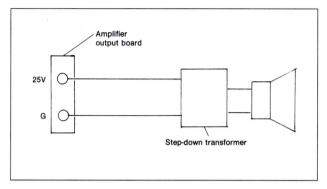

FIGURE 21.49
High-voltage speaker system.

of quality than a low-voltage system, and (3) they reduce the effects of inductive interference.

The high-voltage transmission system steps up the voltage of the output signal at the amplifier. When the high-voltage signal reaches the speaker cabinet, it is first passed through a step-down transformer, which decreases the voltage to a level that will not burn out the speaker (nominally 3.2 volts), as shown in Figure 21.49. If the step-down transformer is not used, the voice coil of the speaker will probably be destroyed.

Determining the proper loading of the amplifier and speakers in a high-voltage system isn't difficult. The relatively high voltage of the signal pragmatically nullifies the effects of the impedance in the system. When connecting a speaker or speakers to the system, simply make sure that you do not exceed the output wattage of the amplifier with the total wattage of the transformer and speakers attached to the system. Since, in any system, the low-wattage speakers will not be as loud as the high-wattage speakers, the system can be designed to take advantage of this phenomenon. Figure 21.50 shows a typical stage monitor system. The dialogue is picked up by an omnidirectional mic and sent to various locations around the theatre. The higher-wattage speakers are normally located in the makeup and dressing rooms, where the ambient noise level is fairly high. The lower-wattage speakers are used in the quieter offices and box office. A multispeaker high-voltage system can also be used to distribute sound throughout an auditorium. The higher-wattage (louder) speakers are placed on stage, and the lower-wattage (quieter) speakers are distributed in various locations about the auditorium. While this configuration does blanket the auditorium with sound, it has its challenges. Unless some type of time delay is added to the speakers farthest from the stage, it may appear to audience members sitting nearby that the sound is emanating from those speakers rather than from the stage. Also, this system does not allow the loudness levels of the individual speakers to be adjusted during the run. To have effective loudness control, each speaker must be driven by its own amplifier.

The step-down transformers used with high-voltage speaker systems normally have several different input taps (terminals) that can be used to vary the wattage associated with the speakers. They also have additional taps that are used to match the impedance of the transformer to the impedance of the speaker.

The contemporary theatre is truly an exciting place to be for someone interested in sound design, simply because what were formerly regarded as "rules" for the "proper" use of sound and music in the theatre have been thrown out, to be replaced with an exciting atmosphere of experimentation and dynamic growth.

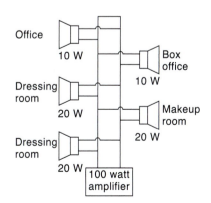

FIGURE 21.50
Typical application of a high-voltage speaker system.

Chapter 22

Drawing and Rendering

Drawing and rendering are the primary visual-communication methods used by theatrical designers. Every designer must be able to draw and render with ease and facility. During the production meetings, designers frequently communicate their ideas with quickly drawn pencil sketches—the costume designer's preliminary sketches and the scenic designer's thumbnail sketches. After the concepts have been discussed and developed, the designers create renderings that provide color representations of the appearance, character, and flavor of the designs.

It is also important that you learn how to draw and render on a computer. Both methods are important. But it is absolutely essential that you be able to draw and paint—well and with ease and facility—by hand. This chapter will demonstrate some of the materials and techniques that are common to this skill.

There are literally as many styles of drawing and rendering as there are designers. Every good designer will ultimately develop a distinctive style for creating scenic or costume sketches. Rest assured, however, that no beginning designer ever just sat down and magically began to draw and paint. Personal style develops after a great deal of time, practice, and effort. Before you begin to practice, you need to learn about the basic materials and techniques of sketching and rendering.

 ## Materials

Designers use a wide variety of materials to create their sketches and renderings. These materials can be roughly divided into two categories: the material being applied—pencils, inks, paint, pastels, or markers—and paper.

Pencils

Almost any pencil can be used for sketching, but different pencils have different characteristics. Hard-lead drafting pencils such as a 3H, 4H, or 5H make crisp, sharp-edged lines, whereas soft-lead drawing pencils such as the 3B or 4B make darker, wider, and softer-edged lines. Ordinary pencils such as the Number 2 tooth-marked Ticonderoga used for taking notes in class can also be used for sketching.

Which type of pencil you choose depends on the subject matter you'll be drawing, the type of paper on which you'll be working, and personal preference. However, it is important to practice with all types of pencils on all types of papers. Experimentation is the only way to learn about the different characteristics of each type of pencil and paper, which works well with which, and which ones you prefer.

There are two general types of colored pencils—hard and soft. As might be expected, the hard pencils produce sharp lines and are good for linear effects, whereas the softer pencils, such as Eagle Prismacolor, produce softer lines. Watercolor pencils can be used to produce a pigmented line which, when overlayed with a water wash, creates a tint of the same hue.

Inks

Some designers use inks for making preliminary and thumbnail sketches and outlining detail on renderings. Frequently, these ink drawings are made with inexpensive drawing and drafting pens such as those manufactured by Pilot, Expresso, and Itoya-Nikko. These pens are available in a variety of nib widths and flexibilities. Traditional artist's pens and inks are also preferred by some designers because of the larger variety of nibs that are available. Bottles of drawing inks, manufactured by Pelikan, Carter's, and Higgins, are available in a relatively narrow range of colors.

Paint

Costumes and scenic sketches or renderings have traditionally been painted with transparent watercolor paints. Although this practice continues, most designers use other materials as well.

Watercolor   Watercolor paint is a pigment mixed with water to create a transparent paint. It is the traditional medium for theatrical rendering, because transparent watercolor provides the sketches with a luminescent quality which closely approximates the appearance that costumes and scenery will have under stage lights. If too much pigment is added to the mix, the watercolor becomes opaque, the dried surface of the painting will have an uneven gloss, and the luminescent quality of the rendering will be lost.

Watercolor pigments are available in three types—tube, cake, and liquid—as shown in Figure 22.1. The tube colors are emulsified pigments of approximately the consistency of well-chilled sour cream. The cake colors are manufactured in hard blocks of watercolor pigment. The liquid watercolors are packaged in small bottles of highly saturated hues.

Both tube and cake watercolors provide the same high-quality pigment, so the choice of which to use is basically a matter of personal preference. Tube colors are a little more convenient for painting a large expanse, such as a sky in a scenic rendering. Similarly, the cake colors are a little more convenient if you need only a small amount of paint to provide trim color on a costume sketch. The third type of watercolor shown in Figure 22.1, Dr. Martin's Watercolors, is a liquid of extremely strong saturation and brilliance. Because these paints are already liquid, they mix very easily and always remain transparent.

Designer's Gouache   Designer's gouache is an opaque watercolor. It is available in tubed form in a wide range of hues similar to those of transparent watercolor. Designer's gouache closely resembles the **matte** reflective properties and colors of scene paint. When thinned sufficiently, the paint becomes transparent. The primary differences between designer's gouache and transparent watercolor are that gouache has a matte finish regardless of whether it is mixed to an opaque or transparent consistency and that watercolors seem to have a little more **life.**

FIGURE 22.1
Watercolor pigment is available in tube, cake, and liquid forms.

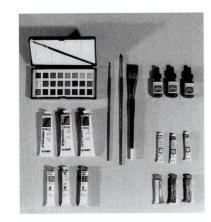

matte: Dull, nonreflective.

life: Brilliance, visual depth, and sparkle.

gloss: Highly reflective, mirrorlike.

spine: The relative stiffness of bristles; good watercolor bristles will flex easily but will also have enough spine to remain erect when fully saturated with paint.

Acrylic   Acrylic paint is very versatile. It can be thinned with water to the consistency of watercolor and can be used for the same purposes. When it is used as a substitute for watercolor or designer's gouache, the only significant difference is that the acrylic leaves a slightly **glossy** surface whereas the watercolor and gouache finishes are matte.

Brushes   It is a truism that you should buy the best brushes that you can possibly afford. With this proviso in mind, most artists would agree that the best watercolor brushes are made from red sable. The next best alternative is the synthetic bristles made to duplicate the characteristics of sable, such as Sabline.

Red sable and high-quality synthetic bristles, such as most manufacturers' student line of brushes, carry watercolor pigment easily, have good **spine,** and cling together when wet. Brushes other than these do not have these qualities, and they will not allow you to do your best work. Consequently, you're wasting your money and your time if you buy them.

While the number and type of brushes that you purchase are matters of choice, you will need brushes of at least two sizes with which to begin. The size of artist's brushes is indicated by numbers—the higher the number, the bigger the brush. The number is normally printed on the handle of the brush. A No. 3 brush can be effectively used for most detail work, and a No. 7 can be used for laying in most washes. A No. 12 brush is very handy for creating large, smooth washes.

Pastels

There are two primary types of pastel, chalk and oil, as shown in Figure 22.2. Colored pencils are also shown, because even though they are not made of pastel, they are used in basically the same manner. Ultimately, the way in which an artist uses any tool is a matter of personal choice, but each type of pastel has specific working characteristics.

Chalk Pastels   Chalk pastels are formed into square or round sticks that have approximately the same consistency as blackboard chalk. The square sticks are about 3½ inches long, and the round sticks are about 6 inches. The square sticks are generally more useful for theatrical sketching, because you can draw a relatively sharp line with the edges of the stick as well as a smooth wash with the flat surfaces.

Chalk pastels are available in three hardnesses: soft, medium, and hard. The brilliance of the color is linked to its hardness—the harder the stick, the less brilliant its color. Soft- and medium-consistency chalk pastels are extremely useful for laying down a smooth background color or a graded wash (which smoothly varies in hue from top to bottom or side to side). Medium and hard pastels are useful for detail work.

Oil or Wax Pastels   Oil or wax pastels have a slightly greasy feeling, because they are manufactured with a soft wax binder. The wax makes them very easy to blend. If you are planning to use oil pastels in conjunction with watercolors, you will need to remember to "paint first and pastel second," because the wax prevents paint from adhering to the paper.

Markers

A number of different markers and marking pens are available. The principal differences are in the shape and material of the tip and the nature and characteristics of the paint or ink contained in the marker (Figure 22.3).

FIGURE 22.2
Pastels, colored pencils, and associated materials.

PRODUCTION INSIGHTS
Blending with Pastels

Both chalk and oil pastels can be blended using either paper or felt blending stumps. The figures show some blending techniques. In addition to the commercial paper and felt blending stumps, newsprint, toilet paper, facial tissues, or your fingers can also be used.

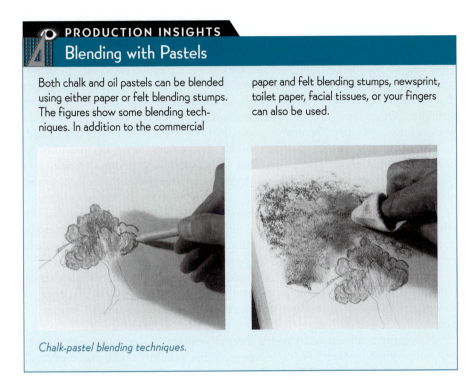

Chalk-pastel blending techniques.

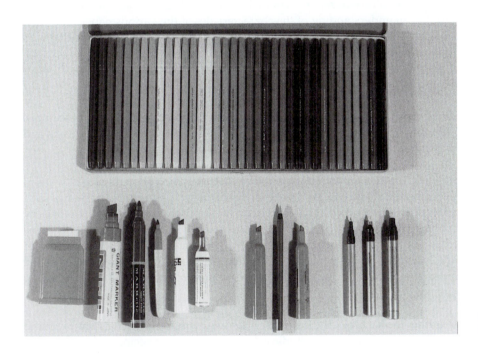

FIGURE 22.3
Markers.

The majority of these markers, such as the Magic Marker brand, contain a permanent semitransparent ink that dries very quickly and is generally available in a limited range of colors. Several lines of artist's markers contain watercolor ink that is more transparent than this permanent ink. Watercolor markers are also available in a much wider range of colors. Both types of marker can be used very effectively for detail work on renderings.

Another type of marker contains a lacquer-base metallic paint. Generally available in silver, gold, bronze, and copper, these markers are very useful for applying metallic detail or highlights to renderings.

illustration board: Watercolor paper mounted on a pressboard backing.

hot-press finish: A slick, smooth texture achieved by pressing paper between hot rollers; this treatment leaves a thin layer of oil, which makes the paper unsuitable for use with transparent watercolor; works well with designer's gouache, acrylic, pencils, and markers.

cold-press finish: A slight surface texture achieved by pressing paper between cold rollers; no oil residue results, so the paper can be used with transparent watercolor, designer's gouache, acrylic, markers, or pencils.

rough finish: A pebble-grained texture achieved by cold-pressing paper with a textured roller or by other techniques; suitable for painted and pastel renderings having little intricate detail.

tooth: A term used to describe the surface texture of a paper.

pixel: A picture element; the smallest discrete part of an electronically projected picture, as on a computer monitor.

Paper

Most final scenic and costume sketches are drawn or painted on some type of watercolor paper or **illustration board.** Illustration board is simply watercolor paper that has been mounted on a stiff pressboard backing to keep it from bending or wrinkling. Other types of paper such as charcoal or velvet paper can be used for work with pastels, pencils, and markers, but they don't work well with paint.

There are three primary surface finishes for watercolor papers and illustration board. A **hot-press finish** is very slick and smooth. The **cold-press finish** has a slight texture similar to a heavy bond typing paper. **Rough-finish** paper has a very noticeable texture.

Your choice of which paper to use should be dictated by the medium in which you plan to work. The hot-press finish is good for opaque paints, pencils, and markers. The cold-press papers work well with all media. The rough-finish papers are particularly well suited for pastels and watercolor.

Matte boards (hot-press illustration board with colored surfaces) are also interesting surfaces for designer's renderings, particularly if you are planning on working with any of the opaque media such as designer's gouache, pastels, or pencil.

Newsprint is often used by both scenic and costume designers for their thumbnail and preliminary sketches. It is inexpensive, has a slightly roughened **tooth,** and is a receptive surface for softer pencils, soft-nibbed markers, and soft pastels.

To determine which paper is suitable for a particular project, you will need to develop an understanding of the characteristics of the various papers and their surfaces. This knowledge can be gained only by playing and experimenting with the various media on the different papers and illustration boards.

Computer Drawing

There are a variety of drawing programs, and they contain a number of features. Generally, they can be divided into two generic types: painting programs and drawing programs.

Painting Tools   Painting programs such as Adobe Photoshop (Figure 22.4A) and Corel Painter (Figure 22.4B) are generally used for nontechnical drawings such as renderings and sketches. Technically, these programs create bitmap objects. A bitmap object is viewed by the computer as a collection of **pixels,** each pixel corresponding directly to one or more "bits" of computer memory including its color and location within the picture.[1] The structure of a bitmap image facilitates the creation of blended or soft-edged images commonly associated with sketching and painting.

Drawing Tools   Objects created with drawing programs such as Strata Studio Pro (Figure 22.5) and/or 3D Studio are object-oriented or vector images. A vector-based program views each object in a picture as a mathematical calculation. If you create a background, then draw other objects in the foreground, you can point and click on one of the foreground objects and move it around in the drawing without affecting the background. When an object is moved, the computer recalculates its position.[2] This quality enables the operator not only to change the position of the object within the picture but also to rotate the object about its var-

[1] Peter Jerram and Michael Gosney, *Multimedia Power Tools,* 2nd ed. (New York: Random House/Verbum, 1995), p. 89.
[2] Ibid.

(A)

(B)

FIGURE 22.4
(A) On-screen view of Adobe Photoshop, an image editing program. Software: Photoshop by Adobe Systems Incorporated. (B) On-screen view of Painter, an image editing program. Software: Painter™ by Corel Corporation.

ious axes to see what it looks like from all sides. Vector programs can be used to create sketches and renderings, but their forte is in the creation of drawings which contain multiple objects that may need to be manipulated independently and that require relatively hard-edged lines.

Most of these drawing and painting programs contain both two- and three-dimensional functions in the same program. The actual drawing can be done with a mouse or with a **digitizing tablet** (Figure 22.6). The first digitizing tablets

digitizing tablet: An electromechanical device that converts the pressure of a stylus on a flat plate (tablet) into binary information that can be understood by the computer.

FIGURE 22.5
On-screen view of Studio Pro, a drawing /
painting program. Software: Studio Pro by
Strata, Incorporated.

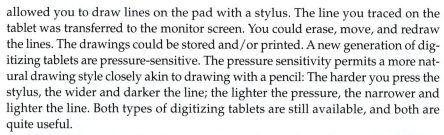

scan: To use a digitizing scanner to convert
existing artwork, photos, or drawings into
binary information.

allowed you to draw lines on the pad with a stylus. The line you traced on the
tablet was transferred to the monitor screen. You could erase, move, and redraw
the lines. The drawings could be stored and/or printed. A new generation of digitizing tablets are pressure-sensitive. The pressure sensitivity permits a more natural drawing style closely akin to drawing with a pencil: The harder you press the
stylus, the wider and darker the line; the lighter the pressure, the narrower and
lighter the line. Both types of digitizing tablets are still available, and both are
quite useful.

Most of the current drawing programs include color palettes ranging from a
minimum of 256 hues to over 1.6 million specific colors. These programs also
allow you to select specific surface textures (e.g., wood, paper, cloth, skin, plastic, and steel) to "wrap" around the objects you are drawing or modeling. The
majority of drawing programs also allow you to design the lighting for your
drawings. The software enables you to select the location and intensity of the
light(s) that are illuminating the object you're drawing. This feature automatically
results in the projection of shadows which aid the three-dimensional quality of
the drawings.

Drawing programs can be used in several ways. Original sketches can be created with a program such as Poser, or hand-drawn sketches or research illustrations can be **scanned** into the computer. Various color combinations and textures
can be quickly "tried out" on the sketches. Three-dimensional drawings allow
you to see all sides of costumes and sets from any seat in the house. Computer-
drawn sketches generally have not replaced hand-rendered drawings and designs at this time but more designers are using computer sketches than ever
before. As the technology advances, it has become more and more difficult to tell
the difference between hand- and computer-drawn designs. The advantages that
computer drawings offer the designer are many and ever-increasing. Which
method is better? It really doesn't matter. The reality is that whichever method
provides the best visualization of the designer's intention will be the appropriate method to use. But the caveat "know how to do both" still applies.

FIGURE 22.6
A digitizing tablet, which can be used to
"draw" images on the monitor screen.

PRODUCTION INSIGHTS
The Scanner

A scanner allows you to enter an existing drawing/photo/picture into a computer. The scanner functions much like a copying machine. You put the picture in the scanner, which digitizes the information and transfers it to the computer and onto the screen. In addition to working with preexisting artwork, you can create an original sketch by hand and scan it; then you can play with its color, outline, and texture to quickly see what effect these changes have on the overall design.

While you can purchase stand-alone scanners, many printers now have four-in-one capability — printing, scanning, faxing, and copying. At the time of this writing the stand-alone units generally have better resolution and work a little faster than the four-in-one units.

Drawing and Rendering Techniques

The following suggestions will familiarize you with some of the basic techniques that are used with the various media. Try the suggested application techniques. Doodle with the pencils, paint, pastels, and markers. Have fun with them. After you've worked with each medium separately, try combining them. Whatever else, be sure that you have fun, because you will improve only with practice, and you will practice only if you're having fun.

Sketching

Scenic, costume, and property designers need to be able to make quick, clear sketches. Thumbnail drawings and preliminary sketches are presented and modified during the production meetings, and almost all renderings begin with pencil sketches.

Initially, almost everyone feels intimidated by the idea of sketching. But some simple hints may help you improve your ability to sketch.

In Chapter 5 we learned that lines are evocative, that they contain meaning. But what is that meaning, and how is it expressed? In theatrical sketching, the lines that define the shape, texture, and detail of costumes, sets, and props are actually representations of the materials that will be used to build the designs. This is the first principle of theatrical sketching: Lines must reflect the qualities of the materials they represent. For example, the quality and character of the line(s) used to create a costume sketch should reflect the psychological qualities of the character as well as the weight, texture, and characteristics of the fabric and materials from which the costume will be made. Similarly, the lines used to describe a set should

(A)

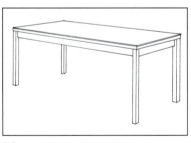

(B)

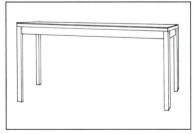

(C)

FIGURE 22.7
Draw what you see, not what you think you see (review the text for details).

be evocative of the wood, metal, fabric, and so forth from which it is constructed. This first principle leads to a second: You must be intimately familiar with the physical characteristics of the materials you're drawing. To accurately sketch a chiffon blouse or heavy woolen cape, you must know the hand of those fabrics—what they feel like, their weight, their draping characteristics, and so on. Sets are made from various types of woods, metals, fabrics, and plastics, each of which has its own physical characteristics. Some are rigid, others flexible; some are rough, others smooth and polished. The set designer must know and understand those characteristics before he or she can create an accurate representation of them.

A related, third principle states that you must know what you're drawing before you can draw it. To draw a chiffon blouse, you must be able to see what it looks like—the shape and fullness of body, sleeve, collar, and cuff; whether it has button closure down the front or back or no buttons at all. To create a realistic Victorian drawing room, you have to know what one looked like. This type of understanding comes from doing the research described in the design process (Chapter 2).

When you follow these three principles, something magical happens as you begin to draw. Your brain, programmed with all the background information it needs, guides your hand and a finished representation of the concept, which actually looks like the object you envisioned, just seems to appear on the paper. But this magic doesn't happen instantly. It takes practice—lots of practice. But it is a skill that all designers must master, and it is only mastered through repetitive practice.

A sketch does not need to, nor is it supposed to, create a photographic likeness of a person or object. Sketching creates a simplified view that shows the basic appearance and, of equal importance, the spirit or character of the object.

A major stumbling block that many people encounter when learning to sketch is that they try to draw what they think they see rather than what they actually see. Figure 22.7A shows a photograph of a table. Because people know that the top of a table is its most useful surface, they tend to draw the top of the table as the most dominant visual element, as shown in Figure 22.7B. They're not drawing what they see. If you really look at the photo of the table, you'll see that the top is only a narrow sliver compared with the overall size of the table. Figure 22.7C is a sketch that was made after careful observation of the photo of the

(A)

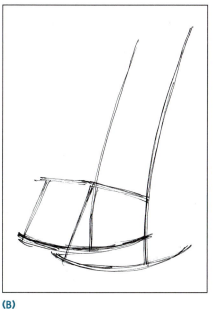

(B)

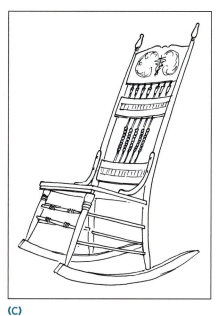

(C)

FIGURE 22.8
Sketching techniques (see text for details).

table. Notice that even though the sketch doesn't show every detail, it does provide an accurate representation of the table, and it also gives you a feeling about its nature or character.

All sketches are based on three principal elements: thematic lines, line angles and intersections, and proportions. Most objects are composed of more than one thematic or predominant line, like the rocking chair shown in Figure 22.8A. The intersection of these thematic lines allows you to use a fairly easy method to accurately lay out the proportions of an object. While you're noting the angle of intersection of the thematic lines (the chair back, legs, seat, rockers, and the floor), also note the relative position where those line intersections take place. On the rocking chair, notice that the seat intersects the back just a little more than one-third of the way up the back. Also notice that the seat itself is just a little bit longer than the distance from the seat to the rockers. This "ratio technique" generally reduces a beginning artist's anxiety (which allows you to be more creative), because it depersonalizes the sketching process. You're no longer "drawing a chair," you're simply observing lines of intersection and re-creating them. An accurate sketch of the rocking chair, Figure 22.8B, can be made simply by using these observations as a guide. The rest of the detailing of the sketch, Figure 22.8C, is based on the same type of observational techniques. The locations of the various solid and spindle elements of the chair are determined by observing their relative positions on the model and then, using the ratio technique, drawing them on the sketch.

Figure Drawing

It is imperative that designers be able to sketch the human figure easily. For costume designers, this requirement is obvious. If clothes are to fit the body in a natural and realistic manner, the costume designer must draw the figure so that it looks natural and realistic, then the clothes follow easily. For scenic designers, the figure-drawing requirement is less obvious, but many designers like to place a human figure or two in their sketches, models, or drafting plates to provide a readily understandable scale reference.

Some designers believe it is important that a figure have a readily identifiable face. Others do not. However, almost all costume designers agree that a visually

FIGURE 22.9
Quick figure sketches use a few lines to capture the flavor and personality of the character.

dynamic sketch—one in which the figure, and consequently the costume, appears to be in motion—is an important aid in representing the character of the costume.

The quick figure sketch in Figure 22.9 is used to capture the flavor and personality of the character. Accomplished with just a few strokes, the quick sketch is the visual distillation of the designer's thoughts, ideas, and research about the character, and it provides a visual description of that character's personality. In costume design, the quick sketch can be considered analogous to the lighting designer's lighting key in that it provides a touchstone to which the designer refers as the figure and subsequent costume design are being developed.

Every costume design needs to begin with a figure drawing. If the body doesn't look right—isn't in proper proportion, doesn't reflect the personality characteristics of the role—then the design of the clothes placed on that body will be similarly flawed. Proportion is arguably the single most important element in figure drawing. If the proportions aren't correct, the figure won't seem natural. Reasonably normal proportions are achieved if the male is about 8½ heads high and the female about 8 heads high, as shown in Figure 22.10. Study the distances and relationships between the various body parts. Notice that the center of the chest is about one head height below the chin, the shoulders are about two heads wide, and so on. A sense of balance and stability is achieved when the figure's head is directly above its center of support, as shown in Figure 22.11. Notice that this sense of balance is achieved because the body's mass is evenly divided on either side of the center of balance. Notice also that the body pivots around its natural hinge points—spine, shoulders, elbows, wrists, hips, knees, ankles, and so forth—to create this balance.

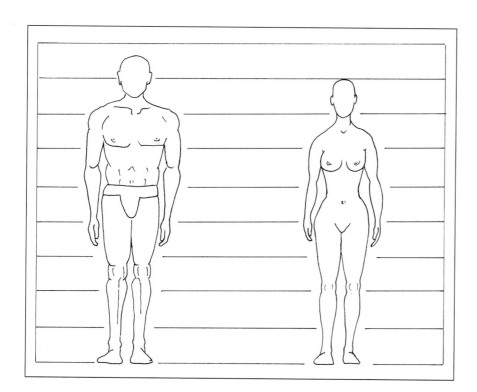

FIGURE 22.10
Proportions of male and female figures.

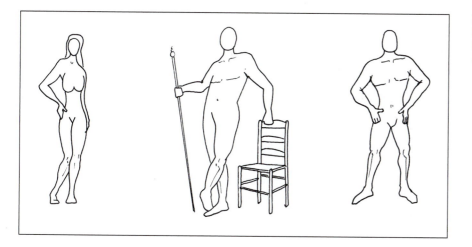

FIGURE 22.11
Costume design figures should appear to be dynamically balanced (see text for details).

To provide the best possible view of the costume, designers draw most costume figures standing with one or both arms extended away from the body in a manner that will provide a view of sleeve detail. Naturally, the particular pose chosen should reflect the personality and nature of the character being portrayed. Deviations from this convention are appropriate when they will provide a better view or understanding of how the costume will look and work in the production.

Proficiency in figure drawing is not achieved easily. It requires study and practice. Designers should become familiar with the skeletal structure of the body and how the various muscle groups work to animate it. And they must practice. Take life-drawing courses, carry a sketch pad, and draw during any idle time. For further study of basic anatomy and figure drawing, see the Selected References at the end of the book.

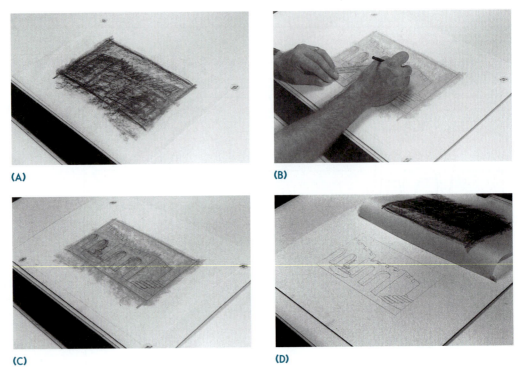

(A)

(B)

(C)

(D)

FIGURE 22.12
Graphite-transfer technique. Cover the reverse side of the sketch with soft graphite and set it (see text for details) (A). Turn the drawing over and trace the sketch (B and C) to transfer the linework to the watercolor paper or board (D).

Graphite Transfers

Watercolor and pastel renderings and sketches usually begin with a pencil drawing. It is fairly standard practice to draw the design on tracing vellum, since the vellum is fairly rugged and will be able to sustain a fair amount of erasing as the sketch is modified. Figure 22.12 explains the process of graphite transfers. After the sketch is completed, turn the vellum over and cover the back side of the sheet with **graphite.** (A soft stick is used for this purpose.) To prevent smearing, set the graphite by daubing thinned rubber cement over it. Use a cotton ball as your dauber. Tape the drawing, face up, to the illustration or watercolor board, and trace the outline of the sketch. (If you use a fine-point ballpoint pen with red ink, it will be very easy to see where you've been as you are tracing the drawing.) As you trace the outline of the sketch, you will be transferring the design to the illustration board. It's much easier, and considerably less messy, to use Saral graphite transfer paper instead.

You may be tempted to employ the carbon paper used for making copies in typing instead of going through the rather laborious task of "graphiting" the reverse side of the tracing vellum. If you are planning on using a transparent medium such as watercolor, try to resist this temptation, because the carbon paper graphite is very dark and will bleed through any transparent paint that you may apply to the paper. If you are planning on working with opaque media, however, the colored transfer papers typically used by costumers to transfer pattern outlines will work very nicely. Colored transfer paper is usually available at most fabric stores.

A light table provides another good way to transfer the original to watercolor paper. The original is taped to the watercolor paper then placed on the light table. Light shines from the table through the "sandwich" allowing you to trace the original sketch onto the watercolor paper.

graphite: A soft carbon similar to the lead in a pencil; sticks can be purchased in most art supply stores.

Scanning

One of the most nerve-wracking experiences in the rendering process is when you've completed your pencil sketch, transferred it to the watercolor paper, and you're ready, for the first time in your life, to add color to the sketch. For many students their first reaction is, "Gulp . . ." A great deal of this stress can be eliminated if, rather than painting the original, you scan the pencil art and print multiple copies on the appropriate paper. That way if you botch your first attempt you have backups. Actually, a number of seasoned designers use this technique. They find it useful for trying out different color combinations or application techniques. Experimentation is frequently a good thing. Try mixing pastels (use them for the cyc or background) with watercolor (for details), or add detail to a watercolor sketch with watercolor pencils or artist's markers. After you practice a bit, and experiment with some of the techniques outlined in this chapter, you'll discover that the thought of coloring your sketch isn't nearly as daunting as it once was.

Watercolor

A **wash** can be laid down wet or dry. A wet wash is made by wetting the area to be painted with water before applying the paint, as shown in Figure 22.13. Using your brush, paint the outlined area with water, let it dry until the area has a uniformly dull finish, and then apply the paint. A wet wash conceals brush strokes a little better than a dry wash.

Since watercolor is a transparent medium, you'll need to remember that the whites and light colors are achieved by letting the paper show through. Because of this characteristic, it is normal procedure to build up a watercolor rendering from light to dark. This simply means that you paint the light areas first, then move to those of middle tone, and finish by painting the darkest details or objects. Applying each hue individually is also a normal technique in watercolor painting. After each coat has dried, additional layers can be built up over the original coat to deepen or change its hue or add texture or detail *if* the previous work has been sealed with a **workable fixative.** Fine detail work can either be applied over the watercolor washes after they have dried, and fixed, or the area where the detail is to be applied can be left unpainted when you are putting in the wash. Detail work can also be applied directly on top of a dried transparent wash with opaque media such as designer's gouache, acrylic, pastels, or markers.

If you have some intricate detail that will be silhouetted against a large wash area, you can "paint" the detail area with rubber cement or masking fluid before laying in the wash. Masking fluid is preferred since there's less chance of damaging the paper. After the wash has dried, peel off the rubber cement, or dried masking fluid, to expose the unpainted paper, and paint in the detail work.

Pastels

The design can be transferred to the pastel paper or illustration board using the graphite-transfer technique.

Oil or wax pastels, which are very easy to blend, give a smooth, opaque finish that somewhat resembles a drawing done with crayons. Chalk pastels give a chalkier, luminescent finish. Most theatrical designers prefer working with chalk pastels, because they can be used with watercolor whereas oil pastels cannot. (The oil in the wax pastel causes the watercolor to bead up and dry in little blobs rather than a smooth wash.)

wash: The covering of a relatively large area with a smooth layering of paint; a smooth wash consists of only one color; a blended wash is created by smoothly segueing from one color to another.

workable fixative: A spray that seals colors in place. "Workable" indicates that paint can effectively be applied on top of the fixative.

(A)

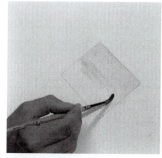

(B)

(C)

FIGURE 22.13
Applying a wet wash with watercolor. First wet the area with water (A). When the water has partially dried (the paper will have a uniform dull sheen), smoothly spread the watercolor across the area (B) to create a smooth wash of color (C).

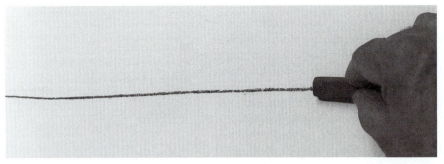

(A)

FIGURE 22.14
Pastel-application techniques. (A) A straight line. (B) A smooth wash. Pastels can be used to lay down background washes (C). Be sure to use drafting tape to mask areas to be left "unwashed." Spray the drawing with workable fixative (D) to lock the pastel to the paper.

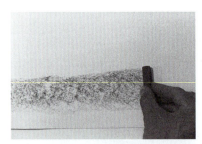

(B)

(C)

(D)

How you actually apply the pastel to the paper has a great deal to do with the finished appearance of the design. Chalk pastels will leave a definite line when applied using an edge, as shown in Figure 22.14. A smooth coverage over a large area can be accomplished by using a softer blend (soft or medium hardness) and the flat side of the pastel stick.

Once the pastel has been applied, it can be blended using felt or paper blending sticks, tissue, or your fingers. Stick pastel can also be erased (although not completely) with a kneadable or soft pink eraser.

If you don't want to get the pastel on a particular area of the drawing, mask off that space with drafting tape. Large areas can be effectively masked using paper held in place with drafting tape. Be sure not to use masking tape, which will leave a slightly gummy residue on the paper when it is removed. Additionally, the adhesive on masking tape is sufficiently strong that it can pull the finish surface layer right off the paper!

Chalk pastels are basically colored chalk. The image they leave on the paper is made of chalk dust and is very easy to smear. Although this characteristic is handy for blending two or more colors, a spray fixative is needed to prevent the picture from being smeared after it is finished.

A workable fixative enables you to create several layers on a pastel rendering. If you first draw and blend the background and then spray it with fixative, you can draw the foreground detail without smearing the background work. Each successive layer should be sprayed, and when the rendering is complete, it should be sprayed again. Be sure to use workable fixatives; their finish won't affect the application of additional layers of pastel.

Pencils and Markers

Colored pencils and pens as well as watercolor or oil markers can be used to good effect for both scenic and costume renderings.

The watercolor drawing pencils, which are hardened watercolor pigments, can be used to sketch in or add detail. The edge of the line can be softened by painting it with water, as shown in Figure 22.15.

Artist's markers are available in a full range of hues and saturations. The ink has the same transparent properties as watercolor paint, whereas the oil markers are generally translucent or opaque. Either type of marker can be used in a variety of ways to achieve any number of interesting effects.

Combined Media

To be able to select the appropriate visual expression for a specific design concept, a designer should feel free to use and combine a wide variety of rendering materials, styles, and techniques. The rendering for a soft, ethereal, dye-painted scrim is probably best achieved with chalk pastels, watercolors, or a combination of the two. The sketch for a costume with a sequined bodice and a long, flowing diaphanous skirt could be effectively realized with watercolor or designer's gouache and fine-line markers or pen and ink. A nonrepresentational setting of abstract forms in strongly contrasting colors might best be expressed by cutting the forms from colored construction paper and pasting them to a representation of the stage space. Ultimately, the selection of which medium, or combination of media, to use for a specific rendering is the designer's choice, and those choices will be more varied if the designer is familiar with a number of media and rendering techniques.

As with any craft, your personal ability to use this information about rendering will improve only with practice. Take courses in drawing, life drawing, pastel sketching, and watercolor painting in your school's art department to help you learn the many techniques and media that can be used to visually communicate your design ideas. As you become more familiar with the materials and techniques of sketching and rendering, you will discover that your ability to manipulate them is improving as well.

FIGURE 22.15
Combining media can produce interesting results. The building masked in the pastel drawing shown in Figure 22.14 is unmasked (A), and the detail is sketched in and colored with watercolor pencils (B), which are blended with a brush and water (C). After the water has dried, additional detail is sketched in with pens (D) and markers to create a drawing with an interesting appearance of depth (E).

(A)

(B)

(C)

(D)

(E)

Appendix A

A Revised Standard Graphic Language for Lighting Design

The material in this appendix is the current draft of a revision to the USITT Recommended Practice for Theatrical Lighting Design Graphics. Please note that as of this writing this revised standard is a work in progress and has not been adopted by the USITT. It is included in this edition because it contains new information and symbols, as well as modifications to the symbols for some existing instruments, and it shows where the standard is probably headed. Additional changes may be made to this draft before it is adopted as the new official USITT standard. But I felt it was important to provide the most up-to-date information possible, and this draft of the proposed revision provides that information.

0.0   PREAMBLE

The original Graphics Standard Board noted that a standard is an example for comparison and an authority, which serves as a model. It should be noted that this model cannot hope to cover all possible situations encountered during the drafting of a light plot and thus should be viewed as a guide that theatrical lighting practitioners use to create their drawings. This document therefore represents a "recommended practice." This document does not seek to represent a specific manufacturer of lighting equipment, but suggests common instruments in general use. The result is a group of generic instrument types that can be adapted to specific uses as necessary rather than an attempt to present a symbol for each luminaire available.

The purpose of this document is to establish a standardized language among lighting designers and anyone else who needs to understand or execute the design. In practical terms, this document is intended to provide guidelines so that anyone, ranging from technicians who hang the luminaires to other members of the production team, can clearly understand the intent of the lighting designer.

1.0   INTRODUCTION

USITT, or modified ANSI, two-line thickness standard drafting practices should be followed. Legibility and consistency should determine the choices made in both CAD and hand-drafted drawings. Luminaire outlines should take visual precedence over all other information on lighting drawings.

The graphical representation of a lighting design normally consists of two categories of documents: the Light Plot and the Lighting Section. Preferably, the documents are produced in $\frac{1}{2}'' = 1'$-0'' scale. Other scales, such as $\frac{1}{4}'' = 1'$-0'', 1:25 or 1:50 for those doing drawings in SI (metric), may be chosen or after considering the size of the architectural space, the overall size of the document, the size of reproductions, the number of individual luminaires and their numeric attributes that must be seen. A complete lighting design requires additional paperwork such as schedules and data sheets. Generally, the light plot should include all information necessary to assure clear understanding of the designer's intentions.

1.1   Special Considerations for CAD drawings

Computer assisted drawings should follow the same recommended practice as those drawn by hand. However, three additional considerations should be made: Layer designation and line weight color assignment must be coordinated with other members of the production team who are using the same document to create other drawings. This avoids confusion between the draftspersons or the end users. When a lighting graphic symbol is created with "labels," attention must be paid to the relative orientation of both the symbol and its associated text. When a symbol is inserted into a drawing, the direction of the symbol may approximate the focus direction, while the associated text should be properly oriented with the rest of the text in the drawing. The luminaire symbols that are included in some computer applications may be specific to various manufacturers' equipment, rather than the generic symbols provided in this document. Nevertheless, the size and designation of the luminaires used should follow these symbols as closely as possible.

2.0   THE LIGHT PLOT

The Light Plot is a composite plan drawing that provides the most descriptive possible view of the luminaires so that the production staff can most efficiently execute the design intent. It may consist of more than a single plate; however, all plates should be the same size to facilitate reproduction. Standard architectural conventions are often followed in this presentation. Distances between front of house hanging positions and the playing area can be compressed in a presentational light plot.

2.1   Information Contained in the Light Plot

Normally, the light plot should include all information necessary to assure clear understanding of the designer's intentions. The location and identification data of every luminaire, accessory, and specialty unit should be represented on the light plot, along with the following information:

- The centerline
- A lineset schedule when appropriate
- A ruler or some other indicator of distance left and right of centerline in scale
- A ruler indicating onstage distances up and down stage (or the 90° axis to centerline) in scale
- A drawn representation of the edge of the stage where applicable
- A drawn representation of the edge of the playing area where applicable
- Basic scenic elements
- All scenic masking
- All architectural and scenic obstructions
- The proscenium arch, the plaster line, smoke pockets or other architectural details necessary to orient the lighting design in flexible spaces
- Trim measurements for movable mounting positions should read from the stage level surface (or other common point of reference) to the pipe (or mounting position)
- Trim heights to boom positions measure from boom base to side arm.
- Identification (label) of hanging/mounting positions
- The legend or instrument key designating symbol type and notation in the light plot
- The title block
- Sightlines

Additional information may include:

- Lighting areas
- Template key
- Color key
- Liability disclaimer
- Union stamp

2.2   Luminaire Symbol Information

The luminaire symbols used on the light plot should represent the approximate size and shape of the luminaires in scale (except where computer applications supply more specific symbols). The default spacing between symbols is 18" (or 45 cm) to allow for adequate focus range of each luminaire. When the symbols are placed in relative locations other than default, dimension lines or other measur-

ing device must be added between the symbols to indicate the distance and facilitate mounting the luminaires. It is acceptable to visually orient the angle of each drawn luminaire to either focus points or 90° axes. Normally, each symbol should be accomplished by the following information:

- Luminaire number
- Indication of focal length or beam angle as part of the symbol
- Indication of any accessories such as templates, irises, scrollers, top hats, barn doors, etc.
- Channel (or control designation)
- Axis notation for PAR lamps

Additional information may include:

- Focus (or purpose designation)
- Wattage (at least for arc source)
- Circuit and/or dimmer number or space for the electrician to add this information
- Indication of "two-fers"
- Color notation
- Color notation for scrollers
- Template notation

2.3.1   Designation and numbering of conventional mounting positions

- Front of House (FOH) positions begin numbering from the position closest to plaster line.
- Onstage electrics number from downstage to upstage.
- Onstage booms number from downstage to upstage.
- All hanging locations not intersecting centerline are subnamed by their location relative to centerline. Ladders, box booms, booms, and such are divided between stage left and stage right; stage left listed first.

2.3.2   Numbering luminaires within conventional mounting positions

- Each separate device requiring line voltage or a control signal receives a unique whole number. If the device is an attachment altering the beam of an instrument, it will often not receive its own whole number, but rather the host instrument's number and an alphabetical letter.
- Luminaires on transverse mounting positions are numbered from stage left to stage right.
- Luminaires on booms or other vertical hanging positions are numbered from top to bottom, downstage to upstage.
- Luminaires mounted on FOH positions parallel to centerline should number starting with the units farthest from plasterline (downstage to upstage).
- Luminaires mounted on positions non-parallel to centerline (box booms) should number starting with the units closest to centerline.

2.3.3   Designation and numbering of mounting positions in non-proscenium venues

- Pipe grid positions should be designated by numbers on one axis of the grid and by letters on the other axis.
- Other atypical mounting positions may be designated by compass points or numbering in a clockwise manner.
- Mounting positions that repeat (bays, etc.) should be numbered from a consistent starting point.
- Other atypical hanging positions should be designated in any fashion that is sensible to the electricians. Luminaires hung in these positions should be numbered in an intelligible fashion compatible with other luminaire designations on the plot.

3.0   THE LIGHTING SECTION

The lighting section is a sectional view in which the cutting plane intersects the theatre, typically, along the centerline, but may intersect any plane that best illustrates the mounting positions. This drawing provides the most descriptive view of the hanging positions relative to the architectural and scenic elements of the production. While it may be appropriate to compress distance (horizontal or vertical) in a presentation section, doing so in the working version reduces its effectiveness.

3.1   Information Contained in the Lighting Section

The purpose of the lighting section is to communicate spatial information and relationships of all other elements relative to the lighting design. The following information should be represented on the lighting section:

- Definition of where the section is "cut"
- Stage floor, deck or "vertical zero" location (indication of which one is being used as reference zero)
- Proscenium, smoke pocket, or the "horizontal zero" location
- Back wall or upstage limitation of the performing space
- Vertical audience sight points and/or sight lines
- Downstage edge of stage floor and/or edge of playing area
- Architectural details necessary to orient the lighting design in non-proscenium spaces
- All hanging positions including side elevation of booms, ladders, etc.
- Trim height for all hanging positions that can change height
- Identification of all lighting positions
- Architectural or scenic obstructions
- Sectional view of scenery
- All masking
- Title block

- Scaled representation of the luminaire that determines batten height mounted in each position
- Human figure (or "head height") in scale

Additional information may include:

- Vertical ruler in scale
- Horizontal ruler in scale
- Defined distance to other elements not shown on the drawing (to follow spot booth, other sight lines, etc.)
- Liability disclaimer
- Union stamp

4.0   TITLE BLOCK

Acceptable locations for the title block are

- Lower-right-hand corner of the drawing
- Vertically spanning the right side of the drawing

4.1   Information Contained in the Title Block

To be placed in the order deemed most important by the lighting designer:

- Name of the producing organization
- Name of the production
- Name of the venue
- Drawing title
- Drawing number (i.e., "1 of 4")
- Predominant scale of the drawing
- Date the plate was drafted
- Designer of the production
- Draftsperson of the drawing

Additional information may include:

- Location of the venue
- Director of the production
- Other members of the production team
- Lighting assistant and/or Master Electrician
- Date and revision number
- Approval of the drawing
- Contact information (telephone and fax numbers e-mail addresses)

5.0   LEGEND OR INSTRUMENT KEY

Placement is acceptable in any location that does not conflict with other information.

5.1   Information Contained in the Legend or Instrument Key:

- Pictorial representations (symbols) of all luminaires and devices shown on the plot with identifying descriptions of each.
- Designation of all notations associated with each luminaire

- Color manufacturer designation (i.e., R = Roscolux, L = Lee, G = Gam, etc.)
- Template manufacturer designation (when applicable)
- Wattage (total luminaire load) and/or ANSI lamp code
- Symbols for any accessories: Templates, irises, color scrollers, top hats, barn doors, etc.

Additional information may include:

- The luminaire manfacturer
- Representation of "two-fers"
- Indication of voltage
- Beam spread (in degrees) for each luminaire type

6.0   SYMBOL GUIDELINES

These guidelines represent a selection of standard generic symbols that accurately represent the size, shape, and functional properties of stage luminaires. Further differentiation or notation may be necessary to distinguish between luminaires of approximately the same size. This may include shading the symbol, making the "front" of the symbol a heavier line, and other various individual techniques. Detailed luminaire symbols specific to each manufacturers' products and supplied by computer drafting programs may be substituted, provided they allow the specialized markings needed to exactly specify the luminaire's functions and provided they are properly indexed on the light plot.

These symbols are presented as a guideline. Specific choices should be considered to differentiate between different manufacturers of the same type of luminaire. It is USITT policy not to specify any manufactures in the symbol Guidelines.

Because of the number and complexity of attributes in automated fixtures, each designer must determine a logical notation system for the luminaire used.

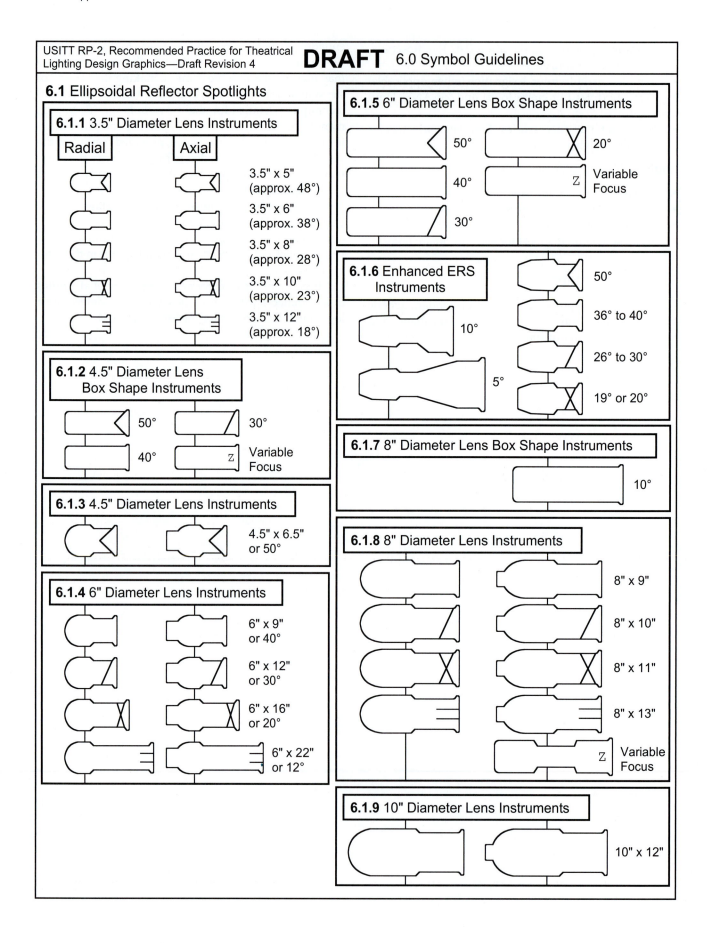

USITT RP-2, Recommended Practice for Theatrical Lighting Design Graphics—Draft Revision 4

DRAFT 6.0 Symbol Guidelines

6.1 Ellipsoidal Reflector Spotlights

6.1.1 3.5" Diameter Lens Instruments

Radial	Axial	
		3.5" x 5" (approx. 48°)
		3.5" x 6" (approx. 38°)
		3.5" x 8" (approx. 28°)
		3.5" x 10" (approx. 23°)
		3.5" x 12" (approx. 18°)

6.1.2 4.5" Diameter Lens Box Shape Instruments

50°   40°   30°   Variable Focus

6.1.3 4.5" Diameter Lens Instruments

4.5" x 6.5" or 50°

6.1.4 6" Diameter Lens Instruments

6" x 9" or 40°
6" x 12" or 30°
6" x 16" or 20°
6" x 22" or 12°

6.1.5 6" Diameter Lens Box Shape Instruments

50°   20°   40°   Variable Focus   30°

6.1.6 Enhanced ERS Instruments

10°   5°   50°   36° to 40°   26° to 30°   19° or 20°

6.1.7 8" Diameter Lens Box Shape Instruments

10°

6.1.8 8" Diameter Lens Instruments

8" x 9"
8" x 10"
8" x 11"
8" x 13"
Variable Focus

6.1.9 10" Diameter Lens Instruments

10" x 12"

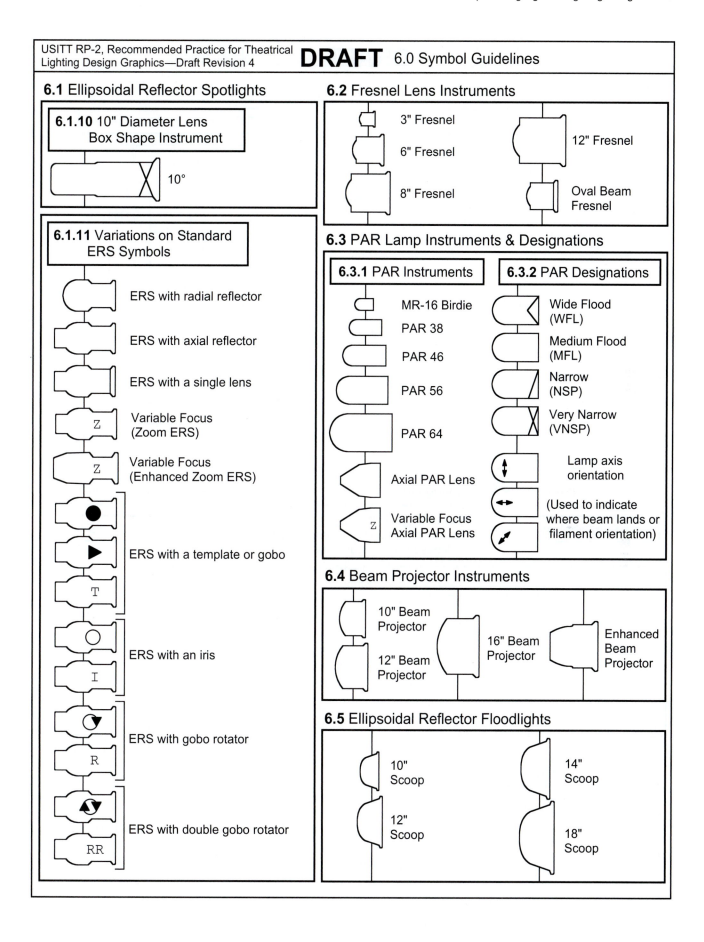

6.1 Ellipsoidal Reflector Spotlights

6.1.10 10" Diameter Lens
Box Shape Instrument

10°

6.1.11 Variations on Standard
ERS Symbols

ERS with radial reflector

ERS with axial reflector

ERS with a single lens

Variable Focus
(Zoom ERS)

Variable Focus
(Enhanced Zoom ERS)

ERS with a template or gobo

ERS with an iris

ERS with gobo rotator

ERS with double gobo rotator

6.2 Fresnel Lens Instruments

3" Fresnel

6" Fresnel

8" Fresnel

12" Fresnel

Oval Beam
Fresnel

6.3 PAR Lamp Instruments & Designations

6.3.1 PAR Instruments

MR-16 Birdie

PAR 38

PAR 46

PAR 56

PAR 64

Axial PAR Lens

Variable Focus
Axial PAR Lens

6.3.2 PAR Designations

Wide Flood
(WFL)

Medium Flood
(MFL)

Narrow
(NSP)

Very Narrow
(VNSP)

Lamp axis
orientation

(Used to indicate
where beam lands or
filament orientation)

6.4 Beam Projector Instruments

10" Beam
Projector

12" Beam
Projector

16" Beam
Projector

Enhanced
Beam
Projector

6.5 Ellipsoidal Reflector Floodlights

10"
Scoop

12"
Scoop

14"
Scoop

18"
Scoop

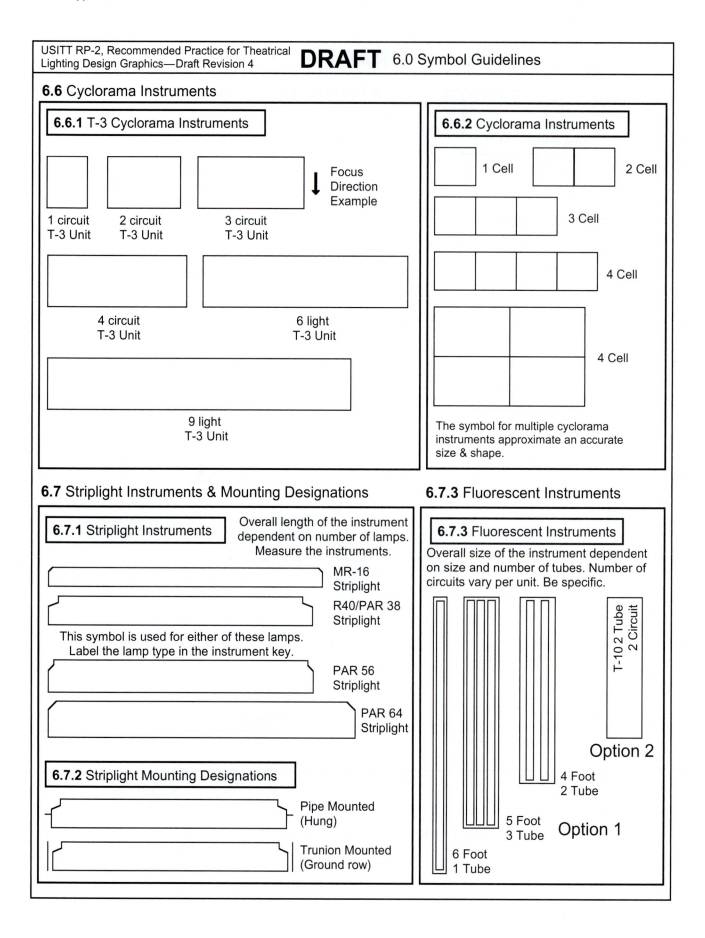

6.6 Cyclorama Instruments

6.6.1 T-3 Cyclorama Instruments

Focus Direction Example

1 circuit T-3 Unit

2 circuit T-3 Unit

3 circuit T-3 Unit

4 circuit T-3 Unit

6 light T-3 Unit

9 light T-3 Unit

6.6.2 Cyclorama Instruments

1 Cell

2 Cell

3 Cell

4 Cell

4 Cell

The symbol for multiple cyclorama instruments approximate an accurate size & shape.

6.7 Striplight Instruments & Mounting Designations

6.7.1 Striplight Instruments

Overall length of the instrument dependent on number of lamps. Measure the instruments.

MR-16 Striplight

R40/PAR 38 Striplight

This symbol is used for either of these lamps. Label the lamp type in the instrument key.

PAR 56 Striplight

PAR 64 Striplight

6.7.2 Striplight Mounting Designations

Pipe Mounted (Hung)

Trunion Mounted (Ground row)

6.7.3 Fluorescent Instruments

6.7.3 Fluorescent Instruments

Overall size of the instrument dependent on size and number of tubes. Number of circuits vary per unit. Be specific.

T-10 2 Tube 2 Circuit

Option 2

4 Foot 2 Tube

5 Foot 3 Tube

6 Foot 1 Tube

Option 1

6.8 Automated Luminaires

Symbols for Automated Luminaires should approximate size, shape, and swing radius.

6.8.1 Fixed Bodies

Moving mirror instrument

6.8.2 Moving Yokes & Heads

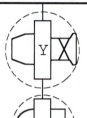

Moving Yoke (Shown with Enhanced 19°)

Moving Head Wash Luminaire

Moving Head Spot Luminaire

Zero Reference Point as specified by Designer

Moving Head Spot Luminaire

External Moving Mirror Device

6.9 Practicals & Special Units

Practical Luminaire

35 mm Slide Projector

The symbol for Special Effects instruments approximates an accurate size & shape.

6.10 Follow Spot

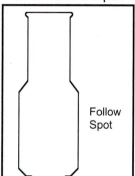

Follow Spot

6.11 Symbols for Circuitry

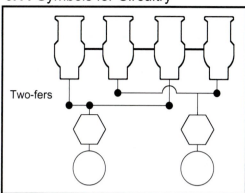

Two-fers

6.12 Symbols and Layout for Lighting Booms

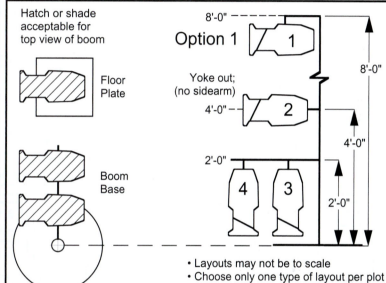

Hatch or shade acceptable for top view of boom

Floor Plate

Boom Base

Flange Mount

Option 1

8'-0"

Yoke out; (no sidearm)

4'-0"

2'-0"

8'-0"

4'-0"

2'-0"

1

2

4 3

• Layouts may not be to scale
• Choose only one type of layout per plot

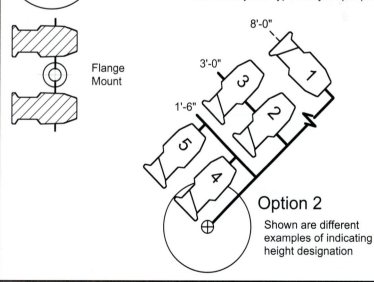

8'-0"

3'-0"

1'-6"

1

3

2

5

4

Option 2

Shown are different examples of indicating height designation

6.13 Accessory & Ancillary Symbols

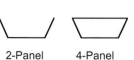

2-Panel Barn Door | 4-Panel Barn Door | Top Hat | Half Hat | Scroller | Scroller | Douser/ Dimming Shutter | Sightline

6.14 Luminaire Notation

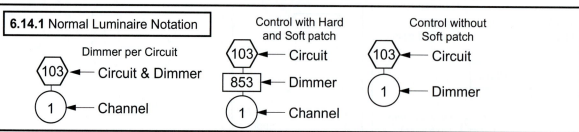

6.14.1 Normal Luminaire Notation

Dimmer per Circuit
103 ← Circuit & Dimmer
1 ← Channel

Control with Hard and Soft patch
103 ← Circuit
853 ← Dimmer
1 ← Channel

Control without Soft patch
103 ← Circuit
1 ← Dimmer

6.14.2 Normal Luminaire Notation

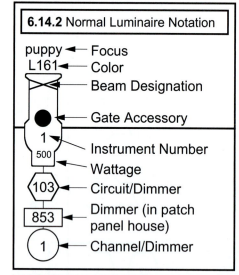

puppy ← Focus
L161 ← Color
Beam Designation
Gate Accessory
1 ← Instrument Number
500 ← Wattage
103 ← Circuit/Dimmer
853 ← Dimmer (in patch panel house)
1 ← Channel/Dimmer

Notation shown on any plot is a case-by-case basis. It is not necessary to include all categories, when the combination runs the risk of making the plot's appearance cluttered.

6.14.4 Notation for Instruments with PAR Lamps

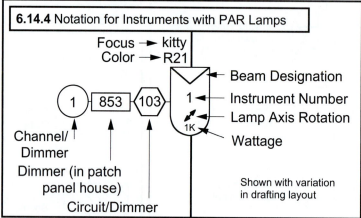

Focus → kitty
Color → R21
Beam Designation
Instrument Number
Lamp Axis Rotation
Wattage

Channel/Dimmer
Dimmer (in patch panel house)
Circuit/Dimmer

1 — 853 — 103 — 1 / 1K

Shown with variation in drafting layout

6.14.3 Normal Striplight and Cyclorama Light Notation

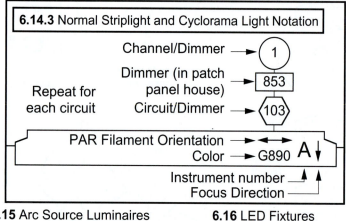

Channel/Dimmer → 1
Dimmer (in patch panel house) → 853
Circuit/Dimmer → 103
Repeat for each circuit
PAR Filament Orientation →
Color → G890   A↓
Instrument number ↑
Focus Direction ↑

6.14.5 Notation for Followspot Boomerang

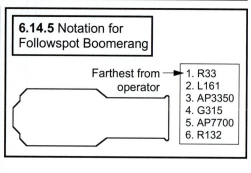

Farthest from operator →
1. R33
2. L161
3. AP3350
4. G315
5. AP7700
6. R132

6.15 Arc Source Luminaires

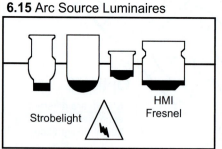

Strobelight
HMI Fresnel

6.16 LED Fixtures

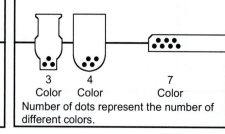

3 Color   4 Color   7 Color
Number of dots represent the number of different colors.

6.17 Scene Machine

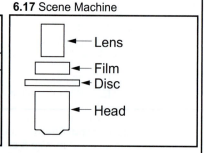

← Lens
← Film
← Disc
← Head

6.18 Line Weights

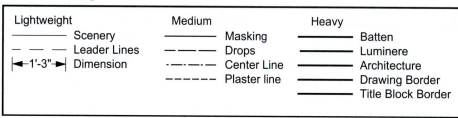

Lightweight	Medium	Heavy
——— Scenery	——— Masking	——— Batten
– — — Leader Lines	— — — Drops	——— Luminere
⊢1'-3"⊣ Dimension	–·–·– Center Line	——— Architecture
	– – – – Plaster line	——— Drawing Border
		——— Title Block Border

Appendix B

Tape Decks and Production Tape Layout

TAPE DECK

A tape deck transports the magnetic tape on which music and sound effects are recorded. There is a subtle distinction between a tape deck and a tape recorder. A tape deck is simply a transport mechanism for the tape; a tape recorder is a self-contained unit with a built-in amplifier and speaker so that it can be used to play back the sound without the need for an external amplifier and speaker.

The tape deck has several functions, which are illustrated in Figure A. The **heads,** which implant electrical data on the recording tape, are vital to the functioning of the tape deck. Top-quality decks appropriate for use in theatre sound have three or four heads. Less expensive models normally have only two heads.

Regardless of the number of heads on the tape deck, they all work in the same way. The head is basically an electromagnet made of a ring of iron, as shown in Figure B. There is a small gap in the ring at the point where the recording tape contacts the tape head. (The gap isn't open; it is filled with a nonconductive metal to prevent it from snagging the tape or filling with dust.)

When an electronic signal from a microphone or other source is fed to the wire wound around the bottom of the iron ring, it creates a magnetic field across the gap at the top of the ring. When the tape deck is recording, the strength of the magnetic field across the gap in the head will vary in a pattern that mimics the voltage variations of the electronic signal.

The configuration of a three-head deck is always the same. The erase head is located on the left, the record head is in the middle, and the playback head is on the right. The erase head feeds an ultrasonic (a sound frequency above the range of human hearing) signal to the tape. This effectively scrambles any previously recorded information. The record head encodes magnetic information on the tape in a pattern that mimics the electronic signal generated by the microphone or other source. The playback head is actually a reverse of the record head. The varying density of the magnetic field recorded on the tape creates a corresponding signal of varying voltage within the playback head. This signal, which is theoretically identical to the signal that was fed to the record head, is then sent on to the various equalizers and amplifiers to be turned into sound waves.

If a tape deck has a fourth head (which is somewhat rare), it is dedicated to monitoring the tape.

Aside from providing the capability to erase, record, and play back the magnetically stored data, the tape deck must be capable of smoothly transporting the tape at a constant speed. Although a wide variety of tape speeds are available— $^{15}/_{16}$, $3^3/_4$, $7^1/_2$, and 15 inches per second (IPS)—most theatrical second designers prefer to use $7^1/_2$ IPS. This speed provides a high quality of sound reproduction (approximately 20–20,000 Hz) with an acceptable level of tape consumption. A speed of $3^3/_4$ IPS can be used for background effects and low-level preshow "Muzak" tracks on which its lower-frequency range (approximately 50–12,000 Hz) won't adversely affect the production. If the sound equipment is of extremely

head: A very high quality electromagnet on a tape deck or tape recorder that is used to implant, retrieve, or erase electrical data from audio tapes.

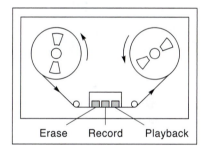

FIGURE A
Tape-deck heads.

Erase   Record   Playback

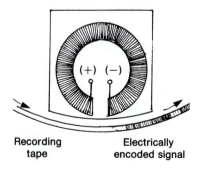

Recording tape   Electrically encoded signal

FIGURE B
How a tape head works (see text for details).

FIGURE C
Monophonic, stereophonic, and quadra-phonic tape tracks.

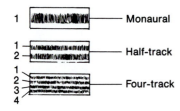

1 ———————— Monaural

1 ————
2 ———— Half-track

1 ————
2 ————
3 ———— Four-track
4

FIGURE D
Otari stereo analog tape deck. Courtesy of Otari.

high quality and tape consumption isn't a budgetary consideration, 15 IPS is often used, because it does provide the highest level of frequency response.

Anywhere from one to three or more motors are used in various models of tape decks to transport the tape. Generally speaking, the more motors the better, simply because the individual motors can be devoted to specific functions (the various playing speeds, fast forward, rewind) rather than having one motor provide all functions through some type of gearing mechanism.

A variety of track configurations are used on tape decks, as shown in Figure C. Generally speaking, the more tape that comes into contact with the head, the better the sound. Most professional-quality theatre sound is recorded on full track (for monaural recording), or half-track stereo (for stereo), or four-track (for quadraphonic sound).

Almost all theatre sound that is not recorded as a computer file is recorded on ¼-inch reel-to-reel tape decks, because these commercial- or studio-quality decks (Figure D) are readily available and the tape is fairly easy to handle and edit.

PRODUCTION TAPE LAYOUT

Tape—whether analog or digital—is still a viable and effective method of production sound playback. Figure E illustrates the layout pattern for a typical production sound tape. A 4- to 5-foot-long piece of white or colored leader tape clearly marked with the word *head* and the name of the production is located at the beginning, or head, of the tape. The first sound cue is spliced to this piece of leader. The point on the magnetic tape at which the sound begins is placed ½ inch from the splice. The tape containing the first cue is cut about 1 foot after the sound of the first cue has ended. The end of the first cue is spliced to a 2-foot piece of white or colored leader tape. *Cue 2* is marked toward the end of this leader tape near the splice for the second cue. The point at which the sound for the second cue begins is again located ½ inch from the splice. The pattern of leader, cue, leader, cue is repeated until either the reel is full or the cues for the show are completed. After the last cue on the tape, attach another 6- to 8-foot piece of leader marked with the name of the production and the word *end* in several places. Be sure that this "tail" is long enough to allow the machine to be stopped after the last cue has ended and before the leader comes off the reel. It will make the job of rewinding

FIGURE E
A typical production tape layout.

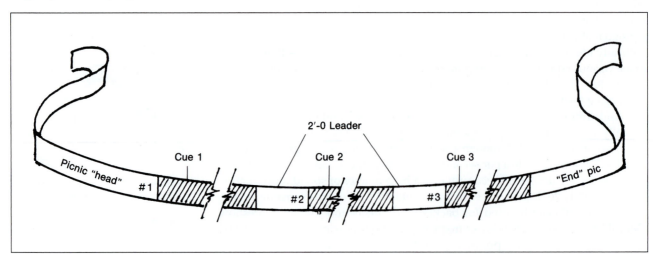

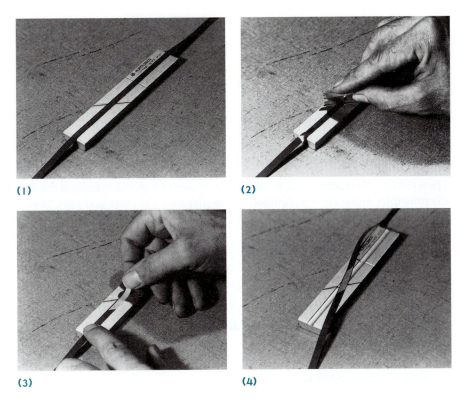

(1)   (2)

(3)   (4)

FIGURE F
Audio tape splicing techniques. (1) Place uncut tape in a splicing block (magnetic face down). (2) Cut the tape with a single-edge razor blade. Be sure the blade isn't magnetized. (3) Tape the splice with mylar splicing tape. (4) A finished splice.

the tape considerably less frustrating if you don't have to rethread the machine. Figure F provides instructions on how to splice ¼-inch audio tape.

Every reel of tape that is used on a production should be clearly marked with the name of the production and the tape deck on which it will be played. If more than one reel is to be used on any deck during the show, the sequence (*1 of 2, 2 of 3*, and so forth) should also be marked on those reels.

Appendix C

Building and Covering Wooden-framed Soft Flats

The following instructions are for the construction of a wooden-framed flat. But the principles involved—the guidelines for placement of stiles and rails, as well as the spacing of togglebars—are equally applicable to the construction of studio and metal-framed flats.

To build a standard wooden flat 14 feet tall and 4 feet wide, you can follow a standard procedure outlined in fifteen steps:

1. Select good, straight white pine 1×3 or 1×4 ("B or better" or "C select") for the rails, stiles, and toggle bars.

2. Trim and square the end of one of the boards, and cut two pieces 4 feet long for the rails. (Note that the rails are cut the full width of the flat.)

3. Trim and square the boards, and cut the two stiles 14 feet (the height of the flat) minus the combined width of the two rails.

4. Square the boards, and cut two toggle bars 4 feet (the width of the flat) minus the combined width of the two stiles.

5. Before you begin to assemble the flat, cut the keystones and cornerblocks.

6. Although a flat can be assembled using mortise and tenon or halved joints for extra strength, most shops use butt joints when putting flats together. Butt the stiles against the edge of the top and bottom rails.

   Assembling the flat in this manner means that the rail will be the only framing element making contact with the floor when the finished flat is set upright. If the flat were assembled with the end of the stile touching the floor, it would be splintered and broken whenever the flat was moved or skidded along the floor.

7. Use a framing square to make sure that the corner joint between the rail and stile is square. Lay a cornerblock on top of the joint with its grain running perpendicular to the line of the joint (parallel to the grain of the stile), and inset ¾ inch from the outside edge of both the rail and stile. Secure the cornerblocks (as well as the keystones or straps) with coated staples, or power-driven screws. This routine is repeated for each corner of the flat.

8. Center the toggle bars at 4 feet 8 inches and 9 feet 4 inches so that they will be equidistant from the top and bottom of the flat and from each other. Use the framing square to make sure that the toggle bars are square to the stile, and secure them with keystones that are also inset ¾ inch from the edges of the stiles.

9. When the flat is wider than 3 feet, diagonal corner braces made of 1×2 are placed in the upper and lower corners of the same side of the flat. Secure these corner braces with plywood straps ripped in half and angle cut so that they can be inset ¾ inch from the outside edge of the flat.

10. To cover the flat, you will need to turn it over so that it is lying on the cornerblocks and keystones (Figure GA). Stretch a piece of heavyweight muslin (128- or 140-thread count) over the frame. The muslin should be

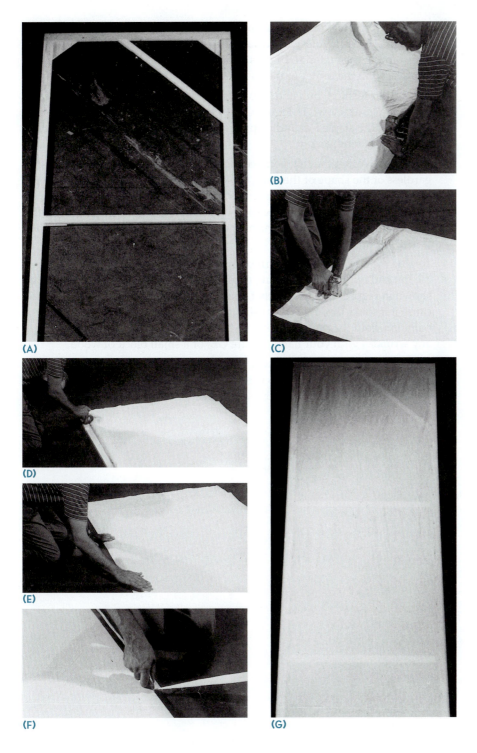

Figure G
Flat-covering technique. (A) The smooth front side of a flat frame. (B) Lay fabric slightly wider and taller than the flat frame over the frame. (C) Staple the fabric to the inside edge of the face of the flat. (D) Glue the fabric to the frame, and smooth the fabric onto the frame with your hands (E) or a small block of wood. Trim the excess fabric with a matte knife (F) after the glue has dried. (G) The finished flat.

slightly larger than the height and width of the flat, as shown in Figure GB. Using a hand stapler, attach the muslin along the inside edge of the face of one of the stiles. Place the staples about 1 foot apart.

11. Move to the center of the other stile, and pull the muslin until it barely sags across the face of the flat. Staple it on the inside edge of the face of that stile. Be sure that you don't stretch the muslin until it is tight; you need to allow room for fabric shrinkage when you paint the muslin. (On a 4-by-14-foot

flat, the completely tacked muslin should just brush the work surface underneath it.) Work your way toward the end of the flat, alternately pulling and stapling the material. Do this in both directions from the staple that you placed in the center of the stile.

12. In a similar fashion, pull and staple the fabric to the inside edge of the face of both rails, as shown in Figure GC. If there are any wrinkles or puckers in the fabric, the staples should be pulled and the fabric restretched until the wrinkles are removed.

13. To finish covering the flat, you need to glue the muslin to the frame. Regardless of the shape of the flat, you should glue the covering only to the face of the rails and stiles. If the covering fabric is not glued to any internal pieces (toggle bars, corner braces), it will be able to shrink evenly when the flat is painted. This uniform shrinkage will result in fewer wrinkles on the face of the finished flat.

14. To glue the cloth to the flat, turn back the flap of muslin around the edge of the flat and apply a light coating of glue to the face of the stiles and rails, as shown in Figure GD. Be sure that you use a thorough but *light* coating, because if it soaks through the muslin, it may discolor or darken the ensuing paint job. Fold the muslin back onto the wood, and carefully smooth out any wrinkles with your hand (Figure GE) or a small block of wood.

15. After the glue has dried, you will need to trim the excess fabric from the flat. The easiest way to do this is to pull the fabric tight and run a matte knife down the edge of the flat, as shown in Figure GF. Figure GG shows a finished soft-covered flat.

Glossary

1-inch centers: the centers of adjacent elements, such as holes, are spaced 1 inch apart.

4-in/2-out: a mixer device with four inputs and two outputs.

6-inch centers: those spaced 6 inches apart.

18-inch centers: those spaced 18 inches apart.

Accessory: in costuming, anything other than clothing that is worn or carried, including wigs, hats, footwear, jewelry, and similar items.

Acoustics: the sound-transmission characteristics of a room, space, or material; also, the science that studies these qualities.

Acrylic: a plastic most readily identified by its trade name Plexiglas; available in rigid sheets and in liquid form (for use as a casting resin).

Acting areas: those areas of the stage on which specific scenes, or parts of scenes, are played.

Additive color mixing: the transmission of light of varying hues to the eye and the brain's interpretation of the ratio of the light mixture as a specific hue.

Adjustable arc-joint pliers: long-handled pliers with a series of jaw pivot points that provide a variety of jaw-opening ranges; used for gripping square and round objects with a great deal of leverage; also known as alligator pliers.

Adjustable-end wrench: generally known by the trade name Crescent Wrench, the adjustable-end wrench has smooth jaws that adjust to fit almost any small to medium-sized nut; used to tighten bolts and nuts.

Adjustable wood clamps: a wooden clamp with two adjustable faces; the jaws can be adjusted to various angles that are useful in holding furniture frames while the glued joints are drying.

Aerial perspective: an optical phenomenon in which objects that are farther away appear less sharply in focus and less fully saturated in color.

Air caster: a nonwheeled caster that lifts objects and holds them up using high-volume, low-pressure compressed air; three to four air casters are used to raise most objects; the one-foot-diameter air caster, load rated at 2,000 pounds, is the standard size used in theatrical production.

Aircraft cable: extremely strong, flexible, multistrand, twisted metal cable; ⅛-inch aircraft cable is frequently used for flying heavy scenery because it has a breaking strength of approximately one ton.

Allen wrench: an L-shaped piece of steel rod with a hexagonal cross-sectional shape; used for working with Allen-head screws and bolts.

Alligator pliers: *see* adjustable arc-joint pliers.

Ambient: surrounding or background.

Ampere: the unit of measurement of electrical current.

Amplifier: a device used to boost the signal received from a transducer to a level that will drive a loudspeaker.

Amplitude: synonym for loudness.

Analog: in electronics, a circuit or device in which the output varies as a continuous function of the input.

Analogous colors: colors that are adjacent to each other on the color wheel; also known as related colors.

Aniline dye: transparent pigment made from aniline, a poisonous derivative of benzene; characterized by brilliant hues and full saturation; a strong solution can be made by putting one teaspoon of dye into a quart of boiling water.

Animal glue: a natural glue (a by-product of the meat-packing industry) used for securing muslin to flat frames and as a binder in dry pigment and binder scene paint.

Anvil: a heavy, solid metal device with variously shaped faces; used in conjunction with a mechanic's or blacksmith's hammer for shaping metal.

Appliqué: a decorative item attached to a basic form.

Apron: the flat extension of the stage floor that projects from the proscenium arch toward the audience.

Arc: an electric current that leaps the gap between two closely placed electrodes.

Arc welder: a welder that uses an electrical arc to melt the metals being welded. The approximately ⅛-inch-diameter electrode melts and flows into the welding zone to provide filler metal.

Arena stage: a stage completely surrounded by the audience.

Armature: a basic skeletal form that holds the covering materials in the desired shape or alignment.

Artistic director: person responsible for the major artistic decisions of a theatrical production company—hiring of production personnel, selection of season, and so on.

Assignable: In this case, the property of being able to be assigned; e.g., an assignable input may be connected to any output or any number of outputs.

Asymmetrical balance: a sense of equipoise achieved through dynamic tension created by the juxtaposition of dissimilar design elements.

Atom: the smallest particle of a chemical element that retains the structural properties of that element.

Atomic theory: a generally accepted theory concerning the structure and composition of substances.

Attenuate: to decrease or lessen.

Auditorium: the seating area from which the audience observes the action of a play.

Auger bits: spiral-shaped bits designed to be used with a brace; used for drilling holes (¼ inch to approximately 2 inches in diameter) in wood.

Backing: flats, drops, or draperies placed on the offstage side of doors and similar openings to prevent the audience from seeing backstage.

Backpainting: literally to paint on the back. You paint the back, or reverse, side of the scenery or drop.

Backsaw: a fine-toothed (twelve to fourteen teeth per inch) crosscut saw with a stiffening spine on its back; used with a miter box to make accurate miter cuts.

Balance: the arrangement of parts of a composition to create a sense of restfulness; also, to adjust the loudness and equalization levels of individual signals while mixing, to achieve an appropriate blend.

Balanced line: a sound cable in which two insulated conductors are wrapped in a braided or foil shield.

Bald cap: a latex cap that covers a person's hair.

Ball peen hammer: a hammer made of hardened steel with a round ball on the back of its head; used for bending and shaping metal and seating rivets.

Baluster: a vase-shaped vertical member that supports the handrail of a staircase rail.

Band saw: a stationary power saw with a narrow continuous loop (or band) blade that passes through a table which supports the work; used for making curvilinear cuts.

Banister: the vertical member that supports the handrail of a staircase rail.

Bar clamp: similar to a pipe clamp except a notched bar is substituted for the pipe.

Barn door: an accessory for a Fresnel spotlight whose movable flippers are swung into the beam to control it.

Base coat: the first coat of the finished paint job; provides the basic color for the ensuing texture coats.

Bass-reflex speaker enclosure: an insulated box with a carefully designed hole or port in front that synchronizes the phase of the rearward speaker excursion with its forward excursion to reinforce the bass frequencies.

Batten: a wooden dowel or metal pipe (generally $1\frac{1}{4}$ to $1\frac{1}{2}$ inches in diameter) attached to the onstage lines from a rope-set or counterweight system. Scenery is attached to the batten.

Batten-clamp drop: a drop that can be quickly attached to or removed from a batten by the use of batten clamps.

Battened butt joint: two pieces of lumber butted end to end with a small piece of similar width attached directly above the joint.

Beam angle: that point where the light emitted by an instrument is diminished by 50 percent when compared with the output of the center of the beam.

Beam projector: a lensless instrument with a parabolic primary reflector and a spherical secondary reflector that creates an intense shaft of light with little diffusion.

Belt clamp: a woven nylon belt with a ratchet device to tighten the belt around the work; used to clamp irregularly shaped objects.

Belt sander: a handheld, portable power tool that uses belts of sandpaper for rapid sanding of (primarily) wood.

Bench grinder: a stationary stand- or bench-mounted power tool consisting of an electric motor with shafts extending from either end; various grinding and buffing wheels, as well as wire brushes, can be mounted on the shafts to perform a variety of grinding, buffing, and polishing functions.

Bench sander: a stationary stand- or bench-mounted, power tool that consists of a combination of a belt and a disk sander; used to bevel or smooth the surface or edges of wood and some plastics.

Bevel protractor: measuring device similar to the combination square except that the angle of the blade is adjustable; used for marking angles between 0 and 90 degrees.

Bevel set: a measuring device similar to a tri square except that the angle between the blade and handle is adjustable; used for transferring angles from one piece of work to another.

Bidirectional: two directions; a microphone pickup pattern primarily receptive to the front and back.

Binder: an adhesive in paint that "glues" the pigment and fillers to the painted material after the vehicle has evaporated.

Blackout: When the stage is completely dark. The stage lights are out and no other lights are on.

Bleeding: the capillary migration of an applied dye or paint to an area outside the area to which it is applied.

Blend: a combination of more than one type of fiber, blends are created to take advantage of the best properties of all fibers in the blend.

Blocking: the actors' movements on the stage.

Block out: in makeup, to cover with soap, spirit gum, wax, material, or preformed plastic film so that no hair is evident.

Block plane: a small plane with a shallow (approximately 15 to 20 degrees) blade angle; used to smooth across the grain of wood.

Blueline: to copy drawings made on tracing vellum; the lines are printed in blue or, sometimes, in black; also known as the diazo process.

Blueprint: a drawing-reproduction technique in which the background is blue and the lines are white; frequently used as a misnomer for blueline.

Board foot: a unit of measurement equivalent to a piece of stock lumber that is 12 inches long, 12 inches wide, and 1 inch thick.

Board operators: the electricians who run the light board during rehearsals and performances.

Bobbinet: a transparent, open, hexagonal weave material; used as a glass substitute, diffusion drop, net backing for cutout drops, and similar applications.

Bobby pin: a hair pin made of springy flat metal wire bent in a tight U shape. The legs—one straight, the other wavy—touch each other and provide the clamping power to hold the hair in place. Generally used with shorter hair.

Bodice: the upper part of a woman's dress.

Bogus paper: a heavy, soft, absorbent paper; similar to blotter paper.

Bolt cutter: heavy-duty shears with a great deal of leverage; used to cut through bolts and mild-steel round stock up to $\frac{1}{2}$ inch in diameter.

Book: to fold hinged flats together so that they resemble a book.

Book ceiling: two large flats about the same width as the proscenium arch, stored in a booked position in the flies; when needed to create a ceiling, they are opened and lowered onto the walls of the set.

Boomerang: (1) a rolling scaffold with several levels; used for painting vertical scenery; (2) a device to hold color media in a followspot.

Borderlights: any lights hung above the stage, behind the borders (horizontal masking pieces). In this context the borderlights were striplights—long, narrow, troughlike fixtures usually containing eight to twelve individual lamps.

Borders: wide, short, framed or unframed cloth drops suspended over the stage to prevent the audience from seeing above the stage. In the Restoration theatre, borders normally matched the decorative treatment on the wings and drops. In modern practice, borders are frequently made of black, unpainted velour.

Bottom hanger iron: flying hardware; a metal strap iron with a D ring at the top and a hooked foot at the bottom; used at the bottom of heavy flats to support the load under compression.

Box: to pour paint back and forth between buckets to ensure a complete and uniform mix.

Box-end wrench: a wrench with a closed, toothed head that must be fit over the head of the bolt or nut; used to tighten bolts and nuts.

Box nail: nail with a narrower shaft than a common nail, to reduce the chance of splitting the lumber.

Brace: a hand-cranked drill used for turning auger bits; used for drilling large-diameter holes in wood.

Brace cleat: bracing hardware attached to the stile on the back of a flat to provide means for securing a stage brace to the flat.

Breathes: a term that defines a material's ability to transmit heat, air, and water vapor.

Brocade: fabric similar to damask but lighter in weight; woven patterns achieved by weaving high-luster yarn into a matte-finish background can be either raised or flat; used for making costumes, upholstery, and decorative drapery.

Bulb: the Pyrex glass or synthetic quartz container for a lamp filament and gaseous environment; synonymous with envelope.

Burn: to record on a CD.

Butcher paper: a medium-weight brown paper, available in 36-inch-wide rolls; also known by its trade name, Kraft paper.

Butt joint: a wood joint; two pieces of wood are square cut and fit together end to end, end to edge, edge to edge, end to face, or edge to face.

Butt weld: a welded metal joint; the pieces being welded are joined edge to edge.

Cabinet drawing: a type of detail drawing that subscribes to the principles of oblique drawing except that all depth measurements are reduced by one-half or some similar ratio, such as 1:4.

Call: to tell specific crew members when to perform their cues.

Canvas head block: a block of material in the shape of a head, covered with canvas. Wigs are pinned to it for styling and storage.

Capacitance: the electrical capacity of a condenser, or capacitor.

Carcass: the foundation structure of something, for example, the framework of a cabinet.

Cardioid: a heart-shaped pickup pattern that primarily picks up sounds in front of, and slightly to the sides of, the microphone.

Card stock: a thick cardboard, similar in thickness to 3-by-5 notecards and file folders.

Carpenter's level: a 2- to 3-foot piece of wooden, steel, or aluminum I beam with glass-tube spirit levels at either end and the middle; used to determine true horizontal and vertical.

Carpenter's rule: *see* folding wood rule.

Carpenter's vise: a vise for holding wood; attached to a workbench, one or both faces are covered with hardwood to prevent the vise from scratching, denting, or marring the surface of the work.

Carriage: the part of a stair unit that supports the tread and risers.

Carriage bolt: a bolt whose upper face has a rounded surface and whose under-side has a slightly tapered square collar a little wider than the diameter of the bolt shaft; used to join wood to wood or wood to metal.

Cartooning: the process of transferring line work (and color blocks) from the painter's elevations to the scenery.

Casein: a natural or synthetically derived phosphoprotein—a chief component of milk.

Casein paint: a paint with a casein binder; has good covering power, is water-resistant when fully dry, and can usually be thinned with a ratio of between two and four parts water to one part paint concentrate.

Casket lock: a heavy-duty hidden lock used to hold platforms together and for similar applications.

Cassette tape: audio recorder tape, also used in computer storage.

Caster: a wheel/axle device attached to platforms and the like to make them roll; casters for theatrical use should have hard rubber tires, a load rating of at least 300 pounds, and sturdy construction.

Casting resins: any number of liquid plastics used for casting forms in molds.

Cavea: Roman term for auditorium.

C clamp: a clamp composed of a U-shaped frame with a threaded shaft; work is clamped between a pressure plate at one end of the U and the toe of the shaft; used for a wide variety of jobs, such as holding work together while parts are being assembled or while glue joints are drying.

Ceiling plate: flying hardware; a flat metal plate with an O ring in the center; attached to the primary structural members of ceiling flats to provide a means of attaching the flying lines to the ceiling.

Centerline: a leader line that runs perpendicular to the set line from the midpoint or center of the opening of the proscenium arch.

Center-line section: a sectional drawing with the cutting plane located on the center line of the stage and auditorium; used to show the height of the various elements of the stage and theatre and any pertinent set pieces.

Center punch: a pointed tool made of hard steel; used for indenting shallow holes in wood and metal.

Centrifugal force: force that moves away from the center; for example, the circular motion of electrons spinning around a nucleus generates centrifugal force.

Chalk line: a metal or plastic housing holding a long piece of twine and filled with dry scenic pigment; used for marking straight lines.

Channel control: an electronic patching system in which one or more dimmers can be assigned to a control channel, which in turn controls the intensity level of those dimmers.

Character: the distinctive qualities, traits, and personality of a person, place, or thing. Also, the emotional quality (e.g., soft, hard, harsh, sensuous) of a line.

Chiffon: a sheer, usually translucent, cloth frequently made from rayon or silk; used for scarves and diaphanous blouses and gowns.

Chopper: *see* shutter.

Chroma: *see* saturation.

Chuck: the adjustable jawed clamp at the end of a drill that holds the drill bits.

Circuit: a conductive path through which electricity flows; also, to connect a lighting instrument to a stage circuit.

Circuit breaker: a device to protect a circuit from an overload; it has a magnetic device that trips open to break circuit continuity.

Circular saw: a portable circular-bladed saw; the angle and depth of cut is variable; used to cross- and angle-cut as well as rip stock and plywood.

Claw hammer: a hammer with two sharply curved claws projecting from the back of its head that facilitates nail removal; used for driving nails.

Cleat: a piece of wood used to brace, block, or reinforce.

Clip art: digitized pictures that can be transferred, or clipped, from the original program into a document on which you are working.

Clothesline: a small-diameter cotton rope; not used for raising or suspending loads, but is the standard rope for lash lines and is used as the operating rope for traveling drapes (travelers).

Clout nail: a wedge-shaped nail made of soft iron used to attach cornerblocks and keystones to the frame of a flat; it is driven through the wood onto a steel backing plate, which curls the end of the nail back into the lumber.

Club: in context, refers to night clubs in which high-energy music (live or recorded) is the prime attraction.

Coated box nail: a box nail with an adhesive applied to the shaft that tightly bonds the nail to the wood.

Cobbler: one who makes shoes.

Cold chisel: a chisel made of hard steel; used for cutting or shearing mild steel and nonferrous metals.

Cold-press finish: a slight surface texture achieved by pressing paper between cold rollers; no oil residue results, so the paper can be used with transparent watercolor, designer's gouache, acrylic, markers, pencils, pastel, and so forth.

Collage: a picture made of various materials (e.g., paper, cloth) glued on a surface; can include drawn or photographic images as well.

Color: a perception created in the brain by the stimulation of the retina by light waves of certain lengths; a generic term applied to all light waves contained in the visible spectrum.

Color frame: a lightweight metal holder for color media that fits in a holder at the front of a lighting instrument.

Color media: colored plastic, gel, or glass filters used to modify the color of light.

Combination square: a 12-inch steel rule with a movable handle angled at 45 and 90 degrees; used for marking those two angles, and the rule can be used for measuring.

Commando: a lightweight cotton fabric with a short, feltlike, almost matted pile; available in two weights and widths, the heavy-weight is suitable for stage drapery; the material face is generally too susceptible to wear for use as an upholstery fabric; also known as duvetyn.

Common nail: nail with a large head and thick shank; used for heavier general construction.

Complementary: two hues that, when combined, theoretically yield white in light or black in pigment; colors that are opposite to each other on a color wheel. In practice, mixing complementary pigment colors results in complex dark grays, not true black.

Composition: an arrangement of parts to create a whole.

Compound curves: a surface that curves in more than one direction (like a ball) or changes the radius of its curve (like a playground slide.)

Compressor: a pump that drives air into a tank; the output pressure from the tank is controlled by a valve called a regulator.

Concentric revolving stages: a revolving stage with, usually, two sections, one rotating inside the other.

Concert: in context, primarily refers to touring rock and country western shows.

Condensing lens: a device that condenses the direct and reflected light from a source and concentrates it on the slide-plane aperture of a projector.

Conduit: thin-wall metal (aluminum or steel) tubing; used as a housing for electrical wiring and decorative stage material.

Conduit bender: a tool for bending conduit.

Cones: nerve cells in the retina that are sensitive to bright light; they respond to red, blue, or green light.

Connecting strip: an electrical gutter or wireway that carries a number of stage circuits; the circuits terminate on the connecting strip in female receptacles.

Constructed sound: any sound created by editing, manipulating, or changing previously recorded sounds.

Construction adhesive: also called panel adhesive. An adhesive contained in a caulking tube; dispensed with a caulking gun. Available in a number of formulations for use in gluing wall panels to studs (wood to wood), Styrofoam to wood, wood to metal, and so forth.

Construction calendar: a calendar that details when various technical elements of a production will be constructed.

Construction crew: those who build the set, move it into the theatre, and set it up onstage.

Construction line: in a two-line-weight system, a thick line 0.5 mm thick (in pencil) or 0.020 to 0.025 inch thick (in pen).

Contact cement: an adhesive for bonding nonporous surfaces together; surfaces bond as soon as they come in contact with each other.

Continental parallel: a platform made of a folding framework of nonvariable height; the top and center supports are removable; the frame folds into a more compact unit than does the standard parallel.

Contrast: the juxtaposition of dissimilar elements.

Coping saw: a lightweight handsaw composed of a U-shaped frame with a narrow, fine-toothed (sixteen to eighteen teeth per inch) replaceable blade; used for making curvilinear cuts in thin plywood and lumber.

Corduroy: a cotton material whose pile ridges, called wales, alternate with a low-luster backing; available in a wide variety of wale widths and depths; heavier weights are used for upholstery, while lighter weights are used in costuming; waleless corduroy is similar to a short-nap velour, with similar uses.

Cornerblock: a triangular-shaped piece of ¼-inch plywood used to reinforce the joint between a stile and a rail of a flat.

Corner brace: a diagonal internal framing member that helps keep a flat square.

Corner plate: an L-shaped piece of ¹⁄₁₆-inch galvanized steel, predrilled for use with flat-head wood screws; used to reinforce corners of doors, windows, and so on.

Corrugated fasteners: corrugated strips of metal used primarily to hold lightweight frames together.

Costume designer: person responsible for the design, visual appearance, and function of the costumes, accessories, and makeup.

Costumer: person responsible for the construction of the costumes and supervision of the costume shop.

Cotton canvas: a durable lightweight, coarse-weave material; used for covering platforms and making ground cloths.

Cotton duck: a lightweight cotton canvas; used more in costumes than scenic construction.

Cotton linters: the short hairs covering the cotton seed.

Cotton rep: a tough cotton fabric with a ribbed finish similar to a narrow, short-nap corduroy; good for stage draperies, costumes, and upholstery.

Counterweight arbor: a metal cradle that holds counterbalancing weights used in flying.

Crash: in reference to hard drives, to become inoperative. Data cannot usually be retrieved from a hard drive that has "crashed."

Crepe: a thin, crinkle-finished, soft cloth usually made from rayon, silk, or fine cotton; frequently used for women's blouses.

Crescent wrench: *see* adjustable-end wrench.

Crosscut saw: a handsaw with an approximately 26-inch blade whose angle-sharpened teeth bend outward so that the kerf is wider than the blade; designed to cut across the grain of the wood. Crosscut saws with ten to twelve teeth per inch are suitable for most scenic purposes.

Crossover network: an electronic device that splits the signal from the amplifier into frequency ranges most appropriate for use by woofers, midrange speakers, and tweeters.

Crowbar: a round metal bar with flattened metal claws similar to those on a claw or rip hammer on one end and a tapered wedge on the other.

Cue: a directive for action, for example, a change in the lighting.

Cueing: designing the light cues. Manipulating, and recording, the distribution, intensity, movement, and color of the lights for each cue to create the appropriate look for that moment in the play.

Cure: to harden and reach full strength (in reference to adhesives).

Cut awl: a portable power saw with a reciprocating blade mounted in a swiveling head; available with a variety of blades to make intricate curvilinear cuts in materials ranging from fabric to wood, paper, and plastic.

Cut list: a list of the color media required for the lighting design for a particular production categorized by hue and size; used to assist in ordering and cutting the color media for a lighting design.

Cutoff saw: a semiportable stand-mounted circular-bladed power saw that can be equipped with a wood or metal cutting blade for square and angle cutting of lumber or metal stock; can be set up for cutting either wood (wooden table without holding clamps) or metal (metal table with holding clamps); also known as a motorized miter box.

Cutout line: *see* silhouette.

Cutter: person who pins patterns to fabrics and cuts the material.

Cutting plane: the plane at which an object is theoretically cut to produce a sectional view.

Cyanoacrylate cement: a powerful, rapid-bonding adhesive that will bond almost anything; generically known by the trade names Super Glue, Krazy Glue, and so forth.

Cyc light: a lensless instrument with an eccentric reflector used to create a smooth wash of light on a cyc or skytab from a close distance.

Cyclorama: a large drop used to surround the stage.

Dado head: a specialty circular saw blade consisting of a set of toothed blades that sandwich a chisel-like chipper. The blades smooth-cut the outside edges of the kerf while the chipper gouges out the wood between the blades. The distance between the blades is variable; used with table and radial-arm saws.

Dado joint: a wood joint made by cutting a notch or groove in the face of one piece of lumber to receive the edge of another piece of stock.

Damask: a rich-appearing cloth with raised patterns of high-luster yarn that are normally woven into the matte finish of the background cloth; used for making costumes, upholstery, and decorative drapery.

Dead hang: to suspend without means of raising or lowering.

Dead lift: to lift without counterbalancing.

Decibel: a unit for expressing the intensity of sounds; an increase or decrease of one decibel is just about the smallest change in loudness that the human ear can detect.

Decking: the covering surface of a structure on which people will walk.

Decorative prop: any item that is used to enhance the setting visually but is not specifically touched by an actor, such as

window curtains, pictures, doilies, table lamps, bric-a-brac, and so forth.

Delay: refers to the time interval that the second part of a split time fade follows the first.

Demi-mask: a mask, normally mounted on a stick, that covers half the face.

Denim: a coarsely woven cotton or cotton blend twill.

Designer's cue sheet: a form used by the lighting designer to record pertinent information (dimmer levels, timing, "go" point, and so forth) about every cue in the production.

Design style: a recognizable pattern of compositional elements that provides a distinctive reflection of the social and political history of the time.

Detail drawings: drawings that describe the detail of objects. Usually drawn in a fairly large scale, normally between ¾ inch = 1 foot and 1½ inches = 1 foot.

Detailing: trim, appliqués, buttons, ribbons, braid, and so forth attached to a garment to enhance its appearance.

Diagonal cutters: pliers with beveled cutting faces on the jaw rather than flat gripping faces; used for cutting soft wire.

Diffuse: to soften the appearance of light by using a translucent filtering element to scatter the light rays.

Digital tape recording: a form of recording in which the audio information is stored on the magnetic tape as binary information rather than an analog signal.

Digitizing tablet: an electro-mechanical device that converts the pressure of a stylus on a flat plate (tablet) into binary information that can be understood by the computer.

Dimension: the relative length and width of a line.

Dimmer: an electrical device that controls the intensity of a light source connected to it.

Dimmer circuit: an electrical circuit terminating on one end at a dimmer. The other end terminates at either a patch panel or onstage. Synonymous with stage circuit when it terminates onstage.

Director: person responsible for interpreting the script, creating a viable production concept, and directing the actors.

Discrete: separate and complete; in context, pertaining to information represented by binary code.

Distress: to create a worn or aged appearance as with fabric, wood, or metal.

Distributed dimming: a concept in which dimmers are placed at the point of use—close to where the fixture to be dimmed is located—rather than in a centralized dimmer rack.

Double-headed nails: nails with two heads; they are driven into the wood until the lower head is flush with the surface, leaving the upper head exposed so that it can be pulled out easily; used for scaffolding or any temporary structure that needs to be dismantled quickly.

Double plano-convex lens train: two plano-convex lenses placed with their curved surfaces facing each other; creates a system that has a shorter focal length than either of its component lenses.

Double whip: a block and tackle configuration that provides a 2:1 mechanical advantage.

Douser: a mechanical dimming device used in followspots.

Dowel: a short cylinder of hardwood, usually birch.

Doweled joint: a butt joint that is internally supported by dowel pegs.

Drape: a vertical element of heavy fabric that frames the sides of a window or an archway.

Draw to scale: to produce a likeness that is a proportional reduction of an object.

Dremel tool: a hand-held router similar to a dentist's drill that can be equipped with a number of bits for grinding, cutting, or carving of wood, metal, and plastic.

Dress: to place decorative props such as curtains, doilies, knickknacks, or magazines on the set to help make the environment look lived in and provide clues to the personalities of the characters who inhabit the set. Also, to work with hair or a wig to create a specific style or look.

Dressers: costume-crew personnel who assist actors in putting on their costumes.

Dress rehearsal: a run-through with all technical elements, including costumes and makeup.

Drill press: a stationary bench or stand-mounted power drill with a variety of speeds. The chuck will generally hold bits up to ½ inch in diameter.

Drop: a large expanse of cloth, usually muslin or scenic canvas, on which something (a landscape, sky, street, room) is usually painted.

Drop box: a small connecting strip, generally containing four to eight circuits, that can be clamped to a boom or a pipe.

Drum winch: in this case, a motorized system in which steel cables are wound around a drum or cylinder and the taking up, or letting out, of the cables is controlled by the rotation of the drum. Each drum winch is equipped with a motor, gearbox, and brake.

Dry brushing: a painting technique frequently used to create a wood-grain appearance; done by lightly charging a brush and lightly stroking it across the surface of the work.

Drywall: gypsum board typically used to cover interior walls in home construction; normally (½ inch thick although other thicknesses are available.

Ducted-port speaker enclosure: a speaker enclosure similar in operational theory to the bass-reflex enclosure except that a tube of specific diameter and length is substituted for the open hole, or port; it reinforces bass frequencies.

Dust mask: a device covering the nose and mouth that filters particulate matter from the air.

Dutchman: a 5- to 6-inch-wide strip of cloth of the same material as the flat covering; used to hide the joints between flats in a wall unit.

Duvetyn: *see* commando.

Effects head: a motor-driven unit capable of producing crude moving images with a scenic projector.

Electric: any pipe that is used to hold lighting instruments.

Electrical current: the flow or movement of electrons through a conductor.

Electrical potential: the difference in electrical charge between two bodies; measured in volts.

Electric glue pot: a thermostatically controlled pot used for melting animal glue.

Electric hand drill: a portable, hand-held power drill; some models have variable-speed and reverse controls; it generally accepts bit shanks up to ⅜ inch in diameter.

Electricians: those who work on the stage lighting for a production.

Electrician's cue sheet: a form used by the board operator that contains the primary operating instructions for every lighting cue in the production.

Electricity: a directed flow of electrons used to create kinetic energy.

Electric screwdriver: a portable, hand-held power tool that resembles an electric hand drill; equipped with a variable-speed motor, a clutch, and a chuck that holds a screwdriver tip; used to insert and remove screws.

Electron: a negatively charged fundamental particle that orbits around the nucleus of an atom.

Electronics: the field of science and engineering concerned with the behavior and control of electrons within devices and systems, and the utilization of those systems.

Elevator stage: a large elevator used to shift large scenic elements or whole sets

between the area beneath the stage and the stage.

Elevator trap: a small elevator used to shift small pieces of scenery, or an actor, from the basement underneath the stage to the stage or vice versa. Usually no larger than 4 × 4 or 4 × 6 feet. Also known as a disappearance trap.

Ellipsoidal reflector floodlight: a lensless instrument with a conical ellipse reflector; used for lighting cycs and drops; also known as a scoop.

Ellipsoidal reflector spotlight: a lighting instrument characterized by hard-edged light with little diffusion; designed for long throws, it is manufactured with fixed and variable focal-length lenses; the light beam is shaped with internally mounted shutters.

Emery cloth: fabric whose surface has been coated with abrasive grit; used for smoothing wood, metal, and plastic.

Enamel: an oil-, lacquer-, or synthetic-base paint that has a hard surface and excellent covering power. It is usually formulated so that it dries with a smooth satin or gloss finish.

Envelope: the Pyrex glass or synthetic quartz container for a lamp filament and gaseous environment; synonymous with bulb.

Epoxy: an extremely strong, waterproof plastic most frequently used in the theatre as an adhesive and casting resin.

Epoxy-resin adhesive: a two-part epoxy-base adhesive available in a variety of formulations that enable the user to do gluing, filling, and painting.

Equalizer: an electronic device that selectively boosts or attenuates specific frequencies or ranges of frequencies.

Extra: a non-speaking part. A person who provides "visual dressing" for the scene.

Eyebrow mask: a thin piece of plastic film or latex glued over the eyebrow; also known as an eyebrow block.

Fade-in: a gradual increase; in lighting, usually from darkness to a predetermined level of brightness. Synonymous with fade-up.

Fade-out: a gradual decrease; in lighting, usually from a set level of brightness to darkness.

Fader: a device, usually electronic, that effects a gradual changeover from one circuit to another; in lighting it changes the intensity of one or more dimmer circuits; in sound it changes audio circuits or channels.

Fade rate: the amount of time it takes for a fade—either fade-up or fade-down—to be completed.

False proscenium: a rigid framework covered with drapery material that is used to adjust the height and width of the proscenium arch. Sometimes unframed drapes are used to create a false proscenium.

Faux finish: using techniques with paints/varnishes to create the illusion of a particular type of surface or material, for example, painting wood to look like metal or stone.

FEL lamp: lamps made in the United States are designated with a three-letter code that specifies all design criteria such as wattage, voltage, filament and base type, color-temperature-rated life, and so forth, FEL specifies a very specific 1,000-watt lamp.

Felt: a material made by matting together short fibers by the use of heat, water, and light pressure.

Ferrule: the metal part of a brush that binds the bristles to the handle.

Field angle: that point where the light output diminishes to 10 percent of the output of the center of the beam.

Filament: the light-producing element of a lamp; usually made of tungsten wire.

Filler: a material that creates opacity (covering power) in paint.

Filler rod: a metal piece of the same composition as the material being welded; used to replace the metal lost during welding or to fill a hole or groove in the work.

Fillet weld: a welded metal joint; made when the edge of one piece is welded to the face of another; both sides of the joint should be welded.

Fill light: the light or lights that fill the shadows created by the key light.

Finish nail: a nail with a slender shaft and minute head; designed to be driven below the surface of the wood so that the nail head can be hidden.

First electric: the onstage pipe for lighting instruments that is closest, from the onstage side, to the proscenium arch.

Five-quarter lumber: a specialty lumber, straight grained and free from knots, that is 1¼ inches thick.

Fixture: *see* lighting instrument.

Flange weld: a welded metal joint; similar to a butt weld, except the edges of the material are bent up; the weld is made by melting the upturned flanges.

Flannel: a lightweight, loosely woven material usually made from soft-finish wool, wool blend, or cotton thread; used for men's and women's suits, trousers, and shirts.

Flat: a framework, normally made of wood or metal; usually covered with fabric, although a variety of other covering materials may be used.

Flat-head wood screw: common screw with a flat head that is beveled on the underside to easily dig into the wood; used for attaching hardware (hinges, doorknobs) and joining various wood elements together.

Flexible glue: animal glue with glycerine added.

Floor line: the base of the vertical plane in a perspective drawing. For a proscenium sketch, it is usually drawn across the stage in contact with the upstage edge of the proscenium arch; in a thrust drawing, it is normally placed just outside the auditorium end of the thrust; in an arena sketch, it is usually placed in the aisle closest to the observer.

Floor painting: painting scenery—flats, drops, and so forth—on the floor rather than standing up or attached to a paint frame.

Floor plate: bracing hardware; a block of wood with a non-skid material (foam, rubber) attached to the bottom; the foot of a stage brace is attached to the top of the floor plate, and weights (sandbags, counterweights) are piled on to keep it from moving.

Floor pocket: a connecting box, usually containing three to six circuits, whose top is mounted flush with the stage floor.

Floppy disk: a thin piece of plastic coated with metal oxide, used to record the information stored in a computer's memory.

Fluorocarbons: a family of tough, durable, low-friction, nonstick plastics best known by the trade name Teflon; used in the theatre as a bearing surface where its slippery qualities can be used to advantage.

Flush: smooth, level, even.

Flux: a chemical that reduces surface oxidation and thus aids in soldering or welding.

Fly: to raise an object or person above the stage floor with ropes or cables.

Fly cyc: a single drop, hung on a U-shaped pipe, that surrounds the stage on three sides.

Fly gallery: the elevated walkway where the pin rail is located.

Fly loft: the open space above the stage where the scenery and equipment are flown.

Focal length: the distance from the lens at which light rays converge to a point; for lenses used in stage lighting instruments, the focal length is usually measured in even inches.

Focus: to direct light from the lighting instruments to a specific area.

Folding wood rule: a 6-foot wooden rule, composed of twelve segments that fold into a unit 7½ inches long; used for measuring lumber in scenic construction.

Followspot: a lighting instrument with a high-intensity, narrow beam; mounted in a stand that allows it to tilt and swivel so that the beam can "follow" an actor.

Font: a particular style or design of typeface.

Footlights: lights placed along the front edge of the stage.

Forced perspective: a process that creates apparent depth in a set by angling the horizontal line.

Foreshortening: representing the lines of an object as shorter than they actually are in order to give the illusion of proper relative size.

Form: space enclosed within a line or lines that meet or cross; also, elements that have similar physical characteristics, such as arena theatres, thrust stages, proscenium stages, and so forth.

Found theatre spaces: structures originally designed for some other purpose that have been converted into performing spaces.

Framing square: a large steel L, typically 16 inches on the bottom leg and 24 on the vertical leg; used for checking the accuracy of 90-degree corner joints.

Free electron: an electron that has broken away from its "home" atom to float free.

French enamel varnish (FEV): a mixture of dye and shellac; made by mixing alcohol-based leather dye (e.g., Fiebing's Leather Dye) with shellac that has been reduced (1:1) with denatured alcohol.

Frequency: the rate at which an object vibrates; measured in hertz (cycles per second).

Fresnel lens: a type of step lens with the glass cut away from the convex face of the lens.

Fresnel spotlight: a spotlight that produces a soft, diffused light; the Fresnel lens is treated on the plano side to diffuse the light.

Front elevation: a front view of each wall segment of the set, including all detail such as windows, doors, pictures, and trim.

Front-of-house: the area in an auditorium that is close to the stage.

Front projection screen: an opaque, highly reflective, usually white material used to reflect a projected image; the projector is placed on the audience side of the screen.

Full-scale drawings: scale drawings made actual size.

Functional model: a three-dimensional thumbnail sketch of a scenic design; normally built on a scale of ¼ or ½ inch to 1 foot; usually made from file folders or similar cardboard; also known as a white model.

Funnel: an accessory for a Fresnel spotlight that masks the beam to create a circular pattern. Also called a snoot or top hat.

Fuse: a device to protect a circuit from an overload; it has a soft metal strip that melts, breaking circuit continuity.

Garbage or slop paint: any paint left over from previous paint jobs; the various paints are mixed and neutralized to create a medium-gray or light-brown hue; frequently used for a prime coat.

Gel: (1) to put a color filter into a color frame and insert it in the color-frame holder of a lighting instrument. (2) generic name for the color media used in lighting instruments.

Gesso: plaster of Paris in liquid state; approximately the consistency of sour cream; dries to a hard plaster finish.

Gimp: an ornamental flat braid or round cord used as trimming.

Glaze: a transparent, usually lightly tinted, layer of thin paint.

Gloss: highly reflective, mirrorlike.

Gobo: a thin metal template inserted into an ellipsoidal reflector spotlight to create a shadow pattern of light.

Graded base coat: a base coat that gradually changes hue or value over the height or width of the painted surface.

Grand drape: the curtain that covers the opening of the proscenium arch.

Grand rag: slang synonym for grand drape.

Grand valance: a teaser or border made of the same material as the grand drape. Used in conjunction with the grand drape, it masks the scenery and equipment just upstage of the proscenium arch.

Graphic equalizer: an equalizer with individual slide controls affecting specific, usually fairly narrow, segments of the sound spectrum; so called because the position of the individual controls graphically displays a picture of the equalization of the full sound spectrum.

Graphite: a soft carbon similar to the lead in a pencil; sticks can be purchased in most art supply stores.

Grid: a network of steel I beams supporting elements of the counterweight system.

Grid transfer: transferring a design from an elevation to the scenery by use of a scale grid on the elevation and a full-scale grid on the scenery.

Grommet: a circular metal eyelet used to reinforce holes in fabric.

Grommet set: a hole punch, a small anvil, and a crimping tool; used to seat grommets.

Ground plan: a scale mechanical drawing in the form of a horizontal offset section with the cutting plane passing at whatever level, normally a height of four feet above the stage floor, required to produce the most descriptive view of the set.

Ground row: generally low, horizontal flats used to mask the base of cycs or drops; frequently painted to resemble rows of buildings, hedges, or similar visual elements.

Group: the grouping of two or more dimmers/channels under one controller.

Gusset: a triangular piece of material used to reinforce a corner joint.

Hacksaw: an adjustable frame handsaw with an extremely fine-toothed (twenty to twenty-five teeth per inch) replaceable blade; used for cutting metal.

Hair pin: a piece of round metal wire bent in a slightly opened U shape. Used with longer hair than bobby pins.

Halved joint: a wood joint made by removing half the thickness of both pieces of lumber in the area to be joined so that the thickness of the finished joint will be no greater than the stock from which it is made; also called a halved lap joint.

Hand: the quality and characteristics of a fabric that can be evaluated or defined by a sense of touch.

Hand drill: a hand-cranked device used for spinning drill bits; used for making small-diameter holes in wood.

Hand power grinder: a portable, hand-held version of the bench grinder; useful on pieces that are too heavy or awkward to be worked with the bench grinder.

Hand power sander: a slightly less powerful version of the hand power grinder; equipped with a flexible disk that provides backing for sanding discs of varying grit; used for rough sanding of wood, metal, and plastic.

Hand prop: a small item that is handled or carried by an actor.

Handrail: the part of the stair rail that is grabbed with the hand; supported by the banister and newel posts.

Hanger iron: flying hardware; a metal strap with a D ring at the top; the hanger iron is attached to the top or bottom of the back of a flat, one end of a line is attached to the D ring, and the other end is attached to a counterweight batten.

Hanging: the process of placing lighting instruments in their specified locations.

Hanging cards: small segments of the light plot, typically pasted onto cardboard so it can be carried in an electrician's pants pocket, that detail all of the hanging information about a specific location such as the first electric or down left boom.

Hanging crew: those responsible for the hanging, circuiting, patching, focusing, and coloring of the lighting instruments; they are under the supervision of the master electrician.

Hanging positions: the various locations around the stage and auditorium where lighting instruments are placed.

Hang out: in this instance, hang out means that most wrinkles will disappear from the fabric if it is hung up.

Hang tag: the small label usually attached to the cardboard core of a bolt of fabric that indicates the percentages of various component fibers.

Hardboard: generic term for composition sheet goods such as Masonite and particle board.

Hard covered: covered with a hard-surfaced material such as plywood. The hard surface is frequently covered with a fabric before painting.

Hard drive: a computer storage device. A spinning magnetic or optical disk on which data are stored and from which data can be retrieved.

Hard teaser: the horizontal element of the false proscenium; usually hung from a counterweighted batten so that its height can easily be adjusted.

Hardware: the physical elements of the computer and the various electronic equipment, printed circuit boards, and so forth inside the computer.

Harmonics: frequencies that are exact multiples of a fundamental pitch or frequency.

Harmony: a sense of blending and unity that is achieved when the various parts of a design fit together to create an orderly, congruous whole.

Head: (1) a housing that holds scenic-projector lenses in fixed positions to project images of a specific size; (2) a high-quality electromagnet on a tape deck or tape recorder that is used to implant, retrieve, or erase electrical data from audio tapes.

Head block: a multisheave block with two or more pulley wheels, used to change the direction of all the ropes or cables that support the batten.

Header: a small flat that can be placed between two standard-sized flats to create a doorway or window.

Heat gun: a high-temperature air gun, visually similar to a handheld hair dryer.

Heat welding: the use of a heat gun to fuse two pieces of plastic.

Heavy-duty hand drill: similar to the electric hand drill, but with a heavier-duty motor; the chuck will generally accept bit shanks up to ½ inch in diameter.

Hinged-foot iron: bracing hardware similar to the rigid foot iron but hinged so that it can fold out of the way for storage.

Hole saws: saw-toothed cylinders of hardened steel with a drill bit in the center that is used to center the saw in the work; used with a power drill to make holes from ¾ inch to 2 inches in diameter in wood that is 1½ inches thick or less.

Holidays: sections of a painted surface that appear lighter than the rest of the surface because the area is either unpainted or the paint was too lightly applied. Areas where the painter took a holiday.

Home page: a site or addressable location on the Internet which contains information about (generally) a particular service, interest group, resource, or business.

Homespun: a coarse, loosely woven material usually made from cotton, linen, or wool.

Honeycomb paper: a manufactured paper product with a hexagonal structure similar to a honeycomb.

Hookup sheet: a sheet containing pertinent information (hanging position, circuit, dimmer, color, lamp wattage, focusing notes) about every lighting instrument used in the production. Also known as an instrument schedule.

Horizon line: in perspective drawing, a line representing the meeting of the earth and the sky; normally drawn parallel to the top or bottom edge of the paper.

Horizontal offset section: a section drawing with a horizontal cutting plane; the cutting plane does not remain fixed—it varies to provide views of important details.

Horn: a dispersion device attached to the front of a pressure driver to direct the sound emitted by the pressure driver into a specific pattern.

Hot-melt glue gun: a handheld electric tool that heats sticks of adhesive to make rapid-hold bonds on a wide range of materials, such as wood, plastic, paper, cloth, metal, dirt, sand, and so forth.

Hot mirror: a glass dichroic filter that reflects the infrared spectrum while allowing visible light to pass.

Hot-press finish: a slick, smooth texture achieved by pressing paper between hot rollers; this treatment leaves a thin layer of oil, which makes the paper unsuitable for use with transparent watercolor. It works well with designer's gouache, acrylic, pencils, and markers.

Hot spot: an intense circle of light created when a projector lens is seen through a rear projection screen.

Hot-wire cutter: a tool for cutting foam; it consists of a wire that is heated to incandescence.

House: synonym for auditorium.

Hue: the qualities that differentiate one color from another.

Hypercardioid: a directional, narrow, elongated cardioid pickup pattern that all but eliminates pickup from anywhere except directly in front of, and for a short distance immediately behind, the microphone.

Illustration board: watercolor paper mounted on pressboard backing.

Image of light: a picture or concept of what the light should look like for a production.

Immersion heater: an electric heater that can be immersed in a bucket of liquid to heat it; used for heating water for starch mixtures, aniline dye, flameproofing solutions, and so forth.

Impact wrench: a power-driven tool that uses sockets to tighten or loosen bolts or nuts; may be either electric or pneumatic.

Impedance: resistance in an AC circuit; the only difference between impedance and resistance is that impedance is defined as resistance to the flow of an alternating current.

Improved stage screw: bracing hardware; an improved version of the stage screw consisting of a steel plug, threaded on the outside and inside, that is inserted into an appropriately sized hole drilled into the stage floor. The screw screws into the plug, and the plug can be removed and a piece of dowel inserted into the floor to fill the hole.

Infinite-baffle speaker enclosure: an air-tight, heavily insulated box that absorbs the sound waves produced by the rearward excursion speaker; it is inefficient and requires a high-wattage amplifier to achieve satisfactory sound levels.

Inner above: the elevated area located directly above the inner below in the Elizabethan theatre.

Inner below: the curtained area at the upstage edge of the playing area in the Elizabethan theatre.

Instrument schedule: a form used to record all of the technical data about each instrument used in the production; also known as a hookup sheet.

Intensity: the relative loudness of a sound.

Iris: a device with movable overlapping metal plates, used with an ellipsoidal reflector spotlight to change the size of the circular pattern of light.

Irregular flat: a flat having nonsquare corners.

Isometric drawing: a scaled mechanical drawing that presents a pictorial view of an object on three axes; the primary axis is perpendicular to the base line and the other two project from its base, in opposite directions, 30 degrees above the base line.

Jack: a triangular brace.

Jig: a device used to hold pieces together in proper positional relationship.

Jog: a flat less than 2 feet wide.

Joists: parallel beams that support flooring.

Kerf: the width of the cut made by a saw blade.

Keyhole saw: a handsaw with a narrow, tapering blade of ten to twelve teeth per inch; used for making curvilinear cuts in plywood and lumber.

Key light: the brightest light on a particular scene.

Keystone: a wedge or rectangular-shaped piece of ¼-inch plywood used to reinforce the joint between a stile and toggle bar of a flat.

Keystoning: the linear distortion created when a projector is placed on some angle other than perpendicular to the projection surface.

Kit-cutting: to cut *all* the individual pieces needed to make something *before* assembly is started; like a model airplane kit.

Lacquer: refined shellac or varnish with quick-drying additives.

Lag screw: large wood screw with a hexagonal or square head; used in situations where bolts are not practical, such as attaching something to a wall or floor.

Laminating: the process of gluing thin pieces of wood together to make a thicker piece.

Lap joint: a wood joint made when the faces of two pieces of wood are joined.

Lap weld: a welded metal joint; made when the pieces being welded are overlapped.

Lashing: a method of joining scenery; a piece of ¼-inch cotton clothesline (lash line) is served around special hardware on adjoining flats to hold them together.

Lash-line cleat: lashing hardware secured so that the pointed end projects over the inside edge of the stile.

Lash-line eye: lashing hardware with a hole through which the lash line passes, attached to the inside edge of the stile.

Lash-line hook: used for same purposes as a lash-line cleat, but has a hook instead of a point; used on extra-wide stiles or in situations that preclude the use of a lash-line cleat.

Latch keeper: *see* S hook.

Latex: a natural or synthetic liquid plastic with the flexible qualities of natural latex or rubber; bonds well and is flexible.

Latex cement: a milky-white flexible cement.

Latex paint: a paint with a latex binder; has fair to good covering power, may or may not be water-resistant, and can be thinned very little, usually no more than one pint of water per gallon of paint.

Lathe: a stationary, stand- or bench-mounted, variable-speed power tool that rapidly spins wood so that it can be carved with the use of special chisels. Can be used to turn foam.

Lauan: also known as Philippine mahogany; ⅛-inch lauan plywood is strong and quite flexible; commonly used as a flat-covering material and for covering curved-surface forms.

Leader line: in a two-line-weight system, a thin line 0.3 mm thick (in pencil) or 0.010 to 0.0125 inch thick (in pen).

Leaf: the movable flap of a hinge.

Legitimate theatre: refers to plays that rely on the spoken word to convey the message. Does not include musicals, reviews, dance, opera, or concerts.

Legs: narrow, vertical stage drapes used for masking.

Lensless projector: a projector that works by projecting a shadow image without a lens, such as the Linnebach and curved-image projectors.

Life: in rendering, the qualities of brilliance, visual depth, and sparkle.

Life mask: a plaster mask of a person's face. A negative mold is made by covering the person's face with plaster of Paris or alginate. The negative mold is used to make a positive cast that is the life mask.

Lift jack: a jack equipped with swivel casters, used to pick up and move platforms.

Lighting area: a cylindrical space approximately 8 to 12 feet in diameter and 7 feet high; lighting areas are located within acting areas to facilitate creating a smooth wash of light within the acting area.

Lighting cue: generally, some type of action involving lighting; usually the raising or lowering of the intensity of one or more lighting instruments.

Lighting designer: person responsible for the appearance of the lighting during the production.

Lighting grid: a network of pipes, usually connected in a grid pattern, from which lighting instruments and other equipment can be hung.

Lighting instrument: a device that produces a controllable light; for example, an ellipsoidal reflector spotlight or a Fresnel spotlight.

Lighting key: a drawing that illustrates the plan angle and color of the various sources that are illuminating the image of light.

Lighting rehearsal: a run-through, without actors, attended by the director, stage manager, lighting designer, and appropriate running crews to look at the intensity, timing, and placement of the various lighting cues.

Lighting sectional: a composite side view, drawn in scale, of the set showing the hanging position of the instruments in relation to the physical structure of the theatre, set, and stage equipment.

Lighting template: a guide for use in drawing lighting symbols.

Light plot: a scale drawing showing the placement of the lighting instruments relative to the physical structure of the theatre and the location of the set.

Limited run: a production run of predetermined length, for example, two weeks, six weeks, and so forth.

Line: the wires in low-voltage control systems; frequently called "lines" rather than "wires."

Line level: a signal voltage range, approximately .75 to 1 volt; specified as a voltage range rather than one particular voltage because the voltage and current of the signal vary with the intensity and frequency of the sound.

Line level setting: the electronic equivalent of a loudness setting for the line level signal. An optimum line level signal would be loud enough to be distinctly heard by the next equipment in line—the power amplifier—but not so loud as to introduce distortion.

Linen canvas: an excellent flat-covering material; extremely durable, it accepts paint very well and doesn't shrink much; expensive.

Line of vision: the vertical line drawn from OP to the floor line in a perspective grid; it represents the line of sight from the observer to the vertical plane.

Liner: in makeup, any saturated color that is used as rouge, as eye shadow, or to create other areas of highlight or shadow.

Lining: painting narrow, straight lines; done with lining brushes and a straightedge.

Livery: identifiable clothing associated with a specific occupation or trade.

Load: a device that converts electrical energy into another form of energy: A lamp converts electrical energy to light and heat; an electric motor converts electricity to mechanical energy.

Load-in: the moving of scenery and associated equipment into the theatre and their positioning (setup) on the stage.

Loading platform: a walkway suspended just below the grid where the counterweights are loaded onto the arbor.

Locking pliers: generally known by the trade name Vise Grip, locking pliers are available in a wide variety of sizes and configurations; used for gripping and holding, the size of the jaw opening and amount of pressure applied by the jaws are adjustable by the screw at the base of the handle.

Locking rail: a rail that holds the rope locks for each counterweight set.

Loft block: a grooved pulley mounted on top of the grid, used to change the direction in which a rope or cable travels.

Long-nose pliers: pliers with long tapering jaws; used for holding small items and bending very light wire; also called needle-nose pliers.

Loudspeaker: a transducer used to convert an electrical signal from an amplifier into audible sound.

Mac: the hardware, operating systems/software, and peripherals based on the Apple Macintosh computer.

Machine bolt: bolt with a square or hexagonal head used to attach metal to metal.

Machinist's vise: a vise with toothed steel faces; used to hold and clamp metal; can be used to hold wood, but the serrated steel faces will mar the surface unless protective blocks of wood are used to sandwich the work.

Main drape: synonym for grand drape.

Mallet: a hammer with a wooden, plastic, or rubber head; the wooden and plastic mallets are generally used for driving chisels; all three can be used for shaping thin metal.

Managing director: person responsible for the business functions of a theatrical production company—fund-raising, ticket sales, box office management.

Manila rope: a strong, yet flexible rope; used in the theatre for raising and suspending loads and as the operating line for counterweight systems.

Mansions: small scenic representations of the standard locations (heaven, hell, garden, palace, etc.) used in medieval plays.

Margin line: an extra-heavy-weight line that forms a border for the plate ½ inch in from the edge of the paper.

Mask: to block the audience's view—generally, of backstage equipment and space.

Masonite: a registered trade name for a sheet stock made from binder-impregnated wood pulp compressed into 4-by-8-foot sheets.

Mass: the three-dimensional manifestation of form.

Master electrician: person responsible for ensuring that the lighting equipment is hung, focused, and run according to written and verbal instructions from the lighting designer.

Master seamer: person responsible for costume construction and direct supervision of costume crews.

Matte: dull, nonreflective.

Matte knife: *see* utility knife.

Mechanical perspective: a picture, in scale, drawn with drafting tools, that provides an illusion of depth.

Mechanic's hammer: a hammer with a heavy, soft metal head; used for shaping metal.

Merrow machine: a machine that, in one operation, sews a seam, cuts both pieces of fabric about ¼ inch from the seam, and makes an overcast stitch on the edge of both pieces of fabric to prevent raveling.

Metal file: any file with very fine teeth; used for smoothing metal.

Microcassette tape: audio recorder tape for use in small cassettes; used in computer storage.

Microphone (mic): a transducer used to convert sound waves into electrical energy.

Mid-range speaker: a speaker designed to reproduce the middle range of audible frequencies—roughly 200 to 1000 Hz.

MIG (metal inert gas) welder: a welder that focuses a flow of inert gas (usually carbon dioxide or argon) on the welding zone to prevent or reduce oxidation of the weld; the electrode is a thin piece of wire automatically fed through the welding handle from a spool stored in the housing of the power unit.

Mike: (verb) to pick up a sound with a microphone; to place one or more microphones in proximity to a sound source (instrument, voice).

Mild steel: a medium-strength, easily worked ferrous metal that is easy to weld; the metal most commonly used in stage construction.

Milliner: one who constructs and styles hats.

Miter: an angle that is cut in a piece of wood or metal, usually in pairs, to form a corner.

Miter box: a guide used with a backsaw to make accurate angle cuts in wood.

Miter joint: similar to a butt joint, but the edges to be joined are angle, rather than square, cut.

Mix: to blend the electronic signals created by several sound sources.

Mixer: an electronic device used to mix the output of a variety of sources and route the blended signal(s) on to other equipment; it can be used for both recording and playback.

Model: an object that is being used as the subject of a mold casting.

Mold: a matrix used to create a form.

Molding cutter head: a heavy cylindrical arbor in which a variety of matched cutter blades or knives can be fit; used with a table or radial-arm saw to cut decorative molding.

Monkey wrench: a heavy-weight, smooth-jawed adjustable wrench for use on large nuts or work that is too large for an adjustable-end wrench.

Monofilament line: a single-strand, transparent, monofilament line; sold as fishing line in sporting goods stores; also known as trick line.

Mood: the feeling of a play—comic, tragic, happy, and so forth.

Mortise: a square hole; used in conjunction with a tenon to make a mortise and tenon joint.

Mortise and tenon joint: a wood joint made by fitting a tenon (square peg) into a mortise (square hole).

Mortise drill bit: a drill bit housed inside a square hollow chisel; used with a drill press to make square holes.

Motorized miter box: *see* cutoff saw.

Mouse: an electromechanical device that controls the movement of a cursor on the computer screen; used by the operator to provide directives to the computer program.

Mullion: a vertical crossbar in a window.

Multiplex: (1) to transmit two or more messages simultaneously on a single channel or wire. (2) to carry out several functions simultaneously in an independent but related manner.

Muntin: a horizontal crossbar in a window.

Muslin: a flat-surfaced, woven cotton fabric.

Nail puller: a tool with a movable jaw on one end for grasping nail heads and a movable slide hammer on the other to drive the jaws into the wood to grasp the nail; used to pull nails out.

Needle-nose pliers: *see* long-nose pliers.

Neutralization: subtractive color mixing; the selective absorption of light as the result of mixing complementary pigment hues; the creation of gray.

Neutron: a fundamental particle in the structure of the nucleus of an atom; possesses a neutral charge.

Newel post: the post at the bottom or top of a flight of stairs that terminates the handrail.

Nicopress tool: a plierlike tool that crimps Nicopress sleeves onto wire rope or cable to make permanent, nonremovable friction clamps.

Nonrepresentational design: a style in which the portrayed elements do not represent physically identifiable objects.

Nonspecific musical effect: any sound effect that does not reinforce a readily identifiable source such as a doorbell or telephone.

Notched joint: a wood joint made by cutting a notch from a piece of lumber; the size of the notch is determined by the width and thickness of the other piece of stock that the notch will receive.

Noxious: harmful to one's health.

Nucleus: the central part of an atom, composed of protons and neutrons.

Nut driver: tool similar in appearance to a screwdriver with a cylindrical socket instead of a slot or Phillips head; used for tightening small hex (six-sided) nuts.

Objective lens: a device used to focus a projected image on a screen or other surface.

Oblique drawing: a scaled mechanical drawing with one face of the object, drawn as an elevation, placed at right angles to the observer's line of sight; the remaining faces project from the elevation to the right or left using a 30- or 45-degree base line.

Ohm's Law: the law that states: As voltage increases, current increases; as resistance increases, current decreases.

Oil stone: an abrasive composite stone, usually with different grits on opposite faces; used for sharpening knives, chisels, and other cutting tools.

Omnidirectional: in all directions; a spherical microphone pickup pattern.

Open-end wrench: a wrench with non-adjustable U-shaped jaws on both ends; the opening between the jaws is of a specific width to grip bolts and nuts of specific diameters; used to tighten bolts and nuts.

Orchestra: the circular area on which the majority of the action of the play took place in a Greek theatre.

Orchestra pit: the space between the stage and the auditorium, usually below stage level, that holds the orchestra.

Orthographic projection: a series of elevations, drawn to scale, that show each side or face of an object.

Overlay: a garment, usually made of lace or a similar lightweight, semitransparent fabric, designed to lie on top of another garment.

Oxford cloth: a flat-surfaced cotton or cotton-blend material frequently used for making shirts.

Oxidation: a chemical reaction between metal and air that forms a thin, discolored "skin" over the work that effectively prevents heat transfer. Oxidation adversely affects the strength and conductivity of both soldered and welded joints.

Pageant wagon: a staging convention used during the medieval period. Basically, a bare platform backed with a plain curtain mounted on a wagon. The wagon could be pulled from town to town.

Paint chip: a small rectangle of paper or thin cardboard painted in a specific hue.

Paint crew: persons responsible for painting the scenery and properties; they are under the supervision of the scenic artist.

Painter's elevations: elevations of a set painted to show the palette and painting styles to be used on the actual set.

Pan: to rotate an object about its vertical axis.

Panel adhesive: an adhesive product, such as Liquid nails, packaged in a caulking tube and intended to be dispensed with a caulking gun.

Paper clad: both sides covered with paper.

Paperclay: a non-toxic modeling material that can be sculpted, molded or shaped, and air dries to a hard finish that can be carved or sanded.

Papier-mâché: a process of building up a form by laminating wheat-paste-soaked strips of newspaper; also available commercially in a powdered form to make a paste suitable for forming in molds.

Parametric equalizer: an equalizer in which individual frequencies or custom-designed bands of frequencies can be programmed for boost or attenuation.

Paraskenia: long, high walls that extended on either side of and parallel with the skene of the Greek theatre.

PAR can: a holder for a parabolic aluminized reflector (PAR) lamp; creates a powerful punch of light with a soft edge; the PAR 64 is commonly used for concert lighting.

Particle board: a sheet stock composed of small wood chips and sawdust mixed with a glue binder and compressed into 4-by-8-foot sheets; it is quite brittle, so it cannot be used as a load-bearing surface.

Patch: to connect a stage circuit to a dimmer circuit.

Patch bay: a cross-connect or patch panel for sound.

Patch panel: an interconnecting device that allows one to connect any stage circuit to any dimmer.

Pattern maker: person who makes patterns based on information contained in the costume designer's sketch, notes, and instructions.

PC: the hardware, operating systems/software, and peripherals based on the IBM personal computer (PC).

PDA — personal digital assistant: a hand-held computer used for making/keeping notes, schedules, phone numbers, and similar functions.

Perspective-view base line: the bottom edge of a perspective drawing.

Phillips-head screwdriver: *see* screwdriver.

Photomontage: a composite picture made by combining several separate pictures; can include nonphotographic images as well.

Piano wire: extremely strong wire made from spring steel; frequently used for flying scenery because of its strength; should not be sharply bent as this significantly reduces its strength.

Picture frame stage: a configuration in which the spectators watch the action of the play through a rectangular opening; synonym for proscenium arch stage.

Picture hook and eye: hooks and eyes that facilitate rapid hanging and removal of decorative draperies.

Piezoelectricity: voltage produced when pressure is placed on certain crystals.

Pig: a loosely woven bag containing powdered eraser material.

Pigment: material that imparts color to a substance such as paint or dye.

Pilot hole: *see* starter hole.

Pinch bar: a flattened metal bar configured like a crowbar.

Pin rail: a horizontal pipe or rail studded with belaying pins; the ropes of the rope-set system are wrapped around the belaying pins to hold the batten at a specific height.

Pipe: a counterweighted batten or fixed metal pipe that holds lighting instruments.

Pipe clamp: a threaded pipe with a movable end plate and an adjustable head plate; used for clamping furniture frames and similar wide objects. A bar clamp is similar except that a notched bar is substituted for the pipe.

Pipe cutter: a tool used for making clean right-angle cuts through steel tubing of half-inch and larger diameters.

Pipe wrench: similar in shape to the monkey wrench, the pipe wrench has jaws that are serrated to bite into the soft metal of pipes; used for holding or twisting pipes and their associated couplings.

Pit: (1) the ground in front of the stage where the lower-class audience stood to watch the play in Elizabethan theatres; (2) in twentieth-century theatres, a commonly used abbreviation for orchestra pit.

Pitch (print): the size of a particular typeface.

Pitch (sound): the characteristic tone produced by a vibrating body; the higher the frequency of vibration, the higher the pitch.

Pixel: a picture element; the smallest discrete part of an electronically projected picture, as on a computer monitor.

Plan angle: the ground-plan view of an object.

Plane: a knife-edged tool used to smooth or round the edges or corners of wood.

Plano-convex lens: a lens with one flat and one outward-curving face.

Plaster line: in drafting, a leader line extending across the opening of the proscenium arch.

Plate: a sheet of mechanical drawings, drawn to scale.

Platea: the open acting area in front of the mansions of the medieval stage.

Playback system: devices used to play recorded sound; usually composed of some combination of a turntable, a tape deck, a CD player, or a computer; an equalizer; an amplifier; and a speaker.

Playwright: person who develops and writes the script.

Plotter: a printer used to produce computer-generated drafting sheets and drawings on large paper.

Plug: a wooden insert used to replace a knothole or other imperfection in the surface layer of a sheet of plywood.

Plush: fabric similar to velveteen but with softer and longer pile; common drapery and upholstery fabric.

Ply-metal: refers to TEK screws specifically designed to attach plywood to metal. The flat head of the screw is typically driven flush with, or slightly into, the top surface of the plywood.

Plywood: a sheet stock made by laminating several layers of wood; its superior strength is created by alternating each successive layer so that its grain lies at a 90-degree angle to the layers immediately above and below it.

Pneumatic nailer: a compressed-air-powered tool similar in appearance to a pneumatic stapler but using clips of adhesive-coated nails rather than staples.

Pneumatic stapler: a compressed-air-powered stapler capable of driving staples with legs up to 1½ inches long; adhesive-coated staples are generally used for assembling flat frames, putting tops on platforms, and similar functions.

Pointing and clicking: pointing: using a mouse to move the on-screen cursor to a specific location; clicking: using a button on the mouse to initiate an action. Thus, "pointing and clicking" refers to using a mouse to initiate a specific action.

Polyethylene: a class of plastics that, in solid form, have a characteristically slick, waxy surface; polyethylene film is frequently used as a drop cloth and can be used as a projection surface; polyethylene foam, generally known by the trade name Ethafoam, is flexible and is available in sheets, rods, and tubes.

Polystyrene: a class of plastics with a variety of formulations useful in theatrical production; high-impact polystyrene sheeting has a hard surface and is moderately flexible, fairly strong, and somewhat brittle. It is used in vacuum forming; polystyrene foam is commonly known by the trade name Styrofoam; it is available in sheets and is frequently used as decorative trim.

Polyvinyl alcohol (PVA): a water-soluble synthetic thickener/adhesive.

Polyvinyl chloride: a family of plastics that are, in solid form, characteristically strong, lightweight, and rigid; PVC water pipe can be used for a variety of functional and decorative purposes; also available in sheet, rod, and other forms.

Polyvinyl glue: a white liquid adhesive that resembles white glue; has excellent adhesion to porous surfaces and good flexibility.

Pop riveter: a tool used to secure rivets in thin metal.

Position: relative placement of objects within a composition.

Potential: the difference in electrical charge between two bodies; measured in volts.

Power amplifier: *see* amplifier.

Power hacksaw: stationary power tool for cutting metal; a horizontal reciprocating metal-cutting blade is used to cut through various types of metal stock.

Power pipe cutter: a stationary stand-mounted power tool for cutting and threading metal pipes with diameters from approximately ½ to 2 inches.

Power ramp up: the time it takes for power to increase from "off" to "on." A sudden ramp up causes filament hum. A gradual ramp up reduces the level of hum.

Preamplifier: an electronic device that boosts the level of a signal, without alteration or reshaping, to the requisite input signal level of the next piece of equipment in a sound system.

Preset sheet: a form used by the electrician to record the intensity levels for each dimmer during major shifts in the lighting.

Pressing cloth: a cloth placed between the iron and the fabric being pressed.

Pressure driver: a unit housing a large magnet that vibrates a thin metallic diaphragm to create mid-range and high-frequency sounds.

Primary colors: hues that cannot be derived or blended from any other hues. In light the primaries are red, blue, and green; in pigment the primary colors are red, blue, and yellow.

Prime coat: the first layer of paint; applied to all elements of the scenery to provide a uniform base for the rest of the paint job.

Producer: person who selects the script, finds financial backing, and hires all production personnel.

Production concept: the creative interpretation of the script, which will unify the artistic vision of the production design team.

Production design team: the producer, director, and scenic, costume, lighting, and sound designers who, working together, develop the visual/aural concept for the production.

Production manager: coordinator of production scheduling and administrative/logistic details of a multishow theatrical season.

Production meeting: a conference of appropriate production personnel to share information.

Production model: a scale model similar to a functional model but fully painted and complete with furniture and decorative props.

Production style: a recognizable pattern of elements, both visual and intellectual, based on social and political history, used to create the environment for the production of a particular play.

Production team: everyone working, in any capacity, on the production of a play.

Profile: *see* silhouette.

Prompt book: a copy of the script with details about each actor's blocking as well as the location, timing, and, as necessary, action, of all set, prop, light, and sound cues.

Propane torch: an open-flame torch powered by propane gas; used for heavy-duty soldering and heat shaping of thin-gauge steel.

Properties: such elements as furniture, lamps, pictures, table linens, bric-a-brac, and window draperies that provide the finished set with visual character.

Property crew: those who construct or acquire all props and run (organize, shift, store) props during rehearsals and performances.

Property master: one responsible for the design, construction, and finishing of all properties.

Prop table: a table, normally located in the wings, on which hand props are stored between onstage use.

Proscenium: a stage configuration in which the spectators watch the action through a rectangular opening (the proscenium arch) that resembles a picture frame.

Proskenium: a columned arch that supported a porchlike projection from the upper floor of the skene in the Greek theatre.

Prosthetic device: in makeup, a device such as a false nose, beard, or other appliance that is added to the face to change the actor's appearance.

Proton: a fundamental particle in the structure of the nucleus of an atom; possesses a positive charge.

Pull: to remove a costume from storage for use in a production.

Push-drill: a hand-powered drill that uses a springloaded shaft to spin the drill bit when one pushes downward on the handle; for light usage, it uses bits from ⅟₆₄ to ³⁄₁₆ inch in diameter; useful for making starter holes.

Push-drill bits: steel bits with sharp points and straight fluted indentations running up the sides of the shaft; used with the push drill to drill narrow holes (⅟₆₄ to ³⁄₁₆ inch in diameter) in wood.

PVA: Abbreviation for *both* polyvinyl acetate and polyvinyl alcohol. Both substances are adhesives, but their chemical formulae are different. Polyvinyl acetate is opaque or translucent if thinned. It is the primary ingredient in white glue. Polyvinyl alcohol is a transparent liquid that, in theatrical production, is primarily used as a base in some specialty scene painting techniques.

Pyroxylin: Celastic is the trade name for a pyroxylin-impregnated felt material that becomes extremely limp when dipped in acetone; when the ace-tone evaporates, the pyroxylin stiffens the felt so that it will hold its molded shape.

Quadraphonic: a sound system composed of four discrete sound channels.

Quality: the nature or intrinsic properties (e.g., straight, curved, jagged) of a line.

Radial-arm saw: a circular-bladed stationary power saw; the motor and blade are suspended from an arm above a table; the height and angle of the blade are adjustable. Primarily used for cross and angle cutting, this versatile saw can be used for ripping and trim molding as well.

Rail: a top or bottom framing member of a flat.

Raked stage: a stage that is higher at the back than the front.

Ratchet winch: a device used for hoisting that consists of a crank attached to a drum. One end of a rope or cable is attached to the drum, the other end to the load; turning the crank moves the load; a ratchet gear prevents the drum from spinning backward.

Rat-tail file: a file with a circular cross-sectional configuration; depending on surface finish it can be used for smoothing wood, metal, or plastic; also known as a round file.

Rear elevations: scale mechanical drawings that show the back of flats depicted on front elevations.

Rear projection screen: translucent projection material designed to transmit the image through the projection surface; the projector is placed in back of the screen.

Related colors: *see* analogous colors.

Repeatablility: the ability to exactly repeat an action. Usually associated with the precision control offered by computers.

Representational design: a style in which the portrayed elements represent some recognizable object, such as a room, a forest, or a street corner.

Resistance: the oppositon to electron flow within a conductor, measured in ohms; the amount of resistance depends in part on the chemical makeup of the material through which the electricity is flowing.

Respirator: a mask covering the nose and mouth that filters out gases as well as particulate matter; the type of filtering medium used determines the type of gases removed from the air.

Reverberate: to reflect in a series of echoes.

Reverberation: a multiple reflection of a sound that persists for some time after the original source has decayed.

Revolve: large, circular platform that pivots on its central axis; also called turntable.

Revolving stage: generally refers to a revolve that is built into the stage floor as part of a theatre's permanent equipment.

Rhythm: the orderly and logical interrelationship of successive parts in a composition.

Rigid caster: a caster that cannot swivel or rotate.

Rigid foot iron: bracing hardware; an L-shaped piece of metal, one leg attached to the bottom of the flat, the other secured to the floor with a stage screw that is inserted through the ring at the end of the leg.

Rip bar: tool similar to a crowbar, but the nail-removing claws have more curl for better leverage.

Rip hammer: a hammar with two relatively straight claws projecting from the back of its head that can be used for prying or ripping apart previously nailed wood; used for driving nails.

Rip saw: a handsaw with an approximately 26-inch blade whose chisel-sharpened teeth bend outward so that the kerf is wider than the blade; designed to cut parallel with the grain of the wood. Rip saws have fewer teeth per inch than a crosscut saw has.

Riser: the vertical face of a stair.

RMS wattage rating: a system (root-mean-square) providing an accurate picture of the energy-dissipation characteristics of sound equipment.

Rods: nerve cells in the retina that are sensitive to faint light.

Rope set: a counterbalanced flying system in which ropes are used to fly the scenery. Sandbags are tied to the offstage end of the ropes to counterbalance the weight of the scenery.

Rough finish: a pebble-grained texture achieved by cold-pressing paper with a texture roller or by other techniques; suitable for painted and pastel renderings having little intricate detail; can be worked with other media as well.

Roundel: a glass color medium for use with striplights; frequently has diffusing properties.

Round file: *see* rat-tail file.

Round-head wood screw: screw with a head that has a flat underside and a rounded upper surface; used when having the top of the screw flush with the surface of the work is not desirable, as when attaching thin metal or fabric to a wood frame.

Router: a portable, handheld power tool that uses a chisel-like rotating bit (25,000 RPM) to shape or carve the surface or edge of the piece of wood; primarily used for shaping decorative moldings and trim pieces.

RTV (room temperature vulcanizing) silicone rubber: a compound used to make flexible molds.

Running: controlling or operating some aspect of production.

Running block: a block and tackle system that provides a 2:1 mechanical advantage.

Running crew: those responsible for operating lighting equipment and shifting scenery and props during rehearsals and performances.

Saber saw: a portable power saw with a reciprocating blade; used for making curvilinear cuts in wood and plastic.

Sandpaper: paper whose surface has been coated with abrasive grit; used for smoothing wood and plastic.

Satin: a stiff, heavy fabric with a smooth, shiny finish on the front and a dull finish on the back; if patterned, the design is usually printed on rather than woven in; used for making costumes, upholstery, and decorative drapery.

Saturated polyester: a plastic used to form the fiber from which polyester fabrics such as Dacron are made; also used to form films such as Mylar.

Saturation: the relative purity of a particular hue.

Scaenae frons: an elaborately decorated facade or wall that was located at the rear of the stage in the Roman theatre. Its historical antecedent was the skene of the Greek theatre.

Scale: a black, scaly coat that forms on iron when it is heated for processing.

Scan: to use a digitizing scanner to convert existing artwork, photos, or drawings into binary information.

Scarf joint: two boards joined lengthwise by making a shallow angle cut approximately 18 inches long in the face of each board; the joint is secured by gluing and screwing or bolting.

Scene shop foreman: person responsible for supervising the crews who build and rig the scenery and some of the larger props.

Scenic artist: person responsible for the painting of the scenery and properties.

Scenic designer: person responsible for the design and function of the scenery and properties.

Scenic projector: a high-wattage instrument used for projecting large-format slides or moving images.

Scoop: *see* ellipsoidal reflector floodlight.

Score: to cut partially through.

Scratch awl: *see* scribe.

Screwdriver: a tool for inserting or driving screws; the standard screwdriver has a narrow blade for work with standard screws; the Phillips-head screwdriver has a four-flanged tip that matches the crossed slots of the Phillips-head screw.

Screw nail: nail with a threaded shaft that rotates as it is driven into wood; used for jobs that require greater holding power.

Scribe: a sharp metal tool used to mark wood, metal, and plastic; also called a scratch awl.

Scrim: a drop made from translucent or transparent material.

Scumbling: a blending of paints of several hues or values to create the appearance of texture; done with brushes.

Secondary colors: the result of mixing two primary colors.

Secrets: the name used to describe the stage machinery in medieval times.

Sectional: a drawing, usually in scale, of an object that shows what it would look like if cut straight through at a given plane.

Sectional angle: the angle of intersection between the axis of the cone of light emitted by an instrument and the working height—usually the height of an average actor's face (about 5 feet, 6 inches)—of the lighting areas.

Self-tapping: screws that drill their own pilot holes as they are power-screwed into wood or metal. The screws have an auger-like tip that drills a smaller diameter hole than the screw threads.

Set: to prevent smearing or smudging. Once a greasepaint makeup design is finished, it is locked in place with a coating of powder.

Set line: in drafting, a leader line that extends, parallel with the proscenium arch, across the farthest downstage point(s) of the set.

Set prop: a large, movable item, not built into the set, that is used in some way by an actor, such as a sofa, floor lamp, table, and so forth.

Setting: to help lock the dye into the fiber of the fabric; to reduce or prevent the dye from being rubbed off the fabric.

Shade: a color of low value; usually created by mixing one or more hues with black.

Sharkstooth scrim: an open-weave material used to make transparent scrims.

Sheer: a thin gauze curtain that hangs across the opening of a window to soften the sunlight and obscure the view into a room.

Sheet-metal screw: a pan-head or hex-head screw used for joining sheets of metal.

Sheet stock: a generic term that applies to lumber products sold in sheet form, such as plywood, Upson board, and Masonite.

Shellac: a generally clear glossy coating made of resinous material (lac—the secretions of certain scale insects) suspended in wood alcohol; also known as spirit varnish.

Shift: to change the position of the scenery, props, or stage equipment.

Shift rehearsal: a rehearsal, without actors, where the director, scenic designer, technical director, and stage manager work with the scenery and prop crews to perfect the choreography and timing of all scenic and prop shifts.

Shim: scrap wood or metal used to raise adjacent parts so that they are level or fit together as designed.

S hook: an S-shaped piece of steel strap used to hold stiffening battens on the back of wall units that are made up of two or more flats; also called a latch keeper.

Show control: the use of computer-controlled, motorized, devices to shift scenery, almost always in view of the audience.

Show file: a digital file containing all the music and effects cues, in sequence, for an entire production. Variously called show tape, sound file, production show tape, or production sound file.

Show portal: a false proscenium that visually supports the style and color palette of a particular production.

Shutter: a lever-actuated device used to control the height of the top and bottom edges of a followspot beam; also called a chopper.

Shutter cut: the shadow line created by the edge of the shutter when it is inserted into the beam of light emitted by an ERS.

Shutters: movable upstage scenic elements used to create a visual backdrop. Essentially wide painted wings, shutters were mounted in grooved tracks and slid into view from either side of the stage. Performed the same function as, and predated, drops.

Shuttle stage: a long narrow wagon that moves back and forth across the stage, like a shuttle in a loom; used for shifting scenery.

Sight line: a sighting extending from any seat in the house to any position on stage.

Sight-line drawing: a scale drawing (plan and section views) of sightings that extend from the extreme seats (usually the outside seats on the front and last rows of the auditorium) to any position on the stage; used to determine how much of the stage and backstage will be visible from specific auditorium seats.

Silhouette: the general outline of form; frequently used to refer to the shape of a garment, set, or prop. The quality and character of the line determines the evocative characteristics of the resultant form. Also known as a profile or cutout line.

Sill iron: a strap of mild steel attached to the bottom of a door flat to brace it where the rail has been cut out.

Single-hand welding: a technique in which one hand holds the welding handle and the other hand is not used.

Single whip: a block and tackle configuration that changes the direction of travel of the line but provides no mechanical advantage.

Size coat: a paint coat used to shrink previously unpainted scenic fabric and to fill the weave of the fabric.

Size water: a mixture of approximately 1 cup of hot animal glue and 1 tablespoon of Lysol (or 1 cup of white glue) per gallon of warm water; the amount of binder in the size water depends on the weight of the pigments being used.

Skene: originally a wall or facade to hide backstage action in Greek theatres. By the end of the fifth century B.C., the wall had evolved into a two-story building.

Skid: a low-profile substitute for a wagon; usually a piece of ¾-inch plywood on which some small scenic element is placed.

Skin: a top or bottom plywood covering for a platform.

Sky drop: a large drop made to be hung flat, without fullness; used to simulate the sky.

Sky tab: synonym for sky drop.

Slide-plane aperture: the point in a projection system where a slide or other effect is placed.

Slide projector: a reasonably high output instrument capable of projecting standard 35 mm slides.

Slip-joint pliers: common pliers with an adjustable pivot point that provides two ranges of jaw openings; used for clamping, gripping, bending, and cutting light wire.

Slipstage: a stage wagon large enough to hold an entire set.

Smooth base coat: a base coat that has no texture.

Smoothing plane: a large, heavy plane with a blade angle of approximately 25 to 30 degrees; used to smooth parallel with the grain of wood.

Socket set and ratchet handle: sockets are cylindrical wrenches used with a ratchet handle; the reversible ratchet handle allows one to tighten or loosen nuts without removing the socket from the nut; used to tighten or loosen nuts and bolts in confined spaces or where other wrenches might not fit.

Software: the programs (sets of electronic instructions) that perform various functions such as word processing, drafting, and three-dimensional modeling.

Solder: a metal alloy made of lead and tin.

Soldering: the process of forming a low-strength bond in metal by flowing a molten metal over a joint area.

Soldering gun: a quick-heating, trigger-activated soldering iron that physically resembles a pistol.

Soldering iron: a device to heat solder and the item to be soldered to the point where a good bond can be made.

Soldering pencil: a low-wattage soldering iron.

Sole: the bottom plate of a plane, with a slot through which the tip of the blade projects.

Sound crew: those who record and edit sound and who set up and run any sound equipment during the production.

Sound designer: person responsible for the design, recording, and playback of all music and sound effects used in a production.

Sound mixer: an electronic device used to adjust the loudness and tone levels of several sources, such as microphones and tape decks.

Sound plot: a list describing each sound cue in the production.

Sound reinforcement: the amplification of specific live sounds, usually actors' voices or musical instruments.

Sound scoring: background music and/or effects tracks that play at a low loudness level throughout a scene or scenes.

Soundscape: the sound environment. The sound effects, music, and reinforcement being used at any particular moment in a play.

Source: the origin of electrical potential, such as a battery or 120-volt wall outlet.

Source light: the apparent source of light that is illuminating a scene or an object.

Spackling: a paste used to fill small holes in walls.

Spade bits: *see* wood bits.

Spattering: the process of applying small drops of paint to a surface; done by spraying paint with a garden sprayer or slapping a lightly charged brush against the heel of one's hand to throw paint drops at the scenery.

Specifications: clarifying notes that explain the building materials, textures, or special effects to be used in a design or other project.

Spectrometer: a device for measuring specific wavelengths of light.

Spidering: running a cable directly from the dimmer to the instrument; also known as direct cabling.

Spindle chuck: a device used to hold wood in a lathe.

Spine: the relative stiffness of brush bristles; good watercolor bristles will flex easily but will also have enough spine to remain erect when fully saturated with paint.

Spirit: the manner and style in which a play is presented to the audience.

Split time fade: a fade in which the fade-up and fade-out are accomplished at different rates or speeds.

Spoke shave: a small plane with a wide, narrow, slightly rounded sole and a steeply angled (approximately 30 to 35 degrees) blade; it is pulled rather than pushed across the surface of the wood; used to soften or round sharp edges rather than to smooth flat surfaces.

Spray cone: the shape or pattern of paint emitted from the nozzle of a spray gun.

Spray gun: a pistol-like device that shoots out a cone of paint.

Spreading: *see* bleeding.

Stage: the area where the action of the play takes place.

Stage brace: an adjustable wooden or aluminum pole that is attached to a brace cleat on the back of a flat to hold it vertical.

Stage business: a specific action, also known as a "bit," performed by an actor during the play.

Stage circuit: an electrical circuit terminating on one end in a female receptacle in the vicinity of the stage. The other end is connected to a dimmer or a patch panel. Synonymous with dimmer circuit when it terminates at a dimmer.

Stage crew: those who shift the sets and, sometimes, props during rehearsals and performances.

Stage house: the physical structure enclosing the area above the stage and wings.

Stage manager: person who assists the director during rehearsals and manages all backstage activity once the play has opened.

Stage screw: bracing hardware; a coarse-threaded, large, hand-driven screw used to anchor a foot iron or the foot of a stage brace to the stage floor; leaves ragged holes in the stage floor.

Stage worthy: strong enough to withstand the use inflicted on them when used on the stage, for example, sofas/chairs that are stood and/or danced on; tables that break apart during fights, and so forth.

Standard parallel: a platform made of a folding framework of nonvariable height; the top is removable and the frame folds like a giant parallelogram for storage.

Staple gun: a tool with a spring-driven piston used to drive staples; used in upholstery, in attaching muslin to flat, and so forth.

Staples: U-shaped fasteners sharpened at both ends; used to attach wire, rope, cording, chicken wire, screening, and similar materials to supporting wooden frames.

Starter hole: a small hole bored into a piece of wood or metal to hold the tip of a screw or drill bit; also called a pilot hole.

Stencil brush: a short, squat brush with a circular pattern of short, stiff bristles; the bristles are pressed onto, rather than stroked across, the work, to prevent the paint from bleeding under the edges of the stencil.

Stencil paper: stiff, water-resistant paper used for making stencils.

Step-down transformer: a transformer whose output voltage is lower than its input voltage.

Step lens: a plano-convex lens with the glass on the plano side cut away in steps that are parallel with the plano face.

Step motor: an electric motor whose movement consists of discrete, angular steps rather than continuous rotation. Precise movement is achieved by programming the motor to run, in either direction, for a specific number of steps.

Step-up transformer: a transformer whose output voltage is higher than its input voltage.

Stereo: two distinct sound channels; a stereo system is composed of two discrete monaural systems.

Stiffening batten: a length of 1 × 3 attached to a multiflat wall unit to keep it from wiggling.

Stile: a vertical side member of a flat.

Stippling: in scene painting, a texturing technique, similar in appearance to spattering, but leaves a heavier texture; stippling is done by touching a sponge, feather duster, or ends of a brush to the surface of the work. In makeup, a texturing technique in which makeup is applied by touching the skin with a textured surface, usually a stippling sponge. Similar to stippling in scenic painting.

Stitcher: one who sews costumes together.

Stock: regular-sized lumber that can be purchased from a lumberyard.

Stock furniture: furniture items owned by the producing organization and held in storage until they are needed for a production.

Stock set: scenery designed to visually support a generalized location (garden, city street, palace, interior) rather than a specific one.

Stop block: a small piece of scrap wood attached to the stile of a flat to prevent flats from slipping past each other when lashed together in an inside corner configuration.

Stop cleat: metal tabs used to prevent flats from slipping past each other when they are being lashed in an outside corner configuration.

Stove bolts: bolts smaller than carriage or machine bolts and with threads on the entire length of the shaft; used for attaching stage hardware, hinges, and similar items that require greater fastening strength than screws do.

Stovepipe wire: soft-iron wire approximately $\frac{1}{16}$ of an inch in diameter and generally black; very flexible but has little tensile strength; used for tying or wiring things together; is not strong enough to be used for flying scenery.

Straightedge: a thin piece of wood, usually 4 to 6 feet long, with a handle attached in the center; used as a guide while painting straight lines.

Straps: rectangular strips of ¼-inch plywood used to reinforce butt joints on the interior support elements (toggle bars, diagonal braces) of flats; substitute for keystones.

Stream-of-consciousness questioning: asking whatever relevant questions pop into your mind in the course of a discussion.

Street makeup: makeup worn in everyday life.

Strike: taking down and/or destruction of the set following the conclusion of a play's production run.

Striplight: a long, narrow troughlike instrument with three or four circuits controlling the individual lamps; each circuit is normally equipped with a separate color; used for blending and creating color washes; also known as an x-ray.

Style: specific compositional characteristics that distinguish the appearance of one type of design from another; for example, realism, expressionism, surrealism, and so forth.

Stylization: the use of specific compositional elements characteristic of a particular style or period that create the essence of that style or period.

Subtractive color mixing: the selective absorption of light by a filter or pigment.

Supernumerary: an actor, normally not called for in the script, used in a production; an extra; a walk-on.

Surform blade: a thin, disposable strip of spring steel honeycombed with sharpened protrusions projecting from its surface; the serrated blade face doesn't leave a smooth surface, so the wood generally has to be smoothed with sandpaper.

Surform tools: tools that use the Surform blade—planes, files, routing bits, and gouges.

Sweat off: when an actor's face perspires, some makeups will run. These makeups are said to "sweat off."

Sweep: a wooden curvilinear form frequently used to outline an arch or irregular form in door- and window-flat openings.

Swivel caster: a caster that swivels or rotates around a vertical axis; the bearing plate should have a ball-bearing swivel.

Symmetrical balance: correspondence in size, form, and relative position of parts on either side of a center dividing line; mirror-image balance.

Synthesizer: a musical instrument that creates sound electronically; can be used to create a close facsimile of instrumental, vocal, or natural tones.

Table saw: a circular-bladed stationary power saw; the blade projects upward from the underside of a table; the height and angle of the blade are adjustable; used to rip lumber, plywood, and other sheet goods.

Tack hammer: a lightweight hammer with a small magnetized head for inserting tacks and a large face for seating them; used only with tacks.

Tap and die: tools used to cut threads on pipe and rod stock; the tap is used to cut internal threads; the die cuts external threads.

Tape deck: a magnetic-tape transport mechanism used to record an electrical signal on magnetic tape; also used to play back that signal; does not contain a playback amplifier or speaker.

Tape measure: a retractable, flexible metal rule housed in a plastic or metal case; used for measuring in general stage work.

Tape recorder: a magnetic-tape transport mechanism used to record and play back an electrical signal on magnetic tape; it has a built-in playback amplifier and speaker(s).

Teaser: a short, horizontal drape used for masking the flies; synonym for *border*.

Technical director: person responsible for supervising the construction, mounting, rigging, and shifting of the scenery and properties.

Technical production: all organizational and procedural aspects of the construction, painting, and operation of scenery and properties.

Technical rehearsals: run-throughs in which the sets, lights, props, and sound are integrated into the action of the play.

Tenon: a square tab projecting from a piece of stock; used in conjunction with a mortise to make a mortise and tenon joint.

Texture: the relative roughness or smoothness of the finish of an object.

Theatrical gauze: a fine mesh weave, similar to cheesecloth, but the threads are thicker and the weave is slightly tighter; 72 inches wide; used for apparition effects and applications similar to sharkstooth scrim.

Theatron: the steeply raked seating area for the audience in a Greek theatre.

Theme: the repetitive use of similar elements to create a pattern or design.

Throw distance: the distance the light travels from its hanging position to the center of its focus area.

Thrust stage: a stage projecting into, and surrounded on three sides by, the audience.

Thumbnail sketch: a small, quickly drawn rough sketch, usually done in pencil, that shows the major outline, character, and feeling of an object but doesn't show much detail.

Tie-off cleats: special cleats used in pairs approximately 30 inches above stage level to tie off the line after the flats have been lashed together.

Ties: strips of material (usually 36-inch pieces of ½-wide cotton tape, or 36-inch shoestrings) used for tying stage drapes to battens.

Tilt: to rotate an object about its horizontal axis.

Timbre: the distinctive quality of a sound that distinguishes one voice, musical instrument, or sound from another of the same pitch and intensity.

Tin snips: scissorlike tools used for cutting thin metal.

Tint: a color of high value; usually created by mixing one or more hues with white.

Tip jack: two (or more) large interconnected jacks that are fitted with swivel casters; normally used for moving wall units.

Toggle bar: an interior horizontal framing member of a flat.

Tone: (1) a color of middle value achieved by mixing one or more hues with black and white; (2) a generic term referring to the intensity of the component frequencies contained in any particular sound.

Tooth: a term used to describe the surface texture of a paper.

Tormentor: the vertical flats that form the side elements of the false proscenium.

Toxic: poisonous.

Tracing paper: translucent paper used for drafting.

Transducer: a device that converts energy from one state into another, such as a microphone or loudspeaker.

Transformer: a device that changes voltage in an electrical system.

Travel: to move horizontally relative to the stage floor, as with a drape that opens in the middle and is pulled to the sides.

Traveler: any drapery that moves or opens horizontally; generally, travelers are composed of two sections of stage drapes covering the full width of the proscenium; the sections split in the middle, and each section retracts in an offstage direction.

Tread: the horizontal surface of a stair unit—the part on which you walk.

Trick line: *see* monofilament line.

Tri square: a small, rigid, hand square with a steel blade and steel, composition, or wooden handle; used as a guide for marking 90-degree angles across narrow (under 6 inches) materials.

Trompe l'oeil: literally "to trick the eye." An illusion of three-dimensionality created with paint.

Truss: an engineered beam in which a downward force at any point on its top will be distributed over its full width by a series of interlocking triangles that channel and redirect the downward force into a horizontal force.

"Tubed" building adhesive: an adhesive product, such as Liquid Nails, packaged in a caulking tube and designed to be dispensed with a caulking gun.

Tubing cutter: a tool used for making clean right-angle cuts on steel and nonferrous metal tubing ½ inch and smaller.

Tumbler: a narrow (¾ inch thick by 1 inch wide, or 1 × 3) piece of stock used as a spacer when three or more flats are going to be booked.

Turntable: *see* revolve.

Tutu: the short, stiff skirt frequently worn by ballerinas.

Tweed: a rough-surfaced woolen fabric in plain, twill, or herringbone weave of two or more shades of the same color; used for men's and women's suits and trousers.

Tweeter: a high-frequency speaker generally designed to reproduce from approximately 1000 to 20,000 Hz.

Twill: a weaving pattern that results in parallel diagonal lines or ribs; a flat surfaced, durable, heavy cotton fabric used for making dresses, men's suits, and work clothes.

Twist-drill bits: drill bits made of mild steel, filed to a point, with spiral indentations in the shaft to carry away material being removed from the hole; used for drilling holes of approximately $1/64$ to $1/2$ inch in diameter in wood, plastic, mild to medium steel, and nonferrous metals.

Two-fer: an electrical Y that has female receptacles at the top of the Y and a male plug at the bottom leg of the Y; used to connect two instruments to the same circuit.

Two-handed welding: a technique in which the torch or welding handle is held in one hand and the filler rod in the other.

Unbalanced line: a sound cable in which a single insulated conductor is wrapped in a braided or foil shield.

Unbleached muslin: a cotton fabric commonly used to cover flats; available in a variety of widths from 72 inches to 33 feet; for scenic-construction purposes, it should have a thread count of 128 or 140 threads per inch.

Undercut: an indentation in a form that leaves an overhang or concave profile, such as the nostrils on a mask of a face.

Unified aniline dye: a coal-tar-derivative dye formulated to work on both animal- and plant-derivative fibers.

Unit set: a single set in which all of the play's locations are always visible and the audience's attention is usually shifted by alternately lighting various parts of the set.

Unsaturated polyester: a liquid plastic generally used as a casting resin and as the bonding agent to create the multipurpose material known by the trade name Fiberglas.

Upson board: a sheet stock composed of a paper pulp and binder compressed into 4-by-8-foot sheets.

Urethane: a class of plastics that have a variety of formulations: flexible foam, rigid foam, and liquid casting resin. Because of toxic fumes emitted when working with urethane foams, their use is not recommended.

Utility knife: a metal handle with a usually retractable replaceable blade; used for a variety of jobs including cutting cardboard and trimming fabric from the edges of flats; also called a matte knife.

Vacuforming: the process of shaping heated plastic, usually high-impact polystyrene, around a mold through the use of vacuum pressure.

Valance: a horizontal element at the top of a drapery arrangement that covers the curtain rod.

Valence shell: the outermost plane of orbiting electrons in the structure of an atom.

Value: the relative lightness or darkness of an object.

Vanishing point: the point on the horizon to which a set of parallel lines recedes.

Varnish: a transparent coating made of synthetic or natural resinous materials suspended in an oil (oil varnish), alcohol (spirit varnish), or synthetic (polyurethane, vinyl acrylic) vehicle.

Vehicle: the liquid medium — water, oil, lacquer, and the like — in which pigments, fillers, and binders are suspended to create a paint mixture; after the paint is applied, the vehicle evaporates.

Velour: a thick, heavy material with a deep pile; generally made of cotton or cotton/nylon blends; heavier weights are used for upholstery and draperies; lighter weights can be used in costuming.

Velum: an awning covering the cavea (auditorium) of a Roman theatre; also known as a velarium.

Velvet: a rich, lustrous material with a soft, thick pile; frequently made of rayon with a cotton or cotton-blend backing; used in dresses, coats, upholstery, and draperies.

Velveteen: fabric possessing the same general characteristics as velour but much lighter (6 to 8 ounces); used in upholstery and costumes.

Ventilate: a method of tying hair to the net foundation of a wig, mustache, or beard. The technique is similar to that used in hooking rugs.

Vinyl acrylic concentrates: highly saturated pigments with a vinyl acrylic binder.

Vinyl acrylic paint: paint made with a vinyl acrylic binder; in scene painting, thinned vinyl acrylic concentrates (two parts water to one part concentrate) are mixed with an opaque white base to create tints and are mixed with a transparent base for fully saturated hues; after curing for 24 hours, the paint is highly water-resistant; can be thinned with up to ten

parts of water depending on particular application.

Void: an unfilled, empty space.

Volatility: in computers, loss of electronic data when a computer loses its power supply.

Volt: the unit of measurement of electrical potential.

Wafer board: a sheet stock composed of large chips of wood mixed with a binder and compressed into 4-by-8-foot sheets; stronger and cheaper than plywood; can be used for the same purposes as plywood.

Wale: visible, usually narrow, ridges in the surface of a fabric caused by a variation in the weaving pattern.

Walk the cues: to move about the stage as the light cues are being run so the light will be falling on a person rather than on a bare stage.

Wall pocket: a connecting box similar to a floor pocket but mounted so that its face is flush with a wall.

Wardrobe crew or staff: those crew members such as dressers and wardrobe-repair personnel who work during the dress rehearsals and performances.

Warp: the vertical threads in a fabric.

Wash: the covering of a large area with a smooth layer of paint. A smooth wash consists of only one color; a blended wash is created by smoothly segueing from one color to another.

Watch tackle: a block and tackle system that provides a 3:1 mechanical advantage.

Web browser: a software program that enables you to preview and access sites on the World Wide Web.

Weft: the horizontal threads in a fabric.

Welding: the process of making a high-strength bond in metal by heating the parts to be joined to their melting points and allowing the parts to become fused together.

Welding rod: a rod, usually coated with flux, that serves as the positive electrode in arc welding.

Wheat paste: a mixture of unrefined wheat flour and water; used for attaching dutchmen and for similar low-strength gluing.

White glue: commonly known by the trade name Elmer's Glue-All, white glue is a casein or milk-based glue used extensively in scenic and property construction.

White model: *see* functional model.

Whiting: a white powder extender, basically low-grade chalk, used to increase the covering power of dry pigment and binder paint.

Wig cap: a skull cap of thin, tight-fitting mesh material. Used to cover and compress the wig-wearer's hair.

Wigmaker: one who makes, styles, and arranges wigs.

Winch-driven system: a System that uses a motorized or hand-powered winch to move a cable; frequently used to move wagons or skids across the stage or to turn small revolves.

Wings: (1) tall cloth-covered frames or narrow unframed drops that are placed on either side of the stage, parallel with the proscenium arch, to prevent the audience from seeing backstage. In the Restoration theatre, wings were usually painted to match the scene on the up-stage drop. (2) The off-stage space adjacent to the stage in a proscenium arch theatre.

Winglights: lights hung on either side of the stage, usually concealed by wings (vertical masking pieces). In this context the winglights were striplights—long, narrow, troughlike fixtures usually containing eight to twelve individual lamps.

Wire-crimping tool: specialty pliers whose jaws are designed to pressure-clamp solderless connectors to electrical wire.

Wire frame: lines used to define the shape of an object.

Wireless microphone: a microphone system that uses a short-range FM radio transmitter and receiver instead of a cable to send the signal from the microphone to the mixer.

Wire nails: small finish or box nails with very slender shafts; used for attaching delicate decorative moldings or panels to larger scenic elements.

Wire strippers: specialty pliers used for removing insulation from electrical wires.

Wood bits: paddle-shaped bits primarily for use in drilling wood, although they can be used in some plastics; must be used in a power drill; also known as spade bits.

Wood chisel: a steel blade sharpened at a 30-degree angle; used for gouging, paring, or smoothing wood.

Wood file: a file with medium-sized teeth; can be flat on both faces, flat on one face and curved on the other, or round; used for smoothing wood and plastic.

Wood rasp: an extremely coarse-toothed file; usually has one flat and one rounded face; used for rough shaping of wood.

Woofer: a low-frequency speaker with a frequency range from approximately 20 to 150–250 Hz.

Work: the object on which work is being performed.

Workable fixative: a spray that seals colors in place. "Workable" indicates that paint can effectively be applied on top of the fixative.

Working sectional: a drawing showing the sectional angle for a lighting instrument; used to determine its trim height; not to be confused with a lighting sectional.

Work light: a lighting fixture, frequently a scoop, PAR, or other wide-field-angle instrument, hung over the stage to facilitate work.

Worsted: a tightly woven, smooth-surfaced fabric of wool or wool blend; used for men's or women's suits and trousers.

Wrecking bars: generic name for the class of metal tools used to pry wood apart and remove nails.

Writable CD: a CD on which data can be recorded, and read, by the user.

X-ray: *see* striplight.

Zoom ellipse: an ellipsoidal reflector spotlight with movable lenses that allow the focal length and beam-edge sharpness to be varied.

Selected References

ACOUSTICS AND ARCHITECTURE

Beranek, Leo L. *Music, Acoustics and Architecture.* Robert E. Krieger Publishing, 1979.

Burris-Meyer, Harold, and Edward C. Cole. *Theatres and Auditoriums.* Reinhold, 1949.

Burris-Meyer, Harold, and Lewis Goodfriend. *Acoustics for the Architect.* Reinhold, 1957.

Mullin, Donald C. *The Development of the Playhouse.* University of California Press, 1970.

SCENIC/PROPERTY DESIGN AND CONSTRUCTION

Arnold, Richard L. *Scene Technology.* Prentice-Hall, 3rd ed., 1993.

Baldwin, John. *Contemporary Sculpture Techniques: Welded Metal and Fiberglass.* Reinhold Publishing, 1967.

Bay, Howard. *Stage Design.* Drama Book Specialists, 1974.

Bellman, Willard F. *Scene Design, Stage Lighting, Sound, Costume and Makeup.* Harper & Row, 1983.

Birren, Faber. *Creative Color.* Schiffer, 1987.

Bryson, Nicholas L. *Thermoplastic Scenery for the Theatre, Vol. 1: Vacuum Forming.* Drama Book Specialists, 1972.

Crabtree, Susan, and Peter Bendart. *Scenic Art of the Theatre: History, Tools and Techniques,* Focus Press, 2nd ed., 1998.

Gillette, A. S., and J. Michael Gillette. *Stage Scenery.* Harper & Row, 3rd ed., 1981.

Glerum, Jay. *Stage Rigging Handbook.* Southern Illinois University Press, 2nd ed., 1997.

Gottshall, Franklin H. *How to Design and Construct Period Furniture.* Reprinted by Bonanza Books, original copyright 1937.

Kenton, Warren. *Stage Properties and How to Make Them.* Drama Book Specialists, 1978.

Meyer, Franz Sales. *Handbook of Ornament.* Dover Publications, 1957.

Meyers, L. Donald. *The Furniture Lover's Book: Finding, Fixing, Finishing.* Sunrise Books, E. P. Dutton, 1977.

Neuman, Jay Hartley, and Lee Scott. *Plastics for the Craftsman.* Crown Publishers, 1972.

Parker, W. Oren, Harvey K. Smith, and R. Craig Wolf. *Scene Design and Stage Lighting.* Holt, Rinehart and Winston, 7th ed., 1996.

Payne, Darwin Reid. *Theory and Craft of the Scenographic Model,* rev. ed. Southern Illinois University Press, 1985.

Pecktal, Lynn. *Designing and Drawing for the Theatre.* McGraw-Hill, 1994.

Taylor, Douglas C. *Metalworking for the Designer and Technician.* Drama Book Specialists, 1979.

The Painter's Journal: A Forum and Resource for Scenic Artists in Theatre. www.paintersjournal.com

The Scenic Artist's Forum. Scenic_Artists_Forum@Yahoogroups.com

LIGHTING DESIGN AND PRODUCTION

Bellman, Willard F. *Lighting the Stage: Art and Practice.* Harper & Row, 1974.

Gillette, J. Michael. *Designing with Light.* Mayfield Publishing, 4th ed., 2003.

Parker, W. Oren, Harvey K. Smith, and R. Craig Wolf. *Scene Design and Stage Lighting.* Holt, Rinehart and Winston, 6th ed., 1990.

Pilbrow, Richard. *Stage Lighting.* Drama Book Publishing, 1991.

Rosenthal, Jean, and Lael Wertenbaker. *The Magic of Light.* Little, Brown, 1972.

Warfel, William, and Walter A. Klappert. *Color Science for Lighting.* Yale University Press, 1981.

COSTUME/MAKEUP DESIGN AND PRODUCTION

Anderson, Barbara and Cletus. *Costume Design.* Holt, Rinehart and Winston, 1984.

Barton, Lucy. *Historic Costume for the Stage.* Baker's Plays, 1963.

Corey, Irene. *The Mask of Reality.* Anchorage Press, 1968.

Corson, Richard. *Stage Makeup.* Prentice-Hall, 8th ed., 1990.

Cunningham, Rebecca. *The Magic Garment: Principles of Costume Design.* Waveland Press, 1994.

Ingham, Rosemary, and Elizabeth Covey. *The Costume Designer's Handbook.* Heinemann, 1992.

Ingham, Rosemary, and Elizabeth Covey. *The Costume Technician's Handbook.* Heineman, 3rd ed., 2003.

Pecktal, Lynn. *Costume Design: Techniques of Modern Masters.* Watson-Guptill, 1993.

Prisk, Berneice. *Stage Costume Handbook.* Greenwood, 1979.

Russell, Douglas. *Costume History and Style.* Prentice-Hall, 1982.

Russell, Douglas. *Stage Costume Design: Theory, Technique and Style.* Prentice-Hall, 2nd ed., 1985.

Waugh, Norah. *The Cut of Men's Clothes 1600–1900.* Theatre Arts Books, 1964.

Waugh, Norah. *The Cut of Women's Clothes 1600–1930.* Theatre Arts Books, 1968.

SAFETY

A.C.T.S. *Arts, Crafts, and Theatre Safety.* http://www.artscrafts theatersafety.org

Rossol, Monona. *The Artist's Complete Health and Safety Guide.* Allworth Press, 3rd ed., 2001.

Rossol, Monona. *Stage Fright: Health and Safety in the Theatre.* Allworth Press, 1991.

Rossol, Monona. *Health and Safety Guide for Film, TV and Theatre.* Allworth Press, 2000.

SOUND DESIGN AND PRODUCTION

Collison, David. *Stage Sound.* Drama Book Publishers, 1982.

Davis, Gary, and Ralph Jones for Yamaha. *Sound Reinforcement Handbook.* Hal Leonard Corporation, 2nd ed., 1989.

Heil, Bob. *Practical Guide for Concert Sound.* Melco Publishing, 1976.

Leonard, John A. *Theatre Sound.* Theatre Arts/Routledge, 2001.

DRAFTING FOR THE THEATRE

Dorn, Dennis, and Mark Shanda. *Drafting for the Theatre.* Southern Illinois Press, 1998.

Morgan, Harry. *Perspective Drawing for the Theatre.* Drama Book Specialists, 1979.

Payne, Darwin Reid. *Computer Scenographics.* Southern Illinois University Press, 1994.

Sweet, Harvey, and Deborah M. Dryden. *The Complete Guide to Drawing for the Theatre.* Allyn & Bacon, 2nd ed., 1994.

Warfel, William. *Handbook of Stage Lighting Graphics.* Drama Book Specialists, 1974.

PERIODICALS

Lighting Dimensions
Entertainment Design
Theatre Design and Technology

Credits

Chapter 9, pp. 174–175. "Design Inspirations: Scenic Design": Daryl Davis, excerpts from "Time Travel" from *Stage Directions* (December 2003): 30–32. Reprinted with the permission of *Stage Directions*, www.stage-directions.com.

Chapter 9, pp. 182–183. "Design Inspirations: Scene Design": Mel Gussow, excerpts from "Onstage Magic with Water" from *The New York Times* (July 28, 1998): E1, E3. Copyright © 1998 by The New York Times Company. Reprinted with permission.

Chapter 11, p. 266. "Design Inspirations: Scenic Production": Si Morse, excerpt from "Hooping It Up" from *Stage Directions* (March 1999): 9–11. Reprinted with the permission of *Stage Directions*, www.stage-directions.com.

Chapter 14, p. 345. "Design Inspirations: Lighting Design": Arnold Wengrow, excerpts from "Thomas Lynch: Far East Marks This Designer's Latest Scenic Transformation," from *Entertainment Design* (March 1999): 38–41. Copyright © 1999 by Theatre Crafts Association. Reprinted with permission.

Chapter 14, p. 350. "Production Insights: Drafting for Lighting Design": Based on USITT, "Revised Standard Graphic Language for Lighting Design" (1991). Copyright © 1991. Reprinted with the permission of USITT.

Chapter 14, p. 372. "Design Inspirations: Lighting Design": Ann Anderson, excerpts from "Nothing in Excess" from *Stage Directions* (November 2003): 51–53. Reprinted with the permission of *Stage Directions*, www.stage-directions.com.

Chapter 16, p. 392. Table 16.2: "Comparison of Same Wattage/Different Output Lamps" from OSRAM Sylvania, Inc. Reprinted with permission.

Chapter 18, p. 447. "Design Inspirations: Costume Design": Amy Reiter, excerpts from "Designing Women" from *Entertainment Design* (May 1999). Copyright © 1999 by Theatre Crafts Association. Reprinted with permission.

Chapter 18, p. 450. Figure 18.5: "A Sample Costume Chart," courtesy Dianne J. Holly.

Chapter 18, p. 452. "Design Inspirations: Costume Design": David Johnson, excerpts from "Prince of Attire" from *Entertainment Design* (July 2003): 32. Copyright © 2003 by Theatre Crafts Association. Reprinted with permission.

Chapter 18, p. 460. "Design Inspirations: Costume Design": David Barbour, excerpts from "I Want My Mummy" from *Entertainment Design* (February 1999): 5–6. Copyright © 1999 by Theatre Crafts Association. Reprinted with permission.

Chapter 21, p. 540. "Design Inspiration: Sound Design": based on Abe Jacobs, "On Sound: The Art, the Technology, and the Facilitator" from *Entertainment Design* (Spring 2003), Eddy Theatre Product Guide, A Special Supplement: 1. Copyright © 2003 by Theatre Crafts Association. Reprinted with permission.

Appendix A, pp. 562–570. "A Revised Standard Graphic Language for Lighting Design". Reprinted with the permission of USITT.

Index